THE GLOBAL PUBLIC RELATIONS HANDBOOK

LEA's Communication Series

Jennings Bryant / Dolf Zillmann, General Editors

Selected titles in Public Relations (James Grunig, Advisory Editor) include:

Austin/Pinkleton • Strategic Public Relations Management: Planning and Managing Effective Communication Programs

Culbertson/Chen • International Public Relations: A Comparative Analysis

Dozier/Grunig/Grunig • Manager's Guide to Excellence in Public Relations and Communication Management

Fearn/Banks • Crisis Communications: A Casebook Approach, Second Edition

Grunig • Excellence in Public Relations and Communication Management

Grunig/Grunig/Dozier • Excellent Public Relations and Effective Organizations: A Study of Communication Management in Three Countries

Ledingham/Bruning • Public Relations as Relationship Management: A Relational Approach to the Study and Practice of Public Relations

Lerbinger • The Crisis Manager: Facing Risk and Responsibility

Spicer • Organizational Public Relations: A Political Perspective

For a complete list of other titles in LEA's Communication Series, please contact Lawrence Erlbaum Associates, Publishers at www.erlbaum.com

THE GLOBAL PUBLIC RELATIONS HANDBOOK
THEORY, RESEARCH, AND PRACTICE

EDITED BY

KRISHNAMURTHY SRIRAMESH
NANYANG TECHNOLOGICAL UNIVERSITY, SINGAPORE

DEJAN VERČIČ
PRISTOP COMMUNICATIONS, LJUBLJANA, SLOVENIA

LAWRENCE ERLBAUM ASSOCIATES, PUBLISHERS

Senior Editor:	Linda Bathgate
Editorial Assistant:	Karin Wittig-Bates
Cover Design:	Sean Trane Sciarrone
Book Production Supervisor:	Eileen Engel
Full-Service Compositor:	TechBooks

This book was typeset in 10.5/12 pt. Times, Italic, Bold, and Bold Italic.
The heads were typeset in Engravers Gothic, Zapf Humanist and Revival.

Lawrence Erlbaum Associates, Inc., Publishers
10 Industrial Avenue
Mahwah, New Jersey 07430

Library of Congress Cataloging-in-Publication Data

The global public relations handbooks : theory, research, and practice / edited by
Krishnamurthy Sriramesh, Dejan Verčič.
    p. cm.
  Includes index.
  ISBN 0-8058-3922-4 (cloth)—ISBN 0-8058-3923-2 (pbk)
    1. Public relations—Cross-cultural studies—Handbooks, manuals, etc.
  2. Intercultural communication—Handbooks, manuals, etc.
  I. Sriramesh, Krishnamurthy.   II. Verčič, Dejan.

  HM1221.G57   2003
  659.2—dc21

                      2003048349

Lovingly dedicated to the memory of
Sriramesh's father
Sri K. N. Krishna Murthy

Contents

Contributor Biographies

Andréia Athaydes earned a bachelor's degree in public relations from Federal University of Rio Grande do Sul, Puerto Alegre. She graduated as a communication and political economy specialist from Pontifical Catholic University of Rio Grande do Sul, Puerto Alegre, and has a master's degree in management and strategic marketing from the University of Business and Social Sciences of Buenos Aires, Buenos Aires, Argentina. Between 1998 and 2001, Andréia Athaydes acted as general secretary and president of the Regional Council of Public Relations Professionals of Rio Grande do Sul and Santa Catarina. Currently, she coordinates the Commission of Integration with Latin América of the Federal Council of Public Relations Professionals. She is also director of the Lutheran University of Brazil's Social Communication Program. Among her teaching areas are communication ethics and legal issues, communication strategies and tactics, projects' development, and news media planning and production. From 2000 to 2002, Athaydes participated of the Ministry of Education's Commission of Teaching Specialists of Social Communication, evaluating public relations programs in various states of Brazil. As a professional, she worked for education and health institutions.

Badran A. Badran is a training director at the Center for Media Training and Research and an associate professor with the College of Communication and Media Sciences, Zayed University, Dubai, UAE. He served as acting director of the Department of Public and Cultural Relations at Zayed University. He holds a PhD in communication studies from the University of Massachusetts, Amherst, a MA in journalism from Indiana University, Bloomington, Indiana, and an International Certificate in Travel and Tourism from Oxford University, Oxford, England. He has published papers and book chapters in public relations, tourism promotion and publicity, population communication, and communication and media in the Middle East.

Günter Bentele is a full professor at the University of Leipzig, Leipzig, Germany. In 1994, he was invited to serve as the chair for public relations at the University of Leipzig, a first for any German-speaking country. Prior to joining the university, he was associate professor for Communication Science and Journalism (between 1989 and 1994) at the University of Bamberg. After his State's Examination in German Literature and Linguistics (1974), he became assistant professor at the Free University (1974–1989). In 1982, he wrote his dissertation about an evolutionary theory of signs; in 1989, he wrote a second dissertation (for the German Habilitation) discussing the problems of journalistic objectivity and media credibility. He has served as a guest professor in Lugano and Zurich (Switzerland), Jyvaeskylae (Finland), Riga (Latvia), and Klagenfurt (Austria) and was a visiting research scholar at Ohio University in Athens, Ohio. Between 1995 and 1998, he served as president of the German Association for Communication and Media Studies. He authored and coauthored nine books; edited or coedited 20 more; and wrote over 130 articles in the fields of public relations, communication theory, journalism, media system analyses, media semiotics and film studies, communication ethics, and other fields.

Constance Chay-Németh is an assistant professor at the School of Communication and Information, Nanyang Technological University in Singapore. Her areas of specialization include public relations, issues and crisis management, health communication, and critical and postmodern studies. She is currently interested in studying the effects of the knowledge economy on public relations and knowledge management. Among other professional duties such as reviewing articles for the *Journal of Public Relations Research*, Constance has also worked with public relations consultancies in the United States and Singapore.

Ni Chen is an assistant professor of communication at the Hong Kong Baptist University (HKBU), Hongkong. Before joining the faculty at HKBU, she worked as an assistant professor at universities in the United States. She earned her PhD in mass communication–journalism at Ohio University, Athens, OH in 1992. She is the author and coauthor of refered journal articles, book chapters, and conference papers. She is the coeditor of a book entitled *International Public Relations: A Comparative Analysis*. She is a board member of International Association of Business Communicators (IABC) Hong Kong Chapter. She advised Public Relations Student Society of American chapters at two universities in the United States and is now the faculty advisor to the student chapter of IABC at HKBU. In addition, she is a member of the Editorial Board for *American Review of China Studies*. She keeps close contacts with colleagues at universities in Mainland China, serving as their life-long distinguished guest lecturer.

Simon Cliffe is currently working in Melbourne, Australia, as a market research consultant with Roberts Research Group, focusing on customer satisfaction within service industries. Previously he worked on projects including public transport brand strategy development. He completed a master of commerce (hons) in marketing at the University of Auckland, Auckland, New Zealand, where he focused in 2001 on the adoption of a sponsorship-based branding strategy for the marketing of services. His academic interests include public relations, brand strategy, services marketing, and stakeholder management.

Hugh M. Culbertson is professor emeritus in the E. W. Scripps School of Journalism, Ohio University, Athens, OH. He coauthored a widely used text, *Fundamentals of News Reporting*, in addition to *Research Methods in Mass Communication* and *Mass Communication Theory and Research*. He is senior author of *Studying the Political, Social and Economic Contexts of Public Relations: A Book of Theory and Cases* and is senior coeditor of *International Public Relations: A Comparative Analysis*. Culbertson has authored or coauthored more than 55 articles in refereed journals, along with 10 published monographs and book chapters dealing with varied topics in public relations and mass communication. In 1990, the Public Relations Society of America (PRSA) named him Educator of the Year. In 1985, he received the Pathfinder Award for excellence in research from the PRSA Research and Education Foundation. In 1976, Hugh Culbertson was named Outstanding Graduate Faculty member at Ohio University, Athens, OH. He directed the "Foundations" section of the PRSA Body of Knowledge project in the late 1980s and early 1990s. Also, he has served on the advisory boards of the *Journal of Public Research Research* (formerly the *Public Relations Research Annual*), *Journalism and Mass Communication Quarterly, Newspaper Research Journal*, and *Public Relations Review.*

Vincent Defourny is UNESCO's web chief editor. He joined UNESCO Paris headquarters in 1997. For 5 years, he worked as program and project evaluation specialist trying to use evaluation as an organizational learning tool. After being closely involved in the elaboration of a new communication strategy for UNESCO in February 2002, he was designated to create and lead a new web editorial coordination unit. Defourny holds a PhD in communication studies from the Catholic University of Louvain, Leuven, Belgium, where he served in the 1980s as assistant lecturer and in the 1990s as visiting professor. He presented papers at conferences and lectured at various European universities. Along with his academic activities, he has worked in France, Belgium, and Spain as a consultant for private companies as well as for public and nonprofit organizations. He has managed a series of projects in the field of corporate communication, human resources training, quality deployment, and change management. From 1981 to 1984, he volunteered in Uganda where he worked in the field in educational and on community-based development projects. Defourny published his doctorate thesis on strategic management of communication and wrote articles on other public relations issues. He is also coauthor of two books on quality management.

Maria Aparecida Ferrari, is the director of the School of Journalism and Public Relations at the Methodist University of São Paulo, Brazil. She is also an associate professor at the Department of public relations at the University of São Paulo. From 1982 to 1995, she worked as a public relations practitioner and consultant with national and multinational companies in Brasil and Chile. She received a PhD in public relations from the University of São Paulo (2000) and a MCS in public relations from the University of São Paulo (1993).

Bertil Flodin has close to 40 years of experience in public relations. This includes practical experience as public relations executive for corporations, nongovernmental organizations, and governmental offices. He spent 12 years as an associate professor and an associate dean at the Department of Journalism and Mass Communication at the University of Gothenburg, Gothenburg, Sweden. Bertil Flodin is the proud recipient of the Gothenburg University Pedagogic Prize, which he received in 1995 for his excellence in teaching. For the past 5 years, he has worked as a full-time public relations consultant. His assignments have involved strategic communications counsel in crisis communication, public affairs, business intelligence and knowledge management, internal communication, civic information, and the education of professional communicators. Bertil Flodin was involved in the creation of crisis communications plans for companies, wrote a handbook on crisis communications for public authorities, and published a number of research reports on public relations and crisis communication.

Larissa A. Grunig is professor at the University of Maryland, College Park, where she has worked since 1978. She teaches public relations and communication research. She has received the Pathfinder Award for excellence in research, sponsored by the Institute for Public Relations; the Jackson, Jackson, and Wagner Behavioral Science Prize; and the Outstanding Educator Award of the Public Relations Society of America. She was co-founder and co-editor of the *Journal of Public Relations Research* and has written more than 200 articles, book chapters, monographs, reviews, and conference papers on public relations, activism, science writing, feminist theory, communication theory, and research. She was a member of an international grant team, sponsored by the IABC Research Foundation, investigating excellence in public relations and communication management. The newest Excellence book won the 2002 PRIDE award sponsored by the Public Relations Division of the National Communication Association. Dr. Grunig also serves as a consultant in public relations.

James E. Grunig is a professor of public relations in the Department of Communication at the University of Maryland, College Park. He is the coauthor of *Excellent Public Relations and Effective Organizations: A Study of Communication Management in Three Countries, Managing Public Relations, Public Relations Techniques,* and *Manager's Guide to Excellence in Public Relations and Communication Management.* He is editor of *Excellence in Public Relations and Communication Management.* He has published over 215 articles, books, chapters, papers, and reports. He won three major awards in public relations: the Pathfinder Award for excellence in public relations research from the Institute for Public Relations Research and Education, the Outstanding Educator Award of the Public Relations Society of America (PRSA), and the Jackson, Jackson and Wagner Award for behavioral science research of the PRSA Foundation. He also won the most prestigious lifetime award of the Association for Education in Journalism and Mass Communication, the Paul J. Deutschmann Award for Excellence in Research.

Vivian Hirsch is Brazilian chief executive officer and vice-president for Latin America of Edelman Public Relations Worldwide. Hirsch is specialist in strategic planning and crisis management. She has 20 years of experience as director of public relations for government agencies and corporations, such as Monsanto and American Express. Since 1994, she has directed public relations agencies. Vivian Hirsch is fluent in Spanish, English, German, and French.

Takashi Inoue is chief executive officer of Inoue Public Relations. He graduated from Waseda University, Tokyo in 1968, majoring in marketing and administration. After a stint in marketing at Yamaha Corporation (formerly Nippon Gakki Company, Ltd.), he founded Inoue Public Relations in 1970. Takashi Inoue was the first public relations professional to be actively involved in the high-technology industry, beginning with Intel and Apple Computer in the late 1970s and early 1980s, which coincided with the beginning stages of a keyboard-based culture in Japan. He is one of only a few Japanese public relations consultants to have achieved an international reputation as a spokesperson for Japan, a reputation built up over 31 years as Inoue Public Relations has worked with an extensive range of industries, including telecommunications, computers, financial, automotive, pharmaceutical, aerospace, and business-to-business and government relations. Over the past 2 decades, he has been especially active and involved in United States–Japan trade-related issues, helping to avert possible crisis situations in the telecommunications, semiconductor, and automotive industries. In 1997, his company won the International

Public Relations Association's top award, the Golden World Award for Excellence in Public Relations, for work the company carried out in connection with deregulation of the automobile parts aftermarket in Japan. He also has edited *An Introduction to Public Relations*, the first comprehensive book on public relations in the Japanese language and one of the best-selling books in Japan, reaching the Top 10 list of *Nikkei Business* (the premier business publication in Japan).

Kevin L. Keenan is an associate professor and director of Graduate Studies in the Department of Journalism and Mass Communication at the American University in Cairo, Egypt. He earned his PhD in Mass Communication from the University of Georgia, Athens. Keenan's teaching and research interests include communication theory and mass media content and effects. His work appears in the *International Journal of Advertising, Journal of Advertising Education, Journalism and Mass Communication Educator, Journalism and Mass Communication Quarterly, Public Relations Review*, and elsewhere. He is active in several professional organizations and has presented over 50 scholarly papers at academic conferences. He has worked in the advertising agency and public opinion research business and currently serves as a consultant for a variety of local, national, and international clients.

Yungwook Kim is an assistant professor of Communication at Ewha Womans University, Seoul, South Korea, where he teaches government public relations, crisis management, and international public relations. He received a PhD in public relations from the University of Florida, Gainesville. His research focuses on international public relations, public relations evaluation, integrated marketing communication, and crisis management. He taught at Illinois State University prior to his current position. He was appointed as a recipient of the Smart Grant sponsored by Institute for Public Relations and Ketchum Public Relations Worldwide in 1998. His research appears in the *Journal of Public Relations Research, Public Relations Review, Corporate Communications: An International Journal, Business Research Yearbook, Journal of Promotion Management, Journalism and Mass Communication Quarterly, Journal of Broadcasting and Electronic Media, Journal of Asia Pacific Communication*, and *Journal of Business Ethics*. He wrote a Korean book titled, *Understanding Crisis Management: Public Relations and Crisis Communication.*

Michael Kunczik is a professor at the Institut fuer Publizistik (Institute of Communications), Johannes Gutenberg University, Mainz, Germany. He researched mass media effects (especially effects of media violence), international communication, public relations, mass media and social change, media economies, journalism (especially ethics in journalism). Among his many publications are *Images of Nations and International Public Relations, Media Giants: Ownership Concentration and Globalization,* and *Concepts of Journalism: North and South* (also in Portuguese and Spanish).

Ryszard Ławniczak, is a professor at the Poznań University of Economics, Poznań, Poland. He was visiting professor at University of Melbourne (1991) and California State University, Fresno (1984 and 1991). He is an expert in the fields of international public relations, foreign economic policies, and comparative analysis of economic systems, and he is the author of *Transition Public Relations*. He also serves as the economic advisor to the president of the Republic of Poland and is the vice-president of the Western Chapter of the Polish Public Relations Association.

Shirley Leitch is a professor of Corporate Communication and executive director of the University of Waikato Management School, Hamilton, New Zealand. She has over 20 years of experience researching and practicing public relations. Her research has focused on external communication, particularly the areas of corporate identity and public discourses. She is well published in the international literature on public relations, communication, and marketing. She is also the author of a book on the New Zealand news media. Her most recent work had been on the role of discourse in change management within the public sector.

Juan-Carlos Molleda is an assistant professor of public relations of the University of Florida College of Journalism and Communications, Gainesville, FL. Molleda's research interest is in international corporate public relations and public relations practices and education in Latin America. He has conducted research in Brazil, Colombia, Costa Rica, Venezuela, and the United States. His main teaching subjects are public relations principles, campaigns, research, international perspective, and communication management. Juan-Carlos received his BS in social communication (1990) from Universidad del Zulia, Maracaibo, Venezuela, an MS in corporate and professional communications (1997) from Radford University, Radford, VA, and a Doctor of Philosophy, PhD degree in journalism and mass communications (2000) from the University of South Carolina, Columbia, SC, where he also coordinated applied communication research projects. Between 1987 and 1993, he obtained the majority of his work experience from a Venezuelan financial consortium, acting as manager of advertising and promotions, manager of corporate communications, manager of public relations, and chief of information and media relations.

Judy Motion is a senior lecturer in the University of Auckland Business School, Auckland, New Zealand. She has a doctorate in public relations from the University of Waikato, Hamilton. Her research is interdisciplinary and broadly concerned with public relations, marketing, and public policy issues. Her research perspective is critical post-structuralist and deals with identity, sociocultural impacts and the environment. Judy is the Australasian associate editor of the *Journal of Communication Management* and a member of the editorial boards of the *Journal of Public Affairs* and the *Australian Journal of Communication*. Her work is published in numerous journals including *Media Culture & Society, Journal of Communication Management, Political Communication, Public Relations Review,* the *Asia Pacific Public Relations Journal* and the *Australian Journal of Communication.*

Jurica Pavicic is an assistant professor of marketing, marketing strategy and marketing for nonprofit organizations at School of Economics & Business, University of Zagreb, Zagreb, Croatia. He received his BSc, MPhil, and PhD from the University of Zagreb. Jurica Pavicic has professional and academic interests in marketing and all aspects of applied nonprofit marketing, management, and communication. He is currently working with nongovernmental organizations, companies, and research associations to study marketing communications in transition economies. He has published over 20 articles in academic and business journals and other scholarly outlets, including the *British Food Journal, Nase Gospodarstvo*, and *Ekonomski pregled.* He also participated in more than 20 international conferences.

Cornelius Pratt is communication coordinator in the Office of Communication, United States Department of Agriculture (USDA) Forest Service, Washington, DC. Prior to joining the USDA, he was full professor (1994–2002) in the Department of Advertising at Michigan State University in East Lansing, MI. In 1999, he served as a Fulbright Senior Scholar at three southern African institutions: the University of Zambia, Evelyn Hone College of Applied Arts and Commerce, and the Zambia Institute of Mass Communication Educational Trust all located in Lusaka, Zambia.

Ronél Rensburg is currently head of the Department of Marketing and Communication Management at the University of Pretoria, Pretoria, South Africa. She is also chairperson of the School of Management Sciences in the Faculty of Economic and Management Sciences at the same university. She previously lectured in the Department of Communication at the University of South Africa, Pretoria and was director of Corporate Communication and Marketing at the same university. Ronél Rensburg is also a change communication consultant (particularly for organizations on the African continent). She currently does research on a variety of corporate current communication issues, including public relations, political communication, rhetoric, and speech communication. Ronél Rensburg a bachelor's degree in Communication; honors degree in Communication; master's degree in Communication, and a doctorate in Communication Science. She has published books and articles on corporate communication, speech communication, political communication, and corporate social investment and public relations.

Amy Rudgard is head of European public relations for LEGO. Until November 2002, she was head of European Consumer Practice at Weber Shandwick (based in London), where she was responsible for building the agency's consumer practices across its wholly owned offices in 10 European countries. For nearly 10 years, she advised multinational companies in the United States and Europe on building brand image, managing reputations, and influencing consumer opinions. She specializes in developing and managing international campaigns tailored to meet the needs of multinational and multicultural constituents. She previously worked with organizations such as Estee Lauder, Simon & Schuster, TNT, and Unilever. Most recently, she advised the mobile and wireless products division of Siemens, overseeing the company's global public relations program in conjunction with advertising and new media to change perceptions of the brand, build awareness of the company's products, and promote its wireless products. In 4 years of working together, Siemens has seen a significant increase in its brand awareness, a jump in market share from Number 7 to Number 4 worldwide, and Weber Shandwick has twice been shortlisted for Best International Public Relations Campaign by *PR Week* and the Institute of Public Relations (IPR). Amy also led the international program in 10 countries to promote real cork stoppers in wine on behalf of the Portuguese Cork Association. An American, Amy Rudgard has a degree in Spanish from Pennsylvania State University, State College, Pennsylvania.

Betteke van Ruler is an associate professor of communication science at the Free University of Amsterdam, Asterdam, Netherlands. She also holds a chair in communication management at the University of Twente. She earned a PhD in social sciences from the University of Nijmegen, Nijmegen. Her research focuses on the relation between organization and communication and on the practice of communication management. She is a well-known consultant on questions of professionalization of public relations and communication management in the Netherlands, and she is the coordinator of the European Network of Public Relations Researchers, a secretary of the Public Relations Division of the International Communication Association, a member of the board of the European Communication Association, and a member of the European Public Relations Body of

Knowledge Group, chaired by Dejan Verčič. Her work published in *Public Relations Review, Journal of Communication Management, Journal of Public Relations Research*, and in many Dutch scientific and professional journals. She recently published the *Bled Manifesto on Public Relations.*

Waldemar Rydzak, is a lecturer at the University of Economics in Poznań, Poznań, Poland. One of the leading Polish specialists in the area of crisis management, he is the author of Poland's first dissertation on that subject. He is founding president of the public relations agency PRELITE. He is a member of the Polish Public Relations Association.

Krishnamurthy Sriramesh is an associate professor in the School of Communication and Information at the Nanyang Technological University, Singapore. He received his PhD from the University of Maryland, College Park in 1992. He began his teaching career as an assistant professor in the Department of Communication at Purdue University, West Lafayette, IN, where he stayed for 6 years. He then moved to the Department of Public Relations at the University of Florida, Gainesville, FL, where he was an assistant and then associate professor (with tenure) for $4^1/_2$ years. After that he joined the Nanyang Technological University as a senior fellow and then accepted an associate professor position. He has won two faculty teaching awards, one each from Purdue University and the University of Florida. At the University of Florida, he also won the Faculty Research Award and the Golden Gator Award for excellence in research. He has presented research papers and invited talks in the United States, Mexico, Germany, Slovenia, Poland, the Philippines, Singapore, Malaysia, Egypt, South Korea, Israel, and India. He serves as the associate editor (Asia) for the *Journal of Communication Management* and is a member of the editorial board of the *Journal of Public Relations Research, Journal of Marketing and Communication Management*, and the *Journal of Information and Knowledge Management*. He also serves as a member of the Advisory Board for the Communication and Public Relations Program of Trisakti International Business School in Jakarta, Indonesia. He has published refereed research articles in *Public Relations Review, Journal of Public Relations Research*, and *Journal of Communication Management*. He also has contributed chapters to *Excellence in Communication and Public Relations Management* and *International Public Relations: A Comparative Analysis*. Currently, he is editing a book on public relations in Asia (Prentice-Hall).

Ana Taklac is a teaching and research assistant of marketing and marketing communications at the University of Zagreb, Faculty of Economics, Marketing Department. She holds a MSc in psychology from the University of Zagreb, Zagreb, Croatia and is currently finishing her PhD in public relations. She recently returned from the University of Maryland, College Park, MD where she spent two semesters as a visiting Fulbright scholar. Her major research interests are focused on attitudes and attitude change in public relations. She has published and coauthored more then 15 papers in the area of public relations and marketing communications, and she also participated in leading international conferences.

Jacek Trębecki, is a lecturer at the University of Economics in Poznań, Poznań, Poland, and founder of public relations agency PRELITE. He was a journalist with *Marketing Serwis* monthly. He is a specialist in the art of rhetoric, development of information messages, and the evolution of social strategies and campaigns. He is a co-owner of the public relations agency PRELITE and a practitioner in the fields of public campaigns and establishing media relations.

Katerina Tsetsura is a doctoral candidate in public affairs and issue management in the Department of Communication at Purdue University, West Lafayette, IN. Her research interests are the development of public relations theory and practice in Russia and countries of Commmonwealth of Independent States (CIS) and Eastern Europe, problems of international ethics in public relations, and social construction of identities of female public relations practitioners in Eastern Europe.

Judy VanSlyke Turk is director of the School of Mass Communications at Virginia Commonwealth University (VCU), Richmond, VA. Prior to joining VCU in March 2002, she was founding dean of the College of Communication and Media Sciences at Zayed University, U.A.E. (United Arab Emirates) a position she held for $2\frac{1}{2}$ years. Previously, she was dean of the College of Journalism and Mass Communications at the University of South Carolina; Columbia, SC director of the journalism and mass communications program at Kent State University; Kent, OH and a faculty member at the University of Oklahoma, Louisiana State University, Baton Rouge, LA and Syracuse University, Syracuse, NY. She is past president of the Association for Education in Journalism and Mass Communications (AEJMC) in the United States. She was chair of the Teaching Standards Committee in 1992 and also is a former chair of AEJMC's Council of Divisions and its Public Relations Division. In addition, she is a past chair of the Public Relations Society of America's (PRSA's) College of Fellows and is a member of the Steering Committee of the Commission on Public Relations Education. She was named Outstanding Public Relations Educator in 1992 by the PRSA. She is coeditor of *Journalism Studies* and a member of the editorial advisory board for the *Journal of Public Relations Research* and *Journalism and Mass Communications Quarterly*. She is coauthor of *This is PR: The Realities of Public Relations* and coeditor of a collection of international public relations case studies developed as a project of the Public Relations Division of AEJMC. She has consulted and lectured on public relations, journalism, and mass communications curriculum issues in Eastern Europe, the Newly Independent States, the Baltics, Russia, the Middle East, and Asia.

Dejan Verčič is a founding partner in Pristop Communications, a communication management consultancy based in Ljubljana, Slovenia, and assistant professor for public relations and communication management at the University of Ljubljana. Among his clients are governments, domestic and international corporations, and associations. From 1991 to 1993, he led the foundation of the Slovenian News Agency—Slovenska Tiskovna Agencija (STA). He holds a PhD from the London School of Economics. In 2000, he received a special award from the Public Relations Society of Slovenia for his contributions to the development of public relations practice and research; in 2001, he was awarded the Alan Campbell–Johnson Medal for outstanding service to international public relations by the United Kingdom Institute of Public Relations. Since 1994, he organizes the annual Lake Bled International Public Relations Research Symposia, and he is active in the European Public Relations Body of Knowledge project. He has published articles in *Public Relations Review* and edited a book on *Perspectives on Public Relations Research*. He is president of the European Public Relations Education and Research Association for 2003.

Timothy N. Walters is assistant professor of Communications and Media Sciences at Zayed University, Dubai, United Arab Emirates (U.A.E.). Prior to joining Zayed University in the fall of 2001, he was a faculty member at the University of Louisiana, Monroe, Louisiana. He taught at several foreign institutions including the Budapest University of

Economic Sciences, Budapest. He worked professionally in the print and publications businesses for more than 20 years. He consulted and lectured internationally and was a guest speaker for the Fulbright Commission. He was a member of the editorial review committee for *Public Relations Review* and served as a reviewer of the Mass Media and Society Division of the Association for Education in Journalism and Mass Communications. He has won several top paper awards and was a Council for Advancement and Support of Education (CASE) award winner. He has coauthored several books. His most current project is a *Bridging the Gulf: Communications Law in the UAE*, an English language primer addressing the legal system in the United Arab Emirates, freedom of expression within the context of an Arabic/Islamic society, rules for journalists, and personal protections including defamation.

Stefan Wehmeier received a PhD in communication studies from Münster University, Germany. He works as an assistant at the Department of Public Relations, Institute for Communication and Media Science, University of Leipzig, Leipzig, Germany. In 1998 and 1999, he worked as a public relations practitioner and journalist. His main research focus is public relations theory and television economy.

FOREWORD

Never has cross-cultural communication been so important to different types of organizations (such as governments, corporations, and non-governmental organizations) as it is today. Since the end of World War II, the United Nations and its specialized agencies, such as UNESCO, were the main practitioners of transnational communication, which was an integral part of how they fulfilled their respective missions. A few multinational corporations, mainly from the western world, also engaged in cross-cultural communication. However, in the past decade, cross-cultural communication has become an important focus for a larger number and a wider variety of organizations.

Even the most experienced organizations face challenges when they need to engage in cross-cultural communication, not least because the relationship between an organization and its environment is never static. UNESCO was created to be a permanent worldwide forum of intellectual and ethical exchange and a laboratory of ideas. In 2001, the 188 Member States decided to place all the activities of the current Medium-Term Strategy (2002–2007) under a unifying theme, namely: "UNESCO contributing to peace and human development in an era of globalization through education, the sciences, culture and communication." The context of an ever-globalizing world requires UNESCO to keep its practice of cross-cultural communication under constant review, especially with a view to encouraging a spirit of knowledge-sharing, which is vital for building knowledge societies that are open, inclusive, and equitable.

And democratic. Press freedom, free speech, and the free flow of information are essential for democratic debate to take place. UNESCO is strongly committed to defending and promoting these values and principles. We believe that democratic debate needs to be nurtured and that all members of society—individual and institutional, public and private— can contribute to its cultivation. We recognize, moreover, that the new information and communication technologies (ICTs) have great potential to generate exciting opportunities for opening up avenues of exchange, debate, and discussion. At the same time, the exercise of democratic freedom implies certain responsibilities too. As the "voices" of organizations and groups pursuing their specific interests and ideas, professional communicators find themselves at the interface where institutional concerns and public responsibilities meet.

In an age when there is talk of an inevitable "clash of civilizations," when ill-judged remarks can ignite the tinder-box of popular opinion, when the stereotyping and stigmatization of "the other" can suddenly destroy community relations built up over decades, there is a premium on intercultural dialog within and between societies. There is a corresponding need for sensitivity to these matters by organizations and individuals operating in multicultural, multi-faith, and multi-ethnic environments. The ethics and practice of public relations should be attuned to the new demands of the global situation. The code of practice of public relations, of course, must be a matter of professional self-regulation, but it is not difficult to see where particular emphasis might be placed—for example, respect for the views of others, the active cultivation of mutual understanding, developing the capacity to listen, and sensitivity to local cultures and community values. UNESCO would encourage public relations professionals to reflect increasingly on their practices in the perspective of intercultural dialog and communication. This *Handbook*, with contributions from 35 researchers and scholars hailing from 20 countries, is designed to help that process of reflection.

This publication should prove beneficial to public relations and communication professionals who need to operate in diverse regions of the world. Moreover, it should prove very useful to students and research scholars specializing in international public relations. Indeed, the *Handbook* is to be especially commended for its treatment of the international dimension of public relations, a dimension which highlights the vital importance of cultivating intercultural understanding and dialog. By discussing public relations practice not in isolation but as a function of the political, sociocultural, economic, media, and activist environment in which global organizations must operate, this volume points the way toward fresh approaches to public relations in this age of accelerating globalization.

KOÏCHIRO MATSUURA
DIRECTOR-GENERAL,
UNESCO

Preface

The twentieth century was undoubtedly the era of democratization and concomitant development of more scientific and sophisticated forms of public relations, particularly in the United States and countries of Western Europe. The 1990s also was the decade of globalization because of the founding of the World Trade Organization and the formation of many regional and trans-region blocs such as NAFTA, the European Union, Asia-Pacific Economic Cooperation (APEC, founded in 1989), and Asia-Europe Meeting (ASEM). Economic cooperation was the primary focus behind the formation of these trading blocs and has resulted in significant increases in cross-national trading and communication. Consequently, public relations professionals have been thrust into managing some, if not most, of this transnational communication.

The need for a comprehensive body of knowledge that will help public relations practitioners operate strategically in this global context prompted the conceptualization of this book. There can be little debate that public relations professionals and students (as future professionals) can greatly benefit by increasing their knowledge of global public relations concepts and practices. In addition to describing various public relations practices across all regions of the world, there is a dire need to contextualize such practice by linking public relations practices with sociocultural variables. We hope that in taking such an approach, this book lays the foundation for establishing a holistic body of knowledge based on a comprehensive conceptual framework. We believe that the contributors to this book, as seasoned public relations scholars, consultants, and practitioners, are in a very good position to describe the state of public relations in their country or region as well as relate such practice to relevant sociocultural variables. We hope this book will be the harbinger of many attempts that will build on and refine the framework and contents of this book.

Producing this book has not been easy, a process that was spread over two years. A volume of this scope could never have been completed without the cooperation of colleagues dispersed throughout the world. So, we would like to thank all the contributors for their diligence in providing state-of-the-art information and for striving to adhere to the framework described in Chapter 1 as much as possible. Special thanks are extended to His Excellency Koichiro Matsuura, Director-General of the UNESCO, for graciously agreeing to write the Foreword for the book. Linda Bathgate and Karin Wittig Bates of Lawrence Erlbaum Associates deserve thanks for their patience and cooperation in seeing a project of this magnitude to fruition. Krishnamurthy Sriramesh would like to thank his family, and colleagues and students at several universities for helping him in various ways over the years and in the conceptualization and production of this book. Dejan Verčič would like to thank his colleagues at PRISTOP Communications for the pleasure of working with them and for their cooperation during his work on this book.

KRISHNAMURTHY SRIRAMESH
DEJAN VERČIČ

INTRODUCTION

The scholarly body of knowledge of public relations has grown significantly in the last 25 years and continues to evolve toward establishing itself as a strong discipline. Although this is an encouraging development, the growth of this knowledge has been very lopsided because the focus of theory building has been confined predominantly to the United States and a few Western European countries. The descriptions of public relations practices from other countries outside of the United States are limited to a few countries of Western Europe and Asia. Consequently, there is a scarcity of empirical evidence about public relations practices in other regions of the world. Until recently, editors of scholarly journals welcomed manuscripts that described how public relations was practiced in a particular country for their "international perspective." But increasingly, editors and reviewers of the few journals that publish public relations research have begun to reject manuscripts about public relations in other countries that are "merely descriptive." This also has contributed to the low number of published studies about public relations practices in other regions of the world, further stifling the growth of the body of knowledge in this domain. Finally, much of the literature on public relations from Latin America is not published in English and therefore has not received wider circulation. The result is that the existing body of knowledge of public relations is either completely silent or makes only cursory references to current public relations practices and the potential for future public relations initiatives in regions such as Asia, Africa, Latin America, the Caribbean, and Eastern Europe.

It is difficult to overstate the importance of a global perspective of public relations practice and scholarship, because this profession has truly become a global enterprise. I question whether there is such a thing as *domestic* public relations anymore because of the international outreach of organizations of all sizes and types as a result of the recent spurt in globalization. I believe that in the new millennium, *every* public relations professional must have a multicultural and global perspective in order to be effective, and such an outlook should not be considered the domain only of *international public relations specialists* anymore. It is apparent from the chapters in this book that several factors have contributed significantly to increasing the transnational activities of organizations around the world, thereby globalizing public relations practice as well.

DEMOCRATIZATION AND PUBLIC RELATIONS

The democratization of the world, especially in the latter half of the 20th century, has forced organizations of all types in many regions of the world to consider giving greater importance to public relations and communications management. It is hard to fathom that in 1900 the world did not have a single truly democratic country that had universal suffrage! However, by the end of the 20th century there were 119 electoral democracies that were home to 58% of the global population. Of these, 85 countries (covering 35% of the world's population) were classified by the Freedom House (2000) as liberal democracies. This process of democratization hit a crescendo in the 1990s when the former Soviet bloc countries embarked on the journey toward pluralism. As a result, not surprisingly, these and other emerging democracies around the world have witnessed a significant growth in public communication, much of which will have to be managed by public relations professionals. Examples of the relationship between democratization and the development of public relations is evident in several chapters of this book that describe the infusion of "modern" public relations by the United States and its allies in countries such as Japan (Chapter 4), South Korea (Chapter 6), and even a Western European nation such as Sweden (Chapter 12) especially after the end of World War II but also in different stages since then. A similar trend is reported from many other countries whose economies are in transition, as will be discussed presently.

NEW COMMUNICATION TECHNOLOGIES, TRADING BLOCS AND PUBLIC RELATIONS

The rapid expansion of new communication technologies such as satellite television and the Internet has increased the dissemination of information about products, services, and lifestyles around much of the world. Coupled with the freedom that accompanies democratization, the result has been a significant increase in the global demand for products and services, as well as global suppliers who can meet this demand. As a result, countries in Africa, Asia, the Middle-East, Eastern Europe, and Latin America have already become, or will soon become, major centers of manufacturing as well as consumption requiring the organizations of these countries to trade and communicate with a global audience.

The formation of multinational trading blocks such as NAFTA, EU, ASEAN, APEC (Asia Pacific Economic Conference) and ASEM (Asia Europe Meeting) has also contributed to shrinking the global market, thereby increasing organizational activities among and between trading blocks. These trading blocks continue to expand by attracting more countries into their fold. For example, the proposed expansion of the EU (announced in October 2002) will result in many former Soviet-bloc countries entering this once bastion of Western European democracy. Two of the 10 countries that are potential candidates for entry into the EU in 2004–Poland (Chapter 13) and Slovenia (Chapter 14)–are discussed in this book.

These factors have contributed to a significant spurt in global communication placing public relations practitioners at the forefront of managing the relationships among people of varied nations and cultures on behalf of organizations of all types. Therefore, it is essential for public relations professionals to prepare themselves to meet the challenges of communicating with publics of various countries and cultures. Not confined to communicating only with domestic audiences anymore, public relations professionals can greatly benefit from a comprehensive body of knowledge that is also multinational and multicultural. As discussed in Chapter 25, public relations educators who are saddled with the awesome responsibility of helping educate future professionals should also benefit from a body of empirical evidence about public relations practices in a global context, which can be provided only by having a comprehensive body of knowledge of global public relations.

Although the importance of a comprehensive body of knowledge of global public relations is undeniable, currently such a body exists only in its most basic form. Efforts to gather empirical evidence about public relations activities in different countries based on strong theoretical and methodological underpinnings only began in the early 1990s. Most of the studies in this book have described the public relations practices of specific countries by using one, or both, of two conceptual foundations: J. E. Grunig's models of public relations and Broom and Dozier's public relations roles–concepts developed in the United States. However, even this body of research is confined only to a few countries of Asia and Western Europe, a chasm that needs to be bridged. As described in the chapter on Brazil (Chapter 17) and Chile (Chapter 18), much of the published work on public relations in Latin America is in Portuguese or Spanish limiting its global utility.

While acknowledging the important contributions that these pioneering studies have made in advancing the knowledge of public relations in a global setting, I believe the time has come to make earnest efforts to widen our analyses to include all regions of the world, refine our description of the public relations practices in these regions, and go beyond description. There is a need to make cross-national comparisons of public relations practices by engaging in multinational studies based on a common conceptual framework. There is also a dire need to extend our analyses of public relations in different regions by going beyond a couple of conceptual or theoretical underpinnings and also exploring how contextual variables external to the organization (such as culture, political system, economic system, and media system) influence public relations activities in various parts of the world. Among other things, such linkages will increase the predictive capabilities of the body of knowledge of global public relations. For professionals to engage in strategic public relations management in a global setting, it is essential that they have the benefit of such a body of knowledge that helps them predict the outcome of their strategies vis-à-vis the organization's environment rather than learning by making mistakes each time.

THE FRAMEWORK FOR THE BOOK

All the above factors were the catalysts that brought about the conceptualization of this book and helped provide the blueprint and the country-specific chapters. Contributors of the country-specific chapters were charged with two basic tasks. First, they had to describe the status of the public relations profession in their country or region, helping to increase our knowledge and understanding of the profession in other regions of the world. In providing these descriptions, among other things, authors were asked to describe specific public relations practices, the knowledge level and professionalism of practitioners, the impact of professional associations on social responsibility and ethics of professionals, the status of public relations education in the nation, challenges being faced by the public relations industry, and the extent to which organizations used strategic public relations management, including measurement and evaluation. It is interesting to note that this task seemed to pose little or no challenge to any of the contributors. One reason could be that the fledgling body of knowledge of global public relations consists almost exclusively of descriptive studies, which do provide at least the basic blueprint for similar approaches. I hope that readers will find that this book has included a wider range of factors that can be used to describe the public relations profession in a country.

The second major task that contributors were assigned was to link the public relations practices in their country to the sociocultural environment of the country using the framework described in Chapter 1. This task appeared to be a greater challenge primarily because of the paucity of empirical evidence on the linkage between public relations and sociocultural variables in most regions of the world. As a result, despite their expertise and earnest efforts, contributors have had varying degrees of success in providing empirical data on the variables in the framework, as well as making informed linkages between these variables and public relations practice. The efforts of contributors in responding to this challenge deserve to be lauded because of the novelty of using this approach given the diversity and scale of countries covered in this book. I hope the framework provided in Chapter 1 will be the conceptual underpinning for future studies, which can also refine and extend the framework. One of the primary purposes of this book will have been served if it encourages a greater number of studies to go beyond describing public relations in specific regions and also use sociocultural variables to contextualize public relations practice. Providing this linkage will not only become easier but also more refined as a greater number of studies adopt the framework provided in Chapter 1.

GLOBALIZING PUBLIC RELATIONS PEDAGOGY

Another significant goal of this book was to extend the discussion of public relations by including contributions from every continent. Our field is in dire need of such a holistic perspective, which is bound to benefit professionals, scholars, and students in various ways. Therefore, in addition to contributions from the United States and countries in Western Europe, this book has included chapters from five countries in Asia, Australasia, two countries in Africa (and a conceptual piece on sub-Saharan Africa), two countries in Latin America, and three former Soviet-bloc countries. Attempts at getting a few more contributions from Africa and possibly one more from Latin America did not bear fruit primarily because potential contributors reported that they had no empirical or even anecdotal data that would help them link public relations with the sociocultural variables described in Chapter 1. This is evidence, if indeed one is needed, of the extent of hard work that remains to be done in putting the building blocks in place for a comprehensive body of knowledge of global public relations.

In identifying the format for the country-specific chapters, I wondered whether contributors should describe the sociocultural environmental variables (culture, political system, economic system, and so on.) of a country first and then contextualize their description of the public relations practices of that country in light of those variables. After much thought, I decided that because there is a distinct lack of empirical evidence on *all* the contextual variables from most regions of the world, it was prudent to describe the public relations profession of each country first and then relate public relations practices to environmental variables as far as possible. After all, currently we lack even descriptive data on the public relations industry from many regions of the world despite the utility of such information. Future anthologies of global public relations may very well find it useful to describe the sociocultural variables first and base their description of the status of public relations in a country based on these contextual variables.

ECONOMIES IN TRANSITION

The former Soviet-bloc countries are generally described as economies in transition. Using the term "nations in transit," the Freedom House studied the extent of democratization in the 27 former communist countries of Central and Eastern Europe and Eurasia. In its latest report, the study has divided these countries into three groups based on the extent of democratization, labeling them as consolidated democracies, transitional governments, and consolidated autocracies (Karatnycky, 2002). The survey classified 10 of the 27 nations in transition as consolidated democracies, 14 as transitional governments, and 3 as consolidated autocracies that displayed "no momentum toward meaningful political liberalization" (p. 16). Poland (Chapter 13) and Slovenia (Chapter 14) were classified as consolidated democracies, clearly showing that they are fertile ground for public relations practices. In terms of the economy, 9 of the 27 countries including Poland and Slovenia were listed by the Freedom House as consolidated market economies. Interestingly, Karatnycky also made a link between civil society activism, one of the infrastructural variables (along with political system and the level of economic development) included in the framework described in Chapter 1.

As noted in the preceding paragraphs, the economies of many more countries around the world are changing from regulated to market-oriented structures especially as a result of the WTO regime, which makes them economies in transition as well. China (Chapter 2) is a good example although one has seen much more economic transformation than concomitant political pluralism there. Singapore (Chapter 5) is also an economy in transition that has developed fast into an "Asian Tiger" and continues to reinvent itself by attempting to become a Knowledge-Based Economy (KBE).

PUBLIC RELATIONS: AN INDUSTRY IN TRANSITION

There is clear evidence in a majority of chapters of this book that the public relations industry around the world is also evolving from publicity-oriented practices into varying degrees of professionalization and sophistication. Even the United States, popularly considered to be the leader in the field, "is well beyond [its] rudimentary beginnings" but "not there yet," according to L. A. Grunig and J. E. Grunig, authors of Chapter 16. Chen and Culbertson characterize the public relations profession in China (Chapter 2) as an "adolescent" that is undergoing "growing pains." A similar description of the profession is evident in Chapter 3 where authors Badran, Turk, and Walters describe the industry in the UAE as "coming of age." There is little doubt that in most of the countries covered in this book, democratization and economic liberalization have resulted in public relations being accorded a greater role by decision makers of organizations. This is bound to spur more professionalism of the practice over the next decade. Globalization has also resulted in the influx of multinational corporations and public relations agencies into new markets, which has helped push the industry in these countries to greater professionalism as seen in Singapore (Chapter 5), South Korea (Chapter 6), the Republic of South Africa (Chapter 8) and Chile (Chapter 18).

SUMMARY OF CHAPTERS

Chapter 1 describes the conceptual framework that contributors of the country-specific chapters were asked to follow in presenting their data. As noted earlier, in addition to describing the public relations profession in their respective countries, authors were required to link public relations practices with variables related to organizations' operating environment. These variables are: the infrastructure variables of a country (consisting of the political system, economic system, level of development, and level of activism in the country), culture, and the media environment. Although these variables are interrelated, it is useful to make distinctions and assess the nexus between them and public relations. This framework needs to be replicated by other studies and refined so that ultimately we will have descriptive and prescriptive studies of global public relations. Because there is a distinct lack of case studies from other countries, authors were also asked to describe at least one case study that in some way typifies the public relations profession in their country. I hope that in the next years, there will be many more case studies on global public relations.

In Chapter 2, Ni Chen and Hugh Culbertson discuss the development and current status of the public relations profession in China. The authors state that the profession, which is about 20 years old, grew rapidly in the 1980s with primary emphasis on interpersonal communication typified by the personal influence model, in contrast to the early years of public relations in the US where mass media played a greater role. However, the profession declined in the early 1990s but is on the upswing again, mirroring recent changes in the country. The mass media now have a greater role in the public relations activities of organizations in China, in part because of an overall growth of the media industry itself and also the media's receptivity to the contributions from public relations.

In Chapter 3, Badran Badran, Judy VanSlyke Turk, and Tim Walters note that in a short span of 30 years, the public relations industry has grown robustly in the United Arab Emirates, parallel with the economic development of the country (one of the infrastructural variables). The UAE is also an interesting case study of a political system (another infrastructural variable) that is a federation with seven rulers none of whom is democratically elected. Citizens have the opportunity to give feedback to their ruler directly through the age-old system known as *majlis*, which often leads to consensus decision making after much debate, according to the authors. The authors conclude that providing publicity and disseminating information continue to be the two primary public relations objectives for organizations in the country.

Takashi Inoue comments in Chapter 4 that public relations was not welcome in Japan primarily because of cultural factors. In fact, there is no Japanese equivalent for the term *public relations*, which is a phenomenon in many other regions of the world as well. Public relations was introduced to Japan by General Douglas Macarthur as part of the democratization process of the country. The author also discusses the recent transition in organizational culture in Japan because of the bursting of the "economic bubble" in the 1990s, the appreciation of the yen, and the impact of information technology and globalization. This has created a need to shift management methods from the "seniority system," "lifetime employment," and "group decision-making process" that had been established in Japanese culture and institutions to a culture that values "openness," "fairness," and "speed"–characteristics that traditionally did not exist in Japanese firms.

In Chapter 5, Constance Chay discusses the status of the profession in Singapore and the effects of the influx of many multinational PR agencies in the 1980s as well as the country's shift to a knowledge-based economy in the 1990s. The author notes that the dominant coalitions (organizational decision makers) of most organizations in Singapore continue to emphasize media relations and positive publicity thereby relegating public relations to a supportive role as a subsidiary to marketing. As a result, the profession is mired in the "pre-professionalism" stage typified by one-way publicity-oriented communication with situational ethics. However, the author adds, a change in political philosophy and the rapid globalization of organizations and the increase in import of foreign talent have induced the profession to begin the move toward a "professional" stage of strategic management of public relations.

In Chapter 6, Yungwook Kim also describes the public relations profession in South Korea as being in a stage of transition. For several decades, the profession was strongly influenced by the government, which led to public relations being called *Gong Bo* (public information function by the government). The profession then adopted the term *Hong Bo* signifying the positive publicity-oriented media relations function that also used the personal influence model. The 1988 Seoul summer Olympic games heralded greater democratization as a result of which the public relations profession in South Korea has begun the transition toward greater professionalism and sophistication.

Chapter 7 discusses public relations in Australasia–Australia and New Zealand. Interestingly, authors Judy Motion, Shirley Leitch, and Simon Cliffe note that in spite of the cultural, economic, and historical differences between these two "friendly rivals," the development and growth of the public relations profession in Australia and New Zealand has been similar. For example, the early public relations practitioners in both countries began their careers as journalists as there were no formal means of training public relations professionals. The authors note the dramatic gender shift in the profession in both countries since the 1950s, with approximately 60% of public relations professionals currently being women. The authors also note that activism has been a major force in both countries, providing public relations professionals challenges and opportunities.

Ronel Rensburg notes in Chapter 8 that both the environment for practicing public relations and the industry itself are evolving in the Republic of South Africa, another evidence of a profession in transition in different regions of the world. The author notes that the earliest forms of public relations in the region cover a wide spectrum of activities such as the "middle-man" who arranged marriages and negotiated dowry to traditional music, dancing, and drums that were used as means of communication–a reference to the impact of culture on public relations. The author notes that the modern public relations industry faces stiff competition and encroachment from management consultants, auditing firms, advertising agencies, and market research institutions. The author states that the Public Relations Institute of Southern Africa is the only public relations association in the world to obtain the International Standards Organization's (ISO) 9002 certification.

In Chapter 9, Kevin Keenan, who has taught in Egypt for six years and conducted research there, notes that although the term *public relations* is familiar to most Egyptians, it is misunderstood. For the most part, public relations in Egypt is restricted to hospitality and customer relations or giving the organization a "smiling and friendly face." Because public relations is often not distinguished from advertising or marketing in universities or organizations, sales and marketing often become the primary functions of public relations professionals. The chapter also notes the direct relationship between media buying and media access. The author notes that with the influx of multinational corporations, there has been a recent trend in the public relations industry to become more professional.

Guenter Bentele and Stefan Wehmeier, authors of Chapter 10, give a comprehensive historical account of public relations in Germany. They note that throughout history and up to modern times, political, social, and economic factors have had an immense influence on the development and current structure of the public relations in Germany. As in many other countries in Europe and Asia, Germany's public relations industry was heavily influenced by American influence after World War II. The authors note that until the late 1960s, public relations was perceived as "advertising for trust" in Germany. But the notion of dialog between organizations and publics began to take root in the 1970s. From 1985, there has been a "boom" in the public relations field. The authors offer a variety of definitions of the term public relations reflecting various perspectives of the profession in German society. They forecast a robust professionalization of the public relations profession as well as its education and scholarship in Germany in the near future.

Bettke van Ruler begins Chapter 11 by characterizing the public relations industry in the Netherlands as a "stable industry" whose primary mission is to engage in *voorlichting*–enlightening–stakeholders. This, according to the author, is indicative of the strong influence that the era of "enlightenment" that began in France and Germany in the 18th century has on the public relations profession. The author also notes that the term *public relations* is not widely used any more in the Netherlands except in a negative context (e.g., "this is bad PR for you"). Most public relations practitioners instead use the terms *corporate communication, communication management*, or *communication* to refer to their activities, stressing the "management" aspect of *voorlichting*. It is refreshing to note that unlike most other countries covered in this volume, organizational decision makers in the Netherlands consider public relations to be an important management function that adds value to organizational activities.

Bertil Flodin notes in Chapter 12 that an "elaborate history" of the public relations profession in Sweden is yet to be written. This is true of many countries around the world, clear evidence of how much more work needs to be done in this field. As in many countries, modern public relations began in Sweden after World War II. According to the author, the 1990s witnessed an "explosion" in demand for public relations, which helped the industry develop rapidly. Today, Sweden has among the highest number of public relations professionals per capita in the world even though the average Swede continues to view the profession negatively largely because of the portrayal of the profession by the media.

In Chapter 13, Ryszard Lawniczak, Waldemar Rydzak, and Jacek Trebecki discuss the growth of public relations in Poland, another society in transition from a communist/socialist state to a democratic one, and from a command economy to a market-oriented one. The authors state that despite this transition in political and economic philosophy, the public relations industry in Poland is plagued by the baggage of communism. Public relations is commonly perceived as suspicious propaganda and the fear exists that publicizing the work of corporations, especially their economic success, might bring on additional tax sanctions (a socialistic vestige). The authors also state that public relations has facilitated and accelerated the political and economic transition of the country.

Dejan Verčič describes the public relations industry in Slovenia in Chapter 14. Slovenia is the youngest of the 17 countries represented in this volume. The author dates "modern" public relations in Slovenia to the relatively "liberal" era of the 1960s when it was one of five Yugoslav republics. But from early 1970, when Yugoslavia became even more restrictive, public relations was labeled "politically incorrect" and disappeared until 1989, a clear link between political philosophy and public relations. The author also notes the transition of the industry from propaganda focused image management to a relational, stakeholder management of public relations in recent times, a development strongly influenced by United States theory and practice.

In Chapter 15, Katerina Tsetsura highlights the enormous geographical, political, economic, and cultural diversity of Russia, one of the largest countries in the world. Consequently, the nature of public relations practiced and the status of public relations education also varies greatly among the various "meta-regions" of Russia. The author notes that modern public relations in Russia is less than 20 years old, has its origins in journalism, and has been developing rapidly. She also notes that public relations practice and education is dominated by government relations and political communication. The chapter also discusses the contrasting perspectives in Russia of "black PR" (political communication and propaganda) and "white PR" (ethical, strategic public relations).

In Chapter 16, Lauri Grunig and Jim Grunig report on the "maturation" of the public relations industry in the United States. They present a set of principles for effective public relations practice that they and their associates in the *Excellence Project* have developed. To apply these criteria effectively, organizations must have a dominant coalition that values public relations and empowers it. In addition, the public relations unit must have the knowledge base and professionalism to effectively apply these criteria. The authors state that in the aftermath of the attacks on September 11, 2001 and the corporate scandals that have rocked the financial markets, a public relations profession that is based on solid research and theorizing and enacted by educated, professional communicators is more important than ever. Among other things, the authors chart the development of public relations in the United States from its emphasis on press agentry/publicity in the early days to a relatively more professional practice today. They conclude that public relations in the United States is still typified by press agentry and although the profession is developing, it is far from becoming truly professional, strategic, and ethical.

Juan-Carlos Molleda, Andréia Athaydes, and Vivian Hirsch chart the evolution of public relations in Brazil in Chapter 17. The authors note that Brazilian public relations can be divided into four periods represented by the pioneers, the professionals, the academics, and the researchers. In 1967, Brazil became the first country to pass a law to regulate the industry, requiring that individuals must have a public relations degree and be licensed by the states' regional councils to practice public relations legally in the country. However, this has not raised the reputation of the profession in the eyes of Brazilians because journalists with no formal public relations education can still operate as public relations officers. The authors note that most organizational decision makers in Brazil continue to view public relations solely as a media relations function, equating public relations success to media advertising equivalency. However, they contend that because of democratization and increase in the economic stability of the country, the public relations profession will continue to professionalize.

In Chapter 18, Maria Aparecida Ferrari notes that even though public relations began in Chile in the 1950s, it began to develop only in the 1990s, owing to democratization and globalization. Public relations has been overshadowed by journalism and suffers from a low status in society. The author notes that 17 years of military rule in Chile has had a lasting impact on the society and culture, causing people to be indifferent to social and political issues. This also has resulted in people developing an individualistic and self-centered outlook— another confirmation that environmental factors affect the development of public relations. The author notes that public relations does not receive the support of organizational decision makers and continues to be viewed only as a publicity function, often executed through personal contacts typified by the personal influence model.

The final section of this book has contributions that focus on the transnational public relations practices of foreign governments, NGOs, and agencies and corporations. In Chapter 19, Michael Kunczik discusses at length the historical and current trends in image cultivation by nations with the help of transnational public relations. The author notes at the very outset that not all the strategies and techniques of such image cultivation are readily obvious to an observer because many nations deliberately mask such activities some times even using secret service agents. He notes the "chameleon-like" approach to international image cultivation where the source of messages often adapts to the surroundings to become unobtrusive. The author quotes Edward Bernays to contend that public relations and propaganda are synonyms, a statement that is bound to bring vociferous rebuttals from some of the contributors to this book, among others. The author states that most countries treat mediation of foreign policy as being closely connected with public relations. He gives several examples from historical times to modern times including the infamous "Nayirah" story from the Gulf War of 1991. The chapter also discusses the use of terrorism to gain media attention, in keeping with recent trends.

In Chapter 20, Vincent Defourny describes the transnational communication activities of, as well as the challenges faced by, UNESCO. He notes that since its inception, UNESCO has focused almost exclusively on writing skills in recruiting public information officers, which has attracted a large number of former journalists. The author notes that when these recruits are required to write articles conforming to the communication strategies of the organization, they begin to view public information and public relations as "unprofessional journalism," one that lacks objectivity. He also observes that despite its international outreach, UNESCO is strongly influenced by the French classical school of thought (perhaps because of its location) and the Cartesian view that it is possible to provide a complete and objective representation of the world. However, the author notes that the organization has been making strides toward improving its communication strategies and activities beginning with the new communication strategy it adopted in 2001.

Cornelius Pratt, author of Chapter 21, discusses how the public relations activities of transnational corporations can be used to respond effectively to the challenges of sustainable development in Sub-Saharan Africa. The author uses stakeholder theory, corporate social performance, and sustainable development to argue that global organizations should apply these constructs ethically to respond more effectively to the challenges posed by the environments in which they operate. The author recommends that corporations operating in sub-Saharan Africa should be cultural relativists and co-opt indigenous cultures into their practices in ways that will foster the common good of all stakeholders and not merely the short-term benefits of the corporation.

In Chapter 22, Amy Rudgard discusses the activities of international public relations agencies, a topic that is not discussed much in public relations scholarly publications or books. The author observes that although these days many agencies claim "international public relations" as one of the services they can offer clients, currently there are probably only a dozen agencies that can truly offer international public relations services from "conceptualization to implementation, via [a] network of offices and professionals at local market level." She then gives a brief history of a few of the leading international agencies noting that it is only in the 1950s that the first international public relations agency activity began when Hill-Knowlton and Burson-Marstellar began operating in Europe. Transnational PR agencies have contributed more than any other source for international PR because they have the international network of resources that in-house PR departments do not possess. The author also gives a detailed set of reasons for organizations to choose the service of international PR agencies, that should prove very useful to a wide audience.

In Chapter 23, Dejan Verčič discusses the public relations practices of transnational corporations. He reviews literature that explains that although TNCs are the primary beneficiaries of the current globalization trend, individual countries are not going to lose their economic sovereignty. The author concludes that because international public relations is practiced in complex environments, one has a greater chance of witnessing "Best Practice" public relations in the international realm than in domestic public relations.

Ana Tkalac and Jurica Pavicic, authors of Chapter 24, describe the activities of NGOs. The authors refer to NGOs as Robinhoods who take it upon themselves to do the altruistic and socially responsible activities that other types of organizations ignore. In keeping with the globalization trend since 1990, there has been a spurt in the number of international NGOs. Although public relations is a key tool for NGOs, the public relations literature is eerily silent on the public relations activities of NGOs either in domestic or international spheres. The authors link the concept of "civil society" to the activities of NGOs but also provide examples where NGO status is misused by groups such as religious cults and terrorists. They also discuss many facets of NGOs such as misappropriation of funds by NGOs, over bureaucratization of NGOs especially with age, and the challenge and pressure put on NGOs to measure up to unrealistic expectations.

Chapter 25 is an epilogue to the book focusing on one of the primary themes–the need for multiculturalism in public relations practice, pedagogy, and education. I believe that public relations has not kept pace with the rapid globalization that has occurred since 1992 and the existing body of knowledge of public relations is not multicultural. As a result, public relations education around the world (including in the United States) suffers in different ways. Students in the United States and some countries in Western Europe (to a lesser extent) receive little, if any, information on public relations in other regions of the world. Students in other regions of the world such as Asia, are exposed only to literature from the United States, thereby robbing them of the need to contextualize public relations practice to local norms. Therefore, there is a dire need for literature on public relations from around the world.

THE FUTURE

The future for public relations at a global level is bright as ever for all the reasons described above. The challenge for scholars is to provide the industry with the knowledge base that can help propel the profession toward greater sophistication and effectiveness. This knowledge base should be useful to current and future practitioners. I hope this book has contributed to establishing the framework for a comprehensive body of knowledge of global public relations by not only covering a wide spectrum of countries from diverse regions of the world but also by providing perspectives on transnational public relations practices. This was possible because of the hard work of the authors who are either leading scholars of public relations or leading public relations professionals (or both scholars and practitioners) with many years of experience. I thank the authors for their efforts, especially in trying to adhere to the framework described in Chapter 1 as far as possible. It bears mentioning that in selecting contributors, special attention was paid to their familiarity with the sociocultural environment of the country. As a result, in the case of all but two chapters, at least one of the authors of a chapter is a native of the country. Although the authors of the chapters on Egypt and Chile are non-natives, they have developed a keen awareness of the societal factors of those countries because of an extended period of residence in those countries (six and seven years respectively). They have taught and conducted research on public relations in each country respectively during their extended stays.

I would like to end with a personal note. I lost my father mid-way through this project, a loss from which my family and I will never recover completely. My father always tried to instill in me the right values so that I would become a better human being, and he did so with the utmost love and understanding, something I did not credit him for adequately when he was alive. Himself an educator (he taught English, Geography, History and Civics in high school), he had advised me to be caring to my students and helpful to my colleagues. I know he would have been proud of this book for its global scope, contents, and authorship. I am sorry that he is not physically here to see it published.

When I mentioned to my co-editor Dejan that I would like to dedicate the book to the memory of my father and asked him if he would also like to make a dedication to someone, he responded that the book should be "dedicated only to the memory of your father." I thank Dejan for his generosity. I extend my deepest gratitude to my grieving mother for her caring, understanding, and unstinted support throughout my life and thank my two brothers and sister for always being there for me.

REFERENCES

Freedom House (2000). Democracy's century: A survey of global political change in the 20th century. Available at: *http://www.freedomhouse.org/reports/century.html*, retrieved on January 18, 2003.

Karatnycky, (2002). Nations in transit 2002: A mixed picture of change. *http://www.freedomhouse.org/research/ nitransit/2002/karatnycky_essay2002. pdf.* Retrieved on January 23, 2003.

KRISHNAMURTHY SRIRAMESH

1

A Theoretical Framework for Global Public Relations Research and Practice

Krishnamurthy Sriramesh
Dejan Verčič

As described in the Introduction, there is very little empirical evidence on the nature of public relations in many regions of the world. We believe that the body of knowledge of international public relations is so young that it is very important to have descriptive accounts of public relations practice from individual countries. But we also believe that it is equally important for this body of knowledge to be able help predict the best way to practice public relations in a particular country or region. This is best done by identifying relationships between public relations and other relevant variables. Therefore, in planning this book, we asked contributing authors to not only describe public relations practice in their countries but to attempt to make informed linkages between environmental variables and the profession. We believe that identifying the impact of environmental variables on public relations practice helps increase our ability to predict which strategies and techniques are better suited to a particular organizational environment.

We believe that the framework presented in this chapter, which was followed in each of the 17 individual country chapters, can be a good starting point in exploring the relationship between organizational environments and their public relations practices. We also recognize that as we begin to build the body of knowledge on international public relations, other variables may emerge. We note that because there is little empirical evidence on the linkage between environmental variables and public relations practice from most regions of the world, currently, we can only conceptualize the linkage between these variables and public relations or base our analyses on anecdotal evidence. Nevertheless, in our opinion, this is a significant first step toward building a comprehensive knowledge base of international public relations.

BACKGROUND

We relied on the three-nation study commonly known as the *Excellence Project* (J. E. Grunig, 1992b) in proposing a three-factor framework for this book that attempts to link environmental variables with public relations practice. Based on the Excellence Project, Verčič, L. A. Grunig, and J. E. Grunig (1996) identified nine generic principles that, they argued, could be used to set up global public relations practices. The authors also suggested that five environmental variables can be used by public relations practitioners to design public relations strategies specific to a given country. The five variables are: political ideology, economic system (including the level of development of the country's economy), degree of activism (the extent of pressure organizations face from activists), culture, and media system (the nature of the media environment in a country).

Culbertson and Jeffers (1992) highlighted the importance of what they called social, political and economic contexts (SPE) to public relations practice at the same time that the Excellence Study was underway, but they did not explore these contexts internationally. As a follow-up to their initial article, Culbertson, Jeffers, Stone, and Terrell (1993) explained SPE contexts as follows:

> As we write this, our definition of elements in the SPE context is still evolving.... As we studied, the social context occupied us more than the political and economic ones. Perhaps this stemmed in part from the fact that, on the whole, we were trained in communication and social psychology not in political science or economics.... However, as we proceeded, we decided there was a deeper reason. Consideration of the political context focuses on gaining support from officials—on power relationships having to do with clients and the public at large. And economic context has to do largely with the distribution of resources. (p. 5)

We agree with J. E. Grunig (1992b) and Culbertson et al. (1993) that these environmental variables have a significant impact on public relations. We note, however, that despite the significance of these variables, 11 years later, few studies have empirically linked environmental variables with public relations. The only exception is culture, which has been linked to public relations, either conceptually or based on empirical evidence, by a few studies in the past 11 years (e.g., Huang, 2000; Rhee, 1999, 2002; Sriramesh, 1992, 1996; Sriramesh, J. E. Grunig, & Dozier, 1996; Sriramesh, Kim, & Takasaki, 1999; Sriramesh & Takasaki, 1999; Sriramesh & White, 1992). The linkage between other environmental variables and public relations remains to be empirically investigated, providing public relations scholars with a challenge and an opportunity.

In this chapter, we present the logic behind linking these variables with public relations and suggest ways of operationalizing each variable as a prelude to future studies. In doing so, we collapsed these five variables into three factors: a country's infrastructure, media environment, and societal culture. We describe each of these three interrelated factors and conceptually identify their relationship with international public relations.

INFRASTRUCTURE AND INTERNATIONAL PUBLIC RELATIONS

We believe that three infrastructural ingredients are key to international public relations: a nation's political system, its level of economic development, and the level of activism prevalent in that country. Each of these variables influences the nature of public relations practiced in a country and each is very closely interrelated, which is why we have collapsed them into one factor. However, we do recognize that each of these factors influences and is influenced by a country's culture and media environment—the other two environmental factors that will be reviewed later in this chapter.

Political System

A country's political system influences its social structure. There is little doubt that public relations practice thrives on public opinion, which would lead one to conclude that only pluralistic societies offer an environment that is conducive for practicing strategic public relations. Available evidence (some of which is described in the chapters in this book) suggests that in societies whose political systems do not value public opinion, the nature of public relations is not sophisticated and tends to be one-way propagandistic in nature. However, democracy comes in many forms as is evident in the fact that almost each of the 192 current member states of the United Nations claims to be a democracy. These countries are able to make the claim because they have their own definitions of what democracy is or should be. As described in the Introduction to this book, comprehensive reports such as the one from Freedom House Karatnycky, A. (2002) are indicative of the variability in the definition and practice of democracy around the world. Such descriptions are invariably helpful to international public relations scholars and professionals.

As noted in the introduction, since the beginning of the 1990s, the world has been evolving rather rapidly, with many countries undergoing political, economic, and societal changes. In particular, many former Soviet bloc countries have embarked on the road toward democratization and market reforms and now have economies in transition. These countries are currently in various stages of democratization and market reforms, offering varied opportunities and challenges to public relations professionals. For many of these countries, the transition has neither been smooth nor consistent. Because the political environment determines the nature of public relations one can practice there, it is essential to conduct comparative research on the linkage between various political ideologies and public relations, a relationship that is yet to be empirically explored in most countries— including countries in transition.

Political ideology is closely linked to economic development because political conditions affect economic decision making and vice versa in every country. Furthermore, the dynamics between political and economic systems often determine a nation's stability and further economic development. Examples abound of how lack of economic development often leaves a society mired in a web of illiteracy and poverty, preventing strong democratic political institutions from taking roots.

Typically, three types of political systems have been used in the past: Western industrialized democracies (the First World); Communist states (Second World); and the predominantly non-Western, developing countries (Third World). The collapse of the Soviet Union and its impact on the global power structure, among other things, makes this distinction moot. Furthermore, there are many newly industrializing countries that no longer fit the definition of developing countries but are also not democratic in the Western sense and, therefore, cannot be categorized as belonging to the First World, according to the aforementioned definition (Wilson, 1995).

Simon and Gartzke (1996) differentiated between political environments on a bipolar continuum ranging from democratic to authoritarian. However, this categorization is too simplistic to provide details about the many nuances and the various political and economic challenges and experiences that many countries experience. The world has witnessed significant political changes in recent years. Thus, we should have a more accurate way to classify the political systems of nations. In fact, the 20th century has been a period of democratization of the world. According to the Freedom House, at the beginning of the 20th century, there was not a single country that could be labeled a democracy! Even countries such as the United States and Britain were not true democracies because they did not have universal suffrage at the beginning of the 20th century.

One of the most comprehensive classifications of political systems, one that we prefer over the others, was proposed by the Freedom House in a project titled: "Democracy's Century: A Survey of Global Political Change in the 20th Century" (http://www.freedomhouse.org/reports/century.html#project). This project examined the political systems that governed the world in the 20th century at the beginning, middle, and turn of the century. In doing so, the study offered the following seven types of political systems:

1. *Democracies* wherein multiple parties and individuals compete in open elections to earn the right to rule for a predetermined period (unless there is a constitutionally mandated reason for earlier elections). In democracies, opposition parties have a fair chance of winning power or participate in power sharing as members of a coalition government.

2. *Restricted democratic practices* in which a single party controls key constituencies such as political institutions, the media, and the electoral process to maintain the status quo. Included in this list are countries that deny voting rights based on factors such as gender, race, and socioeconomic status.

3. *Monarchies* consisting of *constitutional monarchies* (a constitution specifies the powers of the monarch often devolving some power to elected and other bodies), *traditional monarchies*, and *absolute monarchies* (where the monarch rules as despot).

4. *Authoritarian regimes* that usually are one-party states or military dictatorships noted for significant human rights violations.

5. *Totalitarian regimes* wherein a single political party establishes total control over the society including intrusion into private life (e.g., Marxist–Leninist and national socialist regimes).

6. *Colonial and imperial dependencies*, which are ruled by large imperial systems, mostly seen in the first half of the 20th century.

7. *Protectorates* that, of their own accord, request protection from a more powerful neighbor or are temporarily placed under protection by the international community.

Using this classification system, Freedom House synthesized the shift in political systems from the beginning of the 20th century, in 1950, and in 1999.

Table 1.1 reveals that in 1900 there were no true democracies in a world that was dominated by monarchies and empires. Twenty-five countries came closest to being labeled as countries with restricted democratic practices (e.g., no universal suffrage), accounting for just 12.4% of the world population. By mid-century, the postwar world had seen the fall of Nazi and fascist totalitarianism and a spurt in decolonization in many parts of the world. In 1950, there were 22 democracies (covering 31% of the world population) and an additional 21 states with restricted democratic practices (11.9% of the global population). However, by the end of the century, democracy had spread to much of the former Communist world and many regions of Latin America, Africa, and Asia, with electoral democracies making up 120 (62.5% of the world population) of the 192 countries that existed then. Note, however, that of these 120 electoral democracies, only 85 (38% of the world's population) were categorized by Freedom House as liberal democracies

TABLE 1.1

Tracking Polity in the 20th Century

	Sovereign States and Colonial Units			Population (Millions)		
	2000	1950	1900	2000	1950	1900
DEM	120 (62.5%)	22 (14.3%)	0 (0.0%)	3,439.4 (58.2%)	743.2 (31.0%)	0 (0.0%)
RDP	16 (8.3%)	21 (13.6%)	25 (19.2%)	297.6 (5.0%)	285.9 (11.9%)	206.6 (12.4%)
CM	0 (0.0%)	9 (5.8%)	19 (14.6%)	0 (0.0%)	77.9 (3.2%)	299.3 (17.9%)
TM	10 (5.2%)	4 (2.6%)	6 (4.6%)	58.2 (1.0%)	16.4 (0.7%)	22.5 (1.3%)
AM	0 (0.0%)	2 (1.3%)	5 (3.8%)	0 (0.0%)	12.5 (0.5%)	610.0 (36.6%)
AR	39 (20.3%)	10 (6.5%)	0 (0.0%)	1,967.7 (33.3%)	122.0 (5.1%)	0 (0.0%)
TOT	5 (2.6%)	12 (7.8%)	0 (0.0%)	141.9 (2.4%)	816.7 (34.1%)	0 (0.0%)
C	0 (0.0%)	43 (27.9%)	55 (42.3%)	0 (0.0%)	118.4 (4.9%)	503.1 (30.2%)
P	2 (1.0%)	31 (20.1%)	20 (15.4%)	4.8 (0.1%)	203.3 (8.5%)	26.5 (1.6%)
Total	192 (100.0%)	154 (100.0%)	130 (100.0%)	5,909.6 (100.0%)	2,396.3 (100.0%)	1,668.0 (100.0%)

Note. DEM = democracy; RDP = restricted democratic practice; CM = constitutional monarchy; TM = traditional monarchy; AM = absolute monarchy; AR = authoritarian regime; TOT = totalitarian regime; C = colonial dependency; P = protectorate.

(*Source*: Freedom House, 2000)

according to a more stringent benchmark that required countries to also respect basic human rights and uphold the law in addition to holding elections.

Among other factors, Freedom House's study highlights the fact that the 20th century has been the harbinger of pluralism in the world. It may be hard to fathom that there was no truly democratic country in the world just a century ago! In a century, the world has come a long way, although much more needs to be accomplished. The study also highlights the fact that, whereas all societies have political institutions, the means for attaining political power varies among countries. Political power may come as a birthright (as in monarchies or the political dynasties in nepotistic cultures), through association with other power elite (as in totalitarian regimes), or through complex political rituals (e.g., elections), which may have various levels of openness and fairness. Although these distinctions do not specifically state it, a number of nations of the world recently leaned toward a theocratic form of governance.

The significance of these shifts to public relations lies in the fact that the Western definition of public relations assumes a democratic political structure in which competing groups seek legitimacy and power thorough public opinion and elections, which is not always the norm in many parts of the world. Particularly difficult to discern are emerging democracies where alternative views may be encouraged in theory but not in practice, resulting in various forms of covert and overt forms of self-, social, and government censorship.

The impact that each of these political systems has on public relations is yet to be fully explored. However, it is clear that, in addition to being an era of democratization of much of the world, the 20th century has by all accounts witnessed the growth of modern public relations. With an increase in the level of democratization of a society (e.g., the United States and Britain) has come a concomitant increase in the level of sophistication of the public relations profession. There is little doubt, however, that strategic public relations flourishes in pluralistic societies. As the succeeding chapters of this book will affirm, democratization has spurred the growth of public relations in many regions of the world. Now is the time to analyze empirically how the other types of political systems affect public relations practices and the impact that public relations has in the process of democratization and in maintaining a particular political system.

Level of Economic Development

Closely linked to a country's political system, a country's economic development provides
public relations professionals opportunities as well as challenges. There is little doubt that
a more pluralistic political philosophy favors greater economic freedom. By extension, developed (market) economies tend to favor strategic public relations more than developing
(managed) ones. However, public relations has yet to be widely considered a core organizational function in organizations of even developed economies. Instead, it languishes as a
superfluous appendage in organizations around the world, including developed nations. As
a result, the predominant mindset is that scarce resources need to be spent on more pressing
needs that are central to an organization's activities and bring tangible returns. Despite
this lacuna, strategic public relations generally thrives in developed countries because the
more developed an economy is, the greater the number of organizational players and the
higher the level of competition among organizations. These multiple suppliers of goods
and services obviously need to compete for public attention, approval, and support—a
prime reason to employ public relations professionals as in-house staff or as consultants.

Furthermore, the political system of a country also determines the extent to which private
entrepreneurship is valued and encouraged. Prior to the establishment of the World Trade
Organization (WTO), most developing countries, even those claiming to be democracies,
had favored managed economies built mostly around public sector enterprises that often
operated as monopolies. In countries with vast public sectors, the government becomes
the primary, if not the sole, relevant public for a public relations professional. Even after
the establishment of the WTO, countries have been slower in switching to market-oriented
systems. But the change from public sector to private sector investment has begun in many
of the 144 WTO members. This is bound to create fresh opportunities and challenges for
the international public relations professional.

As reviewed in the section "The media and public relations," the level of economic
development of a country directly affects variables such as poverty and illiteracy. These two
potent variables have a direct impact on the strategies and techniques that public relations
professionals may use in a country. The lack of an adequate communication infrastructure
also severely challenges the international public relations professional who attempts to
conduct information campaigns in developing nations, where folk and indigenous methods
of communication may be the more effective choice.

Activism

We clubbed activism with political system and level of development because we believe
that the three are closely interrelated. A country's political system has a direct influence on
the extent of activism in that country because only pluralistic societies tolerate activism of
any sort. Furthermore, a country's level of economic development also directly influences
the level and nature of activism in that country. In most developing nations, people are busy
fighting to earn the next square meal for their family, leaving them little time or inclination
for participating in other activities. To the extent that their livelihood is threatened, the
populace of these nations may engage in activism—predominantly labor unionism. As
stated earlier, the 20th century has been a period of democratization of the world. Many
developing nations, particularly Africa and Asia, engaged in massive social movements
to gain independence from colonial rule. But, after gaining independence, the level of
activism in these countries has declined partly due to a lack of democratic traditions but
also due to economic factors.

Activism provides public relations professionals challenges and opportunities. These days, it is not uncommon to find public relations professionals representing both sides of an activist movement. Chapter 24 of this book describes some of the international activities of nongovernmental organizations as activists. The public relations body of knowledge has not paid much attention to the relationship between activism and public relations. Young as it is, the body of knowledge of international public relations has yet to study the linkage between activism and public relations.

L. A. Grunig (1992) stated that activist groups are motivated to "improve the functioning of the organization from outside (p. 504)." Organizations have continued to face increasing pressure from activists groups who often take various names such as pressure groups, special interest groups, or social movements. Whereas activists believe that they force organizations (especially corporations) to be socially responsible by challenging them, organizations seek to gain autonomy from such challenges that usually drain resources from a corporation's bottom line. Mintzberg (1983) contended that almost every type of organization faces pressures from activist groups at one time or the other. In addition to activism against corporations, one encounters activism in other forms.

Social movements have won nations freedom from colonial rule, much of which happened after World War II principally in Africa and Asia. Theocratic activism has also influenced the political and social structures of many nations and continues to be a potent factor today in many regions of the world. The recent spate of terrorism around the world is evidence of theocratic activism. Labor activism has often played a key role in the economic and industrial development of countries. Therefore, it is critical for us to assess the nature of activism prevalent in a society and determine how it influences the public relations activities of that country. The international public relations professional cannot ignore activism on a global level.

Legal System

The legal system of a country is also closely linked to the level of political and economic development and poses many challenges to the international public relations professional. Every culture has its ways of regulating and enforcing behavior among its citizens and organizations. Whereas legal codes tend to be explicit in Western democracies, the legal structure may appear to be more nebulous and embedded in the social or religious codes in many other regions of the world, which means we need to study the impact of theocracies on public relations as well. Table 1.2 depicts ways of operationalizing these infrastructure variables.

CULTURE

Communication influences and is influenced by culture. Most definitions of the term public relations originating in the United States and Europe recognize that communication (both mass and interpersonal) is the foundation of the public relations profession and is a means to the end of building relationships between organizations and their relevant publics (e.g., Cutlip, Center, & Broom, 2000; J. E. Grunig & Hunt, 1984, Verčič, van Ruler, Butschi, & Flodin, 2001). Logically, culture should affect public relations, and public relations helps alter culture.

Despite this logical linkage between the two, it is only in the last decade that public relations scholars have attempted to study the impact of culture on organizational processes (e.g., Huang, 2000; Rhee, 1999, 2002; Sriramesh, 1992; Sriramesh, 1999; Sriramesh &

TABLE 1.2
The Infrastructure and International Public Relations

Political system
   What is the basic political structure? Democratic, authoritarian, or theocratic, totalitarian, other?
   Is there political pluralism in the society?
   Is public opinion valued?
   How strong are the political institutions?
   What role do formal institutions play in political decision making?
   Do organizations have avenues of influencing public policy making?

Economic system and level of development
   What is the level of economic development?
   Is economic decisionmaking centralized in the government?
   To what extent has membership in WTO changed the environment for private investment?
   What is the power of the private sector in determining public policy?
   What is the relationship between the private and the public sector?
   What is the level of technological development that may be relevant to public relations professionals?

Legal
   How strong and independent is the judiciary?
   What is the relationship between the judiciary and the legislative and executive branches?
   Are there specific legal codes dealing with communication activities of organizations?
   Does the country have legal codes to regulate the media?

Activism
   Historically, what role has activism played in a country (e.g., social movements)?
   What is the nature of activism prevalent in a country currently?
   Are labor unions major forces in the society?
   Currently, what tools do corporations use to deal with activism?

Takasaki, 1999). These studies have empirically tested the relationship between this important variable and public relations. But culture is so fundamental to communication that it behooves scholars of international public relations to study how this variable affects the choice of public relations strategies and tactics in different regions of the world. Many more empirical analyses of the linkage between public relations and culture are needed.

Before one can identify the relationship between culture and public relations, one needs to understand the term *culture* and all of its dimensions. Even in the field of anthropology, in which the central focus involves studying culture, there is no universally accepted definition of the term. Kroeber and Kluckhohn (1952) listed 164 definitions of the term and found 300 other variations of these definitions, thus highlighting the malleable nature of this vital concept! Tylor (1871) provided the first comprehensive definition of culture as "that complex whole which includes knowledge, belief, art, morals, custom, and any other capabilities and habits acquired by man as a member of society" (p. 1). For Kroeber and Kluckhohn, the culture concept encompasses a "set of attributes and products of human societies, and therewith of mankind, which are extrasomatic and transmissible by mechanisms other than biological heredity" (p. 145).

Determinants of Culture

Having defined the term culture, one needs to ask how societies adopt one or more cultures. Kaplan and Manners (1972) identified four determinants of societal culture. First, *technoeconomics* refers to the level of economic development of a society, which invariably influences the culture of each society. We already discussed this determinant as the first environmental factor. Technologies such as satellite communication and the Internet continue to play a role in shaping cultures in the modern world and have a direct influence on public relations as well. Second, *social structure* is indicative of the social institutions that define relationships among different members or groups of a society. Feudal, caste, and class stratifications are examples of social structure. Third, *ideology* refers to the values, norms, worldviews, knowledge, philosophies, and religious principles that the members of a society espouse. Historically, humans have fought over religious philosophies, and they continue to do so. Theocracy is increasingly becoming an issue in international relations because of its impact on sociopolitical systems. Fourth, *personality* refers to the traits of individuals of a society based especially on the child-rearing practices of that society as well as acculturation in school and the workplace.

These four determinants continue to play a vital role in determining the formation of culture in modern societies. In turn, societal culture seeps into organizations through employees who have different family and other backgrounds, turning each organization into a unique corporate culture (Sriramesh et al., 1996).

Dimensions of Societal Culture

Having identified the factors that determine the cultures of a society, it is important to understand how culture is manifested in a society before we link these dimensions of culture with public relations variables. Admitting that he had not been able to measure culture completely because of its malleability as well as our shifting conceptual perspectives in understanding it, Hofstede (1980, 2001) identified five dimensions of societal culture.

The first dimension, *power distance*, describes the vertical stratification of a society wherein members of different strata are accorded different levels of importance and status. The class system of feudal Europe and the caste system in India are examples of power distance. *Social mobility*, the ease with which members of lower strata can achieve a higher status in society, is another variable that corresponds to power distance. Typically, societies with lower power distance tend to have relatively higher social mobility and vice versa. Societies with higher power distance also tend to have more authoritarian organizational structures. The second dimension, *collectivism*, refers to the extent to which members of a culture value the individual over the collectivity. The communes of China, for example, clearly place the welfare of the collectivity over that of the individual. In collectivist societies, organizational employees tend to have greater loyalty to the organization and think in terms of group goals rather than individual accomplishments. Individualistic cultures foster more calculative organizational cultures in which individual employees think more in terms of individual benefits rather than the growth of the collectivity.

The third dimension, *masculinity–femininity*, refers to the gender-based assignment of roles in a society. The extent to which gender plays a role in determining one's status in the organization clearly affects all facets of organizational behavior. This is especially true of the public relations profession because of the feminization of the workforce in many countries, as described in some of the chapters in this book and elsewhere (e.g., Grunig, L. A., Toth, E. L., & Hon, L. C., 2000). The fourth dimension, *uncertainty avoidance*, refers to the extent to which members of a culture can tolerate and cope with ambiguity. Humans have used technology (particularly automation), rites and rituals (a facet of corporate culture), and formalization (also an aspect of corporate culture) to cope with ambiguity in organizations. Furthermore, high-context cultures are known to tolerate greater levels of ambiguity than low-context cultures (Hall & Hall, 1990). The fifth cultural dimension, initially labeled *Confucian dynamism* but later renamed *long-term orientation*, refers to the tendency where a collectivity values long-term commitments and tradition. In an organizational context, this orientation results in a strong work ethic among employees who also expect rewards in a more distant future rather than more immediate returns. However, change also occurs more slowly in such cultures as opposed to those with lower levels of long-term orientation where change can occur more rapidly because long-term traditions do not obstruct the process of change.

Scholars have identified other cultural dimensions as well. Tayeb (1988) identified *interpersonal trust*, the propensity among members of a culture to place trust readily in fellow humans, as another cultural dimension. Kakar (1971) found *deference to authority*, where subordinates readily accept a superior, to be particularly evident in many cultures in Asia. Sriramesh and Takasaki (1999) found the Japanese concept of *amae* to be a manifestation of deference to authority. They also identified the concept of *wa* (harmony) as influencing communication among the Japanese.

In public relations literature, J. E. Grunig (1992) used two worldviews, symmetrical and asymmetrical, to explain the logic behind the choice of public relations strategies and processes by organizations. Although he did not use the term *culture* to refer to them, conceptual linkages can be made between these two worldviews and culture because humans are so greatly influenced by their environment (culture), which shapes their worldviews.

Corporate Culture

The review of societal culture leads us to the next important step in identifying the linkage between culture and public relations—identifying the influence that societal culture has on organizational culture or corporate culture. Sriramesh, J. E. Grunig, and Buffington (1992) observed that whereas corporate culture is influenced by societal culture, it is also distinct from it. Organizations in the same societal culture have distinctive corporate personalities, which are often based on factors such as the charismatic leadership of the organization, age of the organization, organizational type, and size. Schein (1985) identified three reasons for studying the culture of organizations. First, corporate culture is highly visible and can be felt by all observers and participants. Next, by understanding corporate culture, one can evaluate organizational performance and gain knowledge of how people behave and perceive it. Finally, corporate culture provides organizational members with a common frame of reference, a key ingredient of cohesiveness in organizations.

Corporate culture has also been referred to as the rules of the game for getting along in an organization and the ropes that members of an organization share. Scholars such as J. Martin and Siehl (1983) also noted that organizations do not always have a single culture. Organizations often have subcultures and countercultures. Certain subcultures may enhance the mainstream culture by advocating loyalty to core organizational values (*enhancing subculture*), be slightly different from the mainstream culture (*orthogonal subculture*), or completely at odds with the mainstream culture of the organization (*countercultures*). If the counterculture of an organization has a charismatic leader, it may threaten the mainstream culture itself and lead to core changes in organizations.

Glaser (1994) stressed cooperative relationships among organizational employees as a key to organizational success. Needless to say, such cooperation can only be found in an organization that also values communication, the concept that is of primary interest to public relations professionals. The author found that after 3 years of enhanced communication, the sample organization that was afflicted with dissension and mistrust was transformed into one where employees had mutual respect for one another and were more open to teamwork. Communication is the underpinning of a strong corporate culture and is the "normative glue" (Tichy, 1982) that holds an organization together.

What impact does corporate culture have on organizational health? DiSanza's (1995) ethnographic study chronicled the problems encountered by organizations with weak cultures. The author studied the employee orientation procedures of a bank and identified serious flaws in communication, which resulted in low employee morale and poor customer service. Weak corporate cultures are more prone to developing the kinds of orthogonal and countercultures that J. Martin and C. Siehl (1983) identified. Holladay and Coombs (1993) conducted an experimental study investigating the role that delivery of a message plays in employees' perceptions of the chief executive officer's charisma. They found that differences in message delivery seriously impacted the credibility of the leader among employees. Therefore, we can conclude that both corporate and societal culture have a significant impact on communication in general and public relations in particular. Studying the impact of culture on public relations processes is of vital importance to the field of public relations.

How can international public relations professionals use this understanding of societal and corporate culture? In other words, what is the linkage between societal and corporate culture and public relations practice? Acculturation, which may take place at home, school, and work, instills in humans the value system that affects their daily lives. The values that managers espouse clearly affect the choices they make in charting organizational strategies including public relations. Similarly, other publics within a society also carry values that in turn influence their receptivity to organizational messages and their perception of and behavior toward the organization and in other public settings. Therefore, we need to operationalize culture as a variable and identify the impact it has on public relations practice in a given society. Note that whereas the contributions of scholars such as Hofstede (2001) are significant and useful, one must also not discount the importance of cultural dimensions that are unique to a particular country. It is important to identify cultural dimensions that are generic across cultures (e.g., the ones Hofstede, 2001 identified) and dimensions that are unique to a particular culture (e.g., the concept of *wa* and *amae* in Japanese culture). Drawing from this review of literature, the factors noted in Table 1.3 provide a good foundation on which to build the linkage between public relations and culture.

THE MEDIA AND PUBLIC RELATIONS

One cannot overstate the critical relationship between the mass media and public relations. There is near unanimity among authors of public relations literature that the media and public relations have a symbiotic, sometimes contentious, relationship. Most public relations practitioners would agree that media relations accounts for a significant portion of their public relations efforts because they wish to use the media for publicity purposes. However, public relations professionals also serve the media by providing them with information subsidies.

Wilcox and Nolte (1997) observed that despite the continued tension between public relations professionals and journalists, the symbiosis in the relationship requires that they maintain "a solid working relationship based on mutual respect for each other's work" (p. 285). Newsom, Turk, and Kruckeberg (2000) stated that for public relations professionals, "good working relationships with media personnel are always important for smooth functioning..." (p. 395). In their book, *On Deadline*, Howard and Mathews (2000) stressed the need to practice strategic media relations as part of an overall program

TABLE 1.3

Culture and International Public Relations

Stratification

What is the level of social stratification in your society?

How does such stratification manifest itself in organizational activities and in public relations?

What is the level of social mobility in your culture?

Uncertainty (low vs. high context)

How tolerant is your culture to uncertainty and ambiguity?

In organizational communication, are meanings explicit in messages or are they based largely on the context of a situation?

Gender-based role identification

To what extent does gender play a role in assigning organizational roles in your country?

How does this affect public relations practice?

Collectivism

In your culture, are the interests of the collectivity valued over that of the individual?

How does this affect public relations activities?

Orientation to life

Is your culture oriented toward short-term goals or long-term ones?

How does such an orientation to life affect organizational activities in general and public relations in particular?

Interpersonal trust

What level of interpersonal trust does your culture allow within organizational settings?

Deference to authority

Does your culture encourage (expect) deference to superiors in social settings?

If so, how does this manifest itself in organizational communication contexts?

Other

What are the other cultural idiosyncracies that are specific to your country that you believe influence public relations practice?

of public relations and proposed several aspects of effective media relations, such as the characteristics of a good spokesperson. Cutlip, Center, and Broom (2000) reiterated that public relations practitioners will find media relations to be an "economical, effective method of communicating with large and widely dispersed publics" (p. 304).

Mass Media and the Images of Nations

Central to the assertions of the aforementioned public relations scholars is their recognition of the power of mass media to influence public opinion and shape public discourse. Mass media have a powerful influence on organizational activities in general and public relations in particular. Larson and Rivenburgh (1991) recognized the potency of mass media by linking media coverage with the international images of nations. The authors studied the television coverage of the opening ceremony of the Seoul Olympics by the British Broadcasting Corporation, the United States' National Broadcasting Corporation, and Australia's TEN network and concluded that a large majority of developing countries received no mention at all during these telecasts, whereas a few developed countries received very positive and extended coverage. The authors concluded that the media do play a powerful role in influencing how individual countries are perceived globally. Typically, developing nations are stereotyped positively by most media, whereas developing countries are generally negatively portrayed. The findings by Larson and Rivenburgh (1991) are of particular relevance to international public relations practitioners who are often called on by developing countries to change the way they are perceived by the public of developed nations.

Kunczik (1993), who discusses at length the use of the media by nations for public relations purposes in chapter 19, studied the news and advertisements of developing countries in German media and remarked: "since most people's scope of experience is naturally very limited, and their knowledge of complex social processes in other countries comes mainly from the mass media, there is always the danger that, due to the process of news selection, there are differences between 'real reality' and 'media reality'" (p. 1).

Kunczik concluded that many developing countries often view fighting negative media stereotyping as a losing battle, one that they often choose not to wage primarily due to a lack of resources. But other developing nations recognize the need to be heard in the developed world as part of their public diplomacy because they desperately need foreign aid from developed countries and loans from world bodies such as the International Monetary Fund (IMF) or the World Bank, which requires support from key developed countries such as the United States. Because of the powerful effects that the media have in shaping public opinion nationally and internationally, public relations professionals have given primacy to media relations. To conduct effective media relations, international public relations practitioners need to understand the nature of media environment in a particular country. Only then can they develop strategies for conducting effective media relations suitable to that environment.

Currently, the only source for understanding different global media environments is the body of literature in the field of mass communication that describes normative theories of global media systems first proposed by Siebert, Peterson, and Schramm (1956) and subsequently revised and enhanced by several authors (e.g., Altschull, 1984; Hachten, 1981; L. J. Martin & Choudhary, 1983; Merrill & Lowenstein, 1971).

The media systems concept is outdated because of significant world changes, especially in the 1990s. For example, the fall of the Soviet bloc obviates the Soviet media theory, and the fall of Communism in all but a few isolated countries makes the Communist media theory of limited use. Therefore, there is a need to reconceptualize the media environment around the world. Sriramesh (1999) proposed a framework of three factors (media control, media outreach, and media access) that should help public relations professionals design media relations strategies that are appropriate to different media environments. Adhering to this framework may make it easier for international public relations professionals to maintain effective channels of communication between their client organizations and relevant media around the world. Furthermore, the framework should help researchers study the nexus between the media and effective public relations practices in different countries.

Media Control

Maintaining effective media relations requires that public relations professionals understand who controls the media organizations in a country and whether such control extends to editorial content. The latest Freedom House survey of media freedom found that 75 countries had media systems that could be classified as free, 50 had partly free media, and 61 were not free (Sussman & Karlekar, 2002). The study found that the number of countries with free media was the highest it has ever been. However, it is interesting to note that 111 countries still have media systems that are either partly free or not free. In his introduction to the 1999 World Press Survey conducted by Freedom House, Sussman (1999) stated that "Not until the fall of the Berlin Wall in 1989 did those areas of the world under Communist domination begin to experience some freedom of the news media" (p. 1). The author also reported that in many regions of the world press freedom was weakened by inexperienced journalists and partisan control of the media. In Freedom House's 2002 survey, there was clear evidence that press freedom was an outcome of more pluralistic regimes.

Around the world, media ownership is limited to a few principal sources depending on the nature of political system and level of economic development of the country, two variables described earlier in this chapter. In developed democracies, it is the capitalistic entrepreneur who invests in the media, sustaining media operations principally through sale of advertisements and relying, to a relatively smaller extent, on revenue from subscriptions. There is minimal direct or indirect fiduciary relationship between the government and media organizations in capitalistic systems. The need to sell news as a commodity is naturally strong in such an environment, leading to interesting choices in coverage.

On the contrary, in developing countries, one can often discern media ownership in the hands of political interests as well as the elites of the society. Maintaining the status quo is often paramount for these media moguls as an incentive to influence media content. The few theocracies of the world provide us examples of the impact of religious interests on media organizations and media content. In most developing countries, the government typically owns the electronic media and often permits private entrepreneurs to own print media.

It is important to recognize that media ownership does not necessarily result in media control. In many developing countries, even though the media may be overtly owned by private interests, they are strictly monitored and controlled through overt and covert means by political or government forces. Sussman (1999) reported that the Freedom House survey had found that "the muzzling of journalists was increasingly accomplished by more subtle, legalistic methods than through violence or outright repression" (p. 1). Government advertisements are a principal method for political rulers to maintain control over media content. Because advertising income forms the bulk of revenue (and, therefore, the basic means of survival) for a large section of private media in many developing countries, this subtle method of control is often very effective. Controlling the supply of the means of production such as newsprint (often imported by the government and sold to media organizations at subsidized costs) is another effective way for governments to maintain their control over privately owned mass media. It is also not uncommon for political rulers of developing nations to own their own media outlets (usually print media) and use them for controlling public opinion with the sole purpose of maintaining the status quo.

Editorial freedom is directly proportional to the level of economic development of a country. It is the lack of resources and infrastructure that have limited editorial freedom in developing nations. In their study of the relationship between press freedom and social development in 134 nations, Weaver, Buddenbaum, and Fair (1985) concluded that "the stronger the media are economically, the less likely the government is to control these media" (p. 113). The reality is that, in most developing countries, economic independence is a mirage for most media outlets, which also results in various limitations on editorial freedom. As discussed in chapter 20, the proposal for a New World Information Order from developing countries was derailed primarily on the basic of media economics and concomitant issues pertaining to editorial freedom.

Media Outreach

Placing a story in the media is often a significant part of the media relations activity for the savvy public relations professional. Merely placing a message in a medium does not offer the "magic bullet" effect of having intended effects on one's audience. Audience exposure to messages is only the first step. Other intervening steps such as message comprehension or changes in level of knowledge and attitude need to be traversed by audiences before changes can occur in their behavior. Recognizing this, international public relations practitioners need to understand the extent of *media outreach* (media saturation) in the countries where they operate as a gauge of message exposure among their audiences. It is safe to assume that most public relations professionals desire to use the media for disseminating information to as wide an audience as possible. Therefore, in their symbiotic relationship of providing information subsidies to media outlets, public relations professionals seek unpaid publicity for their organizations and clients.

However, it is critical for international public relations professionals to note that, despite the perceived power of the media, these purveyors of information may not provide an effective means for wide dissemination of organizational messages in every country. In fact, in most developing countries, media reach a fairly homogeneous, relatively small segment of the total population because of two principal factors: illiteracy and poverty. A country's high rate of illiteracy seriously inhibits the use of the print media. Consequently, media relations in such environments will be limited in scope to specific groups of urban, educated, fairly affluent, middle-class citizens (the elites of the society). To reach the larger populace effectively, the international public relations consultant will have to think of other media that reach out to these untapped publics. In larger developing nations, the lack of infrastructure constrains timely distribution of print media messages to far-flung places.

When illiteracy hinders the dispersion of information through the print media, the next logical alternative for the international public relations professional would be to use electronic media. However, television sets and radios often prove too expensive for a large section of citizens who have limited resources. Inadequate infrastructure, such as lack of rural electrification, also contributes to limiting access to the electronic media for even wealthier rural residents. Therefore, the efficacy of electronic media for conducting public information or other public relations campaigns is open to question. International public relations professionals must recognize that regardless of the sophistication of the media relations they may practice, the efficacy of these efforts is limited to the segment of the population that the media of a country can reach.

However, there are signs of hope for the international public relations practitioner who has to operate in a developing country that has these impediments. Lee (1994) examined the development of mass media in the People's Republic of China since 1949 and found that the country's spurt in economic growth in the 1980s resulted in a sudden increase in television ownership. The author concluded that there seems to be a symbiotic relationship between economic growth and television ownership. He speculated that whereas economic growth has led to increased television ownership, television may also have helped spur economic growth by having unplanned effects such as the creation of demand for products and services, acceleration of electrification in rural areas, and the creation of a diversion keeping people away from "the delicate problems of government and politics" (p. 34).

When local conditions limit the use of Western-style media such as television, radio, newspapers, and magazines, what options do international public relations practitioners have in their effort to reach a wider audience in developing societies? In India, for example, many public information campaigns have used folk media such as docudramas, dances, skits, and plays in rural areas (Sriramesh, 1992). A few multinational companies such as makers of toothpaste have used Indian folk media to publicize their products in rural regions with some efficacy. Similar strategies could be used for effective communication with various publics in traditional cultures in other parts of the world as well.

Pratt and Manheim (1988) critiqued the urban bias that is so characteristic of public communication in most of Africa and other developing regions of the world and called for new communication strategies that empower large, neglected segments of the populace. The authors presented a framework of six integrated agendas for conducting communication campaigns that include the use of traditional, indigenous media. However, it is critical that these traditional media be used judiciously. West and Fair (1993) studied the use of modern, popular, and traditional media in Africa and highlighted the pitfalls of the improper use of indigenous African media (or traditional media) for developmental activities.

Media Access

The flip side of media outreach is media access. Whereas media outreach refers to the extent of media saturation in a society, *media access* denotes the extent to which the various segments of a society can approach the media to disseminate messages they deem important. It is imprudent to assume that public access to the media remains constant across societies. Sriramesh and Takasaki (1998), reporting on the nature of Japanese public relations, identified press clubs as interlocutors between the media and other publics, including corporations that might want to gain access to the media. Japanese press clubs

TABLE 1.4

A Framework for Media Relations

Media control
  Are the media of a given country:
    A part of the private sector?
    A part of the public sector (direct or indirect government ownership)?
    Aligned with political parties?
    Aligned with or controlled by theocracy?
  What is the political philosophy of the country?
  How much control do media owners display over editorial freedom?
  How are controls over editorial freedom exercised?
  Are media messages aimed at selling news and information as a commodity (a capitalistic
    orientation), as a method of national development (nation building), or to further theocratic causes?
  What is the media infrastructure of the country?
  Are there established legal and other structures to protect the media from political pressure?
  What kind of professional standards do media persons have?

Media outreach
  What is the ability of the media to diffuse messages to a wide audience?
  Which segments of the population do the print media reach?
  Which segments of the population do the electronic media reach?
  How does the existing infrastructure of the country affect media diffusion?
  What is the rate of illiteracy in the country?
  What is the rate of poverty in the country?

Media access
  What is the level of access that organizations have to mass media in a particular country?
  If there are gatekeepers between the media and other organizations, who are they and how are these
    gatekeepers selected?
  Do different elements of the society such as activists and corporations have direct access to the media?
  Do the media of the country value information subsidies from public relations professionals or
    agencies?

act as gate keepers between the media and organizations, limiting access by organizations and others to the media.

A savvy international public relations practitioner will recognize that just as an organization's access to the media is critical, so is the extent to which the media are accessible to the organization's opponents, principally activists. As described earlier in this chapter, activism has a profound impact on public relations. L. A. Grunig (1992) stated that although activism contributes to the dynamism of an organization's environment thereby posing threats to its autonomy, activists also provide public relations opportunities to an organization. Organizations are forced to communicate symmetrically when activists use the media to challenge an organization's image in the court of public opinion.

The result is that when the media of a society are accessible to individuals or groups with different points of view, the resulting publicity will increase the fluidity of the environment for organizations. The organization then will be forced to use two-way communication for conducting its public relations activities with a variety of publics, rather than focusing on one or two publics. But if various groups that do not conform to the mainstream ideology are not accorded a forum for publicly voicing their agenda, then the extent of pressure on an organization is drastically reduced, calling for minimal sophistication in public relations. Therefore, understanding the extent to which the media are accessible to various activist and other groups in a society helps the international public relations practitioner by providing, among other things, a gauge on the amount of opposition that the environment might pose.

Table 1.4 identifies criteria that help one assess the extent of media control, media outreach, and media access in a given society.

CONCLUSION

This chapter highlights the need for us to not only describe the public relations profession in different parts of the world but also link them to environmental variables to help improve the efficacy of international public relations practices. We presented three broad environmental variables and the conceptual linkages between these variables and public relations. The 17 country-specific chapters of this book have used this framework in presenting the current status of public relations practice in these countries. Much of the information on the linkage between public relations and environmental variables presented here is anecdotal. However, it is no less important given that this is the first time that such a collective effort is being made. What we need are many more studies that will use the framework presented here and additional ones that might be relevant to gather empirical data linking environmental variables with public relations. The outcome of such cross-national efforts would be a robust body of knowledge of international public relations that can prove beneficial not only to students and scholars but also to professionals.

REFERENCES

Altschull, H. J. (1984). *Agents of power.* White Plains, NY: Longman.

Culbertson, H. M., & Jeffers, D. W. (1992). The social, political, and economic contexts: Keys in educating true public relations professionals. *Public Relations Review, (11),* 5–21.

Culbertson, H. M., & Jeffers, D. W., Stone, D. B., & Terrell, M. (1993). *Social, political, and economic contexts in public relations: Theory and cases.* Hillsdale, NJ: Lawrence Erlbaum Associates.

Cutlip, S. M., Center, A. H., Broom, G. M. (2000). *Effective public relations.* Upper Saddle River, NJ: Prentice-Hall.

DiSanza, J. R. (1995). Bank teller organizational assimilation in a system of contradictory practices. *Management Communication Quarterly, 9*, 191–218.

Freedom House. (2000). Democracy's century: A survey of global political change in the 20th century. Available at: *http://www.freedomhouse.org/reports/century.html*, retrieved on January 14, 2003.

Glaser, S. R. (1994). Teamwork and communication: A 3-year case study of change. *Management Communication Quarterly, 7*, 282–296.

Grunig, J. E., and Hunt, T. (1984) 'Managing Public Relations', Holt, Rinehart, & Winston, New York.

Grunig, L. A. (1992). Activism: How it limits the effectiveness of organizations and how excellent public relations departments respond. In J. E. Grunig (Ed.), *Excellence in public relations and communication management* (pp. 503–530). Hillsdale, NJ: Lawrence Erlbaum Associates.

Grunig, J. E. (1992a). The effect of worldviews on public relations theory and practice. In J. E. Grunig (Ed.), *Excellence in public relations and communication management.* Hillsdale, NJ: Lawrence Erlbaum Associates. pp. 31–64.

Grunig, J. E. (1992b). *Excellence in public relations and communication management.* Hillsdale, NJ: Lawrence Erlbaum Associates.

Grunig, L. A., Toth, E. L., & Hon, L. C. (2000). Feminist values in public relations. *Journal of Public Relations Research, 12*(1), pp. 49–68.

Hachten, W. (1981). *The world news prism: Changing media, clashing ideologies.* Ames, IA: Iowa State University Press.

Hall, E. T., & Hall, M. R. (1990). *Understanding cultural differences.* Yarmouth, ME: Intercultural Press.

Hofstede, G. (1980). *Culture's consequences.* Beverly Hills, CA: Sage.

Hofstede, G. (2001). *Culture's consequences: comparing values, behaviors, institutions, and organizations across nations* 2nd ed.) Thousand Oaks, CA: Sage.

Holladay, S. J., & Coombs, W. T. (1993). Communicating visions: An exploration of the role of delivery in the creation of leader charisma. *Management Communication Quarterly, 6*, 405–427.

Howard, C. M., & Mathews, W. K. (2000). *On deadline: Managing media relations* (3rd ed.). Prospect Heights, IL: Waveland Press Inc.

Huang, Y. H. (2000). The personal influence model and *Gao Guanxi* in Taiwan Chinese public relations. *Public Relations Review, 26*, 216–239.

Kakar, S. (1971). The theme of authority in social relations in India. *Journal of Social Psychology, 84*, 93–101.

Kaplan, D., & Manners, R. A. (1972). *Culture theory.* Englewood Cliffs, NJ: Prentice-Hall.

Karatnycky, A. (2002). Nations in transit 2002: A mixed picture of change. Available at: *http://www. freedomhouse.org/research/nitransit/2002/karatnycky essay2002.pdf*, retrieved on January 14, 2003.

Kroeber, A. L., & Kluckhohn, C. (1952). Culture: A critical review of concepts and definitions. *Papers of the Peabody Museum of American Archeology and Ethnology, 47*(1). Cambridge, MA: Harvard University.

Kunczik, M. (1993, November). *Public relations advertisements of foreign countries in Germany with special reference to developing countries: Results of a content analysis.* Paper presented at the international conference of the Association for the Advancement of Policy, Research and Development in the Third World, Cairo, Egypt.

Larson, J., & Rivenburgh, N. (1991). A comparative analysis of Australian, United States, and British telecasts of the Seoul Olympic Opening Ceremony. *Journal of Broadcasting and Electronic Media, 35*(1), 75–94.

Lee, P. (1994). Mass communication and national development in China: Media roles reconsidered. *Journal of Communication, 44*(3), 22–37.

Martin, J., & Siehl, C. (1983). Organizational culture and counterculture: An uneasy symbiosis. *Organizational Dynamics*, 52–63.

Martin, L. J., & Chaudhary, A. G. (1983). *Comparative mass media ystems.* White Plains, NY: Longman.

Merrill, J. C., & Lowenstein, R. L. (1971). *Media, messages, and men.* New York: Longman.

Mintzberg, H. (1983). *Power in and around organizations.* Englewood Cliffs, NJ: Prentice-Hall.

Newsom, D., Turk, J. V., Kruckeberg, D. (2000). *This is PR: The realities of public relations.* Belmont, CA; Wadsorth.

Pratt, C., & Mannheim, J. (1988). Communication research and development policy: Agenda dynamics in an African setting. *Journal of Communication, 38*(3): 75–95.

Rhee, Y. (1999). *Confucian culture and excellent public relations: A study of generic principles and specific applications in South Korean public relations practice.* Unpublished master's thesis, University of Maryland, College Park.

Rhee, Y. (2002). Culture and dimensions of communication in public relations: An exploratory study of South Korean practitioners. Paper presented to the Public Relations Division at the annual conference of the International Communication Association (ICA), Seoul, South Korea, July 16, 2002.

Schein, E. H. (1985). *Organizational culture and leadership.* San Francisco: Jossey-Bass.

Siebert, F. S., Peterson, T., & Schramm, W. (1956). *Four theories of the press.* Urbana, IL: University of Illinois Press.

Simon, M. W., & Gartzke, E. (1996). Political system similarity and the choice of allies. *Journal of Conflict Resolution, 40*(4), pp. 617–635.

Sriramesh, K. (1992). *The impact of societal culture on public relations: An ethnographic study of South Indian organizations.* Unpublished doctoral dissertation, University of Maryland, College Park.

Sriramesh, K. (1999). The models of public relations in India. Top Faculty Paper presented to the PR Division, AEJMC, August 4–7, New Orleans, LA.

Sriramesh, K., Grunig, J. E., & Buffington, J. (1992). Corporate culture and public relations. In J. E. Grunig (Ed.), *Excellence in public relations and communication management.* Hillsdale, NJ: Lawrence Erlbaum Associates. pp. 577–598.

Sriramesh, K. (1996). Power distance and public relations: An ethnographic study of Southern Indian organizations. In H. Culbertson & N. Chen (Eds.), *International public relations: A comparative analysis.* (pp. 171–190). Mahwah, NJ: Lawrence Erlbaum Associates.

Sriramesh, K., Grunig, J. E., & Dozier, D. M. (1996). Observation and measurement of two dimensions of organizational culture and their relationship to public relations. *Journal of Public Relations Research*, 8, 229–261.

Sriramesh, K., Kim, Y., & Takasaki, M. (1999). Public relations in three Asian cultures: An analysis. *Journal of Public Relations Research, 11*(4), 271–292.

Sriramesh, K., & Takasaki, M. (1998, July). *The impact of culture on Japanese public relations.* Paper presented to the Public Relations Division, International Communication Association, Jerusalem, Israel.

Sriramesh, K., & White, J. (1992). Societal culture and public relations. In J. E. Grunig (Ed.), *Excellence in public relations and communication management* (pp. 597–614). Hillsdale, NJ: Lawrence Erlbaum Associates.

Sussman, L. (1999). *The news of the century: Press freedom 1999.* New York: Freedom House.

Sussman, L. R., & Karlekar, K. D. (2002). *The annual survey of press freedom 2002.* Available at: *http://www.freedomhouse.org/pfs2002/pfs2002.pdf* (Retrieved on January 15, 2003).

Sussman, L., & Karlekar, K. D. (2002). *The annual survey of press freedom 2002.* New York: Freedom House.

Tayeb, M. H. (1988). *Organizations and national culture: A comparative analysis.* London: Sage.

Tichy, N. M. (1982). Managing change strategically: The technical, political, and cultural keys. *Organizational Dynamics, 11*(2), 59–80.

Tylor, E. B. (1871). *Primitive culture.* London: Murray.

Verčič, D., Grunig, L. A., & Grunig, J. E. (1996). Global and specific principles of public relations: Evidence from Slovenia. In H. M. Culbertson & N. Chen (Eds.), *International public relations: A comparative analysis* (pp. 31–66). Mahwah, NJ: Lawrence Erlbaum Associates.

Verčič, D., Ruler, B. van, Butschi, G., and Flodin, B. (2001) 'On the Definition of Public Relations: A European view,' *Public Relations Review*, Vol. 27, pp. 373–387.

Weaver, D. H., Buddenbaum, J. M., & Fair, J. E. (1985). Press freedom, media, and development, 1950–1979: A study of 134 nations. *Journal of Communication, 35*(2), 104–117.

West, H. G., & Fair, J. E. (1993). Development communication and popular resistance in Africa: An examination of the struggle over tradition and modernity through media. *African Studies Review, 36*(1), 91–114.

Wilcox, D. L., & Nolte, L. W. (1997). *Public relations writing and media techniques.* New York: Longman.

Wilson, F. L. (1995). Teaching comparative politics in the 1990s. *Political Science & Politics, 28*(1), 79–80.

PART

I

ASIA AND AUSTRALASIA

2

PUBLIC RELATIONS IN MAINLAND CHINA:
AN ADOLESCENT WITH GROWING PAINS

NI CHEN
HUGH M. CULBERTSON

INTRODUCTION

The People's Republic of China is the world's most populous nation with about 1.3 billion people (Yan, 2000). Also, it is one of the most enduring countries, having remained intact for about 5,000 years. Survival of a state requires ongoing support or, at the very least, lack of effective opposition from sources such as citizens. Thus, such longevity could be viewed in part as a public relations achievement.

The country's history has featured long periods of political stability interspersed with dramatic, sudden, often violent change (Latham, 2000; Schoenhals, 1999). Forces for stability include the teaching of the classic philosopher, Confucius, who advocated that it was functional for societies to have stratification with citizens feeling reverence for their fathers, local and provincial leaders, and ultimately the emperor who was often called the son of God (Ng, 2000, pp. 49–52). The famous sage also focused on the interdependence of people and social roles and the importance of the collective rather than the individual. And, he stressed harmony rather than disruption and order rather than chaos (Lu, 2000, p. 7). Such thinking within the imperial court set the stage for a rather complex, rigid, meritocratic bureaucracy centered around the throne.

Furthermore, China has long been largely a peasant society. Peasants devote much of their life and energy to raising food and simply surviving. Chinese intellectuals and leaders long viewed them as being unable to determine their own fate or contribute meaningfully to social and political processes (Park, 1998). Peasants endured much suffering, which might have induced them to feel a need for change. Only 60 years ago, Chairman Mao

Tse-tung understood the latent power and strength of the vast peasantry (Schramm, Chu, & Yu, 1976, p. 87). Geographic isolation, anger at being exploited and bullied by foreign invaders and traders, and ethnocentric pride have also contributed to resistance to change among the Chinese (Xiao, 2000, p. 169).

In the 20th century, however, change came rapidly, often, and violently. The collapse of the Qing Dynasty in 1911 was followed by a variety of conflicts. The first was among warlords, with Chiang Kai-Shek and the Kuomintang Party eventually getting the upper hand by 1927. The Communist revolt then featured the famous Long March for survival by Chairman Mao and other leaders in 1935. Japanese invasion and partial occupation of the country in the 1930s created great suffering and turmoil as it co-existed with the civil war between Chiang's and Mao's forces. Mao prevailed and established the People's Republic of China (PRC) in 1949.

Mao Tse-tung sought to change Chinese society dramatically with forced farm collectivization and other social and economic experiments. Eventually, he feared that a reactionary bureaucracy was gaining control by the early to mid-1960s under Liu Shaoqi. This fear led Mao to unleash the violent Cultural Revolution which lasted for almost a decade until his death in 1976. By 1979, supreme leader Deng Xiaoping called for "opening to the West" and modernization. He believed China would escape from poverty and exploitation only if it adopted Western technology and economic institutions—and adapted them to Chinese needs and characteristics. At the same time, he sought to ensure political dominance by the Chinese Communist Party (Qiu, 2000).

This two-track approach to governing—including economic change and political stability—has helped create a kind of split personality in the new field of Chinese public relations. The profession first gained a presence in China in the early 1980s (Chen, 1992, p. 7). Mirroring recent change in the country, public relations grew rapidly for a few years only to decline for a time in the early 1990s. Recently, it has grown once more, as noted later in this chapter.

Authoritarian rule, crises, and culture have contributed to closedness in China. Communication has often been one-way—with little careful listening or attention to dissenting viewpoints as emphasized by Western scholars (Dozier, L. A. Grunig, & J. E. Grunig, 1995; J. E. Grunig, 1992). However, recent opening and modernization have contributed to gradual change (Chen & Culbertson, 1992).

In this chapter, we link China's culture to public relations practice in the country. Second, we provide an overview of Chinese public relations. Third, we examine Chinese media—control of them, their reach, and citizen access to them—discussing media relations practice in the process. Fourth, we explore current trends in Chinese society that provide opportunities and challenges for public relations practice.

CHINESE CULTURE AND PUBLIC RELATIONS

According to Kroeber and Kluckhohn (cited in Sriramesh & White, 1992), there is no unanimity about the definition of the term *culture*, with at least 164 definitions of the term in anthropological literature. Culture basically includes a complex, stable pattern of beliefs about what is, what is right, and what is important. These beliefs help shape behavior and thought in many areas. Also, cultural beliefs tend to be viewed as obvious, leading people to take them for granted. Scholars (e.g., Sriramesh & White, 1992; Sriramesh, 1996; Sriramesh, J. E. Grunig, & Dozier, 1996) have argued that culture influences the character of public relations practice within a nation. Research in this area has been framed largely by five dimensions of culture proposed by Geert Hofstede (1984, 2001). These dimensions and their relation to public relations in general are discussed in some detail in chapter 1 of this book. In this chapter, we link these cultural dimensions with public relations in China. Finally, we consider implications of culture, in general, and of certain specific features of Chinese culture, in particular.

Much of Hofstede's early work was completed in the 1960s and 1970s, at a time when mainland China was closed to Western scholars. Fortunately, after China had "opened to the West" in the late 1970s, Michael H. Bond, a professor at the Chinese University of Hong Kong, conducted a parallel project called the Chinese Value Survey. Hofstede and Bond (1984, 1998) found that the first three dimensions (power distance, masculinity–femininity, and individualism–collectivism) were clearly evident in China, in similar though not identical form, much like Hofstede's data from other countries. Long-term orientation appeared to be salient and clearly defined only in China and other Confucian societies, and uncertainty avoidance was evident only in other lands.

Hofstede suggested that uncertainty avoidance is consistent with Westerners' search for truth. In the age of modernity, Westerners have assumed there was truth accessible to reason, empirical observation, and religious faith. In contrast, Asian philosophers doubt that such truth really exists. They focus on virtue—the realm that seems to underlie long-term orientation (Hofstede, 2001, pp. 71, 363; Lu, 2000, p. 10). Hofstede (2001, p. 357) observed that, across nations, the dimensions are quite independent of each other with one exception. Power–distance and individualism correlate negatively ($r = -.77$). In short, collectivist societies tend to be hierarchical—with relatively unquestioning acceptance of strong leadership.

Hofstede (2001) also affirmed that nations tend to be stable on these dimensions. In particular, this holds true in China and India (p. 34). However, Yankelovich (1981, pp. xii–xx) argued that beliefs and values within a culture can change as proponents interact with outsiders and are affected by various social forces. Later, we note some areas of possible change in China over the past 50+ years under the influence of communism and opening to the West.

In general, the dimensions do not seem to converge and correlate increasingly over time. However, increasing wealth does seem to contribute to a nation's individualism (Hofstede, 2001, pp. 432, 454).

Comparing of China with other nations is quite challenging. Hofstede (2001, p. 502) concluded that:

1. China is relatively high in power–distance but low in individualism. As already noted, these two dimensions correlate negatively and strongly across nations in general. And, on these dimensions, China differs dramatically from the United States and other Western democracies.

2. China ranks low in uncertainty avoidance but high in masculinity. On these dimensions, the Middle Kingdom resembles the United States quite closely.

3. China ranks highest, by far, of seven nations compared on long-term orientation. The United States and Great Britain, in contrast, rate low here within a separate batch of 29 countries.

We now examine the dimensions' implications.

The Implications of the Dimensions of Culture

Power–Distance.   China's high power–distance doubtless stems largely from its imperial tradition. As noted earlier, emperors were viewed as sons of God until 1911. In

contrast, the intelligentsia have regarded the millions of peasants in the country as ignorant, passive, and resigned to a life of bare survival (Park, 1998). Confucius argued that
the stability of society was based on unequal relations in which low-level people owe their
superiors respect and obedience in exchange for protection and consideration (Hofstede,
2001, p. 114; Ng, 2000, pp. 51–2).

Communist rule, beginning in 1949, has been very authoritarian. Chairman Mao demanded unquestioning obedience in his effort to build a utopian state. Conversely,
communist ideology points toward an egalitarian, selfless, classless society as an ideal.
Such thinking seems likely to moderate power-distance somewhat. Also, ancient Chinese
philosophers called on intellectuals to question leaders of the state when they erred dramatically (Lu, 2000, p. 5; Shi, 2000).

Turning to public relations, Sriramesh (1996) suggested that higher levels of power–
distance in societies make it difficult for public relations practitioners, as staff workers,
to become part of dominant coalitions that ultimately set organizational policy. Access
to the dominant coalition is seen by many scholars as being important to public relations
excellence (e.g., Verčič, L. A. Grunig, & J. E. Grunig, 1996, p. 37). These conclusions
gain support from two arguments:

1. In societies with high power–distance, power often is based on coercion and referent power,
    with the latter stemming from leaders' charisma and followers' identifying psychologically
    with them. Public relations people, as staff employees operating in behind-the-scenes
    support roles, seldom are in a position to coerce or show charisma.

2. In contrast, leaders in low power–distance cultures often exert influence primarily by
    demonstrating expertise, something that the bright, studious public relations practitioner
    can demonstrate through day-to-day performance (Hofstede, 2001, p. 97).

In another realm, Taylor (2000) suggested that high power–distance creates special
challenges for practitioners. In such societies, people tend to blame leaders quickly when
things go wrong. Even today, Chinese leaders often are perceived as leading under a
"mandate from heaven" akin to that which supported emperors prior to 1911. When bad
things happen, many doubt that the mandate still holds (Lu, 2000, p. 9). This suggests a
particular need to act quickly and decisively in dealing with a crisis and to communicate
leaders' decisiveness.

Hofstede (2001, pp. 97–98) noted that, in high-power–distance societies, leaders tend
to display their status—presumably through such trappings as cheering crowds, fancy
palaces, and luxurious limousines. Such trappings may seem excessive, connoting arrogance, to people from more egalitarian countries such as the Netherlands where leaders feel
at home "slumming" with ordinary folk. In light of this, practitioners from other countries
must remember to show Chinese leaders the respect they feel they deserve. Such respect
for leaders may not come naturally to die-hard egalitarians (Hofstede, 2001, pp. 430–431).

High power–distance also may call into question one important principle of negotiation
emphasized in the United States. Mediators there are called on to ensure that negotiators
focus on contestants' substantive interests, rather than their positions within an organization or community. With high power–distance, however, positions never cease to be
central. One cannot easily put them aside and achieve meaningful discussion (Hofstede,
2001, p. 436; X. Yu, 2000).

Dobson (2002) noted that third-party endorsement, especially by credible authorities
supporting a project or product, is especially important in China. This is due in large part
to the respect accorded to authority figures.

Collectivism–Individualism.   The deep-seated nature of Chinese collectivism is shown by the fact that the Mandarin language has no word corresponding to the English *person-ality* which denotes a personal identity distinct from the society and culture. The Chinese word for human being, *ren*, includes the person's intimate societal and cultural environment (Hofstede, 2001, p. 210). Another sign of collectivist sentiment is the Chinese nomenclature protocol in which a person's family name precedes the given (first) name, defining the status of the individual by linking with the family. Chinese who migrate to the United States surely find it rather painful to Americanize their names by writing surnames last, as demanded by the telephone company and the Social Security Administration.

A major aspect of Chinese collectivism is *guangxi*—one's network of connections and friendships that seem necessary to get most anything, such as a train, a theater ticket, medicine, or a job! Yang (1994, p. 147) suggested that *quanxhi* helped avoid complete chaos during times such as the Great Cultural Revolution of 1966–1976. However, *quanxhi* poses certain challenges for public relations practitioners. These include:

- A need to spend much time developing relationships of trust before one can get down to business and close a deal. Efficiency-oriented Westerners sometimes are inclined to fly in, get down to substantive business right away, and then leave.

- Hiring and promotion of friends and relatives, often with little regard for ability or actual performance. In joint-venture firms, this strikes Western partners as nepotism or favoritism, perhaps leading to morale problems. Talcott Parsons (1951, p. 30) noted that Chinese are particularistic, taking specific relationships and circumstances into account. In contrast, Americans idealize universal standards of evaluation.

- Demands for money when one requests a permit, license, or shipment. Such "back-door" payments are widely viewed as respectful gifts in China. However, they often look like bribes to naive Westerners who must decide how and whether to offer or receive them (Culbertson, 1994).

- A tendency to talk—in rather personal ways—about people within one's company, department, or circle of friends and coworkers. At its best, such talk can be a genuine expression of personal concern and willingness to help. At its worst, however, personal discussion degenerates into hurtful gossip surely of special concern to internal relations practitioners.

- A perception that non-Chinese are outsiders—and perhaps just a bit inferior. Such thinking can seem ethnocentric to non-natives who are affected by such behavior. This poses relation problems for Western suppliers, customers, investors, technical experts, tourists, and joint-venture partners (Brady, 2000). We examine this issue further later in this chapter.

- Giving credit to the group, as well as to the individual, is important. In one experiment, Chinese management trainees performed best when told their performance would be measured for groups of 10 and their names would not be marked on the completed group product. In contrast, U.S. trainees did best when told their work would be measured individually and their names listed. Also, Chinese subjects performed poorly when told their group mates were strangers from all over the country (Earley, 1989). X. Yu (2000, pp. 124–130) noted that feelings of indebtedness, loyalty, and interconnectedness motivate people strongly in Chinese organizational contexts. Throughout the nation, one owes special allegiance to one's fellow residents or community, province, or region, unlike in most Western cultures.

Masculinity–Femininity.   Historically, China has been a male-dominated, patriarchal society. Confucius once said that there are two kinds of people who are very artful, immature, and thus hard to deal with—women and children. According to Confucian ethics, men are superior and women inferior. The popular belief was that man is to woman as the sun is to the moon. He leads, she follows; thus, harmony reigns. Based on this philosophy, women are to obey fathers when young, husbands when married, and adult sons when widowed. Further, China remains, to a degree, a peasant society. In agrarian societies, women, especially those in the countryside and rural areas, generally have little opportunity for education and career growth apart from that of their fathers and husbands. However, Chairman Mao Tse-tung sought to enhance the status and role of women compared with men. "Women are capable of supporting at least half of the sky," he declared in the 1950s.

Since the public relations profession gained recognition as an occupational field in China during the 1980s, women have played a prominent role. They have served often in guest relations. Some fear this lowers the field's status among patriarchal leaders who largely equate public relations with young ladies of charm and beauty (B. Zhu, personal communication, July 11, 1994). However, this is not an obvious, simple conclusion, as discussed later. A masculine society offers at least two challenges for public relations. First, it suggests that male egos be stroked and strength be respected in negotiations. Second, it entails a kind of masculine stubbornness that resists compromise and may even lead to violence. Practitioners must deal with such tendencies in tactful, sensitive ways (Hofstede, 2001, p. 436).

At least one study supports these ideas. In a simulation, experienced business people from 11 countries, including China, negotiated the prices of three commodities. Players from highly masculine, individualistic cultures made high profits—and enjoyed the game—whereas collectivists did not (Graham, Mintu, & Rogers, 1994). We now discuss two rather culture-specific dimensions.

Uncertainty Avoidance.   This dimension seems very complex. And, as noted earlier, it does not show up very clearly in the Chinese Value Survey, although China does rate low, overall, on it. A key notion of Western thought about civic life is that people with differing views must hunt for compromise. If they are to avoid constant turmoil and disruption, they must recognize that no one participant in dialogue is all right or all wrong (Siebert, Peterson, & Schramm, 1956, pp. 39–71). Each person should feel some uncertainty about her or his position. In contrast, Mao Tse-tung, Chiang Kai-Shek, and other Chinese leaders have viewed contests for leadership as fights to the death—with little possibility for compromise or formation of lasting coalitions (D. A. Jordan, personal communication, June 7, 2001).

Recently, more pragmatic leaders have brooked some dissent, but they have cracked down when protests seemed loud and challenging. Such heralded liberalization efforts as the One-Hundred Flowers campaign of the 1950s have led eventually to harsh crackdowns known as Anti-Right Movements (Chu, 1999; He, 2000). Much the same thing occurred with Deng Xiaoping's treatment of student protesters at Tiananmen Square in 1989. Of course, Deng Xiaoping had decreed in 1979 that his country should adopt useful Western ideas and adapt them to China's situation. Surely journalists and public relations practitioners engage in some self-censorship because of uncertainty as to where the boundary between what is and what is not acceptable lies at a given moment. This is discussed further in the section on media control.

Long-Term Orientation.   This dimension really came to the fore in the Chinese Value Survey noted earlier (Hofstede & Bond, 1984). It emphasizes certain features of Confucianism that impact on strategic thinking and tactical planning in public relations. One aspect is its emphasis on patience, hard work, and perseverance. Typical Chinese students in the United States have these attributes. They often study in the library when their American counterparts are visiting bars! Furthermore, they seem inclined to spend an extra term in school—or an extra month working on a thesis—to truly excel. In one study, only 14% of workers in China described leisure time as very important. That compares with 68% in the most leisure-oriented of 23 countries covered, Nigeria (Hofstede, 2001, p. 356).

Clearly, cross-cultural differences in patience can create relational problems. At times, a foreign joint-venture partner expects quick results, whereas a Chinese partner does not. Such differences must be faced, discussed, and worked out early in a business relationship (Hofstede, 2001, p. 446; Mann, 1989).

A related element is a long-standing emphasis on education (X. Yu, 2000, p. 132). Young Chinese prepare with great effort for tests so they can enroll in the best available schools. Education is valued so much in China that students seem shocked when someone questions its importance.

Clearly, public relations people working in China can count on a motivated audience when they communicate within universities and schools. However, a down side to this is that great emphasis is placed by the Chinese on rote memory as opposed to independent thinking. Further, students often fail to ask questions in class because they have been taught that this is disrespectful to the professor or teacher. Orientation in this area seems crucial in educational exchange programs.

Taken together, collectivism and long-term emphasis on virtue contribute to a major idiosyncrasy of Confucian societies—preserving face. In China, loss of face is often considered to be worse than loss of a limb (Hofstede, 2001, p. 354)! This surely motivates people to work hard and be virtuous. Unfortunately, however, it may also lead them to conceal problems and withdraw from relationships to avoid embarrassment. At least one commentator claims AIDS education and prevention in China have suffered because local government officials sought to save face by ignoring the disease (Yanhai, 2000–2001). Communication professionals must work hard to help ensure candor and continued participation or their client organizations may suffer.

When working in China, public relations professionals must plan their activities so that they do not create a situation in which a native might encounter loss of face. Praising people for positive aspects of their work while acknowledging the negative may help. So does providing face-saving alternatives when a job is eliminated or an effort falls short (Goffman, 1971, pp. 95–187). Actions that may seem irrational to a nonnative are often carried out in China to save face. For example, when the nation is accused of human-rights violations, it often charges the accuser of similar violations. Lu (2000, p. 12) suggested this may be a tactic of saving face.

Emphasis on personal relationships (*guangxi*), along with the drive to save face, surely contribute to an oft-mentioned feature of Chinese life—a government based on people, not laws. This does appear to be changing. In recent years the Chinese legislature, known as the Congress of People's Deputies, has enacted thousands of formal laws (Burns, 1999; Yan, 2000). However, such laws generally are applied within the context of particular situations and relationships. That, in turn, complicates life for the public relations practitioner.

We now turn to several lessons relating to culture that should inform public relations strategists and tacticians:

- Luo (1999) found that the greater the cultural distance between China and that of a joint-venture partner, the smaller the venture's chances of success. Obviously partners need to understand each other, along with the common interests and factors that separate them. This poses a real communication challenge.

- At the same time, cultural similarity does not guarantee successful relationships. Many civil wars have been fought by ethnic groups with very similar cultural values. Those who have a long history of violence—or find themselves in what they see as win–lose relationships—frequently do battle with deadly results (Hofstede, 2001, p. 432).

- Relational and communication problems often develop with transnational organizations such as the World Trade Organization or United Nations. Theoretically, such organizations work to support shared values of all member states. However, workers and leaders come from different countries. And, as shown in a study of American journalists, a person cannot easily hang her or his values in the cloakroom when she or he goes to work each day (Gans, 1980, pp. 182–213). Focusing on common values becomes especially difficult when one or a few member-states contribute disproportionate resources, leading some to feel they should gain hegemony (Hofstede, 2001, pp. 432–433). A good deal of communication effort and training are needed to overcome such problems.

- Westerners tend to idealize a free marketplace in which all ideas are expressed. However, Asian concern for face makes this difficult, as noted earlier. Such concerns also have an up side. Discussing cultural differences can polarize people and lead to conflict. After all, culture consists of well-established beliefs about which belief holders have high personal involvement. Questioning such ideas can amount to questioning people's basic identity, a painful process (Hall, 1965, p. 165; Hofstede, 2001, p. 453). Practitioners need great skill and patience when working in this area.

- "White lies" such as excessive flattery, criticized by some Western philosophers as hypocritical and counterproductive (Bok, 1979, pp. 61–2), are seen as acceptable tools in enhancing a person's face and boosting relationships in China (Lu, 2000, p. 16). This may lead to perceptions of insincerity and deceitfulness across cultures.

- Chinese people tend to view problems and other objects as a whole, whereas Westerners analyze parts of that whole and relationships among these parts (Guan, 2000, p. 34). These tendencies seem to complement each other. However, unless each party is aware of this difference, misunderstandings and a lack of respect could result.

It is important to note that this analysis raises several questions and hypotheses regarding the management of cross-cultural communication. Further study is needed to answer them. Next, we provide a broad overview of Chinese public relations as it has developed within this cultural setting.

CHINESE PUBLIC RELATIONS: AN OVERVIEW

Defining the status and scope of public relations in China is not easy. The country, its provinces, and its cities have more than 150 public relations associations. But none covers the entire field or collects exhaustive data about job titles, practitioner qualifications, and so on. Furthermore, the field's boundaries are not clearly defined. Guest relations, translation, and guiding of tours—areas often viewed as separate from public relations in the West—occupy center stage in the PRC. And political strategy, an important focus in Western public relations, seems to be viewed by many as a separate realm in China.

To identify current trends and developments, Ni Chen, the senior author, who has conducted several studies previously in China (e.g., Chen, 1992; Chen & Culbertson, 1992, 1996a), interviewed 10 people working in the field in 2002. Included in the current study were four educators, four government officials, one agency executive, and one corporate communication manager. In this section, we rely extensively on their comments and draw on data from earlier studies. In general, all the participants agreed on the key areas of the current status of public relations in China, lending weight to their views. Hereafter, we refer to the 10 respondents simply as "our informants."

When Ni Chen collected data for her dissertation on public relations between 1990 and 1991, the young field was growing rapidly. Dozens of educational institutions were offering related courses. Agencies were multiplying. And employment opportunities seemed bright (Chen, 1992, pp. 45–53). However, the next few years witnessed a sudden decline in the field, according to our informants. Approximately one third of the public relations departments in large business organizations were eliminated. The number of newspapers and journals dedicated to public relations declined from 33 in 1989 to only 2 a few years later. The Ministry of Education refused to accredit public relations as a major for study in universities, allowing only Zhongshan University in Guangzhou to offer a public relations program on a trial basis.

Why the decline? Informants suggest several likely reasons. The Asian economic slow-down in the mid-90s affected China as well, causing a trimming of budgets. Public relations was subordinate to marketing in the thinking and practice of many firms. Tensions with foreign governments and firms following the government crackdown on students at Tiananmen Square in June 1989 may have contributed to questioning of "Western imports," including public relations. Many felt that public relations practitioners contributed to widespread government and business corruption. Some cautioned that the field had grown too rapidly—with no well-developed foundation based on Chinese needs and concepts.

Within a few years, however, public relations began to grow once again. According to a 2000 survey by the Chinese International Public Relations Association (CIPRA), earnings from public relations services grew from 200 million RMB ($24 million) to over 2 billion RMB ($242 million) within about 3 years. PRC-owned PR firms grew by 30% per annum in the last several years of the 20th century, whereas foreign-owned agencies in the PRC had a growth rate of 15%. The CIPRA survey suggested that the number of practitioners in the country had surpassed 100,000 by the end of the century. Also, the vice-president of Zenith Integrated Communication noted substantial growth in high-technology and other specialty areas.

Why the growth at the dawn of the new millennium? Informants cited several factors:

- Pressure for transparency in the wake of growing concern about government and business corruption. Executives realized they would need to make accounting and other procedures public—or risk prosecution and even execution—in light of anticorruption programs. Such publicizing required public relations expertise.

- An increasing number and variety of media outlets (described later).

- Growing talk of public relations as an important element, on a par with advertising, in the marketing process. Integrated marketing communication gained much attention in academic, corporate, and agency circles.

- Growth of adult education in support of China's focus on economic, social, and political development. Public relations courses showed up increasingly in adult-education curricula.

- Growth of varied businesses and joint-venture firms in combination with a society-wide tendency to decentralize government and business institutions (Wu, 2000). Each organization has its own public relations concerns.

Communication appears to have different characteristics within different sectors of the industry, according to our informants. In small corporations, practitioners operate largely as technicians. In particular, they help firms build images through publicity. In medium-sized organizations, public relations often plays a communication-management role. Emphasis is on facilitating communication between managers and employees—and between client organizations and external publics. In large firms, practitioners become involved in strategic planning. Building corporate culture is a major focus. Corporate image and logo design have become responsibilities of public relations units. However, the study and development of corporate culture remain in their infancy in China.

Turning to government communication efforts, the central government in Beijing often uses the press-agentry model (J. E. Grunig & Hunt, 1984, chapter 2), including propaganda. Certainly officials did so in the wake of the famous crackdown on students at Tiananmen Square on June 4, 1989. Specifically, PRC leaders did the following:

- Held trials of dissidents during the Persian Gulf War in 1991. The United States government and Western media paid little attention because their focus was on Kuwait and Iraq.

- Hosted the 11th Asian Games in September 1990. President Jiang Zemin and Premier Li Peng saw this as a chance to show the world that China deserved respect.

- Spruced up their showmanship in dealing with journalists. For example, President Jiang dressed in a Western business suit and answered Barbara Walters' questions with smiles— and a few English words here and there. Old-timers like Mao Tse-tung and Zhou Enlai would hardly have used such tactics to reach a Western audience (Chen & Culbertson, 1992).

In contrast, local government officials moved toward two-way communication. An early leader of this strategy was Li Ruihuan, then mayor of Tianjin and later a prominent figure at the central leadership compound, the Zhongnanhai, in Beijing. As mayor, Li held public meetings to gather input from the people. He encouraged citizens to express their views to the media. He began a series of annual surveys to measure public opinion about city government. Further, he used people in the media to obtain information from citizens who had been hesitant in speaking to the government (Chen & Culbertson, 1992). More recently, such two-way efforts have become common in commercial centers of southern China, especially in Shanghai, Guangzhou, and Shenzhen, according to our informants. These cities have long been major entry points for new Western ideas (Chen, 1992, pp. 164–169).

Women in Public Relations

As noted earlier, female practitioners play a central role in the field, often acting as translators and guest-relations experts. Some observers equate public relations with beautiful, charming ladies, creating what supporters of the field in China call the "Miss PR" problem. This often implies a professional who lacks drive, professional training, and ability to think strategically (B. Zhu, personal communication, July 20, 1994). Our informants agreed that such thinking stems from executive ignorance about what public relations really is—and what it can contribute to organizational effectiveness. As suggested earlier, such stereotyping is inaccurate. In fact, guest relations and translation require a high level of understanding, dedication, and sensitivity. Further, a survey of 43 female practitioners found that many thought like managers but behaved as technicians in highly constrained settings (Chen & Culbertson, 1996a, p. 294). Stereotypes about women contributed to this tendency (Chen & Culbertson, 1996a). Overall, according to one senior United States practitioner who has worked in China recently, young women appear to be very sophisticated and assertive in their professional activity (Capozzi, 2002).

Our informants reported that female practitioners quite often play management roles in government agencies, emerging nongovernmental organizations, hospitals, educational institutions, and associations that represent women, laborers, and youth. In these organizations, women in charge of external communication and public relations play leading roles in setting and implementing communication policy. However, male as well as female practitioners play only limited parts in setting overall organizational policy.

Certainly female practitioners have gained high standing in some Chinese firms, such as the huge Capital City Iron and Steel Corporation. A former vice-president of Shanghai Foreign Studies University, now the vice-commissioner of foreign trade and economy in the Shanghai Municipal Government, confirmed recently to the senior author that her appointment to this important post was largely due to her demonstrated ability to make major decisions and her skill in communicating them to relevant constituencies. In her new position, she is able to bring issues of policy promotion, image building, and campaign execution to the top level of decision making. Overall, young Chinese women entering the field appear to be very aggressive and sophisticated (Dobson, 2002).

Public Relations Societies

About 150 public relations societies exist throughout China at the local and provincial, as well as national, levels. CIPRA, with over, 1,000 members, seems to have come to the fore, according to our informants. The association seeks to enhance professionalism through case-study competitions, conferences, and surveys. It also has lobbied successfully to define public relations as a recognized occupation within the national occupational classification record. In 2001, CIPRA introduced the first-ever nationwide accreditation exam for public relations practitioners. The association's current president is Li Daoyu, previously China's ambassador to the United States. His stature "rubs off" on CIPRA. However, many continue to see the organization as heavily oriented toward government practice. A second organization, the Public Relations Society of China, is said by our informants to be losing ground largely because of political fighting among its leaders.

Public Relations Education

As suggested earlier, Chinese public relations education has gone through many ups and downs. When we studied the field in the early 1990s, growth and innovation were apparent (Chen & Culbertson, 1996b). A decline soon after that was followed by more recent growth, according to our informants. Change has been so rapid that even if we had the time to study public relations education and the space to report on it fully, our report would be out of date before it came off the press! Therefore, we venture only to make a few generalizations.

First, public relations education in China is diverse. It is offered in departments of journalism or mass communication, in units focusing on speech and interpersonal communication, and in interdisciplinary programs. It is also offered in 4-year baccalaureate-degree programs, in 2-year technical colleges, and through television distance learning aimed largely at older, nontraditional students (Chen & Culbertson, 1996b). Second, professors appear to strike a reasonable balance between theory and practice; although they often fail to link the two very effectively. Western perspectives get attention, as do Confucius and other classic Chinese philosophers. The latter seem important because they suggest a need for caution and compromise in searching for win–win solutions. Also, the classics focus on long-term interests and on respect needed to build lasting relationships. Third, educators rely heavily on guest lectures. Also, they work hard to arrange internships and hands-on experience. These steps seem especially important because many professors, although perhaps learned, lack practical experience.

We now focus on an interesting and long-standing feature of PRC communication, mass mobilization campaigns.

Mass Mobilization Campaigns

Throughout their history, the Chinese Communist Party and government have sought to enhance the character and spirit of the people through mass mobilization campaigns focusing largely on officially designated heroes. No doubt this squares with the long-standing tradition of worshipping emperors and scholars mentioned earlier in this chapter. Chairman Mao, in particular, came to be viewed widely as a God-like figure during the Cultural Revolution (Zhang, 2000). Such campaigns usually present ideal role models and encourage people to emulate them. Perhaps the best known was Lei Feng, a poor peasant soldier who died when a tree fell on him. Lei Feng was presented as a selfless, virtuous, heroic person.

In recent years, such campaigns have sought to combat "spiritual pollution" and other bourgeois evils. For example, a 24-year-old medical student named Zhang Hua was presented as a hero after he supposedly attempted to rescue a 69-year-old peasant from drowning in a polluted pit. Both Zhang and the peasant were overcome by methane gas fumes and later died (Rosen, 2000, pp. 163–164). Not surprisingly, given the current cynical atmosphere in China, Zhang's heroism soon took a beating. Letters to the editors of certain newspapers questioned his validity as a role model. Shangai's *Wenhui Daily* ran a letter arguing that his supposedly heroic act damaged the interests of the state. He was a young person with much to contribute to the "Four Modernizations." The state already had invested much in him. Thus, it was foolhardy and contrary to the state's interests for him to risk his life for an old peasant whose potential for serving the state was limited at best. Furthermore, press reports alleged that Zhang was not a totally unselfish servant of the party and nation. In fact, against university rules for a medical student, he had a girlfriend (Rosen, 2000, pp. 163–164)!

As this example suggests, mass mobilization campaigns often face uphill battles. Primarily, this problem stems from a lack of faith in various institutions and people in China. Many feel the Communist Party really is Communist in name only (He, 2000, p. 128). Thus, it is viewed widely as a vehicle for making a good living, gaining status, and being safe—not as a focus of faith or deep-seated belief in ideals. In recent years, formally designated role models have had major problems. Their portrayal of selfless dedication to the party, its ideals, and the people at large has seemed somewhat at odds with Deng Xiaoping's widely quoted statement that "to get rich is glorious" (Zhang, 2000, p. 67). Their role in standing against corruption has often received only lukewarm support from party members, some of whom have been corrupt (p. 77).

As elsewhere, media play an important part in Chinese public relations. We now turn to an overview of the nation's media, discussing ways in which media outreach, control, and access impinge on public relations practice in accordance with the framework of this book.

MEDIA IN CHINA: AN OVERVIEW

Media Outreach

In China, as in most developing countries, radio has played a prominent role partly because of the high rate of illiteracy (P. S. Lee, 1994). However, recent strides in education have lifted the literacy rate in the PRC to an estimated 81.5%. Further, the gross national product per capita was about 31,400 RMB ($3,800) in 2001. Although low by Western standards, this income level greatly exceeds that of many developing countries and allows the vast majority of Chinese to afford television sets and purchase newspapers, books, and magazines (Presbyterian Mission Board, 2001, p. 180).

Chinese media were decimated from 1966 to 1967. Chairman Mao Tse-tung closed possible opposition voices and sent journalists, as well as other writers and professionals, to work in the countryside during the Cultural Revolution. Magazines declined from 790 titles circulating in 1965 to just 21 in 1970. Newspapers shrank from 343 to 42 during that period (P. S. Lee, 1994).

When the nation regained sanity following Mao's death in 1976, the media began to flourish. By 1988, 1,579 newspapers were distributed openly (Yan, 2000). Nationwide circulation and readership data are not available, but the high literacy rate indicates a huge potential audience. By 2002, 8,000 specialized and general-interest magazines operated, many of them with circulations exceeding 2.5 million (Dobson, 2002). Further, by 1997, 2,000 local radio stations formed a highly developed system, beaming programs to 417 million receivers, about one for every three Chinese people. By 1999, the nation had 400 million television receivers, with almost 90% of all households having at least one set (Yan, 2000). Early in the new millennium, China Central Television's 12 channels reached about 650 million viewers (Dobson, 2002).

Of course, media outlets are not distributed evenly throughout the land. In 1997, for example, Guangdong, the province adjacent to Hong Kong which the central government viewed as a haven for quick development and Western ideas, had 62 newspapers. Guizhou, a nearby but less developed large province, had just 27 (Wu, 2000, p. 49). Further, there is unequal distribution in buying power as well. Twelve million Chinese workers lost their jobs in just 1997, as privitization and reform almost eliminated the *iron rice bowl*—the guarantee of a job and living wage for everyone that Chairman Mao had sought to implement (Schoenhals, 1999).

In an effort to enhance readership, listenership, and viewership, Chinese media have become more lively and varied. Writing also became more timely and less drab after 1976. Magazine covers feature many glamorous ladies. Sensational content has become common. Even *People's Daily*, the official organ of the Chinese Communist Party, almost tripled the categories of news it covered and reduced its politicized writing about revolutionary themes that had dominated during the Cultural Revolution (Chu, 1999).

The Internet has grown rapidly among elite, highly educated Chinese. By 2002, the number of web users in China was estimated at 56 million (Dobson, 2002). Although impressive, this figure amounts to only about 4% of the nation's total population of roughly 1.3 billion. No doubt this figure is growing rapidly. Yet, dependence on other technology limits expansion. At the beginning of this century, only 5% of Chinese households had telephones, and only 2% had personal computers (C. C. Lee, 2000, pp. 20–21).

Media Control

All media in China are owned by the government. For almost the first 30 years of the PRC, content consisted largely of preaching the party line. However, Deng Xiaoping and Jiang Zemin have been more pragmatic, viewing the press as a tool to enhance modernization and reform (FlorCruz, 1999; Hong & Cuthbert, 1991; Kissinger, 1997; X. Yu, 1994). Exposing the incompetency and corruption of technocrats and lower level administrators have been widely seen as helpful in achieving reform (Chang, 1989, pp. 47–50). Of course, journalists are not permitted to criticize top leaders or the Communist Party or the basic political system (Latham, 2000). Every now and then, the authorities fire an editor or close a web site when they fear things may spin out of control (Dahun, 2000-2001). For example, publication of a two-volume book purporting to detail the events leading to the June 4, 1989, crackdown on students at Tiananmen Square led to a strong government reaction. Officials suppressed the book's circulation, searched for sources of media leaks, and began a general security crackdown on activists (Nathan, 2001). The Communist Party and government have railed recently against "spiritual pollution" by Western ideas and against notions of "peaceful evolution" toward a capitalist and/or democratic society (Qiu, 2000, p. 257).

In this context, the government has cut subsidies even to party papers. Publications began to depend heavily on advertising revenues, which skyrocketed from 248 million RMB ($30 million) in 1985 to 13.6 billion RMB ($1.65 billion) a decade later (Pan, 2000, p. 72). In China, as elsewhere, the person who pays the piper calls the tune to a degree! Officials sometimes tolerate coverage that irritates them because they have to rely on media outlets to reach their publics (Rosen, 2000). Decentralization also has helped loosen government control over the press. Publications have become more and more diverse. Increasingly, the central government has had to rely on local authorities to implement political control. Freedom to operate without government control is greater in the social than the political realm, and in smaller departments and agencies than in central ministries (Wu, 2000, pp. 61–62).

Although somewhat chaotic, financially driven press restructuring and expansion also have extended to the Communist Party press. Throughout the history of the PRC, the party has often operated a morning newspaper and an evening paper in any given large city. The morning paper has been controlled quite strictly and has emphasized party decrees and pronouncements. The evening paper has provided a great deal of soft news and entertainment. From 1992 to 1993, the party began "weaning" media outlets from press subsidies to save money. All newspapers became increasingly dependent on advertising and circulation revenue. Partly because of their readable style and focus on ordinary people, evening papers gained in both areas, whereas morning papers declined.

In response, morning papers were allowed to establish "city evening papers" as cash cows to support them. These new papers sprung up in at least 20 urban areas between 1994 and 1998. Operating independently of party supervision, these papers have often become quite sensational. They report on small social problems, such as missing children and prostitution, and shy away from major controversies. They provide a valuable outlet for public relations people who need to disseminate useful information like bus schedules and instructions on how to do a variety of things (Hang, 2001).

It is important to note that the national media are more closely censored than local and provincial media (Ma, 2000, p. 22). Furthermore, party journalists now are mostly college-educated people exposed to non-Marxist ideas. Thus, today's cadres tend to be more critical and independent than their predecessors (Chu, 1999, p. 13). The Internet has brought many foreign ideas to China. The government often regards this as subversive, leading it to view the medium without much enthusiasm. Authorities have done a great deal to regulate the Internet and little to promote use of it (Yan, 2000). Some web sites have been shut down because they were deemed dangerous (Dahun, 2000–2001).

We now turn to practitioner and news-source access to the media.

Source Access to News Media

Until fairly recently, press coverage in the PRC stemmed largely from government and party directives. In 1994, we met with practitioners in a public relations agency in Hangzhou that was owned by the Xinhua News Agency. One host quipped that "It is rather nice working with the media when you and they have the same boss!" However, the growth, popularity, and limited critical role of the media have complicated things considerably. Young reporters often take the initiative in contacting news sources (Chang, 1989, p. 123).

Although sometimes criticized in official circles, *quanxhi* still operates in China, as noted earlier. Reporter–source relations involve gift giving and reciprocal favors dependent in part on family and geographic ties. All of this makes media relations more complex than in the West.

Reporters, editors, and media relations practitioners share a common uncertainty. They must report critically with a concern in the back of their minds that too much criticism of the wrong people could bring official wrath. China has no official censors who tell journalists in advance what crosses the line. Training of reporters and editors helps them censor themselves (Chang, 1989, p. 256). Our informants believed that most press relations people work with journalists in defining all-important "lines" between what is acceptable and what is not. Such collaboration may reduce press criticism of some client organizations.

Organizations in China gain press coverage in the following ways:

1. Often a newspaper will seek financial sponsorship from a news source for editing a special section or writing an in-depth story. Sometimes the sponsor covers travel and other expenses. At other times, the sponsor may bring cash in so-called "red packets" (Pan, 2000, p. 85). In fact, "red packet" has become a code phrase for corruption in some journalistic quarters, and government officials have railed against it. However, it continues, according to our informants.

2. Sometimes an editor receives a commission of 10% to 20% from advertising and sponsorship revenue that her or his special section brings to a newspaper or magazine (Pan, 2000, pp. 85–86). This, in turn, motivates aggressive advertising sales and promotion by media. And, it leads to in-depth coverage of organizations that may spend their advertising budgets at a publication or station.

3. It is not uncommon for newspapers to contract an external party to edit and produce a special insert or section. Often the public relations people who work for the sponsoring party end up writing and editing such sections (Pan, 2000, p. 87).

4. On occasion, a reporter working for a particular paper or magazine may place her or his story in another publication when a policy or administrative fiat precludes publication in the publication she or he works for. Westerners might call this moonlighting (Pan, 2000, p. 92).

Our informants feared that such arrangements may compromise the integrity of the press as well as public relations, especially when sponsorship and other arrangements are not acknowledged for all to see. Many informants called on educators and leading practitioners to create ethics classes that deal with these matters more forcefully.

Reliance on advertising and circulation revenue appears to give the news media some independence from government. However, this independence may be more apparent than real for one basic reason. The government itself is heavily involved in business, often maintaining partial ownership (Sparks, 2000, pp. 35–49). Furthermore, much as in the West, mergers and conglomerates worry advocates of watchdog journalism. Media conglomerates in Guangzhou and elsewhere have components that may receive little hard-hitting coverage because it would "kill the goose that lays the golden egg" (He, 2000, p. 113).

Although not independent of government, the press appears to be playing a modern public relations role rather than a propaganda role these days in China. Coverage is less ideological than 20 years ago. As He (2000) put it, the main mission is not to brainwash or impose an ideology. Rather, it is to boost the party's image and justify its existence. Some refer to the government and party information system as "Publicity, Inc." (He, 2000).

Much as in the West, reporters move back and forth between work in politics, business, and public relations. Such ties help set the parameters of news and press coverage (Wu, 2000, p. 104). In the final analysis, press coverage relies heavily on government sources in China, much as it does elsewhere (Chang, 1989, p. 84; Culbertson, 1997; Culbertson & Chen, 2001).

We now turn to several developments and concerns in modern China that create important challenges and opportunities for public relations.

SOME CHALLENGES AND OPPORTUNITIES

Social and Economic Development

Chinese leaders have tried, at least since the end of the Qing Dynasty in 1911, to lift out of poverty the mass of peasants who accounted for more than one-half of the population. Chairman Mao Tse-tung's Great Leap Forward, featuring the collective operation of huge farms, and his infamous project of the late 1950s to build backyard steel mills were among the drastic steps taken toward this end. During the first 20 to 25 years of the PRC, radio was viewed as a key vehicle for development instruction. Peasants, many of whom were illiterate, would gather in village squares to hear radio programs. Party cadres would be on hand to answer questions, give instructions, and seek peasant commitment for steps designed to reduce suffering and starvation (F. T. C. Yu, 1963, pp. 277–279).

Recently, as word of urban prosperity spread in the countryside, peasants flocked to cities such as Shanghai, Guangzhou, and Beijing by the millions to search for jobs. Such huge "floating populations" have taxed the infrastructure of these cities beyond limits. The government has reacted by taking the following steps:

1. Instituting a family-responsibility system under which farm families could run their own operations and keep more and more of their own profits.

2. Promoting township and village industries that employ farmers driven off the land by improved technology and other factors. These people, it is hoped, would make a living close to home—rather than migrating to the already overcrowded cities.

3. Supporting certain industries and firms through tax breaks, trade fairs, training programs for workers, infrastructure development, and so on (Belcher & Shue, 2001).

4. Taking land from farmers to build special economic zones, highways, and other development-related infrastructures (Guo, 2001).

Such moves have created an increasingly competitive environment for people who, under Communism, had been taught that competition is basically evil. Competition creates losers as well as winners, and losing is especially painful for folks who have endured centuries of upheaval and near starvation. Sometimes government officials have treated the losers in ways which savvy public relations people would object to.

For example, in the rural Banyan Township of remote Yunnan province, things became so desperate that activists went to Beijing to protest that the meager payments they received for land taken from them were unfair. Beijing officials explained that this was a local matter—outside their jurisdiction. The activists were sent to their provincial capital, Kunming. There they were treated courteously, given a free meal to soothe their feelings, and sent home (Guo, 2001)!

In the wake of such cases, many Chinese people have come to see the national government as their savior, whereas local authorities are seen as corrupt, arbitrary, and unfair (Guo, 2001). Clearly, as decentralization occurs throughout the country, local governments must have legitimacy to operate effectively. Our informants saw a great need for public relations counsel at the village and township levels.

Development has gotten much attention from PRC leaders. Given the widespread reach of television today, development-related programs have become common on China Central Television (CCTV), the nationwide network. For example, CCTV arranged for production of an educational soap opera on family planning. Produced at great expense, the program finally went on the air in 2001 after being bumped from the program schedule for 1 to 2 years by network executives (L. Ren, personal communication, February 10, 2002). Such delays surely hamper development planners to a great extent.

Development news has been featured extensively in party newspapers such as *China Daily* (Culbertson, 1997), and in Xinhua News Agency dispatches. In a study of the latter from 1957 to 1988, Elliott (1998) found heavy emphasis throughout on clarification of development plans and policies, instruction about what local officials and citizens could do to implement these plans, and context relating to progress in other regions and previous goals or claims. However, critical assessment of relevance, success, and failure was quite rare—doubtless reflecting the government's dominant role among news sources (Culbertson, 1997) and its desire to promote development in a positive way (Elliott, 1998).

Some scholars of development communication see current trends in the field as moving away from long-standing Chinese practice. China's highly centralized political system seems ill-suited to dialogic, two-way models relying on grassroots input and support (Freire, 1997). Further, the nation's history of systematic nationwide planning deviates from current emphasis around the world on the identity of specific social groups. A focus on economic growth in isolation from other realms also seems inconsistent with new social movements focusing on personal and group identities (Huesca, 2001). Public relations people need to address such issues. However, our informants reported little practitioner effort to date on these matters.

Institutional Changes

The recent openness and resulting reform have led to institutional innovation in the PRC. Three areas require a great deal of public relations expertise. These are social organizations, local elections, and ties with foreign interest groups. We briefly review each of these realms.

Social Organizations.   In recent years, the government and Communist Party have been unable, due partly to a lack of personnel and financial resources, to meet all Chinese social and welfare needs. Thus, officials have permitted the formation of social organizations numbering almost 190,000 according to one published 1996 estimate (quoted in Saich, 2000). These groups operate with various degrees of government support and control (Saich, 2000). Such organizations have been both a blessing and a dilemma for Chinese authorities. The government realizes they are needed but fears they may spin out of control. Crackdowns sometimes occur. In 1998, several leaders of an emerging political party, the Chinese Democratic Party, were jailed for trying to organize in opposition to the Chinese Communist Party. In 1996, the first home for battered women in Shanghai was closed in light of claims that it was improper for a nongovernmental organization to run such a service. The Falungong religious sect was "de-registered" in 1997 after it surprised leaders by organizing a sit-in with 10,000 supporters at the party headquarters in Zhongnanhai (Saich, 2000).

Clearly such organizations need to spell out clearly what they are about and why. Further, government officials must grant such organizations a more stable and well-defined status, as well as opportunities for dialogue. Public relations expertise can certainly help in this process. However, our informants view this as an underdeveloped area of public relations.

Local Elections.   Recent prosperity throughout the country appears to have been accompanied by declining revolutionary zeal and party membership. Beginning in the late 1980s, the national government began addressing this problem by encouraging elections for village leadership so local citizens could choose their own leaders and hold them accountable. The Ministry of Civil Affairs, the agency responsible for local elections, did not collect data on how many of China's 930,000 villages hold elections (Pastor & Tan, 2000). Opinions vary as to how effective such elections have been in the past. Anecdotal evidence does suggest that some of these elections are transparent, contested vigorously, and free in the sense that candidates can speak freely and voters vote in secret (Pastor & Tan, 2000). However, some observers insist that free elections must be built on the foundation of independent branches of government, a free press, and freedom of association. These areas are evolving rather slowly in China. Legislative, judicial, and executive branches do exist. But our informants emphasized that the executive branch tends to dominate the other two branches. Furthermore, the Chinese Communist Party dominates all three branches.

Surveys have been done on the interest among Chinese citizens in politics, their propensity to consume news about it, their interest in affecting it, and their perceptions about the need to reform the nation's political system. Shi (2000) concluded that grassroots attitudes and informal knowledge are as supportive of democracy as those found in some societies widely regarded as democratic. President Jiang Zemin and other national leaders have spoken in favor of local elections, viewing them as a tool in developing Chinese Communist Party leadership. However, some worry that village politicians might spin out of party control (Diamond & Myers, 2000). Therefore, the national government has allocated few resources to supervise and support village-level elections (Pastor & Tan, 2000).

In small villages, candidates usually campaign very informally as they feel they already are well-known in their areas. Perhaps partly for this reason, little planned public relations appears to occur during such campaigns—or for women's groups and labor unions. Our informants see these as areas for future growth.

Ties With Foreign Interest Groups.   Deng Xiaoping called for adaptation of foreign ideas to Chinese needs and contexts. His pragmatism, still embraced by his successors, leads to some zigs and zags that surely pose public relations problems for the government and for international relations.

For example, an organization called the International Education Foundation became affiliated with the controversial Unification Church of South Koreaunder Reverend Sun Myung Moon. Both groups supported efforts in schools to advocate sexual abstinence as the only effective way to control AIDS and other sexually transmitted diseases. Also, both condemned homosexuals. PRC leaders apparently saw this initially as a useful approach in combating evil Western influences. However, when the organization began to gather a following, the government opposed it as anti-Communist—and as somewhat cult-like in ways reminiscent of the Falungong movement (Yanhai, 2000–2001). We now focus on a final area of concern to the Chinese government.

Dealing With Foreigners

Welcoming Tourists. During a 1-month-long lecture tour in the Middle Kingdom, Hugh M. Culbertson, the junior author of this chapter, commented often that Chinese people really wrote the book on hospitality, after experiencing the bountiful banquets and servings of Peking Duck, considerate tour guides, bright simultaneous interpreters, and comfortable accommodations in Western-style hotels and "dormitories for foreign experts." Interestingly, the very title of foreign expert gave his ego a boost! While in China, he truly had the experience of a lifetime. However, he eventually came to realize three things about the hospitality shown him.

First, although genuine, the hospitality was quite scripted. Activities were highly planned. Banquets were elaborate, as were tours and introductions. Activities seldom seemed completely spontaneous, and this became just a bit disconcerting to an American used to spontaneity. Second, arranged activities often seemed to say implicitly, in light of their formality, "We welcome you warmly, but you are not Chinese. We don't want to forget that you are outsiders visiting our country." Such an insider–outsider distinction was emphasized in several ways, such as dual pricing at the Forbidden City and in certain stores, providing Westerners accommodation in hotels where Chinese could not stay, and so on. Third, the government and party seemingly try, often in subtle ways, to control their guests. A word, *waishi*, denotes such an effort to control relations with guests while welcoming and serving them thoughtfully and warmly (Brady, 2000).

These factors did not really bother the American junior author and his American wife. Feelings of separateness and a need for control seem understandable in light of history— the exploitation of China by the West through parts of at least two centuries, Chinese isolation, Chairman Mao's insistence on the need for self-sufficiency, and so on. Nonetheless, if the nation is to attract Western tourists, such cultural differences deserve careful thought.

Cultural Exchange Balance. Chinese students and workers flock to the West in huge numbers. At any one time in the past 20 years, an average of 40,000 PRC students have attended classes in the United States. These students appear to learn and contribute a great deal. However, relatively few Westerners study or live in China for very long. No doubt this reflects in part their low proficiency in Chinese language. Because of its complexity and utter lack of similarity to Western languages, Chinese seems very daunting. That is especially true in the United States where language studies are notoriously weak. Overall, the number of Chinese students in Europe outnumber the European students in China by almost 20 to 1 according to one study (Meissner, 2002). Contemporary communication scholars stress the importance of symmetry (J. E. Grunig, 1992). That implies mutual understanding among participants in an exchange. And such inequities in the balance of exchange seem apt to hinder mutuality.

CONCLUSIONS

Clearly public relations, a very new field in China, is changing rapidly as it defines itself. Western practices do not set well with the Chinese people. In fact, development of the field appears to have been opposite to that in the West, over time, as to communication channels emphasized. In the United States, early public relations practice focused largely on mass media. Recently, however, interpersonal approaches have gained importance due in part to the following:

- Growing emphasis on employees, stockholders, and other internal publics.
- Widespread development of niche marketing and audience segmentation in strategic thinking as well as tactical practice.
- Growth of the Internet and other technologies that facilitate interaction among small, specialized groups.

In mainland China, in contrast, the field began just 20 years ago with great emphasis on interpersonal communication. Guest relations and simultaneous translation were popular public relations techniques. This stemmed in part from the subtleties of *guangxi*, culture-based collectivism, and low credibility of government-owned media. Recently, however, the mass media appear to have gained in importance. Contributing factors include the following:

- Growth in the number, credibility, diversity, and appeal of media, along with media receptivity to public relations pitches and contributions.
- Marketing of products to large and diverse audiences, as growing purchasing power has expanded markets.
- Great concern for appealing to foreign investors and consumers, using international media, as China has opened its doors to the outside world.

More research obviously is needed to document and clarify such trends.

REFERENCES

Belcher, M., & Shue, V. (2001). Into leather: State-led development and the private sector in Xinji. *China Quarterly, 166*, 368–393.

Bok, S. (1979). Lying: Moral choice in public and public life. New York: Vintage Books.

Brady, A. (2000). Treat insiders and outsiders differently: The use and control of foreigners in the People's Republic of China. *China Quarterly, 164*, 943–964.

Burns, J. P. (1999). The People's Republic of China at 50: National political reform. *China Quarterly, 159*, 580–594.

Capozzi, L. (2002, August). *Public relations in China and Japan today.* Teleconference presentation sponsored by the International Section of the Public Relations Society of America.

Chang, W. H. (1989). *Mass media in China: The history and the future.* Ames, IA: Iowa State University Press.

Chen, N. (1992). *Public relations in China: The introduction and development of an occupational field.* Unpublished doctoral dissertation, Ohio University, Athens.

Chen, N., & Culbertson, H. M. (1992). Two contrasting approaches of government public relations in mainland China. *Public Relations Quarterly, 37*(3), 36–41.

Chen, N., & Culbertson, H. M. (1996a). Guest relations: A demanding but constrained role for lady public relations practitioners in mainland China. *Public Relations Review, 22,* 279–296.

Chen, N., & Culbertson, H. M. (1996b November). *Public relations education in the People's Republic of China: A tentative look at the process.* Paper presented at the meeting the Association for the Advancement of Policy, Research, and Development in the Third World, Cancun, Mexico.

Chu, L. L. (1999). Continuity and change in China's media reform. *Journal of Communication, 44,* 4–21.

Culbertson, H. M. (1994, August). *Cultural beliefs: A focus of study in cross-cultural public relations.* Paper presented at the meeting of the Association for Education in Journalism and Mass Communication, Atlanta, GA.

Culbertson, H. M. (1997). China Daily coverage of rural development: A broad window or a small peep-hole? *Gazette, 59,* 105–120.

Culbertson, H. M., & Chen, N. (2001). Nationality 1, audience 0: A study of factors shaping news about the 1997 Hong Kong handover. *International Communication Bulletin, 36*(1–2), 4–19.

Dahun, X. (2000–2001, Winter). Our life-long struggle for human rights. *China Right Forum,* pp. 13–21.

Diamond, L., & Myers, R. H. (2000). Introduction: Elections and democracy in greater China. *China Quarterly, 162,* 365–386.

Dobson, B. (2002, August). *Public relations in China and Japan today.* Teleconference presentation sponsored by the International Section of the Public Relations Society of America.

Dozier, D. M., with Grunig, L. A., & Grunig, J. E. (1995). *Manager's guide to excellence in public relations and communication management.* Mahwah, NJ: Lawrence Erlbaum Associates.

Earley, P. C. (1989). Social loafing and collectivism: A comparison of the United States and the People's Republic of China. *Administrative Science Quarterly, 34,* 565–581.

Elliott, C. (1998). Defining development news values: An examination of press releases from the New China News Agency. In B. T. McIntyre (Ed.), *Mass media in the Asian Pacific* (pp. 72–84). Philadelphia: Multilingual Matters Ltd.

FlorCruz, J. A. (1999). Chinese media in flux. *Media Studies Journal, 13*(2), 42–46.

Freire, P. (1997). *Pedagogy of the oppressed.* New York: Continuum.

Gans, H. J. (1980). *Deciding what's news.* New York: Vintage Press.

Goffman, E. (1971). *Relations in public.* New York: Harper Torchbooks.

Graham, J. L., Mintu, A. T., & Rodgers, W. (1994). Explorations of negotiation behaviors in 10 foreign cultures, using a model developed in the United States. *Management Science, 40,* 72–95.

Grunig, J. E. (1992). *Excellence in public relations and communication management.* Hillsdale, NJ: Lawrence Erlbaum Associates.

Grunig, J. E., & Hunt, T. (1984). *Managing public relations.* New York: Holt, Rinchart & Winston.

Guan, S. (2000). A comparison of Sino–American thinking patterns and the function of Chinese characters in the difference. In D. R. Heisey (Ed.), *Chinese perspectives in rhetoric and communication* (pp. 25–43). Stamford, CT: Ablex.

Guo, X. (2001, June). Land expropriation and rural conflicts in China. *China Quarterly, 166,* 422–439.

Hall, E. T. (1965). *The silent language.* Greenwich, CT: Fawcett.

Hang, C. (2001). China's state-tabloids: The rise of "city newspapers." *Gazette, 63,* 435–450.

He, Z. (2000). Chinese Communist Party press in a tug of war: A political–economy analysis of the *Shenzhen Special Zone Daily.* In C. C. Lee (Ed.), *Communication patterns and bureaucratic control in cultural China: Power, money and media* (pp. 112–151). Evanston, IL: Northwestern University Press.

Hofstede, G. (1984). *Cultural consequences: International differences in work-related values.* Beverly Hills, CA: Sage.

Hofstede, G. (2001). *Culture's consequences: Comparing values, behaviors, institutions, and organizations across nations.* Thousand Oaks, CA: Sage.

Hofstede, G., & Bond, M. H. (1984). Hofstede's cultural dimensions: An independent valuation using Rokeach's value survey. *Journal of Cross-Cultural Psychology, 15,* 417–433.

Hofstede, G., & Bond, M. H. (1998). *Masculinity and femininity: The taboo dimensions of national cultures.* Thousand Oaks, CA: Sage.

Hong, J., & Cuthbert, M. (1991). Media reform in China since 1978: Background factors, problems and future trends. *Gazette, 47,* 141–158.

Huesca, R. (2001). Conceptual contributions of new social movements to development communication research. *Communication Theory, 11,* 415–433.

Kissinger, H. A. (1997, March 3). The philosopher and pragmatist. *Newsweek,* pp. 42–47.

Latham, K. (2000). Nothing but the truth: News media, power and hegemony in south China. *China Quarterly, 163,* 633–654.

Lee, C. C. (2000). Chinese communication: Prisms, trajectories and modes of understanding. In C. C. Lee (Ed.), *Communication patterns and bureaucratic control in cultural China: Power, money and media.* (pp. 3–44). Evanston, IL: Northwestern University Press.

Lee, P. S. (1994). Mass communication and national development in China: Media roles reconsidered. *Journal of Communication, 44*(3), 22–37.

Lu, X. (2000). The influence of classical Chinese rhetoric on contemporary Chinese political communication and social relations. In D. R. Heisey (Ed.), *Chinese perspectives in rhetoric and communication* (pp. 3–23). Stamford, CT: Ablex.

Luo, Y. (1999). Time-based experience and international expansion: The case of an emerging economy. *Journal of Management Studies, 36,* 505–534.

Ma, E. K. (2000). Rethinking media studies: The case of China. In J. Curran & M. J. Park (Eds.), *De-westernizing media studies* (pp. 21–34). New York: Routledge.

Mann, J. (1989). *Beijing Jeep: The short unhappy romance of American business in China.* New York: Simon & Schuster.

Meissner, W. (2002). Culture relations between China and member states of the European Union. *China Quarterly,* 181–203.

Nathan, A. J. (2001). The Tiananamen papers: An editor's reflections. *China Quarterly, 167,* 724–737.

Ng, R. M. (2000). The influence of Confucianism on Chinese conceptions of power, authority, and the rule of law. In D. R. Heisey (Eds.), *Chinese perspectives in rhetoric and communication* (pp. 45–55). Stamford, CT: Ablex.

Pan, Z. (2000). Improvising reform activities: The changing reality of journalistic practice in China. In C. C. Lee (Ed.), *Communication patterns and bureaucratic control in cultural China: Power, money and media* (pp. 68–111). Evanston, IL: Northwestern University Press.

Park, M. (1998). On Lu Xin's attitude toward the masses. *Chinese Culture, 39*(1), 93–108.

Parsons, T. (1951). *The social system.* London: Routledge & Kegan Paul.

Pastor, R. A., & Tan, Q. (2000). The meaning of China's village elections. *China Quarterly, 162,* 490–512.

Presbyterian Mission Board (2001). China: *Evangelism* and *leadership development,* In the 2002 Mission Yearbook. Louisville, Ky. Presbyterian Church U. S. A.

Qiu, J. L. (2000). Interpreting the Dengist rhetoric of building socialism with Chinese characteristics. In D. R. Heisey (Ed.), *Chinese perspectives in rhetoric and communication* (pp. 249–264). Stamford, CT: Ablex.

Rosen, S. (2000). Seeking appropriate behavior under a socialist market economy. In C. C. Lee (Ed.), *Communication patterns and bureaucratic control in cultural China: Power, money and media* (pp. 152–178). Evanston, IL: Northwestern University Press.

Saich, T. (2000, March). Negotiating the state: The development of social organizations in China. *China Quarterly, 161,* 124–141.

Schoenhals, M. (1999). Political movements, change and stability: The Chinese Communist Party in power. *China Quarterly, 159,* 595–605.

Schramm, W., Chu, G. C., & Yu, F. T. C. (1976). China's experience with development communication: How transferable is it? In G. Chu, F. Hung, W. Schramm, S. Uhalley, Jr., & F. T. C. Yu (Eds.), Communication and development in China (pp. 85–101). *Communication Monographs* (Vol. 1). Honolulu, HI: East–West Center.

Shi, T. (2000). Cultural values and democracy in the People's Republic of China. *China Quarterly, 162,* 540–559.

Siebert, F., Peterson, T., & Schramm, W. (1956). *Four theories of the press.* Urbana, IL: University of Illinois Press.

Sparks, C. (2000). Media theory after the fall of European communism. In J. Curran & M. J. Park (Eds.), *De-westernizing media studies* (pp. 35–49). London: Routledge.

Sriramesh, K. (1996). Power distance and public relations: An ethnographic study of southern Indian organizations. In H. M. Culbertson & N. Chen (Eds.), *International public relations: A comparative analysis* (pp. 171–190). Mahwah, NJ: Lawrence Erlbaum Associates.

Sriramesh, K., Grunig, J. E., & Dozier, D. (1996). Observation and measurement of two dimensions of organizational culture and their relationship to public relations. *Journal of Public Relations Research, 8,* 229–261.

Sriramesh, K., & White, J. (1992). Societal culture and public relations. In J. E. Grunig (Ed.), *Excellence in public relations and communication management* (pp. 597–614). Hillsdale, NJ: Lawrence Erlbaum Associates.

Taylor, M. (2000). Cultural variance as a challenge to global public relations: A case study of the Coca-Cola scare in Europe. *Public Relations Review, 16,* 277–293.

Verčič, D., Grunig, L. A. & Grunig, J. E. (1996). Global and specific principles of public relations: Evidence from Slovenia. In H. Culbertson & N. Chen (Eds.), *International public relations: A comparative analysis* (pp. 31–65). Mawhaw, NJ: Lawrence Erlbaum Associates.

Wu, G. (2000). One head, many mouths: Diversifying press structures in reform China. In C. C. Lee (Ed.), *Communication patterns and bureaucratic control in cultural China: Power, money and media* (pp. 45–67). Evanston, IL: Northwestern University Press.

Xiao, X. (2000). Sun Yat-Sen's rhetoric of cultural nationalism. In D. R. Heisey (Ed.), *Chinese perspectives in rhetoric and communication* (pp. 165–177). Stamford, CT: Ablex.

Yan, L. (2000). China. In S. A. Gunartne (Ed.), *Handbook of the media in Asia* (pp. 497–526). Thousand Oaks, CA: Sage.

Yang, M. M. (1994). *Gifts, favors and banquets: The art of social relationships in China.* Ithaca, NY: Cornell University Press.

Yanhai, W. (2000–2001, Winter). A strange love affair. *China Rights Forum,* pp. 3–9.

Yankelovich, D. (1981). *New rules: Searching for self-fulfillment in a world turned upside down.* New York: Random House.

Yu, F. T. C. (1963). Communications and politics in communist China. In L. W. Pye (Ed.), *Communications and political development* (pp. 259–297). Princeton, NJ: Princeton University Press.

Yu, X. (1994). Professionalization without guarantees. *Gazette, 53,* 23–41.

Yu, X. (2000). Examining the impact of cultural values and cultural assumptions on motivational factors in the Chinese organizational context: A cross-cultural perspective. In D. R. Heisey (Ed.), *Chinese perspectives in rhetoric and communication* (pp. 119–138). Stamford, CT: Ablex.

Zhang, N. (2000). Official role models and unofficial responses: Problems of model emulation in post-Mao China. In D. R. Heisey (Ed.), *Chinese perspectives in rhetoric and communication* (pp. 67–85). Stamford, CT: Ablex.

3

SHARING THE TRANSFORMATION: PUBLIC RELATIONS AND THE UAE COME OF AGE

BADRAN A. BADRAN

JUDY VANSLYKE TURK

TIMOTHY N. WALTERS

Much like the country itself, the practice of public relations in the United Arab Emirates (UAE) has undergone a profound evolution during its short history of 30 years. As the country has grown, so too has the practice of public relations. Once no agencies existed, but today global multinational public relations firms have established a presence in the UAE, some with an equity relationship with their local partners, some as fully owned branches of global firms based in the United States or Europe, and others through affiliates. Companies like Team: Young and Rubicam, Gulf Hill and Knowlton, and Burston–Marsteller operate alongside local, smaller companies, competing for the same dollars and dirhams.

Fueling the development of these agencies has been the explosive growth of the country. The simple, clear, and deep understanding of national priorities set by President His Highness Sheikh Zayed bin Sultan Al Nahyan, who has led the country since its formation in 1971, has moved the UAE to a diversified economy with one of the world's highest standards of living. Once petrocarbons dominated, but now the UAE has broadened its economic scope. The federal government has invested heavily in tourism, aviation, re-export commerce, and recently telecommunications, and it has made progress in shifting the UAE economy from its sole dependence on oil.

The practice of public relations has experienced a parallel growth and increase in sophistication. What once was viewed as the domain of good-looking people who received visitors, provided hospitality, and arranged protocol, is now looked at as a business function, dedicated to managing the resources of the organization for achieving organizational goals.

Helping to make the industry more professional is the Middle East Public Relations Association (MEPRA), which was launched in 2001 with the goal of increasing awareness, raising the level of professionalism, and providing a voice for the public relations industry. One of the association's main goals is to assure that its members adhere to a professional code of conduct.

HISTORY AND DEVELOPMENT OF THE COUNTRY

At about 83,000 km^2, the UAE occupies territory a little smaller than state of Maine in the United States or about four fifths the size of Tasmania. The UAE, a union of seven emirates, is a land of stark contrasts, combining natural wonders such as mountains, beaches, oases, and desert with gleaming man-made modern cities (Babbili & Hussain, 1994, p. 294; see also *Dubai Explorer*, 2001). Two geographical features—the ocean and the desert—have long dictated the pulse of life in this region (Babbili & Hussain, 1994, p. 294). Offshore islands, coral reefs, and salt marshes fill the Arabian Gulf coast, whereas gravel plain and barren desert span the vast inland. To the east the Hajar Mountains rise from the desert, lumbering northward into the Musandam peninsula at the mouth of the Arabian Gulf and reaching an apex of 1,527 m at Jabal Yibir. The western interior of the federation, most belonging to Abu Dhabi, consists mainly of desert dotted with oases (*UAE Yearbook*, 2000/2001, pp. 29–30).

The UAE lies in an arid belt extending across Asia and North Africa, bisected by the Tropic of Cancer. Noticeable variations in climate exist among the coastal regions, interior deserts, and mountains. From November to March mean daytime temperatures are 26°C; nighttime temperatures drop to an almost crisp 15°C. In the summer, temperatures can top out at a life-threatening 50°C. An average of less than 6.5 cm of annual rainfall occurs mainly between November and March, makeing the country's rising population dependent on expensive desalinization (*UAE Yearbook*, 2000/2001, pp. 29–30; *Dubai Explorer*, 2001; CIA, 2001). Sand storms often occur usually from the shamal, a powerful wind from the north or west, that kicks up sand during the winter, whereas the hot-tongued khamsin blows hot air and sand during the summer.

Archaeological evidence has painted a picture of human inhabitance stretching back several thousand years, perhaps as early as 5000 B.C. Early records show sophisticated societies that successfully exploited the environment, raising herds of sheep, goats, and cattle where possible, traversing the long "sand sea" trade routes when necessary, and using the 1,318 km-long coastline to dive for pearls and engage in seafaring occupations such as fishing and trading across the gulf (*UAE Yearbook*, 2000, 2001, pp. 42–43, 46, 51–52, 56).

Some premodern forces shaping the UAE are similar to those affecting other regions in the Middle East. These include the tribal system, a form of governmental rule and societal organization reaching back thousands of years. Ibn Khaldun (1332–1406) provided insight into this organization, much of which is as pertinent to society today it was 6 centuries ago (Barfield, 1990, pp. 154–163). Ibn Khaldun observed that the tribal system relied on actual descent and blood or marital ties for the lower ranks and on political ties for the higher ranks. Continued rule was based on respect and veneration (the notion of *asabiyya*) rather than coercion. It still is, although the blend of these principles varies from emirate to emirate (Van Der Meulen, 1997, pp. 21, 33).

During the British occupation, tribal forms of government were encouraged for the sake of domestic tranquility. The consequences of the decision to manage through the tribal system was far-reaching, confirming the rulers' autonomy and power (Van Der Meulen, 1997). When the UAE moved to independence in 1971, these power organizations carried forward. That meant that the structure and the history of the estimated 42 to 45 Arab tribes located within the UAE were reflected in the country's political process. So, by both law and custom, the Supreme Council of Rulers, the presidency, the Council of Ministers, and the Federal National Council respect and confirm the power of the ruling families in each emirate and the ruling families' relationships with the prominent tribes (Van Der Meulen, 1997, p. 10).

The paramount role of the tribes and their rulers has continued to date; consequently, the legitimacy of the families is unchallenged (Barfield, 1990, p. 156; Van Der Meulen, 1997, p. 10). That means any discussion of UAE's governmental structure must begin from the standpoint of internal tribal origins, partly because many members of the extended family hold high governmental and nongovernmental positions (Tibi, 1990; Van Der Meulen, 1997). That also means family names such as Al Nahyan, Al Maktoum, Al Qasimi, Al Mu'alla, Al Nuaimi, and Al Sharqi appear on the rosters of those holding vital governmental and key business positions.

EVOLUTION AND DEFINITION OF THE PUBLIC RELATIONS PROFESSION

The Western model of public relations in the UAE is a new phenomenon that emerged in the early 1970s. As Cutlip and Broom (1985) noted, the term *public relations* has greatly varying connotations in the United States. Sriramesh and White (1992) argued that cultural differences among societies must affect how public relations is practiced by people within different societies (p. 597). In the Arab World, the nature, goals, roles, and functions of public relations are often described as "vague" (Al Enad, 1990, p. 24).

The vagueness has more to do with the traditional view of public relations than the modern one. Traditionally, public relations was used to describe those individuals and departments whose duties usually were restricted to procuring visas, arranging transportation, and performing hospitality functions (Ayish & Kruckeberg, 1999, p. 124). Moreover, many so called "public relations offices" secured contracts for domestic maids from Southeast Asian countries to work in the UAE and provided secretarial services, such as typing and copying documents (Badran, 1994, p. 3).

The Department of Mass Communication at the UAE University (UAEU) surveyed public relations perceptions and activities in public and private organizations in four major UAE cities in 1994 (Badran, 1994). The survey indicated that most respondents viewed public relations as embodying visitor reception and hospitality, protocol arrangements, and information documentation. Very few respondents viewed public relations as part of the institutional decision-making mechanism.

As for perceptions of a professional public relations practitioner, many respondents thought of him or her as good-looking, educated, open-minded, and highly sociable. Almost all placed a high value on building positive images for their organizations and on satisfying the needs and tastes of the general public. Among the functions not considered within the domain of public relations practice in the UAE were planning; counseling management; anticipating, analyzing, and interpreting public opinion; and managing the resources of the organization for achieving its goals (Badran, 1994, p. 9).

Although some job descriptions for public relations officers in public and private organizations today still reflect the early press agentry model of public relations practice, by and large the modern definition of public relations as a management function is taking hold in the UAE. This change was caused by the arrival of professional public relations agencies in the 1970s and the introduction of public relations education in the country in the 1990s. Though programs generally are heavily oriented toward courses on new technologies, communications departments at the University of Sharjah, American University of Sharjah, American University of Dubai, UAEU, and Zayed University teach either public relations or advertising courses or both.

In the Arab world, the advertising and public relations business reportedly dates back to the 1930s. It began in the Levant as a simple industry, catering to basic needs (Ghassoub, 2002, p. 64). The Lebanese civil war in the mid-1970s forced many advertising and public relations professionals to flee Lebanon. Some, like Eddie Moutran, Akram Miknas, Talal El Makdessi, and Ramzi Raad, chose to work in the gulf. These professionals and a few others like Burhan Beidas and Tareq Noor are usually referred to as advertising legends in the Middle East. They founded successful agencies like Fortune Promoseven, Memac, Intermarkets, and PubliGraphics in Bahrain, Saudi Arabia, the UAE, and elsewhere ("Talking Heads," 2001).

According to Joseph Ghassoub, vice president of the International Advertising Association and managing partner of Team: Young and Rubicam, the real explosion came with the boom in satellite television after the Gulf War. The free-to-air satellite channels that began beaming into people's homes and a concurrent boom in the print media led to this upsurge. Since then, Ghassoub (2002, p. 64) contended, advertising and public relations budgets have been growing at an average rate of 15% per year throughout the region. Standard practice in the UAE and the rest of the gulf was the establishment of an all-purpose company that would offer all advertising, marketing, public relations, and below-the-line services. Nowadays, full-service agencies have given way to segmented and specialized operations.

To mark the development and growing sophistication of the public relations industry, MEPRA was launched in 2001 and officially licensed by the government the following year. MEPRA's main role is "to increase awareness and gain real understanding for public relations as an important economic activity in the region, raise the level of professionalism in public relations and provide a unified voice for the public relations industry to advise, inform and educate the Middle East market about public relations practice."

MEPRA's Chairman Sadri Barrage said public relations is becoming much more widely understood by business and government organizations in the UAE and is becoming increasingly recognized as a strategic communications tool. "The market here has still a lot to learn, however, and this is one of MEPRA's main objectives." Nevertheless, he acknowledged that the public relations industry is still facing a great deal of ignorance (S. Barrage, personal communication, March, 2002). One of MEPRA's key objectives is to create educational forums in the region for young nationals to consider public relations as an exciting career opportunity (MEPRA, 2002). MEPRA defines public relations as "the discipline that looks after reputation with the aim of earning understanding and support, and influencing opinion and behavior." According to MEPRA, public relations also embodies the planned and sustained effort to establish and maintain goodwill and mutual understanding between an organization and its publics (S. Barrage, personal communication, March 15, 2002).

STATUS OF THE PROFESSION

Despite its short history of about 30 years, the UAE public relations and advertising market today includes both global players and local agencies. Global multinationals have established a presence in the UAE, some with an equity relationship with their local partners, some as fully owned-branches, and some through affiliates. The largest professional agencies have their headquarters in Dubai, the UAE's center for business and commerce. The capital, Abu Dhabi, has one or two large agencies and a number of smaller agencies. The same is true in Sharjah, the third largest emirate.

Until recently, the main practitioners of public relations and buyers of public relations services have been multinational businesses and institutions. This is not just because of their economic size but also because of their appreciation of the importance of public relations. Organizations in the area are becoming increasingly sophisticated in their use of communications, which in turn is resulting in public relations becoming a more common practice in the region.

Promoseven PR is part of the Promoseven Network and is considered the market leader in the UAE. Promoseven is an affiliate of McCann–Erickson World Group. In a recent *Gulf Marketing Review* survey of local and multinational advertisers, this agency ranked first among agencies and was the agency with the highest awareness level among clients ("Shining Stars," 2001). Promoseven PR provides public, press, and government relations to independent clients and the agency's advertising clients. It provides organizational services of press offices for sporting events and international exhibitions, conferences, and seminars. In addition, it has an Arab media monitoring service and a specialized unit for product launches, conferences, and special events in all the Gulf Coast Council (GCC), Levant, and North African countries (*Promoseven*, 2001).

Promoseven PR reports that only 30% of its clients have appointed them on a project basis, with the remainder either on a retainer basis or a mix of retainer and project. What is interesting is that 10% of its customers also have an in-house unit.

Other major players include Asda'a Public Relations (the regional affiliate of Burson-Marsteller), Memac, Ogilvy and Mather, Team: Young and Rubicam, Gulf Hill and Knowlton, RSCG, and Bates Pan Gulf. These and smaller agencies compete for approximately $25 million spent on public relations annually in the UAE.

These firms consider people, time, and knowledge as the key resources for generating revenue for a public relations consultancy. Generally, UAE public sector organizations adopt one of two solutions for their public relations needs. They either have in-house departments of media or public relations or they outsource public relations services with professional agencies. Those who feel the need for a full in-house department staff it with public relations professionals who perform functions such as media relations, event management, exhibitions, media production, and public opinion research. An example of this group is the Dubai Municipality.

For those who choose to hire a professional public relations agency, the available services are comparable in quality and quantity to anywhere else in the world. For example, Emirates Internet and Multimedia (EIM), a unit of the UAE's sole telecommunications and Internet service provider, is a client of Asda'a public relations. EIM can avail itself of the following services from its public relations firm: perception management, issues management, business-to-business communication, consumer awareness and education, internal communications, media relations, government relations, investor relations, technology communications, media training, crisis communications, corporate advertising, event management, publishing (both print and web-based), and media monitoring.

Jock Wilson, regional director of Promoseven PR, noted that there is a tendency among UAE clients to focus too much on media relations. Public relations, he said, should be "the active management of an organization's reputation to this stakeholders' audience." Stakeholders include employees, customers, investors, suppliers, government institutions, and the media (Mirabel, October 2001, p. 41). Chair of MEPRA Sadri Barrage has confirmed that media relations is the most commonly used public relations function in the UAE. "Most consultancies in our region offer a wide range of services that cover the entire spectrum of public relations activities but depending on the client profile, I would say that media relations remains the cornerstone of our practice" (S. Barrage, personal communication, March, 2002).

Asda'a's Managing Director Sunil John shares this view. "A typical client's view," John said, "is that public relations is a media relations service and is all about press conferences and press relations." He added, however, that this attitude is changing as more clients today look to public relations more as a strategic consultancy (Mirabel, 2001, p. 42). Current public relations services offered include media monitoring and evaluation, lobbying, sponsorships, events, promotions, and competitions. Future growth areas include corporate communications, covering employee and investor relations, crisis management, and the release of financial information.

PROFESSIONALISM IN THE PUBLIC RELATIONS INDUSTRY

According to MEPRA, most local and regional consultancies enjoy a high level of professionalism. Generally speaking, private and public sectors vary in the level of professionalism exhibited. Although the majority of public relations agencies maintain high professional standards, the public sector, which has in-house public relations departments, practices a narrower range of functions with varying degrees of professionalism. The quality of public relations services rendered also varies between the main urban centers of Dubai and Abu Dhabi and the rest of the country. Outside of these two cities, practices are less professional due to the scarcity of skilled and trained professionals.

Several issues face the profession in the UAE. One is price-cutting (undercutting the competition). This is the practice of smaller operators who cater to price-conscious clients. Price-cutting, although not practiced by all, affects standards and leads to price wars. Another issue is the practice of managing accounts for two or more competitors simultaneously, which is perhaps more of a problem in the advertising industry but it also occurs in the public relations industry. Lastly, gifts and other contributions that some public relations agencies and organizations offer to media professionals in exchange for positive editorial coverage raise serious ethical questions. Anecdotal evidence exists of offers of expensive items as "gifts" to reporters and editors in the UAE.

The practice of publishing press releases verbatim is also customary in some UAE publications compared with the West where the media closely scrutinize and edit news releases. MEPRA's chair says that the adherence of its members to the association's professional code of conduct ensures adherence to high ethics. For us, Barrage said, this a crucial matter of survival. "PR ethics . . . are high on the list of any professional discussions we may have" (S. Barrage, personal communication, March, 2002).

INFRASTRUCTURE AND INTERNATIONAL PUBLIC RELATIONS

The Nation's Political System

Seven rulers exercise political power over a federation established in 1971. None of the emirates has any democratically elected individuals or institutions, and their rule has been both tradition based and patriarchal (United States Department of State, 2001). Because political parties and elections are prohibited, the citizens of the UAE cannot change their government democratically. Citizens may express concerns directly to their rulers by traditional means including the *majlis*—a public forum (International Press Institute [IPI], 2000; also see United States Department of State, 2001).

The seven emirate rulers constitute the Federal Supreme Council, the highest legislative and executive body. The council selects a president and a vice president from its membership, and the president appoints the prime minister and cabinet. The cabinet manages the federation on a day-to-day basis. A consultative body, the Federal National Council, comprised of advisors appointed by the emirate rulers, has no legislative authority, but it questions government ministers in open sessions and makes policy recommendations to the cabinet (United States Department of State, 2001).

Each emirate retains control over its own oil and mineral wealth, some parts of internal security, and some regulation of internal and external commerce. The federal government has primacy in matters of defense and foreign policy, some aspects of internal security, and, increasingly, in the supply of government services (United States Department of State, 2001).

The judiciary generally is independent, but political leaders can review its decisions. The legal system of the UAE is based on a constitution approved by the Federal National Council in 1996, replacing the provisional documents that had been renewed every 5 years since the country's creation in 1971 (www.infoprod.co.il/uae2a.htm). Based on tradition, the constitution, and legislation, the legal system of the UAE has been influenced by Islamic, Roman, and French law (www.law.emory.edu/IFL /legal/UAE.htm; also see www.uottawa.ca. world-legal-systems/eng-common.htm). Common law principles have become important in commercial contracts, and Federal Law No. 40 modernized intellectual property law in 1992 (Abu Ghazaleh, 2002; Dubaiinc, 2001; IPR, 2001). Local government varies from emirate to emirate and is very much a product of the country's growth and urbanization. Hence, the largest, most prosperous emirate, Abu Dhabi, has the most complex local government (*UAE Yearbook*, 2000/2001).

One notable feature remaining from the honored past is the custom of the *majlis*. Traditionally, the sheikh or ruler of an emirate was the leader of the most powerful tribe, and each individual tribe, and often each of its various subsections, also generally had a chief or sheikh. Such leaders kept their authority only as long as they could retain the loyalty and support of their people. Part of that process was the unwritten (but strong) principle that the people should have free access to their sheikh by means of a frequent *majlis*, or public council, in which his fellow tribesmen could voice their opinions.

Today, the *majlis* has maintained its relevance. In large emirates, the ruler and several senior family members hold open *majlis*es. In smaller emirates, the *majlis* of the ruler himself, or of the crown prince or deputy ruler, remain the main focus. To these come traditional-minded tribesmen who may have waited months for the opportunity to speak with their ruler directly, rather than to pursue their requests or complaints through a modern government structure.

In the *majlis*, often heated discussions between sheikhs and other citizens cover everything from questions about governmental policy to relations with neighboring countries. On matters more directly affecting individuals, debates occur before a consensus approach evolves. Frequently, that consensus is later reflected in changes in government policy (taken from http://www.iornet.org /newiornet/uae2.htm).

Level of Economic Development

The UAE has undergone a profound transformation from an impoverished region of small desert principalities to a modern state with a high standard of living. The simple, clear, and deep understanding by President His Highness Sheikh Zayed bin Sultan Al Nahyan of national priorities has fueled this growth. Growth flowed from one early decision on managing water:

> The first fundamental change, and the most important...(was) the availability of drinking water. The bringing of water was...important. After (water came) everything started changing. Housing became available when there was none before, then infrastructure and everything else. Our policy was first to concentrate all our efforts to develop this country, and to develop its citizens. (*UAE Yearbook*, 1995, p. 19)

Today, the UAE reflects His Highness President Nahyan's dream. It has an oil-and-gas driven economy with an estimated 2000 gross domestic product (GDP) per capita of approximately $22,800 (in purchasing power parity [PPP]) and Human Development Indicators ranking it in the top portion of the Human Development Index (CIA, 2001; Human Development Indicators, 2001, p. 141; *UAE Yearbook*, 2000/2001). These figures compare favorably to PPP figures of neighboring countries: Bahrain, $15,900; Egypt, $3,600; India, $2,200; Iraq, $2,500; Kuwait, $15,000; Oman, $7,700; Pakistan, $2,000; Qatar, $20,300; Saudi Arabia, $10,500; and Syria, $3,100 (CIA, 2001).

Although overall per capita PPP is high in the UAE, disparity exists between the emirates. Income distribution is skewed toward Abu Dhabi and Dubai, a product of oil and gas production. Abu Dhabi and Dubai have per capita GDPs of $23,929 and $16,094, respectively; Sharjah's is $9,838, Ras Al Khaimah's is $8,076, Ajman's is $6.047, Fujairah's is $7,955, and Umm Al Quwain's is $7,154 (Al Sadik, n.d., p. 203). Thus, economic development in the UAE is much the tale of its two largest cities.

As oil and gas revenues flow from the wellhead, life is lived large with the Emirati equivalent of two cars in every garage because the emirate of Abu Dhabi is generous with its oil revenue. The federal government supports the trappings of an easy life with low-cost education and medicine, high-paying jobs, short working hours, and inexpensive housing loans for nationals. Inspired by the benevolent leadership of President His Highness Sheikh Zayed bin Sultan Al Nahyan who has led the country through its entire existence, the UAE has blossomed in the desert and has taken steps to move away from its oil dependence.

The federal government has invested heavily in tourism, aviation, re-export commerce, and, more recently, telecommunications. It has made progress in shifting the UAE economy from an overdependence on petrocarbons. In 1975, crude oil contributed to about 68% of the total economy. By 1998, that figure had fallen to about 22%. As oil dependence fell, manufacturing grew from less than 1% of the economy in 1975 to 12.4%. Commerce, restaurants, and hotels went from about 9% to about 14% and real estate from 2.5% to 10.5% (Shihab, n.d., p. 253).

In facilitating this shift, the country's leadership has recognized that the UAE must make more of its human resources. Devoid of most natural resources except for petrocarbons, the UAE, particularly the emirate of Dubai, has invested billions of dirhams in high technology. The great dream is that this human capital, with its various skills and abilities, can create income-yielding activities and serve as pillar of the future (G. J. Walters, 2001, p. 82). Technology (and technology-related communication) is a great hope for the future; yet, although it offers promise, it presents significant challenges as well. As information technology science and technology come to propel the economy, that same science and technology will not only provide jobs but gateways to knowledge capable of empowering individuals. This empowerment is sure to challenge traditional notions of society and how that society functions in the UAE.

Level of Activism

In Arab and Islamic societies people serve families and families serve society, with the individual finishing last (Nawar, 2000; Patai, 1983). For most, the rule of the family is the norm. There are no political parties and no freedoms other than those the ruler offers his "family" or those that the head of a household offers his wife and children. Across the UAE, families also share many common characteristics—the first of which is an abiding dedication to Islam. Muslims have experienced no need for the development of secularism, as has the West. Indeed, Islam is not a "matter of religion as Westerners understand it, "said Mary-Jane Deeb, adjunct professor at American University. Islam is perceived by Muslims as a total way of life. "Conservative Muslims see the West imposing an entire system of economic, political and social values that strike at the heart of Islamic way of life. Westerners would consider most of these values secular, but to conservative Muslims almost nothing is secular. The Koran governs everything . . ." (cited in Ringle, 2001 p. C01). Thus, in the UAE Islam is normative, the sustaining force. It permeates the entire society (Lewis, 1994; Patai, 1983).

Besides Islam, other strands of a long, proud history are woven into the tapestry of society. The Arabic language is one strand. It carries with it emotions, feelings, and thoughts, creating an artistic expression of sound and rhythm that Naguib Mahfouz described as "searching for tunes in the air" (Mahfouz, 1986, p. 33). Loyalty and an emphasis on honor, both drawn from a simpler past, are other valued traits (Patai, 1983).

The advent of political Islam has made issues inherent in economic modernization of society a triangulated problem. The government has the power to control and suppress. Some religious fundamentalists fear those who advocate too much change too quickly and are concerned about the destruction of the traditional values they hold dear. Others, anxious for development, advocate enhanced (and Westernized) freedoms (Nawar, 2000). Thus, navigating the shoals of change will require steady hands and a delicate touch as the Emirates comes to grips with the demands of a new economy (see Kristof, 2002).

Legal Infrastructure

Law by itself does not determine how free, pluralistic, or independent the media will be. That is because the interaction between legal and social–cultural institutions define this freedom (Price & Krug, 2000, pp. 8–10). Laws help, of course, but even authoritarian societies have mastered the vocabulary of free expression (and access to that expression) and have written it into their constitutions (see International Constitutional Law, n.d.).

The will of the people and the development of civic society have great impact on the reality of what actually happens (Bryant, 1995; Diamond, 1994; Geremek, 1992; O'Donnell & Schmitter, 1986). Civic society exists above the individual level but below that of the state and is institutionalized and generalized through law, custom, and practice. In civic society, complex networks of economic, social, and cultural practices based on friendship, family, the market, and voluntary association influence daily life (Wapner, 1995). Sometimes, but not always, civic society is a precursor to a democratic state (Bryant, 1995; Diamond, 1994; Geremek, 1992; O'Donnell & Schmitter, 1986).

Such civic forces are in play in the UAE, where kinship and marriage count, and extended family networks wield enormous power in all aspects of life. So anything related to lifestyle becomes inexorably intertwined with family, tradition, religion, and heritage (see, e.g., Essoulami, 2001; Za'Za', 2002).

CULTURE AND PUBLIC RELATIONS

Social Cultural Aspects of the UAE

As explained in chapter 1, culture provides a road map for how an individual should function in society, and the defining markers of that roadway include knowledge, beliefs, art, morals, law, custom, capabilities, habits, and values acquired by individuals in their daily living. We are not born with the knowledge of how to decipher this map. Culture (and its constituent parts) is a learned, shared, compelling, interrelated set of symbols whose meanings provide orientations for members of a society.

A focus on the individual, isolated, and independent is embedded in the values and culture of Western societies such as the United States (Connard, 1996). Traditionally, Arabic and Islamic societies such as the UAE have focused more on the group and on interrelated networks, defined in no small measure by religion and circles of kinship. But the underlying social environments are undergoing change as the UAE moves toward a more urban, diverse, and modern economy. This transition may be producing a transitional society (Connard, 1996).

Women in the UAE, as in other places, have several models of choice for life. One is a three-way model suggesting that those choices are leisure, paid work in the office or unpaid work in the home (Jalilvand, 2000). The UAE government's public policy views women in a dual role. They are both the hand that rocks the cradle and the force that runs the economy. It is the policy of the government to increase the number of women from the current level of about 15% of the workforce to about 50% by the year 2020. As this unfolds, women, and no doubt all of society, will feel the tug of push–pull forces affecting personal and societal values and shaking the traditional model of the household (Jaliivand, 2000, p. 27; also see Iglehart, 1979; Mott & Shapiro, 1983). Some driving forces that are helping to catapult the current pioneering generation of women into the marketplace are the changes in education, the perceived worth of education, the restructuring of the economy, and increasing urbanization. These have a profound effect on the evolving society in the UAE as well.

Perhaps equipoised is the best description of Arabic and Islamic society as it relates to the transitional woman. Much of what has occurred in the UAE since its formation as a nation in 1971 has been the product of the aging President His Highness Sheikh Zayed bin Sultan Al Nahyan whose birth year is listed as somewhere between 1908 and 1915 (Van Der Meulen, 1997 p. 109). Whether the country stays the course after his death is unclear.

Is the UAE undergoing a cultural revitalization? Does the whole culture believe that the old ways do not work best? Or, is there a hard core that will return to traditional mores and ways if the leadership that succeeds His Highness President Zayed is less forward-looking than that of the founding President (Walters, T. & Walters, L., 2002)?

The answers, though unclear, will chart the course for the UAE's future, because of Islam's relationship to all things. Traditional Islamic order asserts that all things spring from the God-given Holy Law of Islam (Lewis, 1994, p. 37). Islamic order does several things: It creates a shorthand for operating in life, impacts a set of values, and establishes order in the family. Moreover, it serves as a reference point so that Muslims can say that something is taboo (*haram*—forbidden) or permitted (*halal*—permissible or allowed).

For conservative Muslims, alteration of core values is nothing less than an attack on their faith. "Brought up in a complex but functioning system of social loyalties and responsibilities, (a conservation male) finds those loyalties, defined by faith and kin, denounced as sectarian and nepotistic, and those responsibilities derided and abandoned in favor of capitalistic acquisitiveness or socialistic expropriations" (Lewis, 1993, p. 39). Many male Muslims will not want to see their supremacy lost in their own homes "to emancipated women and rebellious children" (p. 40). Because children develop within the family and because outside forces are buffeting the family ecosystem, the roles of children and adults could be subject to change.

Qualities of UAE Culture

In many ways, the culture of the UAE has begun to diverge from that of the other countries on the Arabian peninsula. Although they share a common religion, high regard for the family, and similar style of governance, the UAE is at the crossroads of modernization. Higher education is greatly valued because the country's leadership wants to develop the UAE as the high-technology hub of the Middle East. Women have become valued not just as wives and mothers but as potential leaders in the workplace, and as this new generation of educated women evolves, so too must the role of men in the society.

So too will the army of expatriate workers on whom the emirates now depends to fuel the country's growth. Today, Nationals comprise about 20% of the 3 million plus population; natives of India and Pakistan account for more than 60%, and fewer than 2% of the population are European. As the announced policy of emiratization takes hold, these proportions will drastically change. As they do, the nature of the society will change as well.

THE MEDIA ENVIRONMENT

Media Control

With the exception of a few privately owned newspapers and radio stations, the UAE broadcast and print media are owned and operated by government departments or government-controlled organizations. Smaller media working in design, photography, advertising, public relations, and printing, among other areas, are privately owned. There are no media in the UAE that are affiliated with political parties. There are only publications by public and private organizations, licensed professional associations, and other nongovernmental organizations.

Recently, there have been signs of a decline in government subsidy for public media and more dependence on advertising or sponsorship for revenue. In fact, the Ministry of Information and Culture has taken the lead in requiring its own media to play by the rules of the private sector. This is in line with a drive by some emirates, such as Abu Dhabi, to privatize their public institutions in a bid to expand sources of income (www.uaeinteract.com, 2001).

The UAE media scene has seen significant changes in the last decade, led by Abu Dhabi and Dubai's efforts to modernize, expand, and create new media enterprises. Developments include an increase in new media outlets, a reform and modernization of older media, creation of Dubai Media City (DMC), application of intellectual property laws in the country, and a new vision of more freedom and less censorship.

In terms of infrastructure, each of the emirates has its own distinct media set up and runs them based on its particular philosophy regarding public media. Abu Dhabi has transformed its media from local to Pan-Arab, with emphasis on strong news and sports programs. Dubai's focus is on business, entertainment, sports, and promoting Dubai as a tourist destination. Sharjah's public media emphasize Islamic, cultural, historical, and children's programs. The Omran brothers, Abdulla and Taryam, own Dar Al Khaleej for Press, Printing & Publishing Ltd. in Sharjah. It publishes *Al Khaleej*, the best selling Arabic daily in the UAE with a circulation of 96,000 (The Times Group, 2002). *Al Khaleej* is a strong proponent of national issues and Pan-Arab causes.

Ajman TV has positioned itself as a favorite station for quiz and game shows, as well as drama and entertainment for the family. In addition to radio stations broadcasting in Arabic in the northern emirates, there are broadcasts in Hindi, Urdu, Malayalam, and English by stations like Umm Al Quwain, Ras Al Khaimah, Radio Asia, and Asianet (*TV and Radio-Guide*, 2002). These broadcasts are mostly intended for Asian expats from India and Pakistan who live and work in the UAE.

Not unlike many other countries, the UAE guarantees freedom of expression in its written constitution. Article 30 protects "freedom of opinion and expressing it verbally, in writing or by other means of expression shall be guaranteed within the limits of the law" (Human Rights Watch, 1999b). Article 31 guarantees "freedom of communication by post, telegraph, or other means of communication and (that) the secrecy thereof shall be guaranteed in accordance with the law" (Human Rights Watch, 1999b).

However it is Article 7 of the Constitution that gives an idea of what "accordance with the law" really means in the UAE. This article declares Islam the official state religion and Islamic *shari'a* (law) the principal source of legislation (Legal Profiles, Islamic Family Law). *Shari'a* is derived from principles of the Koran, explicated by Ijma, or rules that develop through debate and the resultant consensus of religious leaders (Kabbani, n.d.). So the law in the UAE is religious, not secular.

Although controls exist on the media in the UAE, these media are relatively free, particularly when compared with other gulf states (United States Department of State, 2001). The Minister of Information and Culture, a son of His Highness President Zayed, has been quoted as telling the media to "criticize freely," although there is no evidence that journalists have complied, particularly with respect to Emirati rulers and their extended families (Al Bakry, 2001; Human Rights Watch, 1999b; Owais & Matthew, 2000). Federal Law 15 of 1988 requires that all publications be licensed with the Ministry of Information and Culture and delineates acceptable subjects of reporting.

Reporters have established boundaries themselves, practicing self-censorship akin to prior restraint. Journalists censor themselves on sensitive subjects such as the ruling families, Islam, national security, government policy, religion, and relations with neighboring states. "Freedom without responsibility may invite chaos," Ayesha Ibrahim Sultan, head of the UAE journalists association, said. "Freedom and responsibility have to go hand in hand. If we separate them and allow total freedom, it will lead to chaos . . ." (Rahman, 2001). Freedom, then, is not absolute. It is limited because certain social aspects including the morals and values guiding a society must be considered (Rahman, 2001).

In establishing boundaries for expression, the UAE is no different than other societies. The First Amendment of the United States Constitution does not allow complete freedom, and Article 19 of the United Nation's Universal Declaration of Human Rights has exceptions in which governments can restrict information to protect certain interests such as national security, public order, or health or morals in what amounts to prior restraint (Human Rights Watch, 1999a).

The differences about what constitutes a threat to national security, public order, or health or morals rest in the eyes of the beholder. Stakeholders are considering what the limits should be. In a 1998 editorial, Abu Dhabi-based Al Ittihad urged people to adopt a modern cultural concept of freedom and make responsible decisions in real life. The article called for the formulation of an Arab concept of freedom (UAE Editorials, 1998). Just what that formulation might be remains the subject of vigorous debate. Some social forces have voiced hostility to the very pervasive modern media. The UAE, sensing an economic opportunity, has been more liberal than GCC sister states Saudi Arabia or Kuwait (Dubai Press Club, 2002). On May 10, 2001, His Excellency General Sheikh Mohammed bin Rashid Al Maktoum, Crown Prince of Dubai and UAE Minister of Defense, speaking in rather de Tocquevillean terms at the launch of DMC, said:

> We who live in today's cyber age increasingly understand the importance of information and the media that carries this information. The TV set, the newspaper, the radio and the mobile phone are the tools that allow us to utilize this information. But pause and think. If knowledge is power, then the media that brings it to us is the source of that power.
>
> As we look at the dynamic and fast changing media world around us we are continually reminded of the power of media. Improvements in technology are breathing new life into familiar media like TV, radio and print. New and advanced technologies such as the mobile phone and the computer have expanded the horizons and transfer of knowledge and information, making the world like a small village where people can communicate with each other.
>
> I guarantee freedom of expression to all of you. . . . Let us do so responsibly, objectively and with accountability and in the spirit of the social and cultural context in which we live.
>
> This freedom will allow and encourage the Arab media to return home, to broadcast and publish once again from Arab land, and contribute to this new regional media industry.
>
> Always remember, the human mind, once stretched by a new idea, never returns to its original size. It only grows larger. Media has the power to effect change and evolve. (*Gulf News*, 2001 online 11 May for more information see Wheeler, 2001)

The Federal National Council has echoed this sentiment, offered its support for freedom of expression, and stressed the need to support efforts to guard freedom of opinion and expression as provided by the constitution (Dawood, 2001). Although pursuing knowledge has been (and remains) essential to UAE society and is embodied in the Quran, the UAE walks a tightrope between unfettered information flow and protecting cultural heritage (Babbili & Hussain, 1994).

Media Reach

For generations, oral communication was the preferred form of transferring information and stories, and news was passed down from person to person. This has changed as the UAE has modernized. In the 1970s, only 15% of the population was literate. By 2002, that figure had jumped to about 85%, one of the highest on the Arabian Peninsula. At the same time, education in the UAE evolved too. In the school year 1974–1975, the total number of students enrolled in all levels of education was 60,254, with 520 students enrolled in colleges and universities. By 1994–1995, those figures had jumped enormously. The total number of students enrolled in all levels of education was 480,973, with 20,570 students enrolled in colleges and universities. Today these numbers are even higher (Al Sadik, n.d., p. 203).

As education grew, so too did means of communication. Partly because the UAE had not been a reading society and partly reflecting the development of an economic base for advertising, newspapers were slow to develop in the UAE. Even in the late 1960s, no indigenous newspapers were published, and the few newspapers available were imported. Kawas Motivala began publishing a small bulletin several times a week in 1967, but circulation was low. Two years later, *Al Ittihad* (meaning union) became the first permanent regular newspaper, and by 1971 *Emirates News* began its run (Babbili and Hussain, p. 297).

From these modest beginnings, the print industry has grown to include six Arabic language and three English language daily newspapers and more than 160 magazines and journals. Among these are newspapers such as Abu Dhabi-based *Akhbar Al Arab* (founded in 2000), *Al Ittihad* (founded in 1969), *Al Fajr* (founded in 1975), *Al Wihdah* (founded in 1973), Dubai-based *Al Bayan* (founded in 1980), *Khaleej Times* (founded in 1979), the *Gulf News* (founded in 1979), and Sharjah-based *Al Khaleej* (founded in 1970) and *Gulf Today*. Many of these have online versions.

The broadcast media, much like their print counterparts, have a short history in the UAE. Before independence, the British began the first radio service in Sharjah. Radio Abu Dhabi was the first station to broadcast Arabic programs in 1969. In 1971, installation or commissioning of modern studios in Abu Dhabi and Ras Al Khaimah and commercial stations in Abu Dhabi and Sharjah were completed (Babbili & Hussain, 1994, pp. 299–302). The history of television is much the same. The first black-and-white television pictures were broadcast from Abu Dhabi on August 6, 1969. Two years later, PAL color equipment was instated in Abu Dhabi; Dubai television's first broadcast was in 1972 (p. 304).

In January 1999, His Highness President Zayed issued a decree creating Emirates Media Incorporated (EMI) to replace all existing broadcast services. EMI, which is attached to the Ministry of Information and Culture, controls 6 of the country's 14 radio stations and three of the eight television channels. Based in Abu Dhabi, it is run by a board of nine directors, all of whom are nationals. His Excellency Sheikh Abdullah bin Zayed Al Nahyan, the Minister of Information and Culture, serves as chair (*UAE Yearbook*, 2000/2001, pp. 232–233).

Television is delivered over the air, via satellite, or on cable, offering a surprisingly broad menu of viewing alternatives assembled from across the gulf and around the world. The UAE now has eight satellite-delivered channels plus about 30 free-to-air channels. Because of the country's size and relatively flat topography, over the air radio and television reach most parts of the country, except the Hajar Mountains in the east. Electronic fare also includes Orbit Satellite Television, billed as the world's first fully digital, multi-channel, multilingual, direct-to-home, pay-TV and radio satellite service, with over 30 television and radio channels; Showtime Network Arabia, a satellite pay-TV network for the Middle East offering exciting Western entertainment for the entire family; and ART Network, a Pan-Arab satellite pay-TV network. E-Vision Cable TV, operated by Etisalat, the government-run monopoly telecoms provider, offers a basic service of 63 channel: 28 in Arabic, 16 in Hindi, 16 in English, 2 in English, and 1 in German.

The Emirates News Agency, WAM, is run through the Ministry of Information and Culture. It delivers news and features in Arabic and English to radio, television, and local newspapers and has exchange agreements with more than 20 Arab countries. WAM employs about 180 people inside the UAE in bureaus located throughout the emirates and has offices in cities such as Cairo, Beirut, Damascus, London, Paris, Islamabad, Tehran, Washington, DC, and New York.

The UAE is also working hard to develop new media. Launched in November 2000, multibillion dirham DMC was designed to make Dubai the regional center for media businesses and new technology workers (*UAE Yearbook*, 2000/2001, p. 233). Rising next to it on the 500 carefully manicured and watered hectares are Dubai Internet City (DIC) and Dubai Knowledge Village (DKV) (Quinn, 2002 p. 9).

The DIC was the region's first information technology zone and has been viewed by His Excellency General Sheikh Mohammed bin Rashid Al Maktoum, Dubai Crown Prince and the country's Defense Minister, as a project that would benefit Dubai's economy. In September 2001, an estimated 95% of the DIC area had already been spoken for by leading high-technology firms. According to DMC Chief Executive Ahmed bin Bayat, around 500 companies will be located in DIC by the end of 2002, many of them moving from Europe to Dubai (2000 World Press Freedom Review, 2001).

DKV describes itself as "connected learning community that will develop the region's talent pool and accelerate its move to the knowledge economy" (http://www.kv.ae/about/). DKV hopes to achieve several things:

1. Position the Dubai technology, e-commerce, and media free zone as a center of excellence for learning and innovation.

2. Provide the infrastructure for developing, sharing, and applying knowledge.

3. Lead, promote, and facilitate the use of e-learning in education and training in the region.

4. Develop key initiatives to bridge the talent gap in the region.

5. Work with DIC and DMC companies to develop the skills and know-how of the industry http://www.kv.ae/about/).

The main aim of the multibillion dirham DMC, DIC, and DKV complex is to create a clustered economy comprising educators, incubator companies, logistic companies, multimedia businesses, telecommunication companies, remote service providers, software developers, and venture capitalists in one place. The hope is to create a critical mass for the new economy (Arabiata, 2002).

With excellent countrywide penetration, UAE media have the ability to diffuse messages to a vast audience. Although precise numbers are difficult to obtain, the UAE had 170 daily newspaper copies, 355 radio receivers, 134 television sets, 87 personal computers, and 362 main telephones lines per 1,000 inhabitants in 1997, according to the United Nations Educational Scientific and Cultural Organization. That penetration surely has increased.

If one special communications device accents the Emirati culture and lifestyle best, it is the mobile telephone. One of every two persons in the UAE has a mobile telephone, making it the top cellular phone user in the Arab region and the 11th in the world, according the a study by Dubai-based Al Dhaman Stocks Portfolio. The study showed there are 58.5 mobile phone lines for every 100 people in the UAE, Compared to (estimated) 30.05 in Bahrain, 24.8 in Kuwait, 19.9 in Qatar, 6.4 in Oman, 6.3 in Saudi Arabia, and 2.14 in Egypt (Castillo, 2001; CIA, 2001).

Emirates Internet and Multimedia (EIM), the country's sole Internet service provider, puts the current number of Internet subscribers at more than 210,000 and the number of users at about 775,000. According to an International Telecommunications Union (ITU) report, "The UAE is the most wired nation in the Arab world and one of the top nations of the on-line world. With a customer base of about a quarter million, EIM has around 25 percent of the Internet users in the Arab world." ITU further said: "Thirty percent of the 565,000 households in the UAE have access to the Internet (Emirates Internet & Multimedia, 2002)."

An EIM study showed that 51% of the UAE's Internet subscribers are Asians, followed by expatriate Arabs (19%), Nationals (10%), and Westerners (4%). The study also reveals that 36% of Internet subscribers are women. "Our audience profile ranges from the Generation-Xers to the upper-income audience," observed the study. Up to 40% of the subscribers are in Dubai, followed by Abu Dhabi with 30%; 15% live on the west coast and 10% in the city of Al Ain. This research found that 45% of the subscribers surf the net for 5 to 10 hr per week; another 37% surf for 5 hr a week. Only 18% surfed for an average of 10 hr per week. Officials said the EIM portal generates 7 to 8 million page views a month. "Consumers in the UAE are spending less time on traditional media and more time on the Internet," the EIM report said. On the business front, 45% of businesses have access to the Internet. "At present, there are 55 Internet Surfing Centres (ISC) in the UAE. The number is expected to grow significantly" (Emirates Internet & Multimedia, 2002).

The print media, both local and foreign, reach an estimated 74% of the country's literate population. Print is generally considered to be less influential than television. The more educated, middle- and high-income segments of the population read the print media, and expatriates in particular probably constitute a large segment of the print media's readership.

The electronic media appeal to a larger segment of the UAE population than the print media. Part of the reason is the size of country's younger generation, which constitutes more than one third of the total population and favors television and radio. With the proliferation of satellite receivers, consumers all over the country can view local and international channels, both free and for a fee.

Theaters have proliferated in the UAE in recent years, especially in larger cities. According to the Ministry of Information and Culture, there are more than 40 theater complexes in the UAE, some offering multiscreen venues and state-of-the-art facilities. These offer Arab, Indian, and Western films that are rated by the ministry.

Media Access

Government departments have full access to the UAE media. Officials holding press conferences or issuing press releases usually get media coverage in the country's dailies and broadcast media. Most dailies publish WAM stories describing policies, announcements, or events without editing. Some supplement these stories with their own reporters' accounts as well.

Local businesses are successful in accessing the media in varying degrees. Big companies that hire public relations agencies or who have a professional in-house public relations unit usually get their messages across regularly. Also, specialized media like Dubai TV's Business Channel tries to cover business news generated by such companies every day. For smaller players, the task of gaining access to the media becomes more challenging. Editors will publish press releases sent to them if they think the story is newsworthy. Otherwise, they would rather publish the information as paid advertising. The Letters-to-the-Editor section of newspapers is another outlet for the public and organizations to air their views about local and international issues. UAE readers send e-mails or fax letters containing their views to dailies that edit and publish them regularly. Letters dealing with sensitive internal issues are routinely censored.

Radio listeners and viewers of talk shows on UAE television stations can air their views live on various issues. Many public affairs, religious, health, and variety programs invite audience participation regularly. Some stations also offer gifts to listeners and viewers in a bid to attract more audiences for their programs.

Influences on Public Relations

As in other countries, public relations practitioners are subject to internal and external forces. And, as in all other things in the UAE, the practice of public relations is much the story of Abu Dhabi and Dubai, the twin cities that dominate most things. The major economic and governmental centers are located here and, by extension, pervasive religious and cultural influences emarate. The major media centers are also located here. Thus, Abu

Dhabi and Dubai could, if the ruling families so chose, leave the other emirates further behind because of the vast influence that they have both in the economy and the media.

Besides the possibility of internal threats, public relations practitioners are, as are most others in this smaller nation, subject to the vicissitudes of external forces. If the world economy suddenly crashes or if the khamsin wind brings war, then public relations practitioners, like all others, would suffer greatly. The risk also exists that, faced with the unfamiliarity of a downturn, public relations practitioners might entirely abandon any code of ethics, resorting to the most virulent forms of press agentry.

CASE STUDY: THE BURJ AL ARAB HOTEL

Introduction

Because of the vibrant local economy with an almost constant stream of new business developments, product launches are frequent in the UAE. That means that a product launch, which certainly is representative of the economy at large, is the almost perfect incarnation of public relations in the UAE. Use of the launch of the Burj Al Arab Hotel is an almost perfect representation of what is occurring on the toe of the Arabian Peninsula. First, the hotel launch was one of the first times that a local brand was taken international. Second, the Burj Al Arab Hotel symbolizes the dynamism and the drive of today's UAE. As such, it represents the desire of the rulers of the city to create a symbol that would stand for the "epitome of Arab hospitality" (D. Murphy & D. Ibrahim, personal communication, January 28, 2002).

Agency Background: Fortune Promoseven

Founded in the Middle East in 1968, Fortune Promoseven, which has grown along with the region and its clients, now offers a full range of public relations and advertising services in all major countries of the Middle East and North Africa. With offices in 12 countries and a total of 750 employees, the company had billings of more than $299 million in 2000. Among the services it offers are an independent public relations division that is integrated into the network, a direct marketing division, an independent e-commerce division in three countries, and an independent below-the-line division. The Dubai branch of Fortune Promoseven was founded in 1975.

Although Fortune Promoseven shepherded the Burj Al Arab Hotel through a successful launch, the agency and Jumeriah International, owners and managers of the Burj Al Arab Hotel, later parted company. Fortune Promoseven resigned the account in July 2001.

Client Background: Burj Al Arab Hotel

The Burj Al Arab Hotel was conceived to be not only as a luxury hotel, but a symbol "of the opulence, ingenuity and the Arabian spirit" (Burj Al Arab Hotel p. 7). The product of a government–private partnership directed under the leadership of His Excellency General Sheikh Mohammed bin Rashid Al Maktoum, Dubai Crown Prince and Defense Minister, the Burj Al Arab Hotel (translated from Arabic means Arab Tower) was conceived to be a wonder of the modern world (D. Murphy & D. Ibrahim, personal communication, January 28, 2002). The Maktoum family, who envisioned Dubai as a multifaceted hub of the Middle East, viewed the Burj as a magnificent piece of the overall economic puzzle both as a luxury hotel and as a gleaming symbol of progress.

The builders of this architectural wonder clearly achieved their marketing goals. From its opening on November 2, 1999, the Burj has stood apart from other hotel properties. Clustered with the distinctively wave-shaped Jumeriah Beach Hotel on a man-made island of tranquility and hospitality amid Dubai's economic hustle and bustle, the Burj rises like a sail 321 meters into the sky. From the moment a visitor enters the causeway leading to the hotel, the property's style is self-evident. Guests walk past a flaming fountain at the circular entrance into the soaring 180-m-high lobby with its colorful architectural details, computer-programmed "dancing" fountain, and aquarium.

Two hundred two duplex suites, all of which have floor-to-ceiling windows, each feature a private butler, spectacular views, and the convenience of a reception desk on every floor. Club suites include a private dining room and snooker room, and the Presidential Suites have two bedrooms, a private dining room, lounge, and library. Two themed restaurants are on the property. The Al Muntaba Skyview Restaurant, resting spectacularly 200-m above the Arabian Gulf, offers breathtaking sundown views; the Al Mahara Seafood Restaurant offers dining surrounded by glassed-in multicolored marine life from the gulf (Burj Al Arab Hotel pp. 3–14).

The Public Relations Problem

The public relations problem was an opportunity as well as a marketing problem: An international brand for the Burj Al Arab Hotel had to be established. This marked one of the first times that a local brand had been marketed globally. Usually, it is the other way around: A national or regional brand needs tweaking for introduction into a local market. But the problem was not just taking an established local product global; it was starting from scratch. The Burj was new to the UAE and to the rest of the world, although the operating company, Jumeriah International, was well-known.

The company wanted to create brand awareness and a brand attitude for the property. These twin goals revolved around helping to establish Dubai as a center for Middle Eastern tourism, making the Burj Al Arab Hotel a symbol of modern Arab identity and creating an attitude that the Burj was "dedicated to exceeding the expectations of even the most discerning guests" (D. Murphy & D. Ibrahim, personal communication, January 28, 2002).

Target audiences included the tourism and travel industry trade and consumers. Marketing focused on two consumer groups. The first was business and personal travelers who wanted to be pampered, pleased, spoiled, and comforted at an elite destination. The second was to the average "Joe Soap," not someone who would stay at the hotel, but someone who would come to see it, tour it, have "high tea," and then talk about it afterward.

Research and Fact Finding

Before the planning began in November 1998, Jumeriah International issued a request for proposal (RFP). The primary reason for doing so was the public–private nature of the project. "The politics required an RFP because government money was involved," said Dee Murphy, director of marketing for Fortune Promoseven who in 1999 managed the Burj Al Arab Hotel account. "They really had to open it up" (D. Murphy & D. Ibrahim, personal communication, January 28, 2002). The RFP covered production of a whole range of items, including corporate material for the opening and launch of the Burj Al Arab Hotel (D. Murphy & D. Ibrahim, personal communication, January 28, 2002).

"Developing the public relations plan was all about building relationships," said Murphy (D. Murphy & D. Ibrahim, personal communication, January 28, 2002). Gerald Lawless, chief executive officer and Chief Operating Officer of Jumeriah International, had done a lot of previous business with Fortune Promoseven both at Jumeriah International and for other hotels for which he had worked in the UAE. Fortune Promoseven, part of the worldwide network of McCann–Erickson, had previously done corporate identity work for Jumeriah International.

Once notified that it had won the account, Fortune Promoseven created a dedicated special eight-person project team (although at various times everyone at the agency worked on the launch). Work began 1 year before opening, with countless meetings between hotel and Fortune Promoseven staff. The team spent a full 3 months just researching the Arab culture so that they could capture the spirit of the brand.

The size of the project was monumental. "It was a nightmare of a project," said Murphy. "Strategy sessions drove everyone crazy" (D. Murphy & D. Ibrahim, personal communication, January 28, 2002). Those sessions involved discussion of filling many needs such as publicity for the hotel's launch, all corporate identity materials (from matchbooks to tie pins and menu covers), brochures, photography, advertising, trade show displays, corporate videos, and so on.

Goals and Objectives of the Launch

A major challenge was portraying the Arab world, particularly Dubai, as a modern society with good values, a place tolerant and accepting of diversity, to both the tourism trade and to consumer groups. "Even if their countries are at war, people live and work here with mutual respect," said Mary McLaughlin, media relations manager for Jumeriah International. One of the objectives of the launch was to let people know that "there's positive energy generated by the multiple races and ethnic groups that work so well together" (M. McLaughlin, personal communication, February 18, 2002).

Besides making the trade and consumer groups aware of the brand, another goal was to create a specific brand image. FP7's task was establishing the Burj as a "landmark in luxury and Arabian hospitality" with "grandeur, warmth and personal service" offering an "experience of hospitality without equal" (D. Murphy & D. Ibrahim, personal communication, January 28, 2002).

The Launch

The team assembled in the fall of 1998, and planning and coordination continued until the official opening of the hotel on November 2, 1999. A full range of tactics was used to support the strategy of establishing the brand and creating a brand attitude. A barrage of marketing materials was directed at the targeted consumer and trade audiences. These included publicity for the hotel's launch; all corporate identity materials; and advertising, public relations, trade show appearances, and corporate videos.

But media relations activity was emphasized above all else in response to journalistic clamor for information. Five months before opening, "we began receiving media inquiries," said M. McLaughlin (personal communication, February 18, 2002). And they have not stopped.

Results

For months before the inauguration, Fortune Promoseven fielded media inquiries that created quite a buzz. "Everyone was talking about this amazing wonder," said McLaughlin.

"People were watching and waiting. We had their attention without even seeking it. BBC, Canadian TV, CNN, Discovery Channel and many others in Asia, the Middle East and Europe aired features or documentaries" (M. McLaughlin, personal communication, February 18, 2002). BBC News online waxed prosaic about "the billowing, sailed shaped structure," Architectural Record talked about the people who built the hotel and the products that they used, and Forbes.com described the two royal suites as a "gleeful explosion of all things gold, glittery and marble" while gushing over the hotel. Finally, the 160-page commemorative book became a collector's item published in multiple languages and available for $65. Perhaps more important, the hotel had its application accepted as a member of the Leading Hotels of the World, joining storied company such as The Breakers in Palm Beach; Peninsula hotels in Kowloon, Beverly Hills, and New York; and the Mansion on Turtle Creek in Dallas, TX.

Culturally Distinctive Features of the Case

The marketing program for the Burj Al Arab Hotel shows the relevance of knowing about the culture in building a successful brand around the best aspects of that culture. In Dubai that meant modern, cutting edge, on one hand, but steeped in Arabic tradition and custom, on the other. The campaign also shows that cultural knowledge and successful use of that knowledge derives from using people with local expertise and from establishing a timeframe that allows for research and careful strategic planning.

This case also demonstrates that public relations in the UAE is practiced in a manner adapted to conditions. This was a product launch, an almost classic example of the press agentry approach to public relations. The public information model is also alive and well in the UAE, primarily in the governmental sector—an adaptation that fits the government's goals of educating and informing the public. As yet, these two models are the only incarnations of public relations in the UAE. Whether practitioners and firms in the UAE adopt two-way, asymmetrical or symmetrical models of practice is likely to depend on how the country's business culture evolves and the role and function that public relations occupies in that culture.

REFERENCES

Architectural Record. (n.d.). Burj Al Arab/Jumeriah Beach Resort. http://ArchRecord.construction.com/projects/lighting/Archives/0005Jumeriah.asp.

Abu Ghazaleh. (2002). *Copyright law of the UAE*. Retrieved from http://www.agip.com /laws/uae/c.htm

Al Bakay, A. (2001, October 24). Media told to exercise freedom. *Gulf News*, Section 1, p. 3.

Al Enad, A. H. (1990). Public relations roles in developing countries. *Public Relations Quarterly, 35*(1), 24–26.

Al Sadik, A. T. (n.d.). *Evolution and performance of the UAE economy 1972–1998*. Retrieved from http://www.uaeinteract.com

Arabiata. (2002). *Dubai internet city*. Retrieved from http://www.arabiata.com/Services/cc.htm

Ayish, M., & Kruckeberg, D. (1999). Abu Dhabi National Oil Company (ADNOC). In J. Turk & L. Scanlan (Eds.), *Fifteen case studies in international public relations*. The Institute for Public Relations.

Babbili, A. S., & Hussain, S. (1994). United Arab Emirates. In Y. R. Kamalipour, H. Mowalna, & Y. Kamplipur (Eds.), *Mass media in the Middle East* (pp. 293–308). Westport, CT: Greenwood.

Badran, B. (1994, july). *Public relations in the United Arab Emirates: Public perceptions and academic needs*. Paper presented to the 44th annual conference of the Internal Communication Association, Sydney, Australia.

Barfield, T. J. (1990). Tribe and state relations: The inner Asian perspective. In P. S. Khoury & J. Kostiner (Eds.), *Tribes and state formation in the Middle East* (pp. 153–182). Berkeley, CA: University of California Press.

B.B.C. (1 December, 1999). World's tallest hotel opens its doors. http://news.bbc.co.uk/1/bi/world/middle_east/545949.stm

Bryant, C. (1995). Civic nation, civil society, civil religion. in J. Hall (Ed.), Civil society: Theory, history, comparison (pp. 136–157). Cambridge, MA: Polity Press.

Burj Al Arab. (1999). *Commemorative book.*

Castillo, D. J. (2001, October 6). Staying even more in touch on the move. *Gulf News*, mobile phones advertising supplement, p. 1.

CIA. (2001). *The world factbook 2001.* Retrieved from http://www.cia.gov/cia/publications/factbook

Connard, R. (1996). *The ecology of the family: A background paper.* Portland, OR: Northwest Educational Laboratory.

Creating the right waves. (2002, February 21). *Gulf News Supplement.*

Cutlip, S., Center, A., & Broom, G. (1985). *Effective PR.* Englewood clitts, N J: Prentice-Hall.

Dawood, A. (2001, January 11). FNC declares support for freedom of the media. *Gulf News.*

Diamond, L. (1994). Rethinking civil society: Toward democratic consolidation. *Journal of Democracy, 5*(3), 4–17.

Dubai Explorer 2001. (2001). Dubai, United Arab Emirates: Explorer Publishing.

Dubaiinc. (2001). *Facts and figures.* Retrieved from http://www.dubaiinc.com/

Dubai Media City. (2002, February). *Entrepreneur*, 12–19.

Dubai Press Club. (2002, November 5). *Dubai launches its Media City.* Retrieved from http//www.dpc.org.ae

Essoulami, S. (2001). *The press in the arab world: 100 years of suppressed freedom.* Retrieved from http://www.cmfena.org/magazine/features/100_years.htm

Emirates Internet & Multimedia. (2002). Retrieved from http://www.Emirates.net.ae/

Forbes.com. (n.d.). Burj Al Arab. http://www.forbes.com/2002/03/07/0307font_12.html

Geremek, B. (1992). Civic society then and now. *Journal of Democracy, 3*(2), 3–12.

Ghassoub, J. (2002, April). Risks and rewards. *Arabic Trends*, No. 52, p. 64.

Gulf News online. (2001, May 11). Power of ideas and media.

Human Development Indicators. (2001). New York: United Nations Development Program.

Human Rights Watch. (1999a). *Freedom of expression on the internet.* Retrieved from http://www.hrw.org/wr2k/Issues-04.htm

Human Rights Watch. (1999b, June). *The Internet in the Middle East and North Africa: Free expression and censorship.* Retrieved from http://www.hrw.org/advocacy/internet/mena/

Iglehart, A. P. (1979). *Married women and work.* Lexington, MA: Lexington Books.

International Constitutional Law. (n.d.). Retrieved from http://www.uni-wuerzburg.de/law/info.html

International Press Review. (2000). *2000 world press review: UAE.* Retrieved from www.freemedia.at/wpfr/uae.htm

International Press Institute. (2000). Retrieved from http://www.freemedia.at

IPR. (2001). *United Arab Emirates.* Retrieved from www.infoprod.co.il/country/uae2a.htm

Issa, N. (2001). *Dubai technology, e-commerce and media free zone.* Retrieved from http://www.eworldreports.com/viewarticle.asp?ArticleID=364

Jalilvand, M. (2000, August). *Monthly Labor Review*, 26–31.

Kabbani, S. H. M. (n.d.). *Questions on IJMA' (consensus), Taqlid (following qualified opinion), and Ikhtilaf Al-Fuqaha' (differences of the jurists).* Retrieved from As-Sunna Foundation of America, http://www.sunnah.org/fiqh/ijma.htm

Kristof, N. D. (2002, April 30). Stoning and scripture. *New York Times.* Retrieved from http://www.nytimes.com/2002/04/30/opinion/30KRIS.html

Lewis, B. (1991). *Islam and the west.* New York: Oxford University Press.

Mahfouz, M. (1986). The beggar (K. W. Henry & N. K. H. al-Warraki, Trans.). Cairo, Egypt: The American University in Cairo Press.

Media. (2002). Retrieved from http://www.uae.gov.ae/Government/media.htm

Middle East Public Relations Association. (2002). Retrieved from http://www.dubaimediacity.com/associations.asp

Mirabel, E. (2001, October). Message received? *Gulf Marketing Review*, p. 41.

Mott, F. L., & Shapiro, D. (1983). Complementarity of work and fertility among young American mothers. *Journal of Population Studies*, 239–252.

Nawar, I. (2000, May & June). *Freedom of expression in the Arab world*. Paper presented at the Aspen Institute Conference on Freedom of Statement, Wye River, CO.

O'Donnell, G., and Schmitter, P. (1986). *Transitions from authoritarian rule: Tentative conclusions about uncertain democracies*. Baltimore, MD: Johns Hopkins University Press.

Owais, R., & Matthew, A. P. (2000, November 5). Media City launched as beacon of creativity. *Gulf News*. Retrieved from http://www.gulfnews.com/Articlesv /News.asp?ArticleID=1898

Patai, R. (1983). *The Arab mind*. New York, New York: Charles Scribner's Sons, pp. 307–313.

Price, M., & Krug, P. (2000). *The enabling environment for free and independent media: Programme in Comparative Media Law & Policy*. Oxford, England: Oxford University Press.

Privatization drive to stay, says Khalifa. (2001). Retrieved from http://www.uaeinteract.com

Promoseven Agency Profile. (2001). Dubai, United Arab Emirates: Fortune Promoseven.

Quinn, S. (2002). Teaching Journalism in a Changing Islamic Nation. *AsiaPacific MediaEducation, 11*, 6–21.

Rahman, S. (2001, May 1). Media freedom without responsibility 'may invite chaos.' *Gulf News* online.

Ringle, K. 23 October, 2001. The Crusaders' giant footprints: After a millennium, their mark remains. *Washington Post*, p. C01.

Shining Stars. (2001). *Gulf Marketing Review*,

Shihab, M. (n.d.). *Economic development in the UAE*. Downloadable as a pdf file at http://www.uaeinteract. com/uaeint_misc/pdf/12.pdf

Sriramesh, K., & White, J. (1992). Societal culture and public relations. In J. E. Grunig (Ed)., *Excellence in public relations and communication management* (pp. 597–614). Hillsdale, NJ: Lawrence Erlbaum Associates.

Talking Heads: Advertising Legends in the Middle East. (2001). *Gulf Marketing Review*,

The Times Group. (2002). http://www.indianadsabroad. com/alkhaleej.shtml

Tibi, B. (1990). The simultaneity of the unsimultaneous: Old tribes and imposed nation-states in the modern Middle East. In P. S. Khoury & J. Kostiner (Eds.), *Tribes and state formation in the Middle East*, Berkeley, CA: University of California Press.

TV and Radio-Guide. (2002). Retrieved from http://uaeinteract.com/news/ tv_radio.asp

UAE Editorials: Zayed's talk to FNC stresses freedom of expression. (1998.) Retrieved from http://www.uaeinteract. com/uaeint_main/newsreport/19980106.htm

United Arab Emirates Yearbook 1995. (1995). London: Planet Publishing.

United Arab Emirates Yearbook 2000/2001. (2001). Abu Dhabi, United Arab Emirates: Trident Press and Ministry of Information and Culture.

United Nations. (2001). *Human development report*. Downloadable as a pdf file at http://www.undp.org/ hdr2001/

United States Department of State. (2001). Country report on human rights practices 2000–United Arab Emirates. Retrieved from http://www.unher.com/ and www.humanrights-usa.net/repo45w/unitedarab Emirates.html

Van dee Melen, H. (May 1997). The role of tribal and kinship ties in the politics of the United Arab Emirates. The Platenew School of Law and Diplomacy.

Wapner, P. (1995). Politics beyond the state: Environmental activism and world civic politics, *World Politics*, 47:311–340.

Walters, G. J. (2001). Human rights in an information age. Toronto, Ontario, Canada: University of Toronto Press.

Walters, T. N., & Walters, L. (2002). *Transitional woman? A case study of values in the context of an Arabic/Islamic Society*. Unpublished manuscript, Zayed University, Dubai, United Arab Emirates.

Wheeler, J. (2001, January 21). Dubai launches Media City. *BBC News*. Retrieved from http://news.bbc. co.uk/1/bi/world/middle_east/1128899.stm

Women account for 36pc of Internet subscribers. (2001). *The Khaleej Times*. Retrieved August 27, 2001, from http://uaeinteract.com/news/default.asp?cntDisplay= 10&ID=177#685

Za'Za', B. (2002, January 8). Summit debates freedom of speech. *Gulf News*, Section 1, p. 6.

4

An Overview of Public Relations in Japan and the Self-Correction Concept

Takashi Inoue

INTRODUCTION

The modern history of Japan and the country's progress on the path toward Westernization has not been a monotonous journey. The rapid pace of change has resulted in the country repeating many errors at times, causing immeasurable pain not only to the Japanese but also to neighboring countries. The old national slogan was "strong army, strong country." After World War II, democracy replaced militarism and a cooperative system was established between the political, bureaucratic, and business worlds under the single party leadership of the Liberal Democratic Party (LDP). This system was aided by the diligence of the Japanese, and swift economic activity was shown to the world based on Japan's social system. As a result, in the early 1980s, Japan stood at the forefront of modern industrialized societies and was recognized for the high quality of its products and its mass production ability (Sakaiya, 2002).

However, the economic bubble burst in the 1990s due to the appreciation of the yen and the progression of information technology that propelled the globalization of Japanese companies. This created a need to shift management methods from the seniority system, lifetime employment, and group decision-making process that had been established in Japanese culture and institutions to a method that recognized openness, fairness, and speed—characteristics that traditionally did not exist in Japanese firms (Tsurumi, 1997). Since it was founded as a country, Japan has possessed a unique communications format due to the impact of its homogeneity and the influence of Confucianism. Therefore, its forms of communication have differed from that of the West (Inoue, (Ed.) 2001).

A review of the introduction and development of public relations in Japan tells us that the profession did not evolve ideally. In fact, public relations may not have been sought by the Japanese because of the sociological and economic system of the country. Public relations may only exist in a democracy that also has a free, unregulated economy. Ideally, the practice would be a two-way communications (Grunig, J. E., & Hunt. T., 1984) activity in line with the demands of the current worldwide shift toward globalization. This is also an area in which Japan is extremely weak.

A SOCIOCULTURAL PERSPECTIVE OF THE NATION

Japan, located in Northeast Asia, is a nation of thousands of islands, the four major ones being Hokkaido, Shikoku, Kyushu, and Honshu (where Tokyo is located). The land area is slightly smaller than that of the state of California, with a population of 127 million. Since its birth, the economy had been based on agriculture and fishing. Ancient Chinese culture and politics have also influenced Japan. The Tokugawa (Edo) Era that began in the early 17th century established a closed country policy that built a unique culture and societal system. In the latter half of the 19th century, Japan opened itself to external influence with the arrival of Commodore Perry's black ships (Shiba, 1996). The Meiji Restoration, which opened Japan's doors to the West, introduced European science, technology, and political systems with earnest efforts to build a modern state. Initially, Japan modeled itself after the German brand of constitutional monarchy and established an imperial parliament. It also actively promoted rapid industrialization that enriched the nation and helped build the nation's military.

The end of World War II saw the Japanese economy developing swiftly, becoming the second largest in the world next only to the United States in terms of gross domestic product (GDP). In 1990, Japan boasted the highest per capita income in the world (Masamura & Yamada, 2002). There are nationwide television networks, newspapers, magazines, and other forms of media; most of the major media companies are located in Tokyo. Thus, the efficiency of information dissemination and media access is very high. It covers national and international news extensively.

With an increase in the decline of the birth rate, Japan is facing an aging society like many other advanced countries. The average life expectancy in Japan is the highest in the world for both men and women. During much of its history, religion in Japan has centered on Shintoism and Buddhism. The philosophy of Confucianism was introduced in the 6th century, which deeply penetrated Japanese society up to World War II. As a result, Japanese culture differs from the Christian civilization of the West in many aspects. The Confucian philosophy that respects humility and requires strict hierarchical relationships is in direct opposition with the activities entailed in public relations.

THE EVOLUTION OF PUBLIC RELATIONS IN JAPAN

The history of modern public relations in Japan is rather brief. It starts with the occupation of Japan by the United States in 1945 following Japan's defeat in World War II. Public relations was introduced to Japan without the concomitant growth of democracy and free speech seen in the West. There are no materials that enable confirmation of a systematic introduction of public relations by any external source before World War II. However, Shibasaki (1984) wrote that the South Manchurian Railroad had established an independent Public Relations Section under the direct control of the President's Office that was differentiated from propaganda. Kisaku Ikeda, a representative of the Public Relations Institute, commented that the first in-house newsletter in Japan was published in 1903 by Kanebo for its female factory workers. Due to its popularity, this was then followed by the publication of the first official issue of the newsletter for all employees of the company in 1904 (Ikeda, 1997).

According to Ikari, (Ed.) (1998), as for the first public relations magazines, there are many versions of the origin, but Maruzen is said to have issued a magazine beginning in 1897 and Mitsui Gofukuten (presently Mitsukoshi Department Store) in 1899. The Mitsui public relations magazine was 350-pages long! It contained business information, new textile patterns, trends, and even novels by famous authors of the times, such as Koyo Ozaki (Yamaguchi, 1995). The executives of both companies were individuals who had visited America, and it is clear that they created their public relations magazines in Japan after models from corporate public relations magazines that existed in America in the late 1880s.

The Japanese Government and military authorities first recognized the importance of propaganda for their country following World War I. It was the use of the Manchurian Incident as a pretext for occupying Manchuria (the present Northeastern China) by the Imperial Japanese Army in 1931, a precursor of further aggression on the mainland of China, that changed communication attitudes concerning wartime propaganda. As mentioned in a book on the Tokyo Metropolitan Government's PR activities during WW II, published in 1995, Japan's government and military personnel considered the criticism of Japanese military actions by international society as a total defeat in the propaganda campaign, and top priority was given for the creation of a system to manipulate international public opinion.

Based on this, the Ministry of Foreign Affairs established an Information Committee in 1932, and an organization was formed for planning domestic and overseas propaganda in line with national policy. Following a number of transformations, the Information Bureau was established in 1940. This bureau centralized the information and propaganda operations that had been conducted at the respective ministries and agencies (Tokyo Metropolitan Government, 1995). This is similar to reinforcing public relations functions conducted in the United States during World War I and World War II. However, the one distinct difference is that Japan was not a democracy at that time, and the use of public relations was strictly for manipulating public opinion; it led the Japanese into war.

General Douglas MacArthur and the General Headquarters (GHQ) of the Supreme Commander for the Allied Powers introduced to Japan the form of public relations that had appeared in the United States in the early 20th century as a part of the democratization measures after World War II. Before the Occupation, however, some reference to Public Relations was made by Japanese author Tetsuhiko Tozawa, in 1942 in his book entitled *Theory of Propaganda*, as noted by Ikari, (Ed.) (1998). Tozawa's above mentioned book refers to two books by Edward Bernays (1923), *Crystallizing Public Opinion* and *Propaganda*. On May 3, 1947, with the proclamation of the Japanese Constitution based on democracy, GHQ suggested the establishment of Public Relations Offices to central and local governmental offices through the military government offices placed in each region. This resulted in the establishment of independent public relations departments in governmental bodies throughout Japan. One of the first problems faced was in naming the departments because a Japanese word that fit the term *public relations* could not be found. The responsible parties first gathered information and worked earnestly to understand what constituted public relations. As a result, the most commonly used term became *ko(u)-ho(u)*, which literally means public information (which is widely recognized as a rather primitive stage of public relations today). However, many other words such as *ho(u)-do(u)* (news) and *ko(u)-cho(u)* (public hearing) were also used (Ikari, (Ed.) 1998).

By 1949, most of the government bodies nationwide had established public relations departments, and the Civil Information and Education Section of the GHQ held public relations seminars for the staff of the central government. Although these seminar attendees talked about public relations, they primarily focused on the *ko-ho* (public information) of "how a government should convey measures to the people to nurture healthy public opinion (Hikami, 1951, 1952)." But, at the time, it was difficult to differentiate between the public information officer and public relations officer stationed at every military government office by any means other than their titles. Therefore, because the conditions of the conceptually introduced democracy had not taken roots, the terms *public information* and *public relations* became entwined as if they were synonyms (Inoue, (Ed.) 2001).

Thus, the public relations introduced in Japan began with the governmental offices (public centers) and then continued to the private sector's advertising and securities industries. Initially, private companies used the original Japanese translation of the English term *public relations* as is, but in almost all cases the term *ko-ho* is now used. Unlike propaganda that was used before the war as a means of controlling public perception, the modern form of public relations has sprouted on a foundation of democracy based on the awareness of respecting public opinion and social responsibility.

Soon public relations seminars were also being conducted for the private sector. In July 1949, Japan Advertising Limited and Telegraphic Service Company (known today as Dentsu Inc.) held a summer advertising seminar called "About Public Relations," the first seminar of its kind. In his book titled, *PR (w)o Kangaeru* (Thinking About PR), Shigeo Ogura (1990) referred to the seminar and stated that public relations was positioned as a function of management, a policy issue of management, and as a management philosophy.

Note that although the misunderstandings about the role of public relations continued among government public relations departments, the private sector was striving to expand the correct concept of public relations.

In 1951, the Japan Federation of Employers' Associations (JFEA) sent the first postwar business tour to the United States to study human relations and public relations. Based on this tour, a Public Relations Study Group (unofficial English translated name) was formed within JFEA in May 1953. Furthermore, in 1951, the spread of public relations also peaked with the publication of nine educational books on public relations such as *Public Relations Talk* by Shinjiro Kitazawa (1951), *Ko-ho Theory and Practice* by the Japan *Ko-ho* Association (1951), and *Basic Knowledge of PR* by Yoshiro Sasaki (1951). Interestingly, the rapid rise of modern public relations that had continued since its introduction by the GHQ began to stagnate toward the end of 1952 (Koyama, 1975). As the *Thirty Year History of Governmental Ko-ho* by Cabinet Secretary Cabinet Public Relations Office (1990), a complimentary commemorative booklet, noted: "As GHQ left Japan with the conclusion and implementation of the 1952 San Francisco Peace Treaty, a simplification of public bodies related to public relations and the shrinking of budgeting for public relations was sought as this was perceived to be a good chance to re-study the policies under the Occupation, and also because of the tight financial situation."

However, the *Dentsu Advertising Annual* (1956) described public relations in the following manner: "There were many companies who thought that their public relations were a success just by using a lot of money to make a fancy business report or by running a so-called public relations advertisement (advertorial) in the newspaper." Thus, one can infer that conditions did not allow for proper public relations to be conducted.

Riding the wave of democratization, government-related public relations activities even penetrated local government offices. Presently, there is no government office without a public relations department or a section related to it. However, despite the spread, the content of the activities stagnated until the early 1990s. In contrast, public relations activities conducted by corporations were being nurtured, although its theories and technology were not appropriately adopted. The creation of public relations materials was certainly enhanced by the explosion of newspapers, magazines, and broadcast media.

The trend toward the public issue of stocks began in Japan in the 1950s, causing securities companies to use public relations and advertisements in newspapers to solicit shareholders. This solidified several methods used in corporate public relations. Upon entering the country in the 1950s, the Shell Oil Company joined other Japanese firms, such as Japan Airlines, Matsushita Electric, Tokyo Gas, and Mitsubishi Electric, in establishing public relations departments. Many major corporations followed thereafter in the 1960s and through the 1970s (Ikari, (Ed.) 2001).

Advertorials initiated by advertising agencies became the mainstream form of corporate communications in the 1950s. Matsushita Electric and Sony proactively ran advertorials in newspapers and weekly magazines. At that time the advertorials clearly showed an understanding of the importance of nurturing a corporate image while advancing development and research of marketing technologies. However, they did not put into practice the public relations theories that covered a broader range of areas such as government relations, community relations, investor relations, and media relations. Within the increasing commonality of public relations activities by these companies, although superficial in nature, a strong awareness of a company's social responsibility grew centering on the business world.

The outbreak of the Korean War in 1950 brought special war demands to Japan and led the Japanese economy into a fast recovery. This unfortunate event stimulated the rapid growth of the Japanese economy. In addition, the lengthy period under the Liberal Democratic Party (Ozawa, 1993) created the golden triangle of the political, bureaucratic, and business worlds, which in turn helped transform Japan into a country with rapid economic growth. It also was a period that demanded that products be supplied in large volumes, and marketing methods, such as advertorials, sales promotion, and publicity were instrumental in introducing these new products to the public. Marketing is distinct from public relations. Although marketing plays a role in public relations, a misunderstanding concerning these concepts led people to confuse publicity as being public relations; public relations was equated with marketing.

From the mid-1950s through the early 1970s, the Japanese economy experienced a rapid actual growth rate that exceeded 10% per year (Masamura & Yamada, 2002). This marked the arrival of the era of publicity that was used for providing news materials to the media. Unlike advertisements, the key decision of whether to run publicity as news was to be made by the media. Therefore, various ideas began to emerge as effective strategies linked to marketing became more refined in their application to public relations. However, just as a specific prescription must be made available to introduce new scientific technologies, there was also a need at that time to introduce specific public relations technologies. The impact of not doing so led to further misunderstanding of what public relations should be. Advertising for public relations and publicity activities dramatically developed in line with the advanced economic growth and the expansion of various types of media.

However, in the late 1960s, environmental pollution emerged as a major societal issue, which resulted in penalties for companies pursuing profits under the mass production–mass consumption paradigm. The activities of the government became pronounced in this area with the establishment of the Basic Law for Environmental Pollution Control Law (1967) and the formation of the Environment Agency in 1971. In the business world, the New Year's Address of the Japan Association for Corporate Executives in 1969 emphasized the "formation of a society that respects humanity" as its perspective. The Japanese vernacular daily Asahi Shimbun, morning edition, June I, 1969 reported as top news in their social affairs section that a New York Times article criticized Japanese automakers for doing secret recalls of their defective cars. During that period, Asahi Shimbun, in particular, made a negative campaign against Japanese automakers and their faulty cars of that time. A consensus on the recovery of humanity, meaning less emphasis on corporate interests only, was established (Ikari, Ed., 1998). This transformation of society was appreciated by Japan's middle management, especially in the company PR departments, but it did not extend to the executive level.

ECONOMIC FRICTION AND OVERSEAS PUBLIC RELATIONS

One of the pillars of the economic recovery following Japan's defeat in World War II was the establishment of Japan as a trading country, which resulted in the infusion of overseas public relations activities. In 1958, the Japan External Trade Organization was established. The European Economic Community was also established the same year, which signaled increasing intensity in the competition on the international stage. Consequently, strong interest was paid in Japan to overseas public relations activities along with marketing, including establishing overseas sales networks to promote exports and branding Japanese products among overseas consumers. The total volume of Japanese exports grew rapidly from the latter half of the 1960s through the 1970s. The growth was critically described as a "squall," but the trade balance surplus took root at that time. This also led to international criticism that Japan was not working hard to increase imports, resulting in the beginning of trade friction.

Beginning in the 1970s, in many Western countries including the United States, a movement arose to regulate imports of Japanese products. This was evident in the textile negotiations between Japan and the United States during the 1970s; high-technology friction evident in the communications and semiconductor negotiations of the 1980s; and automobile, automobile parts, insurance, finance, and global environmental issues in the 1990s.

The Keidanren (Japan Federation of Economic Organizations), a business organization for Japanese large enterprises, started its activities in 1948. In 1978, it established the Keizai-Koho Center (Japan Institute for Social and Economic Affairs, which handled the public relations function for Keidanren) to address a number of these issues. They made big efforts to disseminate a strong message that represented the Japanese business community (Ikari, Ed. 1998).

The public relations activities of overseas companies in Japan and the overseas public relations activities of Japanese companies took cultural, traditional, and other differences into consideration and proceeded proactively by disclosing large amounts of statistical data and tactics. In addition to using the mass media to publicize their positions to the public, companies also hired specialists such as lobbyists.

THE BIRTH OF PUBLIC RELATIONS FIRMS

During the latter half of the 1950s through the 1970s, which was a period of rapid economic growth in Japan, many public relations firms were established in anticipation of the coming public relations era. These firms included the Chisei Idea Center, International Public Relations, and Cosmo Public Relations established in the later 1950s and Dentsu PR Center, Sun Creative Publicity, Ozma Inc. Kyodo Public Relations, Prap Japan, and Inoue Public Relations established in the 1960s. However, with the exception of a few public relations firms, the services of most companies through the 1980s consisted of marketing to a large extent. Any public relations activity was centered mostly on publicity targeting the media. Interestingly, these public relations firms could be divided into two types. One type focuses mostly on Japanese clients and provides services mainly in the realm of publicity and event management (90%), and the other type includes international clients and provides a wide array of public relations as well as consulting services with a bilingual staff (10%).

With the intensifying international competition of the second half of the 1970s, foreign enterprises seeking to open the Japanese market strengthened their offensive by employing overseas public relations firms such as Burson-Marsteller, Hill & Knowlton, Ketchum, and Edelman. These consultancies either set up local offices or entered into alliances with Japanese public relations firms to develop their business proactively in the world's second largest market. Their method of approaching public relations conveyed a lot of theory and skill to Japanese public relations firms and greatly contributed to raising the level of public relations in Japan.

In 1980, the existing Japan Public Relations Industry Association and Japan Public Relations Association merged to form the Public Relations Society of Japan. It has conducted various educational training sessions and international conferences, and it has worked to spread public relations in Japan. However, because the annual membership fees are higher than that of similar organizations in other countries, the association has been able to attract only a limited number of members (approx. 430 in 2002).

The future of the public relations industry in Japan is very bright due to deregulation and changes into Japanese accounting standards. It is safe to assume that there will be a rapid increase in the need for risk communications, investor relations, and brand management—areas to which Japanese companies had previously paid little attention.

INCREASED INTEREST IN PUBLIC RELATIONS AMONG ORGANIZATION LEADERS

From the 1980s into the 1990s, burgeoning Japanese economic power made the United States-Japan relationship heat up regarding telecommunications, semi-conductors, automobiles and auto parts (Prestowitz, 1985). The difficulty of conducting public relations activities in such an environment of trade friction is that political negotiations are conducted in a realm that differs from the corporate one. Matters also tend to become emotional, with reports in each country becoming vituperative in content as a consequence of poor and inacurrate communication. Even when trying to spread facts, the side receiving the information reacts sensationally and public relations activities often lose their effectiveness. With this in mind, in some cases public relations specialists have been hired and have facilitated calm negotiations even in a charged atmosphere (see the case study at the end of this chapter).

The collapse of the economy in 1991 has exposed the harmful effects of the close ties between the political world, the bureaucracy, and the business world. The Japanese economy has lost its confidence as it faces the need for structural reforms. During its prolonged economic recession, the Japan Society for Corporate Communication Studies, a scholarly society of public relations, was established in 1995. It focuses on corporate communications and the further research and development of public relations involving scholars and business people, as well as practitioners (with 475 individual and 54 corporate members in 2002). The Society conducted a fact-finding study on corporate communications in June 2002 called the *Survey of Corporate Communication Today.* Interestingly, 90% of the 107 Japanese executives who responded to the survey indicated an interest in public relations, and two thirds of those who are company presidents stated that they directed the public relations activities of their organizations. In addition, 80% of the corporate executives indicated that they seek the opinions of individuals responsible for public relations when setting organizational policies, although the extent to which this is done varies. The report, however, doubts the competency of the executives due to their lack of practical experience in the area of public relations. Apart from this issue, these figures indicate that companies have begun to place more importance on public relations activities. This can particularly be said of major companies with 1,000 or more employees that were the primary sample for the study. The results of this survey on the awareness of Japanese top management about public relations are similar to the results of the following study.

This study was entitled the International Public Relations Association's (IPRA's) Gold paper No. 12 (1997), the Evolution of Public Relations Education and the Influence of Globalization (Survey of eight countries), (Wright and Ikari, 1997). I initiated Gold Paper No. 12 as the chairman of the steering committee. There was assistance from top executives from Japanese large enterprises such as Toyota, Sony, NEC, YAMAHA, and Kikkoman, as well as from many foreign enterprise top executives, PR managers from domestic and foreign companies and independent PR consultants.

UNDERLYING PROBLEMS IN JAPANESE ORGANIZATIONS

Japanese organizations face obstacles when conducting two-way communication in a flat and horizontal communication environment. These problems encompass government as well as corporate scandals. Presently, most Japanese realize that they are not particularly skilled in communications, and corporate executives realize the need to strengthen themselves in this area. Currently, Japanese corporations proactively use public relations functions by consulting with outside public relations consultants when crises occur and entrust day-to-day public relations activities to their in-house public relations departments. The problem in Japan is that although executives realize the need for public relations and act as spokespersons for their organizations, they still do not understand its essence.

Furthermore, not only do corporate leaders fail to understand public relations, but there are few experienced practitioners with specialized public relations education in the organization. One must understand that this lack of understanding and education lies deep in the very structure of Japanese companies where personnel are routinely transferred between divisions every 2 to 4 years due to the rotation system. This creates a situation in which leaders cannot obtain professional advice. Nevertheless, as far as ethical issues are concerned, the organizational leaders' failure to confront this matter makes it difficult for awareness of it to penetrate to the far reaches of the organization. In regard to this important issue, in September 2002, Hiroshi Okuda, chairman of Nihon Keidanren (the Japan Business Federation) noted that corporate ethics are vital and necessary to the management of enterprises.

It is apparent to observers that there are very few qualified public relations practitioners in Japan. Today most of the companies listed on the Tokyo Stock Exchange have their own public relations departments, but in many cases these departments are staffed by people who lack sufficient experience. According to a study of 451 companies (most of them publicly listed) by Toray Corporate Business Research, Inc., in 1999, an average of eight members worked in each of the public relations departments of these companies. There is no statistical data on the total number of the public relations departments in Japanese companies, although it may be safe to assume that there may be around 10,000 full-time practitioners, most with few credentials in the companies.

There are about 150 public relations consulting firms in Japan, which are staffed by about 2,000 full-time practitioners, only 3% of whom are proficient in English! Three Japanese universities have public relations faculties. The recent increase in awareness of public relations has led to the offering of 40 specialized public relations courses in Japanese universities. These numbers are expected to increase in the future. Table 4.1 shows the development of public relations in Japan and its problems.

THE LEVEL OF ACTIVISM IN JAPAN

In the late 19th century, labor disputes frequently occurred in Japan as a result of various movements, such as the people's right to freedom and the poor treatment of overworked female laborers in coal mines and textile plants. This led to the repeated formation of labor unions; around 1920, the full-scale unions of Nihon Rodo Sodoumei, Nihon Nomin Kumiai, and Zenkoku Suiheisha (the movement to free the discriminated community called

TABLE 4.1
Evolution and Problems of Public Relations in Japan

	Characteristics	*Objectives*	*Problems*
1925–1945 Early Showa era End of World War II Dawn of public relations	Propaganda to build up national wealth and military strength	Manipulate the masses	Suppressed free speech and manipulated public opinion
1947–1952 Introduction period of public relations in government by the GHQ	Public information (one-way communication)	To assist GHQ in the implementation of occupation policies	Misunderstanding of the concept and functions of actual public relations. In addition, public relations was mixed up with public information
1950–1963 Educational period on American-style public relations	Advertorial and publicity type (one-way communication)	To assist companies in obtaining social approval	Advertising and public relations became indistinguishable. Focus on advertorials
Latter half of the 1950s–1990 Public relations during the high- growth period	Publicity type (one-way communication at the international level)	Sales promotion for creating a mass production and mass consumption cycle	Excessive focus on marketing public relations and lack of introduction of skills for practicing public relations. Worldwide negative image of Japan developed in the 1970s.
1991–Present Public relations after collapse of the bubble economy	Corporate communication (two-way communication)	Developing a sense of social accountability within the corporate world	Multiple scandals and immature two-way communication

Buraku) were formed. These unions were at the very least influenced by the 1917 Russian Revolution. But labor unions formed much more readily after World War II because of the democratization policies of General MacArthur. The labor union movement during the Cold War period often involved idealistic claims, and national strikes sometimes occurred. In particular, intense fights over wage raises happened every spring especially during the high-growth period of the 1960s and 1970s. However, because Japanese per capita wages became the highest in the world in 1990, negotiations between labor and management have become more cooperative (Masamura & Yamada, 2002). The long recession and restructuring of the economy after the collapse of the economic bubble has also contributed to this amity. Especially in the postwar period, these unions had supported certain political parties and thereby gained vast influence on politics. However, their ability to compel union members to vote in certain ways has weakened in recent times.

The consumerism that occurred in the United States in the 1950s spilled over into Japan and has led to greater rebellion against existing authority. The problems of environmental pollution, toxic chemicals, defective automobiles, and other product deficiencies that began occurring in Japan from the latter half of the 1950s served to heighten various consumer advocacy movements. With the increase in citizens' movements, nonprofit organizations and nongovernmental organizations began to emerge to counter environmental pollution, support developing countries, make international contributions, and establish countermeasures for an aging society. In 1998, the Law to Promote Specified Nonprofit Activities (1998) was passed in the Diet. Currently, 5,000 organizations are registered under the law. Some of these organizations do enter into alliances with various international organizations to conduct their activities.

JAPANESE CULTURE AND PUBLIC RELATIONS

According to the concept of United States anthropologist Edward Hall (1976) on high and low context cultures, he characterized Japan as being a high context one. This implies that the level of cultural codes that is implicitly held among communicators in Japan is high, resulting in a proportional limit on the volume of tangible information that is exchanged. In particular, over the past 2,000 years, Japan has treasured the concept of *wa* (harmony) in which people of a single race live together in an island country. In such a society, objectives are not achieved by individuals competing against each other, but rather people are skilled at achieving objectives through group cooperation. Furthermore, the entry of Confucianism into Japan in the 7th century created a society in which people did not make excuses when they did something wrong. This led to an inability to take responsibility and an inability to explain one's actions or express oneself to others clearly. As a result, misunderstandings and friction often occur when the Japanese interact with people from other countries and cultures.

The Japanese have traditionally placed priority on corporate and organizational profit rather than personal profit, and the image of the Japanese has been that of an "economic animal" with an unseen face. The information technology boom of the 1990s brought about a true globalization of many aspects of the culture, and there was a demand for individual strength and creativity in which the individual role was greater than that of the group. Many people believed that for Japan to obtain the know-how for creating high value-added properties (intellectual property) ahead of China and other Asian countries, it must develop a doctrine that respects an individual's free thoughts and actions. Educational reforms are currently underway to achieve this, stressing the inculcation of sound values (morality) at the high school level, creativity rather than rote learning, and a renewed emphasis on English as an international language to help young people live in the global village.

Although this may be a characteristic of an island nation's culture, when two individuals first meet each other in Japanese society, whether through work or on a more personal level, a lot of time is spent getting to know that person. The relationship rests only on a surface level until one party develops sufficient knowledge about the other; in time, an *amae* (overdependency) structure is developed in which each party tries to depend on the other. Drinking with friends and colleagues after work is one ritual that promulgates this structure. The building of mutual trust with an individual within an organization sometimes leads that relationship to take precedence over the organization (Hampden–Turner, 1997). There is also the influence of Confucian thought, which causes this tendency to be even stronger when there is a hierarchical relationship built around deference to authority.

For example, the surprise attack on Pearl Harbor created a negative image of the Japanese. For a long time after World War II, the country was referred to derogatively as "sneaky Japan." In fact, it was due to a delay caused by Japanese incompetence: The declaration of war was transmitted after the actual start of hostilities in Pearl Harbor. Such a fact has been published in some recent books on the war in the Pacific. The fact that this mistake was covered up by the Japanese and never explained to the international community reflected the prevailing value system of the nation. This value system encouraged a tendency for the intraorganizational hierarchy to submit to authority and a cultural sense of value in which domestic interests or the interests of one's organization (to protect one's own comrades) is placed over international interests. This is based on the Japanese cultural concepts of *haji* (or embarrassment—when one refrains from notifying outsiders of facts when a mistake is made), *amae* (over-dependency), and *wa* (harmony) (Sriramesh & Takasaki, 1999). Consequently, these Japanese cultural traits militate against the openness and speediness that is part of the preferred environment of the public relations world.

The essence of the scandal that led to the Pearl Harbor surprise attack is an absolute value judgment within an organizational setting that led to priority being given to individual personal relationships and the organization. This is almost identical to the frequently reported scandals of recent days. However, in the case of the recent scandals, many have become public through internal indictments, indicating that intraorganizational morals and communications based on a new sense of values have begun to function (Inoue, 2002a, 2002b, 2002c, 2002d). The Pearl Harbor anecdote was mentioned by myself in my Melbourne IPRA World Congress speech in 1988, and the Asahi newspaper reported the same story 6 years after that.

THE MEDIA AND PUBLIC RELATIONS

It is difficult to overstate the importance of the relationship between the mass media and public relations. Many believe that media relations activities are at the core of public relations, which makes the need for a robust relationship with the media vital for organizations and public relations practitioners. Japan, which boasts a large gross domestic product, enjoys diverse media coverage nationwide with a high density population and PR's impact on Japanese society is getting stronger. Developing a good relationship with and a deep understanding of the media is crucial in Japan. Moreover, media analysis using information technologies such as the computer and the Internet such as CARMA® (a company which provides Computer Aided Research & Media Analysis), which enables self-correction of two-way communication, is a vital public relations solution in the increasingly complex 21st century.

JAPANESE MEDIA

Broadcasting in Japan began in 1925 when NHK, the Japanese public broadcasting network, began radio broadcasts. In 1951, the first privately owned radio station was opened. In 1953, NHK started the first television broadcasts, and other private television stations began operating the same year. Presently, NHK covers the entire nation with 49 television and radio stations. In addition, Japan has 139 private television stations (including 5 in Tokyo) and 99 private radio stations. Moreover, Japan has satellite-broadcasting stations that began operation in 1987, digital satellite-broadcasting stations that began in 1996, and small FM stations that cover towns and communities.

As mentioned earlier, the first newspaper was issued in Japan in 1871. Presently, there are five national papers—*Asahi Shimbun, Yomiuri Shimbun, Mainichi Shimbun, Nihon Keizai Shimbun*, and *Sankei Shimbun*—with a combined daily circulation exceeding 71 million copies (including morning and evening editions). The national papers enjoy an enormous circulation: The morning circulation for the *Yomiuri Shimbun* exceeds 10 million copies and that of the *Asahi Shimbun* exceeds 8.3 million copies. The annual circulation for newspapers and magazines is the greatest in the world and totals about 4.62 billion issues. Furthermore, a total of 133 million books are published every year. The network of print and electronic media cover 48 million households throughout the nation.

In addition, the Japanese Constitution rejects suppression of free speech and prohibits political intervention in religion, which frequently occurred prior to the war. The media, with the exception of some industries and specialized papers that depend on advertising revenues, are extremely free in expressing their opinions concerning corporations, political parties, or religious groups. There are also newspapers, magazines, and books that are run by political parties and religious groups, such as the *Akahata* newspaper of the Japan Communist Party, *Komei Shimbun* of the Komeito Party, and the *Seikyo Shimbun* of the Soka Gakkai—a Buddhist group.

As for communication activities, there are almost no government regulations outside of some guidelines on ethics. The Japanese Constitution guarantees freedom of speech, expression, and publication. At the same time, the media have also established ethical guidelines for themselves to protect the interests of the public. Thus, journalism enjoys a high level of freedom and credibility in Japan. The mass media, which emerged from the latter half of the 1950s preaching postwar democratic philosophy, became the fourth most powerful entity in Japan following the political, bureaucratic, and business entities in the 1990s. One perspective on the present social reformation being implemented is that it is driven by the mass media supported by public opinion.

Media Outreach

As already mentioned, the various media sources easily encompass all areas of Japan. Furthermore, 47.08 million people use the Internet, and the usage ratio in Japan for mobile telephones is more than half or up to 54.7%. According to the Ministry of Public Management, Home Affairs, Posts and Telecommunications, (2001), (2002). A highly dense telecommunications infrastructure provides a fast and dependable transmission of information by the media. The media network that covers every square inch of Japan broadcasts information to the Japanese people who have a right to know, and an environment has been established in which people can freely select the information they want.

Media Access

Many companies have their own *ko-ho* (public relations) departments, that contact the media when needed. Public relations agencies build relationships with the media in an effort to use the media on behalf of their clients. Although many companies are beginning to adopt two-way communications as part of their media relations, many continue to use one-way communication when disseminating information that is useful to them. Historically, the Japanese media have sought access to organizational leaders to obtain comments directly from them. There are some cases in which organizational leaders have become personally close to journalists and contacted the media directly, thus ignoring the public relations department. However, this sometimes makes the relationship with the media difficult, especially during times of crises. Nonetheless, public relations departments of Japanese corporations are being strengthened because of the heightened necessity to handle corporate public relations due to globalization, environmental activism, and the introduction of new corporate accounting standards. However, there continues to be a lack of very experienced public relations specialists as mentioned earlier. Consequently, when a scandal occurs, it is magnified because the existing staff is unable to initiate appropriate and fast measures.

Furthermore, as previously explained, Japanese media correspondents usually change their departments every 2 to 3 years, which brings up the constant need to establish new relationships. This is mitigated somewhat due to the press club system that originated in1890 when the Imperial Parliament was inaugurated. Currently, there are about 800 press clubs nationwide that have borrowed space and facilities in the offices of the central government, major political parties, local governments, industry bodies, and major economic organizations.

The Press Club Organization is very exclusive, and fewer than 60 media organizations, including major newspapers, locally strong media, television stations, and wire agencies, are members of a single press club. This system is extremely convenient for the organizations that have a press club on their premises because they can easily disseminate information and messages to their targeted audiences through the media members of their press club. This system worked especially well during the high-economic growth period when organizations that had press clubs were able to achieve their purposes through controlled management of the news, a one-way flow of information. The management of these clubs is done by the club members themselves. As a result, members enjoy autonomy, but the information flow itself is easily controlled by the organizations where each club is located. Press club members mostly have a monopoly on information originating from the organizations where they are stationed.

In the press club system, there are few opportunities for scoops as all the media members of a club are provided with the same releases and briefings by the organizations where the clubs are located. The exclusivity of press clubs and their tradition of keeping non-Japanese out led to intense demonstrations by foreign journalists in the early 1990s, and the clubs started becoming more open. For example, in the press club of the Ministry of Economy, Trade and Industry, there are currently 61 media members including two foreign media (Reuters and Bloomberg). Of these 61 members, 23 media organizations, including Reuters and Bloomberg, have work space for their representatives in the club. The press club of the Ministry of Foreign Affairs has about 10 foreign media members such as the Associated Press, Reuters, CNN, AFP and Bloomberg, in addition to Japanese press members. There are other signs of reform among the press clubs. For example, after the renowned author Yasuo Tanaka assumed the post of governor of Nagano Prefecture, he abolished the press club that had existed in the prefectural offices and changed the rules to allow anyone to attend a media briefing. Increasingly, access to the media has become easier for organizations and persons such as activists.

CONCLUSION

Japan opened up to external influence in the latter half of the 19th century through foreign pressure when Commodore Perry's black ships arrived. Japan's economic growth has been guided by central authorities in a one-way direction and with a top to bottom fiat style of management. This has taken place despite the influence of foreign cultures, science, and technology; the various policies led by the *zaibatsu* (major corporate groupings with an old, industrialist, famous-name founder, such as Iwasaki of the Mitsubishi group and Mitsui of the Mitsui group); the former military plan to catch up with the advanced countries of the West; and the building of a modern democracy under the leadership of the GHQ after Japan's defeat during World War II. However, with emerging societal issues, such as slumping stock prices, the recession, organizational scandals, the collapse of the family, and the increase in violent crimes, the mature Japanese society is still unable to find ways of building a new social system through a structural reform of the present system.

Nonetheless, Japan is now in an era of major transformation on a global scale, as the capitalist doctrine that Japan and the advanced countries of the West pursued during the last century has come to a dead end. The country must shift from an economic development model based on material wealth and build a new model that seeks coexistence with nature and emphasizes a high sense of ethics and wisdom for resolving diverse global problems, such as a lack of food in many nations, population issues, environmental problems, tribal disputes, conflicts between different cultures, and the digital divide. There is a demand for escape from a system that only pursues efficiency and material goods to a system formed from the creation and sharing of a new sense of values that takes into account changes in organizational environments that are horizontal and a two-way process, that accepts failures, respects people, and honors unique cultures and spiritual values.

Presently, information is shared more broadly on a daily basis, and greater speed is sought in handling situations. Within the rapidly changing society and flood of information, the ability to communicate with the targeted public is a critical issue that can mean life or death for a country or corporate body. However, the public may have difficulties in distinguishing the accuracy of the news with the great volume of information constantly being thrown at them. There is a chaotic appearance in the relationship between the information source and recipient. It seems that we are entering an era of unpredictability where humankind experiences rapid changes as never before.

Public relations is the ultimate real-time "software" in which specialists can provide solutions based on a situational judgment within this fast-changing society. The roles and duties of practitioners intermediating between information transmitters, information receivers, and the media are very critical. The key to the future as the problem solver of an increasingly changing and complex society lies in the implementation of a new model of public relations. Its goal should include global peace that strives toward harmonious and prosperous societies in which people are respected. This model consists of two-way communication but also possesses a self-correction function that is one step advanced from the traditional coordination and adjustment function for optimal results.

A final word is appropriate on what I mean by the newly proposed self-correction function. It refers to the ability to reflect on one's past mistake or misjudgment and it also means to make whatever correction is needed as soon as possible to prevent a recurrence of the error or misjudgment and to make a remedy for it when possible. It is not just a passive or superficial understanding of a past mistake or misjudgment, which reflects the old way of thinking. This model that includes the self-correction function envisages a society comprised of newly built values and takes a direction suitable for the 21st century (Inoue, 2002e).

Case Study: Tenneco—Deregulation of the Japanese Auto Parts Aftermarket, by Inoue Public Relations, Tokyo, Japan[1]

Statement of Problem/Opportunity.   Tenneco Automotive, a major American auto parts manufacturer, had made little progress in selling its shock absorbers (including its top-selling Monroe ® brand) in Japan despite its efforts over a 20-year period. Of the 1.5 million after-market shock absorbers sold during 1994 in Japan by automobile owners, Tenneco's share was a mere 3.5%. The company and many industry experts agreed that the closed nature of the Japanese aftermarket was the source of the problem. Tenneco hired Inoue Public Relations (Inoue PR) in early 1994 to find a way to open the Japanese market to their various products, including the Monroe shock absorbers. The campaign was a 3-year program concluding at the end of 1996.

Research.   Inoue PR, working closely with Tenneco's local subsidiary, Tenneco Automotive Japan, conducted extensive research into legislation and regulations affecting the import of automotive products into Japan. It also interviewed 50 industry experts, auto trade journalists, and representatives of auto repair shops, retailers, auto and auto parts industry groups, and government car inspection and registration centers to gather more data on the environment for automotive products. The research disclosed that a web of government legislation spun over a 40-year period establishing standards for car safety and maintenance and the inspection system itself protected the domestic auto-parts aftermarket from imported products. In the process, domestically manufactured auto parts were labeled "genuine original equipment (OE) parts," whereas imported parts were handicapped from the start with the label "non-OE parts." Furthermore, most of the certified auto repair shops were controlled by top Japanese automakers who also had relationships with domestic parts manufacturers. In addition, the operators of the nation's repair shops were culturally conservative, resisting change of any kind. Finally, imported parts were made more expensive by the complexity of Japan's distribution system. Inoue PR compiled these findings into the Tenneco Report.

Planning.   In consultation with Tenneco, Inoue PR set three objectives for the campaign:

1. Secure the deregulation of the Japanese auto parts aftermarket.
2. Once deregulation was under way, find new business partners for the distribution of Tenneco products in Japan.

---

[1]The program was submitted in 1977 to the IPRA Golden World Awards, Category 4: Public Affairs, and it was awarded IPRA's Excellence in Public Relations Grand Prize, which is the top award and the first one awarded in Asia and the Pacific.

3. Because deregulation alone would not ensure expansion in a market that had been heavily influenced by government regulation for more than 40 years, create new demand by re-educating Japanese car owners regarding the purchase of shock absorbers.

To achieve these objectives, Inoue PR developed two key messages. The first, targeted at the government, advocated the idea that deregulation creates new business opportunities in the Japanese aftermarket. The second, targeted at consumers, exhorted them to replace shock absorbers every 30,000 km to enhance driving safety and comfort. The specific audiences among these two broad publics were the key ministries in the Japanese Government, industry groups such as Japan Auto Parts Industry Association, car shops, prospective new distribution channels such as gas stations, and industry experts. Among the media, Inoue PR concentrated on general newspapers, news agencies, business and trade publications, television stations, and the foreign press.

Execution.   In the United States, Tenneco delivered the Tenneco Report to both the United States Department of Commerce and the Office of the United States Trade Representative. It was then presented to the White House. In Japan, Tenneco Japan and Inoue PR submitted the report to high-ranking officials at Japan's Ministry of Trade and Industry (MITI) and Ministry of Transport (MOT), as well as the American Embassy in Japan. Unofficial briefings were also provided to MITI and MOT. Meanwhile, on October 1, 1994, President Clinton declared the United States' intentions to apply Section 301 Trade Sanctions to Japan's auto parts aftermarket. Typically, Inoue PR and the Tenneco Japan office were responsible for lobbying done in Japan, and the Tenneco head office was responsible for the lobbying done in Washington, DC.

Inoue PR had originally planned to release the Tenneco Report at a press conference. However, because the behind-the-scenes efforts with both the Japanese and American governments were proving effective, Inoue PR decided this would not be appropriate. Instead, Inoue PR gave individual off-the-record briefings to Japan's five major newspapers and two major television stations. These media had been dependent on the Japanese government for their information on the auto parts aftermarket, and the briefings opened their eyes to the unfairness of this market to Japanese consumers.

Meanwhile, negotiations between the United States Trade Representative and the Japanese government stalled just before the June 28, 1995, deadline. The United States threatened to enforce sanctions, which had the potential to set off rounds of tit-for-tat retaliation. Under these circumstances, the Tenneco Report proved to be a critical source for both governments in arriving at a settlement. Using information provided during our briefings, the major media wrote articles about the negotiations, which had a tremendous impact on public opinion, putting pressure on the Japanese government to settle.

Once deregulation was under way, Tenneco and Inoue PR, through their connections, approached and proposed distribution partnerships with Toyota Motors, Autobacs, an auto parts chain with 380 outlets nationwide, and Japan Energy—one of Japan's major oil companies with 6,400 JOMO (Joy of Motoring) gas stations nationwide.

To launch the sale of Tenneco shock absorbers at JOMO gas stations, the first press conference in Japan ever held at a gas station was conducted. It featured officials from Tenneco, MITI, and the American Embassy in Japan. It attracted more than 100 Japanese and foreign journalists. Inoue PR also provided a crucial update on the situation in Japan to Dana Mead, chairman & chief executive officer of Tenneco Inc. Mead met with high-ranking Japanese officials to obtain their support for further opening the auto parts aftermarket. Throughout the campaign, Inoue PR arranged more than 20 one-on-one interviews with major Japanese and foreign media and distributed eight press releases gaining extensive quality coverage.

Evaluation. The campaign made great progress toward achieving the objectives. First, on October 20, 1995, Japan's Ministry of Transport, taking unusually quick action, officially decided to exclude four items—shock absorbers among them—from the list of auto parts requiring inspection. This made possible the sale of shock absorbers at locations not certified as inspection stations. Second, prior to the conclusion of the American–Japan negotiations, MITI sent a notice to distributors instructing them not to discriminate against foreign-made products. Third, the Ministry of Transport instructed auto repair shops not to discriminate and to give consumers the opportunity to select the shock absorbers they wanted. Fourth, Tenneco was able to form business partnerships with Toyota, Autobacs, and Japan Energy to distribute Tenneco shock absorbers nationwide.

As a result, the sale of Tenneco's shock absorbers in Japan increased by more than 40% between 1995 and 1996. President Clinton honored the achievements of Tenneco in Japan in an April 1996 White House press conference, marking the successful end of American–Japanese auto negotiations. The Japanese financial newspaper *Nihon Keizai Shimbun* (equivalent to the United Kingdom's *Financial Times* or the United States' *Wall Street Journal*) wrote a special report after the settlement was reached in Geneva between the two countries. The story revealed the existence of the Tenneco Report and its influence on the talks. On January 14, 1997, Japan's authoritative newspaper *Asahi Shimbun* reported on an evaluation of 45 major American–Japanese trade agreements that were made between 1980 and 1996. The study, conducted by the American Chamber of Commerce in Japan, revealed that 13 of these agreements proved to be successful, 18 partially successful, and 10 were failures. The auto parts negotiations were highlighted as a success by the study.

REFERENCES

Bernays, E. L. (1923). *Crystallizing public opinion.* (reprinted in 1961). New York: Liveright Publishing Company.

Cabinet Secretary, Cabinet Public Relations Office, (1990). *Seifu ko-ho 30nenshi no hakkan ni atatte* [The thirty years history of Japanese Government *ko-ho*] Tokyo: Author

Dentsu Advertising Co., Ltd. (Ed.) (1956). *Dentsu kokoku nenkan* [Dentsu AD annual 1956.], Tokyo: Author. p. 450.

Discovered document: Inefficiency was the cause of the delayed Declaration of War announcement to the U.S. by the U.S. Japanese Embassy (1994, November 21). The Asahi Shimbun, front page, morning edition.

Grunig, J. E., & Hunt, T. (1984). *Managing public relations.* New York: Holt, Rinehart & Winston.

Hall, E. T. (1976). *Beyond culture.* New York: Doubleday.

Hampden-Turner, C., & Trompenaars, A. (1997). *The seven cultures of capitalism* (K. Uehara & M. Wakatabe, Trans.). Tokyo: Nihon Keizai Shimbun Sha.

Higuchi, Y., & Ishiwatari, S. (2002). *Globalization.* Tokyo: St. Paul.

Hikami, R. (1951). *PR no kangaekata to arikata* [The concept and practice of PR]. Tokyo: Sekaishoin.

Hikami, R. (1952). *Jichitai ko-ho no riron to gijutsu* [Theory and techniques of public relations in local governments]. Tokyo: Sekaishoin.

Ikeda, K. (1997). *Shanaiho-hyakunenshi* [100 years of in-house publications], April issue, Tokyo: Gendai-keiei Kenkyukai

Ikari, S. (Ed.). (1998). *Kigyo no hatten to ko-ho sen-ryaku-50nen no ayumi to tenbo* [Corporate development and the strategy of public relations—a 50 year history and perspective]. Tokyo: Nikkei BP-Kikaku.

Inoue, T. (2002a, March). Kyogyubyo ni taisho suru kikikanri ho [How to do crisis management to counter the BSE problem]. Opinion leaders' *Seiron Magazine*, *3*, 342–349.

Inoue, T. (2002b). *Mad cows, bad system in Japan. IPRA Frontline, 24*(2) p. 8, 13.

Inoue, T. (2002c). *The need for two-way communications and self-correction. IPRA Frontline, 24*(4) p. 17–18. and the erratum, 2003 March, 25(1) p. 5.

Inoue, T. (2002d). Deficiency of Japanese diplomacy. *Japan Today.* Retrieved May 29, 2002, from http://www.japantoday.com/e/?content=comment&id=191

Inoue, T. (2002e). United States public relations in transition: Analysis of evolution and proposal for a new model. In the Proceedings of the Japan Information-Cultural Society. Vol. 9 No. 1, pp. 61–75.

The Japan Society for Corporate Communication Studies. (2002). *Senryo-ki no ko- ho/shanai-ho* [Public relations/house organ during GHQ occupation]. Tokyo: Author.

The Japan Society for Corporate Communication Studies. (2002). *Survey of corporate communication today.* Tokyo: Author.

The Law to Promote Specified Nonprofit Activities, Ordinance No. 7 of 1998, March 25, Cabinet Office

Kitazawa, S. (1951). *Public relations kowa* [Public relations talk]. Tokyo: Diamond-sha.

Koyama, E. (1975). *Gyosei ko-ho nyumon* [An introduction to government public relations]. Tokyo: Gyosei.

Masamura, K., & Yamada, S. (2002). *Nihon keizairon* [The Japanese economy]. Tokyo: Toyo Keizai Shinpo-sha.

Ministry of Public Management, Home Affairs, Post and Telecommunications, (2001), *Tsushin-riyou-doko-chosa* [2001 Communication usage trend survey]. Tokyo: Author.

Ministry of Public Management, Home Affairs, Post and Telecommunications, (2002), *Joho-tsushin hakusho* [*2002 WHITE PAPER Information and Communications in Japan*]. Tokyo: Gyosei.

Nihon-Koho-Kyokai (1951). *Koho no genri to jissai* [Ko-ho theory and practice], Tokyo: Nihon Dempo-Tsushin-Sha

Ogura, S. (1990). *PR wo kangaeru* [All about PR]. Tokyo: Dentsu.

Ozawa, I. (1993). *Nihon kaizo keikaku* [Plans for Japanese structural reforms]. Tokyo: Kodansha.

Public Relations Association of Japan, (2002). PR techo (*Public relations hand book*). Tokyo: Author.

Prestowitz, C. (1985). Nichibei gyakuten [*Trading places: how we allowed Japan to take the lead*]. (M. Kunihiro, Trans.). Tokyo: Diamond-sya.

Sakaiya, T. (2002a). *Jidaiga kawatta* [The Era has changed] Tokyo: Kodansha.

Sasaki, Y. (1951). *Pr no kiso-chishini* [PR basic knowledge], Tokyo: Toyoshokan.

Shiba, R. (1996). *Kono kuni no katachi* [The shape of Japan, Vol. 6]. Tokyo: Bungei-Syun-Jyu.

Shibasaki, K. (1984). *Kigyo-joho-sanbogaku* [Corporate policy maker], Tokyo: Diamond-sha

Sriramesh, K., & Takasaki, M. (1999). The impact of culture on Japanese public relations. *Journal of Communication Management, 3*, 337–351.

The Basic Law for the Environmental Pollution Control Law No. 132 of 1967. August 3, Ministry of Health and Welfare.

Tokyo Metropolitan Government. (1995). *Senjika tocho no ko-ho katsudo* [Public relations activities of the Tokyo Metropolitan Office during World War II). Tokyo: Tokyo Metropolitan Archives, Tokyo Metropolitan Government Archives.

Tsurumi, Y. (1997). *High speed senryaku* [World class strategy] Tokyo: Sogo-Horei

Wright, D., & Ikari, S. (1997). *The evolution of public relations education and the influence of globalization—survey of eight countries' IPRA gold paper, No. 12, November 1997.* London: International Public Relations Association.

Yamaguchi, M. (1995). *Haisha-no seishinshi* [Psychological history of the defected], Tokyo: Iwanami-shoten.

5

BECOMING PROFESSIONALS: A PORTRAIT OF PUBLIC RELATIONS IN SINGAPORE

CONSTANCE CHAY-NÉMETH

PUBLIC RELATIONS AND THE GEOPOLITICS OF SINGAPORE

The practice of public relations in Singapore may be understood by exploring the relationship between the geopolitics of the island republic and the important role of the government in political, economic, and social engineering. This chapter begins with a brief description of the geopolitical conditions of Singapore and continues with an analysis of the government's role in the political and economic life of the state and its effects on the practice of public relations.

The Republic of Singapore is located 137 km north of the equator. The mainland (606.7 sq km) and 63 offshore islands occupy a total land area of 682.7 sq km. Its immediate neighbors are Malaysia to the north and Indonesia and Brunei to the south. Its population of slightly over 4 million constitutes ethnic groups such as the Chinese (76.8%), Malays (13.9%), Indians (7.9%), and others (1.4%). The four official languages are English (the language of administration), Malay (the national language), Mandarin, and Tamil. Mainstream religions include Buddhism, Taoism, Islam, Christianity, and Hinduism.

In 1819, Sir Stamford Raffles, a representative of the British East India Company established Singapore as a trading port under agreement with the Sultan of Johor and the Malay ruler of the island. In 1824, the Sultan ceded the island in perpetuity to the British East India Company, and the island became a British colony until its occupation by the Japanese colonialists from 1942 to 1945. In September 1945, the Japanese surrendered to the British who resumed colonial control of the island until its independence on August 9, 1965.

The period between 1945 and the early 1960s was tumultuous, demonstrating local activism at its zenith. It is commonly known that local nationalists of the time were battling colonialism, communalism, and Communism. With Communalism came clashes and riots among the different ethnic groups as they became pawns in the hands of colonial divide-and-rule tactics. Communism reared its head in the form of insurgency against the establishment. These insurgent acts were conducted through the use of front organizations such as labor and Chinese school unions. To combat the latter, the British implemented the detention of communist suspects without trial, or what is known today as the Internal Security Act (ISA, 1986).

In 1959, Singapore gained autonomy from the British. The People's Action Party (PAP) has been in power since it was first elected in 1959. Through a series of brilliant political, economic, and social management strategies, the PAP has successfully kept a tight reign over communalism and communism. Today, Singapore's economy ranks among the most competitive in the world economy. In 2000, its per capita gross national product was S$42,212 (Singapore Department of Statistics, 2001). Its next economic lap runs in tandem with the global drive toward a knowledge-based economy (KBE).

EVOLUTION OF PUBLIC RELATIONS IN SINGAPORE

The early models of public relations in Singapore evolved from those used by the British colonialists. They were primarily propagandists seeking to promote the credibility of the British especially after their defeat by the Japanese army in World War II. Publicity and public information were issued from the Department of Publicity and Printing under the British Military Administration (Yeap, 1994). Lord Llyod, the Parliamentary Under Secretary of State for the Colonial Office, best summed up the mission of public relations during colonialism: "It was everywhere of first importance both for British interests and for the colonial interests of the people concerned that we put across with all possible power and persuasion the ideas for which we stand" (cited in Nair, 1986, pp. 3–4).

In the 1950s, the multinational companies entered the oil industry in Singapore. This period also marked the emergence of in-house public relations departments both in the private and public sectors. The government continued with the press agentry and public information models (Grunig & Hunt, 1984) used by the British propagandists. However, now the mission of public relations was to promote national development. The Ministry of Culture and Information recruited individuals professionally trained in journalism and mass communication as public relations personnel. They were responsible for organizing the many public education programs that followed such as the antilitter, antispitting, and speak Mandarin campaigns (Yeap, 1994).

Since the 1980s onwards, more multinational companies and international public relations consultancies have entered the Singapore economy. Local in-house public relations departments and consultancies have also mushroomed. In the 1990s and to date, the Singapore economy has been rapidly globalizing and shifting toward a KBE. With the latter and the entry of many more multinational companies, the public relations industry is in transition—shifting from one-way communication models to two-way communication models and the strategic management of public relations. However, the shift has been slow. The local industry still has much to learn in developing skills, expertise, and knowledge that would prepare it for a global and KBE. Whereas practitioners belonging to international public relations consultancies and public relations departments of larger organizations recognize the importance of public relations as strategic management, those belonging to smaller local organizations continue to focus excessively on the tactics of public relations in media relations, event management, and publicity (Chow, Tan, & Chew, 1996; Tan, 2001; Yeap, 1994).

This shift toward two-way communication and the strategic management of publics also manifests itself in the government's relations with local communities. The Singapore 21 vision, an ongoing government project, advocates the cultivation of a more active citizenry (The Singapore 21 vision, 1997). The vision reflects the opinions of some 6,000 Singaporeans solicited via public forums, surveys, and web site feedback channels. This shift toward symmetry in government–community relations is aptly described by George Yeo, the then Minister of Information and the Arts: "In the old days, the issues were stark, black and white, left or right, up or down . . . bread and butter issues for which there were clear, unequivocal answers. But I think we have passed that stage" (cited in Yeap, 1994).

CURRENT STATUS OF PUBLIC RELATIONS IN SINGAPORE

The public relations profession in Singapore may be said to be in transition from a preprofessional to a professional status. Preprofessionalism is typically marked by an excess of focus on one-way communication models such as press agentry (Gruning & Hunt, 1984), publicity, and the subordination of public relations to a marketing tool "to gain awareness of a client, perhaps to keep TV ratings up or turnstiles clicking" (Culbertson & Jeffers, 1992, p. 54). Professional public relations is a holistic practice. Although it acknowledges the importance of the technical and tactical functions of public relations (e.g., writing press releases and organizing events), more important, it recognizes public relations as a strategic management function. Public relations as strategic management seeks to manage the interactions among organizational knowledge, information, publics, and environmental variables (social, political, and economic infrastructure) to create a win–win situation for the organization and its key publics. "In fact, it can be argued this type of activity distinguishes the true public relations professional from the publicist or hack" (Culbertson & Jeffers, 1992, p. 63).

Dominant Coalitions and Public Relations

The professionalism of public relations, or its lack, is related not only to the strategic or tactical practice of public relations but also to the significance accorded it by the dominant coalitions of organizations. In Singapore, dominant coalitions determine the type of public relations that is eventually practiced. The following paragraphs describe the perceptions of dominant coalitions regarding public relations and their effects on preprofessional and professional public relations in Singapore.

A recent study of the state of public relations in Singapore (Tan, 2001, pp. 8–9) showed that the top four public relations practices performed were media relations (88%), corporate communications and branding (86%), community relations (64%), and government relations (51%). As mentioned earlier, preprofessionalism is characterized by an excessive focus on media publicity. The importance that dominant coalitions attach to media relations and publicity is also borne out by recent e-mail interviews I conducted with 20 public relations practitioners in Singapore.

For instance, one practitioner from an international public relations consultancy said: "Bigger multinational firms have a better understanding about the importance and function of public relations while smaller, especially local, companies may not see any need in it, or they judge results solely through press coverage." Hence, when the number of column inches of press publicity does not match the organization's investment in public relations, the latter is seen as ineffective and a waste of money. Preprofessional public relations often attributes more importance to media publicity than it does to building rapport with key publics.

Other dominant coalitions see public relations in purely tactical and mundane terms. One consultant reported:

> Whilst our clients generally believe that public relations is important and of value to the company, they lack a full understanding of its value. One client still resorts to heavy wine and dine, with so much emphasis placed on superficial matters, e.g., the quality of the paper, the outer appearance of the press kit folder etc, to the point of ignoring strategic and sensible thinking.

The failure to recognize public relations as a strategic function and hence its subordination to a support role is observed by a consultant from an international public relations agency: "Public relations is viewed as a service industry, providing arms-and-legs support on various communications. This is opposed to public relations professionals being viewed as strategic consultants in other countries, especially in the West."

Thus, as long as public relations is still perceived by dominant coalitions to be a tactical function—mundane, peripheral, and publicity centered—it should not be surprising that the public relations industry in Singapore still has one foot caught in preprofessionalism.

Preprofessional Public Relations in Singapore

Preprofessionalism as practiced in Singapore bears specific characteristics. First, public relations is a purely technician role. A practitioner from the in-house public relations department of a government organization observed that practitioners as technicians primarily "book advertising spots," act as "event organisers or even troubleshooters who reply to unfavorable reports/letters." The technician and tactical role of preprofessional public relations in Singapore also extends into its fixation with media relations and publicity. Hence, it is not surprising that practitioners here spend many hours on cultivating good working relationships with journalists, getting them to attend events and press conferences, and writing press releases rather than on strategic management of their clients' affairs.

Second, preprofessional public relations in Singapore is rarely, if ever, strategic and proactive. One practitioner said: "Like most parts of Asia, public relations is still equated with events and other arms- and-legs functions. The strategic element is lost to most clients, including the marketing departments of even many MNCs. . . . " Reactive public relations also implies that local organizations place little importance on environmental tracking in relation to issues and crisis management.

Third, preprofessional public relations in Singapore suffers from a lack of definition and clear conceptualization of the nature and functions of public relations. It is a free-for-all industry wherein public relations is mistaken variously for marketing, advertising, sales, human resource management, lounge hostessing, and the like. One practitioner aptly summed up this dilemma: "This image problem maybe related to the lack of definition regarding what constitutes 'public relations' work in Singapore, where public relations functions are incorporated into various types of job descriptions such as corporate communications, marketing communications, agency & advertising accounts, etc." And because "public relations is still viewed as a sales or marketing function, and often secondary in importance," its practitioners are similarly accorded a low status by many local organizations.

Finally, preprofessional public relations in Singapore is marked by a practice of situational ethics. However, this does not mean that codes of professional ethics do not exist. On the contrary, the Institute of Public Relations Singapore (IPRS) and most multinationals possess their own brands of ethics. For instance, the IPRS observes the code of ethics of the International Public Relations Association. Rather, the problem lies in putting ethical codes to practice in day-to-day public relations conduct and situations. One practitioner aptly summed up this dilemma:

> While almost every reputable consulting firm I know of has a code of ethics, I don't think most consultants pay much attention to ethics on a day-to-day basis. I suppose the only time there are concerns about ethics is when we are pitching for a new client whose business poses conflicts of interest with existing clients. I think, in Singapore we have not yet reached the level of professionalism as in the states or UK. I feel that many of the practitioners here are themselves not clear on the role of public relations, and do not conduct themselves professionally.

The difficulty in performing ethically is further compounded by the lack of power of practitioners for autonomous action. As such, practitioners are tempted to practice situational ethics rather than abide steadfastly to a code of professional ethics. One practitioner observed: "Management at corporate organisations need to understand the function of public relations in order to leverage public relations in reputation management. And, they pretty much determine the level of professionalism in the industry since they pay the salaries or the bills."

Hence, professional ethical conduct is not primarily determined by the public relations industry and its practitioners but dictated instead by the master who pays their bills. Grunig (2000) aptly summed up this dilemma of preprofessionalism: "Professionals, in other words, have the power to carry out their work based on the knowledge and standards of their profession. Nonprofessionals do not have that power. Instead, clients or superiors in the organization tell them what to do—and often those orders violate professional standards" (p. 26).

Toward Professional Public Relations in Singapore

However, there are signs that public relations is rising to a professional status in Singapore, assisted by changing environmental conditions. The government's push toward globalization and a KBE has stimulated the recruitment of more foreign talent to meet the needs of the new KBE.

Imported talent appears to raise the professionalism of the public relations industry in the following ways. First, dominant coalitions formed by imported talent tend to recognize the importance of public relations as a strategic management function. The practitioner from an international public relations agency reported: "The status of public relations has certainly risen slowly but surely over the years. Obviously, MNCs have been at the forefront in recognising public relations as a strategic business management tool."

These enlightened dominant coalitions perceive the strategic importance of public relations in diverse ways. Some practitioners of multinationals see public relations as a "necessary and strategic senior function which must be networked into the regional organization." Others perceive public relations as strategic communication specialists and gatekeepers of organizational information and knowledge. They asserted that public relations practitioners function as "the gatekeeper of company information and a communication channel," while giving "counsel on their communication strategies." Yet other dominant coalitions are said to perceive practitioners "as strategic partners, not just normal resource for e.g., press conference expertise." Overall, enlightened dominant coalitions perceive public relations as being very important because practitioners offer knowledge and experience to companies that lack public relations expertise and contacts. Public relations is also important to dominant coalitions who see practitioners as the link to their public.

In addition, foreign multinational talent brings to the public relations industry diverse knowledge, skills and expertise, as one practitioner from an international public relations consultancy reported: "Global industry leader companies from the US and UK not forgetting closer home from Australia, . . . has brought positive impact because of the generation of new skills and industry expertise knowledge and industry specialist experiences."

Further, a KBE and technology intensive economy also aids in professionalizing public relations in Singapore. One consultant of an international public relations agency suggested that the accessibility of alternative information via the Internet and the potential of cyberactivism have increased the importance of corporate branding as a form of corporate protection:

> The Internet has widened everyone's perception of the power of communications hence it has raised issue of the liability and damaging impact of global networking that can destroy brands or corporations credibility. Consequently, management and clients willingly invest in a sound communications programme, headed by specialists to protect and promote their corporate and product interests.

Others see the development of public relations into specialist and niche areas with the increase of dot.com businesses: "With the onset of internet technology and the overnight boom of dot.com businesses requiring specialist communications promotion. There is more specialist or niche practice expertise available too."

As organizations become increasing affected by the new knowledge-based economy, public relations is slowly moving away from an excessive focus on media relations and publicity. As one practitioner observed: "Now organisations have realised the importance of specialised public relations skills ranging from investor relations to corporate imaging. Certainly more organisations are calling for more strategic usage of public relations even though they may not entirely understand how it works."

Finally, one cannot underestimate the catalytic effect of a turbulent and volatile environment in increasing the professionalism of public relations in Singapore. A few practitioners have observed that the strategic value and importance of public relations increases during crisis situations. One practitioner reported: "On the whole, I find that the image is slowly improving and that management is beginning to regard public relations as a potential area that can make or break a company, especially after recent events such as the SQ006 crash and OUB takeover bids."[1] Yet others suggested: "As a consequence to the Sep 11 events and the increased voice of NGOs, public relations now goes beyond media relations to help organisations manage issues and crisis as well as NGO communication."

As discussed, the functions of managing organizational knowledge, issues, and crises appear to be gaining in importance in Singapore. In fact, the importance of crisis communication is registered by the recent inauguration of the Public Relations Academy in 2002. The academy is run by the Ministry of Information and the Arts for the purpose of

---

[1] The SQ006 crisis involved the crash of a Singapore Airlines plane in Taiwan, November 2000. The Overseas Union Bank (OUB) crisis emerged when the financial representative of the Development Bank of Singapore (DBS) released statements of a defamatory nature regarding the OUB and United Overseas Bank (UOB) board of directors. As a result of this debacle, the DBS issued a public apology and paid the banks S$2 million. The money was paid to local charities.

training top civil servants in more savvy communication with the media and other publics in the event of crisis situations.

Improving Public Relations Professionalism in Singapore

Although there are clear indications of the public relations industry becoming more professional in the future, it remains that this transition to professionalism is slow, lagging behind professionalism in the Western world. To hasten the transition to professional public relations, the industry would need to address the following areas according to a majority of practitioners interviewed.

First, some practitioners have suggested increasing the visibility and profile of the IPRS: "Public relations in Singapore is still in its infancy in some aspects. We lack a reputable organisation in governing the practices of public relations practitioners. The IPRS aims to do something, but it lacks the buy in of key organizations." In other words, professionals need to support each other through membership with a professional body. A recent study showed that most practitioners are not members of any professional associations (Tan, 2001, p. 15). About 53% of practitioners surveyed in consultancies were members of the IPRS. Only 22% of practitioners in private organizations and 16% of those in government agencies were members of the IPRS.

Others suggested the need to improve public relations training and education for practitioners to prepare them for public relations as strategic management beyond technician duties. One practitioner observed: "Some private schools and local training courses are lacking in depth and only manage to cover a brief scope of public relations and how it can be utilised at a higher level." However, a more crucial need lies in changing the way in which public relations is taught to potential practitioners in the local institutions: "The problem, however, is that Asian universities do not teach their students how to think and the exposure of the practitioners is limited because of a lack of reading and reflection." This is a critical shortcoming for practitioners operating within a KBE, with clients demanding more value-added strategic services.

In short, professionalism includes developing the following: (a) sound training in the technical aspects of the profession, (b) cultivating a wide body of interdisciplinary knowledge refined by critical thinking and creative application to organizational problems, and (c) membership to professional associations that would support the practice of professional values and codes of ethics.

INFRASTRUCTURE AND PUBLIC RELATIONS

Earlier, I mentioned that the practice of public relations in Singapore may be understood by exploring the role of the government in economic, political, and social engineering. One political commentator (Yuen, 1999) observed:

> It is usually agreed that nothing much can be done without government approval, support and coordination to marshall the necessary resources.... Once an idea like this takes hold, it is self-fulfilling: any proposal not backed by the government, or by people known to be in favour with the government, would be given little support by everyone else and are consequently likely to fail. (p. 6)

In this regard, public relations practitioners would do well to include the government as one of their key publics whenever engaged in strategic planning and management.

In the past few years, government leaders have advocated a paradigm shift in the Singapore economy—from the old economy of brick-and-mortar businesses to the new economy of knowledge and technology intensive businesses. This paradigm shift is articulated clearly in the speech of David Lim, the Minister of State for Defence and Information and the Arts, during the Prism Awards ceremony.[2] Here are excerpts of his speech indicating impending changes in communication style, issues management, and the nature of "cyber-publics" that are likely to affect the practices of public relations:

> Already, Internet penetration to the homes in Singapore—at 42%, has exceeded the rate of penetration in the US—at 40%. Media companies, both globally and right here in Singapore, will have to adjust their strategies, add new capability and venture into new services and business alliances if they are to keep up. . . .
> Such structural changes to the media industry will also have a big impact on the Public Relations industry. You will have to watch the trends carefully, to catch new opportunities to get your message through, and to capture new audiences. (Lim, 2000)

In this context, it would be pertinent to ask how an economic paradigm shift to a KBE would affect the status and practices of public relations. It is likely that a KBE may also stimulate an increase in government public relations or public affairs, community relations, activism, issues management, and crisis communication. If this is true, it would appear that the transition to professional public relations is given a boost by changing external conditions such as the economy and its attendant effects on the political and social infrastructures of the system. The following paragraphs describe the effects of the government's new economic initiative on public relations practices in public affairs, activism, and organizational practices.

KBE and Public Affairs

In the past decade or so, the political landscape of Singapore has seen significant changes. Although technically labeled a democratic socialist state governed by a parliamentary system, political observers (Chua, 1995; Ho, 2000; Yuen, 1999) have been quick to label the island's political style variously as authoritarian, fascistic, or a benign dictatorship. For instance, one political observer (Yuen, 1999) said: "Singapore is a place that arouses deeply divided feelings among observers. Economically, it is one of the great success stories of this century, but it is also widely seen as an authoritarian state that limits freedom of speech and political rights" (p. 1).

Hitherto, this political style has also translated into a similar style of public affairs, that is, a top-down and paternalistic approach to communication between the state and its constituencies (Chua, 1995). Within such a political framework, consensus is typically valued over dissent and individual interests are subsumed under group interests in the name of economic necessity, pragmatism, and Asian democracy (Ho, 2000).

In this political framework, the business sector plays a minor role in decision making: "Organized business . . . has little formal role in policy making" (Ho, 2000, p. 203). However, personal networking with key government personnel obviously pays off in terms of influencing policy making: "Its influence is largely derived from personal contacts and informal inroads into policy-making circles in Singapore." (S. P. Tan, 1993–94, p. 77).

---

[2]The Prism Awards is conferred annually to individuals and organizations practicing excellent public relations in Singapore.

This use of personal contacts is akin to the personal influence model reported in some Asian cultures (Sriramesh, Kim, & Takasaki, 1999).

In summary, the style of public communication hitherto adopted by the government with its constituencies may be summed up as follows: (a) It typically practices one-way asymmetrical communication. Decision making is monopolized by the government with little participation from the constituencies. The government defines key issues and sets the agenda for discussing them. The task of government public relations practitioners is primarily to inform and educate the masses about government decisions and policies via the pro-government mass media. (b) It promotes consensus rather than confrontation. Constituencies have been socialized to expect the government to take the lead and intervene in solving community problems. This makes for highly passive publics. Perhaps this also explains the excessive importance of media relations in the public relations industry— that is, the media functions as a vehicle for engineering consent with passive publics. (c) As a corollary, the government and its constituencies have yet to develop productive mechanisms for managing conflict and dissensus. This implies the improbability of a two-way symmetrical style of communication with constituencies in the immediate future. For this to occur, it will require drastic changes in the political philosophy and infrastructures of the system.

In spite of this rather bleak scenario, there are emerging signs that the style of government–community relations is changing for the favorable. Demographic changes such as the emergence of a more affluent and larger middle class population, better educated and well-traveled citizenry, the economic paradigm shift to a KBE and its attendant requirements for the development of niche knowledge areas, and critical and creative applications of knowledge to problems and opportunities all seem to contribute to a slowly but surely emerging communitarian democracy (Chua, 1995).

These changing conditions bode well for a more equitable relationship between the government and its constituencies. The Singapore 21 vision is a clear indicator of a change in the government's style of public communication.[3] It suggests the emergence of a two-way communication process between the latter and community publics. It also encourages the formation of a more active citizenry with increasing interest in social responsibility and public debate. To facilitate the latter, the government has created more channels for feedback from its constituencies (Ho, 2000). These include (a) the mass media as channels through which the constituencies may voice their opinions and concerns on government policies; (b) weekly meet-the-member of Parliament (MP) sessions in which constituencies may voice grievances and complaints to the MP; (c) feedback units set up and sponsored by the government to solicit public opinion on public issues; (d) the government's involvement of selected NGOs in the policy-making process; and (e) the use of parapolitical organizations such as community centers, citizens' consultative committees, and town councils to communicate and explain government policies to the constituencies.

In a nutshell, a communitarian democracy requires the establishment of formal institutions, such as a free press and the right of citizens to be consulted, as it does in liberal democracies (Chua, 1995). The emphasis placed on consensus rather than dissensus in communitarian democracies also implies the need to free up the press so that it may reflect

---

[3]The Singapore 21 vision describes five core values for maintaining the prosperity and survival of the nation in the new century. These values include active citizens, strong families, the fact that every Singaporean matters, the Singapore heartbeat, and opportunities for all.

more honestly grassroots sentiments and popular concerns instead of suppressing them. It also implies the need for a free flow of information if citizens are to make well-informed contributions when consulted by the state. Further, it implies the right of citizens to be consulted in policy making if popular consensus is to be achieved. Finally, the shift to KBE also encourages a pluralistic diversity of ideas and the necessity of dissent if creative solutions are to be found to increase the system's performance and survival.

KBE and Activism

These changes to the political philosophy and politicoeconomic infrastructures have made slow but steady incursions into civic life. In the field of public relations, activism is viewed with mixed reactions by practitioners.

For instance, one practitioner said: "Activism is not prevalent in Singapore. Our regional work has encountered activists on environmental, political and trade issues." Others, however, reported increasing activism on different fronts. One practitioner reported an encounter with environmental activism:

> Yes we have, and surprisingly they were rather loud voices, despite our client being a government statutory board. This proves that the local activist groups are starting to grow in strength and courage, as they often see the importance in putting their views and opinions across, and in seeking a change in course of action.

Another reported an emergence of minority shareholder activism: "Activism in Singapore is not as overt as in other markets. However, there is a growing grassroots movement amongst minority shareholder groups which are increasingly getting their views heard, and companies must acknowledge that and deal with it." The rise of minority shareholder activism is also supported by the local media's (Sreenivasan, 2001) advocacy of protection for the latter.

Consumer activism is also emerging. In a recent case, some 5,000 club members filed a class action suit against their town club for misrepresentation and a breach of contract (Tay, 2001). Club members alleged that the club had falsely advertised itself as an exclusive club when it was, in fact, not so.

Perhaps the event that marks the height of recent civil activism lies with the *tudung* issue ("Singapore: Four Muslim," 2002). Local Muslim activists, supported by Malaysian activists have challenged the state's constitutional right in banning the use of the *tudung* (a headscarf worn by Muslim girls and women) at local public schools. The activist who initiated the issue was the president of Fateha.com., an Internet site hosted by a segment of the local Muslim community. Two outcomes of the *tudung* issue have emerged. The first relates to the withdrawal of four Muslim children by their parents from local public schools when they were asked not to wear the *tudung* to school in conformity with the uniform dress code. The second concerns the decision by these parents to sue the state for banning the *tudung* from public schools, an act considered as unconstitutional by the parents. Currently, the issue is still being negotiated between the parents who withdrew their children from the public schools and the state, with intervention from leaders of the Muslim community.

Although these changes in the level of activism are slowly emerging, practitioners would do well not to underestimate the power of increasingly well-educated and vocal young, active publics. It is likely that practitioners conducting government, community, consumer, and employee relations will have to become more responsive to the interests and demands of this segment of young and active publics in the future.

Responding to Activism

How do public relations practitioners in Singapore respond to activism when it does arise, albeit in limited and rather tame forms? Practitioners interviewed suggest several methods. The most popular of which includes a two-way symmetrical communication approach of engagement and dialogues whenever possible. Another suggested a process of compromise and negotiation:

> We made sure that there was consultation of their views and opinions, and provided avenues of feedback such as hotline, briefing sessions with the activist groups, exhibition explaining the rationale of the client, direct communication channels, e.g., brochures specially printed for the activist groups. There had to be some give and take as well, to show the activist groups that we were also listening to their concerns, and that it was not just a one-way communication process. Of course, the client had already prepared in advance to give some leeway regarding some of the issues.

Yet others suggested more aggressive tactics: "The basic tactic is to aggressively inform all audiences about the facts of the case, and engage activists if, and when, appropriate" and to use "issue and crisis management tactics to manage negativity in media reports on client company, product or service."

With the ongoing shift toward a KBE and the extensive use of electronic communication, practitioners anticipate changes in the style of managing activism. The most obvious difference between offline and online media is the increase in the speed of communication that the latter provides. Practitioners suggested two possible effects that may emerge from the latter: (a) Organizations will need to learn to communicate more quickly and accurately to breaking news in the media. Hence, activist access to the media via new electronic technology means a "higher possibility of the media breaking news and organisations would have to be prepared to react quickly." (b) Organizations will need to improve on their ethical conduct, good corporate governance, and transparency. As one practitioner succinctly put it:

> Instantaneous access translates to more competitive reporting which means every journalist will strive to be the first to file a report. Because of the new environment, it is now even more imperative that corporates take on a more proactive role in communicating their business practices and truths to the media. Corporate governance and transparency will help preempt misunderstanding.

Further, practitioners anticipate a major change in the demographics and nature of publics who use the Internet. One potential change is the emergence of a younger and better educated public, perhaps more politically conscious of their rights as consumers and citizens. This compels organizations to become more socially responsible, as one practitioner observed:

> With the Internet, these interest groups have an added media channel that has unlimited reach. Interested publics would also have increased accessibility to the various sources of information. These publics would be in a better position to evaluate claims and challenges

by interest groups. Organisations would also have to increase engagement with these activist publics so understand and address their concerns. The Internet can also be used as a tool to engage these activist publics.

In addition, the Internet also enables activists to target organizational stakeholders more directly than traditional media. One practitioner observed: "Obviously the penetration rate of the Internet into homes and businesses in Singapore provides avenue for direct targetting of stakeholders." This direct activist access to organizational stakeholders allows for rapid national and transnational coalition building to occur. It also suggests the necessity for increased organizational surveillance of the environment and heightened issues-tracking and management systems. One practitioner observed:

> We will definitely have to be more savvy when it comes to issue management; currently the interest groups are still rather passive; they are definitely not as active or strong as the activists in other countries. However, that will change as the local interest groups have easy access to similar groups in other countries—there will be exchange of ideas and strategies in lobbying policy change, etc. We will need to strategise new methods of managing and communicating to the activist groups.

Thus, it is likely that a shift to a KBE will eventually stimulate organizations and practitioners to pay more attention to ethical corporate performance and transparency, speed up their communication transfers with greater accuracy, strengthen environmental surveillance and issues management strategies, and become more socially responsive and symmetrical in their relations with key publics.

Limits to Activism

Although a more vibrant civil society appears to be in the making, political analysts argue that the development of local activism is retarded by the following factors: (a) legal restrictions such as the ISA, which allows the government to detain indefinitely political suspects without trial, and the Societies Act, which bars nonpolitical societies from making political statements against the establishment under the pressure of being deregistered by the government; (b) the institutionalization of out-of-bound (OB) markers that circumscribe what may be said about religious, racial, and political issues;[4] and (c) a culture of self-censorship that stifles dissenting political opinions (Gomez, 2000).

Hence, local activism in its limited forms may be classified into pseudoactivism and real activism. Practitioners described pseudoactivism variously as grassroots activism from environmental councils that are "not a real threat" to the establishment. Pseudoactivism is also associated with NGOs that are "aligned with the government" or have been coopted by the government. Such activist groups would then be tolerated or legitimized by the government. Pseudoactivism may also take the form of front organizations with hidden agendas. One veteran practitioner argued that the latter is activism with a hidden agenda to benefit the activist leaders and not the masses whose interests they represent. Thus, it may be deduced that real activist are those who challenge the established status quo and are less likely to be tolerated by the government.

---

[4]OB markers are implicit rules of censorship. Although they do not clearly define what may not be articulated in the public sphere, they define categories of topics that may not be articulated. These categories include matters pertaining to religion, race, and politics.

In the context of such a sharp demarcation between pseudoactivism and real activism, where do business organizations stand with local activists? One chief executive officer (CEO) from a foreign multinational business operating in Singapore offered his perspective (Faithfull, 2000):

> Currently, there appears to be an assumption in some quarters that business and government stand on one side, and civil society organizations on the other. The latter thus often expresses skepticism about the trustworthiness of business corporations as partners in development, seeing identity of interests between them and the government. According to this view, businesses may be reluctant to enter into cooperation with civil society organizations for fear of objections from the government, that is, if business could overcome and convince the NGOs of its genuine intent in the first instance. Such a skeptical conception of different alliances between the three parties can be a serious obstacle in the way of productive collaboration of all three parties in furthering the interests of the society as a whole. (pp. 87–88)

If this description holds water, it is unrealistic to expect much productive engagement and dialogue to occur between activists and the business sector. This would also mean that two-way symmetrical communication and relations may not occur with real activists who suspect business of being co-opted partners of the government.

KBE and Organizational Practices

Practitioners suggested that a shift to a KBE would affect organizational and public relations practices in various other ways, besides those of public affairs and activism already detailed.

First, a KBE encourages the emergence of active publics. Practitioners suggest that organizations need to engage in more two-way communication practices to productively engage active publics. One practitioner said: "Also, with publics becoming more active, we will need to pursue different communication strategies, and reach out to them more directly."

Second, a KBE creates the need to seek endorsement from regional media organizations as local media lose their monopoly over target audiences. One practitioner noted:

> The publics will be more savvy, and they will have access to different sources of info regarding matters of particular concern to them, especially with the Internet, making it easy to access foreign media. This means that the way we communicate will be all the more crucial—we will need to gain the endorsement of regional media with strong credibility, and not just relying on our local STs [Straits Times] and BTs [Business Times], as people will tend to be more disbelieving.

Third, a KBE changes the tactics of communication in terms of content, channel, and style. For instance, practitioners observed that already more organizations are using the Internet as an added "push technology" to communicate as it "opens up possibilities for more direct targeting other than traditional media." Others suggested that the Internet when "used properly . . . can also provide greater interaction and tracking capability." Yet others noted: "We are already e-mailing journalists more often than faxing. (Some public relations people I know are even sms-sing!)" Also, practitioners have been "directing them [journalists] to downloadable resources on the Internet."

Fourth, the shift to a KBE also reduces costs for organizations and their clients. Practitioners will need to build expertise in niche areas, specializing in online communication strategies and tactics as clients increasing depend on the Internet to reach out to young and Internet-savvy publics. One practitioner observed:

> Yes, the switch does affect the strategies and tactics used by my organization. The organization that I serve now has an interactive and a technology department whose jobs are to give value added services to clients such as web design, online marketing, database marketing, etc. The way we serve our publics is no longer mainly through offline media but through online media which are more cost effective.

Finally, a KBE critically changes the way in which practitioners will need to conceptualize problems and opportunities. The cutting edge no longer appears to be how much one knows but how creatively one applies that knowledge to create value-added solutions to problems. One practitioner put it succinctly:

> I would define knowledge-based economy (KBE) as an economy where all workers are not only content with just problem solving but they have to be more enterprising, innovative and adding value to the economy. Hence, creative and innovative ideas are very much appreciated as they can be transformed for economic gains.

CULTURE AND PUBLIC RELATIONS

Kiasuism is perhaps the quintessential character of Singaporean culture. It may explain the following organizational features in the republic: political caution on the brink of political paranoia and the general lack of entrepreneurial risk taking with regard to innovative ideas and practices.

The word *kiasu* is derived from the local Hokkien dialect. Literally, it means to be afraid to lose out. As one social critic (Chan, 1994) saw it, *kiasuism* takes the following forms in local culture: (a) a conformist and play-it-safe mentality resulting in "a herd mentality where everyone goes after the same things and avoids the same things. No one wants to be different" (p. 71); (b) a narrow and highly materialistic conceptualization of success reducible to the possession of "a piece of property, a car and security in a well-paying job" (p. 72); (c) an education system that tends not to cultivate independent, critical, and creative thinking; and the moral fiber to accept risk taking and challenges; and an unforgiving attitude to failures (p. 73); and add (d) a culture of political paranoia. This chiefly translates into the institutionalization of OB markers and self-censorship.

Thus, an educational system that breeds young students into conformity and a fixation with passing examinations as a means to material success also churns out working adults with similar cautious and conformist mentalities. One practitioner from an international public relations agency observed:

> The problem, however, is that Asian universities do not teach their students how to think and the exposure of the practitioners is limited because of a lack of reading and reflection. . . . Singaporean employees generally have a high standard of education and command of English. But like many Asian countries there is little of the aggression and extrovertion [*sic*] needed in the profession. Ambition is also curbed by an economically sheltered mindset.

This conformist and play-it-safe mentality does not bode well for organizations shifting rapidly toward a KBE. As one practitioner assessed, the new economy requires practitioners to function more as strategic experts and managers of knowledge than as tacticians. This implies the need for practitioners to engage in critical analysis and creative synthesis. The practitioner stated:

> Increasingly the sharper clients want "value added strategic services". In plain English they need advise and ideas on the big picture of things and creative ideas which are essentially an ability to synthesise disparate, seemingly unconnected ideas into something relevant for them. They also want trends, or the ability to spot them and advise on what to do to tap into them.

Kiasuism, which cultivates a culture of political paranoia, is also manifested at the organizational level. Practitioners practice self-censorship: "Even if there are no hard and fast rules, public relations practitioners self-regulate." Others try hard not to infringe on OB markers of ethnic sensitivities: "I think race and religion are two important values that could affect public relations practices. At this moment, especially, these two issues are highly sensitive and public relations practitioners would have to be careful in conveying their messages so they won't cause social disintegration." Yet others are wary of political OB markers: "We urge our clients not to criticize the government in a way that can be construed as inappropriate."

The concern with cultural and ethnic sensitivities may be traced back to the geopolitical and historical conditions described much earlier. Practitioners here recognize the importance of not treading on the toes of the minority groups. In particular, there are efforts at not offending the sentiments and cultural taboos of local and neighboring Islamic constituencies. Whenever possible, practitioners advocate "sensitivities to race and religion [to] be displayed. This is in terms of food served, in speeches, press releases and articles written. We try to create an atmosphere of pleasantry and harmony in all campaigns due to our multi-racial/religion make-up."

In addition to observing the OB markers of race and religion, practitioners also try not to infringe on OB markers pertaining to establishment politics. Giving face to political leaders is a mark of the local culture's deference to those in political authority. One practitioner remarked: "The concept of "face" plays into public relations in that there are often extra sensitivities to consider." Another advised: "Taking note of Government policy and statement helps guide our thinking and advice to clients wishing . . . us [to do] public relations here in terms of angles and approach, which might gain positive media interest."

However, human cultures are typically never static. Even *kiasuism* is likely to change in the distant future as the shift to a KBE encourages greater pluralism and diversity of lifestyles and reduces the local media's monopoly over information. It is certain that the culture of deference to the political elite is already giving way to a desire for more equitable relations between the government and its constituencies.

Economically, these changes may be translated into an adoption of key American entrepreneurial attributes such as: "emphasis on personal independence and self-reliance, a respect for those starting new businesses, [and] acceptance of failure in entrepreneurial and innovation efforts," as articulated by the ex-Prime Minister, Lee Kuan Yew, in a recent public address (Lee, 2002). In short, this is a willingness to embrace risk taking.

THE MEDIA AND PUBLIC RELATIONS

Currently, media relations is the most important public relations activity in the private and public sectors of Singapore. Media relations is the top revenue earner for most public relations consultancies, followed by strategic planning and counseling and then event management (Tan, 2001, p. 12).

The importance of media relations in Singapore takes precedence from the historical model of public relations practiced by the colonialists—practitioners as propagandists for the colonial government. Then and now, the media continue to be powerful vehicles for the dissemination of information on government policies and important agents in engineering consent for state policies among the masses. The media play this role by their agenda-setting function. They possess the power to construct political and social reality for the masses besides reflecting popular opinion to the political elite (Ho, 2000). The importance of the media in government public affairs is reflected in the way in which it is regulated and controlled by the state via licensing, national security laws, and the 1974 Newspaper and Printing Presses Act (George, 2000).

Media Control

What are the effects of the state's control and regulation of the media in the public relations industry? In general, many practitioners agreed that the local media are sufficient for broad outreach to the masses: "Singapore is a relatively small media market so blanket coverage of most stakeholders can be achieved through a few publications." There is apparently no shortage of publication outlets for reaching out to publics interested in technology, women's issues, entertainment, and lifestyle issues. However, just as many practitioners claimed that media outlets are scarce for niche areas such as vertical sector trade publications, medical and health care media catering to the graying population, among many others.

More important, practitioners observed that the monopoly of the local media and its regulation by the state cripples the ability of practitioners to reach out to critical and active publics. That is, although the local media provide sufficient outreach for most target audiences, they lack the credibility and legitimacy to be used as third-party endorsement for special publics. One practitioner noted that the local media's "quality of thinking, analysis and interpretation is below par, and hence [there is] a lack of credibility among the more critical audiences who matter. The international media and internet provide viable alternatives though." In sum, the local media are sufficient and excellent in catering to broad outreach to the masses but fall short where the special publics are concerned.

Media Access

In light of the importance of media relations, it is heartening to note that practitioners are generally able to access the local media easily. Also, media relations are generally cordial, especially for the bigger and more well-established public relations consultancies: "Being a recognized public relations consultancy helps, as the media is aware of the clientele we are handling, and will tend to take us more seriously." It also improves for practitioners who have spent much time and resources in cultivating friendly media relations: "We place great importance on relationship building sessions with the media, to cultivate our media contacts and resources. It is really useful, and we usually are able to rely on these contacts which we have carefully nurtured when we need to contact them."

KBE and Media Relations

Just as a KBE affects the style of government public affairs, activism, and the culture of *kiasuism*, it also affects media relations. Although some practitioners did not anticipate a significant change in the latter, many others suggested that an increase in the use of electronic communication is likely to affect media relations in the following ways.

First, the access of publics to online alternative foreign media is likely to reduce the monopoly of local media. Also, practitioners are able to access alternative media for the dissemination of press releases, third-party endorsement, and the like: "Media industry would have lesser control on releasing certain press releases because public relations firms would have greater media network to send their press releases to. In fact, media industry would have to compete locally and globally."

Second, the shift to a KBE is likely to increase the relationship of dependency between the media and public relations and increase respect for the public relations profession for the following reasons, according to one practitioner:

> With an emphasis on KBE, both the practitioners and the media are expected to be able to have a wider variety of skills beyond the basic, and to provide value-added services—for public relations practitioners, it also means having more in depth knowledge of the particular industry their client is in, and having diverse knowledge across different yet related industries. With that, the media relations would deepen and change, as the mutual need and dependency for one another reaches new heights. With the public relations practitioner displaying a higher level of expertise and skills, more respect to the role of public relations will be accorded, and the media will start to consult the public relations practitioner more frequently. At the same time, the public relations practitioner will no longer be contented to take a back-seat role to the media and play a beggar's role, as he/she will become an expert in the client's business and industry.

In fact, some practitioners observed that public relations professionalism is likely to increase as practitioners play the roles of gatekeepers to organizational information and educators of the media. One practitioner described this greater media dependency on public relations in the following way:

> I think KBE is when content/information becomes the core business rather than playing a supportive role. That is to say, the management of information rather than technical skills possessed by the employees of an organization becomes more important to the organization.
>
> If that is the case, public relations has a more significant role to play as organizations will need professional help to streamline and package the information into readily digestible content. By reducing jargon and reorganizing content, public relations can help journalists understand the issues at hand, who will in turn be able to transfer that knowledge to the readers . . . because there will be so much more information, often brimming with jargon, the media needs public relations more to sift out info that is relevant to them.

Third, because a KBE facilitates direct engagement with target audiences at a lower cost than traditional media, it is likely to encourage the practices of audience segmentation, rather than the indiscriminate targeting of mass audiences. This also implies a potential decrease in the reliance on traditional mass media for outreach to audiences. In a nutshell, the media market is likely to become more fragmented, departing from the monopolistic monolith that is was and is. Practitioners and activist groups would need to become more media savvy in recognizing the strengths and limitations of different media and customizing them for specific interests (George & Pillay, 2000).

Fourth, a KBE puts pressure on journalists and public relations practitioners alike to produce information content that reflects greater critical analysis, independent judgment, and creative thought because local media and public relations practitioners would be competing with the best practitioners worldwide for the attention of increasingly critical and active audiences. One practitioner put it this way:

> A knowledge-based economy would be an environment in which a person has access to various sources of information. Presented with this wide variety of information sources, people selectively choose the information they receive and evaluate information independently. A KBE would encourage journalists to develop more independent thinking as readers, who have access to the same information, would look toward more evaluative, independent writing. Public relations practitioners will no longer be able to feed information to journalists and expect a regurgitation of information.

In sum, although current public relations in Singapore continues with an emphasis on media relations and tactical public relations, other public relations activities are also slowly emerging in importance. They include public relations as a function of strategic management, corporate branding, community relations, public affairs, and issues management. The next section features a case study showcasing the importance of a strategic management of media relations in Singapore.

A CASE STUDY OF SUCCESSFUL STRATEGIC MANAGEMENT OF MEDIA RELATIONS

In 1998, the Ogilvy Public Relations Worldwide office in Singapore was retained by Andrew Tjioe, the President and CEO of the Tung Lok Group, an international restaurant chain, for assistance. Although the restaurant chain is well-known in Singapore and the region for its excellent cuisine, it had hitherto received little publicity. The CEO wanted the agency's assistance in launching a new theme restaurant and publicizing its new culinary consultant from Canada. The agency's initial research revealed that the restaurant company and its chain of local restaurants did not possess a systematic public relations structure. Calls from the media were handled ad hoc from individual restaurants, and restaurant promotions were not well-publicized in the media. These problems compounded the already insignificant publicity that the chain had then been receiving.

The agency adopted a two-pronged strategy to address the organizational and publicity problems. One of its first strategies was to set up a systematic public relations structure for the client's company and restaurants. The agency created a two-way communication system for the client in the following ways: (a) New work procedures were instituted for the restaurants to provide feedback to the agency on restaurant promotions; (b) the agency met with restaurant managers for regular brainstorming sessions during which communication issues and new promotions were discussed; (c) the agency also trained media spokespersons to develop and deliver key messages, manage media inquiries, stock press kits, and manage requests for photo shoots; and (d) the agency served as the center for coordinating media inquiries.

Its second strategy was to increase publicity for the restaurant chain and publicize the launch of the new restaurant and the culinary consultant. Media publicity and the cultivation of media relations took the following forms: (a) Quarterly media events were generated to introduce the client and the restaurants to key journalists; (b) a friendly and open communication with key media personnel was established by inviting journalists to sample the restaurants' products; (c) a media luncheon was organized at the new restaurant to introduce the CEO and the culinary consultant to journalists; (d) regular updates on the new restaurant's products and promotions were sent to the media; (e) to promote the new restaurant internationally, the agency established contact with the Singapore Tourism Board (a government statutory board) to promote the use of the new restaurant as an attractive venue for media meetings with foreign media invited to Singapore; and (f) to broaden the outreach of publicity for the new restaurant beyond the food and beverage industry, the agency customized news pitches for other media outlets in the fashion, business, lifestyle, and interior designer industries. For instance, fashion stylists, editors, and interior design companies were encouraged to use the new theme restaurant as a location for photo shoots.

In all, the agency's aims were to increase the publicity profile of the restaurant chain among local and international media and to promote the new restaurant, its CEO, and the culinary consultant. An evaluation of the agency's efforts demonstrated that it had made a significantly positive impact on increasing the revenue of the restaurant chain and increasing positive publicity for the client and the chain. In the weeks after the launch of the new restaurant, sales soared and the new restaurant reached breakeven in the first month, a record first in the 18-year history of the restaurant chain. With international publicity offered from various media outlets such as BBC, CNBC, *Asian Wall Street Journal*, the *Cosmopolitan* in Germany, the National Radio in Denmark, Reuters, and a host of other international media houses, the new theme restaurant even stimulated international inquires about the potential for franchise opportunities. Six months later with profits still up, in spite of the then Asian economic crisis, a second new restaurant was opened in Singapore. The client and his new restaurant continued to be the talk of town. Local media coverage was extensive and positive. The new theme restaurant stimulated more articles written on theme restaurants, debates in the dailies, requests from top fashion publications to use its location for photo shoots, and interior design magazines to feature the thematic designs of the restaurant in their publications.

Overall, the client and the chain received very favorable publicity from local and international media. And, to crown the glory, the agency was engaged on a retainer basis to manage the entire restaurant chain's public relations program. In 2001, Ogilvy entered its fourth consecutive year of partnership with Tung Lok. Andrew Tjioe, who was voted Tourism Entrepreneur of the Year (2001) said: "We are pleased to continue partnering with Ogilvy public relations. They have provided us with valuable counsel and helped propel Tung Lok, the brand, to the forefront of the F&B [food and beverage] industry" (Four in a Row, November 2000).

ACKNOWLEDGMENT

The work for this chapter would not have been possible without the contributions of public relations practitioners in Singapore. They gave of their valuable time, energy, and resources to enrich the knowledge and practice of public relations. I thank Mathew Yap of BP Amoco, Agnes Chang and Sylvia Yu of Weber Shandwick Worldwide, Sharolyn Choy of Edelman Singapore, Huw Hopkin of Impiric, and many more practitioners who have assisted me in the process of writing this chapter. Last but not least, special thanks and appreciation must also go to Ogilvy Public Relations in Singapore and the Tung Lok Group for permission to feature them in the case study.

REFERENCES

Chan, D. (1994). Kiasuism and the withering away of Singaporean creativity. In D. da Cunha (Ed.), *Debating Singapore* (pp.71–75). Singapore: Institute of Southeast Asian Studies.

Chow, H. W., Tan, S. J., & Chew, K. L. (1996). Organizational response to public relations: An empirical study of firms in Singapore. *Public Relations Review, 22*, 259–277.

Chua, B. H. (1995). *Communitarian ideology and democracy in Singapore*. London: Routledge.

Culbertson, H. M., & Jeffers, D. W. (1992). Social, political, and economic contexts: Keys in educating true public relations professionals. *Public Relations Review, 18*, 53–78.

Faithfull, T. W. (2000). Corporate citizenship and civil society. In Gillian Koh & Giok Ling Ooi (Eds.), *State–society relations in Singapore* (pp. 77–91). Singapore: Oxford University Press.

Four in a Row for Tung Lok and Ogilvy PR. (November 1, 2001). *AdVoice, p. 8.*

George, C. (2000). *Singapore: The air-conditioned nation*. Singapore: Landmark Books.

George, C., & Pillay, H. (2000). Media and civil society. In G. Koh & Geok Ling Ooi (Eds.), *State–society relations in Singapore* (pp. 189–202). Singapore: Oxford University Press.

Gomez, J. (2000). *Self censorship Singapore's shame*. Singapore: THINK Centre.

Grunig, J. E. (2000). Collectivism, collaboration, and societal corporatism as core professional values in public relations, *Journal of Public Relations Research, 12*, 23–49.

Grunig, J. E., & Hunt, T. (1984). *Managing public relations*. New York: Holt, Rinehart & Winston.

Ho, K. L. (2000). *The politics of policy-making in Singapore*. Singapore: Oxford University Press.

Internal Security Act (chapter 143). Singapore: Government Printer, 1986.

Lee, K. Y. (5 February, 2002). *An entrepreneurial Culture for Singapore*. Lecture presented at the Singapore Management University. Retrieved from http://Search.yahoo.com Retrieval date: 17 January, 2003.

Lim, D. (2000). *Speech by Mr. David Lim*. Minister of State for Defence and Information and the Arts, at Prism Awards. Retrieved from http://www.iprs.org.sg/pages/prism.html Retrieval date: 9 September, 2001.

Nair, B. (1986). *A primer on public relations practice in Singapore*. Singapore: Institute of Public Relations and Print N Publish Pte. Ltd.

Singapore: Four Muslim Primary One Students forbidden to wear the Tudung. (30 January, 2002) *Singapore Straits Times*. Retrieved from www.ahrchk.net/news Retrieval date: 17 January, 2003.

Singapore Department of Statistics. Retrieved from www.singstat.gov.sg Retrieved date: 20 November, 2001.

Sreenivasan, V. (31 August, 2001). It's time the law protects minority shareholders. *The Business Times Online*. Retrieved from http://business-times.asia1.com Retrieval date: 9 March, 2001.

Sriramesh, K., Kim, Y., & Takasaki, M. (1999). Public relations in three Asian cultures: An analysis. *Journal of Public Relations Research, 11*, 271–292.

Tan, R. (2001). *The state of public relations in Singapore*. Singapore: Singapore Polytechnic.

Tan, S. P. (1993–1994). *Roles of organized business in public policy making in Singapore: changes and continuities*. Academic exercise, Department of Political Science, National University of Singapore (NUS).

Tay, C. K. (15 April, 2001). Membership does not come with privileges. *The Straits Times Interactive*. Retrieved from http://straitstimes.asia1.com.sg Retrieval date: 17 January, 2003.

The Singapore 21 vision. Retrieved from Singapore Government website: http://www.gov.sg/singapore 21 Retrieved date: 7 March 2000.

Yeap, S. B. (1994). The state of public relations in Singapore. *Public Relations Review, 20*, 373–394.

Yuen, C. K. (1999). *Leninism, Asian culture and Singapore*. Retrieved from http://www.sintercom.org and www.comp.nus.edu.sg/~yuenck/new. Retrieved date: 15 March, 2000.

6

PROFESSIONALISM AND DIVERSIFICATION: THE EVOLUTION OF PUBLIC RELATIONS IN SOUTH KOREA

YUNGWOOK KIM

South Korean public relations scholars, with help from American colleagues, are in the process of describing public relations in South Korea using various theoretical constructs. By all accounts, it is evident that public relations in South Korea is still early in its development and continues to be under the strong influence of the publicity-ridden *hong-bo*. The term *hong-bo*, often used in South Korea as a substitute for the term *public relations*, can be described as disseminating information in a wide coverage using mass media or to make organizations or persons known to the public broadly (J. Park, 2001). *Hong-bo* often refers to publicity activities aimed at evading negative media coverage of organizations. Further, *hong-bo* is deeply rooted in the collaboration between the authoritarian government and the powerful *chaebol* system during the 1970s. Y. Park and M. Kim (1997) defined *chaebol* as "a business group consisting of many companies that are owned and managed by family members in diversified business areas" (p. 97).

Theorizing about public relations in South Korea should logically begin by drawing distinctions between public relations and *hong-bo* because traditional *hong-bo* tactics conflict with the current desire among many professionals for professional practice. Although publicity dominates much of the public relations activities in South Korea, some practitioners do practice more diversified public relations activities such as community relations, crisis management, and investor relations (Y. Kim & Hon, 1998). Although traditional Korean culture represents closed and personalized approaches to communication, the younger generation is more inclined to practice more open communication, seeking long-term relationships between the organization and publics. This, and the entry of multinational enterprises due to rapid globalization, is forcing public relations practitioners in

South Korea to practice more sophisticated forms of public relations (Y. Kim & Hon, 2001). One can conclude that tradition and change are two forces that have influenced current public relations in South Korea. In this chapter I describe the history of public relations in the country and explain the linkage between environmental variables and public relations practice, thus delineating the dialogical interaction between two forces that may lead to more professional and diversified public relations in South Korea.

DEVELOPMENT OF THE FIELD

History

The emergence of public relations in South Korea is deeply rooted in the public information function by the government (often referred to as *gong-bo*). The arrival of American military forces at the end of World War II, after decades of Japanese domination (from 1910 to 1945), helped introduce South Korea to the public information activity by the government (Oh, 1991). The government used the Public Information Department to control public opinion and establish the new policies proposed by the American military government. After the American military government gave way to the newly established South Korean dictatorship in 1948, *gong-bo* was continued to be used to manipulate public opinion until the civil revolution of 1960. Even though what the American military and the South Korean government did was far from professional public relations, the introduction of the public information function (*gong-bo*) to government public relations was a key juncture in the development of public relations. The democratic government initiated by the 1960 civil revolution did not last long. After the 1961 military coup led by General Chung-Hee Park, the nation saw a highly authoritarian rule that eliminated press freedoms (Choe, 1992). The cold-war confrontation between South and North Korea also contributed to such a political climate.

However, a strong governmental drive for industrialization provided immense financial and political support for big companies, which in turn created what became known as the *chaebol* system, a network of conglomerate business groups. The government provided preferential financing to these groups in exchange for illegal political funds (Y. Kim & Hon, 1998). Amidst this collusion, the development of ethical and professional public relations was virtually impossible.

The public relations profession changed significantly in 1988 during and after the Seoul Olympics because of the participation of multinational public relations companies such as Burson–Marsteller and Hill and Knowlton in big government projects (Choe, 1992). The demise of dictatorship and the advent of social democracy during the 1989 civil upheaval provided a fertile ground for the development of professional public relations. Authoritarian processes are no longer effective in the current democratic society in South Korea. Organizations are being forced to take a new perception of public relations in this new environment. These forces of change are typified by increasing globalization, higher degrees of press freedom, the demand for diversified public relations activities, and the growing participation of grassroots citizens in organizational decision making.

In the 1990s, public relations received a boost from scholars who had studied in the United States and returned home to apply their knowledge to study South Korean public relations. The profession also gained significantly with the entry of several multinational public relations companies. Various crisis situations also gave the public relations departments of corporations the motivation to insist on better relationships with diverse publics.

The Current Status of the Profession

It is estimated that almost 200 public relations companies are striving for survival in South Korea (J. Kim, 2001). This increase in the number of public relations companies has lead to an artificial swelling of the public relations industry. Yet, this growth in numbers does not imply a concomitant advancement in the sophistication of public relations services and relationships with client organizations.

Most public relations agencies have actively affiliated themselves with well-known firms such as Hill and Knowlton and Fleishman-Hillard to exchange information and broaden organizational knowledge related to communication and promotion overseas (J. Kim, 2001). Another reason for these affiliations is the increasing challenges resulting from the diversified needs of clients. Leading international agencies also are eager to penetrate the South Korean market, signaling the potential for growth in this market. However, fierce competition among public relations agencies calls for a new set of business standards and ethical guidelines. Low profits resulting from high competition and the lack of sophisticated public relations practices due to an overdependence on media relations are the major limitations of the public relations industry in South Korea (J. Park, 2001).

This growth in numbers has more positive effects than negative ones. Interviews with 24 practitioners and scholars revealed that South Korean companies increasingly appreciate the value of public relations in the pluralistic and integrated society that South Korea has become (Y. Kim & Hon, 2001). Some public relations firms have begun to carve out niches in areas such as crisis management, new technology communication, cyber communication, marketing public relations, public affairs, and investor relations (Rhee, 1999). Crisis management has become a critical part of public relations in South Korea as several big corporations have experienced crisis situations since 1991. One of the most serious cases was the so-called *phenol crisis.* Doosan Electronics, a *chaebol,* discharged a toxic substance known as phenol to the Nakdong River on March 16, 1991, and was confronted with a major lawsuit by those affected by this pollution. (This case is explained in detail at the end of this chapter.) This crisis also instigated the nationwide boycott of Doosan products resulting in the payment of a huge legal compensation. Since that disaster, South Korean companies have realized that they cannot rely solely on their close ties to the government as a strategy for concealing their misdeeds. Instead, they have begun to focus on building relationships with diverse publics as a critical corporate function in a democratic society. They seem to have learned that public relations could offer effective ways of handling crises and, therefore, have begun viewing public relations as a managerial function.

In 1989, the Korean Public Relations Association was established to advance the interests of the profession in South Korea (Choe, 1992). The Korea Public Relations Consultancy Association (KPRCA) was also established in 2000 to prevent public relations companies from conducting unlawful and illegitimate practices (J. Kim, 2001). In 1998, the Korean Academic Society of Public Relations (KASPR), which is the first association for those involved in public relations education, was established. The KASPR publishes the scholarly quarterly journal, the *Korean Journal of Public Relations Research.*

The Models of Public Relations. The established tradition of media-oriented public relations is hard to change in a short time span. In South Korea, as far as organizational information is concerned, personal relationships with journalists rather than news value still determine which stories get published in the media, representing the personal influence model (Sriramesh, 1992; Sriramesh, Y. Kim, & Takasaki, 1999). The public relations activities of Korean *chaebols* have traditionally been restricted mainly to obtaining positive publicity in an effort to counter public criticism about many irresponsible corporate activities.

Y. Kim (1996) surveyed 167 South Korean practitioners to determine which public relations model (J. E. Grunig & Hunt, 1984) they used and the level of job satisfaction among these practitioners. Results showed that Korean practitioners predominantly used the craft models of press agentry and public information. But results also showed that these practitioners aspired to practice the two-way professional models. The study revealed that practitioners who used the two-way models were more satisfied with their jobs than those practicing the one-way craft models. Conveying factual information, or being a neutral disseminator, is a tough task in South Korea because Korean organizations prefer to withhold information. Some practitioners were also found to consider information manipulation as a major public relations strategy attempting to get favorable publicity into the media while keeping unfavorable publicity out of media focus.

Rhee (1999) replicated the excellence study (J. E. Grunig, 1992) and found that South Korean public relations practitioners are primarily involved with media relations. However, results from her study also showed that these practitioners recognized the importance of mutual understanding as well as persuading the public, which is the essence of the two-way models. Yoon (2001) also found that practitioners working for public relations agencies have more symmetrical worldviews than practitioners of their clients. This implies that agency practitioners can function as powerhouses for making the field more professional.

However, results of another study indicated that existing public relations theories, developed largely in the United States, do not fit the public relations function in South Korea perfectly (Y. Kim & Hon, 2001). Qualitative interviews with 24 chief executive officers (CEOs) and public relations executives in South Korea revealed the pitfalls of applying Western models of public relations to the South Korean situation as explained by a mass communication professor interviewed for the study:

> Public relations in Korea is struggling to get to the stage of the public information model but the progress is very tardy because of other environmental factors surrounding the organization such as the level of democracy, government-business collusion, and the pre-modern press system. The slow development of public relations models has made public relations practitioners skip the developmental stage of the public information model. Even though public relations activities are not based on the belief in disseminating true information, they are trying to conduct research before a public relations program and look at the outcome of attitude surveys about publics. Also many companies describe the purpose of public relations as mutual understanding between an organization and publics. (Y. Kim & Hon, 2001, p. 271)

This indicates that the two-way models are already being used to some extent by South Korean public relations practitioners. But, for the most part, the press agentry/publicity model is the most prevalent. However, if this essay takes into consideration the media's unbalanced reporting habits in South Korea, public relations practitioners do not bear all of the responsibility for the dominance of press agentry. Some practitioners in government and public relations agencies said that they have tried to publicize accurate stories about their organizations or clients, rather than trying to manipulate information. It is evident that they know that, in the long run, disclosing and distributing accurate information is better than concealment.

In addition to J. E. Grunig's four public relations models, other models (J. E. Grunig, L. A. Grunig, Sriramesh, Huang, & Lyra, 1995) were revealed during the interviews. Some comments indicated that the personal influence and cultural translation models reflected some important aspects of public relations in South Korea. Public relations practitioners value personal network in resolving organizational conflicts with publics. For example, practitioners turn to networks such as alumni associations, personal links, family members, and relatives and friends for help when organizational problems arise. In-group solidarity, a characteristic of Korean culture, can be reinforced through give-and-take interactions. One corporate public relations director talked about personal influence:

> A unique business background exists in every country. Personal influence is very important under the Chaebol system. The strategies of the Chaebols' PR departments tend to be defensive to avoid criticism from the press and negative coverage. In this case, if a public relations practitioner has an acquaintance or the closeness of friendship with a reporter or a gatekeeper, he can ask to take an unfavorable article out or minimize the size of the headline or article. For continuing this relationship, practitioners have to prepare regular gifts and provide *Ddukgab* (money for buying Korean cake, sometimes similar to bribery) (Y. Kim & Hon, 2001, pp. 273–274).

Foreign businessmen in South Korea often refer to public relations practitioners as consultants and rely on them for help in understanding the unique business practices of South Korea, an indication of the cultural translator model. The trend toward globalization will only add momentum to the use of the cultural translator model.

INFRASTRUCTURE AND PUBLIC RELATIONS

Social, Political, and Economic Contexts

As already mentioned, the replacement of dictatorship with social democracy has contributed to the development of public relations in South Korea. After General Park's coup in 1961, the military government did not encourage a wholesome relationship between the organization and publics through open and reciprocal communication. The government gave favors to *chaebols* in exchange for political funds. For their part, although the *chaebols* led the economic development, they did so under political policies that benefited them greatly. The South Korean media occasionally exposed the alliance between the government and *chaebols* as government intervention resulted in civil protests under the authoritarian regime. However, the media lacked sufficient freedom, and in exchange for securing information sources and achieving financial stability, they often failed to cover certain sensitive issues. The *chaebols*, backed by the government's industrialization drive, did not care for the other publics except the media. All these circumstances created *hong-bo*, explained earlier (Jo, 2001; Rhee, 1999).

Emphasis on government public relations and crisis management is a key to understanding public relations in South Korea. In the United States, it is against the law for the government to spend appropriated money on public relations efforts to gain support for government projects (Wilcox, Ault, Agee, & Cameron, 2000). However, there are no regulations or laws that block public relations activities by government agencies in South Korea. Instead, the government has invested money in significant public relations projects. Public relations by the government can be characterized as developmental public relations because of its emphasis on national development projects, such as spurring industrial drive, in developing countries.

The development of social democracy, the 1988 Seoul Olympic games, and the effects of globalization are key factors in the development of public relations in South Korea. However, the Asian economic crisis of 1997 has altered the optimistic observations and cast doubts on the development of public relations in South Korea. The South Korean government could not secure enough financial resources to repay its debt and sought assistance from the International Monetary Fund. The government-led economic system, including *chaebols*, came under great pressure in this dynamic international business environment, resulting in the collapse of several *chaebols*. The government began economic reforms including the modification of the *chaebol* system because neither the government nor the *chaebols* could adjust to the openness of a global environment.

Therefore, one can conclude that the introduction of political democracy in 1987 and the economic crisis of 1997 has brought about some maturity to the South Korean business environment. However, South Korean business practices still possess serious weaknesses. Despite its efforts, the government has not succeeded in revamping the *chaebol*-oriented economic system completely. Other factors contributing to the failure include fierce labor disputes and the growing chasm between the haves and have-nots, leading to conflicts between the two.

The South Korean legal system protects the right of free speech fully even though it harbors a conservative orientation, a vestige of previous authoritarian regimes. Youm (1996) noted that the South Korean press has evolved from being a voluntary servant of the regime to a harsh critic since the democratic reforms of the 1987 civil democratic movement. Thus, there are no statutory obstacles to freedom except National Security Laws that prohibit association with North Korea. Most trade associations in the mass communication industry have voluntary regulations prohibiting unethical and illegitimate practices. For instance, the KPRCA and the Korean Advertising Agency Association have voluntary ethical codes of conduct. Related to public relations, social customs and cultural uniqueness may be more important for optimal practices than legal fundamentals.

ACTIVISM AND PUBLIC RELATIONS

The conspicuous characteristic of the current South Korean society is the advent of the civil activism era. Civil activism has been reinforced through the democracy movement that protested the authoritative ruling of the military regime. Also, labor movements for better work conditions have stimulated empowerment of civil movements and led to the birth of diverse nongovernmental organizations (NGOs). NGOs are taking an active role in policy making and often oversee and object to the wrongdoings of the government and *chaebols* (Cha, 2001).

By 1999, there were over 2,000 NGOs in South Korea, with a total membership of 20,000. The typical dues-paying member of an NGO is young and educated. The number of NGOs had been increasing drastically since the 1987 uprising for democracy. Statistics show that 70% of NGOs were established after the 1987 democratic movement. This spurt can be attributed to social democratization, maturation of the grassroots democracy, and active participation in political decision making.

However, NGOs are not financially independent from the government. Their public relations strategies revolve mostly around garnering media publicity for their causes. They often use sensationalism to invoke media interest. They seem to prefer the win–lose strategy, such as illegal protests and premature accusation without prior conversation, over the win–win strategy, such as public hearing and dialogue with the organization. Cha (2001) argued that NGOs and the targets of their attacks could have a win–win relationship through two-way and balanced communication. However, if the two-way symmetrical model is used by NGOs, it may be interpreted as a compromise with the socially unjustified in South Korean society. This may be why they shun such mutually negotiated outcomes, another indication of the impact of culture on public relations activities.

Pressure from NGOs forces organizations to engage in ethical and more transparent public relations practices. Many South Korean organizations that practice unethical public relations feel constrained to establish a wholesome relationship with NGOs. The notion that only the powerful utilize public relations to maintain the status quo has been introduced to scholarly research with the development of NGOs and activist public relations.

Several examples illustrate the power of activist groups in South Korea. In 1998, activist groups opposed to the construction of a dam across the Dong River in the province of Kangwon made the government reevaluate and ultimately cancel its construction plans. In April 2000, an activist movement to oust unfit candidates from politics produced successful results in National Assembly elections. The Citizens' Alliance (an NGO) succeeded in preventing 59 of 86 candidates whom it had opposed from getting elected. In February 2001, mounting pressure from activist groups for media reform led the National Tax Administration and the Fair Trade Commission to investigate the tax evasion case and unfair trading practices by media companies. In April 2002, the Citizens' Coalition for Economic Justice, one of the biggest civic movements in Korea, demanded prosecutors to investigate the scandals involving President Kim Dae-jung's two sons. Increasingly, activist groups have begun to influence all sectors of the Korean society as a third power (political and economic interests are the other two).

CULTURE AND PUBLIC RELATIONS

South Korea is identified as a society with high power distance, high collectivism, less tolerance of uncertainty, high masculinity, and high Confucian dynamism (Hofstede, 1980; Hofstede & Bond, 1987). Confucianism, a main philosophy among South Koreans, has been a widely discussed key to understanding Korean culture (Hofstede & Bond, 1987; K. O. Kim, 1997; Yum, 1987a) and communication styles (Yum, 1987a, 1987b). Harmony based on recognizing individual inequalities is pursued, and individual interest can be sacrificed for the benefit of a society (Kincaid, 1987). This subjugation of personal objectives and loyalty to authority have been the guidelines for maintaining spiritual harmony in Korean society since the adoption of basic Confucian principles during the Lee dynasty in the 14thcentury (Yum, 1987a).

Challenging tradition and breaking established rules by social members have been considered inappropriate communication behaviors. The rule of propriety among social members has priority over ethical judgment (Yum, 1987a). In this context, personal connections or selective treatment through favoritism takes precedence over professionalism (Yum, 1988). Particularly, the lack of professional practices based on vocational conscience has worked toward establishing a bad reputation for the public relations field in South Korea.

Yum (1988) described this characteristic in her study comparing East Asian and North American communication patterns. She categorized five Confucian-based dimensions of interpersonal relationships that she observed in East Asia: particularism (devising particular rules depending on the relationship), reciprocity, the in-group and out-group distinction (different treatment for in-group members and out-group members), the role of intermediaries (the need for persons who can introduce new relationships), and the overlap of personal and public domains (blurred distinction between personal and professional relationship). Yum (1988) also categorized four impacts of Confucianism on South Korean communication patterns: process orientation (as opposed to focusing on communication outcomes), differentiated linguistic codes (different languages used depending on people and situations), indirect communication emphasis (as opposed to explicit communication), and receiver-centered communication (emphasis on listening).

The impact of Confucian culture on public relations remains ambivalent. Huang (2000) insisted that Confucianism blocks ethical public relations practices and develops a unique cultural characteristic, *gao guanxi* (exploiting personal relations or human network not unlike the personal influence model), that implies a negative manifestation of Confucian principles. However, Rhee (1999) argued that collectivism and Confucianism are correlated positively with public relations excellence in South Korea. Confucianism may foster social harmony through individual sacrifices. However, relationships among parties in such a society turn into superficial and disharmonious ones. If public relations excellence is achieved through collectivistic harmony, interpersonal liberation or social reform could be restrained. Such interpersonal and critical aspects of public relations are imperative in this context. The impact of Confucianism on public relations requires more study and also demands more interdisciplinary cooperation.

The South Korean socioeconomic system follows the American capitalism model to a large degree. Yet, marked differences exist in corporate cultural norms and the public relations practices between South Korean and American companies. American companies have more freedom to communicate compared to South Korean companies. Traditional Confucian standards in South Korea value social harmony and indirect communication based on diverse linguistic codes rather than the free flow of communication (Kincaid, 1987). Y. Kim and Hon (2001) identified four Confucian rules based on interviews with 24 South Korean public relations professionals: indirect communication, the family chief orientation, the Confucian worldview, and face saving.

Indirect Communication

Information is best delivered through personal gatekeepers. One related notion is, 'A metaphor is better than a direct exhibition.' South Korean publics tend to mistrust information announced officially by organizations, thereby requiring public relations practitioners to communicate indirectly through interpersonal channels. Indirect communication is one of the four effects of Confucianism on South Korean communication patterns (Yum, 1988). However, South Korean business leaders have realized that keeping a low profile is not always beneficial to their company's operations. They have found this to be especially true after experiencing several crises. Thus, this cultural norm of concealing and remaining silent is fading to some extent.

Family Chief Orientation

Kincaid (1987) explained the Eastern spiritual belief as "the subjugation of individual interest and inclination to a strong hierarchical authority" (p. 6). In South Korean society, communication functions to achieve this spiritual harmony at the expense of individual wants. As is typical of most Asian countries, all social systems are hierarchical in South Korea (Yum, 1988). For example, parents have absolute power over other family members. This hierarchy extends to the social family (considering a social organization as a family) as well. Thus, a top manager, the father figure in a professional setting, can regulate the communication system of the organization without interference and mandate the organization's stance on issues. Public relations practitioners can only afford little input because all communication processes depend on the family chief's decision. One communication director described how this system affects public relations:

> All important decisions are made by the chairmans of *Chaebols*. The educational function of public relations department is very weak because most CEOs do not consider public relations an important function of company management. But this is very interesting. Even though most CEOs underestimate the effectiveness of public relations, the importance of public relations is drastically increasing. This is partly because of crisis situations. No other department can handle the crisis situation better than public relations. However, the main reason for having public relations still is its function of deflecting bad news and the CEO's dependence on the personal information network of public relations practitioners. (Y. Kim & Hon, 2001, pp. 276–277)

Confucian Worldview

As Yum (1988) indicated, Confucianism has defined appropriate behaviors for specific situations without regard to the changing patterns brought on by new social systems. The inflexibility of Confucianism makes values such as personal contacts and loyalty to one's organization to be unquestioned. Confusion over legitimate public relations activities could be attributed to the characteristics of Confucianism itself. Although South Korean public relations practitioners generally have displayed considerable moral standards and loyalty (Y. Kim, 2001), their primary allegiance has been to their organizations. Thus, ethical standards often are determined by in-group agreement. Loyalty to the organization sometimes makes public relations activities more complicated because employees' faithfulness is often related to personal bonds and group memberships. This tension is explained by the in-group/out-group distinction that Confucianism imposes on communication (Yum, 1988).

Face Saving

South Koreans try to save face in interpersonal relationships, which extends to the social level as well. Even though it could be beneficial to their business, South Korean public relations practitioners seldom take advantage of competitors' vulnerabilities. Most of the time, a company that criticizes other companies would be an outcast in that business circle. Yet, organizations have often attacked their competitors by releasing unfavorable information about them to the media (Sriramesh et al., 1999). Saving anothers' face as well as that of oneself should be a prime consideration in public relations practices.

THE MEDIA ENVIRONMENT

Most print and broadcasting companies have been affected by the 1997 financial crisis that sank the South Korean economy into recession. Most press companies depend on advertising income. Thus, the reduction in advertising during the 1997 crisis caused serious managerial difficulties. The financial crisis also created a strong impact on editorial emphasis and reporting patterns of journalists. The business section has been reinforced, and articles on topics such as business reconstruction and induction of overseas capital have been highlighted. Furthermore, the South Korean press has put great emphasis on the issue of economic reform.

Internationalizing and reconstructing the economic system is on the national agenda to revitalize the South Korean economy after South Koreans identified the lack of understanding in international affairs and the *chaebol*-oriented monopoly system as the major causes of the 1997 crisis. Globalization and reconstruction also have become the focus of media coverage among the South Korean press. Such business-oriented media content has become an opportunity for the public relations field.

In 2000, the Ministry of Culture and Tourism reported that South Korea had a total of 112 daily newspapers and 1,999 weekly magazines. However, 10 Korean-language national dailies and 2 English dailies are the major competitors at the national level, whereas many regional newspapers serve regional markets. *The Chosun Ilbo, Dong-A Ilbo*, and *JoongAng Ilbo* are influential national print media. *The Hangeorye Sinmun* is influential among comparatively young and progressive readers. *The Korea Herald* and *Korea Times* are the only two English newspapers in South Korea. There also are several business dailies. *The Yonhap News* is the only news agency that feeds news to dailies and broadcasting companies.

The Ministry of Culture and Tourism also reported that broadcasting services were provided by the Korean Broadcasting System (KBS) with 25 subsidiary stations, the Munwha Broadcasting Corporation (MBC) with 19 subsidiary stations, the Seoul Broadcasting System (SBS), and 8 specialized commercial broadcasters (EBS, CBS, BBS, PBC, FEBC, WBS, TBS, and TBN). Cable television is operated by 29 program providers and 77 stations.

Television has higher approval ratings than newspapers about news credibility, and the Internet is emerging as a new agenda setter, as described by the Korea Press Foundation Report of 2001:

> While television gained more approval in 2000 than in 1998, the comparative rating for newspapers declined. It is particularly noteworthy that newspapers' influence dwindled by more than a half in two years, and in usefulness ratings they lagged behind Internet. What is new is the Internet's rapidly growing role as a tool of mass communication. Its success is significant in that it reflects the growing consumer aspirations to be heard vis-à-vis government and traditional mass media and highlights a potentially crucial role to be played by individual consumers in new system of checks and balances. (http://www.kpf.or.kr, 2001).

Media Control

The print media are privately owned. The government retains a marginal indirect ownership through public funding, but it has minimal influence over the print media, especially after social democratization. Private owners have almost complete control over the employment of reporters, operation of editorial desks, and even editorial content. Private owners control major dailies such as *The Chosun Ilbo, Dong-A Ilbo*, and *JoongAng Ilbo*. Media control by private owners has become a serious dilemma in the democratizing media environment. Powerful media owners have obstructed undistorted communication and influenced editorial content. Conflicts between the print media and the government over tax evasion by media owners in 2001 brought into focus the problem of unprincipled ownership of a section of the print media. Media control by private owners fosters systematic distortion in the development of public agenda and obstructs the development of professional public relations in South Korea.

Although in principle the South Korean press is free from government and other external influences, various political and business interest groups do influence editorial content. *Chaebols* are one of the primary groups that are able to wield such influence. Some *chaebols* own media companies and participate in management decision making. Most media companies depend on advertising revenue provided by *chaebols.* Consumer and civic groups also have their agenda for press reform. One example is the anti-*Chosun Ilbo* movement initiated by civic groups to condemn the paper's cold-war mentality. The 2001 Korean Press Foundation Report analyzed:

> The anti-Chosun movement is remarkable in that it does not merely represent an outburst of grievances against a particular newspaper but bring into focus the deep-rooted structural flaws of the country's newspapers. The anti-Chosun movement, as an exercised form of consumers' legitimate right, has served the worthy purpose of establishing an active watchdog function over media for general consumers. (http://www.kpf.or.kr, 2001).

The South Korean television channels include the government-run KBS 1, KBS 2, and Educational Broadcasting System (public channel); semigovernment sponsored MBC; and private SBS and eight provincial broadcasting companies. The Korea Broadcasting Commission regulates the broadcasting industry legally. The purpose of regulation lies in public interest, not governmental control of the media. Most television programs need postbroadcast appraisal to assess whether their content is in the public interest.

In general, the government does not control journalistic content prior to broadcasting. However, the print and broadcasting media often display a strain in relations with each other, as the print media believes that the government influences the editorial content of broadcast media to attack print media.

Media Outreach and Access

The print and broadcasting media diffuse similar messages to South Korean people repetitively. Therefore, accessing information is not a difficulty. Provincial broadcasting companies and regional newspapers also report on the regional news. With a high rate of literacy and education, South Korean people also utilize the Internet for information gathering. The problem lies in information selection, not information outreach.

South Korean newspaper readers are becoming sophisticated, critical, and have high expectations for the quality of information. There is little argument that reporters need better and greater amounts of information from public relations practitioners if their papers are to remain competitive (*Advertising Yearbook*, 2000). This situation may eventually lead to symmetrical relationships between public relations practitioners and journalists, as stated by a professor of mass communication:

> The newspaper industry has faced fierce competition among itself because the number of papers has increased since 1992. This competition has provided a good opportunity for PR practitioners to cater to reporters' need to attract readers with more interesting and newsworthy stories. This is surely a chance for public relations. (Y. Kim & Hon, 2001, p. 280).

The introduction of cable television and local broadcasting has led to greater competition in the telecommunications industry and enlarged media outreach. The dominance of advertising by a few national network companies has declined in this new environment.

Smaller and newer companies have more marketing opportunities. Similar to what occurred within the newspaper industry, the proliferation of broadcasting channels causes the increased dependence on information from news releases and demands cooperation with public relations practitioners to save production costs. Public relations practitioners have easy access to the media. However, the level of access depends more on personal networks than professional relationships.

It is important to note that South Korea is one of fastest growing countries in the world on Internet use among its population. The number of Internet users has been growing drastically in recent years due to the fast growth in penetration of broadband. The number of Internet users reached 1 million in 1997 and surpassed 10 million in 1999. According to the 2001 Nielsen/Net Ratings Global Index for January, more than half of the population in South Korea has access to the Internet. Furthermore, South Korea leads the world in terms of the number of households with Internet access, and it has the fourth largest Internet-reliant population in the world. A high penetration of broadband Internet access and a sophisticated telecommunication infrastructure make such wide usage of the Internet possible.

Cyber media is emerging as an alternative to newspapers and broadcasting. As the 2001 Korea Press Foundation Report described:

> Consumers' approval rating of the press that had declined in 1998 turned upward in 2000. The good news, however, is attributed to Internet service that has outdone television broadcasting services and newspapers in approval rating. Thus, the Internet has come to stay as a very satisfactory mass media. The most noticeable among the Internet news services was "OhmyNews." Launched in February 2000, OhmyNews has done much to differentiate itself from other forms of mass communication. (http://www.kpf.or.kr, 2001).

Public relations practitioners are increasingly utilizing the Internet as a direct medium to reach target publics. The South Korean government created the cyber spokesperson and distributes information directly to citizens (http://www.allim.go.kr). Many companies also utilize the Internet for direct communication with the public. Newspapers and broadcasting channels also create home pages on the Internet to enhance their interactivity.

CONCLUDING COMMENTS

Social democratization brings with it the development of public relations. The South Korean-style *hong-bo*, which focuses heavily on media relations and personal connections with journalists, is not effective in the rapidly changing democratic South Korean society. The changing economic, political, and legal system provides organizations with more opportunities to practice professional public relations. The traditional communication characteristics of the East are now being combined with the individualistic perspectives of the West as the South Korean public relations industry adapts to new environmental demands.

Although there continues to be a shortage of experienced public relations professionals, and public relations agencies rely heavily on foreign clients, optimism for the public relations industry has been growing among practitioners in South Korea. The demand for public relations services by South Korean companies is increasing along with a concomitant increase in their understanding of the benefits of public relations (J. Kim, 2001). The real potential for growth may lie in the retention of agency services by large-scale South Korean companies. South Korean companies need to build positive long-term relationships with key publics and are beginning to formulate long-term public relations strategies and invest in them. Another encouraging aspect of South Korea's public relations industry is the swelling ranks of enterprising practitioners (*Advertising Yearbook*, 2000).

In the scholarly world, the KASPR spearheads the establishment of Korea-accustomed theories and their applications to the industry (Rhee, 1999). Scholarly journals deal with many topics such as the organization–public relationship, evaluation and measurement, crisis management and image restoration, and ethical issues. With a deep-rooted tradition of activism, public relations studies on NGOs, governmental public relations, and nonprofit organizations have produced prolific discussions. Absolute democracy and free press will contribute more on the development of this trend.

Case Study: Doosan Phenol Crisis Management

In March 16, 1991, an unidentified odor was detected in the tap water in the southeastern area of South Korea. The Environmental Bureau's investigation led to the discovery of the toxic substance, phenol, in the water. A government investigation team discovered that phenol had accidentally leaked to the Nakdong River from Doosan Electronics Company, a member of the Doosan *chaebol* group, that manufactures PCI board for computer chips.

Environmental groups and residents of the southeastern area challenged the Doosan group. Many government officials of the local Environmental Bureau and related workers were charged as a result of the investigation. A large demonstration took place in front of the headquarters of the Doosan group. The National Supermarket Association initiated a campaign to boycott Doosan products. This caused a major reduction in the sales of the Doosan group as a significant portion of its products were sold at supermarkets. Over 10,000 people, including pregnant women, filed a lawsuit against the group. Incredibly, in April 23, 1991, phenol was again found to have leaked from the Doosan Electronics Company, resulting in the forcible resignation of the chairman of Doosan group.

The Doosan group handled this situation very poorly because South Korean *chaebol* conglomerates had traditionally solved such problems by personal networks and collusion with the government. However, this was not possible because of the changed situation due to social democratization. The government could not protect the *chaebol* groups any more and had to accede to the demands by activists for an impartial investigation. Media sensationalism worsened the situation further. Doosan's crisis management strategies were too dated to handle the situation in the changed atmosphere. Doosan did not announce the outbreak of the incident right away but rather tried to conceal the situation. It prevented access to the information rather than providing the media with accurate information. This created many rumors that proved to be detrimental to Doosan. The result was a complete loss to Doosan.

Ironically, this became a monumental incident for the development of public relations in South Korea. *Chaebol* groups have, therefore, started to recognize the need for proactive public relations and reinforced their public relations function. Many *chaebol* groups have experienced major crises, and crisis management became a salient function. This trend is related closely with social and political democratization in South Korea. Publics do not tolerate corporate wrongdoings and unprincipled governmental intervention anymore as they once did under the authoritative regime. One CEO of a public relations firm commented on this new changing pattern:

> After experiencing a big crisis situation, some companies appointed the head of the public
> relations department as a vice president. This means public relations began to participate in
> the process of corporate decision-making. Traditionally, public relations practitioners had

been perceived as a speechwriter, publisher for an organization, or a post-journalist job. But, with social democratization, many companies came to the realization that they should prepare for a crisis situation against a reinforced social watchdog system. Crisis management is a very important factor that enhances public relations at the managerial level. (Y. Kim & Hon, 2001, p. 281).

Organizations, including corporations and the government, have learned that communicating with their publics and winning their understanding is a prerequisite for success. Public relations practitioners have also started playing a managerial role due to frequent crises and open communication demanded for ethical practices. Doosan appointed a public relations vice president for the first time in South Korea and began to communicate with publics, including consumers, community members, NGOs, and governmental officials, on various issues. They also exerted much effort in environmental protection with reinforced safety measures. Doosan's new programs include (a) devising proactive and comprehensive risk-management system, (b) training public relations practitioners to deliver the organization's key messages and to coordinate the public's demands, and (c) introducing environmentally friendly products and production systems. Doosan has regained its market share as a result of such new programs.

REFERENCES

Advertising yearbook. (2000). Seoul, Korea: Jeil Communications.

Cha, H. W. (2001). *The win–win strategy of public relations by NGOs (Korean).* Unpublished doctoral dissertation, Ewha Womans University, Seoul, Korea.

Choe, Y. (1992). *Hyundai PR Eeron* [Modern public relations theory]. Seoul, Korea: Nanam.

Grunig, J. E. (1992). *Excellence in public relations and communication management.* Hillsdale, NJ: Lawrence Erlbaum Associates.

Grunig, J. E., Grunig, L. A., Sriramesh, K., Huang, Y., & Lyra, A. (1995). Models of public relations in an international setting. *Journal of Public Relations Research, 7,* 163–186.

Grunig, J. E., & Hunt. T. (1984). *Managing public relations.* New York: Holt, Rinehart, and Winston.

Hofstede, G. (1980). *Cultures consequences: International differences in work-related values.* Beverly Hills, CA: Sage.

Hofstede, G., & Bond, M. H. (1987). The Confucius connection: From cultural roots to economic growth. *Organizational Dynamics, 16*(4), 4–21.

Huang, Y. (2000). The personal influence model and Gao Guanxi in Taiwan Chinese public relations. *Public Relations Review, 26*(2), 219–236.

Jo, S. (2001, June). *Models of public relations in South Korea: The difference between HongBo and public relations.* Paper presented at the International Communication Association conference, Washington, DC.

Kim, J. (2001, September). The status and future of the Korean public relations industry. *Goanggogye-Donghyang (Korean Adverting Information)*, 21–23.

Kim, K. O. (1997). The reproduction of Confucian culture in contemporary Korea: An anthropological study. In T. Wei-Ming (Ed.), *Confucian traditions in East Asian modernity* (pp. 202–227). Cambridge, MA: Harvard University Press.

Kim, Y. (1996). *Positive and normative models of public relations and their relationship to job satisfaction among Korean public relations practitioners.* Unpublished master's thesis, University of Florida, Gainesville.

Kim, Y. (2001, June). *Ethical standards and ideology among Korean public relations practitioners.* Paper presented at the Korea Academic Society of Public Relations conference, Seoul, Korea.

Kim, Y., & Hon, L. (1998). Craft and professional models of public relations and their relation to job satisfaction among Korean public relations practitioners. *Journal of Public Relations Research, 10,* 155–175.

Kim, Y., & Hon, L. (2001). Public relations in Korea: Applying theories and exploring opportunities. *Journal of Asian Pacific Communication, 11*(2), 259–282.

Kincaid, D. L. (1987). *Communication theory: Eastern and Western perspectives.* San Diego, CA: Academic Press.

Nielson/Net Ratings Global Index (2001). New York: A. C. Nielson. http://www.nielson-netratings.com

Oh, D. B. (1991). *PR communication gae-ron* [Introduction to PR]. Seoul, Korea: Nanam.

Park, J. (2001). Images of "Hong Bo (public relations)" and PR in Korean newspapers. *Public Relations Review, 27,* 403–420.

Park, Y., & Kim, M. (1997). *Understanding Korean corporate culture.* Seoul, Korea: Ohrom.

Rhee, Y. (1999). *Confucian culture and excellent public relations: A study of generic principles and specific and applications in South Korean public relations practice.* Unpublished master's thesis, University of Maryland at College Park, College Park.

Sriramesh, K. (1992). Culture and public relations: Ethnographic evidence from India. *Public Relations Review, 18*(2), 201–212.

Sriramesh, K., Kim, Y., & Takasaki, M. (1999). Public relations in three Asian countries. *Journal of Public Relations Research, 11,* 271–292.

The Korea Press Foundation Report (2001). Seoul: The Korea Press Foundation. http://www.kpf.or.kr.

Wilcox, D. L., Ault, P. H., Agee, W. K., Cameron, G. (2000). *Public relations: Strategies and tactics* (6th ed.). New York: Longman.

Yoon, Y. (2001, August). *Public relations worldview and conflict levels in the client–agency relationship.* Paper presented at the meeting of the Association of Educators for Journalism and Mass Communication, Washington, DC.

Youm, K. H. (1996). *Press law in South Korea.* Ames, Iowa: Iowa State University Press.

Yum, J. O. (1987a). Korean philosophy and communication. In D. L. Kindaid (Ed.), *Communications theory: Eastern and Western perspectives* (pp. 71–86). San Diego, CA: Academic Press.

Yum, J. O. (1987b). The practice of *Uye-ri* in interpersonal relationship in Korea. In D. L. Kindaid (Ed.), *Communications theory: Eastern and Western perspectives* (pp. 87–100). San Diego, CA: Academic Press.

Yum, J. O. (1988). The impact of Confucianism on interpersonal relationships and communication pattern in East Asia. *Communication Monograph, 55,* 374–388.

7

Public Relations in Australasia: Friendly Rivalry, Cultural Diversity, and Global Focus

Judy Motion
Shirley Leitch
Simon Cliffe

INTRODUCTION

As discussed in chapter 1, in recent years, public relations practice has gone global. The strong influence of this globalization is especially evident in New Zealand and Australia. In this chapter we discuss the commonalities as well as the unique features in public relations practice in the two countries. The relationship between the two countries might best be described as a "friendly rivalry" in all spheres. Sporting contests between the two nations, particularly on the rugby field, are fiercely competitive, and victory is highly prized. However, the two nations have always assisted one another during times of crisis and have fought alongside one another in the major conflicts of the 20th century. In public relations, this cooperation can be seen in the joint conferences and the frequent interchanges among practitioners of the two countries. The multinational status of many public relations companies also means that practitioners in New Zealand and Australia find themselves working for the same global companies. Weber Shandwick, Hill and Knowlton, and Burson Marsteller are a few of the many large consultancy chains that operate in both countries. The presence of these consultancies ensures that the standard of public relations in New Zealand and Australia reflects international best practice, whereas competition from local providers ensures that public relations is adapted to fit local circumstances and priorities. This chapter addresses the challenges of distance, bicultural and multicultural policies, activism, technology, and media fragmentation that have influenced the development and practice of public relations in New Zealand and Australia.

History, Geography, and Culture of New Zealand and Australia

The independent nations of New Zealand and Australia, positioned in the southwest Pacific, are often collectively referred to as Australasia. New Zealand lies about 1,000 km to the east of Australia. Australia is situated between the Pacific and Indian Oceans and has Indonesia and Papua New Guinea to the north. Both New Zealand and Australia are relatively sparsely populated, with 3.7 million (statistics New Zealand, 2002) and 19 million (Australian Bureau of Statistics, 2002) inhabitants, respectively, most of whom dwell in urban areas. English is the major language in both countries, although New Zealand also recognizes Maori, the language of the indigenous people, as an official language. Both nations have currencies based on the dollar, but they operate independently. Despite the many similarities between these geographically close neighbors, there also are many differences, especially in politics, economics, and culture.

History has been one point of commonality between the two nations that were once British colonies which, though modern democracies, still recognize the British queen as nominal head of state. The two nations routinely cooperate in a wide variety of areas in the international arena. For example, during World War I, Australia and New Zealand formed a joint army corps—the Australia and New Zealand Army Corps (ANZAC)—to help the allies on the European front. The ANZACs and the hardships they endured constituted an important moment in the formation of each country's distinct national identity (Molony, 1988; Sinclair, 1991). The spirit of cooperation embodied by the ANZACs also defined the notion of mateship, which has been especially predominant within Australian culture ever since.

New Zealand is an archipelago consisting of two main islands: the North Island and the South Island, where the majority of the population resides. It has an indigenous Maori population who have settled in the country since approximately 1000 AD. Discovered by Dutch explorer Abel Tasman in 1642, and circumnavigated by Captain James Cook in 1769, New Zealand was settled predominantly by European traders and whalers, soon to be followed by missionaries who arrived in the early 1800s (Sinclair, 1991). The Treaty of Waitangi, signed in 1840, ceded sovereignty of the land from the Maori to the British empire. This has dominated race relations and continues to do so in the new millennium (Sinclair, 1991). As a British colony, most of the new immigrants after 1840 were of British extraction, which has resulted in the development of close cultural, political, and economic ties with Great Britain. New Zealand once simply adopted British foreign policy as its own and served primarily as a far-flung British farm, producing food and other agricultural products for the British market. These close ties between Britain and New Zealand resulted in New Zealand's almost unquestioning involvement in both world wars. With the adoption of the Statute of Westminster in 1947, New Zealand became a politically independent nation and a member of the British Commonwealth.

In the latter half of the 20th century, New Zealand's biggest challenge had been to combat its declining standard of living relative to other countries (Dalziel, 2002). Like Australia, New Zealand is a member of the Organisation for Economic Co-operation and Development (OECD). OECD's member countries are committed to a market economy and pluralistic government and work to coordinate international and domestic policies in recognition of an increasingly globalized world (Organisation for Economic Co-operation and Development, 2002). In the 1950s, New Zealand was ranked as one of the most prosperous nations in the world (Sinclair, 1991), but its ranking fell to 23rd in the OECD by the beginning of the new millennium. The entry of Britain into the European Economic

Community in the 1970s led to dramatic reductions in the volume of agricultural exports from New Zealand to Britain. The loss of this market caused enormous economic and cultural upheaval in New Zealand and forced the nation to shift its focus from being "Britain's farm" to becoming a distinct nation with its own identity. New Zealand is now a fully participating member of the Asia–Pacific region but has struggled to regain its former economic position.

Australia is the smallest continent but the sixth largest country in the world. The indigenous Aboriginal tribes have inhabited the continent for at least the last 20,000 years. Britain began colonization of Australia in 1788 when Captain Arthur Phillip of the British Royal Navy landed at Botany Bay. Originally, Australia's main role was to serve as a penal colony for Britain's ex-convicts who were the settlers in the early days of the nation (Molony, 1988). Australia did not become a fully integrated colony until 1901 when the various colonies became federated. One of the first actions of the new federal government was to design a "White Australia Policy," which was intended to preserve the Anglo-Celtic heritage of the British settlers (Molony, 1988 p. 294). The policy was made more attractive by the blending of imperial and nationalistic sentiments that proclaimed that Australia's vast empty spaces could support an immense population. World War II revived the old catch-cry, "populate or perish," and a vigorous campaign was launched to encourage immigration from all parts of Europe. Thus, the emphasis shifted from seeking Anglo-Celtic immigrants to seeking immigrants from a variety of European nations. Over the next 4 decades, ethnic diversification gradually intensified with large numbers of Greeks, Italians, and other nationalities, for whom English was not the first language, settling in Australia (Molony, 1988). The 1980s brought heated debates on the relative merits of publicly funded programs for assimilation and for multiculturalism. Between World War II and the late 1980s, approximately 500,000 refugees and displaced persons arrived in Australia. By the 1980s, a quarter of Australians were immigrants, hailing from 120 different countries (Molony, 1988). Today, like New Zealand, Australia has accepted the economic and strategic significance of the Asia-Pacific region given the retrenchment of its traditional European trading partners and has been able to maintain a relatively high standard of living.

Evolution of the Profession

Despite the cultural, economic, and historical differences, public relations has evolved in remarkably similar ways in New Zealand and Australia. The profession began in both countries when journalists, mostly men, began to conduct media relations on behalf of organizations or clients. In New Zealand, the profession's birth can be traced to an historic meeting in the Auckland Star Hotel in 1954 when a group of demobilized military press officers formed what was to become the Public Relations Institute of New Zealand (PRINZ) (Motion & Leitch, 2001). Because of the size of Australia, public relations institutes began at different times in different states and subsequently joined to form the Public Relations Institute of Australia (PRIA). Public relations practitioners in New South Wales became the first to form a professional body in Australia, 5 years earlier than their New Zealand counterparts (Singh & Smyth, 2000). They were followed in 1952 by their colleagues in the state of Victoria. Today, Australia has divisions of PRIA in every state as well as a national body.

In the early years of the profession, almost all public relations practitioners began their professional lives as journalists before entering public relations. There were no opportunities for training public relations professionals in either Australia or New Zealand, an issue recognized by pioneering public relations practitioners. In fact, sharing their knowledge of public relations was the first priority of those who attended the inaugural session of PRINZ in 1954 (Motion & Leitch, 2001). They resolved to circulate whatever books or papers they had among members of the group and actively seek relevant information, particularly from the United States and Europe, which were seen to be leading the development of the field of public relations. In the days before airmail and the Internet, New Zealand and Australia were very isolated from the rest of the world. Newspapers and periodicals took months to arrive by sea and were out of date before they were distributed. There were few opportunities for local practitioners to meet counterparts from other countries. The advent of affordable and regular air services was an important step in exposing the profession in both countries to the ideas of the rest of the world. Air travel made it possible for New Zealanders and Australians to attend conferences and seminars and to learn from a broader range of experiences. However, the significance of the impact of air travel on the development of public relations is probably dwarfed by that of the Internet. For geographically isolated nations, the Internet offers instant access not just to information but also to professional networks.

Status of the Profession

There is no requirement for public relations practitioners to belong to their respective professional associations. Thus, anyone—regardless of education, experience, or understanding of ethics—is able to use the title *public relations consultant* and profit from it. It is difficult to estimate the total number of practitioners who are not members of professional bodies due to the diversity of job titles that are in use. Corporate communications manager, business communications manager, corporate affairs consultant, media relations specialist, press officer, in-house journalist, external relations director, and executive assistant are just a sample of the titles given to or adopted by practitioners. By electing to join either PRINZ or PRIA, practitioners demonstrate their commitment to the development of public relations as a profession with a body of knowledge, accreditation systems, and a code of conduct for ethical practice.

It is estimated that $A250 million is spent annually on public relations in Australia (Tymson & Lazar, 2002, p. 39). Similar figures are not available for New Zealand. In April 2002, PRINZ had a membership of 653, and PRIA's was 2856. The demographics of the members of both associations bear striking similarities. In both countries, approximately 60% of practitioners are women (Peart, 1998; Singh & Smyth, 2000; Tymson & Lazar, 2002). This figure is indicative of the dramatic shift that has occurred since the 1950s when public relations was practiced almost entirely by men. Peart (1998) noted that the older the practitioners were, the more likely it was that they would be male. Singh and Smyth (2000) referred to this gender shift as the "feminization of public relations" (p. 392) and noted some issues associated with feminization, including disparities in salaries based on gender. However, given that men still dominate the senior ranks of public relations in both countries, the full impact of feminization remains to be seen as more experienced female practitioners move into these higher paying positions. Peart's (1998) data suggest that length of experience, rather than gender, is the primary explanation for existing salary disparities. This finding is reinforced by Singh and Smyth (2000) who noted that at least one study in Australia had concluded that women in entry-level positions were earning more than their male counterparts.

Practitioners of both countries face similar professional issues. One of these—technology—has been alluded to already. Technologies, including the Internet, e-mail, databases, mobile telephones, and personal computers, have all had a significant impact on public relations. These technologies were either not invented or were not available in a form or at a price that was accessible when senior practitioners entered the profession. However, technology is only one area of significant change for practitioners. According to Singh and Smyth (2000), Australian public relations is fast becoming a strategic function with ties to the senior levels of management within organizations. This shift from the tactical to the strategic has increased the range of skills and knowledge that practitioners will need to acquire in order to succeed in the profession. A survey by the PRIA showed that major job duties were promotions and publicity (59%), counselling and consulting (52.1%), management (40%), writer/editor/publications (47.2%), internal communications (30.9%), and government relations (27%; Tymson & Lazar, 2002, p. 51).

Professional Education for the Public Relations Industry

The introduction of education and training programs for public relations and the expectation for entry-level practitioners to have relevant training is an important development for the profession, much of which has occurred over the past 2 decades. Nearly 90% of practitioners who took part in a New Zealand study conducted by Peart (1998) had tertiary qualifications. Similar findings resulted from an Australian Committee for Economic Development (CED) study conducted in 1997 (Singh & Smyth, 2000, p. 393). There are no data about the number of practitioners with public relations education, but, given the recent spurt in public relations education, it is likely that a significant proportion of the younger practitioners have some formal public relations education. Thus, the typical public relations practitioner of the future is likely to be a woman with a relevant degree or diploma in public relations.

Formal public relations education began in New Zealand in the late 1960s at Wellington Polytechnic. This part-time course was a joint initiative with PRINZ and was well-supported by the capital city's practitioners, many of whom worked for the government or in the head of offices of New Zealand's largest companies (Motion & Leitch, 2001, p. 661). Now there are degree and diploma courses in public relations at most tertiary institutions in New Zealand. In addition, there are numerous short courses in the area, often offered with the support of the PRINZ. A similar situation exists in Australia with both the tertiary education sector and the PRIA actively offering a range of courses and qualifications for both existing as well as new practitioners (Tymson & Lazar, 2002, p. 38). The major difference between the two nations is that, although PRIA operates an accreditation system for public relations qualifications, PRINZ has a less formal system. Although programs offered in any discipline by New Zealand universities and polytechnics must undergo a stringent approval process, this process is largely overseen by other educationalists, and there are only informal, limited, and piecemeal opportunities for industry input.

Public relations education has been accompanied by a growth in research and scholarship published in local journals such as the *Asia Pacific Public Relations Journal*, the *Australian Journal of Communication*, and *Media International Australia incorporating Culture and Policy*. Reflecting the international trend, public relations theory development in New Zealand and Australia is moving from the predominant systems approach to rhetorical, critical, and poststructuralist approaches.

Practitioner Accreditation

The absence of an accreditation system by PRINZ in New Zealand may be partly explained by the fact that there is a competing organization to which some New Zealand practitioners belong. The strength of this organization in New Zealand—the International Association of Business Communicators—has its roots in the split that occurred within PRINZ following the introduction of accreditation examinations for practitioners (Motion & Leitch, 2001). The accreditation examinations were intended to distinguish full members from associate members of PRINZ. They were not compulsory, and practitioners could continue to belong to and take part in PRINZ activities irrespective of their accreditation status. However, some senior practitioners were unhappy with the suggestion that they needed an examination system administered by their peers to determine their membership status and, therefore, resigned from PRINZ. An accreditation system exists in Australia under the aegis of the PRIA but does not appear to have led to a similar split. There are no data on the number of practitioners who have gained accreditation in the two countries. However, a study by CED in Australia found that about 20% of respondents had gained PRIA accreditation by 1997 (Singh & Smyth, 2000, p. 393). The majority of those surveyed—over 70%—were members of PRIA, suggesting that the majority of PRIA members are not accredited. Peart's (1998) study of senior New Zealand public relations practitioners found that the majority—56%—were accredited members of PRINZ. However, Peart's sample was skewed toward more experienced professionals who are more likely to be accredited.

Codes of Ethics

Accreditation, either of individuals or programs, has the potential to generate controversy. It is only surpassed in this regard by professional codes of ethics or professional practice. Both PRINZ and PRIA operate under such codes, and their content and application have always been the source of lively debate within the profession. In Australia, two separate codes are in operation. The first is the Consultancy Code of Practice, which delineates the general standards to which a consultancy should adhere, a framework within which client relations should be conducted, and a set of guidelines for fees and income. The "General Standards" section of the code begins with the instruction that a registered consultancy: "Accepts a positive duty to observe the highest standards in its business practice and in the practice of public relations; promote the benefits of public relations practice in all dealings; and improve the general understanding of professional public relations practice" (Public Relations Institute of Australia, 2001). This section of the code also states that a registered consultancy: "Adheres to the highest standards of accuracy and truth, avoiding extravagant claims and unfair comparisons and gives credit to ideas and words borrowed from others." There is no legal requirement for any Australian consultancy to either affiliate with PRIA or apply the Code of Practice. However, PRIA operates a register of consultancies in each Australian state, and only those consultancies that adhere to the code are able to list their services. PRINZ operates a similar register for New Zealand consultancies. However, there is no Code of Practice determining which consultancies may or may not list their services. Thus, the PRINZ register serves solely as a reference guide for those seeking to employ a consultancy, a function that could potentially lead to embarrassment for PRINZ in the event of poor or unethical practice by a listed consultant.

The PRINZ Code of Ethics was developed in response to concern over an ethical issue that focused media attention on the profession. Codes of ethics or of public relations practice evolve differently in different countries partly in response to the cases that the ethics committees of the relevant professional bodies confront. In New Zealand, the profession faced a major problem following disclosures in the book entitled *Secrets and Lies: The Anatomy of an Anti-Environmental PR Campaign*. The book, written by two environmental activists, Nicky Hagar and Bob Burton (1998), mapped the role that a prominent New Zealand public relations consultancy had played in assisting the continuation of logging of native forests. The book accused the consultancy of a range of activities including spying, lying, media manipulation, and undermining the democratic process. Such accusations often bring the entire profession of public relations into disrepute and create problems for all practitioners. Given that membership of PRINZ and PRIA is not compulsory, it is difficult for these associations to censure practitioners who choose not to operate within the boundaries of the relevant ethical code. Such practitioners can elect not to join the bodies or can simply resign when controversy erupts to put themselves and their work outside of the jurisdiction of ethics committees.

A new PRINZ code was developed to highlight that public relations practice is a form of advocacy and stress the importance of making the right judgment in balancing corporate and societal obligations: "We must balance our role as advocates for the individuals or groups with the public interest. We must also balance a commitment to promote open communication with the privacy rights of individuals and organisations." (Public Relations Institute of New Zealand, 2002). The code was modeled on that of the Public Relations Society of America and outlined a set of values and beliefs that guide behavior and decision-making processes. These values are advocacy, honesty, expertise, independence, loyalty, and fairness. The code then defines the principles and standards for the practice of public relations in New Zealand. Members are required to balance advocacy and honesty as well as openness and privacy, disclose conflicts of interest, abide by the law, and act in a professional manner. The differences between the codes reflect the lessons learned by the two organizations based on the different situations they have encountered.

Overall, the PRIA code is the more extensive of the two, containing 15 sections compared with the 5 in the PRINZ code. The additional concerns of PRIA primarily relate to the activities of consultancies, with a prohibition on linking fees with results and on seeking payment for unspecified work. The practices of consultancies have clearly been a more prominent issue in Australia than they have been in New Zealand. The PRIA code also requires its members to share information and experiences with one another to assist in the improvement of the general body of knowledge in public relations. Members are barred from misrepresenting their accreditation status in relation to the institute and are also required to act in accordance with the aims, regulations, and policies of the institute. Thus, PRIA is more overt in requiring that members comply with PRIA's standards. PRINZ is, therefore, more prescriptive in its requirements for members in relation to society, whereas PRIA is more concerned with relationships among members and between members and their clients. Both PRIA and PRINZ are members of the Global Alliance for Public Relations and Communications Management (GA) among countries practicing public relations throughout the world. The GA collaborates with a mission to enhance the public relations profession throughout the world. It will, for example, provide opportunities to network, examine ethical practices, and develop a universal accreditation system. A comparison study of codes of ethics was undertaken in February 2002, and the GA is now exploring opportunities to create a global code of ethics.

INFRASTRUCTURE OF NEW ZEALAND AND AUSTRALIA

As mentioned in the overview of this chapter, although both countries are parliamentary democracies with close historical connections to Britain, New Zealand and Australia have developed quite different political and economic systems. However, like other members of the Commonwealth, the two countries have derived their legal systems from British law, and much legislation is still tied to the original British statutes.

An Overview of the New Zealand and Australian Political Systems

New Zealand's parliamentary democracy is based on the British parliamentary model, with legislative power vested in a single house of representatives whose members are elected via universal suffrage every 3 years. The party, or coalition of parties, that holds a majority in the house form the government, with the leader of the dominant party becoming prime minister. The prime minister selects ministers of parliament to form a cabinet, which is the central organ of executive power. The New Zealand Constitution is a combination of both statute and convention, with convention generally taking precedence when there is a conflict between the two.

The Australian system, however, can be described as an amalgam of the British and American political systems. Like New Zealand, it is a parliamentary democracy with the Queen of England as the formal Head of State. However, like the American system, Australia is also a federation of states, and the division of power between the federal government and the state governments is explicitly laid down in a written constitution. The Australian Federation has a three-tier system of government—federal, state, and local. At the federal level, it is based on a two-party system in which the party or coalition of parties with the majority in the House of Representatives forms the government.

The British monarchy is represented in both countries by a governor–general appointed by the monarch at the recommendation of the respective New Zealand and Australian governments. The governor–general has limited powers, but he or she does have the responsibility to protect the constitution and to act in case of a constitutional crisis. Both countries have a tradition of egalitarianism, with New Zealand being one of the first countries to award women's suffrage in 1893 followed closely by Australia in 1894. At present both countries maintain universal suffrage for those age 18 and older.

The New Zealand Political System

In 1993, New Zealand voted to replace its First Past the Post (FPP) system with a Mixed Member Proportional Representation electoral system (MMP) system. Essentially, the MMP system is a proportional voting system in which each voter has two votes: one to elect their representative and one for their preferred party. Parliament currently consists of 67 electorate seats, and 53 party list seats; thus, voters are able to vote for their preferred electorate representative as well as their preferred party. There is a stipulation that for a party to win any list seats it must garner at least 5% of the party list vote or win at least one electoral seat. Elections are held every 3 years.

Historically, under the FPP system, New Zealand politics had been dominated by two major parties, the New Zealand Labour Party (center left) and the New Zealand National Party (center right). Other minority parties include The Association of Consumers and Taxpayers (ACT), the Green Party, the New Zealand First Party, and the United Future Party of New Zealand. Since the inception of the MMP electoral system in 1996, the two major political parties have dominated New Zealand politics, but the MMP system has required them to share power with minority coalition partners. In the current government, the Labour Party was forced to enter into coalition with the left-wing Alliance Party to gain a governing majority in Parliament. The change to the MMP system was based on the rationale of broadening the base of representation in Parliament, thus making Parliament more representative of the wider views of the electorate. In real terms, it has broadened the power base from the executive to the wider members of Parliament, which has made lobbying and power brokering a lot more important and influential in the machinations of government. Lobbying government on behalf of organizations has, therefore, become an important role for public relations consultancies (Aggett, 1996). Weaver and Motion (in press) argued that in New Zealand public relations practices are associated with the neo-liberal political economy where public interest has been subsumed by corporate and market interests. However, a change in government can signal a change in the role of public relations. The current labor-alliance government is more cautious in its use of public relations and has internalized the role, whereas the opposition (National Party) overtly uses public relations consultants.

There has been a high level of political activism in New Zealand. In recent times, the visit by nuclear-powered or armed ships to New Zealand ports, land claims by the Maori, and environmental issues such as genetic engineering have been the major sources of controversy. In the mid-1980s, the government responded to the majority viewpoint that opposed visits by nuclear ships, declaring New Zealand a nuclear-free zone. This effective ban on the warships of allied countries has been a continuing source of strained international relations, particularly between New Zealand and the United States. It has also caused difficulties between New Zealand and Australia and reduced the level of military cooperation between the two countries. More recently, in 2001 the Government held a Royal Commission of Enquiry into genetic engineering. The outcome of the enquiry was to tighten the rules that governed genetic-engineering experiments and trials but not to ban such activity. This issue continues to be a source of controversy in the country as well as a source of votes for the Green Party.

Political activism over a range of issues is, therefore, a continuing concern not only for the government but also other organizations in New Zealand. They must negotiate in an attempt to broker acceptable compromises with a range of stakeholders who often hold strong, often conflicting views. Public relations practitioners are frequently deployed to manage stakeholder relations particularly when political issues are involved. However, public relations practitioners in New Zealand have not always dealt with sensitive political issues in a way that has brought credit on the profession. For example, the tactics used by one consultancy to discredit environmental activists opposing the logging of native forests (Hagar & Burton, 1998) and by another to prevent publicity about mutations occurring in genetically modified salmon (Weaver & Motion, in press) seriously damaged the reputation of public relations as a profession. As already discussed, these incidents have led PRINZ to rewrite its code of ethics and have made professional ethics an important topic for debate in national forums.

The Australian Political System

The Australian electoral system is based on the principles of one person, one vote, and one value. Under the Commonwealth Electoral Act, (Commonwealth of Australia, 2002) Federal elections for the House of Representatives and the Senate are conducted using a preferential voting system, which ensures that a majority of voters have some say in the election of the government, even if their party of choice is not elected. Voters must indicate their preference for every candidate by essentially rank ordering their choices; failure to do so means their vote is not counted. Voters may use ticket voting in the Senate, for which only a mark is required against the name of a political party or an independent, and preferences are then distributed according to that party's official list.

Australian federal politics shares one major commonality with New Zealand in that it has largely been dominated by two major political parties: the Australian Liberal Party and the Australian Labour Party. However, the preferential voting system does encourage minority representation in Parliament, which has made coalitions important in gover-nance. Australian minority political parties include the Australian Democratic Party, the Green Party, the National Party, and the One Nation Party. The multilayered nature of the Australian system, with dual houses in both the states and in the national parlia-ment, presents both challenges and opportunities for public relations practitioners. The complexity of the system ensures that there are multiple points at which public relations practitioners engaged in lobbying activities can attempt to influence the political process. However, this same complexity makes it possible for influence at one level to be countered at a higher level or thwarted at a lower level by opposing lobbyists.

Many of the same issues that divide New Zealanders have also been a source of po-litical activism in Australia, becoming a source of work for Australian public relations consultants. Australia has witnessed a strong environmental movement in areas such as protesting the logging of native forests, the destruction of the environment caused by widespread mining in central Australia, and genetic engineering—particularly of foods. Race relations has also been a contentious issue in Australia. The Aboriginals of Australia do not have the equivalent of the New Zealand Treaty of Waitangi, as a result of which the issue of indigenous land rights has become more complex for both the government and the judiciary system. There are also strong vestiges of traditional beliefs on the White Australia Policy on immigration, and the One Nation Party has emerged as the political voice of this viewpoint. More recently, the current Government regained power in 2001, partly because of its strong stance against refugees from Afghanistan and Asia, who arrive by boat on Australia's northern coastline, by denying them entry.

An Overview of Australasia's Economic Systems

Over the last half century, despite the close economic ties between New Zealand and Australia, Australia has maintained greater economic growth and a higher standard of living than New Zealand in the OECD rankings. The two countries entered into the Closer Economic Relations Agreement in 1983, which has seen the transformation of Australasia into a free-trade zone. Australia benefits from approximately $A7 billion worth of exports to New Zealand, whereas New Zealand exports only over $A5 billion worth of goods to Australia. Much of Australia's trade is dependent on mineral resources and agriculture combined with a growing manufacturing base, whereas New Zealand is very rich in fisheries and agriculture, which contribute to approximately 60% of its export earnings. There is an ongoing discussion about the possible integration of the two economies in the future.

Both countries have highly educated populations, largely because primary and sec-ondary school education is both free and compulsory. Tertiary education is subsidised by the state, and the majority of students study in state-funded tertiary institutions. Both countries possess modern telecommunications systems. The Internet and mobile phone penetration rates in Australia and New Zealand rank among the highest in the world. The availability of broadband is currently an issue confronting the governments of both nations.

The New Zealand Economy

Historically, there has been a large degree of government intervention in the economic of New Zealand. However, there has been a systematic liberalization of the economy and deregulation since 1984. Dalziel (2002) explained these reforms:

> Within a year of change of government in July 1984, interest rates were deregulated, international capital restrictions were removed, the currency was floating freely in foreign exchange markets, and most agricultural subsidies and tax incentives were being phased out. Over the next decade and a half, domestic market regulations were comprehensively reformed in favour of contestability and competition, all import quotas were eliminated and a timetable was set for reducing tariffs to zero by 2006. In 1989, price stability was designated the sole statutory objective of monetary policy. In 1991 labour legislation was radically transformed from a corporatist, union based framework to a decentralised individual based contracts system. Since 1994, the Fiscal Responsibility Act has prohibited budget deficits "on average" over a reasonable period of time. Approximately US $10 billion worth of state assets were privatised between 1988 and 1999, and all remaining central government trading departments have been restructured along the lines of private sector corporations. Social welfare income support entitlements were significantly cut back in 1991, while income tax rates were reduced in 1996 and again in 1998. (pp. 31–32)

Since Dalziel (2002) wrote this piece, the 1991 Employment Contracts Act has been replaced by a more moderate Employment Relations Act, which has attempted to bring the corporate–union relationship back to a more comfortable equilibrium (Rudman, 2002). The top tax rate has also been raised, and some of the cuts to social welfare payments have been reinstated. However, the bulk of the economic reforms remain in place, and they have transformed New Zealand from being one of the most controlled to one of the most deregulated economies in the world. These reforms have resulted in significant economic and social change and upheaval within New Zealand, with a lot of the economic power now focused on the private sector and a much greater emphasis being put on individual responsibility. Deregulation has resulted in numerous public relations opportunities in strategy-oriented work, such as stakeholder relations and corporate identity programs.

The gap between the rich and poor in New Zealand continues to widen. But, compared with the high unemployment figures over the last decade, the current unemployment rate is low at 5.4%. The gross domestic product (GDP) for 2001 was approximately $65 billion (in United States dollars), with the annual growth rate at a modest 2.4%. New Zealand's relatively small population ensures that the country is very dependent on its export earnings. Currently, the economy is in a buoyant state, registering the highest levels of business confidence and consumer spending since the mid-1990s. This buoyancy is largely based on high international prices for agricultural commodities, which are not sustainable over the long term. The government is attempting to reduce New Zealand's reliance on commodities by building what has been called the *knowledge economy*. The longer term economic outlook for New Zealand may well depend on the success or otherwise of this policy, and public relations has played an important role in the policy's implementation. For example, a series of high-profile conferences—most notably the Catching the Knowledge Wave Conference in Auckland and the Innovate Conference in Christchurch—have been staged in an attempt to focus the attention of business and government leaders on the creation of the knowledge economy. Significant media and publicity work was undertaken around these conferences, including live coverage on Sky television, to ensure that the events were available to a wide audience and could provoke national debate around the key economic issues.

The Australian Economy

Although following the reforms of other OECD countries, Australia chose not to move so sharply away from the Keynesian economic model as New Zealand had done. Perhaps the more complex political system to be found in Australia functioned as a source of resistance against such rapid and radical change. Whatever the reasons for moving so slowly, the Australian economy has consistently outperformed the New Zealand economy over the last $1\frac{1}{2}$ decades. Over the past 5 years, Australia's government has played a more interventionist role in the economy, and it has made structural reforms, albeit more gradually than occurred in New Zealand. A key area of the Australian government's structural reform program since 1996 has been the promotion of a more flexible labor market. Significant reforms to workplace relations have included a move from centralized wage fixing to enterprise bargaining. Strong economic growth and moderate wage and price pressures have ensured sustained employment growth. In the last 2 years, however, employment has grown by more than 2% per annum. In March 2001, the unemployment rate was 6.5%, a 4.2% drop from the previous decade's peak unemployment level of 10.7%. GDP is approximately $450 billion (in United States currency according to 2000 estimates). (Australia bureau of statistics, 2002) One of the reasons for Australia's continuing economic strength is the enormous mineral wealth found on the continent. This natural resource has provided the backbone of the Australian economy.

In both Australia and New Zealand, there is a need for investor relations. Tymson and Lazar (2002) outlined the importance of financial public relations in Australia and New Zealand, highlighting the need for merger and acquisition strategies, investor relations, lobbying, and promoting financial products aimed at the consumer market.

An Overview of Australasia's Legal Systems

The legal systems of New Zealand and Australia are based on English common law. In both countries, the judicial branch is separate from the legislative branch to maintain the independence of the judiciary from political interference. However, due to their constitutional differences, the way in which the New Zealand and Australian legal systems manifest themselves is different.

The New Zealand Legal System

In New Zealand, the separation of the judicial and legislative branches has made the judiciary the only source for interpreting and applying the laws enacted by Parliament. The courts in New Zealand are increasingly taking a more independent stance and have begun to play a more significant constitutional and political role with respect to public and administrative law. In addition, some members of the legal community have begun to challenge the traditional doctrine that Parliament may pass any law not binding future Parliaments, contending that certain common-law rights might override the will of Parliament.

New Zealand law is administered by the Department of Justice through its courts. The hierarchy of courts in New Zealand in ascending order (from lowest to highest recognized level) is the District court (which includes disputes tribunals, family courts, and youth courts), the High Court, the Court of Appeal, and the British Privy Council, which can review Court of Appeal cases. Recently, there has been some debate in New Zealand regarding the relevance of having a foreign court involved in the New Zealand legal system. Of particular note, special legislation and land courts—in the form of the

Waitangi Tribunal—have been provided for Maori people, particularly for land claims derived from the Treaty of Waitangi. Over the past 2 decades, hundreds of millions of dollars have been paid out to Maori tribes, known as *iwi*, in recognition of past injustices in relation to the seizure of Maori land by the Crown. Law enforcement is the responsibility of the New Zealand Police Department, a cabinet-level department largely independent (with respect to law enforcement) of executive authority.

A good working knowledge of New Zealand law ensures that public relations professionals can avoid liability and accurately advise clients. Legislation that directly impacts on the practice of public relations includes the Treaty of Waitangi Act of 1975, the Fair Trading Act of 1986, the Broadcasting Standards Act of 1989, the Resource Management Act of 1991, the Defamation Act of 1992, the Human Rights Act of 1993, the Privacy Act of 1993, and the Employment Relations Act of 2000. (Mulholland, 2001).

The Australian Legal System

The Australian Constitution confers the legislative, executive, and judicial powers of the Commonwealth on three different bodies, which are established by the Constitution: Parliament, the Commonwealth Executive, and the Federal Judicature. The demarcation of the branches of government is vague in that there is no strict demarcation between the legislative and executive powers of the Commonwealth. Only the Parliament can pass laws, but these laws often confer on the Commonwealth Executive the power to make regulations, rules, and bylaws in relation to matters relevant to a particular parliamentary act. However, the separation between the judicature on the one hand and the Parliament and the Executive on the other is strict. Only a court may exercise the judicial power of the Commonwealth. In contrast to New Zealand, in Australia, the administration of the law is largely in the hands of the states, each of which has a series of courts culminating in a supreme court. Between them, these courts have comprehensive responsibilities extending to all matters of state and most matters of federal jurisdiction. The states also manage the police, although there is a federal Commonwealth police force that performs general police duties in the Australian Capital Territory and is the principal agency for the enforcement of federal laws. However, for the following matters, the federal judicature take precedence:

- Matters arising directly under any treaty.

- Suits between states, between persons suing or being sued on behalf of different states, or between a state and a person suing or being sued on behalf of another state.

- Matters in which the Commonwealth of Australia or a person suing or being sued on behalf of the Commonwealth of Australia is a party.

- Matters between states, between residents of different states, or between a state and a resident of another state.

- Matters in which a writ of mandamus or prohibition—which concern judicial review of administrative action—is sought against an officer of the federal government or of a federal court. The High Court shares some of its jurisdiction under this section with the Federal Court of Australia. (Attorney-General's Department, n.d.)

Furthermore, in contrast to New Zealand, Australia abolished the ability to appeal to the Privy Council in 1986. In recent years, Australia has also held a referendum on whether or not the British Queen should continue to be head of state. The referendum decided that the connection should remain, but the issue continues to be debated within Australia. In

Australian public relations practice, it is essential to be familiar with relevant legislation because of the potential for liability or negligence. Relevant legislation covers areas such as contracts law, the Design Act of 1906, the Copyright Act of 1968, the Trade Practices Act of 1974, the Australian Broadcasting Act of 1983, the Trademarks Act of 1995, and the Electronic Transactions Act of 1999. Laws relating to business practices, defamation, and lotteries and competitions vary from state to state. The challenge of understanding the law and identifying potential legal problems is, therefore, more complex for Australian public relations practitioners because of the dual systems.

CULTURE AND PUBLIC RELATIONS

Sociocultural Aspects of New Zealand and Australia's Cultural Identities

According to Hall (1996), identities are never unified and, in modern times, are increasingly fragmented and fractured. They are never singular but multiply constructed across different, often intersecting and antagonistic, discourses, practices, and positions (p. 4). Our aim in this section is not to present a unified, essentialized version of cultural identity, but rather to highlight some of the ways that commonalities and shared characteristics are represented in cultural discourses. These commonalities and characteristics serve as points of identification (Hall, 1996) that may be articulated and sutured to form cultural discourses. We now deal with elements of each culture in turn, focusing on cultural elements that are pertinent to understanding the cultures and the public relations practices in both countries.

Although both New Zealand and Australia were originally settled by indigenous people and later became British colonies, significant differences in cultural identity are evident. Both nations emerged as a result of the colonization of indigenous people, but whereas New Zealand has attempted to make financial reparations to these natives, Australia has not (Power, 2000). Maori culture has had a strong influence on the culture of New Zealand. Pacific Island and Asian cultures are also increasingly influencing the New Zealand way of life; so, although New Zealand has a bicultural policy, it has a multicultural focus. Australia, in contrast, is officially multicultural, but the role of the Aboriginal people in the Australian economy and cultural identity is marginal. Cultural identity is thus a political, strategic, positional concept, and bicultural or multicultural policies enable governments to adopt a rhetoric of being considerate to all people or of focusing on indigenous people.

Maori culture is characterized as cooperative, and the *whanau* (extended family) structure of Maori society has influenced an acceptance of cooperation and consensus, as well as a capitalist individualistic approach, in New Zealand society. The Maori have endeavored to save their language and culture by setting up preschool *kohanga reo* (language units) that serve as the starting point of instilling cultural pride and knowledge among their children. The fostering and acceptance of Maori values and knowledge may, however, be contrasted with the disproportionate number of Maori who are poor, face ill health, and appear frequently in crime statistics. As a consequence, the Maori are discursively constructed as either entrepreneurial or welfare dependent.

The national *Pakeha* (New Zealander of European descent) identity has been based on a number of myths: egalitarian society, a heroic settler society, and good old rural values surviving in the suburbs (Bell, 1996). Although traditionally a male-dominated society, a unique recent feature of New Zealand society is that women have succeeded to move to the highest levels. New Zealand was one of the first countries to grant women the right to vote, and currently women hold the four top positions in New Zealand: Prime Minister, Governor General, Attorney General, and Chief Justice. New Zealanders are colloquially referred to as *kiwis*, the name of a flightless native bird. Generally, New Zealanders are characterized as resourceful, self-reliant, outdoors people. Sports play an important part in the New Zealand psyche; for many years, rugby was the predominant sport, with the elite rugby team, All Blacks, attaining iconic status. Rugby is perceived as a sport for the "average bloke." New Zealanders love the water, and from the days of Kupe, the first explorer to reach New Zealand over 1,000 years ago, New Zealanders have had a passion for sailing. Innovation and technology adoption are considered important features of New Zealand culture. For example, competing for and winning the prestigious America's Cup resulted in a number of technological innovations. In addition, New Zealanders are some of the highest mobile phone and Internet users per capita in the world (Tourism New Zealand, 2002). Sensitivity to Maori cultural values, gender equity issues, and environmental management are requisite features of New Zealand public relations practice.

Australian Aborigines were nomadic people who were able to survive in the harsh desert conditions of Australia. The arrival of European settlers led to a dramatic decline in the indigenous population because of conditions of genocide, repression, social and cultural disruption, and dispossession. Australia has not offered Aboriginal people economic settlement for the suffering caused by their colonization. The Prime Minister of Australia, John Howard, refused to apologize on behalf of the Australian government for past injustices done to the Aboriginal people. Power (2000) claimed that an apology would "make people feel more secure that Australia is not now a racist country, it would expunge a sense of guilt and shame that many Australians feel ... the policy of separating children from their Aboriginal parents on racist grounds has been judged by an appropriate body to involve 'gross violations of human rights'" (p. 202). A number of Aboriginal people are beginning to succeed based on Western criteria. However, overall, these people suffer from ill health and welfare dependency. Increasingly, White Australians are questioning the treatment of Aboriginal people and advocating reconciliation and reparation.

The White Australian identity has been based on myths of convict colony, the bronzed lifeguard, and outback hardships. The multicultural nature of Australia and the contrast between urban and outback life make it difficult to categorize Australian culture. Australians are widely regarded as friendly, open people with a dry sense of humor. Generally, New Zealanders are considered more reserved and introverted whereas Australians are considered more extroverted.

Tourism discourses market Australia as a land of contrasts, which also applies to the people: Aborigines, farmers, successful business people, beautiful models, actors, immigrants, and surfers. Australians are recognized for their musical, sporting, and artistic achievements. From opera to rock, Aussie rules to netball, Aboriginal art to Australian film, Australians have succeeded in a global market. Sports are considered the national religion, and both men and women excel in a vast number of sports including Australian rules football, rugby, cricket, hockey, netball, and swimming.

It is difficult to generalize about the impact of culture on public relations practice in the two countries as there is no empirical data on this relationship. But, in general, mostly Western global business practices prevail. However, public relations practice within New Zealand and Australia reflects the multicultural nature of the two countries. Within both countries, conferences address issues of multiculturalism, and there are public relations consultancies that specialize in intercultural communication from Maori, Pacific Island, or a variety of ethnic perspectives.

Hofstede's Dimensions in New Zealand and Australia

The Hofstede's work (1983, 1985) is a useful starting point for a discussion of organizational–cultural dimensions and their implications for the practice of public relations in New Zealand and Australia. The four value dimensions identified by Hofstede and discussed in Chapter 1 do generally apply to both New Zealand and Australia. But the model does tend to act as an essentializing discourse, neglecting the nuances of bicultural and multicultural policies. New Zealand and Australia were both classified similarly by Hofstede. He identified both countries as having a low power distance and weak uncertainty avoidance. Hofstede considered that small power distance plus weak uncertainty avoidance leads to viewing the organization "as a 'village market,' that is an ad-hocracy . . ." (p. 353). The author did qualify his view with the observation that the purpose of an organization may also impact on the value system. Obviously, with bicultural and multicultural nations, a variety of organizational models will be present. Hofstede also classified the two countries similarly as being individualistic and masculine, with achievement, self-interest, self-actualization, and assertiveness as some of the norms present in the two countries. The difficulty with this generalization is that conducting business with Maori organizations would require a different approach based on collectivism and relationship-oriented values. The corporate cultures of New Zealand and Australian organizations may also be mediated by the impact of globalization and the origin of multinational organizations.

THE MEDIA ENVIRONMENT

Media Control

The media in both New Zealand and Australia are partly state owned and partly owned by the private sector. The state's involvement is in the area of broadcasting, with the state owning radio and television channels in both countries. The majority of radio and television channels are, however, in the hands of the private sector. The private sector also owns and controls all Australian and New Zealand newspapers. Control of public sector broadcasting is vested with independent boards so as to avoid charges of political interference in or the censorship of program content. The notion of a free press is a recognized and protected part of the democratic political culture of both countries. Thus, public relations practitioners have unfettered access to journalists when they are attempting to communicate the views of their clients or employers.

The democratic ideal of the free press centers on the notion that the media are public watchdogs who monitor political processes and societal activities. It might be argued that this ideal lies at the core of the ongoing commitment to public sector broadcasting because profitability, rather than public service, provides the *raison d'etre* for the private sector. Moreover, as the media become increasingly multinational, their ability to function as a key component of a national—as opposed to global—culture is increasingly brought into question. Major global media companies have significant holdings in New Zealand and Australia. One company–Independent Newspapers Limited, in which Rupert Murdoch's News Limited has a 50% stake–owns all but two of New Zealand's major daily newspapers. In Australia, two companies—News Limited and Fairfax—control all but 3 of the 33 metropolitan newspapers. Such large holdings are more efficient than multiple smaller companies as they are able to share production facilities and journalistic resources through the syndication of stories across multiple media outlets in different Australian states or regions of New Zealand, among other things. However, these efficiencies have come at the price of a reduction in journalistic pluralism with fewer and fewer journalists employed in both countries to cover the news.

In Australia, the government is currently in the process of relaxing the rules governing cross-media ownership in the same market. In the past, these rules have functioned to prevent one company from owning significant portions of the print and broadcast media that serve the same market. The proposed changes would, for example, enable Kerry Packer's company, which owns the Nine Television network and a large stable of magazine titles in both New Zealand and Australia, to also control a major metropolitan newspaper. A relaxation of the rules would enable media companies to offer attractive packages to advertisers that would cover multiple media. Such packages are likely to make it even more difficult for media that are independent of the major companies to compete for advertising dollars, the media's primary source of revenue. However, note that, in both New Zealand and Australia, the domination of traditional media markets by the major companies is already almost complete. At the same time, the Internet is providing a significant threat to traditional media by offering a forum that is characterized by its diversity, its interactivity, and by a low cost structure that makes it widely accessible. Although the traditional media still function as the major source of news and are themselves moving to offer more online offerings, the Internet offers an alternative source of public information for those who choose to seek it out. Perhaps ironically, it is this development of alternative electronic media that has served as a justification in Australia for the cross-ownership law change (Cunningham & Romano, 2000).

In New Zealand, the major recent legal change in relation to the media has gone in a direction contrary to that in Australia. Rather than seeking to strengthen the private sector media, the New Zealand government has sought to strengthen the role of public sector broadcasting through, for example, introducing a 23-point charter that will require state television to offer quality programming that caters to minority interests, including those of the indigenous Maori population. The charter will also require state television to make greater use of local programming. Currently, the two state-owned free-to-air channels are run primarily as profit-making enterprises that compete directly with private sector channels. Under the new charter, they will still be required to run profitably, but profit will no longer be the main or sole objective. Thus, although there are no moves in New Zealand to hinder the growth of the private sector media, the government has decided to ensure that local content that addresses issues of concern to New Zealanders remains freely available.

One significant difference between New Zealand and Australia is that in the latter newspapers have been more likely to display or be accused of displaying a clear bias towards one of the major political parties. Such bias is commonplace in countries such as the United Kingdom in which the public are able to demonstrate their political commitment by, for example, purchasing the *Guardian* newspaper if they support the Labour Party. If a diversity of viewpoints is represented in a freely available range of media products, then it might be argued that such bias in individual newspapers is not necessarily injurious to the goals of a democratic society. One reason for the absence of such demonstrable bias against one or the other of the two major political parties in New Zealand newspapers is arguably that it would run counter to the profit motive. That is, in New Zealand, only one newspaper dominates in each of the major metropolitan areas. The exception—the capital city of Wellington—boasts both a morning and evening daily newspaper owned by the same company. Given the small size of the market, New Zealand newspapers appear to have settled for the mainstream in that they favor neither of the major parties. However, there is also evidence that they put few resources into representing viewpoints from outside of the mainstream of the political center left or center right (Leitch, 1990). Thus, according to Leitch, public relations practitioners working for mainstream organizations or clients have a far easier job in terms of ensuring that their employer's views are represented in the media than do those working for more radical organizations.

Media Outreach

New Zealand and Australia can both be characterized as media saturated countries. Indeed, Australian media scholar Henry Mayer wrote in 1980 that: "You cannot escape from pollution by holding your nose. There is no refuge from the mass media and their effects. Even if you never touch a paper or switch on TV or radio, most people do all three so frequently that the media affect you through them. (cited in Tiffen, 1994, p. 3)

All but a small minority of homes in both countries possess television sets and are, therefore, able to access the multiple free-to-air television channels as well as the satellite pay-TV channels offered by Rupert Murdoch's global network. In New Zealand, for example, some 14% of the population subscribe to the Sky television network, which brings in international programming including CNN. Newspaper readership is declining throughout the Western world, and New Zealand and Australia are no exception in this respect. In the face of growing competition from other media for advertising revenue, the number of newspapers has been reducing in both countries. The implication of this fragmentation of the news audience across multiple media to public relations practice is that it is becoming increasingly difficult and costly to communicate with the masses. However, the increasing specialization of media products means that it is becoming easier to target messages to particular publics who, for example, subscribe to niche publications or Internet newsgroups. Given the focused nature of most public relations work, the ubiquitous, yet fragmented character of the media in New Zealand and Australia is generally a boon to public relations activity.

Media Access

As is the case in most democratic, capitalist countries, access to media is easily available to those who can afford to pay for it. Organizations with resources are able to purchase both advertising and advertorial space or airtime to ensure that their views are heard. However, there are media outlets in both New Zealand and Australia that provide access for organizations with limited resources and minority points of view. For example, the digital television station, BIGTV, run in conjunction with the University of Waikato in Hamilton, New Zealand, provides a forum for local groups to address their community. However, such access shows on radio and television have limited audiences, and few resources are available to assist groups in producing good quality productions.

The media in both Australia and New Zealand are highly dependent on public relations practitioners for many of the news stories they publish. This dependence has been created in part by the declining number of journalists employed by news organizations as they seek to increase profits or reduce costs. Public relations practitioners clearly provide a subsidy to the media by providing free copy that often requires little editing. The reliance of the media on public relations practitioners has also been partly a result of the increasing number of practitioners employed by organizations to handle their media relations. In 2002, for example, the New Zealand government spent more than $N2 13 million on public relations. A spokesperson for one government ministry—Debbie Chin, the Director-General of Health—defended the expenditure, stating that the use of public relations staff reflected the public's right to know what officials and politicians were doing: "This interest reflects the public's right to know. Our approach is to be open and helpful to the media and to recognise they are an important conduit to the general public" (Scanlon, 2002, p. 1). Thus, public relations practitioners have become an established and accepted component of the news-gathering process.

CASE STUDY: 0800 SMOKEY—A PARTNERSHIP APPROACH TO AIR POLLUTION

The following case study is an example of the use of public relations by a major city to help deal with air pollution in New Zealand.

Background

With a population of 1.2 million, Auckland is the fastest growing region in New Zealand. Rapid growth has exacerbated transport problems in Auckland, which has poor systems of public transport and a motorway network that approaches gridlock during peak hours. Although the air is still clean in comparison with that of other major cities, the recent decline in air quality has been of concern to both residents and the local government. Responsibility for monitoring the region's air quality lies with the Auckland Regional Council (ARC), a government environmental agency. Since monitoring of air quality began in 1991, air quality has deteriorated, and levels of pollutants that exceed World Health Organization safety guidelines have been recorded. ARC research showed that over 80% of the air pollution problem in the region was the result of motor vehicle emissions. Moreover, car ownership has been growing at twice the rate of the population, and there is almost one car for every two people in the region.

ARC scientific research attributed the air pollution from vehicles in the region to poor vehicle maintenance, low fuel specifications relative to other developed countries, and the lack of appropriate legislation on the quality of cars being imported from overseas. Market research conducted by the ARC indicated that, although people did attribute pollution to smoky vehicles, they also incorrectly thought that industry was to blame. The challenge for the ARC was to design a campaign that informed Aucklanders of the issues and educated them on the actions they could take.

Campaign Objectives

The objectives of the 0800 Smokey campaign were to:

1. Raise awareness that motor vehicle emissions caused over 80% of the air pollution and that vehicle owners should tune and regularly service their vehicles.

2. Promote the 0800 SMOKEY hotline and web site where people could report smoky vehicles.

3. Give the air quality issue a public context so that the ARC could influence government fuel quality and vehicle import legislation.

The Campaign: Stakeholder Partnerships and Education

The 0800 Smokey campaign was predominantly a public education advertising campaign aimed at raising the awareness of the air pollution problems. A partnership approach was adopted by the ARC to involve key stakeholders and to keep the campaign within the limited resources and budget. Colenso BBDO, an international advertising agency, agreed to provide the creative material on a pro bono basis. The ARC formed a partnership with the Motor Trade Association, a group of automotive repair garages, so that vehicle owners could get a free inspection of their exhaust emissions. Transit New Zealand, a crown entity that directs transport policy and funding, permitted the ARC to use its electronic motorway road signage to promote the campaign. Local businesses were approached and asked to initiate a regular servicing and tuning of their fleet vehicles; replace older fleet vehicles; provide teleworking opportunities; and provide incentives for staff to tune their vehicles, use public transport, or car pool. As a result of its stakeholder partnerships, the ARC was able to run a mass advertising campaign that had local business support and offered free vehicle inspections.

The advertising campaign asked Aucklanders to tune their vehicles and *dob in* (report) those who had a smoky exhaust by calling an 0800 hotline telephone number. A number of key messages were designed:

- "If you see a smoky vehicle, dob it in."
- "Auckland's air pollution exceeds world health standards. Tune your vehicle."
- "If your exhaust smokes for more than 10 seconds, you're poisoning Auckland."

The campaign was launched on Queen Street, the main street of Auckland's business district, with a special event and a number of publicity exercises. Actors had a mock protest wearing gas masks, fire alarms were placed on poles, and stickers placed on shop window mannequins and parking meters that stated, "You're breathing Auckland's filthy air for another . . ." [time indicated on meter].

The launch was widely covered on prime time news programs. The launch message was reinforced by a television commercial that opened with a close-up shot of a billboard that stated, "Our carbon monoxide levels are nearly as high as Auckland's. Tune your vehicle." A wide-angle shot was then used to show that the billboard was on New Zealand House in London with red double-decker buses in the foreground. That shot was replaced by another billboard stating, "Auckland's air pollution exceeds World Health Standards. Tune your vehicle." The comparison of Auckland and London's pollution served to highlight the seriousness of the problem and create controversy and debate through the contradiction of the clean green image that New Zealand has promoted for many years. Controversy was also generated through the use of the word *dob*. A social welfare campaign that encouraged people to report welfare infringements had been termed *dob in a beneficiary* and been very unpopular. Ironically, although this campaign aimed to make people take personal responsibility for air pollution, one of the primary ways in which they were encouraged to do so was by reporting other defaulters.

Evaluation

More than 57,000 calls were made to the 0800 SMOKEY hotline during the campaign. One year later, 2002, 500 calls per week were still being received on the hotline. More than 27,000 vehicles were dobbed in, and 3,000 vehicles were dobbed in 3 times or more. The worst offender—a used diesel-powered car recently imported from Japan—was dobbed in 73 times. Fifty eight per cent of the dobbed in vehicles were diesel powered, but diesel vehicles make up only 14% of the New Zealand vehicle fleet.

A recent telephone survey found that 85% of respondents expressed concern about the impact of exhaust fumes on the environment, an indication that public recognition of the issue remains high. In March 2001, the 10-s smoke law was introduced that allowed police to fine motorists with visible vehicle smoke emissions. This focus on emission levels, rather than on targeting of the mode of transport Aucklanders used, is one explanation of the positive response to the campaign. The long-term solution—a shift to less-polluting public transport—remains to be addressed and is likely to be far more controversial. Given the love affair that New Zealanders have with their cars, convincing them to turn to trains and buses will be a significant challenge for a future public relations campaign.

REFERENCES

http://www.oecd.org/EN/document/0, EN-document-0-nodirectorate-no-13-26640-0,00.html, 30 April, 2002

http://www.stats.govt.nz/, April 29, 2002

http://www.abs.gov.au/ausstats/abs%40.nsf/94713ad445ff1425ca25682000192af2/1647509ef7e25faaca2568
    a900154b63!OpenDocument, April 29, 2002

Aggett, M.-J. (1996). Health lobbyists eye up corridors of power. *New Zealand Doctor, 16*, 1–4.

Ansley, G. (2002, April 15). Australia targets New Zealand weaknesses. *The New Zealand Herald*, p. C1.

Bell, C. (1996). *Inventing New Zealand: Everyday myths of pakeha identity*. Auckland, New Zealand: Penguin.

Cunningham, S., & Romano, A. (2000, May). W(h)ither media influence? *Media International Australia, 95*,
    19–28.

Dalziel, P. (2002). New Zealand's Economic Reforms: An Assessment. *Review of Political Economy, 14*(1),
    31–46.

Hagar, N., & Burton, B. (1998). *Secrets and lies: The anatomy of an anti-environmental PR campaign*. Welling-
    ton, New Zealand: Craig Potton Publishing.

Hall, S. (1996). Introduction: Who needs an identity? In S. Hall & P. du Gay (Eds.), *Questions of cultural
    identity*. (pp. 1–17) London: Sage.

Hofstede, G. (1983). National cultures in four dimensions: A research-based theory of cultural differences
    among nations. *International Studies of Management and Organization, 13*(1/2), 46–75.

Hofstede, G. (1985). The interaction between National and organizational value systems. *Journal of Manage-
    ment Studies, 22*(4), 347–357.

Leitch, S. (1990). *News talk*. Palmerston North, New Zealand: Dunmore Press.

Molony, J. (1988). *The Penguin history of Australia* (2nd ed.). Ringwood: Penguin.

Motion, J., & Leitch, S. (2001). New Zealand perspectives on public relations. In R. Heath & G. Vasquez (Eds.),
    Handbook of public relations (pp. 659–663), Thousand Oaks, CA: Sage.

Peart, J. (1998, May). The state of public relations. *Marketing Magazine*, 32.

Power, M. R. (2000). Reconciliation, restoration and guilt: The politics of apologies. *Media International
    Australia Incorporating Culture and Policy, 93*, 191–205.

Scanlon, G. (2002, January 24). PR costs civil service $13 million. The Dominion, p. 19.

Sinclair, K. (1991). *A history of New Zealand* (5th ed.). Auckland, New Zealand: Penguin.

Singh, R., & Smyth, R. (2000). Australian public relations: Status at the turn of the 21st century. *Public Relations
    Review, 26*(4), 387–401.

Tiffen, R. (Ed.). (1990). *Mayer on the media: Issues and arguments*. Sydney, Australia: Allen & Unwin.

Tymson, C., & Lazar, P. (2002). *The new Australian and New Zealand public relations manual*. Chotswood,
    Australia: Tymson Communications.

Weaver, C. K., & Motion, J. (2002 in press). Sabotage and subterfuge: Public relations, democracy and genetic
    engineering in New Zealand. *Media, Culture and Society. 24*(3), 325–343.

PART

II

AFRICA

8

PUBLIC RELATIONS IN SOUTH AFRICA: FROM RHETORIC TO REALITY

RONÉL RENSBURG

PREVIEW

In South Africa, the public relations field is still characterized by its search for identity, legitimacy, and professional recognition. Nevertheless, South Africa is a new democracy, and public relations practice is essential to democratic societies. In South Africa, the role of public relations practitioners—in all spheres of business—is shaped by the dynamics of an ever-changing and developing society. In this chapter I describe the practice of public relations in South Africa and examine the cultural, developmental, economic, and sociopolitical complexities that impact on the work and effectiveness of public relations practitioners and consultants. Although the chapter mainly consists of factual information, some of the views, expressions, and interpretations are my individual opinions.

PUBLIC RELATIONS IN SOUTH AFRICA: AN OVERVIEW

History and Development of the Country

The Land

The Republic of South Africa occupies the southernmost part of the African continent, covering a surface area of 1,219,090 square km. It has common boundaries with the republics of Namibia, Botswana, and Zimbabwe; the Republic of Mozambique and the Kingdom of Swaziland lie to the northeast. Completely enclosed by South African territory is the mountain kingdom of Lesotho. To the west, south, and east, South Africa borders on the Atlantic and Indian Oceans. Isolated, 1,290 km southeast of Cape Town in the Atlantic, lie Prince Edward and Marion Islands, annexed by South Africa in 1947 (Government Communication and Information Systems [GCIS], 2001/2002).

In South Africa one finds the world's strangest and most dramatic landscapes; a unique wealth of animal and plant life; a treasure of gold, diamonds, and other minerals; and a kaleidoscope of fascinating cultures. The country is also the home of big game, and the Kruger National Game Park is known throughout the world.

South Africa is divided into nine provinces, each with its own legislature, premier, and provincial members of executive councils. Each of the provinces features its own distinctive landscapes, vegetation, and climate. The provinces are the Western Cape, the Eastern Cape, the Northern Cape, the Free State, North–West, Gauteng, Mpumalanga, KwaZulu-Natal, and the Limpopo (see Appendix Table A8.1).

The People

According to *Statistics South Africa* (2001), the country's population in 2000 was estimated to be 43,686 million, of which 22.7 million were women. The population was classified as follows: 76.7% African, 10.9% White, 8.9% Black, and 2.6% Indian or Asian. The South African population consists of the following groups: the Nguni people (including the Zulu, Xhosa, and Swazi), who account for two thirds of the population; the Sotho-Tswana people, who include the Southern, Northern and Western Sotho (Tswana); the Tsonga; the Venda; Afrikaners; English; Coloreds; Indians; and people who have immigrated to South Africa from the rest of Africa, Europe, and Asia and who continue to maintain their native cultural identity. A few members of the Khoi and San also live in South Africa. South Africa has 11 official languages: Afrikaans, English, isiNdebele, isiXhosa, isiZulu, Sepedi, Sesotho, Setswana, siSwati, Tshivenda, and Xitsonga. Recognizing the historically diminished use and status of the indigenous languages, the government is taking positive measures to elevate the stature of these languages. The official language used in government and business is English.

Almost 80% of South Africa's population adheres to the Christian faith. Other major religious groups are the Hindus, Muslims, and Jews. Freedom of worship is guaranteed, and official policy is one of noninterference in religious practices. Because the traditional religion of the African people has a strong cultural base, the various groups have different rituals, but there are certain common features. A supreme being is generally recognized, but ancestors are of far greater importance, being the deceased elders of the group. They are regarded as part of the community, indispensable links with the spirit world, and the powers that control everyday affairs. These ancestors are not gods, but because they play a key role in bringing about either good or ill fortune, maintaining good relations with them is pivotal, and they have to be appeased regularly by a variety of ritual offerings.

History

Many believe that humankind had its earliest origins in Africa. South Africa is rich in fossil evidence of the evolutionary history of the human family, going back several million years, from the discovery of the Taung child in 1924 to the latest discoveries of hominid fossils at the Sterkfontein caves (recently declared a World Heritage Site). South Africa has been at the forefront of palaeontological research into the origins of humanity. Modern humans have lived in the region for over 100,000 years. The Khoi and the San (the Hottentots and Bushmen of early European terminology), collectively known as the Khoisan and often thought of as distinct peoples, were the first people to roam the southern part of the African continent. Thereafter, other people arrived in South Africa.

The Early Inhabitants.   About 2,000 years ago, Bantu-speaking agro-pastorals began arriving in southern Africa, bringing with them an Iron Age culture and domesticated crops. These farmers spread out across the interior plateau and adopted a more extensive cattle culture. Chiefdoms arose based on control over cattle, which gave rise to patronage and, hence, hierarchies of authority within communities. At several archaeological sites, there is evidence of sophisticated political and material cultures, based in part on contact with the East African trading economy. These cultures, which were part of a broader African civilization, predate European encroachment by several centuries.

The Early Colonial Period.   European seafarers, who pioneered the sea route to India in the late 15th century, were regular visitors to the South African coast during the 1500s. In 1652, the Dutch East India Company set up a station in Table Bay (Cape Town) to service passing ships. Trading with the Khoi soon turned into raiding and warfare. Beginning in 1657, European settlers (French, Dutch, and Portuguese) were allotted farms by the colonial authorities in the arable regions around Cape Town. These settlers expanded northward from the 1830s on, and they provided a myth of the "empty land" which Whites employed to justify their domination over the subcontinent in the 20th century. They became known as *Afrikaner Boers.*

The British Colonial Era.   In 1795, the British occupied Cape Town as a strategic base, controlling the sea route to the East. The Cape Colony was integrated into the dynamic international trading empire of industrializing Britain. By the 1800s, the British brought in settlers and expanded their colonization across the rest of South Africa. During the Anglo-Boer War (1899–1902), British and Boer forces fought for supremacy of the land. The impact of this war has had a seminal influence in the development of Afrikaner nationalist politics. The Boer leaders played a dominant role in the country's politics for the next half of the century. The Union of South Africa came into existence in 1910.

Segregation and Apartheid.   Government policy in the Union of South Africa did not develop in isolation but against the backdrop of Black political initiatives. Segregation and apartheid assumed their shape, in part, as a response to the African's increasing participation in the country's economic life and their assertion to political rights. The African National Congress (ANC), founded in 1912, became the most important organization drawing together traditional authorities and the educated elite in common causes. In its early years, the ANC was concerned with constitutional protest. Worker militancy emerged in the wake of World War I and continued through the 1920s. In 1948, the National Party (NP), with its ideology of apartheid that brought an even more rigorous and authoritarian approach than the segregationist policies of previous governments, won the general election. In 1961, the NP government under Prime Minister Hendrik Verwoerd declared South Africa a republic, after winning a Whites-only referendum on the issue. It also withdrew from the British Commonwealth and a figurehead president replaced the queen as head of state. Racial categories were assigned to the people of South Africa. Under the architects of apartheid a theory of multinationalism was created. This was indeed a separate development wherein the South African population was divided into artificial ethnic nations, each with its own homeland and the prospect of independence. Forced removals from White areas affected some 3.5 million people, and vast rural slums were created in the homelands. Jobs were reserved for Whites only, and many Black people were denied the opportunity to progress in the work environment. The people of the homelands had to carry passbooks to migrate and travel to their work in the cities.

The End of Apartheid and the Birth of a Democratic South Africa.   Mass protests, acts of terrorism, and other forms of internal resistance and the employment of harsh sanctions by the United Nations eventually led to scrapping the pass laws in 1986, lifting the ban on liberation movements, and the release of political prisoners like Nelson Mandela in 1990. South Africa's first (in 1994) and second (in 1999) democratic elections saw the ANC emerge as the leading party. South Africa had a new democratic government and a new president in Nelson Mandela. In 1999, Thabo Mbeki succeeded Mandela. Freedom of movement and social mobility of people were guaranteed by the new government. South Africa indeed has had a very complex, and at times confusing, history.

Evolution and Definition of Public Relations as a Profession

Evolution

The evolution of public relations on the African continent, in general, and South Africa, in particular, goes back decades, if not centuries. The application of certain public relations techniques originated at the dawn of African civilization. In ancient Egypt the Pharaohs proclaimed their achievements through word-pictures on impressive monuments. According to Nartey (1988, p. 25), the concept of public relations was practiced in Africa long before the era of colonialism. He drew a parallel between the task of a public relations practitioner and that of a spokesman at the chief's seat of power in traditional South African villages. According to tradition, no African chief or elder statesman spoke directly to a visitor who called at the chief's seat of power. This, incidentally, is still the case in some remote and traditional rural areas of South Africa. All interactions and communication were channeled through a spokesman, a linguist, or an interpreter—sometimes this was one person. Individuals who were appointed to such offices were known to be well-versed in the customs and traditional practices of the village. Such individuals assumed eminent positions and were highly respected by the people. According to Nartey (1988), the concept of public relations also expressed in the African marital affairs such as arranged marriages and *lobola* (bride price)—the African equivalent of dowry, where the parents of the bridegroom would provide cattle (or other goods of commercial value) to the bride's family. At the initial stages and throughout the negotiations of a marriage contract, the go-between or the middle man plays a crucial role in the success of the union. Public relations is also expressed in the use of traditional music, dancing, and the beating of drums to communicate to the inhabitants of the traditional African village. Thus, the concept of public relations is neither alien nor a practice that arrived with colonialism, commercialization, or Western media imperialism. It has been around for centuries on the African continent—in a different format.

According to Lubbe (cited in Lubbe & Puth, 1994, p. 3), two major approaches can be taken when reviewing the historical development of public relations in South Africa. The first is a *systems approach* that illustrates the increasing scope of the practice of public relations in conjunction with the political, social, and economic development of the country. The second is a *structural approach* that depicts the professionalization of public relations in terms of the establishment of professional bodies in the public relations industry. The history of public relations development is well documented in the United States, Great Britain, and a few European countries, as mentioned in the introductory chapter. However, in South Africa, the development of public relations as part of the social and economic development, as well as its establishment as a fully fledged strategic management function in business and industry, has not yet been comprehensively documented and researched. The development of public relations in South Africa has also not been without international influence in terms of practice, research, education, and training—even terminological nomenclature. The phases of development from its initial phase of fundraising, publicity, and press agentry to its more sophisticated level of information dissemination and providing counsel to management coincide with the profession in the United States in particular.

The development of public relations in terms of its professionalization in South Africa, however, has been well documented since the establishment of the Public Relations Institute of Southern Africa (PRISA). The practice of public relations in South Africa is the most advanced compared with the other 14 countries in the southern African region where the profession is served by only a few practitioners, and the industry is growing in size (Rhodes & Baker, cited in Lubbe & Puth, 1994, p. 287).

Defining Public Relations

The PRISA has adopted the following definition of public relations: *"Public relations is the management, through communication, of perceptions and strategic relationships between an organisation and its internal and external stakeholders."* (Mersham, Rensburg, & Skinner 1995, p. 3) This definition emphasizes the fact that public relations should be a deliberate and intentional part of an organization's policy. It is a conscious effort to provide information and create goodwill. Public relations is designed to influence, gain understanding, propagate information, and ensure feedback from those affected by the organization's activities. Messages are tailored to reach identified target publics in accordance with a definite set of objectives (Mersham, Rensburg, & Skinner, 1995).

The definition offered by PRISA has been widely accepted in South Africa among public relations practitioners and scholars alike. It has merit and helps to explain the nature, role, and intention of public relations. However, Mersham et al. (1995, p. 12) contended that South Africa (as well as Africa) needs to continue to seek more substantial and theoretical insights into the place of public relations in the domain of communication science in a developing region. The authors also believed that insights are needed into how the design of communication models can assist in both the application and execution of effective public relations practice, particularly in the context of South Africa.

Status and Image of the Profession: the Search for Legitimacy Continues

In South Africa, much has been done in recent years to bring luster to a profession and academic field in search of legitimacy. Although public relations has undergone extensive change in terms of its activities and its growing importance in modern South African life, it suffers as a result of its unfortunate and pejorative past reputation. Public relations in South Africa may be described as being in a transitional phase. It tries to reconcile and situate its activities within the form of an ethical science. In doing so, it strives to adopt a broader, more humane social vision in which accountability to its stakeholders is given full importance. In spite of substantial changes in the focus and operation of public relations during the last 2 decades, the term public relations has been both misused and misunderstood since the early 1950s. It continues to be incorrectly associated with propaganda, press agentry, and manipulation, and it is often confused with advertising, marketing, and promotion. Practitioners are still suspected of disseminating incomplete, distorted, and biased information, and being the faceless image brokers and spin doctors for rich and powerful individuals, politicians, causes, and organizations.

During the past 2 decades, but particularly after 1994, strenuous efforts have been made by practitioners, academics, and PRISA to stress the scientific nature of the many activities public relations comprises (Cullingworth, 1990; De Beer, 1993; Mersham, 1993; Mersham et al., 1995; Nel, 1993).

The Professionalism of the Public Relations Industry in South Africa

South Africa is far more advanced than other African countries as far as PRISA is concerned. The overall impression is that in South Africa the practice of public relations is also relatively advanced, if not yet fully understood by clients and organizational leaders. But the industry faces a lot of competition from many disciplines that are infiltrating into areas that were traditionally considered to be the domain of the public relations practitioner. Management consultants, auditing firms, advertising agencies, and market research institutions now include the areas of communication consultation—compiling annual reports, product and service brochures, and entire social marketing campaigns and even conducting communication audits. International consultancies are entering the region, and the public relations industry in South Africa needs introspection and self-evaluation on a regular basis. Table A8.2 (see Appendix) shows the industry's current strengths and weaknesses (Rhodes & Baker, cited in Lubbe & Puth, 1994, p. 288).

PRISA started formally in Johannesburg in 1957, although public relations people had been talking about some kind of association for a number of years. The 23 founder members met at the University of the Witwatersrand (Johannesburg), and a chairman was elected. The progress of PRISA as an association is chronicled in Table A8.3 (see Appendix).

PRISA is the first and only public relations association in the world to obtain the International Standards Organization's 9002 certification. PRISA offers a career path for public relations practitioners and encourages skills development in line with the South African Skills Development Act (Act 97 of 1998, South Africa Yearbook 2001/02: 48). Students and practitioners can use PRISA's registration levels to plan their lifelong learning through a Continuing Professional Development Program. PRISA's registration levels can also be used to identify top-notch communicators who will add value to any organization's bottom line. The globally recognized accredited public relations practitioner (APR) is a well-qualified, widely experienced expert who operates at a strategic senior management level. Table A8.4 (see Appendix) states what PRISA strives for and what it offers its members.

The Public Relations Consultancy Chapter (PRCC) is made up of a voluntary committee with a chairman and office bearers. The PRCC's objectives are as follows:

- To unite consultants countrywide under the PRISA umbrella.
- To provide a forum for networking and professional development.
- To gain credibility for public relations consulting nationally.
- To professionalize the public relations consulting industry.
- To align the industry with the aims of development of the country.
- To foster links with allied industries and international consultants.

The PRCC's activities include the following:

- Organizing networking and professional development functions.
- Facilitating the employment and training of disadvantaged public relations practitioners in established consultancies.

- Lobbying and liaising with government.
- Publishing standard client–consultancy and employment contracts for members.
- Presenting the PRISM Award for outstanding public relations consultancy practice.

The public relations consultancies in South Africa and PRISM Award categories are shown in Tables A8.5 and A8.6 (see Appendix), respectively.

The Role of Universities and Colleges in Furthering the Public Relations Profession

Although communication science is offered in most of the large universities like the University of South Africa, the Rand Afrikaans University, and the universities of the Free State, Natal, Port Elizabeth, Potchefstroom, these universities have public relations as a specialization area in their communication science courses or as part of their marketing courses. However, the University of Pretoria is offering a degree course in communication management with a specific focus on public relations. Most of the colleges and technikons in the country offer diplomas, certificates, and courses in public relations. PRISA also has a student chapter for students studying public relations–the Public Relations Student's Chapter (PRSC). There is ongoing research into the national and global issues of public relations as a science and a profession, and a variety of scholars and students are scrutinizing the existing body of knowledge of public relations in a developing world.

Public Relations as Viewed by the Dominant Coalition in Organizations

The theory of public relations emphasizes that public relations is a management function aligned with all the other major functions of the organization such as marketing and financial management. The public relations or corporate communication department of an organization should ideally have a public relations manager or director with input in the formulation of corporate policy and strategy and decision-making authority. The subordinates and specialists in this department should be the technicians, providing technical and expert support in the implementation of public relations programs. In practice, however, the role and function of public relations is often seen only in terms of technical aspects and is relegated to a low status in the organizational structure (Lubbe, cited in Lubbe & Puth, 1994, p. 27).

In some organizations the status of the public relations practitioner or executive is low—reporting to the marketing director in the marketing department where public relations is still being viewed as part of publicity and promotion. The dominant coalition in organizations, notwithstanding numerous strategic sessions and research efforts by leading practitioners and scholars, still regards public relations practitioners as public relations or public affairs officers who are no more than salespeople, tourist guides, special events organizers, personal assistants, or front counter staff. Organizations in South Africa are mainly looking for technicians, not strategists. This stance should not be criticized too harshly by scholars and practitioners. After 1994 organizations are having to cope with cumbersome strategic plans and scenarios and are now looking for pragmatic implementation for these strategies. The technicians can deliver this implementation and produce tangibles. In research in progress, Steyn (2000) found that there is a significant degree of difference between chief executive officer's perceptions and their expectations of the public relations function and the role of public relations practitioners in organizations.

Public relations departments in South African organizations are called by a variety of names such as Corporate Communications, Public Affairs, Corporate Affairs, Public

Relations and Development, Corporate Communication, Marketing Services, and even lately Relationship Management. This is mainly an attempt to capture the essence of what concerns these departments. Note, however, that the term public relations is still the most acceptable and most often used term in this country; it encompasses all of the communication activities with which organizations are normally involved.

A current trend in many South African organizations, large and small, is to outsource the public relations functions and activities to consultancy firms. These organizations may not feel the necessity of having a fully fledged public relations department or even a full-time public relations practitioner. Consultants are called in when specific communication problems or needs arise.

PRISA, together with Research Surveys (a market research group in South Africa), conducted a survey of all corporate PRISA members in 1992, trying to determine, among other things, what they spent on public relations activities annually. The research showed a close correlation between the size of the organization and the amount it spends on public relations. What was and still is of concern, however, is that there are many large organizations in South Africa with frighteningly small public relations budgets (in comparison to the advertising budgets), a reflection of the lack of clout the industry had with management before 1994. This state of affairs, unfortunately, has not changed substantially since then.

Another part of the 1992 research dealt with where organizations rank public relations disciplines for the past 5 years and for the next 5 years. The results of this part of the research are reflected in Table A8.7 (see Appendix; Rhodes & Baker, cited in Lubbe & Puth, 1994, p. 287). Some of the other areas of importance to the future of South African organization are government communication and relations, political action relations, cause-related public relations, regulatory compliance, and risk management communication.

It becomes clear that the public relations industry in South Africa has its strengths and weaknesses. The strengths, however, are still limited. There are very few specialists and too many generalists in the industry. The industry will have to embark on an environmental scanning exercise to determine and take advantage of new opportunities that emerge from the changing environment. It will take some time to correct the poor image the industry has, and it will also take time to convince fully the dominant coalition in South African organizations of the merits and pivotal importance of public relations as a strategic management function.

INFRASTRUCTURE AND INTERNATIONAL PUBLIC RELATIONS

South Africa's Political System

As mentioned previously in this chapter, South Africa has a democratic political system since 1994 when the first all-inclusive elections took place that brought an end to the apartheid regime. These democratic elections have had wide-ranging effects on all South Africans. One of the most significant is that the extensive coverage of the elections by the world's media has underlined the importance of the global connectivity for ordinary people. This has introduced a wider set of global values, trends, and integrative movements than were possible during the apartheid years of isolation. During the 1994 elections, an estimated 5,000 international observers, representing nearly every country around the globe, were present in the country. Observer status was granted by the Independent Electoral Commission (IEC) to 77 international organizations, including the world's largest intergovernmental organizations—the European Union (EU), the United Nations

(UN), the Organization of African Unity, and the Commonwealth—and many other nongovernmental organizations. More than 1 billion rand (R) was allocated in 1994 to the IEC in support of its logistics to carry out a credible election. Public relations programs and voter education efforts were in abundance. The IEC allotted equal media space and time to all political parties in the elections. It was at this point that South Africa's reentry into a host of new global relationships was signaled for the first time (Mersham et al., 1995, p. 20).

This intense world interest, which elaborated and foregrounded the many components and positions of the global dialogue, was mirrored in the South African media and the daily conversations of all South Africans. The ANC—then under the leadership of Nelson Mandela—had a landslide victory, which was repeated in the follow-up elections of 1999. The ANC as a political institution is extremely strong and has been since its inception among many South Africans; it is backed by foreign countries where it operated when it was banned as a political movement (and labeled a *terrorist organization*) by the previous apartheid regime. There is political pluralism in South Africa and ample opportunities for the free expression of public opinion.

Public relations and democracy are not commonly aligned concepts. However, there are some fundamental links (cf. Hiebert, 1984). First, modern public relations can only function within the fundamental rights of freedom of expression and information. Everyone in a democracy should have the right to be heard. This includes the right to communicate on behalf of a cause, an organization, or an individual. This right is not restricted to the owners of newspapers and controllers of the electronic media or the government. Each individual, pressure or activist group, and institution has the right to seek and use public relations counsel and in most democracies do so. Second, public relations is indispensable in democracies with mass societies and mass communication. The various techniques of public relations were formed organically within the processes of urbanization, industrialization, and mass communication. Today these public relations techniques allow a wide spectrum of interest groups to state their messages in a variety of media in such a way that they have a chance to be heard (Mersham et al., 1995, p. 18). Third, public relations defined as an open communication process can only exist in democratic societies. From 1992 to 1994 and thereafter, the abundance of media conferences and releases by groups and movements previously banned by the state is proof of this. In African governments in which one party or one leader determines public policy, there can be no true role for public relations as we define it. The party or leader may use communication techniques as a form of propaganda or manipulation to keep the people in line, but there would be no room for professional practitioners to practice on behalf of those who wanted to challenge or criticize the status quo or propose different ideas, policies, and procedures. Clearly, these communication practices would be labeled subversive, unlawful, and undemocratic. In the new democratic South Africa this principle might ring true, but since 2000, our neighbor Zimbabwe has had other ideas regarding the right to freedom of expression and the role of open communication. In sharp contrast to South Africa's model and peaceful elections stand the 2002 controversial Zimbabwe elections that, unfortunately, continues to impact very negatively on South Africa and the other counties in the region. While writing this chapter, it became official news that, in spite of international pressure and criticism about the election procedure, Robert Mugabe and his Zimbabwe African National Union Patriotic Front (ZANU-PF) party have—questionably—won the elections. This debate, election, and its outcome are not new concepts in Africa where people are becoming used to the fact that politics is a business.

Fourth, public relations is linked to democracy because everyone has a right to articulate his or her version of the truth. There is no one truth because absolute truth exists only in a one-party, totalitarian state. Public relations as we define it exists in open societies where civil society, business, and government are amenable to freely expressed public opinion and the right to criticize existing and proposed policies. The vision of the Government Communication and Information System (GCIS) in South Africa is to make an indispensable and widely valued contribution to society, working with the government for a better life for all by meeting the government's communication needs and the public's information needs.

The GCIS is facilitating the establishment of Multi-purpose Community Centers (MPCCs) as programs for integrated one-stop government information and service points. This initiative is a partnership between all spheres of government, business, and civil society. By the end of March 2003, 60 of these MPCCs will be operating, at least one in each district or metropolitan council (GCIS, 2001/2002, p. 310). Public relations practitioners will play an increasingly important role in government communication.

South Africa's Level of Economic Development

South Africa has one of the most developed economies in Africa and is definitely the economic leader in the Southern African Development Community (SADC). The member states of SADC are Angola, Botswana, the Democratic Republic of the Congo, Lesotho, Malawi, Mauritius, Mozambique, Namibia, Seychelles, South Africa, Swaziland, Tanzania, Zambia, and Zimbabwe. The eyes of the world have been on South Africa since 1994 not only because of the historic unfolding of the democratic process and the peaceful transition but also because South Africa produces 40% of sub-Saharan Africa's gross domestic product and is viewed by many businesses as the gateway to Africa (Palframan, 1994, p. 1).

Blessed with a wealth of natural resources, the country contains wide disparities of wealth, with obvious implications for broader sociopolitical policy directions. Given its history of inequalities and its location, South Africa is a country whose fate is bound up with that of its neighbors. The recent upheaval caused by the 2002 elections in Zimbabwe and President Mbeki's stance of quiet diplomacy toward President Robert Mugabe have resulted in a drop in South African currency (the rand) to a level lower than it has ever been (nearly 10 rand to the American dollar, 10 rand to the Euro, and 16 rand to the British pound). There is also a resurgence of Afro-pessimism by the international community that South Africa might be taking the same route as Zimbabwe and other impoverished countries in Africa. A further challenge is to translate the positive economic conditions into levels of investment high enough to reduce the country's substantial unemployment level. Unemployment remains South Africa's most formidable challenge. *Statistics South Africa* announced in 2001 that the country's official unemployment rate stood at 26.4%. An increasing number of people are entering the labor market. This situation is exacerbated by a constant inflow of illegal aliens from Zimbabwe, Mozambique, and other poor countries in Africa.

Hundreds of international organizations, especially American companies, left the country during the sanctions era before 1994, but with South Africa's acceptance by the international community, many are returning and new companies are establishing themselves here because of the business potential that the country has to offer. They are still reluctant, however, to commit to tangible physical investment. Nearly everything business does is influenced by the government, which creates and enforces the rules by which business is conducted and determines the climate in which business must function (Sadie, cited in Lubbe & Puth, 1994, p. 250). The need for close relations with government is, therefore, evident. The business sector in South Africa is confronted with great future challenges.

There is currently an international campaign to market the New Partnership for Africa's Development (NEPAD). NEPAD's aim to confirm that African countries take responsibility for democracy, human rights, and rules of law and governance. The program was drafted by President Mbeki, Nigerian President Olusegan Obasanjo, and Algerian President Abdelaziz Bouteflika. The program entails moving away from the continent's broad reliance on loans and aid to self-sustaining development and advancement. Developed countries must respond with debt relief, market access to African imports, private investment flows, and increased development assistance.

However, President Mbeki's and Nigerian President Olusegun Obasanjo's recent backing of Robert Mugabe and their description of the elections in Zimbabwe as "free and fair" has tarnished relationships with the international community. South Africa was severely criticized for its stance in local and international media. Trying to save the situation, Mbeki and Obasanjo attempted to convince President Mugabe to avoid suspension from the commonwealth and to opt for a government of national unity, combining efforts with the opposition of Morgan Tsvangarai and his Movement for Democratic Change. This effort was to no avail, and the commonwealth, via its secretariat (a troika including Australian Prime Minister John Howard, President Mbeki, and President Obasanjo), decided to suspend Zimbabwe from the councils of the commonwealth for a period of 1 year effective immediately. The debate on whether sanctions against Zimbabwe will also be imposed continues.

On the macroeconomics side South Africa is a "model citizen" of the international community, which obviously serves the national interest of the country, and the Mbeki administration has delivered on this front. But South Africa fails to attract sufficient foreign direct investment, and the markets massively oversell its currency. Markets are anticipatory by their nature and are moved by perceptions. And it cannot serve the national interest when Mbeki accuses commonwealth countries of racism because they did not agree with him on Zimbabwe (Mulholland, cited in *Business Times*, 2002). This stance could damage his reputation and that of South Africa, put his plans for Africa's rejuvenation in jeopardy, and threaten the NEPAD dream. It reinforces the underlying fear that South Africa will follow the way of Zimbabwe, and international business is weary to directly invest.

South Africa's Legal Infrastructure

The Constitution of the Republic of South Africa (1996; Act 108 of 1996) is the supreme law of the country, and it binds all legislative, executive, and judicial organs of the state at all levels of government. In terms of the constitution, the judicial authority of South Africa is vested in the courts, which are independent and subject only to the constitution and the law. No person or organ of state may interfere with the functioning of the courts, and an order or decision of a court binds all organs of state and people to whom it applies. The Department of Justice and Constitutional Development is responsible for the administration of the courts and constitutional development (GCIS, 2001/2002, p. 365).

South Africa's constitution is one of the most progressive in the world, and it enjoys high acclaim internationally. The preamble of the constitution states that its aims are as follows:

- Heal the divisions of the past and establish a society based on democratic values, social justice, and fundamental human rights.

- Improve the quality of life of all citizens and free the potential of each person.

- Lay the foundations for a democratic and open society in which government is based on the will of the people and every citizen is equally protected by law.

- Build a united and democratic South Africa able to take its rightful place as a sovereign state in the family of nations.

The only apprehension one might have of the constitution is that it is extremely sophisticated, representing values of a developed society and in cases may run the risk of being in conflict with the traditional belief and value system of the majority of South Africans.

The independence of the judicial system in South Africa has been illustrated on many occasions, and it often rules against government at times. The government, and specifically President Mbeki, is backing the now well-publicized dissident's view (in conjunction with AIDS dissident David Rasnick) that there is no proof that HIV causes AIDS. This stance on HIV/AIDS has caused amazement and anger internationally and confusion locally. The government has also faced numerous court battles with multinational pharmaceutical companies. Supporting Mbeki's dissident AIDS theory, the Department of Health refused to make antiretrovirals available to pregnant mothers with HIV/AIDS. The High Court recently ruled in favor of South Africa's Treatment Action Campaign (TAC) and ordered that the drug nevirapine (viramune) be made available immediately and free of charge for the next 5 years to patients at those health facilities with the support structures to dispense the drug. The government has since appealed to the Constitutional Court, and this debate continuous.

The Promotion of Access to Information Act that came into operation in 2001 gives the right of access to information referred to in the constitution (GCIS, 2001/2002, p. 372). The act generally promotes transparency, accountability, and effective governance of all public and private bodies by, among other things, empowering and educating everyone to do the following:

- Understand their rights in terms of the act and exercise them in relation to private and public bodies.

- Understand the functions and operation of public bodies.

- Scrutinize and participate in decision-making by public bodies that affect their rights.

Although there are policies available for telecommunications, marketing, advertising, and government communication, there are no specific legal codes dealing with communication activities. There are, however, codes of conduct that all of these disciplines have to honor.

The Level of Activism in South Africa

For many years South Africa has been notorious for its apartheid regime. Until the 1940s, South Africa's race policies had not been entirely out of step with those in the colonial world. But by the 1950s, which saw decolonization and a global backlash against racism gathering pace, the state was dramatically opposed to world opinion on the question of human rights. The introduction of apartheid policies coincided with the adoption by the ANC in 1949 of the Program of Action, expressing overt militancy. The program rejected White domination and called for action in the form of protests, strikes, and demonstrations.

A decade of turbulent mass action and resistance to the imposition of still more harsh forms of segregation and oppression followed. South Africa was still the last bastion of White supremacy in Africa.

The Defiance Campaign of the early 1950s carried mass mobilization to new heights under the banner of nonviolent resistance to the pass laws. A critical step in the emergence of activism and antiracism was the formation of the Congress Alliance, including the Indian Congress, the Colored People's Congress, a small White congress (called the Congress of Democrats), and the South African Congress of Trade Unions. The Alliance gave formal expression to an emerging unity across racial and class lines that was manifested in the Defiance Campaign and other mass protests of this period—which also saw women's resistance take a more organized character with the formation of the Federation of South African Women.

The state's initial response was to prosecute more than 150 antiapartheid leaders for treason in a trial that began in 1956, but it ended in acquittals in 1961. Matters came to a head at Sharpeville in 1960 when 69 antipass demonstrators were killed. A state of emergency was imposed, and detention without trial was introduced. Black political organizations were banned, and their leaders went into exile or were arrested. Top leaders still inside the country, including members of the newly formed military wing *Umkhonto we Sizwe* (Spear of the Nation), were arrested in 1963 and tried in the Rivonia Trial. Nelson Mandela and other Black leaders were sentenced to life imprisonment.

The resurgence of resistance politics in the 1970s was dramatic. Armed action from beyond the borders abounded but was effectively contained by the state. A wave of strikes by Black labor unions reflected a new militancy that involved better organization and was drawing other sectors, particularly intellectuals and students, into the mass struggle against the state. The involvement of workers in the resistance took on a new dimension with the formation of the Congress of South African Trade Unions. In 1976 a sustained antiapartheid revolt arose by pupils in Soweto against the use of Afrikaans as the language of instruction in their schools.

From the mid-1980s, regional and national states of emergency were enforced. The Inkatha movement—stressing Zulu ethnicity and traditionalism—came into existence with a large following in the rural KwaZulu-Natal area. Battles for turf between the ANC and Inkatha became a very destructive accompaniment to South Africa's transition to democracy. The state embarked on a series of reforms, like scrapping the pass laws in 1986.

In the late 1980s and early 1990s, acts of terrorism occurred while the international community strengthened its support for the antiapartheid cause. A range of sanctions and boycotts was instituted, both unilaterally and through the United Nations. Faced with an untenable situation, the then-President FW de Klerk had no alternative but to release Nelson Mandela and others in 1990 and to unban the liberation movements—creating the environment for open political negotiations. These acts eventually led to the conception of the South Africa's new constitution (Constitution of the Republic of South Africa Act 108 of 1996, in South Africa yearbook, 2001/02, p. 299).

In 1994 the new democratic South Africa was born and many of the liberation and social movements—like the ANC—became political parties. The history of activism in South Africa before 1994 was mainly politically driven and had a moral high ground because of protests against unfair laws that warranted the causes.

There are a number of activist groups currently operating in the country—ranging from environmentalists, anticrime groups, antirape groups, antiabuse of women and children groups, to AIDS activists. In most cases, these activists have valid causes, and they usually address them through recognized channels, at times without valid response and action taken by government. These activist groups demonstrate in public, but they have to apply for permission to do so via procedural regulations. If their nonviolent resistance approaches are not met, these groups usually turn to legal action and the constitution. The AIDS activist group, TAC, recently had a victory in the High Court where they won the battle against the government's refusal to make antiretroviral drugs available to HIV/AIDS pregnant mothers. The activist groups in South Africa have strong and effective communication networks and make continuous efforts to get their story out—locally and internationally. People Against Gangsterism and Drugs (PAG) is a mainly Muslim activist group that argues that government is not doing enough formally to curb crime, violence, and drug abuse, and in the late 1990s this group turned to violent resistance themselves when they embarked on orchestrated acts of terrorism and vigilantism.

As shown in Table A8.8 (see Appendix), there are formalized and registered labor unions, members, employers' organizations, and bargaining councils in South Africa (Statistics South Africa, 2001).

Labor activism also manifests itself in the workplace. South Africa lost an estimated 1.4 million human days to strikes and stay-aways in 2000. According to labor research consultants Andrew Levy and Associates, 500,000 were lost to shop-floor strikes and 900,000 to stay-aways. The major strike trigger was wages. In 2000, the most active unions were the National Union of Mineworkers, the South African Transport and Allied Workers' Union, and the National Union of Metalworkers of South Africa (cited in GCIS, 2001/2002, p. 173).

Organizations have a variety of tools to handle activists, labor unions, and labor problems in general. Human Resources, Industrial Relations, and Corporate Communication Departments usually have mechanisms in place to deal with dispute resolution.

South Africa and the International Environment

Mersham et al. (1995, p. 10) suggested that South Africa and Africa stand poised to enter a positive new era if the people of the African continent are able to accept the value of learning from mistakes and successes of other countries in adapting to the emerging economic and political challenges of the global village while preserving its own unique identity. As trade barriers between nations are reduced, organizations and institutions have to compete in world markets and international arenas. Government too, is now competing on the world stage of international relations. Globally, we are experiencing a growing trend toward a common culture of agreement on a global civil society. South Africa's transition to democracy not only coincides with these major international developments but also stands as a symbol of global integration and reconciliation, the quest for the demise of Afro-pessimism, and the hope for Black renewal and economic realism on a continent marked by political and economic failure.

CULTURE AND PUBLIC RELATIONS IN SOUTH AFRICA

If there is one feature that characterizes South African society in the new millennium it is that of social change. Therefore, the trends and directions of the change process must be taken into consideration when examining public relations in South Africa. At the same time, there is one factor that underlies all social change—communication.

South Africa is extremely heterogeneous with an abundance of cultures and subcultures in the country. The melting pot concept that works well in countries like the United States, Canada, and Australia, however, cannot be transplanted into South Africa. Given the complexity of cultures and levels of development in South Africa, it also becomes evident that intercultural communication, an area with which the present generation of South African public relations practitioners is still largely unfamiliar, will increasingly require more attention as we move into the new millennium.

The complexity of the South African culture has never been fully understood by Western scholars. Culture and the debate about development, underdevelopment, and globalization walk hand-in-hand in South Africa. One can claim that every area of human and societal activity in its community, national, and international context is part of development. As Mowlana (1987, p. 4) put it: *"In short, development is everything and everything is development."*

Optimists view the recent changes in South Africa as the beginning of a new era of development for both South Africa and the countries of the African continent. One of the keys to this optimism lies in unlocking an effective synthesis of Western development policies with indigenous cultures and environments. South Africa is the perfect laboratory for development. It has survived political transition and is a good mixture of Third and First World, in terms of culture and infrastructure. A question arises: How far should South African cultures adapt to Western conceptions of economic and culturally determined ways of doing things? Conversely, how far can Western development models be adapted to South African cultures? Or can African culture afford to become a substitute for Western culture and ignore First World principles—thus entering into a cultural fight for superiority? Answers to such questions vary. Unfortunately, theoretical research on culture does not frequently investigate economic and political development practices. It is not uncommon to hear that a particular developmental project failed in the African context because it did not take the local culture into account (Mersham et al., 1995).

One of the best-known commentators on African culture, Kenyan political scientist Ali Mazrui, argued that both ideology and technology are rooted in culture and that differences in skills are "profoundly affected by culture" (1990, p. 2). He described traditional African society as "impressive when judged by standards of charity and solidarity (p. 3)" but slow in speed. Africa has "cultures of nostalgia rather than anticipation. (p. 5)" African cultures value prestige instead of achievement where "productivity and effectiveness are less than optimal" (p. 202). More critically, Mazrui stated that African rural culture is a "culture of poverty and indigence" (p. 203). Mersham et al. (1995) argued that Mazrui has perhaps misjudged the mood of African people. Africa has an exploding young population, increasingly exposed to the global worldview and hungrily demanding a second wave of change in political and development spheres (p. 25).

Daniel Etounga-Manguelle (1990, p. 72) spoke of the *principle lacunae* of African culture that *"explains our counter-performance in a world based on other values, including a lack of a critical culture, that is, as system of digestion and assimilation of new cultural events that permit popular culture to progress."* He proposed an African solution that is achieved through a "program of cultural adjustment" (p. 72) carried out by Africans, which would transform their worldview to one more consistent with the values of the developed world.

This idea is not far removed from conception of the African Renaissance. The term *African Renaissance* has been around in African political discourse since the colonial period. The Senegalese intellectual Chaik anta Diop first used the term in the context of the struggle against colonial rule, and it was meant to capture the dreams and aspirations of the people of Africa in their quest for self-determination (Cheru, 2001, p. 2). With the end of apartheid in 1994 and the resurgence of democratic ideals throughout Africa, President Mbeki resurrected the term as South Africa aspired to take a leading role in the economic and political transformation of the African continent. But in Africa many of these plans remain merely as rhetoric. The unfortunate result is that rhetoric (communication) and realities no longer coincide, and Africans fail to face up to the need to become something new while remaining authentically African. For the Africa of the 21st century to succeed, Kabou (1991) stated that it must become rational and pragmatic. Underdevelopment is not a matter only of capital or resources, but it originates "inside the heads of Africans." (p. 61) Boon (1998, p. 61) wrote extensively about tribalism and ethnicity and stated that tribalism exists in the present not only in distant rural areas but also in peoples hearts. Boon suggested that people retreat into ethnicity when they are most threatened. Communities then form communication so that they could get the tribe's perspective on the threat posed by massive change. It becomes difficult to adapt and acculturate.

In South Africa, there remains a deep discord between cultural preservationists and developmentalists on cultural preservation. Those in favor of cultural preservation argue that such a transition should not undermine the fundamental value systems of Black society. In Afrikaner circles the same arguments are heard with regard to the preservation of White Afrikaner culture and the Afrikaans language.

Since 1994, there has been greater social mobility in South Africa and South African organizations, but organizational communication continues to be affected by continuing uncertainty and intolerance in the workplace. Although South Africa is largely a paternalistic society, much has been done to preserve rights of women—particularly in the workplace. South Africa is a country with a strong collectivistic approach. This often leads to conflicts when individual performance is at stake. There is also a lack of interpersonal trust within organizational settings. White workers find the issue of affirmative action difficult to overcome. Nowadays, most organizations in South Africa encourage input by individual workers, and dissent is tolerated when it is not detrimental to the health of the organization. A bottom-up approach instead of a top-down network organization is encouraged—but with mixed results.

Turnbull (1994, p. 12) stated that "the job of the public relations practitioner is to shape the perception, that is, to the world, the reality. And it is that which makes public relations not only the first post-modernist profession but an activity of enormous significance in our culture." Questions concerning global culture, acculturation, media imperialism, the resurgence of cultural and religious conflict, and intercultural communication will increasingly occupy the minds of public relations scholars and practitioners in South Africa in the future. Given the centrality of the public relations practice to development concerns and its pivotal role in organizations in South Africa, it will be essential for the practitioner to grasp the issues involved, irrespective of his or her own cultural orientation or worldview.

A most pressing challenge that public relations practitioners will encounter is to find ways of balancing the traditional cultures of South Africa with Western, colonial influences that have influenced the lifestyle of South Africans but have also had an impact in the workplace. There is an inherent distrust in the broad traditional South African community toward organizations fed by a colonial past and the multinationals. This is a very difficult issue for practitioners to contend with, but the heterogeneous make-up of South Africa will have to be managed in the future.

THE MEDIA AND PUBLIC RELATIONS

Media Control

According to the Bill of Rights of South Africa's Constitution (Act 108 of 1996, South African yearbook, 2001/02, p. 299), everyone has the right to freedom of expression, which includes the following:

- Freedom of the press and other media.
- Freedom to receive or impart information or ideas.
- Freedom of artistic creativity.
- Academic freedom and freedom of scientific research.

Several laws, policies, and organizations act to protect and promote the freedom of the media in South Africa. Press Freedom Day is celebrated on October 19. South Africa now has one of the most effective media systems in the world vis-à-vis freedom of expression. Technical and editorial handling of the print media in South Africa rate among the best in the world, as is advanced broadcasting technology. The Broadcasting Act of 1999 (Act 4 of 1999, in South Africa yearbook 2001/02, p. 121–122) is aimed at developing a broadcasting policy to regulate and control broadcasting to, among other things:

- Contribute to democracy, nation building, the provision of education, and the moral fiber of society.
- Encourage ownership and control of broadcasting services by people from historically disadvantaged communities.
- Ensure fair competition in the sector.
- Provide for a three-tier system of public, commercial, and community broadcasting systems.
- Establish a strong and committed public broadcaster to service the needs of all South Africans.

Several organizations and associations play an important role in maintaining the strength of media. The South African National Editors' Forum (SANEF) was conceived at a meeting of the Black Editors Forum, the Conference of Editors, and senior journalism educators and trainers in 1996. SANEF has facilitated the mobilization of the media in the Partnership Against AIDS campaign and in campaigns to end violence against women and children. At a workshop held at the end of 2001, SANEF members and the government agreed that thorough discussion and analysis were needed to improve relations and reach mutual understanding about the roles and functions of the media and the government in a changing society.

Media diversity in any country is a sign of the level of its democracy. South Africa is on its way to achieving as much diversity as possible. The airwaves were deregulated in 2001, but the print media need to catch up as the monopolistic trend in the ownership of publications in the industry continues.

Media Outreach

Because of the very high level of extreme poverty and illiteracy in South Africa, important messages cannot be diffused to all target publics. Radio is still the medium that reaches publics in the rural areas of South Africa, and print media are available to all in the urban areas. In squatter areas, where electricity is available, people can be reached by electronic media. However, media outreach and access are still closely linked to the levels of development in South Africa.

Van Zyl and Tomaselli (1977), Marchant (1988), Tomaselli (1989), Louw (1989), Kaplan (1990), Morris and Stavrou (1991), Mersham (1992, 1993), and Hooyberg and Mersham (1993), among others, argued for the use of the best satellite technology for development purposes in Africa. Satellite communication can provide the foundation for a cost-effective and more beneficial communication infrastructure for southern Africa. Cellular telephony has the potential to become the great connecter of the people of South Africa—provided that with the eradication of poverty and the culture of non-payment for essential services can be addressed.

After 2 years of intense research, negotiations, and tests, the taxi advertising agency ComutaNet announced in 2002 that, under the auspices of Rank TV, it will present big screen television programs at 10 of the busiest taxi ranks (Cab's parking zones) of South Africa (Sake-Beeld, Thursday, 14 March, 2002). ComutaNet will reach approximately 1.2 million economically active South Africans on a daily basis. With taxis being the favorite form of transportation for about 78% of commuters in South Africa, this new communication medium could become an excellent advertising and public relations vehicle.

Media Access

All South Africans, rich and poor, have access to mass media, notwithstanding their location. At the workplace, it is almost impossible for employees not to be reached by controlled and uncontrolled media of all kinds. In 1997, the office of the Ombudsman was opened in Johannesburg. Members of the public who have complaints about reports in the media can submit their grievances to the Ombudsman. The National Community Media Forum is a network that coordinates and represents the interests of community media initiatives from marginalized communities. The Freedom of Expression Institute was formed in 1994 and had as objective the campaigning for freedom of expression during the apartheid years (GCIS, 2001/2002, p. 130).

Activist groups have direct access to the media, and their causes are often taken up and supported by the mass media in the country. For example, no single day passes without media coverage on the crime levels, the farm murders, the rape of women and children, and the issue of AIDS. The control of the news media by news editors in their gatekeeping role is sometimes criticized but also necessary because of the perceived value of a story and the limitations of time and space. A major influence on the choices made by gatekeepers is the policy and ideology of the particular media organization. Factual information can become distorted. Legal legislation and ethics also influence the choices made by media organizations (Mersham & Skinner, 1999, p. 174). But various editorial columns as well as letters to editors are published to keep controversial debates going—like the HIV/AIDS debate. The openness of debates, particularly in the newspapers, is extraordinary.

There are ways of reaching and communicating specifically to rural publics, which consist of local tribes of mixed ethnic groups with different languages and dialects. Some of these publics might live in remote places and may be beyond the reach of the mainstream mass communication media, and they may pay little attention to radio beyond listening to music. They may also be uninterested in the affairs of the world or the cities and show little interest in news bulletins. There have been numerous arguments for or against the utilization of *oramedia, unconventional,* or *folk media* (media based on the indigenous culture produced and consumed by members of a group). The fact is that utilizing folk media still might be useful in the African environment. Unlike mass media, which reach many people at a time but only have cognitive influence (knowledge, awareness, and interest), unconventional media may only reach a few people at a time but can be an effective relay chain to the mass communication media. These media have visible cultural features by which social relationships and a worldview are maintained and defined. They take many forms and are rich in symbolism. These media must be seen as interpersonal or group media speaking to common people in their own language, in their own idiom, and dealing with problems of direct relevance to the situation (Jefkins & Ugboajah, 1986, p. 33). In South Africa, this device has been used adequately lately to promote all kinds of public relations messages and programs, from family planning to efficient farming, primary health care, adult literacy, and the continuous fight against AIDS. There is a wide variety of these media, but some include puppet shows, village gossip, development, improvisation and industrial theater, oratory, poetry and music, praise singing, weddings, funerals, and political rallies.

Although it is widely assumed that remarkable developments in communication technologies automatically improve communication, unfortunately this is not necessarily true for South Africa. We need to monitor continuously what we are communicating and why. In South Africa education about the interpretation of media content will be just as important as the format in which the publics receive communication messages.

Where would these arguments about media access leave South African public relations practitioners? The product and service scope of public relations in South Africa is broad and expanding fast. The time of the traditional professional who believed that maintaining personal influence with the media and the ability to turn out a readable press release would suffice is over. Today, the profession, like other management disciplines, has to have both specialists and generalists, and it should be able to advise on internal and external communication challenges (Rhodes & Baker, cited in Puth & Lubbe, 1994, p. 287). Lobbying, community networking, industrial theater, the innovative use of the visual medium, and social marketing are all realities with which South African public relations practitioners have to come to terms and use effectively in their changing environment. However, mass media remain important channels and important target publics relations practitioners.

ETHICS AND PUBLIC RELATIONS IN SOUTH AFRICA

Worldviews are powerful, and many public relations practitioners are not always aware of the power that they hold over their behavior and outlook. Grunig (1992, p. 38) contended that public relations should be based on a worldview that incorporates ethics into the process, rather than debating the ethics of its outcomes. Pearson (1989) developed an extensive theory of public relations ethics based largely on the theories of the philosopher Habermas (1984). Pearson (1989, p. 315) argued that the profession needed an approach to ethics that combines "moral conviction and tolerance." When people disagree about what is moral, they debate and attempt to persuade one another.

Ethical public relations practitioners must be totally committed to communicating truthfully. However, in attempting to serve clients or management practitioners, avoid taking extreme positions. They will not mount a communication effort to promote the position of a client or organization that—even if, in some sense, literally truthful—will seriously and wrongly compromise or otherwise be injurious to the legitimate concerns and rights of significant third parties (Martinsan, 2000). This is an excellent ideal but difficult to practice in Africa where hired guns are frequently at work. A recent example is President's Robert Mugabe's efforts to fight against the imposition of possible sanctions against Zimbabwe by the international community. He lobbied the international community against the sanctions by involving his ambassadors to the UN, Washington, DC, and the EU. They talked to American congressmen and the Congressional Black Caucus to try to reject the Zimbabwe Bill. Zimbabwe's representatives in the US lobbied African diplomats based in Washington, DC to oppose the bill, while former American ambassador to the UN Andrew Young and the public relations firm Cohen & Woods International were enlisted by the government to fight impending sanctions. However critical we may be of this situation, Andrew Young and the public relations firm merely provided a specialist service to a client and cannot be associated with the ethical implications of the situation. As proposed in this book, public relations ethics in developing countries is one of the many areas of the field that needs more research.

PRISA has a code of conduct to which all practitioners and consultants should adhere. Table A8.9 (see Appendix) describes the code in detail.

SOUTH AFRICAN PUBLIC RELATIONS CASE STUDY

Park Station Partnership Against HIV/AIDS

This campaign won the PRISM Award for the best campaign of 1999. It was submitted by Ad-Uppe Public Relations on behalf of Intersite and the South African Rail Commuter Corporation (SARCC).

Background

The campaign was a full day AIDS-awareness event held at Park Station, Johannesburg, on World AIDS Day, December 1, 1999. It was based on the success of a similar event at Pretoria Station 1 year before, which was also under the management of Ad-Uppe Public Relations and spearheaded by two of the consultancy's major clients, Intersite Property Management Services and its holding company, SARCC. Both companies are agencies of the Department of Transport, functioning as the owners and managers of metropolitan stations in South Africa.

To achieve maximum impact with limited budgets, Intersite, SARCC, and Ad-Uppe Public Relations invited participation from other parties in a joint venture partnership. The ultimate outcome was the Park Station Partnership Against HIV/AIDS, which was made up of the following:

- Intersite (head office, Northern and Southern Gauteng Regions) (participant and sponsor).
- Gauteng Provincial Government (participant and sponsor).
- Spoornet (participant and sponsor).
- Industrial Development Corporation (sponsorship only).
- Metrorail (participant and minor sponsor).
- LoveLife program (participant only).

Following the previous Minister of Transport's support of the fight against HIV/AIDS and considering that the country's roads and railways are fast spreading the pandemic, the project had the full support of the Department of Transport and Minister Dullah Omar hosted the event.

Objectives and Target Publics

The main objective of the event was to make as many people as possible HIV/AIDS aware. The intended message was twofold: (a) to prevent the spread of HIV/AIDS and to (b) care for those with HIV/AIDS. The target publics of the message were commuters, with specific emphasis on the youth. Hence, Park Station was used because 300,000 people pass through the station each day.

Challenges and Obstacles Overcome

As with any state-driven project, there were budget limitations, and the proposed budget had to be tailored from over R 500,000 to R 330,000. When a final decision to go ahead was made 2 weeks prior to the event, only two thirds of the required budget was guaranteed. However, additional sponsorships were obtained, and costs were tailored accordingly. Ad-Uppe Public Relations donated around R 10,000 worth of time.

On the day of the event there were the usual problems as ministers changed their plans, artists arrived late, and so on. All problems were handled smoothly without the crowd's awareness. The biggest challenge of the project was streamlining the needs, wants, and aspirations of the various organizations and individuals involved. Planning meetings often became heated and, as always, a number of members did not deliver as promised. In all cases, Ad-Uppe Public Relations managed to find solutions to these problems and appease almost everyone.

Strategy

The strategy on the day of the event was to make use of the cross-cultural medium of popular music and celebrities to draw a large crowd and deliver the HIV/AIDS message. People living with HIV gave testimonials to make hard-hitting statements of how real the disease is and how people with AIDS are still people that have to live their lives.

Program Execution and Activities Deployed

Prepublicity. A theme was designed and branded posters, banners, and flyers were displayed and distributed at all major Gauteng stations. A prepublicity media release was issued 2 weeks prior to the event, and invitations were delivered to preferred guests identified by the members of the partnership. These included the entire cabinet as well as provincial and local dignitaries and various industry leaders (potential sponsors for future events).

The Event on Stage. A stage and sound system were set up on the main concourse of Park Station and a full day (from 6:00 a.m. to 6:00 p.m.) program of guests appeared. The day was divided into four sessions:

- Session 1 (from 6:00 a.m. to 10:00 p.m.) featured community disk jockey's (DJ's) young singer Letoya Makhene as master of ceremony (MC) and popular, yet relatively low-key bands.

- Session 2 (from 10:00 a.m. to 1:00 p.m.) was hosted by radio DJ Grant Shakoane. Popular bands attracted a large crowd before Minister Dullah Omar and other guest speakers addressed them. A commemorative candle was lit and 1,600 red balloons were released—one for every new case of HIV reported daily in South Africa.

- Session 3 (from 1:00 p.m. to 4:00 p.m.) included MC Bob Mabena and established music stars performing and addressing the crowd while the preferred guests enjoyed lunch.
- Session 4 (from 4:00 p.m. to 6:00 p.m.) had a very upbeat vibe with popular artists and television stars driving home the message and taking care of the homeward bound commuter traffic.

The Event on the Station.   A team of 200 volunteers, under the guidance of the Gauteng Department of Health, distributed condoms, stickers, and information flyers to commuters on the main concourse thruout the entire day. From 6:00 a.m. til 8:00 a.m., local MECs circulated among the commuter rush, speaking to the people and handing out material. A preferred guest area was set up on the mezzanine level above the concourse, and drinks and a light lunch were served to invited guests. Guests began arriving at 11:00 a.m.

LoveLife used the event to launch their Love Train, which they had parked on one of the station platforms. Preferred guests and others signed their pledges to the fight against HIV/AIDS on the train.

Budget

As already discussed, the budget for the project was extremely limited, and costs had to be kept to a minimum. Sound and stage equipment cost approximately R 80,000; artists' fees were R 65,000; catering for VIPs and workers cost R 38,000; the venue cost R 80,000 (mostly donated by Intersite); visual material were R 31,000, and event management cost R 30,000 (additional time was paid for by Intersite and donated by Ad-Uppe Public Relations). The total budget for the event was R 316,000.

Outcome

The event was a resounding success. All sponsors were satisfied, and the day went off with very few problems. During the lunch hour, an estimated 30,000 people were gathered around the stage. Although a *City Press* article damned the use of music on World AIDS Day, Ad-Uppe Public Relations found it an effective means of reaching a large number of people. The venue was perfect; although there were a lot of hidden logistics behind securing cabinet ministers and controlling large crowds, everything ran smoothly. There was substantial media coverage, both electronic and print (including eTV and SABC1 and SABC 2 news) despite the large number of other initiatives on the same day.

Hundreds of thousands of people heard the message and received background information and condoms to take home with them—which also reached an unquantifiable number of other people. In addition, valuable lessons were learned and contacts made for an even better campaign for 2000. Add-Uppe Public Relations is sure that the Park Station Partnership Against HIV/AIDS made a valuable contribution to the raising of awareness about HIV/AIDS among the people of Gauteng.

CONCLUSION

In this chapter I provided a synopsis of the state of affairs with regard to the evolution of public relations as a profession in South Africa. I also attempted to emphasize the heterogeneous cultural ingredients of South Africa as a country and indicated the level of complexity that public relations practitioners have to confront when operating in a developing world.

APPENDIX

TABLE A.8.1
The Provinces (Statistics South Africa 2001)

Province	Capital	Languages	Population	Area (Square km)	% of Total Area	GGP (1994)	% of Total GDP
Western Cape	Cape Town	Afrikaans English isiXhosa	4.2 million	129,386	10.6%	R81,800 m	14.21%
Eastern Cape	Bisho	isiXhosa Afrikaans English	6.8 million	169,580	13.9%	R29,049 m	7.59%
KwaZulu-Natal	Pietermaritzburg Ulundi (joint)	isiZulu English Afrikaans	9 million	92,100	7.6%	R57,007 m	14.90%
Northern Cape	Kimberley	Afrikaans Setswana isiXhosa	0.873 million	361,830	29.7%	R8,000 m	2.09%
Free State	Bloemfontein	Sesotho Afrikaans isiXhosa	2.790 million	129,480	10.6%	R23,688 m	6.19%
North-West	Mafikeng	Setswana Afrikaans isiXhosa	3.567 million	116,320	9.5%	R21,252 m	5.56%
Gauteng	Pretoria	isiZulu Afrikaans English	7.87 million	17,010	1.4%	R144,359 m	37.73%
Mpumalanga	Nelspruit	isiSwati isiZulu isiNdebele	3 million	79,490	6.5%	R31,175 m	8.15%
(Limpopo)	Polokwane	Sepedi Xitsonga Tshivenda	5.5 million	123,910	10.2%	R14,158 m	3.7%

Note. From Statistics South Africa (2001).

TABLE A.8.2
Industry Strength and Weaknesses

Strengths	Weaknesses
Some in-depth skills	Poor standards
Diversity of skills	Lack of accountability
Flexibility	Low expectations
Can take pressure	Instability
Recognition is growing	Negative image

Note. (Rhodes & Baker, cited in Lubbe & Puth, 1994, p. 288).

TABLE A.8.3

Milestones in the Evolution of Public Relations as a Profession in South Africa

Time	Milestone
1957	Birth of PRISA with 23 founder members.
	First meeting in Johannesburg and PRISA recognized by IPRA (International Public Relation Association).
1958	First PRISA training course for 49 public relations people. First member newsletter.
1959	First PRISA training committee formed. KwaZulu-Natal region formed.
1960	First PRISA library established.
1962	First public relations booklet printed: *Does Your Bark Bite Your Business?* (Members stand at 71.)
1964	The launch of PRISA's comprehensive education and training program in Johannesburg for 50 students. Immediate examination written in Durban and Cape Town. Pretoria region formed. PRISA registered with the Department of Heraldry. Johannesburg region to be called Southern Transvaal.
1965	Fifty students take the PRISA Intermediate Course and 18 pass. First South African public relations handbook written by Malan and L'Estrange. First South African Public Relations Convention in Johannesburg with 100 delegates. Northern Transvaal region established. (Members stand at 150.)
1966	Eighty students started the Intermediate Public Relations Course, 32 wrote the examination, and 18 passed. Western Cape region formed with seven members.
1967	Decision to establish university Communication courses. An Education and Training Committee appointed. Eastern Cape region established.
1968	Committee on Communication formed with Education subcommittee. Communication courses are instituted at universities. First career pamphlet, *Public Relations as a Career*, Johannesburg PRISA is developed. First seven students write the PRISA's Final Certificate examination. First public relations course offered by the Witwatersrand Technical College. First PRISA Gold Medal awarded to Professor Chris Barnard (first heart transplant surgeon). Advisory committee on public relations research established.
1970	First trophy for house journals awarded. Launch of *Communika* (PRISA's official newsletter). Survey undertaken on the status of the public relations profession. (Members stand on 250.)
1971	The University of South Africa starts the first distance education communication courses and enrolls 300 students for the first year. Southern African Association of Industrial Editors (SAAIE) formed. PRISA Code of Conduct published.
1972	The Constitution is revived. Membership tops 300. Inaugural meeting of the Central region.
1973	The University of the Orange Free State starts the Communication degree courses in the new Department of Communication. PRISA's first Communicator of the Year Award.
1974	PRISA opens its first permanent office. Association of Municipal Public Relations Officers started. Presidential chain of office donated.
1975	SAAIE breaks away from the PRISA. First all-Africa public relations conference with Public Relations Society of Kenya and IPRA. Theme: *Communicating With the Third World.* (members stand at 450.)
1976	PRISA Code of Conduct accepted by members. PRISA welcomes its first Black members. Television documentary, *The Image Makers*, on public relations as a career.
1977	PRISA celebrates the first 20 years. The Consultant's Association formed.

(Continued)

TABLE A.8.3
(Continued)

Time	Milestone
1978	PRISA introduces student membership. The National Council produces the first written development plan for PRISA that now has 339 members.
1979	New PRISA logo and membership certificate designed. PRISA survey held on members' needs—100 responses. New Code of Conduct accepted.
1980	Membership increases to 543.
1981	PRISA publishes the *Body of Knowledge* document and all tertiary institutions decide that PRISA should be the examining body for public relations courses.
1982	*Handbook of Public Relations* written by Skinner and von Essen appears. Vaal region established. (Skinner, C & Van Essen (1982))
1985	Public Relations Council of South Africa (PRCSA) is inaugurated.
1986	Launch of Public Relations Council logo. First public relations practitioners accredited. *Communika* wins first prize in the SAAIE house journal competition. In December PRISA signs up its 1,000 member. Management Committee appointed to help run the PRISA.
1987	Official course in the Principles of Public Relations rewritten to meet the needs of the changing market. National Education Committee is reestablished. PRISA is 30 and aims to increase membership and improve services to members. (It now has 1200 members.)
1988	First national education officer appointed. Name returns to the 1957 original. Eighth region—Bophuthatswana formed. PRISA regional assistance program introduced—centralizing mailing and newsletters. PRISA Advanced Principles of Public Relations course designed and presented at main centers. PRISA Basic Principles course packaged and licensed to colleges. (PRISA now has 1,400 members.)
1989	First Head of Education appointed. First strategic planning conference and Education Indaba held. PRISA Professional Development Program was one result. PRISA's Mission Statement published. (It now has 2,000 members.) (Margaret Moscardi)
1991	Academic Conference established at the Pretoria Congress. PRISA is represented at the World Congress in Canada. Transkei region formed. New corporate identity launched for PRISA. Public Relations Consultants' Association closed.
1992	The PRISA Council becomes the accreditation and Ethics Council. First PRISA Management Course implemented.
1993	First academic receives the Educator of the Year Award. The Public Relations Council becomes part of the PRISA. PRISA hosts the first International Public Relations Association (IPRA) congress in South Africa, Cape Town.
1994	The Examination Board (now committee) established. PRISA boasts its first woman president. PRISA embarks on its image campaign. Forty five candidates pass the APR examinations. A new textbook, *Public Relations in South Africa: A Management Reader* (edited by Puth & Lubbe) appears on the shelves. (Isando SA: Heinemann 1994)
1995	Three new courses implemented. PRISA introduces corporate membership. PRISA Consultants' Chapter formed. Another public relations textbook, *Public Relations, Development and Social Investment: A Southern African Perspective* (Mersham et al., 1995) appears.

(Continued)

TABLE A.8.3

(Continued)

Time	Milestone
1996	PRISA Education Directorate becomes PRISA Education Center with its own constitution. Community Relations and Development Course implemented. Namibia region formally inaugurated.
1997	The 3-year diploma in Public Relations is implemented. The infrastructure in the PRISA offices is expanded. PRISA is 40 years old.
1998–2002	PRISA grows in stature with now more than 4,000 members (by January 2002, PRISA had 3,430 student members and 1,300 practitioners). The association moves even closer to the academic institutions when, in 1999, for the first time an academic delivers the keynote address at the annual PRISA Conference on Strategic Scenario Planning for the New Millennium. New and revised relations handbooks by Skinner, Von Essen and Mersham appear. The PRISA Education and Training Center is involved in education and training standards generating bodies and the Skills Development Act structures. The Registration of PRISA Education and Training Center as a Higher Education Institution is formed in 2001. PRISA becomes a founder member of the Global Alliance of Public Relations and Communication Management Associations in 2000. PRISA hosts the Global Alliance annual meeting in South Africa in March 2002.

Note: From *PRISA milestones*, by M. Moscardi, 2002, Johannesburg, South Africa: Director of PRISA. Reprinted with permission by Margaret Moscardi (Executive Director: PRISA).

TABLE A.8.4

Vision and Objectives of PRISA

PRISA's vision: Recognition of the public relations profession, PRISA and its members as key role players in Southern Africa and beyond.
PRISA's mission:
- To establish PRISA as the authority for the public relations profession.
- To foster the professionalization of public relations and communication management in Southern Africa.
- To set and maintain professional ethics and standards among members of the institute.
- To provide dynamic value-added services to members of the institute and thereby to its stakeholders.
- To establish public relations as a strategic management function.
- To continually transform the institute to stay ahead of the dynamic changes in the social, political, and economic environment.
PRISA's objectives:
- To promote a general understanding of public relations and communication management and of the value of its practice and to establish and maintain professional status and dignity for public relations practice among registered members of PRISA, employers and the general public.
- To encourage the observance of the highest standards of professional conduct by registered members of PRISA through adherence to the PRISA Code of Professional Standards for the Practice of Public Relations.
- To protect the interests of all concerned in the event of any complaint of malpractice or nonadherence to the PRISA Code of Professional Standards for the Practice of Public Relations being brought against a registered member through the application of a set of disciplinary procedures.

(Continued)

TABLE A.8.4
(Continued)

<u>PRISA's values</u>: PRISA is continually transformed to meet the needs and challenges of the next millennium by undertaking tasks that are measurable, monitored, performed to time and quality standards, and add value to all stakeholders.

PRISA will implement leadership that is representative of South Africa, accountable and responsible, professional and informed, and visionary.

These (tasks and leadership) will encourage a culture that is professional, adaptable, liberating, open/transparent, empowering, consultative/decisive, value centered, and dynamic.

<u>PRISA's services</u>: The primary role is to represent the profession of public relations and communication management and enhance the status of practitioners. The benefits of this work are enjoyed by all those who practice public relations. But there is also a wide range of services that are provided specifically as a benefit to individual members:

<u>PR hotline</u>	<u>International contacts</u>
Professional advice is available to registered practitioners–either from the national office or through the national executive.	Contact with overseas associations and practitioners is maintained at PRISA and benefits all members.
<u>Consultancy referral system</u>	<u>Networking</u>
PRISA operates a referral system to help members of its Consultancy Chapter. Prospective clients are given a selection of names to approach according to their areas of specialization.	The single most important reason for belonging to a professional body is networking, keeping in touch, business opportunities and professional development.
<u>PR job grapevine</u>	<u>CPD information</u>
This informal job grapevine operates as a contact point between prospective employers and members.	PRISA is the best source of professional development opportunities through its expanded and varied program of seminars and workshops—on a national and regional level.
<u>Accreditation</u>	<u>Regional activities</u>
PRISA offers members the opportunity of obtaining the globally recognized APR certification	Regional networking and professional development programs are offered for members' benefit.

<u>Discounts</u>
Members and students receive substantial discounts.

<u>PRISA's Membership</u>: Research has shown that one of the most important reasons for joining is networking with peers, sharing and gaining knowledge, and benchmarking practitioners against best practice. Registration with PRISA provides the added advantage of gaining a professional status, as well as the globally recognized APR registration, and gives access to all services at substantial discounts. PRISA will assist members in gaining certification from the Services Seta when this process is in place. There are different categories of registration:
- Individual registration—from affiliate to APR.
- Corporate support—organizations or departments with more than five employees.
- Chapters: Student Chapter for individuals studying public relations and a Consultancy Chapter (PRCC).

(Continued)

TABLE A.8.4

(Continued)

PRISA's continuing professional development (CPD): CPD is a global trend and professions around the world have been developing and implementing methods for lifelong learning—at the same time giving senior professionals a formal method of gaining CPD points by contributing their expertise. In essence CPD is a way in which seniors give to and develop the young professional and the young professionals take from seniors and develop themselves. Thus, the profession grows globally, and the status of both the practitioner and the profession is enhanced and its value is firmly established. CPD points will be earned through any or all of these activities:

- Formal further education, completion of formal qualifications.
- Attendance at identified seminars, workshops, and conferences.
- Courses such as time management, and negotiation, and so on.
- Mentoring and coaching.
- Participation in industry and professional bodies.
- Contribution to the body of knowledge, through presentations, the publication of articles, and so on.

PRISA's CPD point system is being finalized now and will become the benchmark for the profession in Southern Africa. It is based on the experience of the IPR in the UK, Public Relations Institute of Australia (PRIA) in Australia, and the Public Relations Society of America (PRSA) in the USA. It follows the guidelines given by the South African Services Seta.

PRISA's awards:

- Vision award: This is an award for developing Black public relations practitioners. It is sponsored by Baird's and Edelmans Worldwide and administered by PRISA.
- President's award: This award is made at the sole discretion of the President of PRISA and is in recognition of outstanding service to PRISA.
- PRISM award for outstanding public relations practice: The Financial Mail PRISM Award is presented to public relations professionals who have successfully blended flair, creativity, and professionalism into public relations programs and strategies that showcase a successful public relations campaign. Presented by the PRCC and supported by the *Financial Mail* newspaper.
- PRISA gold medal award: Awarded in recognition of outstanding public relations service to Southern Africa. Previous winners were Dr. Christian Barnard, Gary Player, President F. W. de Klerk, and President Nelson Mandela.

The purpose of all these awards is to boost standards of professionalism by recognizing and rewarding a clearly defined strategic approach, innovation and creativity.

TABLE A.8.5

Public Relations Consultancies in South Africa

Ad-uppe public relations	Concept communications
Arcay corporate communications	Coralynne & associates
Anthea Johnston & associates	Candid communications
Baird's communications	Corporate communications
Barbara Cousens & associates CC (BC&A)	Debra Anne communications CC
Bay public relations & associates	Fasedemi Newman-Leo Burnett
BSA public relations & event management	Fleishman-Hillard Vallun Wilkins
Bill Paterson (Pty) Ltd	Gillian Gamsy International PR and promotions
Butterfly communications	Gilmark communications
Communications consultants	Grant-Marshall communications CC (GMC)
Cathrall & associates	Grant Thornton Kessel Feinstein
Church Raitt Orr Limited	Harbor public relations & marketing

(Continued)

TABLE A.8.5

(*Continued*)

Image communications	Primary focus
Infokom	Pamela Mgulwa and associates
Integrated communications	Pro-image CC
Joy Cameron-Dow communications CC	Rose Francis communications
Lange public relations	Rosemary Hare public relations
Liz Kneale communications	Sefin marketing communications consultants
Lola Lazarus public relations and promotions (LLPR)	Simeka TWS communications
	Strategic communication consultants
Marcus Brewster publicity	Specialised solutions international
Mandisa communications	Strategic concepts (PTY) limited
Matrix PR & communications consultants	Trish Stewart PR associates (TSPR)
Milkwood communications	

TABLE A.8.6

PRISM Award Categories

Category 1—Overall Institutional
Promoting general relations with all or some publics.

Category 2—Public Service
Promoting societal good with philanthropic motivation (if the principal motivation is a benefit to the sponsor use Category 1 instead).

Category 3—Public Affairs
Specific short-term effort to influence governmental legislation or regulation or to elect a political candidate.

Category 4—Issue Management
Long-term effort dealing with public policy or policies.

Category 5—Emergency
Dealing with a disaster or other unpredicted emergency.

Category 6—Community Relations
Aimed at publics in one or more particular communities in which the company or institution has a special presence or interest.

Category 7—Employee Relations
Designed to increase efficiency or improve morale within the company or institution.

Category 8—Investor Relations
Intended to influence present and prospective investors and the financial community.

Category 9—Product/Service Communication
New product/service or established product/service.

Category 10—Special Event
Concentrated opening, celebration, commemoration, or created event.

Category 11—Environmental
Concerning a real or alleged threat to the environment.

Category 12—Arts
Promoting or fostering the arts by an arts organization or a sponsoring company/institution.

(*Continued*)

TABLE A.8.6

(*Continued*)

Category 13—Other
Aimed at distributors, members, educators, youth, or other special publics.

2001 Financial Mail PRISM Awards has identified a need for the inclusion of communication pieces that highlight technical skills and expertise, such as editing, writing, design, and photography. They recognize the importance of a communication project's goals and measured results and emphasize the creative process of project execution. It has been decided to include the following as additional category:

Category 14—Publications: Employee publications
Production of external or internal publications in all formats except electronic.
    One- to three-color magazines.
    Four-color (or more) magazines.
    Newspapers.
    Newsletters.
    Special publications.
    Posters.
    Calendars.
Judging will be on writing, editing, design (including photography and graphics), and production.

Note. Gold (Campaign of the Year), silver (outstanding public relations practice), and bronze (runner up to silver) are awarded in the PRISM categories.

TABLE A.8.7

Perceived Importance of Current and Future Public Relations Disciplines

Past 5 Years: What is Currently Important?	*Next 5 Years: What Will be Important?*
General corporate pubic relations	Employee relations
Marketing public relations	Community relations
Community relations	Corporate public relations
Employee relations	Marketing public relations
Investor relations	Investor relations
Special events	Issues management
Public affairs	Public affairs
Issues management	International relations
International public relations	Environmental public relations
Crisis communication	Crisis communication
Environmental public relations	Special events

TABLE A.8.8

Registered Unions, Members, Employers' Organizations, and Bargaining Councils, 1999–2000

Year	*Registered Unions*	*Members*	*Employers' Organizations*	*Private Sector Bargaining Councils*
1999	499	3,359,497	260	78
2000	464	3,552,113	252	73

TABLE A.8.9
PRISA's Code of Conduct

Declaration of Principles

We base our professional principles on the fundamental value and dignity of the individual. We believe in and support the free exercise of human rights, especially freedom of speech, freedom of assembly, and freedom of the media, which are essential to the practice of good public relations. In serving the interests of clients and employers, we dedicate ourselves to the goals of better communication, understanding, and cooperation among diverse individuals, groups, and institutions of society. We also subscribe to and support equal opportunity of employment in the public relations profession.

We pledge:

- To conduct ourselves professionally, with truth, accuracy, fairness, and responsibility to the public and toward our colleagues.
- To improve our individual competence and advance the knowledge and proficiency of the profession through continuing education and research.
- To adhere to the articles of the Code of Professional Standards for the practice of public relations.

Code of Professional Conduct

1. Definition

   Public relations is the management, through communication, of perceptions and strategic relationships between an organization and its internal and external stakeholders.

2. Professional Conduct

   2.1 In the conduct of our professional activities, we shall respect the public interest and the dignity of the individual. It is our responsibility at all times to deal fairly and honestly with our clients or employers, past or present, with our colleagues, media communication, and with the public.

   2.2 We shall conduct our professional lives in accordance with the public interest. We shall not conduct ourselves in any manner detrimental to the profession of public relations.

   2.3 We have a positive duty to maintain integrity and accuracy, as well as generally accepted standards of good taste.

   2.4 We shall not knowingly, intentionally, or recklessly communicate false or misleading information. It is our obligation to use proper care to avoid doing so inadvertently.

   2.5 We shall not guarantee the achievement of specified results beyond our direct control. We shall not negotiate or agree terms with a prospective employer or client on the basis of payment only contingent on specific future public relations achievements.

   2.6 We shall, when acting for a client or employer who belongs to a profession, respect the code of ethics of that of other professions and shall not knowingly be party to any breach of such a code.

3. Toward Clients/Employers Conduct

   3.1 We shall safeguard the confidences of both present and former clients and employers. We shall not disclose or make use of information given or obtained in confidence from an employer or client, past or present, for personal gain or otherwise or to the disadvantage or prejudice of such client or employer.

   3.2 We shall not represent conflicting or competing interests without the express consent of those involved, given after full disclosure of the facts. We shall not place ourselves in a position where our interests are or may be in conflict with a duty to a client without full disclosure of such interests to all involved.

   3.3 We shall not be party to any activity that seeks to dissemble or mislead by promoting one disguised or undisclosed interest while appearing to further another. It is our duty to ensure that the actual interest of any organization with which we may be professionally concerned is adequately declared.

(Continued)

TABLE A.8.9
(*Continued*)

3.4 In the course of our professional services to the employer or client we shall not accept payment either in cash or in kind in connection with these services from another source without the express consent of our employer or client.

4. Conduct Toward Colleagues

    4.1 We shall not maliciously injure the professional reputation or practice of another individual engaged in the public relations profession.

    4.2 We shall at all times uphold this code, cooperate with colleagues in doing so, and enforce decisions on any matter arising from this application.

    4.3 Registered individuals who knowingly cause or permit another person or organization to act in a manner inconsistent with this code or are party to such an action shall be deemed to be in breach of it.

    4.4 If we have reason to believe that another colleague has engaged in practices that may be in breach of this code, or practices that may be unethical, unfair, or illegal, it is our duty to advise the institute promptly.

    4.5 We shall not invite any employee of a client to consider alternative employment.

5. Conduct Toward the Business Environment

    5.1 We shall not recommend the use of any organization in which we have a financial interest or make use of its services on behalf of our clients or employers without declaring our interest.

    5.2 In performing professional services for a client or employer we shall not accept fees, commissions, or any other consideration from anyone other than the client or employer in connection with those services, without the express consent of the client/employer, given after disclosure of the facts.

    5.3 We shall sever relations as soon as possible with any organization or individual if such a relationship requires conduct contrary to this code.

6. Conduct Toward the Channels of Communication

    6.1 We shall not engage in any practice, that tends to corrupt the integrity of channels or media of communication.

    6.2 We shall identify publicly the name of the client or employer on whose behalf any public communication is made.

7. Conduct Toward the State

    7.1 We respect the principles contained in the Constitution of the country in which we are resident.

    7.2 We shall not offer or give any reward to any person holding public office with intent to further our interests or those of our employer.

8. Conduct Toward PRISA

    8.1 We shall at all times respect the dignity and decisions of PRISA.

    8.2 We are bound to uphold the annual registration fee levied by PRISA, which fee is payable as determined by registered practitioners at the Annual General Meeting of PRISA.

9. Disciplinary Rules

A registered member who, in the opinion of the Disciplinary Committee of PRISA, infringes the Code of Professional Standards shall be informed in writing. The member deemed responsible for such an infringement shall be given reasonable opportunity to state their defense either in writing or by personal attendance at a meeting of a Disciplinary Committee appointed by the PRISA Board and specially convened for this purpose. Sanctions will take the form of a warning or the practitioner's name will be removed from the register of members. This action will be made public.

REFERENCES

Boon, M. (1998). *The African way: The power of interactive leadership.* (2nd ed.). Sandton, Johannesburg, SA: Zebra.

Cheru, F. (2001). *The African Renaissance and the challenge of globalization* (Working Paper). Geneva, Switzerland: Economic and Social Council of the United Nations.

Constitution of the Republic of South Africa. (1996). (in South Africa yearbook, 2001/2002).

Cullingworth, B. (1990, November). PR comes of age in South Africa. *Review,* 59–61.

De Beer, A. (1993). Journalists could take a leaf from public relations education. *Monitor,* 76–78. Durban, South Africa: The Department of Public Relations and Journalism student publication, ML Sultan Technikon.

Etounga-Manguelle, D. (1990). *L'Afrique: d'un programme d'adjustment culturel?* (Africa: a program for cultural adjustment)? Ivry-sur-Seine: Editions Nouvelle du Sud.

Government Communication and Information System. (Eds.). (2001/2002). *South African yearbook.* Durban, South Africa: Universal Printers.

Grunig, JE. (1992). *Excellence in public relations and communication management.* Hillsdale: New Jersey: Lawrence Erlbaum Associates.

Habermas, J. (1984). *The theory of communicative action* (Vol. 1, T. McCarthy, Trans.). Boston: Beacon.

Hiebert, R. E. (1984). *Introduction.* In B. Cantor (Ed.), *Inside public relations* (pp. xvii–xx). New York: Longman.

Hoogberg, U. & Mersham, G. M. (1993). Mass media in Africa: From distant drums to satellite, in As deBeer (ed.). *Mass media for the nineties:* the *South African handbook of mass communication.* Pretoria: Van Schaik.

Jefkins, F. & Ugboajah, F. (1986). *Communication in industrialising countries* Hong Kong: Macmillan.

Kaplan, D. (1990). *The crossed line: The South African telecommunications industry in transition.* Johannesburg, SA: Witwaters rand University Press.

Kabou, A. (1991). *Et si L'Afrique refusant le devellopement?* Paris: L'Harmatten.

Louw, P. C. (1989). *Communication and Counter Hegemony in Contemperary South Africa. Consideration of a leftist media theory and practice.* Doctoral thesis is, University of Natal, S.A.

Lubbe, B. A., & Puth, G. (Eds.). (1994). *Public relations in South Africa: A management reader.* Isando, Johannesburg, SA: Heinemann.

Malan, J. P., & L' Estrange, J. A. (1965). *Public Relations Practice in South Africa,* Cape Town:Juta.

Mazrui, A. A. (1990). *Cultural forces in world politics.* London: James Curry.

Marchant, H. (1988). *Communication, Media and development.* Durban SA: Butterworths/Does Africa refuse development.

Mersham, G. M. & Skinner, C. (1999). *New insights into Communication & Public Relations.* Sandton, SA: Heinemann.

Mersham, G. M. (1992). *Communication Science in South Africa–The view from Ngoye.* Inaugural Address Kwadlangezwa: University of Zululand Press.

Mersham, G. M. (1993). Public relations: A vital communication function of our times. In A. S. De Beer (Ed.), *Mass media for the nineties: the South African handbook of mass communication.* Pretoria, South Africa: Van Schaik.

Mersham, G. M., Rensburg, R. S., & Skinner, J. C. (1995). *Public relations, development and social investment: A Southern African perspective.* Pretoria, South Africa: Van Schaik.

Moscardi, M. (2002). *PRISA milestones.* Johannesburg, South Africa: Director of PRISA The Institute of Public Relations and Communication management.

Mowlana, H. (1987). *Development: A field in search of itself.* Budapest: International Association for Mass Communication Research.

Nartey, V. (1988). Public relations education and research in Africa. *International Public Relations Review,* 24–28.

Nel, J. J. (1993). From teen to adult. *Communika,* 1.

Palframan, B. (1994). South Africa: Creative alliances work best, *Communication World, 11*(6), 35–36.

Pearson, R. (1989). *A theory of public relations ethics.* Unpublished doctoral thesis, Ohio State University, Athens.

Sakebeeld, Thursday, 14 March, 2002.

Statistics South Africa. (2001).

Steyn, B. (2000). CEO expectations in terms of PR roles. *Communicare, 19*(1), 20–43.

Tomaselli: R. E. (1989). Public Service broadcasting in the age of information capitalism. *Communicate*, 8(2): 27–37

Turnbull, N. S. (1994). Is public relations the first post-modernist profession? *Communika.*

Van Zyl, J. & Tomaselli, K. G. (1997). *Media and change.* Johannesburg, SA: McCraw-Hill.

9

PUBLIC RELATIONS IN EGYPT: PRACTICES, OBSTACLES, AND POTENTIALS

KEVIN L. KEENAN

The Arab Republic of Egypt is located in the northeastern corner of Africa, bordered by Libya to the west, Sudan to the south, and the Mediterranean Sea to the north. The Red Sea borders mainland Egypt to the east, and Israel borders the eastern edge of Egypt's Sinai Peninsula. With a population of 70 million, Egypt is the largest country in the Arab world. The capital city of Cairo, with over 16 million inhabitants, is the center of business, culture, diplomacy, and media in the Middle East.

More than 90% of Egypt's 1 million km^2 area is uninhabited desert, and most of the population resides along the Nile River, which runs the length of the country from south to north. Natural resources include petroleum, natural gas, iron ore, manganese, limestone, and zinc. Agriculture and industry each account for roughly one quarter of Egypt's gross domestic product (GDP) and the services sector makes up the rest, with tourism being an especially important part of the Egyptian economy. Egypt has a trade deficit ratio of 2:1. The country receives substantial foreign aid from the United States, especially after it signed the 1977 Camp David accord with Israel, as well as from the European Union. Through the final years of the 20th century and the beginning of the 21st century, unemployment in the country has hovered between 11% and 12% of the adult population.

Arabic is the official language of Egypt, with English and French understood by many of the upper classes. Approximately 95% of the population is Muslim, and most of the rest are Coptic Christians. Just over half of the population is literate, with the literacy rate for women being lower than that for men. Generally thought of as a developing country, Egypt has been identified as one of several "semiperipheral" nations in the trichotomous approach of world-system theory (McPhail, 2002, p. 17). In world-system terminology, the semiperipheral designation is given to countries that fall between the most highly developed core nations of the United States, Canada, Japan, Australia, New Zealand,

Israel, and the countries of the European Union and peripheral nations, which are the least developed parts of the world, including most of Africa and Latin America and several countries in Asia and the former Soviet Union.

HISTORY AND DEVELOPMENT OF THE COUNTRY AND THE PROFESSION

Although Egypt has a fascinating and documented past extending back 6,000 years, there is little in the history of ancient Egypt that is relevant to modern public relations. Examples of what might be considered the very first forms of agricultural communication can be traced to Egyptian pharaohs (Al-Tohami & Al-Dakoki, 1980) and Alanazi (1996) claimed that something similar to the press-agentry model was practiced as early as 2000 BC in the region that is now Egypt. But clearly, the link between activities in those times and contemporary public relations is not direct. Instead, events and conditions of the last 2 centuries are more important to understanding the practices encompassing, and challenges to the further growth of, the public relations profession in Egypt and will receive the most attention in this chapter.

Beginning in 1798 when the armies of Napoleon invaded Egypt and continuing until the Revolution of 1952, Egypt was intermittently under French control and later under English control. Although this period also included the rule of Mohammed Ali and an era of royal importance under King Fouad and King Farouk early in the 20th century, certain Western influences on Egyptian culture, commerce, and thinking took root during European rule (Botman, 1998; Dykstra, 1998).

By the start of World War I and through World War II, Egypt was essentially a part of the British Empire, with economic and political reliance on Great Britain and British interests having priority in much of what took place in the country. As the role of Britain in Egyptian affairs increased during this period, so did local resentment of such colonialism (Jankowski, 2000). These feelings resulted in a nationalist movement, calls for the expulsion of the British presence, a series of anti-British riots, and a military revolution in 1952 under the command of Gamal Abdel Nasser. Nasser ruled as the president of Egypt until his death in 1970 (Vatikiotis, 1991).

In the half century since the revolution and declaration of independence, Egypt has grown into a position of leadership in the Arab world. During these years, the country has had three presidents, Nasser (1956–1970), Anwar Sadat (1970–1981), and Hosni Mubarak (1981–present), each facing different challenges and concerns, each endorsing different directions and policies, and each in turn having different impacts on the development of public relations in Egypt. Note that all three of Egypt's presidents in the modern era have military backgrounds.

Under Nasser, Egypt adopted a socialist but repressive system of government. Foreign businesses were either expelled or their assets seized, and major industries were nationalized. Political opposition was not tolerated, and numerous cases have been recorded of journalists and opponents being tortured, jailed, or even executed. Political parties, including the Muslim Brotherhood, which had supported Nasser's original coup, were outlawed and thousands of dissidents were imprisoned. During most of the Nasser administration, Egypt was aligned with the Soviet Union. Nasser was a strong proponent of pan-Arabism, and for a brief period from 1958 to 1961, the country was joined with Syria to form the United Arab Republic.

Major accomplishments and activities during Gamal Abdel Nasser's reign as president included taking control of the Suez Canal shortly after the Revolution, the building of the Aswan Dam on the Nile and the resulting changes in electrification and agricultural practices; the United Nations supported military victory over Israel, France, and Britain in 1956; and the rather humiliating defeat by Israel in the Six Day War of 1967. On the whole, however, Nasser's rule was a dictatorship that did little to establish an environment where open expression and the democratic principles necessary for two-way flow of information might flourish. As far as the public relations profession is concerned, his legacy is one that stifled the growth of an open communication system thus limiting the profession principally to propaganda efforts by the government.

When Nasser died in 1970, he was succeeded by his Vice President, Anwar Sadat, who had joined Nasser during the revolution. Under Sadat, Egypt began to liberalize both politically and economically, at least initially. In the early years of Sadat's presidency, many of those imprisoned for political reasons during Nasser's rule were released and restrictions on the formation of political parties were eased. Censorship was reduced for a short span of time, and some amount of press freedom was restored. As will be discussed, in 1977, there was a clampdown on this openness.

On the economic front, Sadat was more open to foreign investment and private sector development than nationalist Nasser. Many in Egypt's upper classes thrived during this period, but conditions for much of Egypt's population did not improve. In fact, ordinary Egyptians suffered due to inflation and other factors related to this openness. In 1977, when government food subsidies were reduced, riots occurred throughout the country prompting the government to quickly reinstate them (Jankowski, 2000).

As a diplomat, Anwar Sadat is certainly best known for the Camp David peace agreement he signed with Israel in 1977. Although international reaction to this move was largely favorable, opinion at home and in the rest of the Arab world was less enthusiastic and hostile among a section of the Egyptian populace. In fact, the backlash among those who disagreed with this move was so great that many of the domestic reforms and moves toward pluralism that Sadat had put in place were reversed. New regulations were reinstated to restrict government criticism and reduced openness and the free flow of information that had characterized the early Sadat years. The combination of dissatisfaction with the poor economic conditions and with the peace accord with arch enemy Israel led to increased unrest in Egypt. This resulted in the rise of a strong Islamist movement and further government crackdowns on open expression and activities deemed threatening to the regime. In 1981, Anwar Sadat was assassinated by a member of the Islamic Jihad, one of the groups targeted by the restrictions put in place during Sadat's final years as president.

In terms of providing an environment conducive to the growth of the public relations profession, the Sadat era can be summarized as a time that offered much promise at the beginning but concluded with repression and limits on expression and activism only slightly less severe than under Nasser. Efforts to establish a private sector economy, encourage open expression, and shifting alliance with the Soviet Union toward the United States and the democratic West would seem like a good start toward a system of democracy, respect of public opinion, and media freedom conducive for modern public relations. But in the end, the Sadat administration reverted to methods of repression and restrictions familiar to Egyptians since their first days of independence.

For the 20 plus years since Sadat's assassination, Mohamed Hosni Mubarak has led Egypt as the country's president. Having served as vice president under Sadat, Mubarak continued the policies of that administration in the early years of his administration. Over time, however, he has put his own mark on Egypt, both domestically and in the global community.

The Mubarak era has seen Egypt's reemergence as a force within the Arab world. After losing favor among much of the region as a result of Sadat's peace with Israel, including the severing of diplomatic relations with most Arab countries and expulsion from the League of Arab States (LAS), Egypt under Mubarak was readmitted to the LAS in 1989, and Cairo currently serves as the headquarters of the LAS. Egypt also took a leadership role among countries of the Middle East in siding with the West during the Gulf War and has led recent regional efforts against terrorism.

Internally, Egypt has faced a variety of issues and opportunities during Mubarak's rule. There has been much discussion and some effort toward further privatizing the economy and introducing competition into industries handled exclusively by the public sector since Egypt's independence. The government has faced varying pressures and threats from Islamist groups and has reacted in ways that have succeeded at times and have brought problems during others. Because it is the Mubarak administration that is leading Egypt into the 21st century, and under whose rule the public relations industry must operate, the following sections concentrate on Egypt under Mubarak. In addition, this chapter focuses on the status of the profession and implications on the profession by environmental factors such as infrastructure, culture, and media systems.

THE EGYPTIAN PUBLIC RELATIONS INDUSTRY

The term *public relations* is familiar to most Egyptians, and jobs bearing that title have existed since privatization became a priority during the last years of the 20th century. However, by Western definitions, the field is rather misunderstood in Egypt and is far less developed than it is in the West or in more progressive parts of the Middle East, such as Lebanon and the United Arab Emirates (Lussier, 2002). In Egypt, public relations is often synonymous with hospitality or customer relations. The industry that is probably most associated with public relations jobs is the service industry. Hotels employ public relations directors responsible for guest services such as arranging airport transportation, hosting dignitaries, and generally putting on a "smiling and friendly face" on behalf of the organization.

There is also a lack of understanding of the parameters of the public relations profession, and confusion exists among Egyptian organizations with regard to the distinctions between public relations, advertising, and marketing (Zaklama, 2001). Most organizations consider sales to be the primary goal of public relations, and there is little interest in or patience for programs or tactics that do not directly contribute to sales. By one estimate, of those individuals who consider themselves part of the public relations business in Egypt, only about 10% are skilled professionals who have a full understanding of the profession in a Western sense (Spiers, 1991). The rest are essentially sales agents of one form or another.

The Egyptian mass media reflect and reinforce the blending of public relations with marketing by linking publicity and news coverage with advertising expenditures. For example, it is accepted practice in Egypt for media use of information contained in news releases and other publicity materials to be contingent on the purchase of advertising space or time. Thus, completely contrary to Western concepts and expectations, publicity truly is paid for in Egypt. An organization either agrees to buy a certain amount of advertising from the publication involved or pays outright for publishing a press release because of the credibility that comes from the information being covered as a news item. Spiers (1991) cited several examples in which media organizations published news stories referring generically to "a pharmaceutical firm" or "a soft drink company" because the organizations involved refused to pay for the privilege of having their company mentioned by name.

The media relations function of public relations professionals in Egypt has traditionally been rather weak and ineffective as well. In part, this is because of the insistence by media gatekeepers that they be compensated for granting access to their audience. It is also an indication of the lack of respect for the profession and the low power public relations practitioners have in deciding their strategies and tactics in most organizations. In addition, it also is probably linked to the fact that most Egyptian public relations practitioners are not considered to be good sources of information by those in the media. As described by one journalist (quoted in Lussier, 2002), "PR departments in Egypt have no power to answer questions on their own. They always have to go back to their superior. They can take your question, and they'll get back to you, but it usually takes days or weeks. It's just not useful for a journalist" (p. 41). Spiers (1991) suggested that problems with media relations are further compounded by the fact that many Egyptian journalists do not work from a permanent office and, therefore, it is difficult to contact them.

Other public relations specialties such as investor relations, sponsorship arrangements, event management, crisis management, and government relations are occasionally found among Egyptian organizations. Lobbying is an underdeveloped tool (Lussier, 2002); as stated earlier, few Egyptian organizations make distinctions between the roles and objectives of public relations and marketing.

Taking these points into account, it is not surprising that the dominant coalitions in most organizations have traditionally not included public relations specialists and, therefore, do not have a very high regard for the contributions that public relations can make to organizational effectiveness. Industry analysts cite many reasons for the underdevelopment of the public relations profession in Egypt and the failure to grasp its purpose and potential. Khorasanizadeh (2001) pointed to the fact that because media and market systems have traditionally involved little or no competition, there has never really been a need for public relations. Stones (1994) proposed that there is a history of government policies and business philosophy in Egypt that actually discourages the sharing of information.

A further factor that likely contributes to the current low status of public relations in Egypt is the lack of formal training in modern theory and practice. Those national universities that include public relations in their curricula generally limit it to a single course in either business or communications departments. At the American University in Cairo, public relations courses are included in an Integrated Marketing Communication specialization. Not surprising, given several of the points already raised, most Egyptian public relations professionals have backgrounds in marketing rather than journalism or any communication area of expertise.

There are some signs, however, of advances in the understanding and sophistication of public relations in Egypt. Zaklama (2001) claimed that a new "mindset" has emerged among leading Egyptian organizations since the last years of the 20th century. The author gave examples of cases in which more sophisticated public relations strategies and techniques have been tried in recent years. These include the use of two-way communication principles by the Egyptian government and the tourism industry in developing public relations approaches in the wake of terrorism incidents in the late 90s and the launching of a successful telecommunications industry during that same period. Recognition that most organizations are likely to have multiple publics each requiring individual attention is also becoming more common, and there is evidence that public relations may finally be emerging as a function distinct from marketing.

As private enterprise continues to increase in Egypt, and as multinational corporations continue to enter the market, there is reason to expect that the worldview that has led to recent advances in the field will continue to spread. International public relations firms, including Brodeur Worldwide, Hill and Knowlton, and Weber Shandwick, have entered into affiliation agreements with local agencies in Cairo. Newly privatized Egyptian businesses in a range of sectors have set up in-house operations intended to treat public relations as something more than just a marketing tool. In their study of the global diffusion of the top 10 international public relations firms, Sriramesh and Verčič (2002) classified Egypt as an emerging nation in terms of factors related to the development of global public relations.

The founding of the Arab Public Relations Society as a modern trade organization has added to the credibility of the profession in Egypt. In October 2002, Egypt hosted the annual conference of the International Public Relations Association, further establishing public relations among Egyptian businesses and decision makers. However, there are numerous obstacles and problems to be dealt with before public relations is fully accepted as an effective and integral organizational function in Egypt. But there seems to be reason for optimism as the country's economic and social systems evolve in the coming years.

INFRASTRUCTURE OF EGYPT

Certain characteristics of Egyptian society and the Egyptian system of government should be recognized as restraints and obstructions to international public relations activities. An understanding of the backgrounds involved and factors related to circumstances faced in dealing with bureaucracies, courts, regulators, and institutions can do much to lessen the barriers faced and to facilitate effective planning of public relations efforts in Egypt. As a country with a developing economy and an important role in regional and global politics, there are opportunities for scholars and practitioners familiar with Egyptian idiosyncrasies to utilize this knowledge to help build a theory of international public relations in addition to considering strategies for conducting effective public relations within Egypt.

Political Structure

Under the constitution passed in 1971, Egypt has a Republican form of government and, in theory, a limited democratic system. The constitution calls for the division of author-ity among the executive, legislative, and judicial branches. In reality, however, it is the president who wields the most power and who appoints key officials to serve in all areas of government. Islam is the official state religion, and at least indirectly, it guides the direction of most decisions and policies.

For administrative purposes, Egypt is divided into 26 governorates, each with a governor who is appointed by the president. But the system is actually quite centralized, with control ultimately resting with the national government in Cairo. In a public relations sense, the little bit of lobbying that goes on in Egypt is usually concentrated in Cairo.

The legislative branch of Egypt's government consists of two bodies, the People's As-sembly of at least 350 members and the smaller Shura Advisory Council. Both the People's Assembly and the Shura Advisory Council are made up of some elected individuals and some appointed by the president.

The concept of political parties and the notions of compromise and exchange, crucial to most democracies and assumed in Western public relations models, are quite limited in Egypt. All political parties must be approved by the government. Although ballots usually include candidates from multiple parties, a single ruling party, the National Democratic Party (NDP), has control of the presidency as well as of both legislative chambers in contemporary Egypt. Since its establishment by Sadat in 1978, the NDP has held anywhere from 70% to 90% of the People's Assembly and Shura Advisory Council, and it is common for those elected as Independents to join the NDP upon taking office. Charges of electoral fraud, corruption, and intimidation are fairly common in Egyptian politics (*Run-Up to Shura*, 2001).

At the executive level, the process of selecting a president involves nomination and approval within the People's Assembly, followed by election in the form of a popular referendum. The term of office is 6 years, with no term limits. In 1999, Hosni Mubarak was elected to his fourth consecutive term, winning 94% support as the only candidate named on the ballot.

The dominant party system that results from this process, with the president designating a portion of the legislature and the legislature in turn nominating the president, is characteristic of many former third-world countries. These emerging democracies commonly end up with power weighted toward the presidency and a government that combines elements of authoritarianism with those of genuine democratic rule. Although there is a place for some limited form of public relations in such a setting, true democracy, with participation and attention to public opinion, has yet to be fully developed in Egypt.

A further indication of the central role of the president in Egyptian government is his executive authority to select (and to dismiss) the country's prime minister, vice-president(s), and the Council of Ministers in charge of overseeing various government responsibilities, industries, and areas of concern. Of these cabinet-level positions, the Ministry of Information is particularly relevant for public relations interests, overseeing the country's media system and serving as the public relations arm of the Egyptian government in a public information sense.

Economic Development

Egypt has the second largest economy in the Arab world, behind only Saudi Arabia. It is a relatively diversified economic system, with oil, tourism, and revenue from the Suez Canal accounting for significant portions of the country's GDP. Agricultural exports and remittances from expatriate Egyptians working abroad also contribute a sizable amount to the economy, as does the $3 billion in foreign aid that Egypt receives annually, most coming from the United States. There is also a substantial hidden economy in Egypt (Roy, 1992), consisting of traditionally undocumented and quasi-illegal activities in several different sectors.

The structure of Egypt's economy has undergone important changes since the days of total nationalism under Gamal Abdel Nasser. It has evolved from the centralized state economy of those times to a system that has much more of a place for private enterprise and, at least in theory, represents a much more fertile setting for the growth of modern public relations practices. Changing from a socialist to a market economy is by no means an easy process, and the country has faced many problems during this period, some of which continue today.

The concept of privatization of large chunks of the economy began receiving lip service in Egypt as part of the open door policy of Anwar Sadat in the 1970s (Gomaa, 1996). It has been expanded as a priority of the Mubarak administration and continues as probably the single most major issue in Egypt's economy in the 2000s. The approach to privatization in Egypt has varied from industry to industry and has evolved over time. In some cases, full ownership of public companies has been sold to private investors, both Egyptian and foreign. In others, only a percentage, often a low percentage, has been sold to private ownership. The range of privatized industries includes banking, construction, hotels, retailing, shipping, and tourism. The government plans to sell additional government-owned businesses working toward the goal of an economy that is 80% privately held by the first years of the 21st century (B. Smith, 1999). This has encouraged a stronger stock market in Egypt.

The public sector in Egypt has a reputation for not being very efficient, and in certain industries, efforts to privatize have been met with low levels of interest among profit-seeking investors. However, privatized industries have seen dramatic improvements in management and marketing (P. Smith, 1999). This appears to bode well for the public relations industry whose value is more likely to be recognized by new organizational leaders.

As might be expected of any economy undergoing radical change from state to market control, there are certain issues and problems that need to be worked out in Egypt. One of these is the increasingly important issue of labor practices and unemployment. Even with the movement toward privatization, over one quarter of Egypt's workforce remains on government payroll, and there are concerns about shifting this large portion of the working population. There are also worries that even a healthy private economy may have trouble supporting Egypt's ever-increasing supply of labor, which looks to increase at a rate of one-half million people per year at least through the first decade of the new century.

Another economic factor of note is the position of small businesses in Egypt. Over 99% of the country's private enterprises have fewer than 50 employees, and the majority have fewer than 10 ("Credit Where," 1999). In addition, most entrepreneurs do not own their own property. This has resulted in a system in which business owners are not able to take advantage of economies of scale and lack collateral for expanding and improving their operations. In facing what amounts to a near daily struggle to remain solvent, these small businesses may consider public relations something of an unaffordable luxury. If the profession is to further establish itself in Egypt, this issue needs to be addressed.

Egyptian businesses of all sizes operate in an economic environment that remains overly bureaucratic and somewhat protectionist in its outlook. Tariffs on imported products average 15%, among the highest in the world. Licenses, permits, taxes, and regulatory rituals can be extremely frustrating, and these laws often make little sense to the outsider. What results is a situation that does little to encourage outside investment in the Egyptian economy.

Legal System

Whereas the Egyptian government and economic systems have changed in ways that are seemingly favorable to the growth of modern public relations, the judicial system has been less progressive. Relying on a combination of Islamic, Ottoman, French, British, and Soviet laws, along with presidential decrees and special "emergency laws" that are passed with some regularity, the Egyptian legal system is often contradictory and inefficient. As a result, it is not uncommon for the simplest of legal contentions to become entangled in the courts for 10 years or more. Judges commonly consider as many as 1,000 cases a day, and postponements are the rule rather than the exception.

The Supreme Constitutional Court is the highest body of the Egyptian legal system, and it oversees issues related to the constitution and resolves cases that have been passed up from lower courts. Beyond that, the Egyptian judiciary consists of two principal branches, the Courts of General Jurisdiction and the Administrative Courts System, each with a rather complex, if not always logical, group of subcourts. One writer characterized the Egyptian system of laws and regulations as "enmeshed in their ancient cobwebs" and described a legal bureaucracy in which it can take 77 separate procedures in 31 different government offices just to register property (B. Smith, 1999, p. 4)!

Although calls for reform are fairly common and blame for the state of Egypt's legal system is often directed at the dominance of the executive branch over the legislature and the judiciary, the current structure is entrenched and is not likely to be overhauled anytime soon. Practitioners and scholars of public relations must recognize that the system they will encounter in Egypt is unlike that of most Western countries. Planners should take into account the delays and inefficiencies characteristic of Egyptian courts and should be aware of the thick bureaucracy involved.

Level of Activism

The subject of activism is a sensitive one in Egypt. Although the country's constitution allows certain rights and protections for all citizens, there is also a history of intolerance and severity in controlling and punishing dissidents. Many of the activities that would be considered legitimate activism in Western democracies are not allowed in Egypt. These prohibitions and their enforcement tend to vary depending on the area or issue at hand. For public relations purposes, it is important to understand the types of issues over which activism is likely to be tolerated as well as the varying enforcement of curbs against activism.

Although restrictions on social and activist movements may seem to be advantageous to businesses fearing activist reaction to their policies or practices, such restrictions also contribute to an environment that stifles expression and promotes repression of the environment as a whole. The result is a situation in which an organization may not have to worry much about activists but may worry about the limited options for involvement with issues of interest to it (issues management).

Among the realms of activism particularly constrained in Egypt are what some would consider basic civil rights of expression, assembly, and association. Reports from Amnesty International (Egypt: Amnesty International, 2002), Human Rights Watch (Human Rights Watch, 2002), and the United States State Department ("Country Reports," 2002) all are critical of the Egyptian government for its heavy-handed methods of dealing with activism. These include closing down newspapers, banning books, outlawing public demonstrations, taking measures to silence trade union representatives and other activists, and placing severe limits on Islamist political activity. Recent examples of government infringement that have attracted international attention include the jailing of a noted sociologist for research work deemed to be "undermining the dignity of the state" (Del Castillo, 2001, p. 53), alleged discrimination against Coptic Christians (Gauch, 1995) and homosexuals (Hammer, 2002), a respected writer being ordered to divorce her husband for making statements considered anti-Islamic (Gauch, 2001), and the passing of a law that places nongovernmental organizations under state control (Mekay, 2000).

However, there are also areas in which activism has been tolerated and is successful in accomplishing various objectives. Feminist groups have used activist methods in campaigns to stem the practice of female circumcision in Egypt (El-Gibaly, Ibrahim, Mensch, & Clark, 2002). Consumer boycotts have become an accepted and widely employed tool for expressing disapproval of an organization's actions (Howeidy, 2001) or the policies of foreign governments (Hanafi, 2002). Thus, although the potential for activism exists in Egypt, public relations planners would do well to recognize that it depends very much on the particular situation, topic, and publics involved.

EGYPTIAN CULTURE

The people of Egypt come from a variety of ethnic and historic subcultures including the more African Nubians of the south, the nomadic Bedouins, and Berber descendents in the western desert. Despite this diversity in background, Egypt has a rich and deep national culture, which most subgroups are proud to share. Egyptian culture is conservative and among the most diverse in the Arab world.

Probably the two characteristics that best distinguish Egyptian culture are the importance of family and the central role of religion. Nearly all aspects of life in Egypt revolve around the immediate and extended family, with marriage, children, and kinship having particular priorities in all social, educational, recreational, and work-related matters. Women are generally responsible for child care and maintaining the family household, whereas men are expected to provide full financial support, even if that entails working multiple jobs or temporarily separating from the family and moving outside of Egypt to earn a sufficient income (Haikal, 1993).

The place of religion, primarily Islam but also Christianity for the Coptic minority, is so important that it is hard to separate it from basic Egyptian culture. Both Muslims and Christians are very religious people in Egypt. Daily life involves a routine of prayer and devotion to the tenets of one's beliefs; even in the noisy city of Cairo, the broadcast sermons and praying from neighborhood mosques and the ringing of church bells are heard as a constant part of the background. Religious holidays are major celebrations in Egypt, with special importance given to the 1-month-long holy period of Ramadan, a time in which Muslims fast every day during daylight hours and indulge in a daily *iftar* meal at sunset. Ramadan is also a time for charity, with mosques, community groups, and even Christian churches often sponsoring *iftars* for the poor, neighbors or employees, and others. Some more astute organizations have begun to recognize the spirit and meaning of such activities in Egypt and include *iftars* and Ramadan festivities as part of their strategies for dealing with various publics. Ramadan is also the prime season for advertising campaigns in Egypt, as television audiences during this season are more than twice as large as during the rest of the year (Keenan & Yeni, 2002).

In terms of Egypt's dimensions of culture suggested by Hofstede (1980, 1998), little formal study has been done. It appears to a keen observer that the country is stratified socially, it tends toward masculinity and collectivism, it uses high-context communication in most settings, and deference to authority is expected in both social and business contexts.

To elaborate briefly on these points, the stratification of Egyptian society is distinct in terms of education, income, and general standard of living. Gaps between the haves and the have-nots are great and, interestingly, are mostly accepted by both groups. This may be due in part to religious beliefs and the Arabic phrase, "en shah Allah," meaning basically that things are as God meant (willed) them to be.

There is an increasingly large middle class in Egypt, but social mobility is not a defining quality of the culture. Public relations programs based on individual or group mobility motives that might work in the West will not necessarily succeed in Egypt, and it is probably more important for planners to consider the social class of their target publics in Egypt than it is in most other parts of the world.

On the dimension of individualism–collectivism, Egyptian culture values the society and the family over the individual. This collectivism is evident in the rabid patriotism of most Egyptians, the level of charity to help others (again influenced by Islam's teachings), and even in common Cairo street scenes and village settings where citizens cooperate toward a common group goal.

Egypt fits the profile of a masculine culture as laid out by Hofstede (1998)—men are generally assertive, and women are expected to be modest—and there are clear distinctions between the roles and expectations of genders. The masculine nature of the culture runs deep, with male children being a special source of pride in most families. Certain occupations including most of the professions, senior-level management, and high-ranking government and church positions, continue to be almost exclusively the domain of men. In addition, Egyptian laws include elements that discriminate between women and men.

As with most collectivist societies, in Egypt, communication tends to be high in context; people share a wider range of cultural understandings and symbols than in individualistic societies and take more meaning from certain settings and communicators. Combined with the high power distance or deference for authority found in Egypt, the culture is one in which people sort of know their place in a way that might seem inappropriate and unfair to outsiders, especially those from cultures on the other end of the context–power distance continuum.

Both within an organization and for dealing with external publics, it is crucial that public relations practitioners consider these and other cultural factors. It is also important for those whose interest is more scholarly to recognize the characteristics and structure of Egyptian culture in carrying out research on public relations in the country. Unless one is sensitive to the particular nature of the culture and to the interaction of factors such as those discussed here, professional and academic ventures are not likely to have much success. With such sensitivity, the Egyptian culture is one in which there are rich opportunities for public relations work and study.

MEDIA IN EGYPT

The beginnings of modern mass media in Egypt date from 1798, when Napoleon Bonaparte established the first mass circulation newspaper in Alexandria (Dabbous, 1994). Today, the Egyptian press includes national daily and weekly papers and regional publications centered in the larger cities. Magazines have evolved from simple tabloids to a range of full-color, glossy publications to be found on the nation's newsstands in the early years of the 21st century. A limited selection of foreign newspapers and magazines is also available in the country though they tend to be a little outdated by the time they reach Egyptian audiences, especially in the case of foreign dailies.

Radio was introduced in Egypt in 1926 and passed through a stage under Nasser as an important propaganda tool for nationalization and for pan-Arab causes. In contemporary Egypt, AM and FM radio stations offer a full array of programming formats. In 1960, the Radio Corporation of America assisted the Egyptian government in setting up a television system (Gher & Amin, 1999). As of 2002, there are two national broadcast television stations and seven stations with local or regional transmission. There is also one cable television system operating in Cairo, and over 1 million Egyptian households have access to satellite television (Elghawaby, 2000).

As expected, most Egyptian media are in Arabic. There is a daily newspaper and a weekly newspaper in English, and daily newspaper in French. There are also a number of weekly and monthly magazines in English. One of Egypt's television stations, Nile TV, broadcasts both in English and French, and there are several radio stations that have foreign language programming at least part of the day.

Media Control

Since the time of Nasser, Egyptian media have been state-owned or state controlled. The privatization of Egypt's economy has not really included the mass media industry, although some have suggested that the process will just be slower as far as the media are concerned (Napoli, Amin, & Napoli, 1995). With new media such as the Internet and satellite television making inroads, the government is less able to maintain control over what Egyptians view. The result has been a limited loosening of controls, with some private, advertising revenue-supported, publications being permitted. This is true especially among the relatively small circulation English language magazines. Private investment has also been permitted in the operation of Egyptian cable television (Boyd, 1999), and licenses have been granted to private television channels on the government-owned satellite, NileSat (Wahby, 2002).

Despite such developments, Egyptian media remain under government control for the most part. Rugh (1987) described the Egyptian media system as an example of what he called the "mobilization" (p. 31) model of government control, in which the state oversees all media, dictates policy and content, hires and fires media personnel, and exercises strict censorship standards.

The three largest, and most influential, newspapers in Egypt, *Al-Ahram, Al-Akhbar*, and *Al-Gomuhuria*, all remain government owned, as do the English and French language dailies, the primary regional papers, and the country's radio and television stations. In the print segment, an "opposition press" exists but is heavily regulated through laws, taxes, and licensing procedures. Publications that go too far in opposing the government or run content deemed inappropriate to religious and cultural norms are summarily shut down.

In cases when Egyptian media are not owned outright by the government, control is maintained by indirect means such as the supply of newsprint and the distribution of publications, which are under government control. Advertising is also a means of government power in that at least for the print media, the largest advertising spenders are traditionally public sector enterprises (under government control), and the largest advertising agencies in the country are government owned.

The government agency that oversees the ownership, control, and regulation of all media in Egypt is the Ministry of Information. The Egyptian Television and Radio Union, within the Ministry of Information, is responsible for planning, decisions, and implementation of policies related to the broadcast media.

Media Outreach

There are certain factors that should be taken into account in targeting different segments of the Egyptian population, but with proper planning and familiarity with the country, all can be reached through one medium or another. The characteristics and advantages inherent in different media are of course important in public relations work, but in some cases they must be sacrificed in Egypt due to circumstances and obstacles that limit media options for reaching particular groups.

The major national newspapers in Egypt are distributed throughout the country. The largest of these, *Al-Ahram*, has a circulation of over 1 million, and the combined circulation of all Egyptian papers is around 3 million (Gher & Amin, 1999). It is important to recognize, however, that illiteracy remains a problem in Egypt, especially in areas outside the population centers of Cairo and Alexandria. The fact is, that with nearly half of the country's population unable to read, newspaper readership is naturally low, as stressed in chapter 1 of this book. Currently, the low rate of literacy is a priority of the Egyptian government and various nongovernmental organizations. As a result, there is reason to hope that as the portion of the population with reading skills increases, so will the reach of the country's newspapers.

Magazines face the same literacy dilemma as newspapers, and with their typically higher cover price, they also have an audience size that is limited by basic economic affordability in some cases. Although no single Egyptian magazine has a very large circulation, magazines do a good job of reaching narrow audience niches. Magazines specializing in sports, entertainment, religion, women's topics, and other specialized areas are popular among different segments. Distributed through the same *Al-Ahram* newsstand system as Egyptian newspapers, major magazine titles are available throughout the country.

The electronic media offer the greatest opportunity for reaching large audiences and all segments of Egyptian society. Especially with the national radio and television stations, broadcast disseminated messages can be expected to cross boundaries of literacy and socioeconomic status. At the dawn of the 21st century, nearly all Egyptian households have both radio and television receivers, and in areas where television penetration to individual households is low, there is a tradition of communal viewing in neighborhood cafes or village coffee shops. The growth of satellite television among the upper and middle classes has diverted some of the audience that was recently held by domestic channels (Hafez, 2001), but the popularity of certain Egyptian programs and serials and the reputation of special Ramadan programming continues to attract substantial viewership among all classes of society and is even exported and popular throughout the Middle East.

A somewhat unique aspect of Egyptian media outreach involves a category that Dabbous (1994) referred to as "external media services" (p. 70). These include a variety of government-produced radio programs aired outside of the country, the Nile TV channel aimed at foreign audiences, and international distribution of *Al-Ahram* newspaper. Public relations implications of such media include the potential ability to reach expatriate Egyptian publics and the fact that certain messages and media content may "bleed" beyond national borders.

Media Access

The predominant government control over Egyptian media has some obvious impact on the access afforded to those media. One of these is that government organizations and causes have a special advantage in gaining access. By extension, organizations who toe the government line are also much more likely to be permitted access than those with no shared interests or those who oppose the government in some way. Considering this point, government relations practices can be especially important in Egypt; at some level, an overlap of government and media relations should probably be taken into account.

An additional point concerning access to Egyptian media is the confusion between publicity and advertising described earlier in this chapter. As long as it is accepted practice to require either the purchase of advertising or direct payment to the media for media access via releases and other methods, Western conceptions of public relations' role in acquiring media space or time will bear no relation to reality in Egypt. Decisions ought to be made early in public relations planning as to whether an organization is willing to pay for access or will seek other ways through media gatekeepers in Egypt.

Less direct means of gaining media access include letters to the editor, talk shows, audience call-in shows on radio or television, and program-length television infomercials, although the scale and acceptability of such methods are restricted and those involving controversial topics are likely to be heavily censored. For addressing upscale publics composed of Internet users, satellite subscribers, or those exposed to foreign media, there may also be occasions when media strategies might choose to circumvent Egyptian media entirely if access is overly problematic.

In conclusion, the areas of media outreach and media access are closely tied to media control in Egypt. Although the future may see changes in the structure and flexibility of Egyptian media systems, the reality of things now is that the government is all powerful in allowing access and determining who and what will be included in the country's media. Public relations professionals would do well see this as a starting point for planning work to achieve media access.

Considering the current state of factors covered here and the ongoing changes in Egyptian society and business practices, there is reason to think the public relations profession will continue to grow in Egypt. Some obstructions will remain that may constrain this growth, and it is not likely that Egyptian public relations will ever mirror the Western model completely. But as the economy continues to move in the direction of privatization and as the government, Egyptian culture, and the media become more welcoming of the conditions that accompany the privatization, public relations will find an environment where it is increasingly welcome and necessary. In the years ahead, Egypt will offer regular opportunities for public relations consultants to help develop the public relations industry in Egypt and for scholars to study the profession and its development and train future professionals.

CASE STUDY: COCA-COLA EGYPT

Understandably, soft drinks are quite popular in Egypt. The country's dry, hot climate is certainly responsible for their basic appeal. But Egyptians are also notorious for having a sweet tooth. In addition, Islam's prohibition of alcoholic drinks makes soft drinks the beverage type of choice for social gatherings and celebrations.

There are several local soft drink brands on the market, but, like almost everywhere else in the world, the leading sellers are Coca-Cola ® and Pepsi Cola. However, unlike most other countries, in Egypt, Pepsi has always had a larger market share than Coke. In fact Egyptians refer to any soft drink generically as a *Pepsi* (or with colloquial Egyptian pronunciation, as a *Bebsi*) in the same way the term *Coke* is sometimes used to include any and all soft drinks in the United States.

Coca-Cola has been available in Egypt since 1945, but it was nationalized under Nasser and was produced by government-owned bottling plants until 1994 when the Coca-Cola Bottling Companies of Egypt was formed as part of the country's privatization policy. Since then, the company has faced a number of obstacles, including the already established Pepsi Cola as a privatized soft drink bottler in Egypt, occasional consumer boycotts with the identification of the product as a symbol of American imperialism, and a general perception in the Arab world that "Coke is for Jews; Pepsi is for Arabs" (Mikkelson, 1999). But with updated production plants, improved distribution and marketing, and a modern approach to public relations, Coke has made substantial inroads to the point where the brand's current market share is nearly equal to that of Pepsi.

Since its privatization, Coca-Cola Egypt's public relations activities have focused on community service and what most would consider a two-way symmetrical philosophy of emphasizing feedback through research of relevant publics and a recognition that the company must make certain adjustments in its Egyptian operations. Specific efforts have included an employee literacy program that has produced a 100% literacy rate among its 8,000 workers; campaigns in which a portion of all money earned from product sales goes to select charities in Egypt; and sponsorships and participation with nonprofit projects in the areas of education, health, youth sports, and the environment.

In 2000, the company was faced with a potentially devastating situation when a rumor spread through Egypt that Coca-Cola was anti-Islam. A charge was made that if the Coca-Cola script logo was viewed upside down and in a mirror, it read as "No Mohamed. No Mecca." Given the deep importance of religion in all areas of Egyptian life, the supposed message degrading Islam's prophet and the religion's holiest place caused outrage and an instant drop in sales of Coke products nearing almost 20%. Literature decrying the company and calls for its ouster from the country circulated in mosques, schools, and on the streets of cities and villages throughout Egypt. In certain jurisdictions, authorities ordered that all Coca-Cola signage and advertising be removed.

Coca-Cola Egypt's response to this rumor, whose original source was never determined, was immediate, culturally sensitive, and reasoned. The company requested to meet with Egypt's Grand Mufti Sheik Nasser Farid Wassel, the highest religious figure in the country, and also arranged for an official panel of Islamic scholars to consider the matter. Note that in meeting with the Grand Mufti, Coca-Cola's approach was less to plead their case than to seek the input and opinions of the respected religious leader. The convening of the scholarly panel was also done in conformity with tradition and established procedures of Islam.

The outcome of Coca-Cola Egypt's decision to involve local religious experts was that both the Grand Mufti and the group of scholars ruled there was no substance to the rumor of the Coke logo being anti-Islam. The Grand Mufti announced this opinion publicly and went on to scold those who were disseminating the rumor for behavior not befitting their religion and for risking the jobs and welfare of thousands of Egyptian Muslims employed by Coca-Cola.

In the aftermath of this crisis, Coca-Cola took the step of providing its sales force and delivery truck drivers with copies of the Grand Mufti's statement to display and distribute among businesses and customers. The company also followed up with an advertising campaign in which verses from the Holy Koran were included as part of their message, running alongside the recently controversial Coca-Cola logo. Within just a few weeks, Coke regained its prerumor sales level and was once again challenging Pepsi for leadership in the Egyptian soft drink market.

This case shows just how crucial it is for international public relations practitioners to understand what underlies the culture and structure of individual countries. Through no recognizable fault of their own, Coca-Cola had to face perhaps the most serious accusation any company can endure in an Islamic nation. By realizing the severity of the situation and by working with the country's religious leaders in a respectful and cooperative manner, Coca-Cola Egypt managed to avert serious damage and proclaim their innocence and contribution to Egypt's economy.

REFERENCES

Alanazi, A. (1996). Public relations in the Middle East: The case of Saudi Arabia. In H. M. Culbertson & N. Chen, (Eds.), *International public relations: A comparative analysis* (pp. 239–256). Mahwah, NJ: Lawrence Erlbaum Associates.

Al-Tohami, M., & Al-Dakoki, I. (1980). *Principles of public relations in the developing nations.* Beruit, Lebanon: Da Alama'arefa.

Botman, S. (1998). The liberal age, 1923–1952. In M. W. Daly (Ed.), *The Cambridge history of Egypt, 1798–1801* (pp. 285–308). Cambridge, England: Cambridge University Press.

Boyd, D. A. (1999). *Broadcasting in the Arab world: A survey of the electronic media in the Middle East.* Ames, IA: Iowa State University Press.

Country reports on human rights practices: Egypt. (2002, March 4). U.S. Department of State. www.usis. usemb.se/human/2001/neareast/egypt.html

Credit where credit is due. (1999, March 20). *The Economist,* pp. 9–10.

Dabbous, S. (1994). Egypt. In Y. R. Kamalipour & H. Mowlana (Eds.), *Mass media in the Middle East: A comprehensive handbook* (pp. 60–73). Westport, CT: Greenwood Press.

Del Castillo, D. (2001, April 13). Egypt puts a scholar, and academic freedom, on trial. *Chronicle of Higher Education*, pp. A53–A55.

Dykstra, D. (1998). The French occupation of Egypt, 1798–1801. In M. W. Daly (Ed.), *The Cambridge history of Egypt* (pp. 113–138). Cambridge, England: Cambridge University Press.

Elghawaby, A. (2000, March). Egypt: Satellite dishes abound. *World Press Review*, p. 11.

El-Gibaly, O., Ibrahim, B., Mensch, B. S., & Clark, W. H. (2002). The decline of female circumcision in Egypt: Evidence and interpretation. *Social Science and Medicine, 54*(2), 205–221.

Egypt: Amnesty International Report 2002. Retrieved August 12, 2002, from web.amnesty.org/web/ar2002. nsf/mde/egypt

Gauch, S. (1995, February 24). Egypt's Coptic Christians endure harassment by Muslims. *Christian Science Monitor*, p. 10.

Gauch, S. (2001, June 18). Egyptian feminist faces stiff penalty for statements deemed anti-Islamic. *Christian Science Monitor*, p. 9.

Gher, L. H., & Amin, H. Y. (1999). New and old access and ownership in the Arab world. *Gazette, 61*(1), 59–88.

Gomaa, S. S. (1996). The civil debate over privatization in Egypt: Conflicting interpretations and goals. In W. Badran & A. Wahby (Eds.), *Privatization in Egypt: The debate in the People's Assembly* (pp. 179–209). Cairo, Egypt: Center for Political Research and Studies.

Hafez, K. (2001). Mass media in the Middle East: Patterns of political and social change. In K. Hafez (Ed.), *Mass media, politics, and society in the Middle East* (pp. 1–20). Cresskill, NJ: Hampton Press.

Haikal, F. (1993). Family life in modern Egypt. In J. Malek (Ed.), *Egypt: Ancient culture, modern land* (pp. 172–181). Norman, OK: University of Oklahoma Press.

Hammer, J. (2002, February 16). *One man's tale*. Retrieved August 1, 2002 from www.msnbc.com/news/708876

Hanafi, K. (2002, July 22). Egypt: Protest groups boycott United States products. *Islam Online*. Retrieved August 1, 2002 from, www.corpwatch.org/news/PND.jsp?articleid=3148

Hofstede, G. H. (1980). *Culture's consequences: International differences in work-related values.* Beverly Hills, CA: Sage.

Hofstede, G. H. (1998). *Masculinity and femininity: The taboo dimension of national cultures.* Thousand Oaks, CA: Sage.

Human rights watch world report 2002: Egypt. Retrieved August 15, 2002, from www.hrw.org/wr2k2/ menaz.html

Howeidy, A. (2001, April 26–May 2). Secure a victory and move on. *Al-Ahram Weekly On-line*. Retrieved September, 2002 from, www.ahram.org.eg/weekly/2001/531/eg7.htm

Jankowski, J. P. (2000). *Egypt: A short history.* Oxford, England: Oneworld.

Keenan, K. L., & Yeni, S. (2002, August). *Ramadan advertising in Egypt: A content analysis with elaboration on select items.* Paper presented to the Association for Education in Journalism and Mass Communication Conference, Miami, FL.

Khorasanizadeh, F. (2001, April). Sector survey: Marketing and PR. *Business Today Egypt*, pp. 51–58.

Lussier, A. M. (2002, August). The wages of spin. *Business Monthly: The Journal the American Chamber of Commerce in Egypt*, (Vol. 18) 38–45.

McPhail, T. L. (2002). *Global communication: Theories, stakeholders, and trends.* Boston: Allyn & Bacon.

Mekay, E. (2000, September 11). Denial. *New Republic*, pp. 16–17.

Mikkelson, B. (1999). *Red, white, and Jew.* Retrieved January 26, 2003 from www.snopes.com/cokelore/ israel.asp

Napoli, J. J., Amin, H. Y., & Napoli, L. R. (1995). Privatization of the Egyptian media. *Journal of South Asian and Middle Eastern Studies, 18*(4), 39–57.

Roy, D. A. (1992). The hidden economy of Egypt. *Middle East Studies, 28*(4), 689–711.

Rugh, W. A. (1987). *The Arab press: News media and political process in the Arab world.* Syracuse, NY: Syracuse University Press.

Run-Up to Shura Council election marred by a wave of arrests. (2001, December 11). News release from Amnesty International. Retrieved August 1, 2002 from www.amnestyusa.org/news/2001/egypt 05152001.html

Smith, B. (1999, March 20). New and old. *The Economist*, pp. 1–4.

Smith, P. (1999, July/August). Egypt sells off. *Middle East*, pp. 33–36.

Spiers, P. (1991, September). It's not advertising: What is it? *Business Monthly: The Journal of the American Chamber of Commerce in Egypt*, (Vol. 7) 32–33.

Sriramesh, K., & Verčič, D. (2002). *The innovativeness–needs paradox and global public relations: Propositions on the need for international PR subsidies.* Paper presented to the International Communication Association Conference, Seoul, Korea.

Stones, L. (1994, June). The art of image building. *Business Monthly: The Journal of the American Chamber of Commerce in Egypt*, (Vol. 10) 27–30 .

Vatikiotis, P. J. (1991). *The history of Modern Egypt: From Mohamed Ali to Mubarak*. London: Weidenfeld and Nicolson.

Wahby, E. (2002, July). Satellite stations cross red lines. *Business Monthly: The Journal of the American Chamber of Commerce in Egypt*, (Vol. 18) 32.

Zaklama, L. (2001). Public relations Egyptian style. In M. Terterov (Ed.), *Doing business with Egypt*, (pp. 98–103) London: Kogan Page.

III

EUROPE

10

From Literary Bureaus to a Modern Profession: The Development and Current Structure of Public Relations in Germany

Günter Bentele
Stefan Wehmeier

INTRODUCTION

The Federal Republic of Germany with nearly 82 million inhabitants is the country with the highest population in middle Europe. It covers a 356,790 km^2 area. The North Sea and the Baltic Sea border the national territory to the north, and the Alps border the territory to the south. There are no such natural borders on the east and west. The northern neighbor is Denmark, and Poland and the Czech Republic are the eastern neighbors. The predominantly German-speaking nations Austria and Switzerland border Germany to the south, with France, Belgium, Luxembourg, and the Netherlands bordering on the west. Around 7.3 million foreigners (approx. 9% of the total population) live in Germany. The country ensures freedom of religion. In 2000, the Protestant and Catholic churches had around 27 million members each, with 2.8 million Muslims forming the next largest religious community.

HISTORY OF PUBLIC RELATIONS IN GERMANY

The development of public relations in Germany was shaped by numerous historical conditions. Political, economic, and social influences have had an impact on the evolving public relations profession in Germany. We emphasize the changing political history of Germany since the beginning of the 19th century because the type of state changed several

TABLE 10.1
Periods of German Public Relations

Pre-history: Official press politics, functional public relations, development of instruments	
Period 1 (mid-19th century–1918) Development of the occupational field	Development of the first press offices in politics and firms, war press releases under the conditions of censorship, first public campaigns
Period 2 (1918–1933) Consolidation and growth	Fast and widespread growth of press offices in different social fields: economy, politics, municipal administration
Period 3 (1933–1945) Media relations and political propaganda and the Nazi Regime	Party-ideological media relations within political propaganda. National and party-related control and direction of journalism, media relations, and inner relations
Period 4 (1945–1958) New beginning and upturn	Postwar development, upturn and orientation to the American model starting in the early 1950s, development of a new professional self-understanding under the conditions of democratic structures (public relations defined as distinct from propaganda and advertisement), fast development of the professional field predominantly in the economic sphere
Period 5 (1958–1985) Consolidation of the professional field in the Federal Republic of Germany and establishment of a socialist public relations in the German Democratic Republic (GDR)	Development of a professional self-consciousness, 1958 foundation of the professional association DPRG, which initiated private training programs. Simultaneous with the developments in West Germany, a type of socialist public relations developed in the GDR from the mid-1960s.
Period 6 (1985–present) Boom of the professional field and professionalization	Strong development of public relations agencies, professionalization of the field, beginning and development of academic public relations education; improvements in the training system, scientific application and enhancement of the instruments; development of public relations as a science

Note. From Bentele 1997: 161

times from the German Alliance during the German Reich to the Weimar Republic, followed by the Nazi Regime, World War II, and the establishment of two German states (one democratic and one socialist), which eventually reunited in 1990. These turning points are also reflected in the periodical structure of German public relations history (see Table 10.1), which is closely related to the general historic periods.

The Press and Freedom of the Press Until 1914

The defeat of France by Napoleon in 1806 officially sealed the end of the Holy Roman Empire. After the Congress of Vienna, this German Empire was succeeded by the German Alliance. It constituted 39 states and existed until 1866. Above all, the claims of sovereignty of some principalities lead to a strong particularism within the alliance (Schieder, 1999, pp. 98–107). A strong and powerful central power was missing, and there was no freedom of the press. For example, on October 18, 1819, the censorship dictate in Prussia since December 1788 was renewed (Koszyk, 1966, p. 59). Only after the failed March Revolution in 1848 was censorship abolished in some states. However, the rulers still kept powerful means of pressure on printing products that they disliked. The most important institute were the granting and cancellation of concessions based on the whims of the rulers (Koszyk, 1966, pp. 120–126).

The German party-related press, such as the social–democratic press, developed under these conditions until the founding of the German Reich in 1871 (Koszyk, 1966, pp. 127–208). Otto von Bismarck, who was prime minister from 1862 and chancellor of the Reich from 1871, tried to either prohibit or exploit the press. Bismarck's treatment of the press was a mix of banning newspapers, legally persecuting journalists and publishers, and manipulating media content (Koszyk, 1966, pp. 229–250).

After the founding of the German Reich, a few more rights and journalistic freedoms were granted by the *Reichspressegesetz* (Reich press law). As a result, the German press experienced an upturn, but it also was an opportunity for advertising gazettes and mass press products of a rather cheap and apolitical character. In 1914, the number of daily and weekly newspapers was around 4,200, and the number of copies printed is estimated to have been 18 million (Pürer & Raabe, 1996, p. 22). This extensive development of the press also caused national organizations and businesses to put more effort into public relations. During this time, public information and public manipulation were often strongly intertwined.

State Press Politics, Municipal Public Relations, and the Evolution of Business-like Public Relations

In 1841, the *Ministerial-Zeitungsbüro* (governmental bureau of newspapers) was established in Prussia as the first political press department. Its function was not only to inform and observe the press but also to avoid negative articles in the media (known as wrong press reports) and the impression of overt censorship (Nöth-Greis, 1997). After the official abolishment of censorship in 1848, the communicative functions of the succeeding institutions such as *Literarisches Cabinet* (Literary Cabinet; 1848–1859), *Centralstelle für Presseangelegenheiten* (Central Office of Press Affairs; 1850–1860), and *Literarisches Büro* (Literary Bureau; 1860–1920) shifted to the observation of the press, the internal information of the Prussian government, and international press relations. However, particularly under Bismarck, this shift included a more subtle influence and control of the press. For example, officious (or government-friendly) newspapers were financially supported (Koszyk, 1966, p. 229ff; Nöth-Greis, 1997). This practice of keeping in leading strings of the press by the government continued after the founding of the German Reich and after the already mentioned liberalization of the press through the Reich press law. Further, the *Pressedezernat des Auswärtigen Amtes* (Press Department at the Office of Foreign Affairs), founded in 1871, had task observation and information of the press and its manipulation. The first corporate press department was established by Alfred Krupp, the founder of the famous steel company, Krupp, in 1870, 4 years after Krupp had seen the necessity to hire a literate. The duty of this literate was to read newspapers from around the world that the organization saw as important as well as to write articles, brochures, and correspondences to publicize the corporation and its products (Wolbring, 2000).

Admiral Alfred von Tirpitz engineered one of the most important public campaigns of the German Reich in his quest to build a strong German Naval fleet. At the end of the 19th century, the German economy developed rapidly, and a section of the political and military elite desired to extend German influence by colonizing new territories. This section of the power elite wanted to counter the dominance of the British Empire by building a strong navy that could not only colonize new lands but also protect German merchant ships. Tirpitz and his supporters had to first convince a majority of the political class, the Kaiser, and the population that this was the right thing for Germany. Tirpitz used different kinds of publicity instruments such as posters, lectures, speeches, and press reports to persuade the relevant target groups. By arguing his case from an economic standpoint, he finally was successful in changing public opinion (Kunczik, 1997, pp. 111–116). Whereas the "fleet campaign" had some manipulative characteristics, the public relations activities at the municipal level mainly were informative. They mostly focused on developing and maintaining relationships with local publics and carrying on the tasks of the cities, thereby actually performing community relations (Liebert, 1997, p. 88).

Besides the political changes of the 19th century, the economic and technical progress also shaped the development of public relations in Germany. Coal mining and the steel industry became pivotal foundations of the German heavy industry and electronics, and chemistry became an innovative growth industry. Alfred Krupp, Emil Rathenau, and Werner von Siemens simultaneously became leading businessmen as well as architects of public relations (Wolbring, 2000; Zipfel, 1997).

In the course of industrialization, friction developed between the powerful trusts and wealthy business families and the evolving working class. Along with industrialization and urbanization, social hardship appeared, which demanded actions from politicians and businesses. Consequently, the late 19th century witnessed the first steps toward social legislation and the first efforts at human relations, such as employee magazines, pensions, sports and singing clubs, and recreation homes for children. The motivation for these moves originated from the ethical pretense of numerous businessmen viewing themselves as fathers of a family of workers on the one hand while fearing strikes and rebellions on the other.

In addition to these internal communication practices, there were early accounts of external communication instruments in companies like Krupp, AEG, and Siemens. Krupp used the First World Exhibition in 1851 in London to present his own efficiency and to show off the biggest steel cube. AEG had already begun systematical analysis of press clippings since the beginning of the 20th century.

Public Relations From World War I Until the Nazi Dictatorship

During the World War I, there was one outstanding national public relations campaign— the loan campaign to raise funds for financing the war. Corporate public relations also was affected by the war, with companies morally supporting their employees on the front with employee magazines (Heise, 2000). At the end of the war and the establishment of the democratic Weimar Republic, public relations made great strides in Germany. A significant number of press offices and news bureaus came into being, and the economic boom of the Twenties convinced the businessmen to carry out active public relations (Kunczik, 1997, pp. 166–182, 290–307).

In contrast, the national socialism (1933–1945) period represented a step backward for the entire field of public communication. Under the Nazi dictatorship, the media were brought in line and exploited to advance the Nazi doctrine. The national socialist state made great propagandistic efforts, and the oppressed media (press, broadcasting, and film) served as loudspeakers of political and ideological content. Although there had existed a relatively diverse and independent media system in the Weimar Republic, public information activities under the Nazis was centralized under the Reich Ministry of Public

Information and Propaganda. The media were cleared of Jewish journalists, and strict penalties were introduced to punish people who did not write stories that pleased the Nazis. Needless to say, the entire system of public communication gained a propagandistic character. Although external media relations and internal information in governmental organizations, associations, communities, cultural institutions, and companies still existed during the Nazi dictatorship, these activities often employed a propagandistic communication style. During this period, German public relations pioneers Carl Hundhausen and Albert Oeckl got their first experience in advertising and public relations. Ivy L. Lee, who at the beginning of the Nazi regime was counselor to a subsidiary of the IG Farben, represented the connection between the development of public relations in Germany and the United States (Kunczik, 1997, pp. 298–301).

From the End of World War II Until Today

After World War II, the public relations field in West Germany was reborn. The American influence on West German society was also widely felt in the development of postwar public relations. Besides German advertising and public relations agencies, branches of American agencies also started to operate in West Germany and bring with them their view of public relations. This, to a certain extent, only meant revitalizing practices that could not be carried out during the Nazi regime. Carl Hundhausen and Albert Oeckl represented both continuity and new beginning for the public relations profession in West Germany. Both of them had already been active in public relations during the Nazi dictatorship, and now they played a crucial role in the development of the profession in the first 2 decades after the war. One of their central achievements was the founding of the professional association of public relations, the Deutsche Public Relations Gesellschaft (DPRG) or the German Public Relations Association. Carl Hundhausen and, later, Albert Oeckl were chairmen of this organization for many years (Binder, 1983).

Until the late 1960s, a rather simple understanding of public relations was dominant in Germany. Public relations was interpreted as advertising for trust. Information and the creation of attention were understood to build trust in organizations and to draw the attention of the media to their products and images. It was only in the early 1970s that an understanding of public relations as the dialogue with different target groups started to develop. The end of the so called economic miracle, resulting in social tensions, and the appearance of environmental activism turned customers into demanding groups with whom dialogue needed to be established. A boom of financial and human resources has been witnessed among public relations agencies since the middle of the 1980s. In addition, public relations was introduced in universities and polytechnics (*Fachhochschulen*), resulting in the intense discussion of ethical standards and the scientific foundation of the field (Bentele & Liebert, 1998, pp. 78–80; Kunczik, 1999).

CHARACTERIZING PRESENT STRUCTURES OF THE PUBLIC RELATIONS FIELD IN GERMANY

The Image of Public Relations

The image of the public relations field varies among different publics. Because public relations is hardly felt directly by the general public, it has a rather diffuse image in contrast to journalists and the media as well as chairmen of companies and other high-ranking persons in organizations who can react directly to public relations activities. Journalists often have an ambivalent image of the public relations field. On one hand, they recognize that public relations is indispensable as a professional information source; on the other hand, they continue to harbor negative expressions such as "PR gags" or "PR pretense" or "typical PR" (these expressions refer to exaggerations or entertaining events with only little content). Especially true of members of the dominant coalition such as the boards of companies, the image of communication experts has significantly improved over the last few decades. In the 1960s expressions like *Sektglashalter* (someone who only holds champagne glasses in his or her hands) or *Frühstücksdirektor* (someone who has a director's position but only dines with guests) were still used to characterize the public relations profession in a negative way. Today, the necessity of communication management and the need to employ well-qualified academics are mainly unquestioned although not yet recognized universally in the country. The bigger an enterprise, the more readily public relations is accepted as an independent function by the organization, preferably combined with other communication functions (Bruhn & Boenigk, 1999, Haedrich, Jenner, Olavarria, & Possekal, 1994). Professional communication experts are treated as partners and as colleagues "on the other side of the desk" by journalists.

Definitions and Different Public Relations Concepts

Just as there are many definitions of terms such as *philosophy, communication*, or *sociology*, there are many definitions of the term *public relations* in Germany. In 1951, Carl Hundhausen (1893–1977) defined public relations as "letting the public or its parts know about yourself in order to advertise for trust" (Hundhausen, 1951, p. 53). Albert Oeckl (1909–2001), who in the 1950s rediscovered the German term *Öffentlichkeitsarbeit* that had been in use in 1917, described public relations as "working *with* the public, working *for* the public, working *in* the public." He continued that "working means the intended, planned, and continuous effort to build mutual understanding and trust and to care about it" (Oeckl, 1964, p. 36). Twelve years later, he defined *Öffentlichkeitsarbeit* as "information + adaptation + integration" (Oeckl, 1976, p. 52). Following a definition by Grunig and Hunt (1984, p. 4), Bentele (1998) described public relations as the "management of information and communication processes between organizations on the one side and their internal and external environments (publics) on the other side. Public Relations serves the functions of information, communication, persuasion, image building, continuous building of trust, management of conflicts, and the generation of social consensus" (p. 33).

To structure the countless definitions in a logical way, different perspectives of public relations should be defined. Bentele (1998, p. 27 ff) distinguished three *starting perspectives* (Who defines public relations?) and three *target perspectives* (How is it defined?). The three starting perspectives are (a) the *everyday life perspective*, (b) the *professional perspective*, and (c) the *scientific perspective*. The target perspectives are the *activity related, organizational*, and *society related* (see table 10.2).

It is not surprising that there are different definitions within the professional perspective. But in the academic perspective, two clearly different perspectives can be distinguished: the *organizational* perspective (subdivided into the communication studies and the business studies perspectives) and the society-related perspective (i. e., public relations is seen and analyzed as a functional element of our modern information and communication society).

Every-day life perceptions of public relations frequently focus not only on neutral fields of activities of public relations practitioners (e.g., providing information) but also on judgments. Those can be positive (e.g., public relations is a cool job and an interesting occupation) or negative (e.g., public relations referred to as embellishments, propaganda, or

TABLE 10.2

Different Starting and Target Perspectives of Public Relations

	Activity related perspective	Organizational perspective	Society related perspective
Every-day life perspective	Interesting profession but also manipulation, extenuation, propaganda, media relations	Activities of public relations agencies, public relations departments in companies etc.	No concept
Professional perspective	Information, talk to the public, care for relationships, keep secrets, and manipulation	Task and function of leadership and management	Basic form of public communication
Scientific perspective	Information, communication, persuasion, acquisition of trust, and soon	Communication studies: communication management. Business studies: instrument of marketing, communication politics	Form of public communication, subsystem of the public communication system

Note. From Bentele 1998: 29

manipulation). Conversely, the conceptions of practitioners mostly are positively connoted but often normatively introduced. Nowadays, professional associations usually label public relations as *dialogue*, but this is more of a normative pretense than an empirical proof. Using a scientifically based viewpoint, public relations can be looked at from an activity-related perspective as well as from an organizational and a macrosocial point of view. The organizational–communication studies perspective poses the question: What does public relations generally contribute to organizations (not only businesses)? Another scientific perspective is the study of marketing which uses public relations as an instrument within communication politics. Communication politics itself is seen as just another part of the general marketing mix (besides product politics, price politics, and placement politics). Thus, public relations in this perspective is in principle subordinate to marketing (for more on this point, see the definitions of public relations, marketing, and advertising in the following chapter). From a society-related (macrosocial) perspective, the question arises: Which social function(s) for the entire society are held by all organizational public relations activities (for more details, refer to Bentele, 1998, p. 32; Ronneberger & Rühl, 1992, p. 249 ff)?

Structures of the Occupational Public Relations Field in Germany

To give an account on the present status of the field in Germany, one can draw on a number of empirical studies that offer important insights from different perspectives. However, a representative study that covers the entire field in Germany does not exist. The total number of full-time public relations practitioners in Germany is estimated to be at least 20,000, of which around 40% work in corporate public relations; 20% in organizations, such as associations, clubs, churches, unions, and so on; 20% in institutions (e.g., political administration on national, regional, and local levels as well as courts); and 20% in public relations agencies (Bentele, 1998). Only an estimated 10% of all public relations professionals are members of one of the professional associations (e.g., the DPRG has approx. 1,800 members: about 4,000 PR practitioners are members of the *Deutscher Journalisten Verband, djv* [the German Journalists Association]. The number of public relations practitioners has increased faster than the number of journalists in Germany. In 1973, the leading public relations agencies founded their own association (Gesellschaft PR-Agenturen—the Association of Public Relations Agencies), which presently accounts for about 30 agencies representing nearly 1,500 professionals.

Professionalization. The degree of professionalization of the public location field, which is strongly interconnected with the training facilities, has been increasing since the beginning of the 1990s. Note that the public relations profession is, in general, academically institutionalized, with 70% to 80% of the practitioners having graduated from an institution of higher education (universities or polytechnical institutions). Some have even earned doctoral degrees (Becher, 1996; Merten, 1997). Nevertheless, the proportion of public relations practitioners who possess a high degree of public relations training (e.g., those who took many public relations courses or majored in public relations) is still under 20% (Röttger, 2000, p. 317). As early as the 1960s and 1970s, the DPRG and some private institutions began offering training courses, with several spread over a few weeks. Yet, it is only since the early 1990s that there has been a boom in public relations training. Many courses, sometimes including government support, were offered by a number of private providers to unemployed academics coming from all disciplines. Some of these courses lasted only 1 day or were spread over a few days, whereas others lasted several weeks or went as long as $1\frac{1}{2}$ years. Universities also began to offer public relations-related subjects, which eventually led to several public relations programs at major universities such as the Free University of Berlin and the Leipzig University. In addition, we currently see some public relations programs at vocational polytechnic institutes (Fachhochschulen) and universities (e.g., Hannover and Osnabrück). Equally important is the fact that several professional associations came together to establish a training academy called Deutsche Akademie für Public Relations—German Academy of Public Relations. There are some 40 other private academies and institutes that offer public relations courses, which are also available in evening schools and as distance learning courses. In the future, the function of public relations training is going to shift to the traditional institutions (polytechnical schools and universities), but private institutions will continue to be important for programs that further education (Bentele & Szyszka, 1995; Brauer, 1996; von Schlippe, Martini, & Schulze-Fürstenow, 1998).

Course Content. The content of academic programs as well as that of private institutions is very diverse and covers the entire spectrum of the profession, including courses such as the basics of communication and public relations, the history of public relations and public relations theories, the methods and instruments of practical public relations and communication management (e.g., media relations, investor relations, event management, internal communication, crisis public relations, and integrated communication), methods of evaluation and empirical communication and social research, and ethics. The training programs also cover economic and legal topics relevant to the profession. At universities, students are expected to take a second major or a minor to develop the required competence in a related discipline, such as political science or business. As far as professional ethics is concerned, the existing ethical codes such as the Code of Athens or Code of Lisbon are not well-known by public relations practitioners (Becher, 1996, p. 187; Röttger, 2000, p. 324). Although ethical attitudes are present among individual practitioners, public discourses on ethics are rare among practitioners. At least the Deutsche Rat für Public Relations (the German Council of Public Relations), a self-regulating organization founded in 1985 by the associations in the field, has been relatively active for some years outlining new guidelines and encouraging discourses about the violation of rules or ethical codes by agencies or practitioners (Avenarius, 1998; Bentele, 2000).

Two other noticeable features of the professional field in Germany are the process of feminization and the openness of the profession, to imports from other professions, such as journalism, law, or engineering. As recently as the late 1980s, not even 15% of public relations professionals in corporations, administration, or associations were women (Böeckelmann, 1988, p. 123; 1991a, p. 155; 1991b, p. 189). A survey by Merten (1997) showed that this proportion rose to 42% by 1996. Further, the present proportion of women among the members of the DPRG (43% in 2001) further confirms this process of feminization of the workforce as does the increase in the number of female public relations students at universities and *Fachhochschulen*, which is more than 60% of the student population.

The fact that the public relations field in Germany is still attracting practitioners from other occupations is proven by a 1989 survey of DPRG members as well as by a more recent study by Becher (1996). Both studies showed that approximately 33% of all people interviewed originally came from journalism, approximately 33% came from business or administration professions, and about 15% had previously worked in advertising and market research. Interestingly, about 20% had no other occupation before entering public relations (Becher, 1996, p. 194; DPRG, 1990).

Concerning the question of self-understanding and role models, Böckelmann's (1991b) surveys indicated that most press speakers (79% in corporations; 56% in organizations such as labor unions, churches, political parties, and business associations; and 53% in institutions such as ministries, parliaments, administration of justice, or municipal administration) identified themselves as being representatives of their respective organization. About 54% to 70% thought of themselves as mediators between the organization and the public, and only 12% (businesses) and 29% (organizations) considered themselves to be journalists (Böckelmann, 1991b, p. 176). This could have resulted from the high number of former journalists among public relations practitioners. Empirical data on the self-assessment and external assessment of public relations technicians and managers do not exist in Germany.

Which activities typically dominate the work of public relations professionals? The lion's share of the daily agenda is used for media relations (press reports, press conferences, organizing talks with journalists, etc.). Internal communication is dominated by analyzing the media as well as by producing and organizing internal media, such as employee magazines and using the intranet.

Are there different standards of quality in the different specialties of the profession? Based on our observations and anecdotal data, the highest qualified public relations practitioners can be found in public relations agencies and in the public relations departments of big companies. These departments are generally fully staffed, and the various specialties are well differentiated. The public relations departments of nonprofit organizations, associations, and public institutions (e.g., museums, theaters, and universities) had employees with the lowest qualifications and worst equipment. The need for public affairs and political communication (not election campaigning) has increased over the last 10 years. As a result, the demand for specialized agencies is high. Particularly during election campaigns, parties do establish large communication departments, which are planned strategically and communicate in a differentiated way. Varying quality standards are more prominent between businesses or agencies and the nonprofit and public field than between different branches (e.g., between the car industry and the financial branch or chemistry).

One of the most ardent desires of public relations associations is the highest possible ranking of public relations practitioners within an organizational hierarchy. According to Merten's (1997), survey, 68% of interviewees held a leading position in the organizational structure. A representative survey among businessmen by Haedrich et al. (1994, p. 4) revealed that 26% of all companies ranked public relations as a line function, whereas 71% ranked it as a management function. The same survey also revealed that 33% of responding companies ranked public relations as being in the top level of the corporate hierarchy, 54% ranked it at the second highest level (i.e., directly under the executive level), 12% ranked it at the third level of hierarchy, and 1% graded it even lower. The same study also found that the bigger a business was, the more independence was granted to the public relations departments; this hierarchy level was similar to that in marketing departments or, in some cases, was even higher than the marketing department. At the same time, the subordination of public relations under marketing or at least the mixing of the two tasks is still apparent especially in small and medium-size firms.

In 1997, the wbpr agency surveyed 3,000 businessmen and found that the ranking of public relations within businesses has improved since the 1990 study. According to those interviewed, 16% ranked public relations as very high, 56% ranked it and as high (wbpr, 1997, p. 9 ff). A recent representative survey among companies confirms these older results and indicates that 80% of the heads of communication departments work on the top hierarchical level with 7% of the public relations department heads even serving as members of the board (Zühlsdorf, 2002, p. 215). These results clearly show that today German companies consider public relations to be relatively important. When public relations practitioners or entire communication departments have a rather low status, this may be due to the fact that public relations practitioners have inferior qualifications at the decision-making level. This situation can be improved not only by continuing the process of professionalization and improving practitioner training but also by academically strengthening the professional standards.

Although it is possible to use existing data to identify the frequency of use of various public relations tools, it does not seem to make sense to rank more complex public relations strategies and methods used in Germany. Presumably, wherever there is public relations, there are at least media relations activities. In addition, one can assume that all of the modern methods of public relations are in use, such as employee relations, investor relations as part of financial relations (this has quickly developed over the last 5 years), crisis communication, issues management (Röttger, 2000a), and event management. Some of the more recent trends, especially at the bigger agencies, focus on change communication (i.e., the management of communication by companies undergoing change), issues management, sustainability communication, brand public relations, corporate governance, and impression management (Bentele, Piwinger, & Schönborn, 2001). These specialties are often organizationally differentiated in bigger companies. Public relations agencies that specialize in event communication, environmental public relations, or change communications are often hired by big corporations. The activities of governmental organizations, municipalities, and associations are dominated by routine public relations, whereas new trends, often imported from the United States, are first applied by the bigger corporations.

THE POLITICAL SYSTEM OF GERMANY

The political experiences of the Weimar Republic and the national–socialist dictatorship have influenced the Constitution of the Federal Republic of Germany. The failure of the Weimar constitution is reflected on in the *Grundgesetz* (Constitution) in four inalterable (nonrepealable) principles. Article 79 (paragraph 3), in combination with Article 1 and 20, defines the principle of human and fundamental rights of democracy, federalism, and the constitutional and welfare state. This constitutional nucleus places the *Grundgesetz* not only on a liberal and democratic structure but also dissociates it from the legal positivism of the Weimar Republic under which everything was legal if decided with the support of a majority of votes (Rudzio, 1997, p. 52). The consequences of the failure of the Weimar Republic are evident in the following four constitutional principles.

1. All political institutions are organized within a parliamentary government system. The parliament can claim exclusive and direct political legitimacy both at the federal (*Bund*) and state (*Länder* or land) levels. All other state institutions derive from the *Bundestag* (lower house of the parliament) or the *Landtag* (state parliament). The chancellor is elected by the parliament and can only be dismissed by a no-confidence majority vote or through the election of a successor. Conversely, the federal president has only representative functions. In Germany, there can be referenda though they are restricted to questions on the new organization of the *Länder* (Rudzio, 1997, p. 60).

2. Germany can be classified as an anthropocentric state. In addition to the traditional features of a constitutional state (i.e., the separation of the powers, the independence of the courts, and the equality before the law), the German *Grundgesetz* also emphasizes the crucial role of inviolable human rights. These human rights are directly effective and can be claimed even at the highest Federal Constitutional Court. In material terms, the fundamental rights belong to the liberal–democratic tradition. Basically, there are two distinct groups of rights (Rudzio, 2000, p. 54): (a) liberal defensive rights against the state (e.g., personal protection and human dignity) and (b) democratic participation rights (e.g., freedom of thought and freedom of association). In particular, the latter refers to just another understanding of democracy. Through Article 9, Germany guarantees the freedom of the citizens to organize themselves, whereas Article 5 and others guarantee the freedom of speech. Freely organized interest groups (e.g., activist groups, citizens' initiatives, demonstrations, and corporations) have the right to stand up actively for their interests and thus to influence the development of political objectives. Due to the possibility of free articulation of interests and their organization in interest groups, Germany can be called a pluralistic democracy where, in principle, all interests can be articulated (Rudzio, 2000, p. 69 ff).

3. Liberal democracies are supported by federalism with the balance of power vertically split between the federal government and individual states. The right to participate in the central decision-making processes is granted to the land governments. The individual states apply federal laws and translate them into action. In this respect, an important feature of the German federalism is the close linkage between the federal (central) government and the states (*Länder*; Rudzio, 1997, p. 53).

4. In contrast to the other constitutional principles, the principle of the welfare state is not elucidated explicitly. It does not contain claim over rights such as the right to work, the right to education, or the right to obtain housing. Still, from the welfare principle, one can draw that it is not legal to leave any individual to his or her fate without a minimum of social care. In addition, the legislator can be obliged to do something about social equalization. How this is done is up to the responsibility of the political majority (Rudzio, 1997, p. 54 ff).

For the purpose of the protection of liberal democratic fundamental rights, the constitution allows a number of legal–administrative procedures (e.g., the prohibition of unconstitutional parties and the right to resist against anyone trying to destroy the fundamental order). For this reason, this democracy is also called a resistant democracy. However, these resistance rights do mainly serve preventive functions to minimize the scope for antidemocratic actions (Rudzio, 2000, p. 46 ff).

On the basis of this constitutional nucleus, a central function of public relations can be derived. The information activities conducted via public relations, that is "making public" (publicizing) information, opinions, attitudes, and demands, corresponds with the concept of a functioning liberal–democratic system (Ronneberger, 1977, p. 12). Pluralistic societies live on public discourses that evoke political objectives and mandatory decisions. Public communication processes make mutual control possible, and the discussion of different interests make mutual corrections possible. The overall aim is to achieve a social consensus of interests (Ronneberger, 1977, p. 13).

The political system of Germany has always had a strong influence on the communication style[1] public relations and its organizational forms. The first German Democracy, the Weimar Republic, enabled rapid development of the public relations profession in all social areas. During the Nazi dictatorship (third period of German public relations history), many issues could not be discussed publicly because of censorship by the state; during, the same time period, the public relations style was propagandistic. During the later periods, public relations developed under the framework of a democratic political system including the growth of organizational forms such as public relations agencies.

THE ECONOMIC SYSTEM IN GERMANY

The concept of a social market economy, which has been present in Germany since 1949, is intertwined with the former federal minister of economy and later Chancellor Ludwig Erhard and his counselor, Alfred Müller-Armack. A social market economy is a special type of economy that pursues the synthesis of legitimized economic freedoms with welfare state ideals of social safety and social justice (Pilz & Ortwein, 1997, p. 250 ff). Considerations to join social and political components evolved at the end of the 19th century when social imbalances started to appear as a result of the development of industrial societies.

The idea of this synthesis grounds on theoretical considerations of the *ordoliberalism*[2], but particular intentions of the Christian social doctrine and liberal socialism were also integrated. Due to this concept, the dissociation from the collectivist socialism and an unbounded capitalism was achievable. The social market economy upholds the liberal economic structures that are constituted by private ownership and private autonomy. Consequently, a *Vergemeinschaftung* (nationalization) of the means of production and a centralized economic control are mostly not feasible. The state confines its own actions

---

[1]Communication styles of public relations can be defined as public communication patterns that consist of combinations of different communication forms (language and textual patters, terminology, or argumentation) and the the selection of publicly discussed topics or themes. At least informative, argumentative, persuasive, and propagandistic public relations styles can be differentiated. They are influenced by social and (especially) political structures.

[2]This word is composed from *liberalism* and the Latin word *ordo* or order. Ordoliberalism is the technical term for the neo-liberal school of thinking (Schmidt, 1995, p. 679).

to setting general frameworks. Social justice, personal freedom, and economic efficiency are interdependent elements of a social market economy (Hennig, 1990, p. 59 ff; Pilz & Ortwein, 1997, p. 251 ff).

The general political framework sets out basic *constitutive* and *regulative* elements for economic politics. Constitutive elements consist of the economic competition (i.e., the free competition of supply and demand), free access to markets, the protection of the freedom to make contracts, and the constancy of economic politics that guarantees a reasonable degree of safety for investments to the businesses (Grosser, 1993, p. 10 ff; Lampert, 1990, p. 36 ff; Pilz & Ortwein, 1997, pp. 252–254). However, economic competition can clash with other state objectives (e.g., the right to equal chances), and competition can also be limited by fusion processes. Therefore, state institutions regulate the conditions of particular processes. Regulating elements are the correction of the market-conditioned income distribution by finance politics, the establishment of a system of social protection that provides minimum social standards (wages, working and time regulations, and regulations on working women and children), and the observation and control of monopolizing processes by cartel institutions (Pilz & Ortwein, 1997, p. 252 ff).

After the end of the economic miracle of the 1960s, the economic–political functions of the state were redefined with the introduction of the *Stabilitätsgesetz* (stability act). This law is also known as the *magic rectangle*, referring to its four objectives. The economic activities of both the federal government and individual states are supposed to contribute to a stable price level, a high employment rate, a balanced international trade, and an appropriate economic growth.

The social and economic structures of Germany have developed and changed significantly. The theoretical conceptualization allowed the building of efficient and liberal structures as well as the integration of a high degree of social market economy achievements (e.g., business constitutions) into the everyday economic activities. However, this structure has been watered down in some fields such as agriculture, pensions, and health insurance. It is now apparent that, due to demographic changes, the quantitative limits of the social sector have been reached. The concept of a social market economy is now facing major challenges.

The system of social market economy, together with a democratic political system, has generally enabled and necessitated the use of public relations by all kinds of social organizations, such as corporations, associations, unions, churches, nongovernmental organizations (NGOs), and so on. Furthermore, different influences of the economic system on public relations could be observed during different phases after World War II. During the 1950s for example, when the acceptance of a social market economy was rather limited, a broad information campaign called *Die Waage* (or pair of scales or the idea to have a socially and economically balanced system in society) was initiated to improve the knowledge and the degree of acceptance of this system. The amount of money in the communication (advertising and public relations) budgets of business enterprises depends directly on the level of ecomomic development. The longevity of public relations agencies also depends on the status of the economy. When corporations slash communication budgets, both in-house public relations and agencies suffer. Advertising budgets were slashed 10% in 2001 after many years of double-digit growth rates. There was a shrinking of the advertising and public relations agency sectors in 2001. This negative trend continues in 2002. Stuctrual changes to the economic system have had positive impacts on some sections of the public relations industry. The great number of IPOs (Initial Public Offering) in 2000 and 2001 has increased the demand for investor relations experts, resulting in a short-term paucity for skilled practitioners.

THE MEDIA SYSTEM IN GERMANY

In pluralistic societies, the mass media serve a key function. Being independent from governmental influence, they generate debate in the public sphere by disseminating information about all important events in politics, economy, society, and culture (Rudzio, 2000, p. 483). The most vital precondition is the freedom of the press which is guaranteed in Article 5 of the German constitution. Paragraph 1 of the constitution guarantees "... freedom of the press and the freedom of broadcast reporting on radio and in film" (*Grundgesetz*, 1994, p. 14) that is free from censorship.

Mass media in Germany are assigned a service function, which includes three main tasks: to encourage the development of public opinion, to control the legislature; the government, and their executing institutions as well as the legal authorities (judicature); and to mediate between the citizens and state institutions (Branahl, 2000, p. 20 ff). At the same time, mass media are economic businesses that have to be regulated. One regulating element is the media diversity, which means that preferential treatment is deliberately granted to the print media because the diversity of the print media market ensures the liberal development of opinions or external pluralism (Papier & Möller, 1999, p. 464). In addition, monopolies can be legally prevented (Pürer & Raabe, 1996, p. 260 ff). The legal regulations for the media can be found in the constitution, verdicts of the Federal Constitutional Court, the media laws of the *Länder*, and cartel and copyright laws (Pürer & Raabe, 1996, p. 261).

The media system of Germany used to be strictly divided into the privately owned print media market and the publicly held broadcasting market until the mid-1980s. The individual types of media can be classified into analytical categories such as publicity, periodicity, topicality, and universality. In Germany, the following basic types of print media can be distinguished: daily newspapers, weekly newspapers, magazines, and advertising journals (Noelle-Neumann, Schulz, & Wilke, 2000, p. 382–412). Due to the technical development of cables and satellites, the argument of a technically limited distribution of television and radio programs became obsolete. Private broadcasting was introduced, and this constituted the dual-broadcasting system in Germany in which public and private commercial broadcasting operate side by side (Stuiber, 1998, pp. 517, 707). Public and private broadcasting are subject to different legal regulations. Public broadcasting has to serve public welfare and ensure the fundamental tasks of providing audiences with information, sports, entertainment, and culture. It has a central integrating function because it articulates the interests of minorities and generates public access among different interest groups (Hesse, 1999, p. 115 ff). For this reason, public broadcasting adopts a strict, internal pluralistic concept (*Binnenpluralismus*) wherein every program has to reflect the actual diversity of the society. Official and independent *Rundfunkräte* (broadcasting boards) control whether these normative demands are fulfilled. In these boards, the representatives of socially relevant groups such as political parties, employers' associations, unions, religions, and science are not allowed to conduct censorship, but they can in retrospect judge the plurality of the programs. Public broadcasting is financed by fees and advertising, which ensures their independence from state budgets (Hesse, 1999, p. 178 ff).

Because private broadcasting depends on incomes from advertising, the constitutional demands are less. As an indirect consequence of economic competition, the concession of private broadcasting activities is expected to result in an increasing diversity of offerings thereby providing more choices for the consumer. This demand is met when at least three stations that cover all general interests are distributed all over Germany by at least three media organizations. Under this condition, the total amount of content provided by private broadcasters has to correspond with the diversity of opinions in the society. To prevent a private broadcasting organization from monopolizing segments of the market, a provider is not given a license to acquire another station if one of the existing stations gathers more that 30% of the audience (Papier & Möller, 1999, p. 465). The media institutions of the *Länder* and the commission for the determination of concentration in the media field (Kommission zur Ermittlung der Konzentration im Medienbereich) are supervising this aspect (Hesse, 1999, p. 243).

Included in the dual-broadcasting system are possibilities for citizens' broadcasting in a local area. Due to the federal structure of the radio and television market, the regulations differ from region to region. In North-Rhine Westfalia, for example, citizens are allowed to produce their own radio and television shows to be broadcast on so-called *open channels*. Open channels distribute their content via private media stations, and these stations are obliged to give technical support for producing the journalistic content (LRG NW, 1995). However, due to the low professional standard of these programs, they are not very popular with audiences.

Media Outreach

An exact measuring system makes precise data about media use by the population possible. The average time of media use is 8.5 hr per day, of which 41% (3.4 hr) is for radio and 37% (approx. 3 hr) is for television. The need for information is mainly met by public stations, whereas private television provides entertainment and relaxation. East Germans watch 30 min more television than West Germans, with the former also watching more entertainment programs. Around 40% of the total population uses the Internet for at least 13 min per day. Each day, 80% of Germans spend 30 min reading the newspaper (Media Perspektiven, 2001, p. 102 ff; 162 ff). In 2001, there were 136 *Publizistische Einheiten* or independent, complete editorial offices with political departments. A total of 386 daily newspapers were produced, with 28.4 million sold copies. Adding local and regional editions, the number of newspapers published rises to nearly 1,600. In addition, there were 23 weeklies (1.9 million sold copies), 845 popular magazines (129.7 million sold copies), and 1,094 professional journals (18 million sold copies; Media Perspektiven, 2001, p. 45). Most daily newspapers are sold through subscriptions. However, seven street-selling newspapers (a total of 43 editions) account for a total circulation of 5.7 million copies. Among these, *BILD* is the biggest street-selling newspaper, with 4.2 million copies per day.

The current media system affects public relations in different ways. First, the growth of a large, private broadcasting market gives public relations more opportunities to be recognized by the media and choose the channels. Second, the increasing number of radio and television stations produces a higher number of journalistic activities and a corresponding increase in public relations activities. Third, on the one hand, it is easier to reach certain publics because of the large number of specialized media; on the other hand, it is more difficult to reach the entire population by performing classical media relations activities because the audience is much more fragmented. Generally, it can be stated that one important reason for the growth of public relations in Germany since the beginning of the 1990s is the growth of the private media market. The public relations boom is coupled—and generated to a great degree—with the marketed media boom. One indicator for the growth of public relations in general is the growth in the number of public relations agencies in the 1990s (see Fig. 10.1).

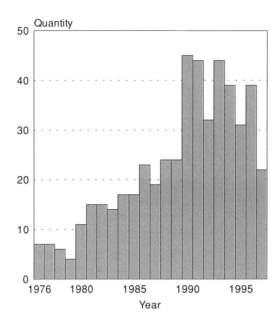

FIG. 10.1.   Start up of public relations agencies and free consultants in Germany between 1976 and 1997 (Fuhrberg 1998: 248).

GERMAN CULTURE

Within German history, several social developments that were crucial to the development of cultural values can be named. For example, the enlightenment of the 18th century destroyed the traditionally organized society and emphasized the individual role of any human being on the basis of universal natural rights. Other examples would be the workers' movements and the industrialization processes of the 19th century, World War I and World War II, establishment of the Weimar Republic, and the national socialism movements.

In the rationalized, mechanized, and individualized industrial Germany that is now developing into an information and knowledge society, there is reasonable consensus about the importance of living realms such as family and health as well as work and success. Conversely, there are numerous different life conceptions that can be classified into two dimensions. First, representatives of traditional values establish their priorities on the family's order, work as obligation, and traditional roles of men and women. Second, representatives of more modern values focus on lifestyles that emphasize the possibility of free and independent self-realization and professional success (Lohauß, 1995, p. 215). Since the late 1960s, the importance of obligation and acceptance values has been decreasing in Germany, whereas the importance of self-development values has been increasing (Klages, 1993, p. 32 ff; 1998, pp. 699–703). Examples of obligation and acceptance values are obedience, order, capability, diligence, modesty, and the will to adjust. Self-development values are emancipation, the right to be treated fairly, hedonism, and individualism (e.g., creativity, spontaneity, and self-realization).

The culture in Germany is not only shaped by this change of values but also by the process of individualization, which basically means the liberalization of human beings from traditional norms and collective relations. The decreased standardization of people by social institutions such as churches, schools, and family corresponds with the decreased affiliation to classes. People have greater opportunities to change their social status due to increased social and cultural mobility. This individualization is apparent not only in the enormous increase of single households but also in very flexible party preferences. However, this increase of individual autonomy causes the need to seek more information because this individualized society offers many choices and thus evokes compulsions to make decisions (Beck, 1986; Ebers, 1995).

Due to this individualized and differentiated society and the increasing role of the media, the requirements from communication activities of organizations have significantly expanded. Individualization has an impact on the organizational culture, implying that employees no longer constitute homogenous groups but rather demand heterogeneous communication to communicate extensively and mediate the organization's interests. Furthermore, external dialogue groups have continuously been differentiated, requiring the external communication of organizational interests to analyze and take into consideration the diversity of partial publics and their cultural values. This is essential for the creation and establishment of understanding of and compliance to the activities of an organization in relevant groups.

CONCLUSION

In this chapter we described that, after a long prehistoric period, the public relations industry in Germany has developed into a differentiated field since the middle of the 19th century, influenced largely by the changes in political systems in the country. The public relations industry also has seen obvious influences by the economic and media systems. Looking at the future of public relations in Germany, it can be stated that the ongoing development of the German society into an information and communication society will have an influence on the field. Public relations will gain importance at two levels in this process—organizational and societal. Public relations departments in organizations will gain importance in comparison with other departments, and public relations as a social subsystem will gain relevance within the society as a whole. This will take place in politics, business, culture, sports, and other aspects of society. Techniques and strategies of communication management will be seen as key competences of the 21st century. Especially through online communication, media will develop further—not only mass media but also public relations—to become an established factor of German society.

Projecting to the future, public relations will be more differentiated and specialized within organizations and agencies. That is, complex and institutionalized public relations specialties such as reputation management, issues management, change communication, and so on will become the norm. This change will also be reflected among agencies. In some parts of the professsional field, the integration of different communication disciplines will increase. The process of professionalization will develop further, which also means that more and more programs in university-level education as well as programs of further education will emerge. The existing research is already on the way to becoming an academic discipline, which Germans call *public relations science*. Discussions about appropriate strategies and techniques as well as about ethics will become more important for the entire field. Although public relations cannot reach the status of the classical professions (e.g., law and medicine) for structural reasons, it will grow to a new type of profession with a stronger scientific foundation. The value and equity of organizational communication as well as techniques to measure it will gain much more relevance, and the need for basic and applied research will increase.

Case Study

An important case in German public relations circles was the public conflict between the petrochemical multinational company Shell and the multinational activist group Greenpeace. The two collided in 1995 over Shell's proposal to sink the Brent Spar oil rig in the open sea. The case is remarkable for several, but three primary reasons:

1. The ability of an activist group (Greenpeace) to gain an extraordinary influence on international public opinion.
2. The role and behavior of the media during a clash of two multinationals.
3. The inept communication management by a global corporation such as Shell.

Short Chronology

In September 1991, Shell shut down the Brent Spar oil storage platform. After contemplating various ways of disposing the platform, Shell decided in 1995 to scuttle it in the open sea. On May 10th, 1995, the Scottish Parliament gave Shell the license to dump Brent Spar in its waters. But Greenpeace activists from Great Britain, the Netherlands, and Germany had already occupied the platform 10 days earlier in an effort to prevent it from being scuttled in the open sea. They demanded that the rig be disposed of onshore to prevent hazard to marine life. This conflict resulted in a dramatic media battle.

On May 12th, 1995, Greenpeace protestors were asked to leave the platform, but they refused, emboldened by many European politicians such as the Danish Environment Minister Svend Auken and some representatives of the European Union who by then had declared their resentment about the plan to sink the platform in open sea. By this time, the government of Iceland urged the British government not to dump Brent Spar in the sea. On May 23rd, Shell put an end to the first occupation of Brent Spar.

On May 24th, the youth wing of the leading German Christian Democratic party (CDU) requested the German consumers to boycott Shell-owned gas stations. Six days later, members of the German parliament joined the protest against Shell. Politicians belonging to the Social Democratic Party also urged Germans to avoid Shell-owned gas stations. In a common statement published on May 31st, the German Fishing Association and Greenpeace protested against the sinking as an environmental disaster. The results of a survey published on June 1st showed that the majority of the German population was against the dumping of Brent Spar in the sea. About 75% of those polled were willing to boycott Shell-owned gas stations to display their sentiments.

On June 12th, Shell moved the platform into the North Atlantic Ocean to sink it, but a ship chartered by Greenpeace accompanied the Brent Spar platform to the site. Politicians belonging to both conservative and liberal parties, as well as representatives of churches and business associations, continued to protest Shell's action and called for a boycott of Shell products in Germany. This intense pressure forced the director of Shell in the Netherlands, Jan Slechte, to admit publicly that his company would open a new discussion concerning the disposal of the platform if the British government demanded it. In a meeting with the British prime minister, German Chancellor Helmut Kohl brought up the Brent Spar as the main issue speaking against sinking the platform, whereas other members of the German Government continued to condemn the proposal to sink it in the open sea. On June 16th, two activists of Greenpeace reoccupied the Brent Spar while other members of Greenpeace continued to inform customers about the sinking at Shell gas stations across Germany, Great Britain, the Netherlands, Belgium, Luxembourg, and Switzerland. On the same day, Peter Duncan, chairman of German Shell, hinted at a press conference that the sinking could be postponed. However, this was followed immediately by a declaration by Dutch and British Shell that the sinking would go ahead as planned.

On June 18th, Greenpeace Germany published analyses of samples taken from the Brent Spar that seemed to prove that, in addition to the materials declared by Shell, it contained an unknown quantity of oil that could be hazardous to marine life if the platform was scuttled in open sea. Greenpeace United Kingdom (UK) blamed Shell for leaving close to 5,500 tons of oil in the platform. Other documents published by Greenpeace resulted in the suspicion that the tank also could contain 4,500 l of the chemical Glyoxal that had allegedly been concealed during the authorization procedure. On June 28th, the Brent Spar was only 24 hr away from the North Feni Ridge, the approved location for scuttling the ship. However, that evening it was published that Shell would abandon plans to sink the platform at the ridge and would instead request authorization to anchor the Brent Spar in the Norwegian Erfjord northeast of Stavanger. After extensive consultations, Shell decided to dismantle the platform and recycle some of its parts. Clearly, Greenpeace had come out victorious in this dramatic public conflict and forced Shell, against all odds, to yield to its pressure. However, Greenpeace's victory was not blemishless in retrospect. Later, the activist group admitted to making a misleading statement about there being 5,500 tons of oil left on the condemned rig and apologized to Chris Fay, chief executive officer of Shell UK. Also, the claim that Brent Spar still contained Glyoxal could not be proved by Greenpeace.

Short Analysis

This very well-documented and systematically analyzed case (Klaus, 2001, Krüger and Müller-Henning 2000, and Vowe 2001) shows some mechanisms of the public sphere and the functioning of public communication. With the help of the media, a global activist group was able to mobilize large publics in different countries to participate in its cause with the help of the media. It is pertinent to add here that one of the themes of this case is that the media and activist groups can form a potent adversary to corporations in particular. The result of the intense media and activist pressure was that there was a temporary boycott of Shell gas stations causing economic damage to these independently owned gas stations and, ultimately, to Shell itself.

The communication strategy of Greenpeace has always been to use a "David-against-Goliath-principle" in which it tries to present itself as the weak David fighting against the powerful Goliath (a corporation). In such conflicts, Greenpeace calculates very consciously that a few minor legal transgressions can and ought to be overlooked if the object of its criticism can be shown to contain a greater amount of immorality. Greenpeace was successful in the Brent Spar case in portraying Shell as an unscrupulous and irresponsible big corporation that favors its own economically motivated interests over that of the environment and society itself.

Shell's own organizational structure proved to be a handicap in its battle. Shell UK was responsible for the decision to sink the oil platform, but Shell Germany was a counterpart of Greenpeace protests in Germany. However, Shell was publicly perceived as a single organization! Shell clearly underestimated the sensitivity of the Germany population toward environmental issues. It also did not fore see the influence that media coverage of the Brent Spar event would have on politicians, including leading members of the conservative

CDU party. At the same time, Shell failed to enter into a dialogue with Greenpeace or display open communication with some of its most important publics. Ultimately, Shell had to submit to public pressure generated through contrived events and dramatized media coverage. The company was forced to recognize remarkable losses in reputation and economic damages. After its decision to abandon the sinking of the Brent Spar platform, Shell ordered an "excuse-me" advertisement to minimize loss of reputation. But in doing so, it also had to concede to having made a big mistake.

The media also learned something from this case. Throughout this issue, and in years prior to it, many journalists were very accepting of Greenpeace press releases as shown by an input–output study done by Rossmann (1993). Today many journalists are more careful in adopting press releases by Greenpeace, which lost some of its credibility by misinforming the media and public about the oil and chemicals supposedly left in the platform. Journalists now have a greater distance to this NGO, which continues to be seen as an important information source.

ACKNOWLEDGMENT

We thank Christian Sommer for his helpful input with the following sections: The Political System of Germany, The Economic System in Germany, The Media System in Germany, and German Culture.

REFERENCES

Avenarius, H. (1998). *Die ethischen Normen der Public Relations. Kodizes, Richtlinien, freiwillige Selbstkontrolle* [Ethical norms of public relations: Codices, guidelines, voluntary self-determination]. Neuwied/Kriftel: Luchterhand.

Becher, M. (1996). *Moral in der PR? Eine empirische Studie zu ethischen Problemen im Berufsfeld Öffentlichkeitsarbeit* [Moral in public relations? An empirical study on ethical problems of the professional field of PR] (Vol. 1). Berlin: Vistas.

Beck, U. (1986). *Risikogesellschaft. Auf dem Weg in eine andere Moderne* [Risk society: Approaching a new modernity]. Frankfurt am Main: Suhrkamp.

Bentele, G. (1997). PR-Historiographie und funktional–integrative Schichtung. Ein neuer Ansatz zur PR-Geschichtsschreibung [PR historiography and functional–integral stratification: A new approach on PR historiography]. In P. Szyszka (Ed.), *Auf der Suche nach Identität. PR-Geschichte als Theoriebaustein* (pp. 137–169). Berlin: Vistas.

Bentele, G. (Ed.). (1998). *Berufsfeld PR* [The professional field of PR]. Berlin: PR Kolleg, Loseblattwerk [collection of unbound papers].

Bentele, G. (2000). Ethik der Public Relations—eine schwierige Kombination? [Ethics of public relations—A problematic combination?]. In *PR⁺ plus Fernstudium Public Relations: Vol. 17, Recht und Ethik für PR* (pp. 29–48).

Bentele, G., & Liebert, T. (1998). Geschichte der PR in Deutschland [History of PR in Germany]. In G. Bentele (Ed.), (pp. 71–100).

Bentele, G., Piwinger, M., & Schönborn, G. (Eds.). (2001). *Handbuch Kommunikationsmanagement. Strategien, Wissen, Lösungen* [Handbook of communication management: Strategies, knowledge, solutions]. Neuwied: Luchterhand.

Bentele, G., & Szyszka, P. (Eds.). (1995). *PR-Ausbildung in Deutschland. Entwicklung, Bestandsaufnahme und Perspektiven* [PR training in Germany: Development, current situation and prospects]. Opladen: Westdeutscher Verlag.

Binder, E. (1983). *Die Entstehung unternehmerischer Public Relations in der Bundesrepublik Deutschland* [The development of businesslike public relations in the Federal Republic of Germany] http://kontakt@orkolleg.com. Münster: Lit.

Böckelmann, F. E. (1988). *Pressestellen in der Wirtschaft* [Press offices in free economy]. Berlin: Spiess.

Böckelmann, F. E. (1991a). *Die Pressearbeit der Organisationen* [PR offices in organizations]. München: Ölschläger.

Böckelmann, F. E. (1991b). Pressestellen als journalistisches Tätigkeitsfeld [PR offices as field of activity for journalists]. In J. Dorer & K. Lojka (Eds.), *Öffentlichkeitsarbeit. Theoretische Ansätze, empirische Befunde und Berufspraxis der Public Relations* (pp. 170–184). Wien: Braumüller.

Branahl, U. (2000). *Medienrecht. Eine Einführung* 3. überarbeitete Auflage [Media law: An introduction] (3rd ed. rev.). Wiesbaden: Westdeutscher Verlag.

Brauer, G. (1996). *Wege in die Öffentlichkeitsarbeit. Einstieg, Einordnung, Einkommen in PR-Berufen* [Paths into public relations: Start, positioning, income in PR professions] (2nd ed.). Konstanz: UVK Medien.

Bruhn, M., & Boenigk, M. (1999). *Integrierte Kommunikation. Entwicklungsstand in Unternehmen* [Integrated communication: On its status quo in businesses]. Wiesbaden: Gabler.

Deutsche Public Relations Gesellschaft (1990). *Auswertung der DPRG-Mitgliederumfrage 1989* [Analysis of the DPRG members survey from 1989]. Bonn: Author.

Ebers, N. (1995). Individualisierung: Georg Simmel—Norbert Elias—Ulrich Beck. *Epistemata: Reihe Philosophie* (Vol. 169) [Individualization: Georg Simmel—Norbert Elias—Ulrich Beck]. Würzburg: Königshausen und Neumann.

Fuhrberg, R. (1998). PR-Dienstleistungsmarkt Deutschland [PR firms in Germany: The German PR service market). In G. Bentele (Ed.), (pp. 241–268).

Grosser, D. (1993). *Soziale Marktwirtschaft—Soziale Sicherheit: Erfahrungen in der Bundesrepublik. Perspektiven im vereinigten Deutschland, Deutschland Report 17* [Social market economy—Social safety: Experiences in Germany. Prospects for the reunited Germany, Germany Report No. 17]. Melle: Ernst Knoth Verlag.

Grundgesetz [The constitution] (32nd ed.) (1994). München: C. H. Beck.

Grunig, J. E., & Hunt, T. (1984). *Managing public relations*. New York: Holt, Rinehart & Winston.

Haedrich, G., & Jenner, T., Olavarria, M., & Possekel, S. (1994). *Aktueller Stand und Entwicklungen der Öffentlichkeitsarbeit in deutschen Unternehmen—Ergebnisse einer empirischen Untersuchung* [Current situation and developments of public relations in German businesses—Results of an empirical study]. Berlin: Institut für Marketing, Lehrstuhl für Konsumgüter-und Dienstleistungs-Marketing.

Heise, J. (2000). *Für Firma, Gott und Vaterland: Kriegserlebnis und Legendenbildung im Spiegel betrieblicher Kriegszeitschriften des 1. Weltkriegs. Das Beispiel Hannover* [For the company, for god and the fatherland: War experiences and the invention of legends in works war magazines of the first world war. Hannover as example]. Hannover: Hahn.

Hennig, B. (1990). Das gesamtwirtschaftliche Zielsystem im Rahmen der Sozialen Marktwirtschaft [The entire economic system of objectives within the framework of social market economy]. In Bundeszentrale für politische Bildung (Ed.), *Wirtschaftspolitik, Schriftenreihe* (Vol. 292, pp. 50–64). Bonn: Bundeszentrale für politische Bildung.

Hesse, A. (1999). *Rundfunkrecht* [Broadcasting law] (2nd ed.). Studienreihe Jura, München: Vahlen.

Hundhausen, C. (1951). *Werbung um öffentliches Vertrauen* [Promoting public trust]. Essen: Girardet.

Klages, H. (1993). *Traditionsbruch als Herausforderung. Perspektiven der Wertewandelsgesellschaft* [The break from traditions as challenge: Perspectives of a value changing society]. Frankfurt am Main New York: Campus.

Klages, H. (1998). Werte und Wertewandel [Values and the change of values]. In B. Schäfers & W. Zapf (Eds.), Handwörterbuch zur Gesellschaft Deutschlands. Bonn: Bundeszentrale für politische Bildung.

Klaus, E. (2001). Die Brent-Spar-Kampagne oder: Wie funktioniert Öffentlichkeit? [The Brent Spar Campaign – Or How the Public Sphere is functioning] In U. Röttger, [ed.] *PR-Kampagnen. Über die Inszenierung von Öffentlichkeit.* (2nd ed., pp. 97–119). Westdeutscher Verlag.

Koszyk, K. (1966). *Deutsche Presse im 19. Jahrhundert* [The German press in the 19th century]. Berlin: Colloquium Verlag.

Krüger, C., & Müller-Hennig, M. (2000): *Greenpeace auf dem Wahrnehmungsmarkt. Studien zur Kommunikationspolitik und Medienresonanz* [Greenpeace on the Reception Market: Studies on Communication Policy and Media Resonance]. Hamburg: Lit.

Kunczik, M. (1997). *Geschichte der Öffentlichkeitsarbeit in Deutschland* [History of public relations in Germany]. Köln et al.: Böhlau.

Kunczik, M. (1999). Öffentlichkeitsarbeit [Public Relations]. In J. Wilke (Ed.), *Mediengeschichte in der Bundesrepublik Deutschland* (pp. 545–569). Bonn: Bundeszentrale für politische Bildung.

Lampert, H. (1990). Die Soziale Marktwirtschaft in der Bundesrepublik Deutschland. Ursprung, Konzeption, Entwicklung und Probleme [Social market economy in the Federal Republic of Germany: Origin, concept, development, and problems]. In Bundeszentrale für politische Bildung (Ed.), *Wirtschaftspolitik, Schriftenreihe* (Vol. 292, pp. 31–49). Bonn: Bundeszentrale für politische Bildung.

Liebert, T. (1997). Über einige inhaltliche und methodische Probleme einer PR-Geschichtsschreibung [On some content-related and methodical problems of PR historiography]. In: P. Szyszka (Ed.), *Auf der Suche nach Identität. PR-Geschichte als Theoriebaustein* (pp. 79–99). Berlin: Vistas.

Lohauß, P. (1995). *Moderne Identität und Gesellschaft. Theorie und Konzepte* [Modern identity and society: Theory and concepts]. Opladen: Leske + Budrich.

LRG NW—Rundfunkgesetz für das Land NordrheinWestfalen in der Fassung der Bekanntmachung der Neufassung vom 24. August 1995 (GV. NW. 1995 S. 994), zuletzt geändert durch Gesetz vom 10. Februar 1998 (GV. NW. 1998 S. 148). Retrieved from http://www.lfr.de/downloads/Lrg-nw.doc

Media Perspektiven. (2001). *Basisdaten. Daten zur Mediensituation in Deutschland 2001* [Basic data: Data on the media situation in Germany 2001]. Frankfurt: Main.

Merten, K. (1997). Das Berufsbild von PR—Anforderungsprofile und Trends. Ergebnisse einer Studie [The professional field of PR—Requirements and trends. Results of a survey]. In G. Schulze-Fürstenow & B.-J. Martini (Eds.), (1994 ff), *Handbuch PR. Öffentlichkeitsarbeit in Wirtschaft, Verbänden, Behörden,* (chap. 3-65, pp. 1–23). Neuwied: Luchterhand.

Noelle-Neumann, E., Schulz, W., & Wilke, J. (2000). *Fischer Lexikon. Publizistik, Massenkommunikation* [Fischer Encyclopedia: Publicity and mass communication] (6th ed.). Frankfurt/Main: Fischer.

Nöth-Greis, G. (1997). Das Literarische Büro als Instrument der Pressepolitik [The Literary Bureau as instrument of press politics]. In J. Wilke (Ed.), *Pressepolitik und Propaganda. Historische Studien vom Vormärz bis zum Kalten Krieg* (pp. 1–78). Köln/Weimar/Wien: Böhlau.

Oeckl, A. (1976). PR-Praxis. Der Schlüssel zur Öffentlichkeitsarbeit [PR practice. The key to public relations]. Düsseldorf; Wien: Ecoh.

Oeckl, A. (1964). *Handbuch der Public Relations. Theorie und Praxis der Öffentlichkeitsarbeit in Deutschland und der Welt* [Handbook of public relations: Theory and practice of public relations in Germany and the world]. München: Süddeutscher Verlag.

Papier, H.-J., & Möller, J. (1999). Presse- und Rundfunkrecht [Press and broadcasting law]. In J. Wilke (Ed.), *Mediengeschichte der Bundesrepublik Deutschland* (Vol. 361, pp. 449–468). Bonn: Bundeszentrale für politische Bildung.

Pilz, F., & Ortwein, H. (1997). *Das politische System Deutschlands. Systemintegrierende Einführung in das Regierungs-, Wirtschafts- und Sozialsystem* [The political system of Germany: A system-integrating introduction into the administrative, economic and social system] (2nd ed.). München/Wien: R. Oldenburg.

Pürer, H., & Raabe, J. (1996). *Medien in Deutschland: Vol. 1, Presse* (korrigierte ed.) [The media in Germany: Vol 1, The press] (rev. ed.). Konstanz: UKV Medien.

Ronneberger, F., & Rühl, M. (1992). *Allgemeine Theorie der Public Relations* [A general theory of public relations]. Wiesbaden: Westdeutscher Verlag.

Ronneberger, F. (1977). Legitimation durch Information [Legitimation by information]. Düsseldorf; Lsien: Ecoh.

Rossmann, T. (1993): Öffentlichkeitsarbeit und ihr Einfluss auf die Medien: Das Beispiel Greenpeace [Public relations and its influence on the mass media: greenpeace as an example]. In *Media Perspektiven* No. 2, 1993 (pp. 85–96).

Röttger, U. (2000). *Public Relations—Organisation und Profession. Öffentlichkeitsarbeit als Organisationfunktion. Eine Berufsfeldstudie* [Public relations—organization and profession. Public relations as organizational function. A study on the professional field]. Wiesbaden: Westdeutscher Verlag.

Röttger, U. (2000a). Issues-Management. Wiesbaden: Westdeutscher Verlag.

Rudzio, W. (1997). Das politische System der Bundesrepublik Deutschland [The political system of the Federal Republic of Germany]. In *Grundwissen Politik Schriftenreihe* (Vol. 345, 3rd ed. rev., pp. 47–89). Bonn: Bundeszentrale für politische Bildung.

Rudzio, W. (2000). *Das politische System der Bundesrepublik Deutschland* (5th ed.) [The political system of the Federal Republic of Germany]. Opladen: Leske + Budrich.

Schieder, T. (1999). *Vom Deutschen Bund zum Deutschen Reich: 1815–1871* (16th ed.) [From the German Alliance to the German Reich: 1815–1871]. München: Deutscher Taschenbuch-Verlag.

Schmidt, M. G. (1995). *Wörterbuch zur Politik* [Political dictionary]. Stuttgart: Kröner.

Stuiber, H. W. (1998). Medien in Deutschland. Vol. 2, Rundfunk, [The media in Germany: Vol. 2, Boardcasting]. Konstanz: UKV Medien.

von Schlippe, B., Martini, B.-J., Schulze-Fürstenow, G. (Eds.). (1998). *Arbeitsplatz PR. Einstieg— Berufsbilder—Perspektiven. Mit einer Dokumentation der aktuellen PR-Bildungsangebote* [Vocation PR: Getting started—professional fields—prospects. Including a documentation of current PR training offers]. Neuwied/Kriftel: Luchterhand.

Vowe, G. (2001). Feldzüge um die öffentliche Meinung. Politische Kommunikation in Kampagnen am Beispiel von Brent Spar und Mururoa [Campaigns for public opinion: Political communication in campaigns, illustrated by the cases of Brent Spar and Mururoa]. In U. Röttger, (Ed.). (2001). *PR-Kamapgnen. Über die Inszenierung von Öffentlichkeit.* (2nd ed., pp. 121–142). Westdeutscher Verlag.

wbpr. (1997). *Wo ist der Schlüssel? Zweite Untersuchung zur unternehmensspezifischen Bedeutung von Public Relations. Eine Untersuchung der wbpr Gesellschaft für Public Relations und Marketing GmbH in Zusammenarbeit mit dem LUMIS-Institut der Universität-GH Siegen und dem Wirtschaftsmagazin Capital* [Where is the key? Second survey on the specific meaning of public relations in businesses. A survey by the PR company wbpr in co-operation with the LUMIS institute at the University Siegen and the business magazine *Capital*]. München/Potsdam.

Wolbring, B. (2000). *Krupp und die Öffentlichkeit im 19. Jahrhundert* [Krupp and the public of the 19th century]. München: C. H. Beck.

Zipfel, A. (1997). *Public Relations in der Elektroindustrie. Die Firmen Siemens und AEG 1847 bis 1939* [Public Relations in the electronic industry: The companies Siemens and AEG from 1847 until 1939]. Köln/Weimar/Wien: Bèohlau.

Zühlsdorf, A. (2002). *Gesellschaftsorientierte Public Relations. Eine strukturationstheoretische Analyse der Interaktion von Unternehmen und kritischer* Öffentlichkeit [Society-oriented public relations: A structural–theoretical analysis of the interaction between businesses and critical publics]. Wiesbaden: Westdeutscher Verlag.

11

PUBLIC RELATIONS IN THE POLDER:
THE CASE OF THE NETHERLANDS

BETTEKE VAN RULER

PREVIEW

In this chapter I draw a picture of the Netherlands and its public relations. The Netherlands is "A fine place to be," (*The Economist*, p. 8, 2002) because "Dutch business is outward-looking and open to new ideas and the rule is common sense." Given such a business atmosphere, one would presume that public relations must have been very successful in the Netherlands. Although Dutch behavior regarding public relations is obviously close to normative, the Dutch public relations industry is not at the level that normative thinking would cast. The question is, why?

I use as many sources as possible to give a broad and deliberate picture of this country and the state of the art and background of public relations as a phenomenon and as an industry. This picture is, however, necessarily subjective, because it is my interpretation of facts and figures as well as my realities and thoughts.

HISTORY AND DEVELOPMENT OF THE COUNTRY

With nearly 16 million inhabitants, the Netherlands is one of the smaller countries of Europe, comparable in population size to Denmark, Greece, and Hungary (about 11 million people), although much smaller in size. The population density is a little over 450 km^2, which is exceeded only by Bangladesh, Taiwan, and South Korea. The Gross Domestic Product (GDP) for the Netherlands in 1998 was 110, whereas the United States' was 145 and Poland's was 38. The Dutch economy rose sharply to an all-time high during the 1990s thanks to an explosive services sector that accounted for almost 70% of the GDP. Employment is high, with less than 5% unemployed in 2001 and just 13% employed by the government. Nevertheless, 800,000 people of the potential labor force of 7 million are not able to work because of long-standing physical or mental illness. All of these people get an income by the state until their 65th birthday, which is based on their latest earned income level. Everyone above the age of 65 gets a state pension in addition to their private pensions. In 2001, 13.5% of the population was over 65. In a few years, this is expected to be about 20% or even higher, which has the potential to challenge the state pension system.

The Netherlands can be seen as a country of reasonable diversity. One third of the population identify themselves as Catholic (passive or active), almost one third as Protestant of some kind, and the remainder as something else or with no religious affiliation (almost one million is muslim). Most people are Dutch for generations, whereas 1.7 million are first- or second-generation immigrants. Although Dutch women are not as emancipated as women in Scandinavian countries, the Index of Gender Development is almost .7, which is rather high (Gallagher, Laver, & Mair, 2001). This Index measures the degree of women's representation in key areas of political and economic life, taking account of the number of women in national parliaments, women's share of earned income, and their levels of occupancy in a range of professions.

Since the 17th century, the Netherlands has been known for its high level of economic and cultural wealth. The country is famous for painters like Rembrandt and van Gogh, and many continents have had contact with the Dutch because of their entrepreneurial nature and business sense. Many argue that the Dutch became successful because they had to overcome the lack of their own natural resources, inducing them to develop an earthy nature, strict work ethics, and a very strong propensity to negotiate and build consensus. At the same time, the Dutch have built the questionable reputation of pretending to know how people in other societies in the world should behave. *The Oxford Dictionary* defines talking to someone as a *Dutch uncle* as "lecturing him paternally"(Hofstede, 1987, p. 5). The expression *Dutch party* shows a certain ungenerous behavior with money. The country is also famous (or notorious) for its liberal behavior on drugs, which is seen—at least by the Dutch themselves—as the best way to cope with this problem: Drugs are illegal, but the use of them is allowed.

Pillarization, Corporatism, and Consensus

The Dutch have always had a strong outside orientation while maintaining a very tight societal concept. This concept is often characterized by pillarization, corporatism, and consensus (Kickert, 1996). Until the 1970s, Dutch society was segmented by four so-called *pillars*: Protestants, Catholics, Socialists, and Liberal-Neutralists. According to Kickert (1996), this ideological stratification started with the successful 16th-century struggle of the Protestant–Calvinist Dutch for separation from the Catholic Habsburg–Burgundy Empire. In the following centuries, Protestantism was the dominant and preferred religion, and Catholics were seen as second-rate citizens. But almost half of the inhabitants were Catholic. The subsequent necessity for Catholics was to establish a countervailing social and political power. At the end of the 19th century, two other groups in the Netherlands— the socialists and liberals—also started their own social structure, and the ideologically based stratification of Dutch society was a fact. Since then, the social organization of the Dutch state (including political parties, trade unions, employer organizations, schools and universities, the media, health, and welfare) has been performed by many organizations, all based on their (legal) status as private foundations or associations belonging to one of the four pillars and headed by a council of amateurs, as delegated by the pillars. As recently as 40 years ago, a Protestant would not shop in a Catholic grocery or listen to the socialist radio. That is why class stratification was never strong. The secularization of the 1960s has "depillared" society to a large extent. Nevertheless, radio and television as well as primary and secondary schools and other public-oriented and voluntary organizations are still partly organized according to pillarization, and societal culture is still based on this reasonably silent segmentation of society.

According to Kickert (1996), the Netherlands can be seen as an almost perfect example of the modern nonstatist concept of what he called *neocorporatism* (see also Hemerijck, 1993). This (European) model emphasizes the interests represented by a small, fixed number of internally coherent and well-organized interest groups that are recognized by the state and have privileged or even monopolized access to the state. The most important groups in a corporatist society are employers, employees, and the state. However, in the Netherlands all kinds of single-issue pressure groups also are involved in the system.

Another characteristic of the Netherlands is its focus on consensus. Many authors stated (see for an overview: Gallagher, Laver & Mair, 2001) that due to this consensus-building focus of the Dutch, pillarization and corporatism never resulted in a strong polarization of society, even in the turbulent 1960s.

EVOLUTION AND DEFINITION OF THE PROFESSION

Evolution

Another characteristic of the Netherlands is its strong roots in Enlightenment, as developed in the 18th century in France and Germany. Enlightenment has strongly influenced the evolution and practice of public relations in the Netherlands. In the 18th century, science and knowledge were no longer seen as the attributes only of the elite but as things that had to be diffused among all members of the society. The means for this diffusion was *voorlichting*, which means enlightening. The idea of *voorlichting* is based on Kant's expression *sapere aude* (which literally means dare to know): "all people must be willing to be informed on what is going on and made enlightened, so that they can take part in the ongoing debate about and development of society." Besides education, *voorlichting* was seen as the main way to help people to be informed. In the 19th century, *voorlichting* was defined as "giving full information to all people to mature and emancipate." (van Gent, 1995, p. 11) However, many people were afraid of enlightening ordinary people, which is why *voorlichting* is also used to show people how to behave as good citizens and to control them. The history of *voorlichting* can, therefore, be seen as a history of the battle between information and emancipation, on the one hand, and education and persuasion, on the other, but always under the ("Dutch uncle") dogma of knowing what is good. In all theories of *voorlichting*, the rather pedantic premise is that it is given for the benefit of the person or group to be enlightened, even when the people involved do not want to be enlightened at all or at least not in this way. This *voorlichting* influenced public relations to a great extent.

Many like to state that public relations was invented in the United States and crossed the ocean together with Marshall Aid after World War II. This is certainly true for the term *public relations* but not for the practice. When industrialization became a fact, industries started to give information about their well-being to the press as well as to the people at large. The government followed soon after and installed departments to inform journalists. However, Dutch journalists wanted direct access to administrators and politicians. Thanks to the strong pillarization of society in which every pillar had its own media and, therefore, its own political contacts, their lobby was successful for a long time, and the departments had to focus only on foreign journalists.

The characteristics of *voorlichting* can still be found in the practice of the public relations departments of business and government today. The evolution of public relations in the Netherlands cannot, therefore, be captured in terms of publicity or press agentry but more so in terms of public information and well-mentioned but patronizing education.

Definition of Public Relations

After World War II, Dutch society had to be rebuilt. It became important to promote business and societal goods, but society had an even stronger aversion to propaganda than before (Katus, 2001). Therefore, there was a strong debate about the ethics of this kind of promotional activity. Thanks to the propensity among the Dutch toward negotiation and consensus, these problems were solved by creating associations. In 1945, the first professional association was established, initiated by a journalist but open to public relations professionals as well as journalists. The goal of this association was to facilitate the exchange of knowledge between journalists and public relations officers (representing various government agencies and businesses) and to take away the fear for political information, which was strongly associated with Nazi's propaganda.

In 1946, the first professional association was followed by the first public relations association called the Association for Public Contact. A forum for press officers of corporations and the government, it was later renamed as the Association for Public Relations in the Netherlands (now called the Dutch Association for Communication). The primary aims of this association were to help knowledge development among practitioners, provide networking opportunities, and help develop an identity for the profession. Since the founding of this association, there has been a strong debate about the definition of the profession influenced by new knowledge of the profession from the United States and the already existing knowledge of *voorlichting.*

To the definition of public relations borrowed from the United States—"the development of good relationships between an organization and its publics" (Groenendijk, 1987, p. 54)—was added a small but, for the Dutch, very essential clause—"most of all by 'voorlichting.'" It was not until 1966 that this sentence was further discussed. In the beginning of the debate in the 1960s, the official definition remained unchanged except that it did not include the clause, "most of all by voorlichting." By that time, however, the relationships between the government and society and between business and society were very much under pressure. The concept of "good relationships" was seen as "too much aimed at harmony" (Lagerwey, Hemels, & van Ruler, p. 137, 1997) and was soon altered into the more neutral expression of "mutual understanding." This definition remained official (at least for the members of the association) until 1996. During this time, government public relations officers were debating whether they were allowed to persuade "and use the techniques of public relations" (Lagerwey et al., 1997, p. 147). The conclusion was that public relations could not be allowed in governmental communication not because of the concept of mutual understanding, but because of its persuasive character, which was imported from the United States. This debate shows that in reality public relations was seen primarily as propaganda and imagery.

In 1998, the Association of Public Relations in the Netherlands merged with two other smaller associations (the Association of Communication in the Netherlands and the Dutch Association of Corporate Journalists) to become the Dutch Association of Communication.

The board concluded that it served no purpose to try to define the field, and the discussion was over.

The term public relations is hardly used anymore. On the one hand, this is because of the negative connotations of the term itself and, on the other, this is because of the one-way and nonscientific orientation of the practice. Nowadays, the term is used only in a negative way to define what can be seen as bad for one's image and by some consultancies that work for American enterprises and use (aggressive) publicity. The most common current names for the field are corporate communication, communication management, or communication. Defining the public relations field, however, is also not seen as useful because of the mindset that communication management is what communication managers do. Such management is, however, still mainly aimed at *voorlichting* (van Ruler, 1998).

STATUS OF THE PROFESSION

The profession of public relations, with its new nomenclature of communication management or corporate communication, is widely accepted. All organizations have communication employees or at least structural contacts with communication consultancy bureaus. Managers see communication as an important or even as a critical factor for success. Recently, an official state commission advised the prime minister on how to cope with communication in the new information age and was very positive about the necessity of good communication management in the public sector (Commissie Toekomst Overheidscommunicatie, 2001). Nevertheless, it is hard to fathom what is meant by *good* in this respect. Even practitioners themselves still call it a diffuse field. But there is no debate on what it is or what it should or could be. Even journalists do not consider it important to debate the practices of communication managers and consultants anymore. There is hardly any debate among professionals about their specific professional ethics. In 1998, the association organized a meeting on ethics and codes. A meager 12 (of over 1,000 members) participated in this meeting. The general conclusion was that a professional code is an old fashioned instrument of no practical significance and that ethics is a situational concept that cannot be debated in general. The discussion has been closed ever since. There is a current debate in the Netherlands about the social responsibility of business as well as on business and societal ethics. The profession is, however, almost totally absent in this debate.

The Visibility of the Profession Within Organizations

A large, representative survey (van Ruler & de Lange, 2000) on the structural representation of communication within organizations with over 50 staff members showed that almost all of these organizations have communication employees and that the responsibility for communication activities is placed at a high level. However, the internal visibility of the profession is very low. Of those responsible for communication activities, less than half (42%) reported to have a job title that relates to communication in one way or another (including external communications, *voorlichting*, public relations, and even advertising). It is no surprise that bearing a communication-related job title corresponds with the presence of a single department coordinating different communication activities, although this correspondence is not complete. Of the over 60% of organizations that reported having a special department to coordinate communication activities, only 55% were headed by a person with some explicit reference to *communication* in his or her job title. The conclusion is that many respondents indicate that there is one special department in which communication activities are coordinated but that these departments are not always led by a real communication manager, a department head, who is named as such. In such cases, the management of communication activities is obviously encroached by another department. Remarkably, if a job title has the word *communication* in it, its hierarchical position is different compared to titles that refer to *marketing*, for example. Staff functions and positions at the middle-management or operational level coincide more often with the use of *communication* in the title, whereas among members of the management team, marketing-related titles prevail. This indicates that communication under the marketing denomination often can be found in a management position. Single communication departments, however, participate less in the board of directors meetings. Obviously, communication management is seen as important, but it is not part of a specialized department at the managerial level.

Another indication of internal visibility is budget. Almost half of the respondents in the study (van Ruler & de Lange, 2000) indicated that either there was no structural budget for communication activities (40%) or that they did not know what this budget was (9%). Communication management is apparently a position at a high level of responsibility, but a structural communication budget is not always available. All in all, communication management may not yet be regarded as being visible within organizations, at least not at a managerial and strategic level, because only 3 of 10 of the organizations in this research comprised a communication department that was visible in the hierarchy as such and had its own structural budget.

PROFESSIONALISM IN THE PUBLIC RELATIONS INDUSTRY

Public relations can be seen as a stable industry in the Netherlands. Of a labor force of about 6 million, public relations accounts for some 30,000 employees with communication duties in organizations, about 50% of whom also have other tasks in personnel, marketing, office management, and other departments. About 25,000 public relations professionals work in public relations consultancies (van Ruler & de Lange, 2000). About 20% of communication professionals are employed in the public sector (government and semigovernmental organizations), as well as at the governmental, provincial, and local levels. The average communication unit employs six people. Marketing communication is included in these figures because it is impossible to make a distinction between marketing communication, advertising, and public relations in the Netherlands. What one calls public relations is mostly seen as (part of) marketing communications, whereas others talk about communication management but actually mean advertising or use marketing communication in such a broad sense that others would call it corporate communication or communication management.

If one were to base their decision on the size of the communication branch alone, one could conclude that public relations has been professionalized. It is questionable, however, whether the profession really meets the traditional criteria of professionalization. Some indicators of professionalism are the educational (knowledge reproduction) system, the knowledge development system, and professional culture. The educational system in public relations is very well-developed at different levels but is focused on the vocational side. There is a well-developed system of education in technical communication activities at a pre-bachelor's as well as at the bachelor's level. At bachelor's level almost all (about 30) professional and scientific universities offer full programs in organizational communication or communication management (with 180 or 240 European credits). Education at the master's level is less developed. There is one university-based master's program in applied communication science (aimed at organizational communication problems); one in corporate communication; one or two in what used to be called *voorlichting*; and one in policy, communication, and organization. There are no doctoral programs in organizational communication or communication management. Researchers of the Netherlands School of Communication Science are much more oriented to mass media and advertising than to organizational communication and communication management. Moreover, there is only one full professor specializing in corporate communication and none specializing in communication management or organizational communication, let alone in public relations. Knowledge production is not at a high level in the Netherlands.

But knowledge reproduction is also not obvious. Of those responsible for communication, 90% have no educational background that has anything to do with communication. This could, of course, be partly caused by the fact that most educational programs have been founded only recently. One could say that lengthy experience could be equalized with higher education. However, 90% of those responsible for communication are in the branch for less than 3 years. It is, therefore, also obvious that it is not a sector for which a special background is needed to get the job. It is also not common to be a member of one of the professional associations. There is a special association for the professionals of the public sector, but only 15% of those eligible actually are members. The Association of Communication has only about 1,000 members from a potential pool of 55,000. There is only one association of consultancies with 40 of 11,500 potential members. These facts lead us to conclude definitively that public relations in the Netherlands is not professionalized.

SUPPLY OF SERVICES IN THE CONSULTANCY SECTOR

The consultancy sector is a booming branch, with approximately 11,500 consultancies. At least three quarters of these are one-person operations. Of the remaining, 90% have fewer than 10 employees. So, it is a large industry with many small businesses. At conferences and in trade publications, the Dutch consultancy sector often claims that it is far ahead in bringing communication management to a strategic level. Van Ruler and de Lange (1999) assessed this claim in their study of the service supply in the consultancy sector. Asked how they typify their own work, professionals working in consulting firms responded that offering communication advice is by far their most common activity, followed by advertising, creative work, and public relations (as in publicity seeking).

Most of the consultancies assessed in the study (van Ruler & de Lange, 1999) had existed for only a short time. One quarter had existed for 2 years or less, and almost half (48%) were less than 5 years old, indicating that this is a young sector. The age of the consultancies correlated positively with their size ($r = .33; p < .01$)—the longer they have been in existence, the larger they are. Does this mean that a consultancy cannot survive if it does not grow? This would imply a correspondence with profitability. One of the outcomes of this study was that the consultancy sector as a whole generates net turnover of more than EUR 4 billion per year. However, profitability per consultancy is low. If the minimal gross income limit is set at EUR 68,000 per employee, then 46% of the larger consultancies and 65% of the one-person consultancies cannot survive, because their turnover lies below this level. If the minimum limit of EUR 110, 000 set by the Vereniging van Erkende Adviesbureaus (VEA) (an association of advertising) is adopted, then fewer than 18% of all consultancies can be expected to survive. There is an almost linear relationship between size and profitability. At the lower limit of EUR 68,000 per employee, a consultancy can survive with seven employees or more; at the VEA standard, a consultancy can survive with 9 employees or more. Thus, the consultancy sector is a young sector with many very small (often one- or two-person) consultancies and their long-term viability is very much at risk. This, of course, has an impact on investments in professionalization.

The Specializations of Consultancies

When asked what their specialization was, although respondents chose the broad denomination of communication most often, advertising, creative work, and public relations were also mentioned (van Ruler & de Lange, 1999). The question is, what are the specializations that the consultancies offer within these denominations? A list of 20 segments of the communication profession was prepared based on a literature review and interviews with directors of consultancies. This list was included in the questionnaire, and respondents were asked to designate the segments they offered. On average the consultancies offered 5 segments, but the individual differences were large: Some consultancies offered only one segment (18%), whereas others offered more than 10 (almost 10%). Predictably, the text consultancies and the creative consultancies had a very limited range of specializations, whereas other consultancies offered a much more diverse range of services. There is, however, hardly any correlation between typification of the supply and the chosen segments.

Aggregate all consultancies, text production scored highest followed by creation and concept development. In the larger consultancies, marketing communication and creation and concept development came first. In the one-person consultancies, text production scores the highest. More strategic issues such as positioning, profiling, and strategic policy advice were mentioned much less frequently. Research was hardly mentioned as a service. Also ethical issues were not apparently regarded as a segment of communication advice. There are not many consultancies that offer advice on strategic issues, but those that do are also more likely to offer research services as well. This applies particularly to the few larger communication and public relations consultancies, not to the consultancies that typify themselves as advertising consultancies. Apparently, providing communicative coaching services is being left to the consultancies that offer organizational advice. It is hardly mentioned in the list of service consultancies delivered in the survey, although it is in demand by communication managers. The supply of communication consultancy, therefore, is limited mainly to tactical and creative (artistic) spheres. The study concluded that the consultancy branch is a sector with a large number of small, relatively young, consultancies. They typically offer services similar to public relations and advertising consultancies and is, above all, tactical and artistic in nature.

INFRASTRUCTURE AND PUBLIC RELATIONS

The Political System

The Netherlands is a constitutional monarchy. The queen opens the parliament every year, but her speech is written by the government. She must sign all legislation, but she has no direct influence on its contents. The queen also has no opinions, at least not in public, and a slip of her tongue to the press is not meant to be made public, although they take the liberty of making these comments public from time to time. The prime minister is politically responsible for everything the queen and her family do or say.

Multiparty System. Similar to Sweden, Dutch politics is highly fragmented. Many parties compete for electoral and parliamentary support, and none of these is in a position to win a working majority on its own. That is why every government is a system of coalitions and alliances. The major parties still represent the ideological pillars of the last century—socialist, liberal, and religious (Catholics and Protestants now work together in one party)—but apart from them, all kinds of interest groups can form their own parties and contest for control of the parliament.

The Polder Model.   According to one of the leading political journalists (Kranenburg, 2001), Dutch politics is an oasis of calm where conflict is seen as counterproductive. Like many others, Kranenburg claimed that this is because no single party has ever come close to approaching a majority in parliament. Therefore, a coalition government is inevitable, and today's enemy can become tomorrow's ally. Ever since World War II, the Christian parties (who merged to form the Christian Democratic Union [CDA]) played a pivotal role in these coalitions, aligning themselves with the Social Democrats at times and with the Liberals at other times. This practice ended in 1994 when the "red" of the socialists and the "blue" of the liberals joined to form a coalition known as *purple*. They got along so well that the coalition continued after the 1998 elections as well. Kranenburg described this coalition between labor and capital as "the Third Way *avant la lettre*" (p. 71) (before the term third way was invented) and a most successful one at that. The former trade union boss Wim Kok became prime minister in 1994 and was worshipped by the business community until he retired in 2002. In 2002, the CDA again became a part of the coalition.

This kind of coalition is said to be a natural exponent of Dutch culture, which for centuries has relied on the practice of consultation and the involvement of as many people as possible in decision making. Every issue bearing even the remotest risk of disagreement has a forum of its own in which all interested parties are represented, whether it be traffic issues, defense matters, or education affairs. Kranenburg (2001) showed that this culture has many repercussions in politics: "The more the relevant bodies agree, the less freedom of movement remains for the politicians". It was under these conditions that the now well-known polder model was born in the early 1980s. (*Polder* is a Dutch word for reclaimed land that is made out of water or swamp) (p. 38). At that time, politicians planned to intervene in the country's wage levels and tackle the high rate of unemployment by sharply reducing labor costs. Facing the loss of their freedom of negotiation, labor unions and employers agreed to a voluntary wage restraint in return for a reduction in work hours. The political establishment had no choice but to acquiesce to this "voluntary" agreement between employers and labor unions.

The Dutch Parliament consists of two chambers—the Lower House and the Upper House. The Lower House has existed for more than 500 years and consists of 150 members elected every 4 years by the voters, under a system of proportional representation. The Upper House was installed in 1815, during a short union with Belgium. Its 75 members, part-time politicians, are elected every 4 years by the members of the provincial executives. In the days of the pillarization voting behavior was very clear. As Gallagher, Laver & Mair (2001) stated, "to speak of the majority of voters at a given election as choosing a party is nearly as misleading as speaking of a worshipper on a Sunday 'choosing' to go to an Anglican rather than a Baptist or a Catholic church" (p. 252). Nowadays, there is a massive decline in party identification, with only 28% of voters identifying themselves with a political party. However, this lack of identification could also be partly caused by the fact that voters have several parties to choose from, within the left as well as at the right wings, with about 20 political parties participating in elections at the national or local levels (Gallagher, 2001, p. 258). However, parties do have to campaign, and many observers comment about the "Americanization of politics" when personalities seem to become more important than party programs.

Dutch politics is boring, European Commissioner Frits Bolkestein, once said in a television interview in the 1990s. During the 2002 elections, politics was no longer boring because of a newcomer, the Late Pim Fortuyn, who started the debate about boring politics and politicians. He was murdered 9 days before the elections, throwing the country in shock. His party did well enough to come second behind the Christian Democrats.

However, all parties are arguing for a revised polder model. In government as well as in business, the usual reaction to important and controversial problems is to form a kind of forum to discuss the issue at hand and look for harmonious solutions. This way of solving problems takes a lot of talking, both inside and outside parliament. Long discussions have always been a part of Dutch culture, but they are only allowed when aimed at compromise and consensus. Moreover, the Dutch hate what they call "fried air," or pompous talk and rhetoric (Vossestein, 2001, p. 80). These factors contribute to making politics dull and seldom really innovative. But, as the Dutch say, "Slowly, slowly, then the line will never break . . . "

Level of Economic Development

The Netherlands is a very prosperous country. Despite its small size, the Netherlands is the world's eighth largest trading nation (Vossestein, 2001). It has experienced an even higher employment growth than the United States in recent years. Along with Ireland, Spain, and Finland, the Netherlands is currently one of the more successful countries in Western Europe (Bomhoff, 2001). The exploitation of its large reserves of natural gas has given the Dutch economy a boost since the early 1960s and made the (former) guilder a very strong and stable currency.

Although the Netherlands has a strong agricultural image abroad, just over 2% of all working people are employed in agriculture (Vossestein, 2001). The Dutch economy is predominantly industrial and most of all service-oriented, with a strong international orientation based on the country's long trading tradition and colonial past. Vossestein (2001) contended that this is reflected in the disproportionately high number of Dutch multinational companies, such as Ahold, Akzo-Nobel, DSM, Heineken, KLM, Philips, Shell, Stork, Unilever, Wolters/Kluwer/Reed/Elsevier, ABN/AMRO, Aegon, ING, KPN, Rabobank, which have its roots (and most of the time also their headquarters) in the Netherlands.

Vossestein (2001) described the Netherlands as a mixture of free market economy and fairly strong government control, although the latter is decreasing. Still, there are many rules and regulations on safety, hygiene, salary levels, workers' rights, protection of the environment, limitations on building, and so on, made by consultation with all kinds of groups and coalitions, even more than in many other nations. Strangely, employers do not seem to treat this as restrictive. "A deeply felt need to have everyone share a decent standard of living has led to a system in which, more than in most countries, the national wealth is distributed to all" (Vossestein, 2001, p. 182).

Taxes are high, with a maximum rate of 52%. Rate of taxation is directly proportional to income levels to moderate the income gap between the rich and poor. There is a largely subsidized public transport system, good-quality housing (even for those who cannot afford it; the local government subsidizes high rents if necessary), comprehensive insurance coverage against medical calamities, social security benefits that are higher than in the Anglo Saxon countries, and a significant contribution to overseas development aid (Bomhoff, 2001, p. 60). Of course, this makes the Netherlands an expensive country in which to live. Bomhoff stated that if the Dutch do not want to be cheap, they will have to be smart, implying that if the Dutch cannot comply with international standards they have to be smart to be able to afford it economically. International research clearly demonstrates, he claimed, that the average quality of education strongly influences the level of economic development that a country can attain. Although education is already at a high level, he believed that a change in thinking at the Ministry of Education is needed to increase competition in education. Teachers' unions continue to remain opposed to variable pay for teachers (all teachers at all levels of education are paid by the government and have the same level-based salary scales). The unions also are opposed to any scheme that aims to reward individual schools that do a good job educating their students. Public opinion, he said, is keenly interested in better primary and secondary education, but methods that have been successful abroad always involve more freedom for school managers, a taboo for the Dutch. Other economists believe that the Dutch advantage in Europe will be challenged because of bad innovative power in this field and that competition in the educational system (and selection) has to be introduced for the Dutch to continue to stay wealthy. This could have its influence on the demand for corporate profiling and image making of the educational system, which is at the moment almost nonexistent.

Legal Infrastructure

All legislation is first introduced in the Lower House of parliament where it is debated and can be amended. If it has been introduced by a minister, a bill may be withdrawn up until the final vote is taken. After passage, it is sent to the Upper House where it is adopted or rejected with no provision for making any amendments.

Gallagher et al. (2001, p. 33) made a distinction between two general types of legal systems: the common law tradition and the civil law tradition. Britain and the United States have a common law tradition. Most European countries, including the Netherlands, have a civil law tradition. The difference is that common law systems rely less on law as act of parliaments and more on the accumulated weight of precedents set by the decisions, definitions, and interpretations made by judges. Many key legal principles and rules are thus established not in statutes made by the legislature but in judgments made by the judiciary. The essential feature of a civil law system is that the ultimate foundation of the law is a comprehensive and authoritative legal code. Upon this foundation is built a superstructure of statutes enacted by the legislature. In civil law systems, judges do not make laws, they merely apply the law. Laws are made by parliament and established as legal code. One of the most cited codes in this respect is the Code Napoléon, which emerged as part of the new order after the French Revolution. This code has greatly influenced the Dutch legal system. In practice, Gallagher et al. (2001) explained, the two systems are becoming blurred: "In the Netherlands, the courts have increasingly become interpreters of the law rather than mere appliers of it, partly because the parliament has been inclined to include in statutes 'vague norms' that leave considerable discretion to the judges. In areas such as euthanasia and abortion, the Supreme Court has in effect produced case laws where parliament was unable to pass detailed legislation" (p. 35).

There is a constitutional right to freedom of speech, but this right does not include advertising. That is why it is forbidden to publish certain kinds of advertisements, for example, for cigarettes or liquor. At the same time, public relations and communication managers in these sectors try to avoid this by looking for what they call *brand communication*; they become sponsors for events to attract people to buy their products. This practice is often criticized, and politicians have frequently tried to find ways to end such sponsorships.

In 1970, an official state committee introduced a draft for a Public Access to Government Information Act, which was meant for all individuals. According to Katus (2001), a Dutch scientist on *voorlichting*, "although the Netherlands is a democratic country, it took ten years before this act came into force, legally recognizing the citizens' rights to government information" (p. 28). This has to do with the already-mentioned fear about keeping all people informed at all times and about all subjects. Still, individuals, mostly journalists, have to threaten now and then to get the information they want, and *voorlichters* (communication officers) continue to clash with politicians and bureaucrats who are less inclined toward openness. However, openness is the norm.

Organizations in the Netherlands are not obligated to give any information to individuals. However, they have to file their annual statement of accounts at the Chamber of Commerce, which is obliged to open its files to any interested party as a matter of public record. Most enterprises make these figures public themselves in annual or biannual statements. Although corporations are required to release financial information to stock holders annually, they tend to do so at least twice a year. The law is, however, not as detailed as in the United States. Currently, a public debate on whether to require all organizations to make annual statements regarding financial matters, their record on environmentalism, and their social affairs is taking place. However, many organizations already publish these kinds of data annually.

Level of Activism

Part of Dutch culture is its socio-ideological pluralism. One consequence of pluralism is that there is rarely a majority opinion on any issue, and even if there is one, there will always be factions or individuals with minds of their own and they want to be heard as well (Vossestein, 2001, p. 66). As a result, activism is rather high in the Netherlands but has a unique character because interest or pressure groups are part of the social and political system instead of being outsiders. On all important aspects of social life such as employment, social security, education, health care, energy, environment, and so on, interest groups are trying to get involved in politics and are very successful at it. According to Deth and Vis (2000) it is obvious that pressure groups play an enduring and important role in the political process in the Netherlands and are "part of the system" (p. 229). The constitutional freedom of association is the legal basis for their existence. The number of activists, their expertise on the issue of concern, and their ability to participate in the public debate is the social basis for their success. Almost all Dutch people belong to one or more pressure groups, and they all donate money for the right causes. Activism is, one can say, institutionalized in the Netherlands.

Pressure groups can target public and private interests. Some are small and active because of one local problem, such as building a new chemical plant in a particular area, whereas others are large and internationally oriented. An important example of a pressure group is labor unions. Although only 25% of employees are organized in unions, unions still negotiate with employers thus helping about 83% of the workforce who work under a collective agreement (Deth & Vis, 2000, p. 213). However, 70% to 80% of all employers are united in employers' associations. This could, of course, lead to much polarization, but this is not the case in the Netherlands. Work stoppage strikes are rarely used as weapons, unlike in Germany, Great Britain, or the United States. The obligation to have a well-functioning work council in which the unions are represented helps to establish good relations.

Other pressure groups (also called *social movements*) are aimed at the public interest. Important examples of this kind of pressure groups are the World Wildlife Fund and Greenpeace, which are both very active in the Netherlands, with over 2 million Dutch donors. These groups have pressured governments on public policy issues for years and have now begun to pressure entrepreneurial decision making on a larger scale, with enterprise struggling to cope with this new phenomenon.

All over the world, pressure groups have become professionalized. They have developed in quantity as well as quality. This leaves the Dutch with a fundamental dilemma of according all groups equal rights to be heard. Challenges for politicians today include how to give all pressure groups equal attention and how to keep fair autonomy in decision making. Challenges for entrepreneurs these days in the Netherlands and around the world is to decide which pressure groups they should give attention to and which pressure groups they can afford to ignore. The Dutch society has accepted that pressure groups have become a fact of life and that, in general, they have a right to be heard.

Pressure groups used to be seen from a collective behavior approach, which observes that pressure disturbs social order. But due to the Dutch culture, activism has never reached a violent state. A prominent anti-institutional action group in the 1960s worked under the striking name of the *Gnomes*. They wanted to change the political as well as the economic system and declared a "Gnome state." They started a political party and won several seats in the local parliament of the city of Amsterdam. Most people liked them, and much of the democratization of the region is based on the disturbance they created during the 1970s. Nowadays, most people in the Netherlands see pressure groups from a resource mobilization view, which recognizes collective action as a normal phenomenon of the political system (van Noort, Huberts, & Rademaker, 1992). Moreover, pressure groups have been allowed greater involvement in decision making in the political field as well as in the corporate arena, as long as they are not too violent in their approach. That is why cooperation is an important strategy of Dutch pressure groups. Van Luijk, a professor on business ethics in the Netherlands, called it "democratization of moral authority" and saw it as a trend (van Luijk & Schilder, 1997, p. 16).

Government and private enterprise are developing an interactive approach to policy development, which has proven to be an interesting strategy to deal with activism. It is seen as the best solution for coping with all kinds of pressure in society, and the recent State Commission on Governmental Communication sees it as the key to public policy making.

CULTURE AND PUBLIC RELATIONS

Social Cultural Aspects of the Netherlands

Because of the interactive nature of many of these environmental variables, the previous sections of this chapter have covered many aspects of Dutch social cultural life. Discussing Dutch culture, some authors spoke of a fragmentation of the society due to increasing individualism. Some even spoke of a *tweedeling* (or segregation or apartheid) of society, denoting a split between the beneficiaries of the booming economy and those left out in the cold (Vossestein, 2001). Although no one is financially destitute in the Netherlands, some are left behind due to exploiting economic opportunities. Examples are single mothers, people with mental problems, old people without children living solely on old-age benefits given by the state, and the homeless. Still, Americans who live in the Netherlands mention the ongoing strong family orientation in much of Dutch society (Vossestein, 2001), and most mention the widely felt right to be subsidized by the state. Still, all kinds of signs of individualism can be found in the Netherlands. Fewer and fewer younger people are volunteering these days. This may be a result not only of individualism but also a sign of an increase in workload and other entertaining avenues to spend free time. Some foreign journalists describe the Netherlands as a (far too) liberal society where people do whatever they like such as indulging in drugs and pornography. This is a nation that finds it perfectly normal for gay couples to be married in the town hall and obtain children by artificial insemination or adoption or for doctors to practice euthanasia legally. Luckily for the Netherlands, investors soon discover that much of this image is half true at best and that there is a lot more to Dutch society than this, argued Vossestein (2001).

According to Vossestein (2001), the basic values of the Dutch are egalitarianism and a high work ethic. The Dutch have difficulty in dealing with hierarchy, always trying to maintain a balance between being aware of the hierarchical aspects of a relationship and not wanting to make that awareness too obvious, he argued. In the Netherlands, common people are the norm, so the elite can be mocked. The elite also do not like to be presented as such. They prefer to be pictured riding their bikes or bringing their children to school not for imagery but for practicing the norm. Although working in the Netherlands is highly competitive, competition is not greatly appreciated. One is certainly not expected to compete at the expense of weaker players or colleagues. "Act normal; that is strange enough" and "Never put your head above the surface level" are widely known expressions. Moreover, those with talent should deploy it for the benefit of all, not just for themselves, according to Vossestein (2001). The Dutch like to see themselves as hard-working people with strong work ethics. Hanging around is not seen as fruitful unless it is seen as being deserved after some hard work. In earlier days, girls were not allowed to sit still but had to do needlework when their normal work was done. This is not normal anymore, but sitting still or watching television for example, is still not seen as constructive behavior. However, the Dutch are known for their short work week of 36 hr and their long vacations, ranging from 3 to 5 weeks each year depending on, among other things, their age. However, some Dutch researchers argued that these achievements are no longer sustainable because of globalization (mostly described as Americanization) of the world (see a. o. Bomhoff, 2001).

Hofstede's Dimensions in the Netherlands

In Hofstede's (2001) terms, the Netherlands can be characterized as a nation with a slightly different culture from its neighbors Germany and Belgium and a very different culture from that of the United States, Asia, and Africa. Hofstede treated culture as "the collective programming of the mind, which distinguishes the members of one human group from another" (p. 25). He found five dimensions—power distance, collectivism, masculinity–femininity, uncertainty avoidance, and Confucian dynamism or long-term orientation—as described in some detail in chapter 1. He stated that the Dutch culture is highly feminine and individualistic wherein low levels of power distance is normal, the people act to avoid or minimize uncertainty, and the members of society have a relatively long-term worldview (Hofstede, 1995, 2001). In feminine cultures like the Netherlands, people prefer to solve conflicts by negotiation and compromise. De Swaan (1989), a Dutch sociologist, stated that Dutch society has evolved from a relative command economy (structured by the pillars) into a full negotiation economy in which all people negotiate about everything. This affinity to negotiate makes itself felt in private as well as in public and organizational life. The Law on Works Councils prescribes deliberations on all organizational policy matters. Labor unions have the right to submit their own candidates for these councils and care for the education of council members. Labor unions have less than 30% membership but negotiate with employers on collective agreements that benefit all employees. The general feeling of employers is that labor unions cause trouble but are natural part of life (Hofstede, 1995, p. 121)—a necessary evil.

Hofstede (1987) stated that the Dutch play eight roles in society. The first role is that of the Dutch uncle, explained previously. The second is the role of the housewife (applicable also to men) with a more than normal aim at caring for personal and social environment. The third role is of the nurse (also equally applicable to men). The fourth is that of the innkeeper, always welcoming but never totally altruistic. An interesting aspect of this role according to Hofstede is that the Dutch practice their uncertainty avoidance not as "strangers are dangerous" but as "strangers are strange," which allows room for tolerating unfamiliar behavior. The fifth role is that of the traveller, which is less chauvinistic and rather internationally oriented. The sixth role is the merchant, the seventh is that of the citizen, and the eighth the farmer's wife who denotes a no-nonsense, no-esthetics, hard-working nature. All of these roles are visible in private as well as in social and economic life, and they can be translated into corporate culture. Although the current trend toward globalization tends to export a more Anglo–American culture, many of these roles can still be found in Dutch daily life.

THE MEDIA ENVIRONMENT

Media Control

Freedom of press is a constitutional right in the Netherlands. Diversity of structure and content is a key principle in the Dutch media system ever since the rise of the mass media at the beginning of the 20th century. At that time, the pillarization was a fact and the new mass media were owned or controlled by the pillars and its social institutions from the start. In fact, the Catholic church, several Protestant churches, the Liberal party, and the Socialist party started their own newspapers and nationwide radio stations because they saw these new media as interesting instruments to socialize their people and develop a bond. In view of the very close relations and interaction between people, religion, politics, and the press, it is not surprising that the Dutch press was and remains an opinion press primarily and not an oppression press. Yellow journalism is hardly visible in the Netherlands.

The first daily newspapers were developed in the second half of the 19th century. Hemels (2000) described how the Dutch press was almost entirely run on the basis of corporatist production principles. To boost circulation and reach and hold onto irregular readers, a new generation of managing newspaper publishers offered their readers a very peculiar extra—free accident insurance. At that time, workers had no accident insurance via their employers and were very happy with this extra. According to Hemels, that is why publishers quickly succeeded in penetrating the market of new readers with this rather unique system of subscriptions, which shows the entrepreneurial side of the Dutch. Although this marketing instrument vanished in 1940, until today, most daily newspapers find their ways to their readers mostly via (yearly) subscriptions.

In 1940, on the eve of World War II the daily press had 70 newspapers, with a total circulation of 500,000 copies. Of these, 32 were Catholic, 6 were Liberal, 5 were associated with one of the Protestant parties, 2 were affiliated with the Social Democrats, 1 was Communist, and 1 was National Socialist; the remaining 23 were somehow independent (Hemels, 2000). This segmentation was even stronger with the other new mass medium—radio. Although radio started as a commercial enterprise (by Philips), it was soon taken over by the pillars. The broadcasting system can be typified as external pluriformity in which all pillars had their own broadcasting organization and shared the two available transmitting radio stations. The usual form taken by organizations belonging to a pillar was that of an association governed by its members or by a foundation with a cooperative board. Until the Media Act of 1988 (van Cuilenberg, 1999) commercial radio and television was not allowed.

After the 1960s, the pillared organizations lost their control in society in general and in their own target groups in particular. Some dailies and weeklies that identified with political parties or special-interest groups totally disappeared, whereas others reinvented themselves and broadened their circulation base. The independent popular press increased its market share enormously. *The Telegraph*, for example, reached an all-time high circulation of 1 million copies per day in 1994 (Hemels, 2000).

However, since advertising on television and radio was allowed in 1967, the printed media had to cope with competition for revenues. As compensation, television and radio have been required to pay a portion of their advertising revenue to the press to keep the highest possible plurality in the press system. A special Trade Fund for the Press, paid by radio, television, and government, subsidizes newspapers and magazines for a certain period if they fail to become or stay commercially independent and obviously add to a multiform media system.

Until the 1960s, five (pillar-oriented) broadcasting organizations had a license to broadcast. After years of political struggle and heated public debate about the future of broadcasting, the *open system* was introduced in 1966—new organizations could enter the system as long as they met the principles of noncommercialism, variety, and membership. The Broadcasting Act (see van Cuilenburg, 1999) made it possible for all kinds of ideological or religious schools of thought to engage in broadcasting. However, they were obliged to deliver a comprehensive programming schedule with reasonable proportions of different program categories and to satisfy the population's cultural, religious, or spiritual needs. Since 1988, commercial radio and television has been legalized. In 2002, Dutch television can be said to have a dual system. The first consists of three public television channels programmed by the old (private) pillars and the newer noncommercial broadcasting organizations (including a Muslim broadcaster as well as a very fundamental Protestant broadcaster and other ideologically based organizations), whereas the second other part of the system consists of about 10 commercial channels. Most commercial stations have been owned by or are subsidiaries of the big multinational media corporations such as Bertelsmann and SBS.

Brants and McQuail (1997) described how government policy has been characterized by constant hesitation and decisional hiccups. With the press, there is a growing fear that a diminishing number of publishers will monopolize the market. The adage "government keeping its distance" and hesitation to interfere in press matters has prevented consecutive Cabinets from taking action, they argued. As far as broadcasting was concerned, the government was aware of the financial opportunities offered by selling airtime to commercial parties and the chance that this money would otherwise cross the border and be lost for the development of original Dutch cultural programming. But there was a traditional hesitation about commercialization, and through traditional ties, it tried to preserve both the existing public system and to create a healthy competitive commercial system. The basis of media policy, which used to be "the widest possible dissemination of information from diverse and antagonistic sources" (van Cuilenburg, 1999, p. 10) is still the basis of the media system but becomes blurred with all kinds of commercial and entertaining variables. Regarding pillarization, van Cuilenburg (1999) concluded that there is no longer pluralism among pillars, but a lot of pluralism does exist within each pillar, although they still officially own many of the broadcasting systems and have informal influence on their actions.

Media Outreach

Van Cuilenburg et al. (1999) discussed the overabundance of the Dutch media. In 1940, the Dutch daily newspaper circulation was 500,000 copies. By 1950, it had reached 2.5 million copies per day distributed to 2.5 million households. Currently, the daily press reaches about 80% of the 6 million households who subscribe to one or more periodicals, resulting in a circulation of almost 5 million copies. Van Cuilenburg et al. called the media market a buyers market wherein media consumption is very elastic, which means that the demand for media is directly or even overproportional to media offers and price. A positive consequence of this kind of a media market is a market-oriented diversity by which the public receives the best service; a negative consequence is a middle-of-the-road type of journalism. The commercialization of the media delivers less openness and diversity of meanings, and these are still norms for quality media. Publishers fear a decline of interest in printed information most of all because of the enormous number of television channels and the increase in time spent watching television. They talk about "de-reading." Their answer is a market-oriented one (Lockefeer, 1999), in which they cater to the needs of target groups by delivering niches of information. This means that professional journalism standards are not the only measures of quality of newspapers, but circulation is an important factor as well. Journalism professors, such as Lockefeer, fear for the quality of journalism, because editor-in-chiefs have recently acquired commercial responsibility for newspapers in addition to content.

Radio and television reach almost all households. In almost all households one can find one, two, or more television sets. There is hardly any household without more than one radio. Knulst (1999) did longitudinal research measuring media consumption for the period from 1955 to 1995. He found that, in 1955, respondents listened to the radio for about 15 hr per week, spent 5 hr per week reading newspapers, and watched television for only 25 min per day (very few people owned television sets). The study contrasted this data with data from 1995 when respondents spent 2.5 hr per day watching television; listening to the radio as a single activity was almost not done anymore and newspaper and book readership had also vastly decreased. People with low levels of education and younger people typically watch commercial television, whereas those with higher education and older people watch public television channels. There has also been a steep decline in the reading habits of the Dutch. In 1955, 21% of leisure time was spent on reading, whereas by 1995 it had dropped to only 9%. Reading was restricted to people with higher education and older people. Bronner and Neijens (1995) found that, for most people, television is no longer the intense experience it used to be and has instead become "the water from the tap"—a part of daily life. For the common person, radio is a medium of entertainment nowadays, although experts still think of radio as an information medium. Daily newspapers are used for information, but younger people turn to newspapers only when they have nothing else to do. Reading magazines is still a rather high intense experience. The Internet shows itself as a medium with high usability for all kinds of information.

Since 1995, much time has been spent on new media. In 2001, 59% of all households have a PC (and 97% of all students have one) and about 47% of these households surf the Internet now and then. The average time spent on the Internet and e-mailing currently is 1.8 hr per week (3.4 hr a week for 12- to 19-year-olds; www.scp.nl). Although there are a lot of workshops for older people and the Internet is promoted for all kinds of people, it is still a tool for younger white boys and men. However, trend watchers believe that in a couple of years the Internet will be as normal as the telephone.

Media Access

Although freedom of speech is a constitutional right in the Netherlands, there is a chasm when it comes to pluralism in media access. There are few constraints for anyone to communicate with journalists, but it is extremely hard to get editorial space. This limitation has little to do with any effort to exclude systematically certain organizations or institutions because publicity seeking is part of the communication game of almost all organizations. Two criteria need to be met to get any access to the media. The first is for publicity seekers to be professional. There are numerous books and courses on how to get media attention. Media relations is a key task of communication managers and consultants, and even very small organizations know how to conduct it professionally. As a result, journalists often complain of information overload. The second criterion is the reputation (credibility) of the source of publicity to deliver interesting and well-organized news, as well as being accessible. Some argue that a few pressure groups or social groups get access to media more readily than others. And some of the *allochtonous* (who are not native Dutch citizens) groups in the Netherlands do not have easy access to the media or are only reported in the news in a stereotypical manner. This is partly due to the sociocultural diversity between journalists and these groups and partly due to commercial reasons. Many of these groups do not read Dutch newspapers or watch Dutch television but read their own newspapers and watch their home country stations via satellite dishes. So they often are not considered a part of the Dutch media market.

CONCLUSIONS AND CASE STUDY

Influences on Public Relations

Based on this review, the following conclusions are drawn about public relations in the Netherlands. First, it is obvious that seeking mutual understanding, as prescribed by the normative theory of public relations, is the normal way of doing business in the Netherlands, as the Dutch are culturally inclined to seek consensus. Note that this is not to be seen as something that has been introduced by public relations. Second, concomitantly, relationship building does not have to be introduced as an instrument because it is what we normally do in the Netherlands. Negotiation is our nature. The Dutch multiparty political system, in which today's enemy can be tomorrow's ally, makes it quite normal to cooperate with natural enemies. The economic system shows that reasonably equal division of prosperity and things like empowering people and management of diversity are part of Dutch economic culture. However, the globalizing economy has challenged traditional ways of behaving.

The legal infrastructure is still founded in the civil law tradition (there are no juries). However, the Dutch fear that it will become normal to bring things *sub judice* (the juridization of society) and the introduction of a claiming culture. This will make life harder and could change the nature of public relations in the future into imagery. Still, image building is not seen as the normal way of doing business, but as the American way. The Dutch like image building as long as they can use it, but the norm continues to be "Never make yourself bigger than you are." Image building is seen by many as untrustworthy; hence, this is not a good path for the public relations society in the Netherlands. Working on identities is increasingly seen as more profitable than working on images. Ron van der Jagt, a leading professional, has written a series of articles advocating this school of thought in the journal of the public relations practice, *Communicatie*. Working on identity as a specialty of public relations, however, should not make professionals neglect the basic roots of public relations as proposed in *voorlichting*, whose primary aim is to enlighten people. For centuries, the Dutch have been keeping each other well-informed as a basic societal principle. However, the boundaries of the concept of *voorlichting* are currently being blurred with concepts such as profiling. It is my opinion that the third conclusion drawn, the most important one, is that if there is a need for a normative theory of public relations, it is on *voorlichting*, which produces an informed society where public opinion is the outcome of deliberation and public debate. That is the current focus of many of the Dutch communication scientists.

Case Study

Be Yourself: The Dutch Approach to Repositioning Unilever on the Recruitment Market by Chris Kersbergen[1]

Unilever, one of the world's leading fast-moving consumer goods companies, pursues a multilocal strategy, which pays special attention to local traditions and cultures for successfully marketing consumer brands. One of the foundations of this multilocal strategy is that 90% of Unilever managers are locally recruited and trained. Those responsible for recruitment and management have the freedom to tailor the presentation of Unilever as an employer to suit local conditions.

In 1999, Unilever Netherlands launched a process to reposition itself on the Dutch recruitment market through integrated employer branding. There are two ways in which one can see clear parallels between this strategy and Dutch culture, as explained in this chapter. First, the values and content of the new employer brand are very Dutch. Second, the process by means of which it was developed is in some ways comparable with the so-called 'polder model.'

Authentic Individuals.   One of the key characteristics of Unilever is its diversity in all its activities and products and brands but, most importantly, in people. But this was not the image the target group top potential university graduates had. They merely regarded Unilever as a large, formal, and uniform company that was only looking for the "smartest boys in the class." This image did not reflect the richness and diversity that this multinational and its employees represented. Moreover, this image was not very appealing to the recruitment market, where potential recruits rated personal development, low hierarchical levels, informal working culture, interesting colleagues, and quality time (private and at work) as most relevant. Research showed that some of the values that Hofstede (1993, p. 5) termed as "typical of the Dutch culture"—feminine and individualistic with short lines of command—were top-of-the-mind criteria for selecting an employer. Potential recruits look for an environment in which they have the space to learn and grow as individuals. Unilever is that environment, but not everyone who should have known that actually did.

This gap between perception and reality has not yet led to recruitment problems, but one must repair the roof while the sun is shining. That is why Unilever, together with communication consultants at Bikker Euro RSCG, began to develop the new Unilever

---

[1]Chris Kersbergen is a partner at Bikker Euro RSCG, a leading Dutch corporate communications consultancy, and has been responsible for codeveloping the employer brand with Unilever since early 1999.

employer brand. The first step was to match Unilever's company values with those perceived as the most relevant by Dutch recruits. These key brand values were communicated through a remarkable corporate-branding campaign consisting of advertising campaigns and a total redesign of all corporate and recruitment material. By using portraits of credible individuals, using more feminine colors, and focusing on authenticity and personal growth (e.g., using a "be yourself" campaign) Unilever was able to show its Dutch side to local recruits. The employer-branding approach has been very successful in attracting existing and new target groups to apply to Unilever.

A Consensus Model for Brand Development.

A Consensus Model for Brand Development.   Apart from the Dutch content and tone of voice of the brand, the process used to develop it was also very Dutch. In the Dutch recruitment market, it is vital to make sure that everything you claim on the outside is a credible reflection of the internal reality. The various networks between students and people working in different companies should never be underestimated. Any graduate thinking of applying to a firm will first contact a friend, family member, or acquaintance who actually works in that company to check "how it really is." After all, you are not just choosing a new toothpaste, you are choosing your working environment and career path for the coming years. So in the recruitment market, and especially in the Dutch network economy, the motto "inside equals outside" rules.

This led Unilever to "involve the involved" in every stage of developing the employer brand, thus making sure that all external claims reflected the internal reality while safeguarding the commitment and support of all Dutch Unilever employees, thus making them ambassadors of the company. Consensus was not a wish but a fundamental necessity to make the campaign credible. Here we can see parallels between the Dutch culture of consensus and coalitions and the so-called polder model.

From the beginning, a group of almost 300 young Unilever managers, all with less than 5 years of experience with the company, were involved in developing the criteria for employer brand fundamentals and the campaign. These young managers became a very cooperative group for the public relations consultants. They witnessed the interviews with students (potential employees) about the image they had of Unilever as an employer and discussed differences between reality and image. When the first visuals of the employer brand were developed, these young managers gave critical feedback. They also contributed in preparing the text for brochures and the web site, and they did the final editing and judging. In many different groups and on many different occasions, this group of young managers actually codeveloped the brand basics and the campaign with the Management Recruitment Department and the agency.

Involvement of senior management was another fundamental factor that contributed to the success of this effort. The Management Recruitment Department showed every proposal to the chief executive officer to get his or her input and consent. Eventually, top management became so involved that they became some of the most enthusiastic ambassadors of the employer brand, conveying that it was not just something from the Management Recruitment Department but part of the corporate story of everyone at Unilever. This not only contributed to making the effort attractive to potential recruits, but it also worked well with current employees. Finally, a lot of attention was paid to informing all other internal and external stakeholders. A special insert in the personnel magazine explained the concepts to all employees before launch. All management recruiters followed special media training focused on explaining the "be yourself" key messages. Finally, all young Unilever managers participated in a pre-introduction day where they were encouraged to translate the campaign messages in their own words.

This consensus model resulted in a very high commitment and an over 90% overall positive evaluation of the "be yourself" campaign among Unilever managers. It helped Unilever become the Number 1 employer of choice in different rankings in 2000 and 2001. But, more important, the "be yourself" philosophy reflects the internal reality and is strongly supported and propagated by Dutch Unilever employees.

REFERENCES

Bomhoff, E. (2001). Not quite smart enough. In *the Netherlands: A practical guide for the foreigner and a mirror for the Dutch*. Amsterdam/Rotterdam: Prometheus/NRC Handelsblad, the Netherlands, pp 58–63.

Brants, J. K., & McQuail, D. (1997). the Netherlands. In B. S. Oestergaard (Ed.), *The media in Western Europe: The Euromedia handbook*. London: Sage. pp. 153–167.

Bronner, F., & Neijens, P. (1999). Hoe beleven mensen hun media? (How do people perceive their media?) In J. van Cuilenburg, P. Neijens, & O. Scholten (Eds.), *Media in overvloed* (Overabundance of media). Amsterdam: Amsterdam University Press, the Netherlands, pp. 118–133.

Commissie Toekomst Overheidscommunicatie. (2001). *In dienst van de democratie. Het rapport van de Commissie Toekomst Overheidscommunicatie* (In the service of democrazy. The report of the Commission on the Future of Government Communication). Den Haag: SDU Uitgevers, the Netherlands.

Cuilenburg, J. van (1999). Het Nederlands mediabestel: Verscheidenheid tussen kartel en concurrentie (The Dutch Media System: a range between cartel and competition). In J. van Cuilenburg, P. Neijens, & O. Scholten (Eds.), *Media in overvloed* (Overabundance of Media). Amsterdam: Amsterdam University Press, the Netherlands, pp. 10–24.

Cuilenburg, J. van, Neijens, P., & Scholten, O. (Eds.), (1999). *Media in overvloed* (Overabundance of Media). *Amsterdam*: Amsterdam University Press, the Netherlands.

Deth, J. W., & Vis, J. C. P. M. (2000). *Regeren in Nederland. Het politieke en bestuurlijke bestel in vergelijkend perspectief* (Government in the Netherlands. The political and administrative system compared). Assen: Van Gorcum, the Netherlands.

Groenendijk, J. N. A. (1987). Public relations in het bedrijfsleven (Public relations in corporations), pp. 49–64. In J. N. A. Groenendijk, G. A. Th. Hazekamp & J. Mastenbroek (Eds.). Public relations & Voorlichting, beleid, organisatie en uitvoering (Public relations and enlightenment, policies, organization and practice). Alphen aan den Rijn, the Netherlands Samson.

Gallagher, M., Laver, M., & Mair, P. (Eds.). (2001). *Representative government in modern Europe*. Boston: McGraw-Hill.

Gent, B. van (1995). Voorlichting in vogelvlucht; bij wijze van inleiding (Overview of enlightenment, an introduction), pp. 9–22. In B. van Gent & J. Katus (Eds.). Voorlichting, theorieën, werkwijzen en terreinen (Enlightenment, theories, methods and fields). Houten, the Netherlands: Bohn Stafleu Van Loghum.

Hemels, J. (2000). Press and broadcasting. In J. Katus & W. T. Volmer (Eds.), *Government communication in the Netherlands*. The Hague: SDU, the Netherlands, pp. 49–69.

Hemerijck, A. (1993). *Historical contingencies of Dutch corporatism*. Unpublished doctoral dissertation, Balliol College, Oxford, England.

Hofstede, G. (1987). *Gevolgen van het Nederlanderschap. Gezondheid, recht en economie* (Consequences of Dutch citizenship. Health, law and economy). Inaugural lecture, University of Maastricht, the Netherlands.

Hofstede, G. (1993). *Images of Europe*. Speech delivered on the occasion of his retirement as a Professor of Organizational Anthropology and International Management, University of Maastricht, the Netherlands.

Hofstede, G. (1995). *Allemaal andersdenkenden. Omgaan met cultuurverschillen* (All dissentient people. How to cope with cultural differences). Amstedam: Contact, the Netherlands.

Hofstede, G. (2001). *Culture's consequences: International differences in work-related values* (rev. ed.). Newbury Park, CA: Sage.

Katus, J. (2001). Government communication: Development, functions and principles. In J. Katus & W. F. Volmer (Eds.). *Government communication in the Netherlands*. The Hague: SDU, the Netherlands pp. 21–36.

Kickert, W. J. M. (1996). Expansion and diversification of public administration in the postwar welfare state: The case of the Netherlands. *Public Administration Review*, *56* (1),

Knulst, W. (1999). Media en tijdbesteding (Time spent on Media) 1955–1995. In J. van Cuilenburg, P. Neijens, & O. Scholten (Eds.), Media *in overvloed* (Overabundance of Media). Amsterdam: Amsterdam University Press, the Netherlands, pp. 101–117.

Kranenburg, M. (2001). The political wing of the "Polder Model." In *the Netherlands: A practical guide for the foreigner and a mirror for the Dutch*. Amsterdam/Rotterdam: Promethuis/NRC Handelsblad, the Netherlands.

Lagerwey, E., Hemels, J., & Ruler, B. van (1997). *Op zoek naar faamwaarde: Vijftig jaar public relations in Nederland* (In search for reputation. Fifty years Public Relations in the Netherlands). Houten: Bohn Stafleu Van Loghum, the Netherlands.

Lockefeer, H. (1999). De krant als baken in een zee van overvloed (The newspaper as beacon in a sea of plenitude)? In J. van Cuilenburg, P. Neijens, & O. Scholten (Eds.), *Media in overvloed* (Overabundance of Media). Amsterdam: Amsterdam University Press, the Netherlands, pp. 54–66.

Luijk, H. van, & Schilder, A. (1997). *Patronen van verantwoordelijkheid: Ethiek en corporate governance* (Patterns of responsibility: Ethics and corporate governance). Schoonhoven: Academic Service, the Netherlands.

Noort, W.J. van, Huberts, L.W., & Rademaker, L. (1992). *Protest en pressie: Een systematische analyse van collectieve actie* (Protest and pressure: A systematic analysis of collective action). Assen: Van Gorcum, the Netherland.

Ruler, B. van (1998). Communication management in the Netherlands. *Public Relations Review*, *26*(4), 403–423.

Ruler, B. van, & Lange, R. de (1999). *Trendonderzoek Communicatieberoepspraktijk in Nederland, Monitor Communicatiemanagement en -advies 1999* (Research of the profession of communication managers and consultants in the Netherlands 1999). Beroepsvereniging voor Communicatie (Association of Communication), Den Haag, the Netherlands.

Ruler, B. van, & Lange, R. de (2000). Monitor communicatiemanagement en—advies 1999: De stand van zaken in de Nederlandse beroepspraktijk. *Tijdschrift voor Communicatiewetenschap*, *28*(2), 103–124.

Swaan, A. de (1989). Uitgaansbeperking en uitgaansangst: Over de verschuiving van bevelshuishouding naar onderhandelingshuishouding (Restriction of curfew and fear for pleasure seeking: On the move from a rule-governed system to a negotiation-based system). In A. de Swaan. (Ed.), *De mens is de mens een zorg* (A human is a human's concern). Amsterdam: Meulenhoff (inaugural address 28.5.79), the Netherlands, pp. 77–99.

Vossestein, J. (2001). *Dealing with the Dutch: The cultural context of business and work in the Netherlands in the early 21st century.* Amsterdam: KIT. the Netherlaands.

12

PUBLIC RELATIONS IN SWEDEN: A STRONG PRESENCE INCREASING IN IMPORTANCE

BERTIL FLODIN

The purpose of this chapter is to introduce readers to the development of public relations in Sweden, discuss the current status of the industry in Sweden, and present some thoughts about the profession's future. At the outset, it is important to recognize that an elaborate history of the public relations profession in Sweden is yet to be written. As such, this chapter provides my personal view of the profession, some of which is based on published information, whereas the rest is based on my 35 years of experience as a public relations practitioner, teacher, and researcher. I begin this chapter with an overview of Sweden as a nation.

CHARACTERISTICS OF SWEDEN

Sweden is a small, highly industrialized country in the northern part of Western Europe. It has less than 9 million inhabitants although it has one of the largest land masses (449,956 km^2) among Western European countries. Sweden is a constitutional monarchy with a parliamentary system of government. As a result, only the king has ceremonial responsibilities as head of state and the parliament sets national policies. The parliament consists of one chamber with 349 members. In the 1998 elections, 149 women were elected to parliament, which is an unusually high proportion compared with the rest of the world. Sweden has a very strong public sector at the national, regional, and local level (Swedish Institute, 1999a).

There are 290 municipalities in Sweden, each with is own popularly elected council. These local councils collect taxes and provide various public services such as schools, child and elder care, housing, and cultural and leisure activities. It is a characteristic feature of the Swedish economy that there is an extensive list of services provided under public auspices. A consequence of this system is that the percentage of taxation is very high.

At the beginning of the 20th century, Sweden was largely an agrarian economy and one of the poorest nations in Europe. However, a rich domestic supply of iron ore, timber, and hydropower enabled the rapid industrialization of the country, transforming it into a modern welfare state (Swedish Institute, 2001). Economic growth was especially strong from the post-World War II period to the middle of the 1970s. During the last 20 years, however, Sweden's gross national product has declined in relation to that of some other European countries. In the early 1990s, Sweden experienced its deepest recession since the 1930s (Swedish Institute, 2001).

After the end of World War II, Swedish politics has been dominated by a power struggle between socialist and nonsocialist groups. Between 1932 and 1976, the Social Democratic Party was in power, either by itself or in coalition with other parties. It regained power in 1994 and remain in power today. Militarily, Sweden is a nonaligned country. One of the implications of this is that it took an extensive period of time and a great many discussions before Sweden was ready to join the European Union (EU) in 1995. As of February 2003, Sweden has not yet made a decision on whether to join the European Monetary Union.

DEVELOPMENT OF SWEDISH PUBLIC RELATIONS

In its modern form, public relations in Sweden began after World War II. In the early days of the profession, media relations was the dominant activity for public relations professionals, which represented corporations and government agencies. In the beginning of the 1950s, several of these practitioners created the Swedish Public Relations Association. In the late 1960s, there was a significant reduction in the number of local governments and an increased interest in active citizenship and democracy. This resulted in a noticeable increase in the number of public relations personnel in the governmental sector as well as the start of a lively debate about what we describe today as asymmetrical and symmetrical communication (Abrahamsson, 1973, 1993). In the beginning of the 1970s, the first courses in communication with reference to public relations were offered at Swedish universities. One of the courses was called *Informationsteknik,* clearly teaching practically oriented techniques as indicated by the title of the course.

After steady progress during the 1980s, the market for public relations exploded during the 1990s, leading up to the new millennium. The tremendous increase in the membership of the Swedish Public Relations Association is an indicator of this development, with a growth in membership from 676 in 1980 to 1,377 in 1990. Today, the association has over 4,400 members. There has been a corresponding increase in the public relations budgets of corporations, organizations, and government agencies as well, particularly in the last decade. It is estimated that public relations spending rose from a total of 4 billion Swedish kronor (SEK) in 1999 to between 5.5 billion and 6 billion SEK in 2001 (Sveriges Informationsförening, 2001a).

Each year, an estimated 4,000 to 5,000 students enroll in communication sciences programs, many of whom have ambitions of entering the public relations profession upon graduation (Högskoleverket, 2001). The public relations profession is becoming more sophisticated to keep pace with rapid globalization, the increase in speed of communication, as well as the expectation that the profession be socially responsible (Flodin, 1999b). The profession is also increasingly perceived as a legitimate and valuable resource by the decision makers in corporations and governmental bodies. As a result, the profession appears to have an interesting future.

CURRENT STATUS OF THE PROFESSION

If we look at the profession from a societal viewpoint, it is evident that the general public does not have an adequate or correct picture of the work performed by committed public relations professionals. In fact, the general perception among the masses is that public relations is merely a publicity activity at best and a concept that encompasses all that is manipulative and propagandistic at worst. To a large extent, this pejorative view of the profession must be considered a reflection of the portrayal of the profession by mass media.

Herein lies the contradiction: The media perceive and describe the profession negatively, whereas public relations professionals produce and deliver a lot of useful information to the media, which the media present to the public daily. Journalists seem to take information subsidies by public relations professionals for granted. One encounters a much more serious and complex understanding of the profession by members of the dominant coalitions of organizations. In a recent study (Sveriges Informationsförening, 2000), the first of its kind in Sweden, 99% of 800 executives in the private and public sector declared that they considered effective public relations a winning concept. The purpose of this study was to obtain a clearer picture of the attitudes among members of dominant coalitions toward public relations and the value these decision makers placed on the profession. The study attempted to ascertain whether members of dominant coalitions had an adequate knowledge of the background, skills, and work assignments of public relations professionals. The sample for the study was diverse, with respondents representing different organizations and industries such as corporations, government agencies, and nongovernmental organizations. Telephone interviews were used to gather data.

The respondents (percentages shown in parantheses after each item) considered the following public relations practices important:

- Creating good relations with stakeholders and publics (88%).
- Advising executives (88%).
- Developing communication strategies (87%).
- Establishing credibility among stakeholders (84%).
- Image creation (83%).
- Crisis management (77%).

This study confirmed that Swedish public relations professionals have established themselves as an important function in the minds of senior managers (57%). Data further revealed that senior managers defined the following competencies relevant to public relations professionals:

- Broad-based competence.
- Sense of design.
- Verbal capacity.
- Good stylistic ability.
- Good social competence.
- Ability to quickly become familiar with situations.
- Good education.
- Keen awareness.
- Excellent communication abilities.

The responses also indicated that senior managers realized the importance of public relations. However, they still do not seem to understand the significant contributions that public relations professionals can have on the overall strategic decision-making process, the business as a whole, and the social intelligence or intellectual capital of the business.

PUBLIC RELATIONS PROFESSIONALS

With 4,400 members from a population of approximately 9 million, Sweden probably has one of the largest, if not the largest, number of public relations professionals per capita in the world. The national association for practitioners—the Swedish Public Relations Association—is strong with a current membership of over 4, 400, making it the second largest in Europe in absolute numbers after the British Institute of Public Relations. The association is very active in a number of areas. It has a highly elaborate professional development program consisting of various communications courses and seminars for members. In addition, it stimulates informal meetings among members working within certain areas (knowledge exchange groups in crisis communication, media relations, etc.). Five years ago, the association started a program exclusively for senior public relations professionals to prepare the professionals to participate in deliberations of dominant coalitions (Sveriges Informationsförening, 2001b).

The Swedish Public Relations Association started in 1996 a research effort on how to measure the impact of public relations (Sveriges Informationsförening, 1996). It also became a partner in a project on how to evaluate the intellectual capital in a company (Nordic Industrial Fund, 2001). A survey of the members of the association (Aldemark, 2001) identified several characteristics of the profession in Sweden. Increasingly, women are dominating the profession. A 1997 survey (Aldemark, 2001) had reported that 70% of public relations professionals were women. However, by 2001, the number had risen to almost 75%. Twenty-five percent of the respondents had the job title of vice president. Most of the respondents (80%) reported that their expertise had been more sought after by their organization in the last 2 years than in the past, a reference to the importance that organizations were placing on the profession. More than 50% of public relations executives were members of the board of management (the dominant coalition) in their respective organizations, another indicator of the significance being accorded to the profession in organizational settings. Of the professionals surveyed, 40% worked in the private sector, 24% in the public sector, 25% in agencies, and 10% in other types of organizations. It was interesting that two thirds of those surveyed worked in the vicinity of Stockholm, the capital. A majority of respondents (85%) had at least a bachelor's degree. When asked about the future, most of the respondents (80%) said that they were convinced that the public relations sector will continue to grow. As far as future growth areas are concerned, respondents believed that strategic planning, profile work, business intelligence, and environmental scanning would be the most important public relations specialities over the next 5 years.

PUBLIC RELATIONS AT UNIVERSITIES

It has been possible to study public relations at Swedish universities since the 1970s although, initially, the number of programs offering it and the number of courses were small. At the beginning of 2001, students were able to take courses in public relations at roughly 12 universities and university colleges (Högskoleverket, 2001). Public relations departments have almost exclusively been situated in programs (schools) of media and communication sciences. In the majority of undergraduate and graduate programs, the number of hours devoted to public relations is rather limited. Ten universities and colleges have specific courses dedicated to public relations. At these institutions, about 15% of the total undergraduate courses (credits) is in public relations, not including credits obtained for doing thesis work (Högskoleverket, 2001). Approximately 40 to 50 exemplary undergraduate (bachelor of arts) theses are produced each year. Postgraduate education in public relations is only represented by two or three universities. There are only three programs (3 years long) at university colleges that focus on professional work in public relations.

The resources available for research in public relations are very limited in Sweden. Presently, there is no full-time professor in public relations and there are no doctoral programs in public relations. Public relations is a growing industry that needs many talented, well-educated young people. There are a large number of students at the undergraduate and graduate levels who want to study public relations. However, the number of qualified public relations teachers is too limited to be able to provide the industry and the students the necessary support and stimulation they need (Dokumentation Information Kultur, 2002). Despite these limitations, about a dozen doctoral students are pursuing research on public relations. Furthermore, about three to five books on the subject are published annually (e.g., Hedquist, 2002; Larsson, 2002; Lidskog, Nohrstedt, & Warg, 2000).

ETHICS AND SOCIAL RESPONSIBILITY

Swedish practitioners have accepted the Code of Athens and the Code of Venice, and they suggested their own ethical codes as well (Sveriges Informationsförening, 2001b). However, these have only existed on paper so far, and very seldom have they been referred to in practice. There also have been no public discussions on the ethics of this industry; so far, almost no public relations practitioner has received sanctions for unethical practices, although it is obvious that practitioners face ethical challenges in their profession regularly (Forsberg, 2001).

At the beginning of the new millennium, some positive signs can be seen in this regard. A number of mentors have accepted to advise younger colleagues on ethical questions, and practitioners have initiated discussions on the subject of social responsibility—an encouraging sign. For example, the Association of Public Relations Consultancies has recently adopted new ethical codes (Föreningen Public Relations Konsultföretag i Sverige, 2002). Even more important is the fact that almost every major Swedish company has adopted communication policies that indicate a strong acceptance of social responsibility and a willingness to use open, transparent, and honest communications. So far there exist no research studies that shed light on whether and to what extent these propositions of high ethical quality are realized in practice.

INFRASTRUCTURE AND SWEDISH PUBLIC RELATIONS

The power of the Swedish parliament has declined during the last decade or so not only because of Sweden's membership in the European Union but also because the Swedish economy is heavily interdependent with the world economy in a globalizing world. Now, in addition to working with the European parliament, Sweden has to work in close cooperation with several other political and economic supranational institutions such as the World Trade Organization and the United Nations (Johnsson, 1999).

An illustrative example is the introduction of commercial television in Sweden. The majority of Swedish politicians did not want commercial television in Sweden. One of their arguments against introducing commercial television was that Sweden already had plenty of commercial messages and advertisements in the print media as well as channels of direct marketing. These opponents also believed that new commercial channels would not match the quality and standard of the public service channels. However, they could not prevent the influx of satellite-broadcast programs from commercial television companies located outside of Sweden. As a result, during the 1990s Sweden saw an influx of terrestrial and satellite television networks, cable television, and commercial radio. For example, 34% of television viewers between 9 and 79 years old watch a Swedish or foreign satellite channel on an average day (Nordicom, 2001). At this point there are few indications that the development of the satellite and cable television networks has had any profound impact on the public relations industry.

Relations between the all levels of the Swedish government and the citizenry can be characterized as being open and transparent. There are numerous opportunities for individuals, groups, and organizations to participate in public debates, and the country has a long tradition of influencing politicians and decision makers. Because of this tradition and the relatively short distance between voters and policy makers (a result of a lack of social stratification), lobbying has only recently expanded in volume and importance as a public relations specialty.

This development escalated even more when Sweden became a member of the EU. One reason for this escalation is that EU bureaucracy is not as transparent as Sweden's is. Furthermore, the complex EU bureaucracy and cultural codes of the EU make it necessary for member countries to have a very specialized knowledge to understand and influence the EU parliament. As a result, it is important to have people who personally know the relevant actors and understand the cultural codes of multiple European decision makers with whom they need to communicate.

Today, the national, regional, and local governments in Sweden use public information as a way of having a dialogue with their stakeholders and publics. These publics can be differentiated along a range of dimensions: citizens, homeowners, shareholders, patients, parents, and environmentalists etcetera. In addition, a great deal of work is being done to communicate with people who have different types of communication problems such as the inability to speak Swedish, not being familiar with the Swedish culture, or being disabled (Landstingsförbundet, 2002).

The political culture in Sweden has affected the public relations profession in a number of ways. The Swedish legislation supports open and free access to information in an attempt to maintain transparency of the government. Examples of this openness can be seen by the way in which the parliament has supported a rich variety of newspapers, public service radio stations, and access to the Internet for everyone for decades. This, in turn, has stimulated the growth and need for a profession in which expertise in media relations is a must. Furthermore, restrictions are not placed on lobbyists, and anybody may call himself or herself a public relations professional and practice the profession.

Swedish political traditions emphasize a strong public sector in which responsibility for schools, health care, and other services are the responsibility of the government. The Swedish public sector is very large; to be able to communicate with the general public and different stakeholders and actors, it is necessary for the public sector to have a large number of public information specialists.

Legal Dimensions

Sweden has a very strong constitutional protection of the rights and freedoms for individuals to express their views without restrictions. The fundamental law of freedom of the press protects the right to publish printed matters without government restrictions and gives citizens the right of access to official documents. The fundamental law of freedom of expression protects this freedom in the media (Swedish Institute, 1999a).

Sweden is believed to have been the first country in the world to establish freedom of the press. In 1776 parliament adopted a Freedom of the Press Act as a part of the Constitution. In 1992 similar legislation was passed for radio, television, film, and other media through the Freedom of Expression Act. The Freedom of the Press Act expressly forbids public censorship of the press as well as other restrictions on publishing and distributing printed matters. This principle is safeguarded with an elaborate combination of measures. First, any periodical appearing four times a year or more must appoint a responsible publisher, who alone is responsible for the content of the publication. Next, the law prohibits the investigation or disclosure of journalists' sources. Finally, the law assures journalists and the public free access to public documents.

Anyone, including aliens, has the right to seek from a state or local government agency any document kept in the agency's files regardless of whether the document is related specifically to the person making the request. Officials are legally required to comply and even to supply copies of the documents requested. This openness is not absolute. Special laws can place restrictions on access as a result of questions concerning personal integrity, the safety of the country, or to prevent criminal acts (Swedish Institute, 1999a).

In practice, this means that journalists check incoming mail daily as a source of accessing different kinds of documents. It also means that public relations practitioners in the public sector always have to base their strategies and tactical work on this principle of openness. The principle of openness in Sweden is unmatched within the bureaucracy of the EU according to Swedish journalists, who have tried to obtain access to EU documents in vain.

This principle of openness also operates within organizations. Sweden has an Employment (Co-Determination in the Workplace) Act (2002), which states that an employer is obliged to inform employees in the organization regularly on matters such as levels of production, the financial health of the organization, and policies regarding personnel. The employer is also required to allow employees the opportunity to examine books, accounts, and other documents. This is governed by the labor union to protect the common interests of its members in relation to the employer (Employment [Co-Determination in the workplace] Act, 2000). This law has been in effect since 1976 and is one of the pillars that make internal communication one of the most important subjects of Swedish public relations practice. By law, this two-way symmetrical communication is forced on every private and public organization.

Presently, the development of information technology (IT) is probably an even stronger force. New media makes available to employees new ways of communicating via the Intranet, the Internet, and e-mail. A recent study of found that 61% of employees interviewed used the Internet daily (Nordicom, 2001). There is general consensus among public relations professionals that different forms of new information technology will be responsible for a significant part of the internal and external communications that they will use in the future. This development is indeed supported by the government, whose ambition is to make Sweden an information society accessible to all (SOU, 2002:20, p. 20).

ACTIVISM

A strong element of Swedish organizational culture during the 20th century has been the understanding between trade unions and employers. This mutual understanding was cemented with a 1930 agreement between trade unions and employers outlining the ways of resolving their differences with a minimum of strikes and lockouts. This consensus model was gradually expanded to encompass the entire political system, which has been characterized by great stability and balance.

Within this system of balance and consensus, activism from different types of social movements and nongovernmental organizations has been witnessed in Sweden. Whether their mission was religious, environmental, or cultural, these activist groups have worked within a democratic system and often have had the support of the parliament and local governments. During the last decades of the last century, new organizations such as Greenpeace and Amnesty International entered the Swedish society and have established themselves as active members of this pluralistic society. For example, Amnesty International has a sponsorship agreement with a Swedish company that produces writing paper.

Until very recently, Sweden had not experienced the use of unconventional or criminal methods by activist groups. Swedish companies had become used to having a dialogue with traditional nongovernmental organizations and supporting them via sponsorships. However, in the last 5 years, activists have been using tactics to grab attention such as climbing on rooftops and chimneys, trying to steal animals from fur farmers, sitting in front of machines that build new roads, sitting in trees to prevent logging, and throwing eggs at ministers. When confronted with this new form of unconventional activist tactics, baffled organizations have often been silent and refused to meet with such activists. Recently, however, corporations and government authorities have been much more open toward inviting activists for constructive dialogues. As one would expect, it is not unusual that these attempts have turned out to be unconstructive and result in dramatic attention-grabbing tactics by activists, who end up being carried away by the police. The most dramatic incident to date took place in Gothenburg when EU held their Summit Meeting in June 2001. Large peaceful demonstrations took place outside the meeting venue, but there were also violent riots resulting in considerable property damage and serious personal injury (Granström, 2002). In the same way that companies track media exposure and market signals, companies track the activities of activists more closely. This means large companies now have the capability to monitor their environments continuously using new media and forecast potential threats to the company's image by activists. They can now plan communications events with activists based on such environmental monitoring. Most often, organizational relations with activists are framed within crisis management and issues management divisions and not included in the day-to-day activities of the company.

CULTURE AND SWEDISH PUBLIC RELATIONS

The majority of public relations practitioners in Sweden during the 1940s and 1950s were men. Over the years, the proportion of women in the profession has grown to almost 75% by current estimates. Over the 10 years, women have occupied a number of strategic executive positions. There are probably few areas within the Swedish labor market where the proportion of women at senior levels is as high as in public relations.

Another cultural aspect that is very visible is the Anglo-American influence on the Swedish society in general and public relations in particular. English is the first foreign language in the Swedish primary school system and is widely understood in the country. As a result, most public relations textbooks are American from authors such as Cutlip, Center, and Broom. Students are also very familiar with the excellence project (J. E. Grunig, 1992). In addition, students read books on topics such as intercultural communication and strategic communications and scholarly public relations journals published in English. I feel that it is unsatisfactory that the Swedish public relations industry, including research and teaching, is so greatly influenced by British and American experiences and ignores the substantive research that is being done in Germany, Denmark, and Austria.

The research in Europe is more oriented toward questions about the role of public relations in an open society (Gerhard, 2000). Often, this research has a critical reflection and does not take a corporate, profit-oriented perspective (Larsson, 2002). Much research is focused on the role of communication in the dialogue between governmental agencies and citizens. Lately, the relations between individual countries and the EU have started to generate interest among researchers, politicians, and decision makers (Organisation for economic co-operation and development, 2001).

Sweden, by tradition, is very open to the world, particularly during the last decade, Sweden has become quite multicultural. By 1998, approximately 19% of the population resulted from immigration (Johnsson, 1999). By extension, public relations practitioners who have an immigrant background would be expected to be commonplace in Sweden. However, this is not the case, probably because the public relations industry has not yet realized the importance of being able to established multicultural dialogue. As Dozier, L. A. Grunig, and J. E. Grunig (1995) suggested, to be excellent and effective, public relations departments must be much more cultural diversified (see Dozier et al., 1995)—a goal that Sweden must strive to achieve.

Strong laws in support of citizens' rights to access information and the relatively small power distance in Sweden are two strong reasons for the very expanded public information service especially among public sector organizations in Sweden. Currently, thousands of public relations practitioners work for the public sector. They do not use propaganda techniques; they use a combination of the two-way asymmetrical and two-way symmetrical communication models first propounded by J. E. Grunig and Hunt (1992). Examples of these types of communications can be found by visiting the web site www.sverigedirekt.se This site provides access to the entire public sector at all levels. The present trend in Sweden and other countries is to involve citizens as partners in policy-making processes (OECD, 2001).

As public relations has grown in strategic importance, Swedish companies have recognized the importance of knowing and adapting their public relations activities to the different cultural environments of their global markets. They have realized that using different cultural values can create problems. For example, a Swedish company that is used to operating under Swedish regulations and work conditions could encounter public relations problems when they have unjudiciously followed the local practices of a foreign country. For example, the Swedish media have often challenged Swedish companies for hiring child labor abroad. As a result, it is not uncommon today for Swedish companies to have very explicit statements about their policy on such matters. For example, Skanska (2002) declared in its Code of Conduct that "... we provide equal opportunities to people without regard to race, colour, gender, nationality, religion, ethnic affiliation or other distinguishing characteristics" (p. 2).

The awareness among Swedish organizations of the fragility of our environment and the need to preserve it has increased over time. Up until the last decades of the 20th century, the annual reports of Swedish organizations only contained financial information. Then a process was started to incorporate information about the activities performed by organizations to contribute to a sustainable environment. Now Swedish companies like to add information about their relations to society in general and to certain stakeholders in particular in an effort to emphasize their social responsibility.

THE SWEDISH MEDIA

Swedish newspapers have traditionally had a very strong readership as the Swedish are among the most avid newspaper readers in the world (Swedish Institute 1999b). Newspapers have held their position of strength partly because of a very elaborate system of state subsidy introduced in the early 1970s. The aim of the system is to provide each region in Sweden with at least two newspapers. As a result, the less popular newspaper in a region can ask for state support to survive. Besides a very high degree of penetration of the market, Swedish newspapers today are characterized by weak ties to political parties and an almost nonexistent relation to religious movements.

Until the middle of the 1980s, the broadcast media were under monopoly state control. Viewer licensing fees financed the operations, and advertising over this medium was prohibited. As a result of the influx of satellite broadcast channels from commercial companies, the broadcasting situation has totally changed in Sweden. Commercial television broadcasting began in Sweden in 1991, followed by the commercialization of radio stations in 1993.

A recent development is the very rapid introduction and adoption of IT technology in general and the use of the Internet in particular in public relations. A study in 2000 found that at least 64% of the Swedish population between 9 and 79 years old had access to a personal computer in their homes of whom 52% had Internet access (Nordicom, 2001a). The study also reported that the typical Swede uses the Internet 65 min per day, and men use the Internet more frequently than women. The study also found that the Internet is used by middle-aged people more often than by people under the age of 14 or over 65, and the well educated use the Internet more than the less educated.

Table 12.1 provides an overall view of the actual media consumption in Sweden and clearly shows that the Swedish population consumes a variety of media. Furthermore, within each media sector, there are signs of very specialized media consumption. In

TABLE 12.1

Percentage of 9- to 79-Year-Old Swedes Who Use
Different Mass Media on an Average Day in 2000

Medium	Percentage
Television	88
Radio	80
Daily newspaper	74
Books	39
Compact disk	37
Weekly magazine	33
Internet	32
Special interest media[a]	32
Text television	31
Evening paper	28
Video	15
Cassette tape	12
Cinema	1

[a]For example, philately and hunting.
Source: Medienotiser 1/2001, Nordicom 2001b, Sweden

addition, the public is exposed to the flow of international news by Swedish and international media such as CNN and BBC. To be competitive, the Swedish media have to be very fast, focus on domestic as well as global issues, provide general as well highly specialized news, and make strategic choices on the degree to which they want to use Internet in their news dissemination. To meet the requirements of the media, Swedish public relations professionals must be able to work with very short deadlines and liaise with national and international media. Furthermore, the field will require highly specialized professionals who can deal with issues such as finance, crisis, legislation, and cultural diversity in a competent way.

The relationship between public relations practitioners and journalists has matured over the years. The earlier unfamiliarity and suspicion between the two has to a large degree been transformed to a professional exchange of information in which both journalists and practitioners are well aware of each other's roles and responsibilities. Of course, this generalization of the industry does not account for many exceptions. In public, however, journalists very often talk about public relations in disparaging terms.

The single most important media development of the last decade both for journalists and public relation practitioners is the rapid introduction and use of the Internet and IT. The amount of information and the speed with which it can be exchanged have created new working conditions for public relations practitioners as well as for journalists (Flodin, 1999a). Today journalists and practitioners exchange information at high speed via the Internet on a daily basis.

The new IT gives professionals the power to create new forms of dialogue with stakeholders and publics and to make all basic information available to the public and to the media. In the long run, this will probably change the working relations between professionals and journalists. Less time will be devoted to the exchange of basic information and more time to proactive and selective efforts.

CASE STUDY: CONSTRUCTION COMPANY SUSPECTED OF CARTEL CONCURRENCE

In March 2001, NCC, one of the leading construction and property-developing companies in the Nordic region, reported seven of its employees to the police for fraud. In the summer of 2001, an anonymous person reported to the Swedish Competition Authority that the NCC was participating in an illegal cartel, an antitrust arrangement with a few of its competitors to lower bids on public tenders. In the morning of October 23, the Swedish Competition Authority suddenly appeared at several of the largest Swedish construction companies to collect data for further investigation. In January 2002, the NCC confirmed at a well-attended press conference that it had participated in this illegal antitrust cartel with some of its key competitors. The press conference resulted in very intensive and negative media coverage. Much of the publicity was of course negative but, as NCC put it, "This is not the time to get good publicity, but to minimize the negative one." The media also began to search for the other members of the cartel.

The press conference was the result of a proactive strategy that the NCC had decided to implement. The key aspects of the strategy were the following: Confirm cartel suspicions, take the initiative, decide when to break the news, be open to internal and external publics, cooperate with the authorities, and supply the media with information. Last but not least was the strategy to take a number of actions to prevent this from happening again, including educating middle management and implementing a compliance program. With this strategy, the NCC wanted to expose the whole affair at one point to prevent a prolonged interest on the subject from the media. The organization also wanted to shift the focus of interest to other actors. The NCC realized that there was an urgent need to rebuild the public's confidence in the board and management of the NCC. In the process, the NCC decided to concentrate on the following key publics: the Swedish Competition Authority, customers, the media, employees, competitors, and the shareholders.

The Swedish Competition Authority was given a full report by the NCC based on an independent investigation by a solicitor's office. The NCC contacted important stakeholders by phone or in person and were given the NCC's version of events. Employees were informed by a combination of Intranet and print media, including a personal letter from the chief executive officer. Just before the press conference, the most important competitors were informed that the NCC intended to break the news about their involvement in the cartel. The first reaction of these organizations was to deny any involvement. Some continue to maintain their innocence. Personal contacts were made with the most important shareholders.

The NCC's own evaluation of public opinion showed that, although a large proportion of the respondents considered the NCC's involvement in the cartel to be serious, a substantial number felt that the NCC had taken care of the situation in a responsible way. Among the employees, the support for the NCC was very strong.

In June 2002, the first phase was over, but the process continues. The NCC awaits court proceedings in 2003, a report from the Swedish Competition Authority, initiatives from other actors, and possible renewed media attention.

The NCC has drawn the following lessons from their crisis:

- It is important to have a powerful crisis management team.
- Organizations have to be prepared for different types of crises.
- Organizations need to solicit second opinions but to keep the initiative.
- Organizations need to scan opinion among important target groups carefully during a crisis.

In conclusion, faced with an embarrassing and dangerous situation, the NCC chose to play by the first rule of the crisis management manual: "Tell it all and tell it fast." So far, this seems to have been a successful strategy, supplemented with the highly demanding ethical standards that NCC has adopted.

REFERENCES

Abrahamsson, K. (1973). *Samhällskommunikation: Om kontakten mellan myndigheter och medborgare* [Public communication: Contacts between authorities and citizens]. Lund: Studentlitteratur, Sweden.

Abrahamsson, K. (1993). *Medborgaren i samhällsdialogen* [The citizen in the public dialogue]. Stockholm: Publica, Sweden.

Aldemark, L. (2001). *INFO 2001 Rapport*. Stockholm: Sveriges Informationsförening, Sweden.

DIK (2002). *Informatörer—ett yrke för framtiden . . . om utbildningarna hänger med* [Public relations officer—a profession for the future . . . if the educations can keep up]. Stockholm: Dik-förbundet, Sweden.

Dozier, D., Grunig, L. A., & Grunig, J. E. (1995). *Managers guide to excellence in public relations and communication management.* Mahwah, NJ: Lawrence Erlbaum Associates, USA.

Employment (Co-Determination in the Workplace) Act. (2000), Sweden.

Flodin, B. (1999a). *Planlagd kriskommunikation* [Planned crisis communications]. Stockholm: Styrelsen för psykologiskt försvar, Sweden.

Flodin, B. (1999b). *Professionell kommunikation* [Professional communication]. Stockholm: Styrelsen för psykologiskt försvar, Sweden.

Föreningen Public Relations Konsultföretag i Sverige. (2002). *Normer för PR-konsultföretagen i PRECIS* [Standards for the Swedish Public Relations Industry]. Retrieved from January 1st, 2003. www.precis. se/standards.

Forsberg, E. (2001). *Sunt-förnuft-konsulter* [Common-sense-consultants]. Örebro: Örebro universitet, Sweden.

Gerhard, J. (2000). Das Öffentlichkeitsdefizit der EU: Theoretische Überlegungen und empirische Befunde. (The public deficit in EU: Theoretical considerations and emperical findings). In B. Baerns (Ed.), *Information und Kommunikation in Europa, Forschung und Praxis*. Berlin: Vistas, Germany.

Granström, K. (Ed). (2002). *Göteborgskravallerna* [The Gothenburg riots]. Report 187. Stockholm: Styrelsen för psykologiskt försvar, Sweden.

Grunig, J. E. (Ed.). (1992). *Excellence in public relations and communication management*. Hillsdale, NJ: Lawrence Erlbaum Associates, USA.

Hedquist, R. (2002). *Trovärdighet—en förutsättning för förtroende* [Credibility A condition for trust]. Stockholm: Styrelsen för psykologiskt försvar, Sweden.

Högskoleverket. (2001). *Utvärdering av medie-och kommunikationsvetenskapliga utbildningar vid svenska universitet och högskolor* [Evaluation of programs in media and communication science at Swedish Universities and University Colleges]. Stockholm: Author, Sweden.

Johnsson, H.-I. (1999). *Spotlight on Sweden*. Stockholm: Swedish Institute, Sweden.

Landstingsförbundet. (2002). *Alla kan vinna* [All may win]. Stockholm: Author, Sweden.

Larsson, L. (Ed.). (2002). *PR på svenska* [PR in Swedish]. Lund: Studentlitteratur, Sweden.

Lidskog, R., Nohrstedt, S. A., Warg, L. E. (Eds.). (2000). *Risker, kommunikation och medier* [Risks, communication and media]. Lund: Studentlitteratur, Sweden.

Nordic Industrial Fund. (2001). *Intellectual capital managing and reporting*. Oslo: Nordic Industrial Fund, Sweden.

Nordicom. (2001a). *Internetbarometer 2000* [Internet barometer 2000]. MedieNotiser 2.2001. Göteborg: Author, Sweden.

Nordicom. (2002). Sveriges 2000 *Mediebarometern 2000*, [Swedish Media barometer 2000]. MedieNotiser 1.2001. Göteborg: Author, Sweden.

OECD. (2001).*Citizens as partners, information, consultation and public participation in policy-making*. Paris: OECD, France.

Skanska. (2002). *Skanska code of conduct*. Stockholm: Author, Sweden.

SOU 2002:20. (2002). *Guide på Internet—ett stöd för medborgarnas möte med det offentliga* [Guide to the Internet—support for the meeting between the citizen and the public sector]. Statens offentliga utredningar. [Swedish Government. official reports] Stockholm: Fritzes. Sweden.

Sveriges Informationsförening. (1996). *Return on communication*. Stockholm: Author, Sweden.

Sveriges Informationsförening. (2000). *Attitydundersökning om informatörer i företag och offentlig sektor* [Survey of attitudes about public relations practitioners in the private and public sector]. Stockholm: Author, Sweden.

Sveriges Informationsförening. (2001a). *INFO 2001 Medlemsundersökning* [Survey among members in the Swedish Public Relations Association]. Stockholm: Author, Sweden.

Sveriges Informationsförening. (2001b). *Nätverk 2001/2002* [Network 2001/2002]. Stockholm: Author, Sweden.

Swedish Institute. (1999a). *General facts on Sweden*. Stockholm: Author, Sweden.

Swedish Institute. (1999b). *Mass media*. Stockholm: Author, Sweden.

Swedish Institute. (2001). *The Swedish economy*. Stockholm: Author, Sweden.

13

PUBLIC RELATIONS IN AN ECONOMY AND SOCIETY IN TRANSITION: THE CASE OF POLAND

RYSZARD ŁAWNICZAK
WALDEMAR RYDZAK
JACEK TRĘBECKI

INTRODUCTION

Since 1989, the Central European country of Poland has been undergoing a political shift toward democracy and an economic transition from a command economy to a market economy. Several features distinguish Poland from the region's other transition economies. First, only those of Russia and the Ukraine exceed Poland's vast area and population. Second, the process of building democracy in Poland began as early as 1956, a process that was supported by the strong Polish Catholic Church, which operated with varying degrees of intensity throughout the period of Poland's socialist economy. Third, Poland's has had a relatively strong private agricultural sector since World War II, with private farmers holding approximately 85% of the country's total farmland. Fourth, private business ownership in the trade, crafts, and service sectors gained significance after 1956. Finally, Poland has a historic role as a pioneer of transformation including applying *shock therapy*—the process of radical transitioning from a centrally planned economy to one dictated by market forces.

History and Development of the Country

Situated in Central Europe, Poland shares its borders with Germany, the Czech Republic, Slovakia, Ukraine, Belarus, Lithuania, and Russia's Baltic enclave. In the north, Poland borders the Baltic Sea. With an area of 312,683 km² (129,725 square miles) and stretching some 650 km (405 miles) from the east to the west, Poland is the ninth largest country in Europe. At the end of 2001, Poland had a population of 38,632,000, ranking 29th in the world and 8th in Europe. The population consists of 48.6% boys and men and 51.4% girls and women. The average life span is 68.5 years for men and 77.0 years for women. Ethnically, Poland remains fairly homogenous, with ethnic minorities accounting for 2.6% to 3.9% of the population. Poland's prevailing religion is Roman Catholicism.

History.   In early times, western Slaves inhabited the territory that is Poland today. Their adoption of Christianity in 966 AD led directly to the establishment of the Kingdom of Poland in 1025. Poland flourished culturally and economically under the reign of the Jagiellonian Dynasty (1386–1572). By the end Jagiellonian rule, its territory enlarged to several times larger than it is today. For the 2 centuries that followed, the nobility elected kings. Their reign brought about the accelerated growth of towns but also frequent wars that reeked havoc on the economy and led to stagnation in rural areas. Efforts to prevent rapid deterioration came much too late. The neighboring countries of Russia, Prussia, and Austria joined forces to take advantage of Poland's military and economic weakness. As a result, they imposed three consecutive partitions in 1772, 1791, and 1795, effectively wiping Poland off the map of Europe. Significantly, in 1775 Poland remained 2.5 times larger than it is today.

Poland did not regain independence until the end of World War I. Between the World War I and World War II, Poland managed to consolidate itself socially, politically, and administratively. In a time of global depression, the economy proved to be the hardest sector to restore. Following Hitler's invasion of Poland, which marked the outbreak of World War II, the country was occupied by Nazi Germany and the Soviet Union. Approximately 6 million Poles perished during the war. Once it was over, Poland again regained independence. This time, however, its sovereignty was severely compromised by Soviet influence and Communist Party control imposed on the government. After decades of phenomenal growth in the 1960s and 1970s, the inherent flaws of its centrally planned economy led to severe market shortages. The consequence was a lower standard of living, growing dissatisfaction, and social unrest, all of which culminated in the establishment of the Solidarity trade union movement headed by Lech Wałęsa. After a series of strikes and a period of martial law, the Communist government agreed to start roundtable talks with Solidarity representatives. The result was the parliamentary election of June 1989.

These events produced a breakthrough in the postwar political history of Poland. During the roundtable talks, the Communists ensured for themselves a formal majority in the lower chamber of the parliament (the *Sejm*). Solidarity, however, gained an absolute majority in the Senate. By autumn, the first non-Communist government in postwar history was established. In late 1989, the new government and the parliament adopted a package of laws and economic policy measures referred to as shock therapy, thereby abandoning its centrally planned command economy.

Although Poland is a democracy and a market economy today, to this day the legacy of a socialist democracy and central planning is manifested in many areas of social life, including the practice of public relations. The legacy can still be seen in three principal areas, as well as elsewhere. First, there is a common perception that public relations is suspicious propaganda. This view stems from the country's past experience with such things as censorship of the mass media, the subjugation of all such media to a single doctrine, and the resulting stereotypical conviction that the press lies. Second, there is a failure in the society to understand the philosophy behind advertising and promotion of products and businesses or building the images of companies and their executives. This problem stems from the fact that all goods manufactured during the socialist economy were readily sold because of severe shortages and lack of competition. Finally, there is a belief in Polish society that corporations, their owners, and their successes are better left unprompted because such high profiles may bring on additional tax sanctions. This view stems from the fact that, for ideological reasons, all privately owned operations were considered suspicious and were fought with the use of ad hoc taxation.

These characteristics have had a significant impact on the development and current status of public relations in Poland. One might argue that political, social, and economic transformations are responsible for having created a demand for public relations services and for the arrival of public relations experts and agencies, mainly from the West. However, public relations has played the role of an important and useful instrument that has facilitated and accelerated the political and economic transition of the country. One may, therefore, postulate that in Poland, as well as in other transition economies, public relations has a fifth transitional dimension in addition to the other four dimensions characteristic of the developed economies of Europe: managerial, technical, reflective, and educational (van Ruler, 2000).

The Evolution and Definition of Public Relations as a Profession

Evolution. As can be easily demonstrated, Poland is among the countries for which the concept of public relations has had a long historical and ethnic tradition. Examples of early forms of public relations in the country include attempts by the Polish nobility and kings to gain publicity. The most famous of these were *the Thursday dinners* held by the last Polish King Stanisaw August to promote arts and science, as well as the match-making customs of Polish peasants.

The history of modern public relations in Poland started with a transition from a centrally planned to a market economy and the shift from socialist democracy to a pluralistic political system that began in the early 1990s. With a track record of a little more than 1 decade, Poland's public relations market is relatively young. Yet, as early as the 1970s during Poland's Communist era, information on public relations trickled into Poland from Western Europe and the United States through Polish researchers who maintained scientific links with the West. The year 1973 marked the publication of the article, "Public Relations in the Socialist Economy" (Żelisawski, 1973), which most likely was Poland's first published article on public relations. Yet, principally, Polish public relations is a product of the country's systemic transformation and the need to communicate about the environmental variables resulting from the transition to a market economy.

The evolution of public relations in Poland has followed two tracks. The first track is that the systemic transformation has created opportunities for establishing broader foreign contacts, thereby allowing for foreign investment and privatization to enter the country. Numerous Western enterprises that recognized the need for public relations services have moved into the Polish market. Some of this demand was satisfied by foreign agencies that established branch offices in Poland. These included Burston Marsteller, which opened its Warsaw office in 1991. One year earlier, however, the first two domestic public relations agencies—First Public Relations and Alcat Communications—were formed.

The second track is that before establishing certain market instruments, mechanisms, and institutions (e. g., the stock exchange) that were absent in the command economy, the Polish government engaged public relations agencies to carry out public information campaigns. An example is the use of such agencies during the levying of direct and indirect taxes and upon the introduction of the national privatization program in the 1990s. Financing for such campaigns has come from foreign sources, mainly from the PHARE fund (Poland and Hungary Aid for Economic Restructuring). Since the Polish public relations market was virtually nonexistent, the government hired Western companies, which relied on the help of Polish consultants. In this way, even though external funds ultimately ended up in the pockets of external contractors, the transformation provided an impetus for the emergence of the Polish public relations industry.

Between 1990 and 1994, only 11 newly established companies claimed to have made public relations their core business. Still, their actual focus was on advertising. Nevertheless, thanks mainly to big government contracts (for the already-mentioned public information campaigns), the first 5 years of public relations evolution in Poland witnessed rapid development of the market, with an annual growth rate of 12%. In 1997, the annual sales of one of the agencies reached a staggering $3.7 million. By comparison, the market's growth from 2000 to 2001 was less than 5% per annum (Łaszyn, 2001).

The years 1995 to 2000 saw further dramatic growth of public relations in Poland. For most of the period, this growth was mainly quantitative. It was not until the late 1990s that actual qualitative improvements were made as the need for crisis communication (in the wake of the Russian crisis of 1998), internal public relations, and investor relations were recognized. Starting in 2000, a growing number of public relations agencies recognized the need for specialization. The formerly fragmented public relations market consolidated through mergers and acquisitions. Many agencies were pushed out of business partly because the first stage of transformations had been completed by then and the government no longer had large contracts to offer to big Western agencies. In addition, many smaller agencies were adversely affected as the economy declined into recession. However, this is when another stage in the development of public relations, one of professionalization and internationalization, began in Poland.

In October 2001 in Berlin, Warsaw-based Business Communications Associates won three Golden World Awards from the International Public Relations Association (IPRA). One of their prize-winning programs was also nominated to receive a United Nations award. In July 2002, in its new strategy for administrative reform drawn up to the European Commission's recommendations given for Polish tax administration, the Ministry of Finance resolved to establish 16 public relations units at local and regional tax offices by January 1, 2004. The ministry's new communications strategy for promoting a good name for tax administration would be developed and implemented in the PHARE 2001 project in close cooperation with French and Swedish experts.

Defining Public Relations.   There is no Polish equivalent for the term *public relations*. Although a great number of attempts have been made at translating this term into Polish, no proposal accurately expresses the idea behind it. Therefore, the English term is commonly used. Another term that is gaining popularity in Polish language is *komunikacja społeczna* (social communication), derived from the English word *communication*. The authors of one of two parts of Poland's most popular textbook on public relations (Kadragic & Czarnowski, 1995) have offered the following informative definition of the term: "Public relations is about information. The information is honest and objective, professional and reliable, complete, fast, media- and public opinion-friendly, ethical and responsible."

The approach seemed very appropriate at the time in view of the need to develop public relations as a separate domain in Poland because at that early stage of the profession, the media and public opinion often confused public relations with advertising. Another reason for adopting the above view of public relations was that many public relations practitioners in Poland were former journalists who commonly used language that is similar to that of the media and that is often misunderstood even while practicing public relations. Another factor affecting the perception of public relations in Poland was offered by Goban-Klas (1995):

> The transfer from a command to a fully privatized and highly competitive market economy was not complete. The predominant approach to doing business was to seek a quick profit, which generates considerable distrust, especially since scams and fraud were commonplace. . . . The government is overly apprehensive about working with the media, revealing its plans and submitting itself to public supervision. In effect, Polish PR campaigns could not be modeled after those developed in other countries, including the United States. (p. 8)

In a textbook published in 2001 which to this day remains the most popular public relations textbook, Wójcik (2001) provided a list of key definitions of public relations from world literature and a list of public relations associations from a range of countries. It appears that the definition most quoted in Poland has been taken from one of the most popular American textbooks, which defines public relations as "a management function that deals with evaluating public attitudes, identifying the policies and procedures of an individual or an organization with the public interest, and planning and executing a program of action to earn public understanding and acceptance" (Cutlip, Center, & Broom, 1994, p. 3).

Status and Image of the Profession

By mid-2002 public relations had become one of the most fashionable professions, measured in terms of the number of and demand for public relations programs at state and private institutions of education. Paradoxically, public relations practices have not been officially included in the list of professions pursued in Poland despite the efforts of the Association of Public Relations Firms, established in 2001, which continues to lobby state administration to recognize the profession.

The public relations profession in the country is dominated by women. Most public relations practitioners are young, well-educated women around 30 years old. According to a mid-2002 ranking of the major public relations agencies by the magazine *Impact* (July/August 2002 issue), half of the chief executive officers of such companies are women. Iskra (2001) reported that when asked why they chose public relations as their profession, most practitioners mentioned the opportunity to be creative and performing diverse tasks. The second most quoted reason was the independence and responsibility associated with the profession. A decent remuneration (at an average of approximately 2,500 euros in 2001) was also among the key reasons for respondents to select a career in public relations. The pay factor has clearly contributed to boosting the demand for postgraduate programs in Poland.

Even today, public relations work is often confused with marketing and press agentry and associated with the misused propaganda by the government. According to the founder of Poland's first public relations agency whose opinion may appear to be too critical:

> Polish PR remains far removed from world practices and often stands in complete contrast to them. This, of course, is due largely to market circumstances as Polish media differ widely from those in the rest of the world—rather than serving the mission of informing the public, the media in Poland frequently yield to the paranoia of concealed advertising. Differences can also be found in the way public opinion reacts—the media in Poland are still expected

to provide sensational rather than informative news, customers make their purchases on the basis of price, not quality. Other differences concern the clients of PR agencies—clients in Poland often expect agencies to manipulate the media, corrupt and blackmail journalists rather than disseminating reliable and honest information. (Czarnowski, 1999, p. 1)

The Professionalism of the Public Relations Industry in Poland

As of mid-2001, public relations services were being offered by some 500 agencies and the approximate annual worth of the public relations market was estimated at $100 million (Łaszyn, 2001). Only about 50 of these agencies are fully professional, offer a wide range of services, operate on a long-term basis, and seek to establish lasting relationships with their clients. Other agencies, typically run by one or two individuals, have been set up by journalists and public relations experts who have chosen to leave their jobs in corporate public relations departments or large public relations agencies. Most of these professionals (85%) are natives.

Even today, only a few foreign public relations agencies such as the Rowland Company and Prisma International operate in Poland. Burson Marsteller, which had operated in Poland since 1991, closed its Warsaw office in April 2001. The move appears to be a failure on the part of the company to adapt to the specific requirements of an economy and society in transition. Nearly all of Burson Marsteller's former Polish employees, who gained experience when the agency operated in Poland, currently head Poland's leading public relations agencies. Burson Marsteller's experience in Poland supports that central theme of this book: environmental variables such as nature of the economy, culture, and media are important predictors of success in public relations.

Poland's leading agencies are affiliated with reputable Western multinational consultancies. These include BCA (which won three Golden Awards in Berlin), Edelman PR World Wide, Sigma, Weber Shandwick World Wide, ComPress, Fleishmann Hillard, United Public Relations, Manning, Salvege & Lee, and Hill and Knowlton. Sigma International was ranked as the public relations agency with the largest sales according to a ranking by the monthly *Impact*, with an estimated $4.5 million in revenues and a staff of 60 (*Rzeczpospolita*, 2002).

The Role of Professional Associations.   The rapid growth of the public relations market in the 1990s has increased the demand for the establishment of a professional association of practitioners. As a result, the Polish Public Relations Association was established in 1994, and it currently has 184 members. Another public relations association, the Association of Public Relations Firms, was established on January 18, 2001, to represent public relations agencies. Currently, this association has 16 leading agencies as members, with 5 others applying for membership in 2002. The mission of the Association of Public Relations Firms is to protect the rights of its members; represent members in dealings with state authorities, state administration, local governments, and other institutions, as well as with corporate and natural persons; and to strengthen the position of and disseminate knowledge on public relations professions. As this association became more professional, it joined international organizations in the public relations industry. In August 2001, the association was admitted to the International Communications Consultancy Organization. In the same year, it signed a cooperation agreement with the IPRA and joined the Polish Confederation of Private Employers. To date, these are the only public relations associations in Poland. In view of the size of Poland's public relations market and its evolution, it is unlikely that any other associations will be established in the near future.

Ethics: The Hot Issue for Public Relations.   Public relations ethics has been debated quite heatedly since the establishment of the Polish Public Relations Association, which adopted a Code of Ethics at its second Congress in 1996. The Association of Public Relations Firms followed suit, drafting its own Statement on Professional Public Relations Practices in 2001. The latter document set out detailed ethical guidelines for its members. The problem with both of the codes is that they are very general and the standards they describe are frequently violated in by public relations professionals. There are three most common violations. The first is the corruption of journalists (Wielowiejska, 2000) and political decision makers. There is a practice of offering material benefits to journalists to influence them, among other things, to include desirable messages in their articles, which is referred to as *nonstandard advertising*. Corruption of political decision makers through unethical lobbying practices is apparent. The second is the unofficial practice by an organization of furnishing the media with anonymous messages aimed at tarnishing the image of the organization's competitors. This practice is referred to as *black PR* in Poland. The third is the use of public relations to acquire funds illegally from state owned- or state-controlled corporations for the purpose of financing the election campaign of a favored political party, for instance.

The Role of Universities and Colleges in Furthering the Public Relations Profession.
The origins of public relations education in Poland go as far back as the early 1970s when the country's first course in public relations was offered by the former Main School of Planning and Statistics. At that time, the course was a lecture given on an elective basis by Professor Krystyna Wójcik, who later authored what today is a primary public relations textbook. Since 1989, this course has been a core requirement in the Economic Journalism specialization program offered by Dr. Agenor Gawrzyał at the Poznań University of Economics. Starting in mid-1990s, teaching public relations has gained popularity in both state universities and private business colleges, which have cropped up in great numbers. The first two textbooks on public relations were published in 1992 (Wójcik, 1992; Zemler, 1992).

Today, public relations programs are offered by almost all major state and private institutions of higher education in the country. For the most part, public relations is taught in universities of economics and in some humanities-oriented institutions. Occasionally, it is also taught in institutes of technology. The majority of such institutions offer public relations at the postgraduate, undergraduate, and graduate levels (mainly to holders of other undergraduate degrees). These undergraduate and graduate programs usually focus on a specialization (e.g., public relations, spokesmanship, public relations, media relations, or communication). These specializations are offered as part of programs in economics, sociology, journalism, political science, management, and marketing. The programs are 3 years in duration at the undergraduate level and 4.5 to 5 years in duration at the graduate level (with 2 years focused on the public relations specialization).

Most common, however, are universities with 2-year postgraduate courses, awarding graduates postgraduate diplomas in compliance with the requirements of the Minister of Education. Graduates of undergraduate programs receive bachelor's degrees, whereas persons completing graduate programs are granted master's degrees documented with proper diplomas. Students who complete specializations in specific majors receive master's or bachelor's degrees in their majors (e.g., sociology or journalism) and a document certifying their completion of a public relations specialization.

Public relations as an area of research is relatively new to Poland. Some of the first public relations studies were conducted in the early 1990s. The investigators behind these studies focused on general rather than specific issues. The first two dissertations in the public relations field completed in Poland were defended in 1995. By 2002, 38 dissertations in public relations were submitted, 14 of which were at the final stage of approval. The first higher level dissertation (*habilitacja*) has been defended in 2002. Paradoxically, as of mid-2002, public relations has not been given the status of a scientific discipline (according to the classification of the Scientific Research Committee). Yet, experts claim that the real growth of public relations as a scientific discipline has yet to come.

Public Relations and the Business Community

Systemic transformations and, in particular, the uncertainties of an economy in transition have forced the business community to revisit its position vis-à-vis public relations. State-owned enterprises were forced to reform their communications policies to get their foreign shareholders to support privatization and retrenching (Ławacz, 1995). Public relations was used in this context as an important instrument to support the transition of large enterprises from the former command to the new market economy.

Nevertheless, the majority of demand for public relations services in Poland has not come from state-owned companies but rather from international corporations and companies controlled by foreign enterprises. The second largest group of public relations customers was a new generation of large Polish private businesses and privatized State Treasury companies ranked in the top 10 of Poland's largest business organizations. The group least cognizant of the need for public relations includes small- and medium-size entrepreneurs and large state-held enterprises that have not yet been privatized.

Large, privately owned, foreign and domestic corporations are quite successful in articulating and advocating their interests by using different types of public relations strategies and techniques. In their efforts to maintain relationships with the parliament, other branches of the government, and trade unions, corporations are able to call on a highly professional group of lobbyists such as the Business Center Club and the Confederation of Private Employers. The latter has managed to obtain an equal representation in the Trilateral Commission within whose framework representatives of the government, trade unions, and employers negotiate on all key regulations pertaining to the labor market. Much less effective in dealing with various activist groups are medium-size and large enterprises that are either owned or substantially controlled by the state. In less severe cases, such as when faced with environmental protests, these enterprises respond by using press spokesmen. More serious situations are dealt with by external consultants or crisis management companies (Rydzak, 2001).

A study carried out in 2000 has helped identify where public relations is housed in corporations operating in Poland (euroPR Agency Study, 2000). Of the companies analyzed, 44% were found to place public relations in their marketing departments, 22% in their sales departments, 15% in their management board offices, and 10% in their advertising departments. Only 5% of the organizations maintained a separate public relations unit with a direct reporting relationship with the management board.

Interesting insights were uncovered by the same study that also analyzed the goals that enterprises have formulated for their public relations function. According to the study, creating and maintaining a good corporate image was a public relations priority for 22% of the companies. Another 19% of companies used public relations to inform external publics, whereas 17% concentrated on maintaining good relations with customers and on increasing sales. Shaping public opinion was found to be a priority for a mere 9% of the companies, whereas 4% of the surveyed companies sought to concentrate on the need to maintain ties with the media and organize campaigns. The smallest proportion (1%) indicated a focus on lobbying and internal communications.

One study found that 40% of employees are not familiar with the concept of public relations and that only 12% of the surveyed understand the difference between public relations and advertising (Trębecki, 2001). The level of education of people responsible for public relations functions leaves a lot of room for improvement. Only 6 (or 45%) hold degrees in public relations. The largest proportion of public relations practitioners (53%) are economists, whereas 23% hold degrees in engineering. Other professionals had specialized in human sciences (12%) and law (approx. 4%).

INFRASTRUCTURE AND INTERNATIONAL PUBLIC RELATIONS

Poland's Political System

Today's Poland is a democratic, multiparty, parliamentary republic. Poland's head of state is the president, who is elected in general elections. The national legislature is bicameral and consists of the Sejm (lower house) and the Senate. The prime minister is nominated and appointed by the Parliament. The Senate has a supervisory function and was reinstituted in 1989 for the first time since the end of World War II. Executive powers are entrusted to the prime minister and his or her cabinet, which is referred to as the Council of Ministers.

Poland's current political system has evolved through structural reforms of the state that were originally launched as a result of the roundtable talks of February 1989. Even then, the need to establish a new constitutional order was recognized as one of the most important tasks of systemic transformation. In April 1989, soon after the conclusion of the roundtable talks, the Polish Parliament amended the 1952 Constitution. The Constitution was again redrafted in April 2, 1997. The new version contained changes such as the deletion of articles referring to the leading role of the Communist Party and the alliance with the former Soviet Union. Poland was redefined as a democratic state governed by the rule of law. Another key change was the adoption of the principle of the freedom of association, which in effect allowed for the formation of new political parties. Together with articles on ownership rights and the freedom to engage in economic activities, these constitutional provisions form the basis of the present political and economic system of the Republic of Poland.

Another result of the systemic transformation was the formation of the new administrative system. On January 1, 1999, Poland was reorganized from 49 provinces to 16 *voivodships* (provinces), with three city governments (Warsaw, Kraków and Łódź). The most important part of the system is that the representatives of the three new tiers of local government (communes, counties, and *voivodships*) are now elected. The changes were considerably expanded, and decision-making functions delegated to the lowest levels.

Ever since Poland held its first multiparty presidential, parliamentary, and local elections, a new need arose for ways to communicate with the electorate. There was increasing demand for expertise in political marketing and public relations. Nevertheless, politicians in the early 1990s were relatively slow to trust the knowledge and suggestions of public relations experts. Their distrust was due partly to the failure of the 1993 election campaign carried out for the Liberal Democratic Congress Party (*Kongres Liberalno-Demokratyczny*) by the reputable agency, Saatchi & Saatchi. The agency was proved to be totally unprepared to deal with the realities of the Polish transition environment. The

Liberal Democratic Congress never made it to Parliament and, in fact, was soon dissolved as an independent party. Some of the reasons for its failure were the unrestrained and uncritical use of American models (street parades with Dixieland bands) before the party had a chance to establish its image. The party also was hurt by its poor election slogan: "millions of new jobs."

The first instance in the newly formed democratic Poland when public relations played a pivotal role was the presidential election of 1995. Lech Wałęsa rejected an offer by communication specialists who wanted to hone his communication skills. Wałęsa told specialists of social engineering and public relations that he could teach them how to build images and that he was going to win the election. However, Wałęsa opponent, the left-wing candidate Aleksander Kwaśniewski, took the opposite strategy and entrusted himself to the care of Jaques Sequel, a French public relations and political marketing expert. Kwaśniewski's complete trust in his advisor led to an election victory and a loss for Wałęsa. The color blue, built up as the symbol during the campaign (e.g., eye and shirt color), has since become the favorite color among Polish politicians. The paradox in the second round of the election was that just 5 years after Solidarity's thumping victory, Poles were witnessing a confrontation between Lech Wałęsa, a world renowned symbol of victory over Communism, and a post-Communist candidate who was an atheist and commonly considered a career maker. The breakthrough in the campaign came with Aleksander Kwaśniewski's appreciation of the power of public relations and particularly with the televised debate, which experts believe was the direct blow that led to Lech Wałęsa defeat.

The outcome of the 1995 presidential election was also of great importance for establishing public relations as a force in the Polish political scene of the early 21st century. In the 2000 presidential election, image consultants were engaged by nearly every candidate, as none wanted to repeat Lech Wałęsa mistake from the 1995 campaign. This essential turnaround in politicians' perceptions of public relations can be seen as a manifestation of not only a change in their way of thinking but also a pragmatic way of coping with competition. In 2002, a trend has emerged among politicians as well as business executives of relying on the services of very professional, but sometimes also rather incompetent, image creation experts.

Another link between the new politics of democratization and the public relations profession lies in the educational role given to public institutions that were set up during the transition (Barlik, 2001). The transformation process has had a profound effect on public administration. Some market institutions, such as the stock exchange and the securities and exchange commission, that were absent in centrally planned economies were created. Equally new were hitherto unknown concepts such as the value-added tax. Public administration was placed in charge of educating the public on how to deal with such novel instruments and institutions of the market economy. In particular, public officials' main tasks were to dispel fears of the adverse effects of capitalism and to drum up public support for the ongoing systemic reform.

All of these goals have been pursued by the relevant ministries since the early 1990s. The ministries have outsourced public educational tasks to foreign companies (e.g, Ogilvy Adams & Rinehart) often using foreign aid funds to finance these campaigns. A case in point is the information campaign (which was the second such information campaign after the tax awareness effort of 1992–1993) launched in 1999 to pave the way for social reforms in local administration, health care, the pension system, and education. The campaign was conducted from September 1998 to February 1999. Most of its total cost of about $1.1 million was financed by foreign aid (*Rzeczpospolita*, 1998).

Today, most public relations campaigns carried out by the central administration are performed by full-time, in-house professionals employed in newly formed public relations departments. The responsibilities of such departments are defined by modifying the job descriptions of former spokespeople who operated even in the socialist era. Some of the work is outsourced to specialized public relations agencies.

The majority of public relations tasks handled by Polish public administration institutions involve some sort of media relations. Therefore, public relations officers at all levels of Polish administration are employed in press relations, promotion departments, and information or public relations offices. In addition to media relations, their key responsibilities include promotion of organizational activities and creating and writing publications and web site postings. At lower levels of administration, public relations responsibilities are commonly placed in the hands of spokespeople.

Poland's Level of Economic Development and its Market Economy Model

Measures of Economic Development. Poland is a developed, industrial, middle-income economy and is classified as an emerging Central European market. Its per capita gross domestic product (GDP) in 2000 was $8,763 using purchasing power parity (PPP) and $4,078 using exchange rates (*Concise Statistical Yearbook of Poland*, 2002). Poland is the world's leading manufacturer of a wide range of goods. The country ranks among the world's top 10 producers of hard and brown coal, copper, and sulfur. It ranks among the top 20 producers of sulfuric acid, television sets, cars, trucks, and power-engineering products.

In 2000, per capita GDP PPP amounted to 39.2% of the European Union (EU) average for the same year, up from under 34% in 1995 (European Commission, 2001). What enabled Poland to catch up in real terms was the fact that it was one of the few transition economies that experienced substantial and sustained growth in the 1990s (6% to 7% per annum from 1995 to 1998). Since the end of the 1990s, however, the growth has slowed to 1% (in 2001). As a result, unemployment has increased rapidly from approximately 12.5% in 1999 to 17.4% at the end of 2001, and it continues to rise. However, one silver lining that influences the standard of living is the fall of the rate of inflation to 1.3% as of June 2002 (*Gazeta Wyborcza*, 2002).

One of the best indicators of economic development, one that is more accurate than GDP, is the Human Development Index (HDI). This index is used by the United Nations Development Programme (UNDPs) as a measure of the quality of life in a nation. A nation's HDI is a combination of life expectancy, adult literacy, and per capita GNP. Former communist countries including Poland rate rather well in HDI rankings as these countries have always had high rates of literacy, even if their GNP is generally low. Measured with the HDI, Poland ranks 38th in 2001 with a life expectancy at birth of 73.1 years (1999), a youth literacy rate of 99.8% (for 15- to 24-year-olds), an adult literacy rate of 99.7% (1999), and a per capita GDP PPP of over $8,000 (UNDP, 2002).

UNDP also relies on a number of other economic growth indicators that provide opportunities and pose challenges for public relations professionals in any country. Examples of such indicators, given here for Poland for 1999, include human skills (the average years of schooling completed by age 15 and above is 9.8), electricity consumption (2,458 kilowatt hours per capita), telephone penetration (365 mainline and mobiles per 1000 people), and cellular mobile subscribers (102 per 1000), internet hosts (11.4 computer systems connected to the Internet per 1000). According to statistics for the first half of 2002, 23% of Poles regularly access the Internet (*Gazeta Wyborcza*, 2002), and 18% of the respondents indicated they use the Internet regularly. Thus, approximately 5,600,000 people access the Internet at least once per month in Poland.

Market Economy Model Implemented in Transitional Poland.

One of the most difficult tasks faced by Poland and other formerly centrally planned economies was to select the best market economy model. When this issue was debated in the early 1990s, neo-liberal economists such as Szomburg (1993) noted that a number of elements in Poland's sociocultural heritage made the Anglo-Saxon model of capitalism best suited for the Polish economic environment. Specifically, what made the model fit Poland so well were Polish qualities such as readiness to take risks, a strong entrepreneurial spirit, the ability to learn fast (mushroming consultancy firms), a deeply ingrained sense of individualism, reluctance to cooperate with others and operate within larger institutional systems, and the propensity to consume (as demonstrated by a skyrocketing demand for Western products, such as cars, satellite television systems, VCRs, cellular phones, etc.). Alternatives to this brand of capitalism included more institutionally and socially oriented varieties that were prevalent in Germany, Sweden, and Japan. However, a number of economists (Fleck & Ławniczak, 1993) have argued that the legacy of the old socialist system lingering in people's minds and in the economy itself, coupled with the fact that the Polish economy was still relatively undeveloped, suggested that Poland was better off selecting the European social market economy model similar to that adopted by Germany.

Poland's final decision on this debate has been written into Article 20 of the redrafted Constitution of April 2, 1997, which stated that "social market economy . . . lies at the heart of the economic system of the Republic of Poland." Despite this constitutional provision, the model that actually prevails in Poland bears more resemblance to the Anglo-Saxon variety. The first Solidarity government applied a neo-Liberal shock therapy strategy that featured a monetarist program of economic stabilization and a liberal doctrine of systemic transformation based on full-scale marketization.

The adoption by Poland of the radical, neo-Liberal, prescription can be explained by:

- "The receptiveness of the Poles to liberal economics, which is evidently not the case in other parts of the region" (Kiss, 1993 p. 50).

- Strong pro-American sentiments.

- The rather successful public relations activities carried out by a number of specific think tanks. These can be described as forms of activism or as organizations aimed at influencing political outcomes and indeed gaining political power or, in other words that have strictly policy advocacy ambitions.

A number of such think tanks, including the Adam Smith Center, the Stefan Batory Foundation, the Center for Socio-Economic Studies (Centrum Analiz Społeczno-Ekonomicznych), the Independent Center for Economic Studies (Niezależny Ośrodek Badań Ekonomicznych), and the Institute for Market Economy Studies (Instytut Badań nad Gospodarką Rynkową), were established soon after 1989. These organizations received funds and know-how from Western governments, institutions, and multinational corporations. Their objective is to carry out scientific research and provide public relations services that promote a liberal economic doctrine. The institutes generate hundreds of documents and publications every year targeted at political decision makers, entrepreneurs, and journalists, or, generally speaking, the so-called *multipliers* who shape public opinion. In the Polish media and, in particular, on Polish television, these institutions seem to

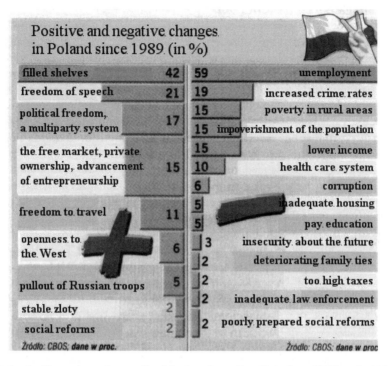

FIG. 13.1. Positive and negative results of the transformation. *Note*. from CBOS study, 1999.

have a monopoly on experts. One of their educational campaigns was conducted in 1992 under the slogan of "Myths about the economy." Materials published in the course of the campaign were published in 18 newspapers, including 13 dailies and 5 weeklies.

The practice of such transitional public relations in today's Poland has helped spread such ideas as the excessive state interference in the economy, the need to replace ideology with economy, privatization as being the key to success, and foreign capital investments always being good for the economy. Such beliefs ran strong practically until 2001 and 2002 which is when unemployment went over the 3 million mark, or approximately 18%. In addition, a growing number of foreign investors (e.g., DAEWOO) filed for bankruptcy and in mid-2002 the world learned of the ENRON and World-Com scandals in the United States. As early as 1999, a Centrum Badania Opinii Społecznej (CBOS) study had explained the balance between the positive and negative results of the Polish transformation, as noted in Fig. 13.1.

These developments have triggered a wave of criticism of the neo-Liberal economic development model. In one critical statement by a journalist, a claim was made that the predominance of neo-Liberal ideas in today's Poland "is not as much an effect of their suitability for the Polish economy but rather of the effectiveness of neo-liberal marketing" (Markowski, 2002, p. 4). Organizations that were promoting neo-Liberal economics launched a public relations campaign of their own to counter such criticism. An example of their response is a large conference entitled, "Foreign Investment—a Driver or Barrier to Poland's Economic Growth," organized in July 2002 by the Polish Confederation of Private Employers (Polska Konfederacja Pracodawców Prywatnych), an organization that had earlier published the "Capitalist Manifesto" (see case study at the end of this chapter).

Legal Infrastructure

The principle sources of law in Poland are the redrafted Polish Constitution of April 4, 1997, legislation passed by the parliament, and subsequent decrees issued by the Council of Ministers or individual ministers. Judicial power is vested in independent courts that answer to the Supreme Court. Civil and criminal cases are tried by juries and by either a professional or a lay judge. The choice of the type of judge to be assigned to a case depends not only on circumstances but also on the kind of court before which the case is brought.

The legal system that has emerged from the systemic transformation in Poland is far from perfect and, as the majority of the Polish population would agree, is in need of extensive modifications and amendments. Public opinion polls regarding the functioning of the justice system carried out in the early 2002 (CBOS, 2002) showed that most of the surveyed believed that Poland suffers from growing crime rates partly because of the inefficient administration of justice. The surveyed attributed inefficiencies of the justice system primarily to poor legislation and corruption and, to a lesser extent, to the fact that judges and prosecutors were intimidated by criminals.

Polish society, however, remains hopeful that one of the positive outcomes of Poland's accession to the EU will be the harmonization of its legislation with that of the community, giving rise to a more effective legal system. (It was announced in October 2002 that Poland and nine other countries may be invited to join the EU in 2004.) Although Poland is not yet a member of the EU, the country concluded the Association Agreement with the Community in December 1991. Poland's obligations under the treaty include bringing foreign trade and investment laws, business regulations, and other legislation into line with European Commission standards. The present legal system and its efficiency problem affect public relations practices in Poland in a two significant ways.

First, the legislature has not yet regulated lobbying. Delays on the issue are constantly reported. The law today allows interest groups to influence the shape of legal regulations. The most powerful of such groups, which represent the interests of foreign armaments, tobacco, pharmaceutical, and alcohol industries, have managed to push through a number of regulations that are not necessarily in the best interest of Polish society at large.

Second, one uniquely Polish example of the impact that legislation has on public relations practice is the ban on concealed advertising that has been written into the new press law. The ban makes it very difficult to provide the public with information, no matter how important and true it may be, if even a reasonable suspicion exists that readers or viewers could be led to discover the name of a company or product involved in the story.

The Level of Activism

Polish activist groups have played a major role in facilitating and accelerating Poland's transition toward democracy and a market economy and continue to do so into the new millennium. At the first stage of the transformation process, these groups contributed mainly by stimulating social initiatives, boosting confidence in the success of revolutionary systemic reforms, fighting for democracy and human rights, and training staff to be assigned to carry out the transition process. Today, NGOs help the society cushion the negative consequences of transformation to a market economy and reinforce and readjust the system of political pluralism and the market economy with a view to building capitalism with a human face.

Historically, activism began with the earliest attempts to liberate Poland from Communist rule. These attempts were made in 1956 when activist groups of rioting workers in

Poznań tried to force the ruling elite to reform the political system using the main slogan, "Yes to socialism, no to corruption." As soon as worker protests in the 1960s induced a certain amount of liberation and democratization in Poland's political system, opportunities opened up for other activist groups. Although such groups were financed to varying degrees and controlled directly by the state and indirectly by the Communist Party, their influence on the systemic transformation in Poland in the 1990s is quite considerable.

A special role in Poland's transition was played by the Association of Polish University Students (ZSP). Its members were given opportunities to learn certain mechanisms of democratic rule, such as direct and secret-ballot voting used in electing officials to the organization's governing body. They were allowed to maintain extensive international contacts with such major-centered student organizations as the Associating Business Administration and Economics Majors and work as interns in developed capitalist countries. In effect, starting from as early as the mid-1960s, Poland's future ruling elite during the transition period began to benefit from the opportunity to engage in international relations and learn about the workings of Western democracies and the market economy. Today, now in their 50s and 60s, these relatively well-educated (many from Western universities as well) former members who also speak several foreign languages have become leaders of political parties, ministers, bank presidents, ambassadors, and other contributors to the success of the Polish transformation.

A special contribution to the Polish systemic transformation, unique in the socialist block, was made by the United Nations Students Association of Poland (SSP ONZ (Studenckie Stowarzyszenie Przyjaciół ONZ)). Its uniqueness stemmed from the fact that, for many years since its establishment in Poland, SSP ONZ was the only youth organization of its kind in the entire socialist block. The advantage of that kind of a monopoly position lies in the very fact that, for many years, acting as sole representatives of socialist countries, representatives of SSP ONZ had been gaining knowledge and experience in international debates and negotiations. This very knowledge is used today to shape the present political and economic system of democratic Poland.

Today's activist and social movements of the Polish transition period can be described as diverse, dependant on available funding, dedicated, and professional. The *Rzeczpospolita* (1999), which is one of the country's two most influential dailies, stated that at the turn of the 20th century: "Non-governmental organizations in Poland are experiencing tough times. Fund raising is not easy, due to sponsor reluctance; earning money is even harder, while state funds are granted not on pragmatic but rather . . . on political considerations. The apparent rule is that governments prefer organizations that are close to them ideologically, a criterion that is far from appropriate."

Because of this ideological slant, organizations that promote liberal ideas of free entrepreneurship (the already-mentioned think tanks and the Confederation of Private Employers) and ideals of a civil society, political pluralism, and integration with the EU (e.g., the Freedom Foundation, Amnesty International, and the Schuman Foundation) are relatively well financed, mostly by foreign sources and the private sector. They can, therefore, afford to maintain in-house experts or engage external consultants to render public relations services in a professional manner.

In the case of other grassroots initiatives and with NGOs engagement in providing social assistance and protecting the environment, public relations efforts are rarely carried out in-house. Instead, the tasks are performed largely by volunteers with little of no training. Nevertheless, some of these organizations in Poland have achieved success unprecedented on the international scene. An example is the Polish public relations achievement of a nonprofit organization conducted by some committed volunteers—the Great Christmas

Aid Orchestra. This unusual project, first launched in 1992, is a special kind of foundation. Journalist Jerzy Owsiak developed the idea of organizing this orchestra in 1991. Each year a concert is held and the event raises funds for a different goal, such as life-saving equipment for newborn babies. The nine events held so far have helped purchase medical equipment worth over $31 million, which was donated to more than 440 hospitals located throughout Poland.

There is little doubt that labor unions have played a central role in the history of the Polish transition. It was the Solidarity trade union (or social movement) that brought down the Socialist and Communist regime. In 2002, in the face of growing unemployment (18% and rising, as already stated), the Solidarity labor union is no longer a major force in society. It was outgrown in terms of importance by OPZZ (Ogólnopolskie Porozumienie Związków Zawdowych), a competing post-Communist trade union. This seemingly paradoxical situation has resulted from a phenomenon referred to by some as the *Solidarity paradox*. This phenomenon describes that, unlike in other post-Communist countries, the Communist system in Poland was abolished by the working class employed in large socialist manufacturing enterprises (e.g., shipyards and mines). It was exactly that section of society that, according to the Communist doctrine, was the mainstay of the system. Meanwhile, however, large and inefficient industrial behemoths were the first to fall victim to the process of market reforms. Governments formed by the Solidarity Party were, therefore, internally torn between their recognition of the need for structural reform and their awareness of the social consequences of such reforms. Both of the competing trade unions now realize the importance of public relations support for their efforts. They use this tool mostly for media relations and, in particular, for dealing with activists and corporations.

CULTURE AND PUBLIC RELATIONS

The value system, standards, and behaviors that distinguish one society from others depend on a country's geographic location and a wide array of natural and historical factors. All of these factors certainly affect the Poles. First, Poland is a predominantly lowland country with no natural borders. Situated between two superpowers, Germany on the West and Russia on the East, Poland has historically served as a corridor for passing foreign armies. This is why, starting in the 17th century, Poland has remained under constant threat of losing its national identity and why so much emphasis has been placed on protecting it. Today Poland has adopted a free market economy and faces tough competition from the West. It also is in danger of losing its cultural values, which is why slogans such as "Polish means good" and "Poland now" that appear on labels against the background of the national flag are increasingly more effective as marketing tools.

The second most important factor shaping Polish culture is the country's history. Several influences from different periods in history have strongly affected the way the Poles perceive the world today:

1. Those tied to the formation of Polish identity have influenced the country since the Polish state first originated. These include the adoption of Christianity in 966, which has made religion a strong influence in both the Polish state and the nation. Poland would wage war against countries representing other religions, such as Islamic Turkey, Orthodox Christian Russia, and predominantly Protestant Germany. Being a real Pole was equated with being Catholic. This association became even stronger during Communism when authorities attempted to secularize the country through force and after Karol Wojtyła assumed the position of the Pope and became Pope John Paul. The Polish brand of Catholicism is

mainly family oriented and underlines the important role of women (e.g., the cult of Virgin Mary of Częstochowa).

2. The influence of the partition is another important factor. During the period when the country was torn between Germany, Russian, and Austria, Poland grew even more devoted to Catholicism and more distrustful of the state and state authorities. Just over 170 years ago, and to some extent during the 5 decades of Communist Poland, the establishment came to be seen as an alien hostile power imposed on the Poles. Civil disobedience and actions aimed at inflicting damage on the state were seen as acts of patriotism and received public support.

3. Another period that strongly affected Poles' collective view of the world was the 5 decades of Socialist Poland. Although sovereign and democratic in theory, Poland remained under Soviet influence during this period, having seen its fate sealed by the Yalta Treaty. Remnants of the old socialist system, based on collectivism, a centrally planned economy, and state regulation of nearly all aspects of the lives of citizens, can be seen to this day. The state has done away with the system of incentives and set up a typically "real Socialism" safety net that has created a special brand of society. Its members, who are in their 50s and 60s, are reluctant to face the challenges of the free market actively, unable to take their lives into their own hands, and incapable of advancing in society. They wait for the state to provide for them. Equally important is their distrust of foreign capital and the capital market. Average workers believe societies are divided into classes that are constantly at war with one another. Rather then recognizing business owners as people whose ideas, effort, and knowledge have helped them succeed, they see them as thieves who built their fortunes by exploiting workers. The cultural legacy of the period is a widespread conviction that everyone is entitled to equal benefits no matter how hard they have worked, what knowledge they possess, and how professional they are. For this very reason, a key task of transitional public relations is to promote entrepreneurship, secure public approval for the concept of private property, and dispel perceptions of entrepreneurs as speculators and exploiters and present them as persons who create jobs and contribute to the economic welfare of the country (see case study). In fact, all major private entrepreneurs in Poland recognize the importance of creating such images and have long maintained teams of public relations experts.

4. The most recent influence comes from the new model of Polish capitalism characterized by growing individualism, Americanization (i.e., the invasion of cheap mass culture imbued with consumerism, violence, and sex), commercialization of life in all of its aspects, and the surge of such new phenomena as gangsterism, unemployment, maximization of profit, and an increasing shallowness in interpersonal relations. The group that best adjusted to these new realities consists of the youth. Paradoxically, however, the beneficiaries of the process of change include Poles in their 50s because many of them have managed to liberate themselves from past political influences.

In analyzing the distinctive features of Polish culture, as fashioned by these factors, one may apply the dimensions of culture proposed by Geert Hofstede (1980). Classified in such a way, Polish society appears to be reluctant to support the government and to trust in its capacity to make a meaningful difference by participating in democratic elections. This is evidenced by voter apathy (the turnout in the presidential elections of 2000 was 61% but dropped to 46.29% in the Sejm elections of 2001) and people's waning interest in politics. Confidence in the transition process also seems to be on the decline. The euphoria of the 1990s, when any change was thought as being for the better, was soon followed by disillusionment and widespread inertia. Economic problems, unemployment, and a growing sense of insecurity provided fertile ground for another wave of populism and collectivism.

History has turned Poles into rugged individualists. Although there is no denying that 5 decades of exposure to a doctrine that advocated collectivism has left a mark especially on the mentality of Poles who are in their 50s and 60s, the tough capitalist competition of the 1990s soon triggered a return to individualism and egoism. However, mainly because of the unusually strong influence of the Polish Catholic Church, the family is cherished in Poland. Poles' devotion to Catholicism was demonstrated during the most recent visit to of the Pope, who drew a record crowd of 2.5 million at an event in Krakow on August 18, 2002. The model of the family promoted by the Church and the political right wing is commonly adopted for practical reasons because in times of insecurity the family remains the only certain source of support. A side effect of such an approach is growing nepotism and a lack of confidence in instruments that promote individuals.

The high esteem in which family values are held in Poland has translated directly into an appreciation of the role of women in Polish society. Respect for mothers and the admiration and adoration of women dates back to the times of nobility and courtly traditions. The period of real Socialism also ensured equal rights and opportunities for women. One of rather famous example of this equalization principle applied in Poland in the 1960s, was the case of appointing women as captains of seagoing vessels. The era of capitalism brought with it a new concept, the businesswoman, who is typically well-educated and very gainfully employed but struggling to reconcile these responsibilities with the traditional role of wife and mother.

Another masculinity–femininity issue can be found in the business environment where the model for solving problems through negotiations is now being abandoned in favor of an aggressive "male" problem-solving mode; an offer to negotiate is often perceived as a sign of weakness. In this context, a special role is played by political parties and trade unions that vie for influence among desperate and disgruntled electorates. This approach creates bidding wars that are won by those parties whose demands are most exaggerated and whose show of strength is most impressive. This system is exploited most effectively by political parties such as the Peasant Self-Defense headed by Andrzej Lepper, a man who rose to his position largely with the help of public relations specialists. This sort of culture puts traditional public relations in a bad light and creates other problems such as the growing distrust of information campaigns, widening income gaps between various levels of society, more extreme attitudes, and, in effect, the perception of traditional public relations tools as governmental propaganda.

THE MEDIA AND PUBLIC RELATIONS

Similar to other Central and Eastern European countries, in the 1990s, Poland saw sweeping changes that affected both the structures of media companies and the rules that governed their operations. Conditions were then created for the media to represent a wide range of views and compete against one another. The state was deprived of its exclusive control over the press, and a number of new private broadcasting companies emerged to compete with public radio and television. Radio and television programming and press offerings became noticeably richer and more diverse. Many of the changes were driven by foreign capital whose presence in Poland proved to be quite fortunate considering how small the budgets of homegrown media companies were at the time. Foreign capital facilitated fast technological and marketing progress. Foreign companies took advantage of the situation and achieved high market penetration, especially in the press sector.

Initially, the emergence of a large number of market-oriented enterprises greatly escalated competition in the media market. Ultimately, however, the market consolidated through mergers and acquisitions, putting both fair competition and diversity at risk. Most recently (in 2002), companies have begun consolidating across media segments (e.g., publishing and radio broadcasting) and emerging into strong multimedia groups. This has given rise to a heated debate over the need to restrict such consolidation. Representatives of foreign publishers have accused the Polish coalition government consisting of Democratic Left Alliance and the Polish Peasants' Party of attempting to constrain the freedom of speech. The government has responded by saying that censorship comes from the market, whose role can be compared to that of a gatekeeper who lets only a select few with sufficient resources have a say in political debates (*Rzeczpospolita*, 2002).

Media Control

The media market has been shaped by a spontaneous and largely unsupervised transition process. Most Polish media have fallen into the hands of and, therefore, under the control of foreign capital. Foreign companies have gained a strong hold over national opinion-forming press controlling Poland's largest dailies, such as *Gazeta Wyborcza* (owned by the American corporation Cox Enterprises, Inc.), *Super Ekspress* (owned by the Swedish group Bonnier), and *Rzeczpospolita* (owned by the Norwegian company Orkla). Magazines catering to women and teenagers are dominated by Gruener + Jahr and Bauer of Germany and Edipresse of Switzerland. The regional and local press also is under the control of Western corporations, especially Passauer Presse of Germany.

Although Western investors have unanimously denied representing the interests of their home countries, parent companies, or other political groups, a strong case can be made to prove that this is exactly what they do. Polish public opinion is increasingly more concerned about the fact that foreign domination of the media results in promoting conservative and neo-Liberal economic views and foreign political and economic interests (*Życie Warszawy*, 1994, *Rzeczpospolita*, 2002). Surprisingly, the most liberal Polish-owned weekly, *Wprost*, known for promoting foreign investments in Poland and other transition economies, published an article criticizing the domination of German investments in the Polish economy, arguing that the government should have a policy enabling the diversification of influence and not allowing the domination of investments from a single country (Nowakowski, 2002). Nowakowski cited banking and mass media as two industries that were predominantly under German ownership. In his opinion, such a situation leads to instances when "in the German bank it will be easier for the German entrepreneur to receive a loan than for his Polish competitor." . . . "On the other hand, in the automobile magazine we can read the 'objective' analysis, from which one can draw a clear conclusion that the cars produced in country of the editor are the best."

Some of the trends seen in the Polish press sector, especially foreign domination of media, have justified governmental efforts to protect the electronic media in Poland. The government has placed stricter controls over the radio and television market by imposing a new system of licensing that includes harsher rules for foreign capital. The Law on Radio and Television Broadcasting provides for the appointment of the National Council for the Supervision of Radio and Television to oversee the radio and television market as well as grant broadcasting licenses. The requirement to disclose any changes in the capital structure of licensed publishers to the council allows the body to monitor market trends on an ongoing basis.

Media Outreach

Thanks to Poland's existing media infrastructure, the virtual nonexistence of illiteracy (.3% in the population segment above 15 years old), and a relatively low poverty rate, the media are capable of disseminating messages practically to the entire population. Daily newspapers reach a relatively unchanging 60% segment of the population; local dailies are the most popular form of press in most provinces. Channel I, which is Poland's most popular radio station, covers the entire country. Channels I, II, and III of Polish radio reach 40% of Poland's population. Public radio in Poland faces strong competition from private stations (most of which are regional and specialize in music and other forms of entertainment) and from private national stations, one of the strongest of which among Polish Catholics is the Catholic radio station Radio Maryja.

Telewizja Polska S.A. (Polish Television), owned exclusively by the state treasury, offers three national channels and one channel abroad via satellite. Channel I of Polish Television is accessible to 98% of the population. Private television, meanwhile, has been steadily gaining market share. In fact, the licensing of private television stations began as early as 1993. In 1997, the ratings of the private station Polsat exceeded those of public television. Many stations in Poland transmit their signals via satellite, which gives them an outreach that transcends Poland's boundary.

Media Access

Throughout the period of Polish transformation, politicians have been warring over access to the media and, particularly, to television. The political victory of the Solidarity faction put an end to the domination of socialist ideology and to state censorship of the mass media. Factors such as excessive public expectations, the deepening stratification of society, and skyrocketing unemployment allowed the leftist coalition of the Democratic Left Alliance and the Polish Peasant Party to rise to power after the 1993 election, which they repeated during the election of 2001. One of the coalition's priorities has been to regain, at least in part, the media access it once enjoyed. Every ruling elite in Poland is well aware of the advantages of controlling the media. Such control can be achieved by acquiring a sufficiently big share in a publishing house or having it managed by people willing to promote their views. Thus, gaining influence over and better access to the media in a market economy requires substantial funds to buy shares and large advertising budgets. Today's market belongs to advertisers for whom the media fight mercilessly.

Public relations professionals and agencies play an important role in providing the media with information subsidies. According to a recent study commissioned by the Association of Public Relations Firms, more than half of public relations practitioners believed that companies are given press coverage in return for placing paid advertisements in a given publication. Over 25% of public relations professionals claimed that press coverage is obtained by bribing a journalist *(Gazeta Wyborcza*, 2002).

All of this shows that direct access to the media in today's transitional Poland differs widely among individual groups of society. Groups such as the government and its institutions (e.g., the Ministry of the Treasury and the Ministry of Finance which publish official announcements in the press), corporations (because of their sizable advertising budgets), and the so-called think tanks among activist groups (which have access to foreign funds and private sponsors) are in a much better position to gain access to the media than the thousands of minor activist groups that deal with issues such as environmental protection, social care, and drug addiction.

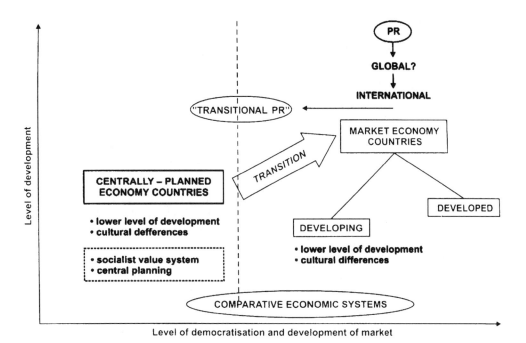

FIG. 13.2. The sources of transitional public relations. *Note.* From *Public Relations Contributions to Transition in Central and Eastern Europe: Research and Practice* (p. 10), by R. Ławniczak (Ed.), 2001, Poznan, Poland: Printer. Copyright 2001 by Ryszard Ławniczak Reprinted with permission.

CONCLUSIONS AND CASE STUDY

Why Transitional Public Relations?

By analyzing Poland as a country in transition, we draw several conclusions. First, Western public relations theory and practice needs to accommodate the unique realities of countries in transition. Second, although one may agree with Verčič's (1996) postulate that there are certain "generic principles of public relations" that may be applicable in every political economic system, we argue that the public relations practitioners in Central an Eastern Europe need to account for the influence of the former and Communist political economic system to a much larger extent. Because of the constraints it previous to efficient use of public relations. Third, the legacy of the former system, as reflected in ways of thinking, the structure of the economy, and the mechanism of resource allocation, has created a unique combination of those constraints on the application of the universal principles of public relations. For this reason, we may speak of *transitional public relations* as a specific brand of international public relations. Fourth, the sources of this concept based on a methodological contribution of the theory of comparative economic systems (Gregory & Stuart, 1985) are presented in Fig. 13.2.

Capitalist Manifesto—A Case Study of Transitional Public Relations

Background. One aspect of systemic transformation in Poland is the state's reorientation from its role as a supervisor protecting the interests of a selected social group to that of a regulator ensuring the proper operation of economic mechanisms. The rationale behind such a reorientation lies in the legacy of the Communist system, which was built on the belief that class struggle is unavoidable, and was committed to ensuring the victory of the working class. Other social groups were thought of as less significant. Private entrepreneurs were described as parasites who lived off the fruit of the toil of workers and peasants. This doctrine was reflected in the official ideology and became the frame of reference for an overgrown administrative apparatus. Restrictions on individual enterprise were written into the law.

Once the systemic transition had taken place, the practice of free enterprise by individual citizens became the cornerstone of the state's economic success. Free enterprise was then manifested by pursuing business through such forms of organization as civil law, joint stock, and limited partnership companies.

State doctrine has also undergone an official change. The state tries to limit its interference in the market and support individual enterprise. High-ranking officials issue statements of commitment to support private business owners. Nevertheless, at its very core, the state apparatus and especially local officials continue to perpetuate old doctrines and portray individual enterprise as a form of exploitation of particular social groups. The approach has led to the imposition of a number of hindrances and administrative barriers for entrepreneurs. The absence of an unambiguous and coherent corporate law has given state officials abundant room to interpret the law at will.

Objectives.   The Confederation of Private Employers (CPE) was established in 1999 to protect the interests of private entrepreneurs. The organization represents private business owners from all industries across Poland. According to its founders, the organization plays a crucial role in securing economic order, as it exercises its statutory right to participate in the formation of law and in public discourse. The CPE's main object is to promote its solutions and integrate them into the body of existing laws. The CPE participates in the work of institutions negotiating Poland's accession to the EU, issues opinions on new legislation, and puts out commentaries on the country's economic situation. Its activities also involve supporting the day-to-day business of its members by, among other things, providing consultations, organizing meetings, and intervening in the ongoing business of employers.

Instrument Used.   One of the most spectacular actions undertaken by the CPE was a campaign to promote the Capitalist Manifesto. The idea came from the Communist Manifesto drawn up in 1847 by Karl Marx and F. Engels for the newly created Communist Association of England; it was to become the party platform and the binding political program. The Communist Manifesto contained the fundamental theses of Marxist political economics, as well as his criticism of the capitalist system and of various currents of socialism of the time. It set out the tasks and goals of the revolutionary labor party and defined the concept of the international proletariat. One of its statements, "Working men of all countries, unite," has become the chief slogan of the Communist Party. In the spring of 2000, over 150 years after the proclamation of the Communist Manifesto, the Capitalist Manifesto of CPE appeared in all Polish press publications. In support of the press campaign, the representatives of the confederations, as well as other promoters of private entrepreneurship, were restating the thesis and the arguments from the Manifesto in their public speeches, presentations in the parliament, meetings with representatives of trade unions, and so on.

Outcome.   Two years after the announcement of the Capitalist Manifesto, the CPE gained the status of one of the most visible and influential lobbying organizations on the Polish political and economic scenes. It has gained equal representation in the Trilateral

Today, private companies in Poland account for:
- 75 percent of Gross Domestic Product
- 70 percent of all employees
- 79 percent of exports

POLSKA **POLISH**
KONFEDERACJA **CONFEDERATION OF**
PRACODAWCÓW **PRIVATE**
PRYWATNYCH **EMPLOYERS**

THE CAPITALIST MANIFESTO

Private businesses have become a driving force behind Poland's growth and prosperity. We, Polish employers and employees, can now reap the benefits of their work. Credit for the success of the Polish economy should be given to all the people who, through their hard work and perseverance, developed their businesses, frequently working from scratch. It should also be given to everyone who efficiently works in those companies today.

Free market mechanisms still need to be fully approved by society at large and by politicians. Without a common recognition of the fact that company growth is fueled by profits, even the worthiest of social and public causes will stand no chance of ever being achieved. Even the most heated arguments about how to divide state funds will not generate economic growth. We want to see new jobs created. We also want the right to pursue happiness rather than having poverty shared equally by everyone. Political declarations alone will not force entrepreneurs to want to develop their companies, pay higher taxes, create new jobs, increase exports or investment spending, because those decisions are based on one fundamental measure - acceptable return. As entrepreneurs and employers, we expect the central and local governments to create favorable conditions for the development of companies. These should be made by ensuring macroeconomic stability, a consistent budgetary regime and making no more promises that cannot be delivered.

It is the duty of both the Parliament and the Government to improve Polish legislation so as to sharpen the competitive edge of Polish companies and products. Let us also seize new opportunities arising with Poland's upcoming accession to the European Union!

WE DEMAND:
- a lower and uniform taxation rate to allow companies to retain funds for future investment,
- a lower cost of labor, including lower social insurance contributions to allow us to increase employment securely in our companies,
- legislation allowing flexibility in industrial relations,
- mandatory social benefits adjusted to match market requirements,
- stable and coherent legislation that is consistently enforced, unaffected by discretionary powers of officials, and that will effectively help curb corruption,
- public offices and institutions aware of their responsibilities towards entrepreneurs,
- equal rights and obligations for private and state-owned companies,
- equal rights for employer organizations and trade unions.

We hereby proclaim this Manifesto, guided by a sense of responsibility for our companies and our employees, for the economic and social development of Poland and concerned about unique opportunities that we cannot afford to lose.

POLISH CONFEDERATION OF PRIVATE EMPLOYERS

CAPITALISTS OF THE 21st CENTURY, UNITE!

pkpp@prywatni.pl!

FIG. 13.3. The Capitalist Manifesto of Polish Confederation of Private Employers. *Note.* Copyright 2000 by CPE. Reprinted with permission.

Committee, thus breaking the monopoly of the Confederation of Polish Employers, which represents predominantly large state-owned enterprises. Not 1 week goes by without representatives of the Confederation of Polish Employers presenting their position on important economic and political issues, promoting entrepreneurship, and shaping a positive image of the private employer before the media, the parliament, and governmental institutions. See Fig. 13.3.

REFERENCES

Barlik, J. (2001). Public awareness campaigns in Poland and Slovenia: Lessons learned by government agencies and PR practitioners. In R. Ławniczak (Ed.), *Public relations contribution to transition in Central and Eastern Europe: Research and practice*. Poznan: Printer Poland.

Czarnowski, P. (1999, July). *Polskie public relations—jakie jest, każdy widzi*. Paper presented at the meeting of the Polish Association of Public Relations. In Warsaw.

Commission of European Communities. (2002). *Regular Report on Poland's Progress Toward Association*, Brussels.

Concise Statistical Yearbook of Poland, Warsaw. (2002).

Cutlip, S. M., Center, A. H., Broom, G. M. (1994). *Effective public relations*. Upper Saddle River, NJ: Prentice-Hall.

Goban-Klas, T. (1995). *Public relations czyli promocja reputacji. Pojęcia, definicje, uwarunkowania*. Warszawa: BUSINESS PRESS.

Gregory, P. R., & Stuart, R. C. (1985). *Comparative economic systems*. Boston: Houghton Mifflin.

Hofstede, G. (1980). *Culture's consequences. International differences in Work-Related Values*. Newbury Park: Sage (new edition 2001).

Iskra, R. (2001). *Public Relations in zwei Kulturen. PR-Verstaendnisse in Deutschland and Polen und eine empirische Bestandaufnahme des Berufsfeldes PR in Warschau*. Unpublished master thesis. University of Leipzig, Germany.

Kadragic, A., & Czarnowski, P. (1995). *Public relations czyli promocja reputacji. Pojęcia, definicje, uwarunkowania*. Warszawa: BUSINESS PRESS.

Kiss, K. (1993). Western prescriptions for Eastern transition. In H. G. Fleck, & R. Ławniczak (Eds.), *Alternative models of market economy for transition economies*. Warsaw: SORUS Press.

Łaszyn, A. (2001). Poland's pr slowdown. *IPRA FRONTLINE*, October 2001.

Ławniczak, R. (2001). Public relations—an instrument for systemic transformation in Central and Eastern Europe. In R. Ławniczak (Ed.), *Public relations contribution to transition in Central and Eastern Europe: Research and practice*. Poznan: Printer.

Markowski, K. (2002). Ekonomicznie poprawni, *Trybuna*, 31.05.2002

Nowakowski, J. M. (2002). Drang nach Osten, *Wprost*, Nr. 1041.

Ruler, B. van (2000). Future research and practice of public relations, a European approach. In D. Verčič, J. White, & D. Moss, *Public relations, public affairs and corporate communications in the Millenium: The future*. Ljubljana: Pristop Communications.

Rydzak, W. (2001). The application of public relations in crisis situations in enterprises in Poland. In R. Ławniczak, R. (Ed.), *Public relations contribution to transition in Central and Eastern Europe: Research and practice*. Poznan: Printer.

Sriramesh, K., & Verčič, D. (2000). A framework for understanding and conducting international public relations. In D. Verčič, J. White, & D. Moss, (Eds.), *Public relations, public affairs and corporate communications in the Millenium: The future*. Ljubljana: Pristop Communications.

Szomburg, J. (1993). Jaki kapitalizm? *Przegląd Polityczny* (Numer specjalny).

Trębecki, J. (2001). The use of media relations by Polish enterprises. In R. Ławniczak (Ed.), *Public relations contribution to transition in Central and Eastern Europe: Research and practice*. Poznan: Printer.

UNDP. (2002). *Human Development Report*.

Wielowiejska, D. (2000). Korupcja mediów. *Gazeta Wyborcza*, 31.03.2000

Wójcik, K. (1992). *Public relations, czyli jak zjednać otoczenie i tworzyć dobra opinię*. Warszawa: Centrum Szkolenia Liderów.

Wójcik, K. (2001). *Public relations od A do Z* .Warszawa: Placet.

Żelisawski, J. (1973). Public relations w gospodarce socjalistycznej, *Reklama* Nr 6.

Zemler, Z. (1992). *Public relations, kreowanie reputacji firmy*. Warszawa: Poltext.

14

PUBLIC RELATIONS IN A CORPORATIVIST COUNTRY: THE CASE OF SLOVENIA

DEJAN VERČIČ

INTRODUCTION

The public relations profession in Slovenia is very young, having developed only in the 1990s. Its emergence, and early advances, are documented by Ašanin Gole and Verčič (2000); J. E. Grunig, L. Grunig, and Verčič (1996); L. Grunig, J. E. Grunig, and Verčič (1997, 1998); L. Grunig and Verčič (1998); Gruban, Verčič, and Zavrl (1994); Verčič (1993a, 1993b, 2002); Verčič, D., L. Grunig, and J. E. Grunig (1993, 1996); Verčič, Razpet, Dekleva, and Šlenc (2000); and Verčič and van Ruler (2002). This chapter merges these previous reports, updates them, and places them in a broader sociopolitical context, in line with one of the primary purposes of this volume.

L. Grunig and Verčič (1998) described the major attributes that affect the practice of public relations in Slovenia:

Slovenia has a population of nearly 2 million people, living on 20.296 km², and making GDP of US$ 21 billion. It is slightly larger in size than New Jersey and has about the same population as the Seattle metropolitan area. The contribution of transportation services alone to the United States GDP equals Slovenia's total GDP. The major difference, though, is that Slovenia is an independent country. It is located in the middle of Europe between Austria, Croatia, Hungary, and Italy. From its capital, Ljubljana, it takes two hours by car to get to Venice, Italy, or five to Vienna, Austria. Slovenia gained its independence from Yugoslavia on June 25, 1991, when it also began a transformation from a closed to an open society.

A decade ago, Thurow (1993) predicted that Slovenia would be at the top of the countries that were part of Yugoslavia. The *Economist* (1997a, 1997b) later confirmed Thurow's statement when it noted that "Slovenia has remained the most prosperous country in ex-communist Europe" (p. 45). In 1999, Slovenia's per capita gross domestic product (GDP) surpassed that of Portugal and Greece (both members of the European Union) and entered the new millennium with a per capita GDP that is more than twice that of any of the Central or Eastern European country (Republic of Slovenia, Ministry of Economic Affairs, 2000, p. 11). On October 9, 2002, the European Commission recommended that Slovenia be one of the ten countries that will be invited as full members of the European Union by 2004. It is clear that the first decade of Slovenia's existence as a nation has been good for the country as well as its public relations industry.

History, Development, and Status of the Profession

A History of Slovenia and Its Public Relations-Like Activities

According to the 2002 census, Slovenia has a population of 1,948,250 (943,994 men and 1,004,256 women) of whom 88% are ethnic Slovenians. The population lives in 688,733 households at an average of 2.8 members per household (Statistični urad Republike Slovenije, 2002). The primary official national language is Slovenian, but Italian and Hungarian are also official languages in the regions where Italian and Hungarian minorities reside. The majority of the population is Roman Catholic. In addition, there are 30 other officially registered religious faiths in Slovenia. Life expectancy is 71 years for men and 79 for women. Table 14.1 presents a brief historical overview of the territory and people of Slovenia.

Every nation can claim that it is a product of public relations–like activities. For ex-ample, similar claims are made about the use of persuasive communication during the American Revolution in the United States of America (Cutlip, Center, & Broom 2000, pp. 103–104; J. E. Grunig & Hunt, 1984, p. 17; Newsom, VanSlyke Turk, & Kruckeberg, 1996, pp. 35–37). Gruban, Verčič, & Zavrl (1994, pp. 10–13) referred to several key events in Slovenian history starting with the Freising Records, probably dating before 1000 AD as the oldest known record of persuasive speech in Slovenian language. A second commu-nication milestone these authors identified was the publication of the first three Slovenian Alphabetical Primers (in 1550, 1555, and 1556) by Primož Trubar, the first Slovenian author to stress the importance of communication. A third was the publication of the first Slovenian popular science paper intended for farmers, artisans, craftsmen, and intellectu-als titled *Kmetijske in rokodelske novice* (Agricultural and Handicraft News) by Kranjska kmetijska družba (the Agricultural Society of Kranj).

The First Trial of Modern Public Relations

The use of contemporary public relations in Slovenia can be traced back to the 1960s, which was a 'liberal' period in communist Yugoslavia. Until 1991, Slovenia was one of the six republics that constituted the former Yugoslavia. During one of his visits to universities in the United States, the founder of communication science at the University of Ljubljana (currently the capital of Slovenia), Prof. France Vreg, met Scott Cutlip and even began translating the second edition of the textbook *Effective Public Relations* (Cutlip & Center, 1960). At the same time, a lecturer at the Department of Communication, Pavle Zrimšek, translated a German book on public relations by Hundhausen (1969). In the early 1970s, final preparations were under way for the introduction of public relations as a separate academic subject to be taught in the Faculty of Sociology, Political Science,

TABLE 14.1

Historical Facts About Slovenia

250,000 BC: The first evidence of human habitation in the territory of the present-day Slovenia

120,000–33,000 BC: Remains from the early Stone Age—the Palaeolithic; among them the oldest musical instrument in the world, found in Slovenia

5,000 BC: Remains found as evidence of a hunting and gathering way of life

3,900 BC: Pile dwellings on the Ljubljana Marshes

1300 BC: Urnfield culture

8th to 7th century BC: Bronze and Iron Age fortifications

4th–3rd century BC: The arrival of Celts; the Noricum kingdom

circa 10 BC: The Roman Empire; the appearance of the first towns

5th–6th century AD: Invasions by Huns and Germanic tribes

After 568: Dominance of Slav people on the territory of Slovenia

7th–11th century: The Duchy of Carantania, the oldest known independent Slavonic state in this area

8th century: The start of conversion to Christianity

9th century: The spread of the Frankish feudal system and the beginning of the formation of the Slovene nation

10th century: The appearance of the Freising Manuscripts, the earliest known text written in Slovene

11th century: The beginning of the development of the Carniola, Styria, Carinthia, and Gorizia regions, and intensive German colonization

11th–14th centuries: The development of medieval towns in Slovenia

14th–15th centuries: Most of the territory of Slovenia including all its hereditary estates is taken over by Habsburgs; in 1456, the Celje counts become extinct—this was the last Slovene feudal dynasty

15th century: Turkish invasion begins

15th–17th centuries: Peasant revolt

1550: Protestantism; first book written in Slovene

18th century: Enlightenment and compulsory universal education

1809–1813: Illyrian provinces

1848: Unified Slovenia, the first Slovene political program

1918: The state of Slovenes, Croats, and Serbs; the kingdom of Serbs, Croats, and Slovenes

1945: The end of the Second World War and the formation of the Federal People's Republic of Yugoslavia

1990: Plebiscite on independence

June 25, 1991: Proclamation of the independent Republic of Slovenia

---

Note. From *Facts About Slovenia* (p. 26), by S. Možina and A. Resman, 2001, Ljubljana: Government of the Republic of Slovenia Public Relations and Media Office.

and Journalism in Ljubljana. Around the same period, some export-oriented companies began experimenting in public relations practice.

However, the 'liberal' period in Yugoslav politics ended in early 1970s and public relations was labeled as 'politically incorrect,' unlike advertising and marketing which were allowed to develop more or less undisturbed both in practice and academia since the mid-1970. As a result, public relations practice with a 'pro-Western leaning' nearly disappeared until 1989. The first academic courses in public relations were offered at the University of Ljubljana only in 1994 (Verčič, 2002).

The First Decade: 1990–2000

The first public relations agency in Slovenia was established in 1989 and 10 practitioners formed the Public Relations Society of Slovenia (PRSS) in 1990. The same year, the first booklet on public relations was published in Slovenian language (Gruban, Maksimovič,

Verčič, & Zavrl, 1990). A year later, the Slovenian chapter of the International Public Relations Association (IPRA) was formed. In 1992, Larissa Grunig and James Grunig, professors of public relations at the University of Maryland, visited Slovenia for the first time and gave a lecture to members of the PRSS. They returned a year later to give the first lecture on public relations at the University of Ljubljana. These visits started an intensive international cooperation between academics and practitioners. Since 1994, when the first international public relations research symposium was organized on Lake Bled, more than 250 top academics and practitioners in public relations from more than 30 countries on five continents have visited Slovenia and exchanged their knowledge and experience. Further, in 1994, the *Excellence in Public Relations and Communication Management* project was replicated in Slovenia and for years its results were used as a benchmark for the development of the profession in Slovenia (Dozier, L. Grunig, and J. E. Grunig 1995, pp. 174–175; Gruban, Verčič, and Zavrl, 1994; J. E. Grunig, L. Grunig, and Verčič 1996; L. Grunig, J. E. Grunig, and Verčič, 1997, 1998; Verčič, 1993a, Verčič, L. Grunig, and J. E. Grunig, 1993; Verčič, L. Grunig, and J. E. Grunig, 1996).

In 1993, the PRSS became a full member of the European confederation of public relations societies—CERP (Confédération Européenne des Relations Publiques—the European Public Relations Confederation) and Slovenia appeared in the *Hollis Europe Book* (a guide to public relations in 35 countries across the European continent) for the first time (Verčič, 1993b). Beginning in 1994, public relations came to be offered regularly as a subject of study at the Faculty of Social Sciences, University of Ljubljana. The following year, the public relations students formed a student section of the PRSS (with members from the two Slovenian universities in Ljubljana and Maribor), with affiliation to the European association of public relations students (CERP Students). In 1996, the PRSS launched its Website (http://www.prss-drustvo.si), and in 1997 organized its first national public relations conference. After the Bled symposia, this became the second regular annual public relations event in Slovenia. In 1998, the Slovenian Code of ethics was adopted leading to a declaration of the ethical unacceptability of hidden advertising. The declaration was initiated by the Slovenian board of IPRA, endorsed by the PRSS, and acknowledged by the Society of Journalists and Marketing Society of Slovenia. In 2000, the PRSS celebrated its 10th anniversary. To mark this milestone, the society began awarding prizes to the best Slovenian cases and the best communicator in management, in cooperation with the Chamber of Commerce and Industry of Slovenia, the Manager's Association of Slovenia, and the Slovenian section of FEACO—the European Association of Management Consulting. By the middle of its first decade in existence, the PRSS had 100 members and by the end of the decade, the number had doubled. It is safe to state that the public relations profession in Slovenia has become an institution (Verčič, 2002).

Definition of Public Relations

The first Slovenian booklet on public relations (Gruban, Maksimovič, Verčič, & Zavrl, 1990) proposed a new translation of the American term "public relations" into Slovenian language: "odnosi z javnostmi." The old term for public relations was *stiki z javnostjo*, which can be literally translated as "contacts with the [general] public." In the 1990s, it was replaced with *odnosi z javnostmi*, whose literal translation is "relations with publics." When the PRSS started a public relations book series in 2002, in cooperation with the major business publishing house GV Založba (with a goal of publishing two books a year, one original and one translation) there was no argument on how the profession is called in Slovenian (Verčič, Zavrl, & Rijavec, 2002). Explanations and defenses of the new term were given in the research report on the Slovenian replication of the *Excellence project* (Gruban, Verčič, & Zavrl, 1994), the first book in the Slovenian language (Gruban, Verčič, & Zavrl, 1997) and the first collection of contributions by practitioners (Gruban, Verčič, & Zavrl, 1998).

The transition from *stiki z javnostjo* to *odnosi z javnostmi* was about the transition from propaganda focused image management to a relational, stakeholder management of public relations. This development was strongly influenced by United States theory and practice (Verčič & J. E. Grunig, 2000). Toward the end of the 1990s, the definition of public relations in Slovenia broadened into "total communication" (Aberg, 1990) between an organization and all its publics (Theaker, 2001) and synchronized with the European approaches (Ruler & Verčič, 2002; Verčič, van Ruler, Bütschi, & Flodin, 2001) that go beyond relational to include discursive and reflective approaches: *celovito komuniciranje* [literally: "holistic communication"] and *komunikacijsko upravljanje* [literally: "communication management"]. Currently, the three terms (*odnosi z javnostmi, celovito komuniciranje,* and *komunikacijsko upravljanje*) coexist in both practice and in academia—their relations and their future are at the moment not decided yet.

A recent study found that typically, Slovenian companies have an average of two public relations professionals (Verčič & Ruler, 2002, p. 7). A linear extrapolation based on this would imply that 7,040 individuals currently work as public relations professionals in the for-profit sector, or approximately 0.05% of the total population. This research also found that 37% of medium and large companies in the representative sample had no specialists in public relations, which means that public relations is practiced by people primarily working in other functional areas (such as general management, human relations, marketing, sales, etc.). In response to questions on the public relations budget, respondents of the study indicated that they spend an average of 16.171 million Slovenian Tolars (SIT) (Euro 74, 675) on public relations annually. With linear extrapolation, the researchers estimated that 57 billion SIT (Euro 263 million) is the total amount of money spent on public relations in Slovenia, amounting to approximately 1.5% of the gross domestic product (GDP) (based 2000 on economic data).

However, one needs to take these numbers with a grain of salt. When asked which department performed the external communication function in their organizations, respondents replied: public relations department (6%), marketing or sales department (31%), no department because the CEO personally attends to this (26%), nowhere and by nobody (25%), and other (12%). When asked which department performed the internal communication function, respondents listed: public relations department (4%), human resources/personnel department (6%), marketing or sales department (19%), the CEO (25%), nobody (26%), and other (20%). When asked which department handles marketing communication (with advertising) respondents replied: marketing and sales department (50%), the CEO (18%), nobody (20%), and other (10%). Respondents also indicated that 60% of the total communication budgets go for marketing communication, 21 for external relations (not primarily marketing), and 19% for internal communication.

Government Practice

In the year 2000, the Government of Slovenia committed itself to implementing the good governance principles defined in the OECD *Citizens as Partners* sourcebook and handbook (see www.oecd.org/puma). The primary principles are accountability (making it possible to identify officials and hold them accountable for their actions), transparency (availability of information about government activities), and openness (seeking and providing appropriate responses). To ensure information society for all and reform of public administration (in line with the aforementioned principles), the government founded a Ministry for Information Society to facilitate the first principle. A position of a Ministerial Counselor in the Office of the Prime Minister was instituted to coordinate work on the second principle. The government as the corporate entity, all the ministries, and many subordinate agencies have Websites (see http://www.gov.si/ and http://www.gov.si/vrs/ang/index-ang.html for general entries, and http://e-gov.gov.si/e-uprava/english/index.jsp for e-Government). To listen to its constituency, the government not only regularly purchases public opinion surveys from the Faculty of Social Science, University of Ljubljana, but also publishes them promptly on the Internet (http://www.uvi.si/slo/aktualno/javnomnenjske-raziskave/pdf/aktualno.pdf). At the center of the government communication structure is the Public Relations and Media Office with 15 professionals, all members of the civil service, and a Director who is also the spokesperson for the government. The director is nominally a civil servant but has been replaced each time a new government has taken office. This office is divided into three departments, one for managing domestic and one for international communication. The third has been given responsibility for managing the Communication Program for Slovenia's Accession to the European Union. Every ministry employs at least one communication professional, with the Ministry of Interior having the largest department with five communication officers in addition to the eight communication officers the police headquarters and a well-organized structure covering the whole country. The Office of the Prime Minister has three communication officers (see Table 14.2). Although the government has built up its public relations capabilities substantially, it still suffers from inadequate strategic and managerial competence.

Consultancies

As already stated, the public relations industry emerged in the late 1980s and early 1990s in Slovenia. By the end of 1990s, it transformed itself into a "total communication" industry, in line with the development of the definition of public relations given above. Pristop Communications was the first public relations agency in Slovenia. Founded in 1990 with a public relations focus, it entered into other fields of applied communication, including advertising, by the mid-1990s. By the end of the 1990s, Pristop Communications had become not only the largest public relations agency but also the largest advertising agency in Slovenia. All other public relations agencies have followed the same path of providing "total communication" to clients. Therefore, currently there is no public relations agency that exclusively offers public relations services in Slovenia. At the same time, all the advertising agencies also started offering public relations services resulting in a convergence from both professions. There is a Slovenian chapter of the international public relations consultancy organization (ICCO—the International Communications Consultancy Organization, the umbrella association for more than 850 consultancies employing more than 25,000 people through their trade associations in 24 countries) with eight members: Imelda, Informa Echo, NT & RC, Prestige, Pristop, SPEM, Studio 3S, and Studio Kernel, none of whom can be classified as an exclusively public relations consultancy. The largest Slovenian communication consultancies are domestically owned by their founders as limited liability companies, are affiliated with one or more international networks and/or multinationals, and operate in other countries but primarily in South and Eastern Europe. They typically employ up to 40 employees (see Table 14.3).

TABLE 14.2

Republic of Slovenia, Public Relations in Government (plus the President and
the National Assembly), April 2002

Institution	People in Public Relations
Office of the Prime Minister	3
Ministry of Agriculture, Forestry and Food	2
Ministry of Culture	1
Ministry of Defense (with the Slovenian Army)	5
Ministry of Economy	2
Ministry of Education, Science and Sport	2
Ministry of the Environment and Spatial Planning	3
Ministry of Finance	1
Ministry of Foreign Affairs	4
Ministry of Health	1
Ministry of Information Society	1
Ministry of the Interior	5
Police	8
Ministry of Justice	1
Ministry of Labor, Family and Social Affairs	1
Ministry of Transport	2
Public Relations and Media Office	15
Office of European Affairs	2 = 59
Office of the President of the Republic	2
National Assembly (parliament)	5 + 7

Several government agencies and offices have their own public relations staff, including Agency for
Agricultural Markets and Rural Development, Agency for Regional Development, Environmental
Agency, Government Centre for Informatics, Office for Drugs, Office of Equal Opportunities, Office
for Legislation, Office for Metrology, Statistical Office.

Note. From communication between Government and Citizens in Slovenia: A report & recommendations
prepared under the auspices of the United Nations Development Programme Regional Bureau for Eastern
Europe and the CIS UNDP RBEC sub-regional project RER/01/003/A08/13 "Improving communication from
Government to Societies," by D. Verčič and A. Ažman, 2002.

INFRASTRUCTURE AND INTERNATIONAL PUBLIC RELATIONS

Political

The Republic of Slovenia is a constitutional parliamentary democracy, with a president
who is directly elected by citizens through a secret ballot. The National Assembly, the
highest legislative body, is composed of 90 deputies also directly elected by citizens
through a secret ballot following the proportional voting system. As a result of the last
parliamentary elections in 2000, the 90 seats in the National Assembly were divided as
follows: Liberal Democracy of Slovenia (LDS) 34, Social Democratic Party (SDS) 14,
United List of Social Democrats of Slovenia (ZLSD) 11, SLS+SKD Slovene People's
Party 9, New Slovenia–Christian People's Party (NSi) 8, Democratic Party of Pensioners
of Slovenia (DeSUS) 4, Slovene National Party (SNS) 4, and Youth Party of Slovenia (SMS) 4. The representatives of the Italian and Hungarian minorities have one seat
each.

TABLE 14.3

Slovenian Communication Agencies by Turnover in 2002

Agency	Turnover in Million Euro
Pristop	15
S Team Ideas Group	14
Mayer Group	11
Studio Marketing J. W. Thompson	9
Futura DDB	9
Prestige Mythos	9
Luna	9
Formitas BBDO	7
Tovarna vizij	5
Votan Leo Burnett	5

Note. From *Marketing magazine*, "Agencije: promet v letih 2001 in 2000 in napoved za leto 2002," *Marketing magazine*, January 30, 2002.

Slovenia's proportional electoral system seems to produce coalition governments. Even though balloting during elections is not compulsory, Slovenia seems to have a high rate of voter turnout with participation of 83% in 1990, 86% in 1992, 73% in 1996 and 70% in 2000 (Lukšič, 2001, p. 43). Although the general feature of the Slovenian political system is that it is a parliamentary democracy with a proportional electoral system, it is specifically a corporativist system:

Slovenian political culture contains strong elements of corporatism. A living being that organizes all the main concepts of the body politic and determines political behavior is the best metaphor for corporative political behavior. According to this concept, the state, politics and society are not and cannot be separated. It is because of the tradition of corporatism that the self-management system in its various ideological forms gained so much credence in Slovenia. The fundamental objective of the corporative culture is the survival of the nation because only through the survival of the nation can the lower or sub-communities survive and, indirectly, the individual as well.

In terms of values in the corporative culture, the highest positions are reserved for the stability of the community, equality, unity, justice, solidarity, order and success.

In terms of interest representation, a system of functional representation is being developed which is essentially a complex network of special interests and professional organizations (a better translation of the Slovenian word would be communities) that are incorporated into the political system in one way or another. Political parties are not accepted as an appropriate representative of social interests because of their inevitable politicization and subsequent distortion of authentic interests. During the course of their history, Slovenians have only rarely warmed to the notion of political parties, most recently during the period from 1989 to 1992. A general antipathy to party politics and to parliamentary government is an important ingredient of corporatism. Social alliances leading to consensus among the carriers of vital interests—such as labor unions and employers, physicians, farmers etc.—is one of the most sought-after values. The form of political activity is not as highly valued as its content. For this reason, legal culture does not play a significant role in corporative political culture. Legitimacy is considered far more important than legality. Moral and religious forms of reflection and practice also hold a privileged position in the corporative model while legal and scientific forms and practices are discriminated against on favor of the first two. (Lukšič, 2001, pp. 75–76)

TABLE 14.4

Formal Structure of the National Council

Representatives of employers	4
Representatives of employees	4
Representatives of farmers	2
Representative of craftsmen	1
Representative of free-lance professionals	1
Representative of universities and colleges	1
Representative of educational system	1
Representative of research activities	1
Representative of social security	1
Representative of health care	1
Representative of culture and sports	1
Representatives of local interests	22
Total	40

Note. From *The political system of the Republic of Slovenia: A primer*, 2001, by I. Lukšič (E. J. Debeljak, Trans.), Ljubljana: Znanstveno in publicistično središče.

The most visible feature of this is the second chamber of the parliament, known as the National Council, which is unique to the political systems of Western democracies. It is composed according to the principle of corporative representation (through special interest and professional organizations, like trade unions, employers' and farmers' organizations, universities and colleges, etc.) and its only foreign counterparts were the former Irish senate and the former senate of the Free State of Bavaria (Lukšič, 2001, p. 22). Table 14.4 gives the formal membership in the National Council.

In January 1992, the European Union (EU) officially recognized Slovenia as a sovereign nation and Slovenia became a permanent member of the United Nations in May 1992. In June 1996, the European Association Agreement was signed between the EU and Slovenia, and Slovenia presented its application for full EU membership. Slovenia is a member of Council of Europe, the World Bank, the International Monetary Fund, and the World Trade Organization (WTO). As already stated, on October 9, 2002, the European Commission recommended Slovenia for full membership in the European Union by 2004. A similar recommendation is expected in a few months to give Slovenia NATO membership.

The major influence of the political system to public relations practice is in operation of corporativist structures that favor negotiation and compromise over overt conflict. For example, employers and employees are obliged to talk, negotiate and compromise at micro, mezzo, and macro levels—within large companies employees are represented in supervisory boards and trade unions have special rights, there are general and special industry by industry collective negotiations on wages and terms of employment, and there is a tripartite system of government, employers, and employee negotiations at the national level. Similar formal structures exist in many other areas, including culture, public media, and so on, institutionalizing at least some relationship-building strategies of public relations.

Economic System

The economic strength of Slovenia is indicated in a statement by the BBC during its reporting of the European Commission's recommendation for Slovenia to become a member

TABLE 14.5

Slovenia's Competitiveness: Strengths and Challenges

Strengths
- Stable macroeconomic environment
- Well-educated labor force and fast expansion of higher education
- High female labor force participation rate
- Low corporate income taxation
- Excellent geographic location and connections
- Modern basic information technology infrastructure
- Developed public research capacities and quality of scientific research
- Availability of good health care services and broad coverage of social welfare system
- Biodiversity, forests, and water resources

Challenges for future development
- Structural reforms and reform of public administration
- High unemployment, inflation, and interest rates
- Low foreign direct investments
- Insufficient adult education
- Heavy tax burden on personal income and high social security contributions
- Low volume on Internet-based services
- Insufficient use of energy and low share of renewable energy resources
- Low co-operation between the private business sector and public research institutions
- Underdeveloped entrepreneurial culture
- High health and social welfare costs

Note. From *Benchmarking Slovenia: An evaluation of Slovenia's competitiveness, strengths, and weaknesses* (pp. 7–8), 2000, Ljubljana: Ministry of Economic Affairs, Republic of Slovenia.

of the European Union: "As the wealthiest country in eastern Europe, the former Yugoslav republic of Slovenia is the easiest new member for the Union to digest. As European Commission sources put it, with just 2 million people and living standards almost on a par with Greece or Portugal, it could join in a fortnight" (Vornic, 2002). Table 14.5 gives an overview of strengths and weaknesses of the Slovenian economy.

Slovenia is a small open market economy with a GDP of US $20 billion in 2000. From 1990 to 1999, the average annual growth rate in real GDP was 2.4%. Currently, the per capita GDP is US $10,000 originating from the service industry (58%), industries (38%, of which manufacturing is 28%), and agriculture (4%). The main export destinations are Germany, Italy, Croatia, Austria, and France (which are also the main origins of Slovenian imports). Slovenia spends 7.8% of its GDP on health and 5.7% on education (*Economist*, 2002, pp. 202–203). Table 14.6 gives an overview of the economy.

Legal System

Slovenia is a constitutional democracy with a division of powers between the executive, legislative and judiciary branches. The constitution states that judges are independent within the boundaries of the constitution and the law. Judges are elected by the National Assembly, which acts on the proposal by the 11-member Judicial Council. The country has one supreme court, 4 higher courts, 11 regional courts, and 44 district courts. There are also specialized courts that deal with matters relating to specific legal areas, such as a Court of Audit that controls state accounts, the government budget, and all of public

TABLE 14.6

An Overview of the Slovenian Economy

Population—mid-1999 (1000 persons)	1,985
Surface area (km^2)	20,720
GDP per capita 1998 in PPS (purchasing power standard)[a]	13,700
GDP per capita 1999 in PPS (purchasing power standard)	14,183
GDP per capita as % of EU15 average, 1998	68
GDP at current exchange rate (billion US$), 2000	20
Exports of goods and services as % of GDP, 1998	57
Imports of goods and services as % of GDP, 1998	58
EU share of total exports (%)	66
EU share of total imports (%)	69
Structure of value added by industry (1998), %	
Agriculture	4
Manufacturing	27
Other industries	10
Services	58
Employment by activities (1998), % share	
Agriculture and mining	7
Manufacturing	31
Other industries[b]	9
Market services	36
Non-market services	18
Proportion of employed persons (1999), %	63.3
Unemployment rate, registered (1999 est.), %	13.6
Unemployment rate, ILO (1999 est.), %	7.7
Investment rate, (1998), % of GDP	24
Investment rate, (1998), % of GDP, EU average	20
General government expenditure, (1998), % of GDP	44
Current account balance, (1999 est.), % of GDP	−2.9
External debt, (1998), million US$	4,959
Foreign exchange reserves, (1998), million US$	4,767
Gross public debt, (1998 est.), % of GDP	25

[a]GDP is expressed by Eurostat in an artificial currency called purchasing power standard (PPS) to enable correct comparison of goods and services produced by different countries.
[b]Other industries: electricity, gas, water, and construction.
ILO (International Labour Organization)
Note. From Republic of Slovenia, Ministry of Economic Affairs (p. 12), 2000; *Economist* (pp. 202–203), 2002.

expenditure. The Human Rights ombudsman is responsible for the protection of human rights and fundamental freedoms in relation to state bodies, local administrative bodies and all those with public jurisdiction (Možina & Resman, 2001, pp. 41–44).

The level of corruption in Slovenia is low compared with other Central and Eastern European countries and some member countries of the European Union. The Transparency International Corruption Perception Index in 1999 placed Slovenia at level 6. Slovenia ranked below Denmark, which was listed at level 10 denoting that it had the lowest corruption rate, and Finland (9.8). But Slovenia was above Belgium (5.8), Hungary (5.2),

Greece (4.9), Italy (4.7), the Czech Republic (4.6), and Poland (4.2) (*Republic of Slovenia*, Ministry of Economic Affairs, 2000, p. 17).

The Slovenian constitution protects the freedoms of speech and association, which can be taken as the legal protection of public relations activities. However, the protection of commercial speech is limited and there exist many restrictions related to the promotion of certain services (e.g, legal, medical), products (e.g., alcohol, drugs, tobacco), and targets (e.g., minors). These are changing as Slovenia harmonizes its legislation with that governing the members of the European Union (so-called *acquis communitaire*) in preparation for entry in the EU.

The constitution also contains a clause on the right to information, which is to be operationalized in the newly proposed freedom of information law. Media legislation is extensive and among other things guarantees not only the rights of journalists (guaranteeing them privileged access to information from public bodies), but also of media audiences (a right to correction of wrong information and a right to publish a response). A special law regulates the operation of the public radio and television systems (including its finances based on compulsory subscription fees). There are many other pieces of legislation that affect the practice of public relations in Slovenia: consumer, financial, government, internal, and media relations are all referred to in specific pieces of legislation. Consumer relations are affected with clauses referring to competition, commercial communication regarding specific products (alcohol, drugs, tobacco), informational rights of consumers, and so on. Financial relations are affected by clauses on transparency of financial markets, protection of small shareholders, operation of the stock exchange, and so on. Government relations are affected by clauses on elections and electoral campaigns, organization of civil service, and freedom of information, among others. Employee relations are affected by clauses on informational rights of employees and their representatives, their representation in company supervisory boards, and so on. Although it is impossible to say that any of those pieces of legislation was adopted with public relations profession in mind, they all do affect public relations practice and a professional consulting and execution in the filed of public relations in Slovenia is impossible without a thorough understanding of the regulatory framework.

Activism

Although it has fewer than 2 million inhabitants, Slovenia has more than 14,724 registered nongovernment organizations (NGOs) of which approximately 10,000 are active to varying degrees (Rončević, 2002, p. 62). The majority of these NGO's are founded around specific interests and professions. They form the backbone of Slovenian corporativism:

> A substantial segment of these so-called interest groups had been acknowledged as vital and important to the state and has been elevated to a special status and institutionalized in the National Council. Following an almost identical process, many interest groups are also represented on the board of RTV, Slovenia's national broadcasting company. The specific interests of employers and employees are separately organized or institutionalized within a social partnership system. Only labor unions representatives are allowed to negotiate with employers and the state on behalf of employees. There are 31 such labor unions. (Lukšič, 2001, pp. 54–55)

In addition to having organized labor, Slovenia also has three large associations that bring together employers: the Chamber of Commerce and Industry, the Association of

Employers, and the Trade Chamber. The past decade also has seen special interest groups actively participating in political elections and having a voice in the legislature. For example, the Green Party focused on environmental issues in the previous National Assembly, while the present Assembly has representations from the Youth Party and the Pensioners Party. Besides all of the interest formally represented in the National Council, there are also 31 registered religious organizations.

It is safe to say that corporativism strongly affects the nature of activism in Slovenia. In the 1980s, the implosion of Yugoslavia and its socialism in the country brought to the surface many so-called social movements that championed causes such as the protection of human rights, the environment, and need for pacifism. The majority of these special interests are currently manifested through formal (coorporativist) channels. Yet, there remain some permanent, but not corporativist activist groups such as the anarchist and anti-globalist factions. Activism also often appears at local levels in reaction to en emerging local issue, but it tends to channel itself into regular formal structures of corporativist social organization. This has an important consequence for public relations practice, because it directly links public relations to formal channels of social interaction.

CULTURE

Currently, there exists only one study linking Slovenian culture with public relations (Verčič, L. Grunig, & J. E. Grunig, 1996, pp. 52–56). Although reported in 1996, this study was conducted in 1993, and was based on lengthy personal interviews by North American researchers with three Slovenian practitioners. The authors acknowledged the many limitations of their study, yet remained convinced of its value stating that it was very helpful because "short of a direct cultural encounter with Slovenians or a deep understanding of the cultural roots of that society, scholars from other parts of the world should gain a useful understanding of the way Slovenians as a cultural group view the universe and thus develop a set of rules and behavior" (p. 50).

The theoretical underpinning for Verčič, L. Grunig, and J. E. Grunig's (1996) study was Hofstede's (1980) work on the dimensions of societal culture, which are described in the first chapter of this volume. Verčič, L. Grunig, and J. E. Grunig (1996, p. 56) found that Slovenian culture was high on individualism, power distance, and uncertainty avoidance. They also stated that "the [Slovenian] culture, which had been relatively feminine, is becoming increasingly masculine with the advent of capitalism." So far as societal culture shapes public relations (Sriramesh & White, 1992), the public relations practiced in Slovenia closely resembles that practiced in Austria and other countries in Central Europe.

The central cultural value in Central Europe is "quality of life," which usually refers to a balance between work and family (or leisure). From this balance is derived a clear division between public and private life, which gives a high protection of privacy even to public figures such as politicians and top corporate managers. On the other hand, this same division supports hard work and an authoritarian corporate culture (we are equal and free after work and outside organizations, but not within them), which complements corporativist political structures (favoring negotiations and compromise among equals—but on a collective, not an individual level). The final result of the "quality of life" doctrine is a hierarchy of values often expressed as health, family, and wealth (in that order). All public relations activities need to be adjusted to this fact of *de facto* dualism between public (social, collectivist) and private (individual alone and in family).

THE MEDIA AND PUBLIC RELATIONS

As described in Chapter 1, it is very important to understand the media system in a nation to understand the public relations practiced in that country. Splichal (1999) noted that "whatever the direction of their influence, the mass media represent the most effective influence system in contemporary society" (p. 8). Slovenia has five national TV channels. TV Slovenija 1 and TV Slovenija 2 belong to the public broadcast system RTV Slovenija. POP TV, Kanal A, and TV 3 are private TV channels. Slovenia has 80 radio programs, of which 6 are national (with Radio Slovenija—Program A1, 1. program, Radio Slovenija— Val 202, 2. program, and Radio Slovenija—Program ARS, 3. program, belonging to the public service RTV Slovenija, and the following being the remaining three: Radio Ognjišče, RGL, and Radio SI), 42 regional and 32 local stations.

Currently, 914 newspapers and magazines are regularly published of which 183 belong to companies, associations, societies, and political parties, and 138 to the trade press. A further 91 are local or regional, 53 concentrate on business, finance, and entrepreneurship, 48 have an entertainment focus, and 47 are education oriented. Of the remaining, 38 focus on general interest and current affairs, 35 on issues that interest children, youth or students, and 35 focus on sports and cars. In addition, 32 publications focus on religion and spiritual culture, 30 are oriented toward family issues, 15 are about home, nature, and pets, and 15 are regular supplements to major print editions. A further 11 are oriented toward computers, 9 focus on gastronomy, restaurants, and tourism, 9 deal with health, 7 with music, film, radio, and TV, and 2 focus on border sciences (Mediana, 2002).

The constitution of Slovenia protects freedom of media and expression. In just over a decade, the nation's media system has been significantly affected by the sea changes in policy such as the liberalization of the print media market, privatization of the media, and the introduction law to regulate new media, media monopolization, and commercialization (Hrvatin & Miloslavljević, 2001, p. 7).

Media Control

After studying the issue of media control in Slovenia, Hrvatin & Milosavljević (2001) gave the following overview:

> The Slovene media market is small, so relatively modest financial resources suffice to es-
> tablish control over it (especially in comparison with the sums involved in the takeovers
> and acquisitions in other European countries). Before the process of media privatization got
> underway, the Slovene state expected the invasion of large European and American corpora-
> tions, similar to what has happened in some other countries in transition. One decade later it
> is possible to conclude instead that a small number of local owners with stakes in numerous
> affiliated companies control the major part of the Slovene market. The concentration is still in
> progress, while cross-ownership ties remain unchanged. It is obvious that the state, or rather
> its supervising institutions, do not have any mechanism (and no interest) to introduce order
> into this field. (Hrvatin & Milosavljević, p. 7)

Four big media companies control 90% of the daily newspaper market in the country. Three of them (*Delo, Dnevnik*, and *Večer*), have their roots in the previous socialist system but were privatized through employee (internal) buyouts and internal distribution of shares after the democratization of Slovenia. The fourth daily newspaper, *Slovenske novice,* was established as a partial bypass company of the employees of *Delo* (who established it as a separate and privately owned company using the intangible assets of their primary employer, *Delo,* to form another newspaper and company to which some of them later moved, while others are still employed in *Delo* but participate in profits of *Slovenske novice* as owners).Three other dailies that started after 1990, *Slovenec, Republika,* and *Jutranjik,* closed down because of poor revenue.

This specific form of newspaper privatization was based on several assumptions. The first was that privatization was a safeguard against government intervention into editorial decisions. Next was the notion that employee (internal) buyout was a protection against foreign takeovers. Article 39 of the Mass Media Act of 1994 also prescribed a dispersed ownership of the media to prevent monopolistic practices (Hrvatin & Milosavljević, 2001, pp. 10 and 17). The final result of these practices was that at the end of 1990s, media ownership on the country consisted of a small number of domestic owners except in television where one American and one Scandinavian corporation seized the two largest commercial TV stations and merged into one (Hrvatin & Milosavljević, 2001, p. 97). In Slovenia, media ownership is balanced by a strong Journalist Society that vigorously protects the professional independence of its members and advocates the profession's focus on public service.

The present structure of media ownership is unstable and it will probably change after Slovenia's entry into the EU (2004). Its current consequences for public relations practice are expressing themselves in often conflicting situations between media owners and journalists. While these conflicts have positive consequences in balancing the powers of both sides, they make the life of public relations practitioners working in media relations very complicated.

Media Outreach

Slovenia can legitimately be called a media-rich society because 97.6% of households own a color television set and 98.6% own at least one radio (Mediana, 2001). In 2001, 48.4% of all households owned a computer. In 2001, the average daily media outreach among the Slovenian population aged 12–65 years was: 81% for television, 68% for radio, 44% for daily newspapers, 32% for outdoor media, and 27% for newspapers and magazines (Cati, 2001). Of the 600,000 Internet users in Slovenia (defined as those who have ever used the Internet) 16% can be classified as daily users (RIS, 2002). It is important to recognize that in Slovenia one can simultaneously use the mass media and the corporativist structure of nongovernmental organizations to reinforce messages in an institutionalized two-step model of public communication (impersonal mass media first and personal influence in corporativist institutions later or vice versa). Taken from this perspective, it can be said that media outreach in Slovenia is practically total.

Media Access

Sriramesh and Verčič (2001, p. 115) stated that "the flip side of media outreach is media access." Although Slovenia has reached media saturation in that it is possible to reach everybody through the mass media, it does not mean that every Slovenian has access to use the media for his or her own publicity purposes. Although the media law gives Slovenians a legal basis on which to seek the right to a public voice, such access is not very common. Currently there exist no studies on the issue of media access from the point of view of public relations in Slovenia. For that reason any conclusions on the topic can only be drawn from other fields of interest that were empirically tested. Based both on the data on media control and on the character of the political system, one can conclude that media access belongs to groups and networks that possess other forms of power (economic or political) which they can transform into media access. Such groups typically are different businesses, special interest, and professional, and political organizations acting alone or in coalitions. Public relations in such circumstances becomes 'relationship management' in the literal meaning of the term. Media access in Slovenia can be said to be general, yet mediated by corporativist structures.

From its emergence in 1990 until today, public relations in Slovenia has become an institutionalized practice that attracts many people and resources. Both social culture and the political system have produced a favorable environment for the development of public relations–like activities. Further impetus for the industry is expected when Slovenia becomes a full member of the EU. While professionalization of public relations is still inadequate by theoretical and normative standards, it can be said to be on pair with the best one can find around the world.

CASE STUDY

Several case studies from Slovenia are available in English. Ašanin Gole and Verčič (2000) published 33 cases from the country that have received international awards. Drapal, Verčič, Peterlin, and Ilešič (2002) have presented a case explaining the successful lobbying of institutions of the EU by Slovenia. The case study presented here is a description of the public communication campaign "Raising environmental awareness in Slovenia" that received the United Nations Award given by the International Public Relations Association (IPRA) in cooperation with the UN. Only one such award is given each year to a project that best meets the working guidelines of the United Nations in the domain of environmental protection, and is fully documented by Verčič and Pek-Drapal (2002).

Problem

In an effort to combat air pollution, the Government of Slovenia established the Environmental Development Fund (Eco-Fund) in 1995. One of the objectives of the fund was to provide low-interest loans to households to help them convert their old dirty heating systems to more environmentally friendly modern systems. During the first year of the project (between June 1995 and May 1996), only 117 households applied for loans under this program. Clearly, there was a need to induce greater participation in the program.

In 1996, the European Commission, through its Phare program, issued a public tender for the 'Pilot testing Phase of the World Bank Air Pollution Abatement Programme.' A Slovenian consortium of four consultancies (ITEO, Pristop Communications, Sistemi Shift, and E-Net) was awarded the contract. The total value of the project was ECU 400,000, of which ECU 154,000 were designated for the public communication campaign. The communication campaign began in May 1996. The initial month was designated as the inception phase, the next 11 months as the implementation phase, and the 13th month as the finalization and evaluation phase.

Formative Research

The formative research consisted of individual and group interviews with the management and staff of Eco-Fund and personal interviews with some members of the target audience (including some enabling organizations such as commercial banks that administered the loan scheme). This was followed by a poll of a representative quota sample of 1,163 households from the population of 645,000 households in Slovenia. J. Grunig's (1997) situational analysis of publics was used for identifying the willingness among the population to enter into a dialogue with the project administrators on the key topics of the project. One important finding of this research was that retirees were very interested in the conversion of their heating systems from coal to gas. It was also found that children were prepared to offer financial help to their elderly parents to cover the costs of conversion.

Campaign Goals

The above formative research enabled the project team to set the following five goals for the communication campaign:

- to train and increase communicative capability of the Eco-Fund management and staff;
- to increase awareness about the loan program in the target population;
- to establish consciousness that it is necessary to convert to environmentally friendly heating systems;
- to establish a mutual understanding and strategic partnership between Eco-Fund and their stakeholders;
- to influence the target population and other enabling groups to do the necessary preparatory work, apply for the loans, take the loans, and convert the heating systems.

Stakeholders

Five groups were identified as critical for the success of the program:

- people with old and environmentally unfriendly heating systems needing conversion;
- enabling groups (banks, contractors, natural gas, and district heating distributors);
- media;
- energy consultants and professional associations;
- political entities (Ministry of Environment, pressure groups, etc.).

Messages

Key messages consisted of:

- financial arguments (favorable loans);
- environmental arguments (to convert to environmentally friendly systems);
- convenience arguments (new energy supplies, e.g., natural gas, as reliable, cost efficient, and comfortable);

- enabling arguments (promoting the need for partnership between all organizations that were incorporated into the program).

Tactical Plan

The following were the key elements of the tactical plan:

- a launch "open day";
- training and seminars for Eco-Fund management and staff;
- advertising;
- live radio talk shows;
- media relations;
- a brochure;
- a toll-free telephone number;
- a national round table on air pollution abatement.

Outcome

In the 10 months of the campaign, the number of loans increased from earlier low take-up level of only 117 to 1896. At the end of the program an evaluative research was conducted and the results were fed back to the Eco-Fund.

CONCLUSION

The case we have presented is typical for public relations in Slovenia in that it includes relationship management in its corporativist version (gaining cooperation of many, including political stakeholders without which any project will fail), high managerial sophistication in the field of public relations conceptualization and research (such as the use of Grunig's situational theory in this practical case), straightforward technical execution, and a professional attitude (that is demonstrated in the final feedback to the client at the end of the project that has value only in future use by the client itself). It is worth noting at the end of this discussion that the public relations industry in Slovenia itself must contain elements of corporativism (with a relatively strong association—PRSS being its visible representation). This chapter has only outlined them. A study on the consequences of corporativism on public relations development remains a project for future research.

REFERENCES

Aberg, L. (1990). Theoretical model and praxis of total communications. *International Public Relations Review* *13*(2): 13–17.

Ašanin Gole, P., & Verčič, D. (Eds.). (2000). *Teorija in praksa slovenskih odnosov z javnostmi/Slovenian public relations theory and practice.* Ljubljana: Slovensko društvo za odnose z javnostmi—Public Relations Society of Slovenia.

Cati (2001). *Medijski Monitor.* Ljubljana: Raziskovalna Družba Cati.

Cutlip, S. M., & Center, A. H. (1960). *Effective public relations: Pathways to public favor* (2nd ed.). Englewood Cliffs, NJ: Prentice Hall.

Cutlip, S. M., Center, A. H., & Broom, G. M. (2000). *Effective public relations* (8th ed.). Upper Saddle River, NJ: Prentice Hall.

Dozier, D. D., Grunig, L. A., & Grunig, J. E. (1995). *Manager's guide to excellence in public relations and communication management.* Mahwah, NJ: Lawrence Erlbaum Associates.

Drapal, A., Verčič, D., Peterlin, I., & Ilešič, T. (2002). Slovenia and the EU: An anti-dumping case. In R. Pedler (Ed.), *European Union lobbying: Changes in the arena* (pp. 143–151). Houndmills: Luk Palgrave.

Economist (2002). *Pocket world in Figures, 2002 Edition.* London: Economist.

Economist (1997a, January 3). Slovenia: Canny survivor. *Economist*, pp. 63–65.

Economist (1997b, November 22). A survey of business in Eastern Europe: Eastern Europe recast itself. *Economist*, (Suppl).

Gruban, B., Maksimovič, M., Verčič, D., & Zavrl, F. (1990). *ABC PR: odnosi z javnostmi na prvi pogled.* Ljubljana: Tiskovno središče Ljubljana.

Gruban, B., Verčič, D., & Zavrl F., (1994). *Odnosi z javnostmi v Sloveniji: raziskovalno poročilo 1994/ Public relations in Slovenia: research report 1994.* Ljubljana: Pristop.

Gruban, B., Verčič, D., & Zavrl, F. (1997). *Pristop k odnosom z javnostmi.* Ljubljana: Pristop.

Gruban, B., Verčič, D., & Zavrl, F. (Eds.) (1998). *Preskok v odnose z javnostmi: Zbornik o slovenski praksi v odnosih z javnostmi.* Ljubljana: Pristop.

Grunig, J. E. (1997). A situational theory of publics: Conceptual history, recent challenges and new research. In D. Moss, T. Macmanus, & D. Verčič (Eds.), *Public Relations Research: An international perspective* (pp. 3–48).

Grunig, J. E., Grunig, L. A., & Verčič, D. (1996). The status of public relations in Slovenia: Extending the IABC's Excellence project. Paper presented to the Global Conference on Education for the 21st Century. Association for the Advancement of Policy, Research, and Development in the Third World, Cancun, Mexico. November, 21–23.

Grunig, J. E., & Hunt, T. (1984). *Managing public relations.* New York: Holt, Rinehart & Winston.

Grunig, L. A., Grunig, J. E., & Verčič D. (1997). Are the IABC's excellence principles generic? Comparing Slovenia and the United States, the United Kingdom, and Canada. Paper presented to the IABC Research Foundation at the 1997 International Association of Business Communicators Conference, Los Angeles. June, 9–11.

Grunig, L. A., Grunig, J. E., & Verčič, D. (1998) Are the IABC's excellence principles generic? Comparing Slovenia and the United States, the United Kingdom, and Canada. *Journal of Communication Management, 2*(4), 335–356.

Grunig, L. A., & Verčič, D. (1998). PR in Slovenia: Doing public relations in a small country in transition in Eastern Europe. In J. Felton (Ed.), *Crises in Wired World: How Does PR Handle the Instant Transmission of Problems Globally? Proceedings of International Symposium 2.* Gainesville, FL: Institute of Public Relations, University of Florida.

Hofstede, G. (1980). *Culture's consequences: International differences in work-related values.* Beverly Hills, CA: Sage.

Hrvatin, S. B., & Milosavljević, M. (2001). *Media policy in Slovenia in the 1990s: Regulation, privatization, concentration and commercialization of the media.* (O. Vuković, Trans.). Ljubljana: Peace Institute.

Hundhausen, C. (1969). *Public relations: Theorie und Systematik.* Berlin: de Gruyter.

Lukšič, I. (2001). *The political system of the Republic of Slovenia: A primer* (E. J. Debeljak, Trans.). Ljubljana: Znanstveno in publicistično središče.

Marketing magazine (2002, January 30). Agencije: promet v letih 2001 in 2000 in napoved za leto 2002.

Mediana (2001). *Mediana BGP.* Ljubljana: Inštitut za raziskovanje medijev, Mediana.

Mediana (2002). *Preglednica slovenskih medijev.* Ljubljana: Inštitut za raziskovanje medijev, Mediana.

Možina, S., & Resman, A. (2001). *Facts About Slovenia,* (3rd ed.). Ljubljana: Government of the Republic of Slovenia, Public Relations and Media Office.

Newsom, D., VanSlyke Turk, J., & Kruckeberg, D. (1996). *This is PR: The realities of public relations,* (6th ed.). Belmont, CA: Wadsworth.

Republic of Slovenia, Ministry of Economic Affairs (2000). *Benchmarking Slovenia: An evaluation of Slovenia's competitiveness, strengths and weaknesses.* Ljubljana: Ministry of Economic Affairs, Republic of Slovenia.

Ris (2002). *Research on Internet in Slovenia.* Retrieved on June 15, 2002, from http://www.ris.org

Rončević, B. (2002). Nekaj nastavkov za sociološko obravnavo nevladnih organizacij. In D. Jelovac (Ed.), *Jadranje po nemirnih vodah menedžmenta nevladnih organizacij* (pp. 45–70). Ljubljana and Koper: Radio Študent, Študentska organizacija Univerze v Ljubljani & Visoka šola za management v Kopru.

Ruler, B. van, & Verčič, D. (2002). *The Bled manifesto on public relations*. Ljubljana: Pristop Communications.

Splichal, S. (1999). Ownership, regulation and socialization: Rethinking the principles of democratic media. *The Public* 6(2): 5–24.

Sriramesh, K., & Verčič, D. (2001). International public relations: A framework for future research. *Journal of Communication Management* 6(2), 103–117.

Sriramesh, K., & White, J. (1992). Societal culture and public relations. In J. Grunig (Ed.), *Excellence in public relations and communication management* (pp. 597–614). Hillsdale, NJ: Lawrence Erlbaum Associates.

Statistični urad Republike Slovenije (2002). Popis 2002: Tabelarni pregled—Slovenija. Retrieved October 10, 2002, from http://www.sigov.si/popis2002/prvi_rezultati_slovenija.html

Theaker, A. (2001). *Public relations handbook*. London and New York: Routledge.

Thurow, L. (1993). *Head to head: The coming economic battle among Japan, Europe, and America*. London: Nicholas Brealey.

Verčič, D. (1993a, December). Excellence project studied in Slovenia. *Communication World* (pp. 9–10).

Verčič, D. (1993b) Privatisation fuels PR growth. In R. Sarginson (Ed.), *Hollis Europe: the directory of European public relations & PR networks* (pp. 389–390). London: Hollis Directories Ltd.

Verčič, D. (2002). Public relations research and education in Slovenia. In S. Averbeck & S. Wehmeier (Eds.), *Kommunikationswissenschaft und public relations in Osteuropa: Arbeitsberichte* (pp. 157–173). Leizig: Leipziger Universitätsverlag.

Verčič, D., & Ažman, A. (2002). Communication between government and citizens in Slovenia: A report & recommendations prepared under the under the auspices of the United Nations Development Programme Regional Bureau for Eastern Europe and the CIS UNDP RBEC sub-regional project RER/01/003/A08/13, "Improving Communication from Government to Societies." (Unpublished Research Report.)

Verčič, D., & Grunig, J. E. (2000). The origins of public relations theory in economics and strategic management. In D. Moss, D. Verčič, & G. Warnaby (Eds.), *Perspectives on Public Relations Research* (pp. 9–58). London and New York: Routledge.

Verčič, D., Grunig, L. A., & Grunig J. E. (1993). Global and specific principles of public relations: evidence from Slovenia. Paper presented to The International Conference on The State of Education and Development: New Directions. Association for the Advancement of Policy, Research, and Development in the Third World, Cairo, Egypt. November, 22–25.

Verčič, D., Grunig, L. A., & Grunig, J. E. (1996). Global and specific principles of public relations: evidence from Slovenia. In H. M. Culbertson & N. Chen (Eds.), *International public relations: A comparative analysis* (pp. 31–65). Mahwah, NJ: Lawrence Erlbaum Associates.

Verčič, D., & Pek-Drapal, D. (2002). Raising environmental awareness in Slovenia: A public communication campaign. In D. Moss & B. DeSanto (Eds.), *Public relations cases: International perspectives* (pp. 167–179). London & NewYork: Routledge.

Verčič, D., Razpet, A., Dekleva, S., & Šlenc, M. (2000). International public relations and the Internet: Diffusion and linkages. *Journal of communication management* 5(2): 125–137.

Verčič, D., van Ruler, B., Bütschi, G., & Flodin, B. (2001). On the definition of public relations: a European view. *Public Relations Review* 27(4): 373–387.

Verčič, D., & van Ruler, B. (2002). Public relations and communication management in the Netherlands and Slovenia: A comparative analysis. Paper presented to the Public Relations Division, 52nd Annual Conference of the International Communication Association: Reconciliation Through Communication, Seoul, Korea, July 15–19.

Verčič, D., Zavrl, F., & Rijavec, P. (2002). *Odnosi z mediji*. Ljubljana: GV Založba.

Vornic, A. (2002). The EU's uneven new contingent. *BBC News, World edition*. Retrieved January 24, 2003 from http://news.bbc.co.uk/1/hi/world/europe/2314659.stm

15

THE DEVELOPMENT OF PUBLIC RELATIONS IN RUSSIA: A GEOPOLITICAL APPROACH

KATERINA TSETSURA

INTRODUCTION

When one hears about the Russian Federation, or simply Russia, he or she evokes his or her own set of social and cultural images of this country. Some think about an economically struggling post-communist country, while others see quite developed and prosperous cities such as Moscow. Some imagine everlasting winters and miserable countryside roads of peripheral Russia, the poverty and continuous struggle of Russian citizens, while others talk about the successful transformation of the communist regime into a democracy, in which a free market economy develops giving rise to a large middle class.

There is no single answer to how today's Russia and Russian society can be characterized. Opposite viewpoints on a number of issues, analyzed by researches in the social sciences and social studies, have been created not only as a result of different perspectives and approaches to evaluations of the transformation of Russia, but also as a result of examining how certain phenomena perform differently in different parts of the Russian Federation. For example, many public relations scholars discussed theory and practice in Russia by solely constructing their arguments on the evidence from one region or even one city. Clarke (2000) did so based on an analysis of public relations practices in Moscow; Guth (2000) based on a study in St. Petersburg; and McElreath et al. (2001) on

Katerina Tsetsura is a doctoral candidate in Public Affairs and Issue Management in the department of Communication at Purdue University. Her research interests are the development of public relations theory and practice in Russia and countries of CIS and Eastern Europe, problems of international ethics in public relations, and social construction of identities of female PR practitioners in Eastern Europe. Comments on this chapter can be sent to: tsetsura@purdue.edu the analysis of public relations practice in Moscow and St. Petersburg. Such analyses are incomplete because they do not provide a holistic perspective on all Russian public relations practices.

Contemporary research in the area of international public relations suggests that cultural factors should be examined when one looks at public relations practices in a particular country (Botan, 1993; Culbertson, Chen, 1996; Taylor, 2001). But because the Russian Federation is one of the largest countries in the world and is diverse geographically, politically, economically, and culturally (Chirkova, Lapina, 2001; Lankina, 2001), it is appropriate to assume that Russian public relations can be theorized and practiced differently in different parts of the country. As demonstrated later in this chapter, this assumption is supported by a number of examples.

This chapter seeks to identify the similarities and differences in public relations theory and practice in different metaregions of Russia. Here, metaregions refer to the groups of federal subjects that form the Russian Federation, which are geographically, politically, and economically different and culturally diverse. There are three large types of federal subjects within the Russian Federation: the republics, the territories, and the regions, which are united into metaregions.

This chapter uses a widely accepted categorization of the federal subjects. Five metaregions can be identified: the European metaregion, which includes federal subjects in the Northern, Central, Central Black-Soil, and Southern areas; the Ural metaregion with federal subjects concentrated in the area of Ural mountains; the Central Siberian metaregion with subjects concentrated in the Central Siberian region; the ZaBaikal metaregion, which includes subjects from the Baikal Lake and ZaBaikal (beyond the Baikal Lake) areas; and the Far East metaregion, with federal subjects from the Far East geographic area. In addition, Moscow and St. Petersburg areas all analyzed as a separate metaregion due to a central role these two cities play in the economic, political, and cultural spheres of Russian society. A detailed discussion on why these two cities can be considered as a separate metaregion will be presented later in this chapter.

These metaregions, each having unique geopolitical particularities, should be taken into consideration when one examines the theory and practice of any social field of study, which is new to Russia. This chapter specifically seeks to analyze how public relations practices differ from metaregion to metaregion in Russia and how this fact affects the development of Russian public relations theory. In doing so, the historical particularities of the development of public relations in Russia will first be discussed to provide an evaluation of the status of the profession in today's Russia. The next section will demonstrate how political, economic, and social idiosyncrasies of different Russian metaregions create and maintain the field of public relations in Russia. Then, the chapter presents an analysis of some characteristics of Russian culture and will discuss some cultural differences which exist within the Russian Federation in relation to public relations practice and perceptions of the field. Finally, the difference in relationship between the Russian mass media in Moscow and mass media in peripheral Russia and public relations practice in the capital and in other Russian cities is presented. A case study presented in the last section of this chapter will illustrate why it is important to evaluate the differences in public relations practice in different metaregions of Russia when one analyzes contemporary public relations in Russia.

HISTORY, DEVELOPMENT, AND STATUS OF THE PROFESSION

The concept of public relations is relatively new to Russians. Not so long ago, few people had heard of public relations and even fewer knew what public relations entails. The public relations field emerged in Russia less than 20 years ago, and has been developing rapidly since then. Scholars from different fields have turned to this new, unexplored area of promise and have examined the phenomenon in some detail providing their own understanding of what public relations is. This rather eclectic scholarship, based on a number of theories from psychology, social psychology, sociology, political science, philosophy, marketing, and journalism created a diversified perspective of public relations, which later became somewhat of a challenge to a new generation of public relations scholars (Tsetsura, 2000a). The lack of unified understanding of public relations reflects the lack of theoretical development of Russian public relations and the diversity of public relations practices in Russia.

The history of the development of public relations in Russia differs significantly from the development of this profession in the United States. This difference is created not only by the youth of the field in Russia, but also by the lack of Russian scholarly works about the theory of public relations. Perhaps, the primary difference in the origins of public relations education in the United States and Russia is the absence of a communication tradition in Russia. In the United States, communication is a key to understanding the field of public relations. However, in Russia, the communication tradition does not exist. Instead, public relations theory is heavily drawn from journalism, whose impact on Russian public relations has to be addressed.

Traditionally, it was journalism and business scholars who began to define and discuss the conceptual frameworks and worldviews of public relations. They continued to argue about the principles of public relations as well as the methods of teaching public relations. Since then, business scholars have concentrated on the management and marketing functions of public relations (which one can call business-type public relations), whereas journalism scholars have focused on the management-communication function (which one can call journalism-type public relations).

After 10 years of active implementation of public relations courses into programs of higher education in Russia, the significant impact of these two areas became obvious. This impact can be identified not only through the existence of the two schools and the scholarly debates about the business or communication nature of public relations, but also through the contemporary curricula for public relations majors.

The popularity of the field motivated many schools to create their own programs where students could study public relations as a major, minor, or area of emphasis. Faculty members who became interested in the area started to promote public relations courses in their departments. The syllabi they created for classes were based heavily on Western sources and were either marketing or communication based, based on which area they had access to, first. In addition, depending on the scholarly background of these educators, public relations education took either a business or journalism path.

Contemporary public relations education in Russia has a strong orientation to journalism or business depending on its location in the university and the expertise of the faculty teaching at specific programs. As a result, the public relations programs at Moscow, St. Petersburg, Voronezh, and Ural State Universities are journalism-oriented and Moscow State Academy of Management, St. Petersburg Electro-Technical University, and Voronezh State Technical University are business-oriented.

The distribution of public relations programs along these two approaches is fairly even, although the distribution of public relations programs itself is uneven across regions. For instance, the Moscow/St. Petersburg region has a number of programs concentrated in one geographical area, as a result of the active development of public relations practices in the Russian capital. The development of public relations in this region is influenced by incredible free-market opportunities in Moscow, the active relationship building activities among universities in Moscow and St. Petersburg, as well as the linkage between these universities and other European and United States universities.

In April 2000, 56 Russian higher education institutions offered majors or emphases in public relations and more than 65 offered one or more public relations courses (Konovalova, 2000). In September 2001, there were more than 60 public relations programs (*PR News*, 2001). Two years ago, the higher education requirements for public relations majors were formed, and the Federal Russian Committee of Higher Education certified public relations as an official major in universities. This committee, a governmental organ, not only creates the guidelines that universities and colleges should follow but also evaluates these institutions for compliance of federal certification standards (Department of Higher Education of Russian Federation, 2000).

However, only a few programs in Russia actually meet these certification standards (Varustin, 2000). The Moscow and St. Petersburg metaregion has a large number of standardized programs because of an active development of relations with universities in Europe and Northern America. Thanks to the number of federal grants and the volume of financial aid from independent foundations, many universities in Moscow and St. Petersburg such as Moscow State University, Moscow State Institute of International Relations, Moscow Humanitarian Institute, Moscow State Academy of Management, St. Petersburg State University, and St. Petersburg Electro-Technical University, can afford to have American scholars lecture and conduct seminars and workshops on public relations theory and practice quite often (Alyoshina, 1997; Clarke, 2000; Guth, 2000; McElreath, Chen, Azariva, & Shadrova, 2001; Newsom, Turk, & Kruckeberg, 2000).

At the same time, universities in other Russian areas such as the European and Ural metaregions, have fewer programs in public relations and generally offer fewer public relations courses. For example, Voronezh State University, Rostov State University (the European metaregion), and Ural State University (the Ural metaregion) are among the few that offer strong programs in public relations outside of the Moscow/St. Petersburg metaregion. The relationships between Western universities and schools outside of the Moscow/St. Petersburg metaregion are not well developed. For example, between 1995 and 1998, only one educational program brought public relations practitioners to Voronezh State University twice to lecture and conduct seminars, whereas Moscow State University had visiting professors generally once every four months during the same period (S. Martin, personal communication, December 2000). In Voronezh, a city in a Central Black-Soil region with a population of one million, only two universities offer public relations as a major, whereas in Moscow and St. Petersburg there are about twenty programs in public relations. Moreover, in the early days, some regions such as the ZaBaikal metaregion did not have comprehensive programs in public relations. Today, however, all metaregions have standard public relations in higher education institutions.

This analysis suggests that public relations has developed differently in different metaregions as a field of study in higher education. As a result, certain metaregions (such as Moscow/St. Petersburg and European metaregions) have more developed public relations education programs than others, partly because they were created much earlier than in other metaregions (V. V. Tulupov, personal communication, December 2000). These early programs started to offer courses in public relations in 1994–1995. In contrast, Ural State University (the Ural metaregion) offered courses in public relations in 1997, and ZaBaikal State Pedagogical University (the ZaBaikal metaregion) and Dalnevostochnyj State University (Far East State University in Vladivostok, the Far East metaregion) in 1999 (I. Boldonova, personal communication, March 2001). Thus, the development of public relations education has different timelines in different metaregions of Russia. This lag in the development of education has affected the development of the public relations profession in different regions as will be discussed in greater detail in the succeeding pages.

The professional side of public relations in Russia is typified by a greater emphasis on certain specific specialties. Political public relations (public affairs), media relations, and corporate relations are the most popular areas in public relations practice. Several Russian scholars have tried to study public relations in Russia but most of these efforts concentrate on a functional description of practices rather than on theorizing about them (see, e.g., Alyoshina, 1997; Maksimov, 1999; Tulchinsky, 1994).

Governmental and political public relations is a leading specialty in Russian public relations practice. Public relations scholarship is concentrated around this area. Today, the majority of public relations textbooks and case studies published by Russian scholars cover political public relations almost exclusively. For example, Pocheptsov (1998) spent much time on analyzing the nature of political public relations and modern practices in the field. Among the most popular books on public relations are ones that offer practical advice on how to organize political campaigns and use public relations techniques in election campaigns (Pheophanov, 2001). Further, political public relations is often analyzed in conjunction with political advertising, clear evidence that Russian scholars do not make a clear distinction between the two (Egorova-Gantman, & Pleshakov, 1999).

Political public relations practice is constantly criticized by the Russian public partly because, unfortunately, the concept of public relations is not well understood and well communicated in Russian society. Moreover, many unethical practices such as black PR (discussed later in this chapter), have provoked negatively oriented discussions and led to public relations being equated with manipulation. The concept of ethical public relations is often seen as an oxymoron rather than a real phenomenon (V. V. Tulupov, personal communication, December 2000).

Corporate public relations is another specialty that is growing in popularity. This area is becoming more popular as the Russian economy grows and Russia increases its presence in the international market. Unfortunately, many textbooks covering this area as well as many corporate public relations courses cover only basic etiquettes or provide simplistic explanations of the role of modern mass media in society with no information on how to practice strategic corporate communication. Further, such chapters are usually included in books on advertising (Pankratov, Bazhenov, Seregina, & Shakhurin, 2001).

As a profession, public relations has been developing rapidly in Russia. A number of public relations courses are now being taught in Russian universities and colleges. A number of public relations departments are also being created in governmental, corporate, and non-for-profit organizations, signifying a parallel growth in the industry as well. No doubt, Moscow is a leading center for the development of public relations. This concentration is the result of three primary factors. As the capital, Moscow is the center of a high degree of political activity. It is also the center of economic development relative to other cities in Russia. Finally, as mentioned earlier in this chapter, Moscow is the hub of public relations education, having been the pioneer of public relations education in Russia. In contrast, most of the other metaregions, continue to struggle to inculcate strategic public relations practices in business mostly because the phenomenon is neither widely known, nor recognized, by leaders of business and government and by publics. Lately, however, this situation has been changing dramatically.

New departments of public relations have been organized in a number of governmental organizations and have now become an integral part of their structures. For instance, the department of press services in the Yekaterinburg Russian Internal Revenue Service office (in the Ural metaregion) produces publicity and advertising campaigns for the local office. One of its latest efforts featured a series of press-releases aimed at changing the attitudes of taxpayers as well as facilitate communication between these publics and internal revenue service workers, using slogans such as: "have a cup of coffee with your tax service agent" (T. Korchak, personal communication, March 2002).

Most not-for-profit organizations also actively use public relations, mostly for fundraising. For example, Voronezh regional teenage nonprofit organization "New View" (the European metaregion) conducted a number of publicity campaigns to promote its programs. Professional public relations associations in Russia also actively seek to promote public relations as a legitimate profession. Among the biggest and most active are: the Russian Public Relations Society and the Russian Society of Advertising Agencies. It is important to note that many Russian advertising agencies offer public relations services as well, as there are only a few agencies that exclusively practice public relations. These public relations agencies mostly concentrate on political public relations, managing election campaigns with special attention to candidates' image-making (Tsetsura, 2000a). The next section describes one of the most provocative issues in modern public relations in Russia: formulation of the image of the public relations field in relations to "black PR" versus "white PR."

"BLACK" VS. "WHITE" PUBLIC RELATIONS

One of the most interesting and provocative discussions in modern Russian public relations theory centers around two contrasting views on public relations: "white PR" versus "black PR." These two terms were introduced in the early 1990s and soon became very popular among professionals and, later, scholars. Ethics is the main reason behind dividing public relations practices to "black" and "white." "Black PR" is associated with manipulative techniques that are expected to be used mostly in the area of political public relations, particularly, in election campaigns. "White PR," in contrast, presents the Western, ethical view of public relations drawing from the *Excellence Project* (Maksimov, 1999), which is described in the chapter on North America in this volume. In media references, as well as discussions among political relations practitioners, the field is often presented in terms of "black" and "white" PR.

Other scholars, however, reject categorizing public relations practices in these stark terms. Instead of dividing public relations on "black" and "white" terms, they argue, "black" public relations is not a public relations at all, but rather it is propaganda (Tulupov, 1996). Many of them point out that "black vs. white PR" discussions exist mainly because the profession has been slow to adopt ethical standards. Novinskij (2000) argued that in Russia, there is no philosophy and ethics of public relations *per se*. Some scholars from the United States contended that "black" public relations cannot exist because "any misuse or abuse of public relations is a question, not of 'bad' public relations of which only an individual practitioner can be held responsible, but rather such misuse or abuse becomes a question of unethical professional practice which is of collective concern and which must be [the] collective responsibility of all practitioners" (Kruckeberg, 1992, p. 34).

One may conclude that public relations professional ethics is not well understood in Russia. Even though Russian professionals have joined associations such as the International Public Relations Association (IPRA), International Association of Business Communicators (IABC), and the Public Relations Society of America (PRSA) that exhort them to follow codes of ethics, these professionals often consider such codes as idealistic and not practical in the Russian environment (V. V. Tulupov, personal communication,

August 2002). Russian public relations professional organizations often face the same problems as their many counterparts in other countries: the accepted codes of ethics are not enforceable and thus are not practiced (Tsetsura, 2001).

Although the problem of enforcing codes of ethics is not a problem faced only by the Russian public relations industry, the attitudes among some Russian public relations professionals toward this important issue are reason for concern. Many Russian practitioners would readily admit that they do not always practice ethical public relations as presented in the code of ethics of the Russian Public Relations Association. They present what in their view is a plausible excuse for ignoring ethical considerations in their professional practice by citing differences in the mentality of Russian society (cultural differences), which makes it difficult for them to practice specific public relations practices (professional differences). Many of them simply say that it is impossible to practice ethical public relations because nobody would pay for it (Maksimov, 1999).

In addition, Russian society fails to recognize the importance of a wide dissemination of information. Heavily influenced by its Soviet past, senior managers of Russian organizations and governmental agencies do not appreciate the importance and benefits of open communication. Ethical concerns connected to the problem of dissemination of information were clearly evident in the case study of Chernobyl by Jaksa and Pritchard (1996) who described what happened when public relations ethics (government public relations in this case) clashed with the appropriateness (or lack thereof) of particular strategies and practices (such as hiding information from a public who had a right to know what happened at the nuclear station on April 26, 1986).

Jaksa and Pritchard (1996) noted that a group of students from the United States who were on a cultural exchange tour to Kiev, which is about 80 miles away from Chernobyl, were in the vicinity of the disaster on the days immediately following the nuclear accident. Along with this group, hundreds of thousands of area residents were not aware of the accident for almost a week as the group continued its trip in the region. Hiding such critical information, obviously under orders from local and federal government officials, has raised a number of ethical questions about the appropriateness of such actions and the right of publics to have access to information that could present a real or potential threat to health and life. Jaksa and Pritchard concluded that those who have access to important and potentially hazardous information, especially in crisis situations, should be held responsible for disseminating it. This case is an illustration that when government information channels are closed because policy makers intend that to be the best strategy, it is impossible for ethical public relations to be practiced. Unfortunately, even today, government public relations professionals often do not address the ethical aspects of free dissemination of information. Ethics stays on the background as far as the practice of government public relations is concerned.

Thus, the discussion of the practice of ethical public relations leads one to address the impact of environmental variables on the profession and its principles. Therefore, it is helpful to address the political, economic, and activist infrastructure in Russia and the influence of these variables on the development of public relations theory and practice in this country.

INFRASTRUCTURE OF RUSSIAN PUBLIC RELATIONS

Political System

Russia can be characterized as an emerging democracy (Guth, 2000). After the collapse of the Soviet Union, it began to actively seek a national political identity as an established democracy by trying to break its traditional domineering and hierarchical political structure. Aron (2001) contended that Russia had made a significant progress in becoming democratic when he noted that "Russia is by far the freest, most democratic nation of all the post-Soviet states" (p. 79). Others are not so optimistic about Russia's progress as a democratic state. For instance, famous writer and activist Solzhenitsyn (2001) argued that Russia has failed in its quest of becoming a democracy: "There exists no legal framework or financial means for the creation of local self-government; people have no choice but to achieve it through social struggle" (p. 68).

It is worth noting that whereas Solzhenitsyn refers to local governments, Aron talks about the central government. One of the essential features of the Russian political system is that whereas there has been progress toward democracy at the federal level, local governments often remain very conservative and non-democratic. They work under the old scheme of centralized government management. At the same time, when local governments gain additional power that is divested by the central government, they often do not know how to handle it (Lincoln, 2001). For Russia, democracy currently is more of a proclaimed goal than a reality. Many metaregions still do not practice democracy in its true sense, and evidence of that can be found in the contents of the many publications from the central and local Russian media (Brown, 2001).

As mentioned earlier, political public relations is one of the most popular areas of practice in all parts of Russia. Election campaigns are developed and implemented by agencies that engage in political public relations and image-making. Often these are the most popular and well-known public relations agencies. Because of democratization and the resulting ongoing election processes in Russia to elect local, regional, and federal governments, public relations professionals are actively involved in political image-making activities.

Many public relations campaigns such as the All Russian Census Campaign 2001 (which now has been moved to 2002 because of budget cuts) are organized and paid for by the Russian government. Independent public relations firms benefit by winning the contracts to create such campaigns. "Image-Land," a Moscow-based public relations and advertising group, won the account to plan and implement the All Russian Census Campaign 2001.

ECONOMIC SYSTEM AND LEVEL OF DEVELOPMENT

As described the beginning of this book, there is an interrelationship between political philosophy and level of development. This linkage is evident in Russia also where one sees the differences in political systems of various metaregions being closely connected with differences in economic development of the metaregions. The Moscow/St. Petersburg metaregion was central to economic development of the country during the Soviet era, and it continues to maintain that leading position today as well. Most of the investments, Russian and foreign, are concentrated in Moscow and St. Petersburg because of their geopolitical closeness to the federal government. The Ural metaregion is the second most developed metaregion because of its distance from the Moscow area, which also helps it serve as a connecting bridge between the capital and Siberia and Far Eastern regions. The Ural mountains divide Russia into European and Asian parts, and the Ural metaregion (particularly, Yekaterinburg) is considered the single most important connection between the two parts.

Equally important is the Central Siberian metaregion, which has rich natural resources such as gas and oil. Traditionally, this region has had a well-developed heavy industry sector. Most of the largest oil production companies are located in this metaregion. Being important players on the international market for oil and gas products, they practice public relations activities such as lobbying and financial relations. But their primary focus continues to be on positive publicity (press agentry model) rather than strategic public relations.

The economy of the European metaregion has also been growing rapidly in the past decade. Big and small businesses are actively growing in the region, but they do not seem too keen on practicing public relations practices. For the most part, large companies, which work on international markets, try to get involved in some public relations activities albeit at the publicity level.

Although many companies can afford to have public relations practitioners, only a few actually hire more than one professional. This one person is responsible for all aspects of the public relations practices of the organization from technical aspects such as writing press-releases to conceptualizing and implementing strategic campaigns that seek to promote organizational activities. Having one person doing all the public relations work is a common practice in different parts of Russia because very often organizational decision makers (the dominant coalition) do not appreciate the benefits of strategic public relations management. Most senior managers consider public relations to be a technical rather than strategic function one that is not so crucial to the effectiveness of the organization.

Many Russian textbooks and professional workshops organized in different parts of Russia promote the idea that public relations is merely publicity-oriented as is seen in the many publications on public relations that describe the profession as limited to publicity-oriented activities such as organizing exhibitions and thematic presentations, news conferences, and special events (Alyoshina, 1997; Pankratov, Bazhenov, Seregina, & Shakhurin, 2001; Pheophanov, 2001). Seminars and workshops are frequently organized to teach professionals how to create and successfully implement plans for conducting special event luncheons, publicity events, and news conferences. Virtually no information is available in Russia on strategic public relations practices and their connection to overall organizational effectiveness. Some Western textbooks, as well as professional seminars and workshops conducted by Western European and American practitioners and educators, emphasize the strategic nature of public relations. For example, the textbook *This is PR* by Newsom, Turk, and Kruckeberg (2000) is translated to Russian and is widely used by Russian educators.

One of the biggest problems, however, is the lack of economic development among many of Russia's metaregions, which has hampered the growth of public relations in these regions. Organizations and companies not only have a poor understanding of the full value of strategic public relations, but they also do not have the financial resources to invest in public relations departments that can plan, implement, and evaluate strategic campaigns.

Level of Activism

The level of activism in a society demonstrates the extent to which publics are prepared to argue for changes and force the implementation of changes in society. Thus, organizational public relations efforts often reflect the extent to which publics are ready to promote and pursue their goals in the society and thereby posing a challenge to organizations. In Soviet Russia, activism was extremely low because it was a punishable crime. As a result, people learned to stay away from activist groups of any kind. Lincoln (2001), in particular, pointed out that in the Soviet Union, "state propaganda applauded the people's participation in state-controlled civic life, but in reality it was every person for himself [herself]" (p. 87).

As a result of past suppression, post-Soviet Russian publics have been struggling to establish and develop activist groups. Today's Russian activism varies among the different metaregions. Generally, the highest degree of activism is seen in the Moscow/

St. Petersburg, European, and Central Siberia metaregions, generally in the form of labor unions. Most of these activists have focused on economic problems such as salaries and benefits. Because the government still has control over many companies, either directly through government subsidies or indirectly through local and federal legal regulations, efforts of activist groups are directed toward the government as well as toward the management. Most labor unions are not well structured and therefore have poor support even among employees.

For the most part, activism has not spread to other sections of the society. Activist ideas often stay among members of the activist groups and are not known among general publics. Many scholars have examined Russian publics in search of explanations for the reticence among Russians to be active citizens. One explanation is that this is a legacy of the Soviet era and is connected to the poor understanding of activism as a phenomenon. Another is that democracy itself is yet to develop in modern Russia. Lincoln (2001) argued that "Russians today simply lack that sense of civic responsibility that underlines the proper functioning of democratic institutions in the West" (p. 86). He continued that Russians do not understand the concept of a democratic society in which citizens are expected to actively participate in the social life and be responsible for their communities and their neighbors. As a result of underdeveloped activism, corporations in modern Russia do not face pressures from activist groups. For the most part, such groups are rarely seen and those that exist are not powerful (Miroshnichenko, 1998).

Legal Structure

As of today, there is no Russian law regulating public relations practices *per se*. However, there are two federal laws that regulate journalism and advertising, in which some public relations practices are also addressed. The first one is the Media Law of Russian Federation, which specifically addresses a problem of journalistic dignity and states that journalists cannot be paid to publish materials as editorials. Such materials can include positive information about organizations and can be considered "hidden advertising" because their goal is to publicize a product or service by paying for such exposure while not specifying it as such in the media. The Advertising Law of the Russian Federation also addresses this problem, but unfortunately, the statute does not specify the difference between hidden advertising and publicity. As a result of misinterpretation of publicity, materials which are based on press releases are often criticized by the federal organ, Antimonopoly Committee, and its regional departments, which are in charge of implementing the Advertising Law.

The Advertising Law defines hidden advertising as the act of promoting products or services through the media (often published in the editorial pages) without clearly identifying such acts as advertising (with a statement such as "This is advertising"). However, many articles, which are written by journalists but based on organizations' press releases, are often also considered as hidden advertising for which journalists do receive legal warnings from the regional offices of the Antimonopoly Committee (Tsetsura, 2000b). One of the biggest problems is that many of those who work in the offices of this Committee are not familiar with the concept of public relations and do know about the nature of publicity. For instance, the head of Krasnoyarsk Regional Antimonopoly Committee (the Central Siberia metaregion) published a manual for his workers on the ways to uncover hidden advertising in which he stated that any material positively describing an organization or a company can be considered as hidden advertising (Tsetsura, 2000b).

This is not such a big problem in the Moscow/St. Petersburg metaregion because the media there are generally better aware of public relations practices and have more exposure to press releases and publicity events. A different problem, paying journalists and editors for publishing publicity-oriented materials, has now risen in this region and has spread to other Russian metaregions as well.

The slang word *zakazukha* describes the act of publishing material favorable to an organization written by a journalist and printed on editorial pages in return for payment by the organization. Money can go directly to a journalist or an editor. A recent study conducted by Promaco Public Relations, a Moscow-based public relations firm, concluded that 13 of 21 Russian national newspapers and magazines were willing to publish a fake press release (without even checking the facts) for a payment of between $200 to $2000 for the service (Sutherland, 2001). Russian laws define this as hidden advertising but the poor enforcement of the law makes it possible for the practice to continue. As of today, neither journalists nor public relations professionals who engage in this practice have been legally challenged for their activities. Further, codes of ethics of journalism and/or public relations are not enforced either further exacerbating the problem creating a strong negative perception of the field of public relations (Tsetsura, 2000b).

In sum, the preceding pages articulated several major particularities of Russian society that have affected the development of public relations in the country. First, democracy is not well developed in Russia. Next, as a result of the 70-year long Soviet legacy, activism is not well understood or accepted by the Russian public. Third, economic challenges and the ongoing political changes in the country have created barriers to the active development of the public relations profession. Next, because organizational managers and their stakeholders do not have a clear understanding of the nature of public relations, public relations is seen as technical rather than strategic organizational function. Finally, the section has offered certain legal and ethical constraints to the development of public relations. The next section discusses the impact of environmental factors on the public relations profession in Russia.

RUSSIAN CULTURE AND PUBLIC RELATIONS

The editors have discussed the conceptual linkage between public relations and both societal and corporate culture. Culture plays an important role in any field, but it is especially important in the field of public relations which actively relies on communication (Sriramesh, & White, 1992). Russian culture affects public relations practices in two distinct ways. First, Russian culture influences the understanding and conceptualization of Russian public relations as a profession itself. Second, different subcultures within Russia influence the choice of specific public relations practices in different metaregions.

Unfortunately, very little research has been conducted in Russia on cross-cultural communication factors (Ting-Toomey, 1999). Much of the existing research in the area identifies Russia culture as being predominantly individualistic, with higher levels of power distance, but low in context, and with low levels of uncertainly avoidance (Gudykunst, Ting-Toomey, & Chua, 1988). It is important to note, however, that because of the differences in cultures among the metaregions, many cross-cultural indices vary from region to region. For example, the European metaregion generally is considered as a Western-oriented culture with high level of individualism, whereas Central Siberia and ZaBaikal metaregions sometimes are classified as Asian-oriented, collectivist cultures (Richmond, 1996). So far, no formal research has been done to evaluate the cultures of different parts of Russia even though the cultural idiosyncracies of different Russian metaregions require closer examination. Such research would surely be useful in defining the linkage between culture and public relations practices in different metaregions.

Today's Russia is a union of people of almost 100 different nationalities with different subcultural backgrounds. One may safely surmise that these differences might influence the perceptions and general understanding of public relations practices among these peoples. However, it is important to remember that as a profession, public relations developed in the Moscow/St. Petersburg metaregion first and was then transported to other metaregions. The misinterpretations and misunderstandings of the profession, which were developed in the Moscow/St. Petersburg region, thus got transported to these other regions also. In the succeeding pages, the relationship between Russian culture and the public relations profession will be discussed.

The cultural norms of Russian public relations might be explained by:

1. the lack of a well-defined history of public relations as a field;
2. the mixture of Western theories with Russian traditions of communication and relationships;
3. association of public relations with other phenomena (such as propaganda, advertising, promotion, and marketing) in Russia; and
4. the perceptions of public relations by Russian publics.

As would be the case with any new professional occupation, public relations faces a number of problems in modern Russia. Many of these problems have resulted from misunderstandings that have occurred throughout the years that public relations has continued to develop as an area of study in Russia. Because Russia was a part of the Soviet Union for more than 70 years, it has a rich history of negative propaganda practices. This fact has a tremendous effect on the ways in which people perceive public relations in modern Russia. In the next section, a language-related problem is analyzed that affects the philosophy of public relations in modern Russia.

In Russia, the negative meaning of "Soviet propaganda" was broadly used in the middle 1980s, during the early years of *perestrojka*. Negative associations and perceptions of propaganda were very common among Russians who had just gotten freedom of speech and were reevaluating their beliefs and values. At the same time, Russian scholars began working on the neutral nature of propaganda, which still remained shocking for most Russian publics. Western authors Pratkanis and Aronson (1991) were among the first educators to present this "neutral" approach, which was actively extended by other Russian scholars. In their book *Age of Propaganda*, Pratkanis and Aronson supported the idea of a synonymous meaning of the words "propaganda" and "persuasion." These authors distinguished the two words by defining one as "mindless propaganda" and the other as "thoughtful persuasion." As a result, the word "propaganda" got back its original neutral meaning: it might be positive (open and honest explanations) or negative (lying, manipulative, based on total inspiration, but not on argued evidence).

The concept, although seemingly acceptable, created problems outside of scholarly discussions. Some Russian publics—overwhelmed by the negative perceptions of propaganda and remembering old definitions of publicity and public relations, which were wrongly translated as propaganda practices early on (Tsetsura, 2000b)—made inaccurate connections implying that the term "public relations" was a synonym of "propaganda." Thus, the discussion about the differentiation between public relations and propaganda, which Western public relations scholars had been engaged in for many years, has become a matter of urgency to Russian scholars.

The relationship between propaganda and public relations might not be so easy to describe in some of the emerging democracies but an examination of their mutual influence and coexistence could create fascinating discussions. It is especially important to continue to examine these issues because of the need to reevaluating communication phenomena and public relations in the multinational context, as is being done in this volume. At the same time, from the Russian standpoint, it is important to distinguish between public relations and propaganda to establish a clear understanding of which public relations practices are ethical. Misinterpretations in translation and a lack of a clear understanding of the public relations profession has led to the formation of negative perceptions about public relations as a field of practice and an object of study.

MEDIA AND PUBLIC RELATIONS

Media relations is the second most popular area of public relations practices in Russia after political communication involving image building for political figures and political candidates. Most public relations practices are concentrated around the production and dissemination of press releases as well as the creation of special publicity events, as Russia has followed the path of many other countries. Media relations has actively developed in all Russian metaregions, and most public relations and advertising agencies outside of the Moscow/St. Petersburg region almost exclusively offer media relations services.

Media Control

In theory, Russian media can be considered to be private. However, the government (through subsidies) and corporations (investment and advertising) have a significant impact on the media. The financial constraints that the Russian media face on a daily basis have put these media in a disempowered situation of dependency on governments and corporations. Of course, editorial freedom becomes one of the major casualties in this context. This section presents several major factors that have contributed to the creation of a framework for media relations in modern Russia.

Russian media have traditionally been divided into two large categories: national and local. The national media have typically had their headquarters in Moscow, and they traditionally have had the best equipment and personnel. During the Soviet period, national media played an important role in the dissemination of information by the government, which tightly controlled these media. Further, local media always looked up to the national media and never opposed them. Even though the political philosophy of the country has changed, some local media have continued this practices of dependency over national media.

Media Outreach

The outreach of Russian media is tremendous. A massive infrastructure of production and distribution of all types of media, print and broadcasting, was developed during the Soviet era. The high rate of literacy in Russia helped the media establish large readership and viewership during the Soviet period. The public relations implications of these two factors is very clear: this media outreach created an opportunity for fast dissemination of information to the whole country.

The Russian publics, especially in Central Siberia, ZaBaikal, and Far East metaregions, tend to trust the media more than those who live in the European and Ural parts of the country (Kay, 2000; Potcheptsov, 2001). Traditionally, the latter ones have been the more politically and socially active, with better developed, and more diverse, media. The publics in these metaregions do not trust the media as much as residents of other regions and they are especially skeptical about the national media in modern Russia. This fact is important to any/one who wishes to conduct media relations in one of these metaregions.

Editorial pages are often viewed skeptically and critically by these publics. Many problems, or perceived problems, arise when a piece written by a journalist was paid for by a company or an organization or just looks like *zakazukha*. The problem of *zakazukha* exists in all metaregions. At the same time, many publications are the result of the active professional and the legitimate collaboration between journalists and public relations people and should be recognized as such. Public relations practitioners in modern Russia try to find new ways of dealing with public skepticism by demonstrating creativity in organizing publicity events and writing feature press releases (I. Boldonova, personal communication, March 2001; T. Korchak, personal communication, March 2002).

In addition to the many concerns already addressed in this chapter, one must discuss and analyze the self-censorship of the Russian media and its impact on the public relations profession. Self-censorship is practiced by Russian media as a result of financial and legal pressures from government officials and corporations. Self-censorship today is probably the biggest problem of Russian media (GDF, 1999; Tsetsura, & Kruckeberg, in press). The tremendous power of financial groups in Russia coupled with the legal paradoxes of Russian laws on freedom of speech created a situation where the media are trapped between competing forces (Tsetsura, 2002). On the one hand, business conglomerates involve the media often in accusing and attacking one another. On the other, federal, regional, and local government officials try to control the media to keep criticism of their out of the public eye. Even though national media may at times exercise some editorial freedom and resist government and corporate pressures (see Belin, 2001, for the famous NTV scandal case), local media do not have any power to resist such pressures. Belin summed up: "Media in the [other] Russian regions face more restrictions than Moscow-based media. Although no formal monopoly on media ownership exists, there is a dearth of small and medium-sized businesses to support private media through advertising" (p. 340).

The problem of editorial freedom among the regional media in Russia is of vital importance to public relations. In the last decade, the federal government has done practically nothing to protect media freedom in the regions. There is no doubt that the local media are highly dependent on local authorities who often directly dictate media content. Brown (2001) argued that:

> Journalists' dependence on those who were subsidizing their newspapers or television channels curtailed their freedoms, while in the republics and provincial Russia the controls exerted by presidents and governors tended to be much more direct and uncompromising. At best, then, this requirement of a democracy, which has already survived turbulent times, remains a fragile growth. (p. 554)

A study that measured freedom of speech in Russia in 1999 found that none of the 88 studied regions, including Moscow and St. Petersburg, had created satisfactory conditions for genuine press freedom to exist. The new federal government was quick to play the role of godfather of local media when Russian president Vladimir Putin signed a law mandating that subsidies to local print media should be paid directly from the federal budget. According to Belin (2001), this new law "could somewhat reduce the print media's reliance on regional authorities, which previously had control over how federal funds were divided locally" (p. 341). The result, one could argue, is that the print media would now begin depending on the federal government's media ministry! In sum, both the national and local media in Russia still have a long way to go to achieve true freedom of speech.

Public relations practitioners should be aware of these constraints and challenges when dealing with Russian media. Specifically, media relations practices should take into consideration that media often exercise self-censorship. Media access is often curtailed and public relations practitioners may frequently find it difficult to access the media. Further, *zakazukha*, cash for editorial publication, is often an ethical dilemma for public relations practitioners.

CONCLUSION

Public relations in Russia has come a long way. This relatively new profession is developing incredibly. Yet, there are many political, social, educational, and cultural peculiarities that can create not only different perceptions of public relations as a field, but also lead to different practices in various metaregions. Contemporary Russian public relations scholars have begun to study and examine these differences so that they can be used to further develop public relations practice and scholarship. In spite of the many problems that contemporary public relations faces in Russia, it continues to be one of the most exciting and fast growing professional areas. Continuous theoretical and practical contributions certainly will help the field grow, and the future of public relations in Russia looks promising.

REGIONAL PUBLIC RELATIONS PRACTICES: A CASE STUDY

This section illustrates some of the concepts and idiosyncracies of Russian public relations practice which, as already stated, vary from metaregion to metaregion. The case study presented here deals with a public relations campaign "KidSoft," whose aim was to promote an annual festival of computer creativity among children and teenagers. The campaign was conceived and implemented in 1998 by the Voronezh regional youth nonprofit organization called "New View" (the European metaregion). The author of this chapter was the head of the public relations department of the organization at the time. This case study demonstrates which public relations practices this nonprofit organization used and how they were adapted to different metaregions, especially to the Moscow/St. Petersburg metaregion.

The "KidSoft" campaign was the biggest project that "New View" had undertaken. The festival had been conducted twice before, in 1996 and 1997. The main feature of the festival was a contest inviting schoolchildren to send their original computer software to the committee. The finalists were chosen by a panel of judges consisting of professional programmers. On the day of the festival, all the finalists were honored with awards, and the winner won a personal computer. There also were a number of small contests and a computer exhibition at the festival. The 1997 festival had attracted about 60 contest participants and about 500 visitors in a single day. In the third year, 1998, the organizing committee of "KidSoft'98" decided to expand the festival by conducting a two-day final event and promoting it at the national level.

Precampaign research showed that enough information was not available to target publics (schoolchildren, volunteers, sponsors, and journalists) about the festival and contests that were a part of the festival. Also, "KidSoft" was unknown outside of the Voronezh region. Further, the fundraising strategies of the client were not well developed, and enough volunteers were not available to help with the organization of the festival. Finally, the media did not pay attention to earlier festivals or to the organization behind the festival—"New View."

Based on this information, several strategies were developed. First, an intense publicity campaign was implemented. Public relations personnel (one full-time specialist, one part-time specialist, and one part-time volunteer) created and distributed press kits to the national, regional, and local media about the festival and about the organization. Seven national media received press kits by mail and three reacted to the kits seeking from the organizational committee more information about the festival and about possibilities of attending the festival. Campaign personnel responded to these reactions with a series of phone calls as well as special news releases via e-mail to these three national media—two broadcasting and one print. Materials about upcoming events were published and aired, and journalists from all three media covered the festival in 1998. All three national media sent representatives to the festival.

It was well-known that the regional and local media in Voronezh do not follow up on press releases and press kits sent to them. So, practitioners personally visited and talked to editors of each medium in order to get publicity and to find journalists who would agree to cover the event. These personal contacts (typified by the personal influence) were proven to be very helpful as journalists from the local media who personally knew public relations practitioners were more willing to publish information.

Fundraising was another big part of this campaign. Efforts included personal meetings with various potential local sponsors. The concept of fundraising was not well developed in Russia, and generally companies did not engage in sponsorship activities. Special hour-long conversations about benefits of sponsorship were developed for potential sponsors.

Volunteer programs were also new to many schoolchildren who were invited through publicity campaigns to participate in the organization of the festival. Many of them did not even know what it means to be a volunteer. Special information sessions about benefits of being a volunteer and a special project "Help KidSoft'98" were implemented. Volunteers were organized in special teams, and each team competed for a grand prize for the best volunteer team. Weekly meetings with workshops on leadership and social activities "Only for our volunteers" were organized.

As a result of these public relations efforts, the number of participants in "KidSoft" increased to more than 100, with participants from seven different regions and three metaregions of Russia. The total number of visitors during the two-day festival reached 4000. In all, 19 national, regional, and local media covered the event, nine of which covered other projects of the organization in separate stories and five of the media published/aired follow-ups on the festival. The number of sponsors doubled and the contest budget was almost tripled.

This public relations campaign had several ingredients that are common to public relations practices in the European metaregion. First, public relations practitioners were actively involved in the local journalistic environment and personally knew journalists, which helped them to get more publicity. Second, practitioners spent a lot of time explaining to various publics such as journalists, sponsors, and volunteers, not only the goals of the project (the festival in this case), but also, more importantly, the *nature of public relations practices per se*. Many asked practitioners about the field of public relations and various practices that are associated with the field. In 1998, there was still a lack of understanding among the general public of what public relations is.

Further, personal meetings with journalists helped promote publicity efforts because most journalists did not know what to do with press kits and news releases. Even today, many journalists from local media hardly see press releases on their desks. Even though practitioners created releases according to national standards, few local journalists wanted to use them as a starting point, preferring instead to base their stories on face-to-face communication with public relations practitioners.

At the same time, journalists from the national media, who were located in Moscow, and from regional media (St. Petersburg youth magazines) were anxious to see press kits and news releases and even requested information in appropriate formats via mail or e-mail. Thus, it was clear that journalists from the Moscow/St. Petersburg metaregion were familiar with media relations practices and expected to have professional relationships with public relations practitioners.

Therefore, one of the major characteristics of Russian public relations is the need to adapt to different publics from different metaregions. When public relations practitioners want to successfully communicate with publics outside of their metaregion, they should know to what extent public relations is developed and practiced in that metaregion. In addition, perceptions and the backgrounds of various publics should be taken into consideration.

Public relations practitioners who plan to work within the Moscow/St. Petersburg metaregion should be ready to practice a Westernized way of public relations; whereas those who practice public relations in other regions should adapt to the well-known and traditionally successful strategies and tactics used in those metaregions. In particular, personal contacts and face-to-face communication are very popular and successful in media relations practices in European and ZaBaikal metaregions (I. Boldonova, personal communication, March 2001) and less popular in Moscow/St. Petersburg and Ural metaregions (T. Korchak, personal communication, March 2002).

REFERENCES

Alyoshina, I. (1997). *Public relations dlja menedgerov i marketerov* [Public relations for managers and marketers]. Moscow: Gnom-press.

Aron, L. (2001). Russia has made a significant progress in achieving democracy. In W. Dudley (Ed.), *Russia: Opposing viewpoints* (pp. 73–82). San Diego, CA: Greenhaven Press.

Belin, L. (2001). Political bias and self-censorship in the Russian media. In A. Brown (Ed.), *Contemporary Russian politics: A reader* (pp. 323–342). Oxford: Oxford University Press.

Botan, C. (1993). A human nature approach to image and ethics in international public relations. *Journal of Public Relations Research, 5*(2), 71–81.

Brown, A. (2001). Evaluating Russia's democratization. In A. Brown (Ed.), *Contemporary Russian politics: A reader* (pp. 546–568). Oxford: Oxford University Press.

Chirkova, A., & Lapina, N. (2001). Political power and political stability in the Russian regions. In A. Brown (Ed.), *Contemporary Russian politics: A reader* (pp. 384–397). Oxford: Oxford University Press.

Clarke, T. M. (2000). An inside look at Russian public relations. *Public Relations Quarterly, 45*(1), 18–22.

Culbertson, H. M., & Chen, N. (Eds.) (1996). *International PR: A comparative analysis.* Mahwah, NJ: Lawrence Erlbaum Associates.

Department of Higher Education of Russian Federation. (2000). *Novyj gosudarstvennyj obrazovatel'nyj standart po spetsial'nosti "Svjazi s obschestvennostiju" (350400)* [New governmental standard in the major "Public Relations." Official document]. Available: http://www.pr-news.spb.ru/

Egorova-Gantman, E., & Pleshakov, K. (1999). *Politicheskaya reklama.* (Political advertising). Moscow: Nikkolo M.

GDF, Glasnost Defense Foundation (1999). *The silent regions.* Moscow: Sashcko Publishing House.

Gudykunst, W. B., Ting-Toomey, S., & Chua, E. (Eds.) (1988). *Culture and interpersonal communication.* Newbury Park, CA: Sage Publications.

Guth, D. W. (2000). The emergence of public relations in the Russian Federation. *Public Relations Review, 26*(2), 191–207.

Jaksa, J. A., & Pritchard, M. S. (1996). Chernobylk revisited. In J. A. Jaksa, & N. S. Pritchard (Eds.), *Responsible communciation: Ethical issues in business, industry, and the professions* (pp. 215–228). Cresskill, NJ: Hampton Press.

Kay, R. (2000). *Russian women and their organizations: Gender, discrimination and grassroots women's organizations, 1991–96.* London: MacMillan Press, Ltd.

Konovalova E. (2000, April). A za PR otvetish' pered . . . sovest'ju. *Electronic version of magazine Sovetnik* [On-line serial]. Available at http://www.sovetnik.ru/archive/2000/4/article.asp?id=2, September 2, 2000.

Kruckeberg, D. (1992). Ethical decision-making in public relations. *International Public Relations Review, 15*(4), 32–37.

Lankina, T. (2001). Local government and ethnic and social activism in Russia. In A. Brown (Ed.), *Contemporary Russian politics: A reader* (pp. 398–411). Oxford: Oxford University Press.

Lincoln, W. B. (2001). Russia's history and culture preclude the creation of a democratic society. In W. Dudley (Ed.), *Russia: Opposing viewpoints* (pp. 83–89). San Diego, CA: Greenhaven Press.

Maksimov, A. A. (1999). "Chistye" i "gryaznye" teknologii vyborov: Rossijskij opyt. Moscow: Delo.

McElreath, M., Chen, N., Azariva, L., & Shadrova, V. (2001). The development of public relations in China, Russia, and the United States. In R. L. Heath (Ed.), *Handbook of public relations* (pp. 665–673). Thousand Oaks, CA: Sage Publications, Inc.

Miroshnichenko, A. A. (1998). Public relations v obschestvenno-politiçheskoj sphere. Moscow: Ekspertnoe buro.

Newsom, D., Turk, J. V., & Kruckeberg, D. (2000). *This is PR: The realities of public relations* (7th ed.). Belmont, CA: Wadsworth/Thompson Learning.

Novinskij, B (2000). PR: nauka ili remeslo? *RUPR* [Online]. Available at http://www.rupr.ru/news/173192.html?section=articles, February 3, 2001.

Pankratov, F. G., Bazhenov, Y. K., Seregina, T. M., & Shakhurin, V. G. (2001). *Reklamnaya deyatelnost.* (Advertising activities). Moscow: Informatsionno-vnedrencheskij tsentr "Marketing."

Pheophanov, O. (2001). *Reklama: Novye texnologii v Rossii.* (Advertising: New technologies in Russia). St. Petersburg: Piter.

Pocheptsov, G. (1998). *Public relations, ili kak uspeshno upravljat'* obschestvennym mneniem. (Public relations, or how to manage public opinion successfully) Moskva: Tsentr.

Pocheptsov, G. (2001). Public relations dlya professionalov. (Public relations for professionals). Moscow: REEFL-Book.

PR News (2001). Online Periodical Journal. [Online]. Available at http://www.prnews.ru/news, November 2, 2001.

Pratkanis A., & Aronson, E. (1991) *Age of propaganda.* New York: W. H. Freeman.

Richmond, Y. (1996). *From nyet to da: Understanding the Russians* (2nd ed.). Yarmouth, ME: Intercultural Press.

Solzhenitsyn, A. (2001). Russia has failed to achieve true democracy. In W. Dudley (Ed.), *Russia: Opposing viewpoints* (pp. 66–72). San Diego, CA: Greenhaven Press, Inc.

Sriramesh, K., & White, J. (1992). Societal culture and public relations. In J. E. Grunig (Ed.), *Excellence in public relations and communication management,* (pp. 597–616). Mahwah, NJ: Lawrence Erlbaum.

Sutherland, A. (2001). PR thrives in harder times. *Frontline, IPRA, 23,* p. 52.

Taylor, M. (2001). International public relations: Opportunities and challenges for the 21st century. In R. L. Heath (Ed.), *Handbook of public relations* (pp. 629–637). Thousand Oaks, CA: Sage.

Ting-Toomey, S. (1999). *Communicating across cultures.* New York: Guilford.

Tsetsura, E. Y. (2000a). *Conceptual frameworks in the field of public relations: A comparative study of Russian and United States perspectives.* Unpublished master's thesis, Fort Hays State University, Hays, KS.

Tsetsura, K. (2000b, March). *Understanding the "evil" nature of public relations as perceived by some Russian publics.* Paper presented at the Annual Interdisciplinary International PRSA Educators Academy Conference, Miami, FL.

Tsetsura, K. (2001, March). *Can ethics in public relations finally become international? Dialogic communication as basis for a new universal code of ethics in public relations.* Paper presented at the 4th PRSA Educators Academy international interdisciplinary conference, Miami.

Tsetsura, K. (2002, April). *Use and abuse of freedom of information: Monitoring freedom of speech in Russian media.* Paper presented at the Central States Communication Association convention, Milwaukee, WI.

Tsetsura, K., & Kruckeberg, D. (in press). Contemporary Russian journalism: problems and opportunities. In A. S. de Beer & J. C. Merrill (Ed.), *Global Journalism*, 4th ed. Longman.

Tulchinsky, G. L. (1994). *Public relations: Reputatsija, vlijanie, cvjazi s pressoj I obschestvennostiju, sponsorstvo*. St. Petersburg: St. Petersburg GAK.

Tulupov, V. V. (1996) . Public relations in Russia as a new social institution. *Speeches of conference "Public relations in Russia today and tomorrow"* (pp. 17–21). Voronezh, Russia: Voronezh State University.

Varustin, L. E. (2000, summer). Sistema obrazovanija public relations pered novym vyborom. *Online newspaper PR News* [On-line serial]. Available at http://www.pr-news.spb.ru/, November 5, 2001.

PART

IV

The Americas

16

PUBLIC RELATIONS IN THE UNITED STATES: A GENERATION OF MATURATION

LARISSA A. GRUNIG
JAMES E. GRUNIG

Writing a chapter characterizing public relations in the United States is daunting. We accepted this invitation with trepidation. We did not write this chapter in an attempt to galvanize opinion within the academic community of public relations worldwide. Understanding that risk, we did our best to avoid the arrogance that so endears North Americans to the rest of the world. Instead, we tried to stake out a position apart from those whose work legitimately might be characterized as ethnocentric.

Most especially, we do not consider public relations professionals and scholars on other continents imitators rather than innovators. Countries like Germany, for example, have a century-plus history of scholarship and practice in the field. Other countries in which public relations has developed more recently, such as Slovenia, already offer a fecund body of knowledge and sophisticated, highly professional practice. Still others, such as South Africa, are developing democracies that often find themselves in crisis; thus, they are pushed to create solutions that their counterparts around the world will emulate. Finally, giants, such as China and Russia, by their sheer size undoubtedly will produce an exceptional body of theoretical and applied work as soon as public relations educational programs there become a critical mass.

In this chapter, we emphasize the importance of the triad of knowledge, shared expectations between the dominant coalition and public relations, and the organizational context in United States public relations practice. To whom do these considerations relate? They relate to nearly 200,000 practitioners who work in this field in the United States, for sure. Beyond that, we believe that the implications of research we have conducted over the last 17 years are significant for public relations colleagues in other parts of the world.

The Excellence theory (Dozier, L. A. Grunig, & J. E. Grunig, 1995; J. E. Grunig, 1992; L. A. Grunig, J. E. Grunig, & Dozier, 2002) seems to work for North America and at least parts of Europe as well.

We offer the criteria we developed and tested in the Excellence study as a set of generic principles for effective public relations practice. These criteria require knowledge and professionalism by the public relations unit. They also require understanding of and support for public relations by senior management. The characteristics of an excellent public relations function can be placed into five categories that are discussed in the following sections.

EMPOWERMENT OF THE FUNCTION

For public relations to contribute to organizational effectiveness, the organization must empower communication as a critical management function. Empowerment of the public relations function subsumes four characteristics of excellent practice. The first three consider the relationship of communication to the overall management of the organization:

- The senior executive in public relations is involved with the strategic management processes of the organization, and communication programs are developed for strategic publics identified as a part of this strategic management process. Public relations contributes to strategic management by scanning the environment to identify publics affected by the consequences of decisions or who might affect the outcome of decisions. An excellent public relations department communicates with these publics to bring their voices into strategic management, thus making it possible for publics to participate in organizational decisions that affect them.

- Communication programs organized by excellent departments to communicate with strategic publics also are managed strategically. To be managed strategically means that these programs are based on formative research, have concrete and measurable objectives, use varied rather than routine techniques when they are implemented, and are evaluated either formally or informally. In addition, the communication staff can provide evidence to show that these programs achieved their short-term objectives and improved the long-term relationships between the organization and its publics.

- The top communicator is a member of the dominant coalition of the organization or has a direct reporting relationship to senior managers who are part of the dominant coalition. The public relations function seldom will be involved in strategic management and public relations practitioners will not have the power to affect key organizational decisions unless the senior public relations executive is part of or has access to the group of senior managers with the greatest power in the organization.

The fourth characteristic of empowerment defines the extent to which practitioners who are not White men are empowered:

- Diversity is embodied in all public relations roles. The principle of requisite variety (Weick, 1979) suggests that organizations need as much diversity inside as outside if they are to interact successfully with all strategic elements of their environment. Excellent public relations departments empower both men and women in all roles as well as practitioners of diverse racial, ethnic, and cultural backgrounds.

COMMUNICATOR ROLES

Public relations researchers (e.g., Broom, 1982; Dozier & Broom, 1995) have conducted extensive research on two major roles that communicators play in organizations—the manager and the technician. Communication technicians are essential to carry out most of the day-to-day communication activities of public relations departments, and many practitioners—especially women (Toth & L. A. Grunig, 1993)—enact both roles. In less excellent departments, however, all of the communication practitioners—including the senior practitioner—are technicians. If the senior communicator is not a manager, it is not possible for public relations to be empowered as a management function. Three characteristics of excellence in public relations are related to the managerial role:

- A strategic manager rather than a technician or an administrative manager heads the public relations unit. Excellent public relations operations must have at least one senior communication manager who conceptualizes and directs public relations programs, or other members of the dominant coalition who have little knowledge of communication management or of relationship building will supply this direction. In addition, the results of the Excellence study distinguished between two types of senior managers: a strategic manager and an administrative manager. Administrative managers typically manage day-to-day operations of the communication function, personnel, and the budget. They generally are supervisors of technicians rather than strategic managers. If the head of public relations is an administrative manager rather than a strategic manager, the department usually will not be excellent.

- The senior public relations executive or others in the public relations unit must have the knowledge needed for the manager role or the communication function will not have the potential to become a managerial function. Excellent public relations programs are staffed by professionals—practitioners who have gained the knowledge needed to carry out the manager role through university education, continuing education, or self-study.

- Both men and women must have equal opportunity to occupy the managerial role. The majority of public relations professionals in the United States are women. Research (L. A. Grunig, Toth, & Hon, 2000) also has established that female practitioners are the best educated in this field and most likely to take advantage of professional development opportunities. If women are excluded from the managerial role, the communication function may be diminished because the majority of the most knowledgeable practitioners will be excluded from that role. When that is the case, the senior position in the public relations department typically is filled by a technician or by a practitioner from another managerial function who has little knowledge of public relations.

ORGANIZATION OF THE COMMUNICATION FUNCTION AND ITS RELATIONSHIP TO OTHER MANAGEMENT FUNCTIONS

Many organizations have a single department devoted to all communication functions. Others have separate departments for programs aimed at different publics such as journalists, employees, the local community, or the financial community. Still others place communication under another managerial function such as marketing, human resources, legal, or finance. Many organizations also contract or consult with outside firms for all or some of their communication programs or for communication techniques such as annual reports or newsletters. Two characteristics are related to the organization of the function:

- Public relations should be an integrated communication function. An excellent public relations function integrates all public relations programs into a single department or provides a mechanism for coordinating programs managed by different departments. Only in an integrated system is it possible for public relations to develop new communication programs for changing strategic publics and to move resources from outdated programs designed for formerly strategic publics to the new programs.

- Public relations should be a management function separate from other functions. Although the function is integrated in an excellent organization, the function should not be placed in another department whose primary responsibility is a management function other than communication. Many organizations splinter the public relations function by making communication a supporting tool for other departments such as marketing. When the public relations function is sublimated to other functions, it cannot be managed strategically because it cannot move communication resources from one strategic public to another—as an integrated function can.

MODELS OF PUBLIC RELATIONS

Public relations scholars (beginning with J. E. Grunig, 1984) have conducted extensive research on the extent to which organizations practice four models of public relations— four typical ways of conceptualizing and conducting the communication function—and to identify which of these models provides a normative framework for effective and ethical practice. This research suggests that excellent departments design more of their communication programs on the two-way symmetrical model of collaboration and public participation than on three other typical models: press agentry (emphasizing only favorable publicity), public information (disclosing accurate information but engaging in no research or other form of two-way communication), or two-way asymmetrical (emphasizing only the interests of the organization and not the interests of publics).

Two-way symmetrical public relations is based on research and uses communication to enhance public participation and to manage conflict with strategic publics. As a result, two-way symmetrical communication produces better long-term relationships with publics than do the other models. Symmetrical programs generally are conducted more ethically than are other models and, as a result, produce effects that balance the interests of organizations and the publics in society. Four characteristics of excellence are related to these models:

- The public relations department and the dominant coalition share the worldview that the communication department should base its goals and its communication activities on the two-way symmetrical model.

- Communication programs developed for specific publics are based on two-way symmetrical strategies for building and maintaining relationships.

- The senior public relations executive or others in the unit must have the professional knowledge needed to practice the two-way symmetrical model.

- The organization should have a symmetrical system of internal communication. A symmetrical system of internal communication is based on the principles of employee empowerment and participation in decision making. Managers and other employees engage in dialogue and listen to each other. Internal publications disclose relevant information needed by employees to understand their role in the organization and to provide employees with a voice to management. Symmetrical communication within an organization fosters a participative rather than an authoritarian culture as well as improved relationships with employees—greater employee satisfaction, control mutuality, commitment, and trust.[1]

ETHICS

Finally, we determined that incorporating ethics and social responsibility into practice is necessary for public relations to achieve excellence. We (L. A. Grunig et al., 2002, p. 554) acknowledged that elaborating on this final principle requires additional research, but even now we understand that public relations practitioners frequently serve as the ethics officers or consciences of their organizations. Why? Public relations is the function that introduces the values and problems of stakeholders into strategic decisions and that establishes a moral element in those decisions.

It may be early to celebrate the implications of the Excellence theory. The project, begun in 1985, was completed with the publication of the third and final book in the series in 2002 (L. A. Grunig et al., 2002). Already, however, it serves as the organizational framework for this book. Results of that research are woven throughout this chapter.

Clichéd though it may be, we contend that at no time in our country's history has public relations counsel based on solid research and theorizing been more important. In the wake of the attacks of September 11, 2001, and financial mismanagement scandals on the part of major United States corporations, the role of corporate conscience (Edelman, 2002) enacted by educated, professional communicators should be central. Some aspects of this societal context encourage that approach to public relations; others, as detailed next, constrain it.

INFRASTRUCTURE

The United States of America is a land of more than 3.6 million square miles (9.4 million sq km) on the continent of North America. It consists of 50 states, 48 of them contiguous. They are bordered by Canada to the north, Mexico and the Gulf of Mexico to the south, the Atlantic Ocean to the east, and the Pacific Ocean to the west. The state of Hawaii is in the Pacific, southwest of California; Alaska is northwest of Canada. There are several territories and possessions in the Caribbean Sea and the Pacific Ocean, in addition to these states.

Washington, DC, is the capital. Other large cities familiar to people from abroad include New York, Los Angeles, Chicago, Houston, Philadelphia, San Diego, Detroit, Dallas, Phoenix, and San Antonio. The population, according to the 2000 United States Bureau of the Census, is 281,421,906. (About 197,000 of these people are public relations practitioners; United States Department of Labor, 1998.) The population is increasingly heterogeneous—creating an immense challenge for public relations professionals and the U.S. organizations that employ them. The primary language is English; although in some cities (e.g., Los Angeles), more students enter the school system speaking Spanish than English as their native tongue.

---

[1]The generic principles of excellence as presented here are taken largely from J. E. Grunig and L. A. Grunig (2001).

Political System

The United States of America is a democracy. Sovereign power is vested in the citizenry as a whole indirectly through elected representatives. Guiding principles of our 2 centuries plus of constitutional self-government include equality of rights, opportunity, and treatment. Equality relates to everyone, without privileges of rank or heredity. Citizens hold dear the notion of the "common people," in reference to political power. (Of course, as Toth's, 2002, essay on postmodern public relations asserted, no single ideology such as democracy exists.)

After the American Revolution in 1776, the states functioned under the Articles of Confederation for 12 years. By1789, representatives of several states had met in Philadelphia and wrote and adopted the more structured Constitution. The United States Constitution calls for three branches of government: executive, judicial, and legislative. (These branches serve as a system of checks and balances on each other.) Congress is composed of two parts. In the Senate, states enjoy equal representation (two legislators per state). Population determines representation in the House of Representatives.

Here is what historian of public relations Cutlip (1995) had to say about the significance of the approval of the Constitution for public relations in the United States:

> The monumental struggle Alexander Hamilton, James Madison, and John Jay waged to win ratification of the United States Constitution, which governs our lives to this day, demonstrates far better than any other public relations campaign the far-reaching effect of public relations' unseen power. Allan Nevins was not exaggerating when he termed this campaign "the greatest work ever done in the field of public relations." (p. 280)

A mere 2 years after its passage, concerned that the Constitution did not protect certain freedoms, citizens pressed for change. The Bill of Rights resulted. The first of these 10 amendments includes the freedoms of speech, the press, and "the right of the people peaceably to assemble" (cited in Jordan, 2002, p. 45). All three aspects of the First Amendment[2] have important implications for United States practitioners of public relations.

Together with its 10 amendments, the Constitution makes possible our advocacy role in public relations. The freedom of speech,[3] freedom of thought, and freedom of assembly all guarantee, in turn, the right of public relations practitioners to represent all points of view in this democratic marketplace of ideas.

However, according to political communication expert Parry-Giles (quoted in Sherman, 2002), democracy is a "vision premised upon interaction between the voter and the leader" (p. 2). At this point in the republic's history, he said, concerned citizens are searching for alternatives to the standard debates and town hall meetings to understand candidates' stances on issues and to stimulate voters to go to the polls. The interaction between political candidates and constituents has become limited for two main reasons, he explained: Politicians want to control the message, and the media that report on the message are imperfect surrogates for the public voice.

---

[2]A good, current reference to the First Amendment can be found in Farber (2002). It includes discussion of the Internet and other electronic media as well as new federal restrictions on soft money in political campaigns and national security issues after 9/11.

[3]There are constraints on these rights, which are discussed in the portion of this chapter that deals with media. Constraints include "fighting words," defamation, and privacy.

Corporate political expression is controlled in the United States, particularly through the Federal Election Campaign Act of 1970. This act limits what organizations—as well as individuals—can contribute to a candidate's campaign. However, corporations can make partisan statements to their stockholders and can sponsor appearances by candidates. Furthermore, they and their unions may help employees contribute to candidates' campaigns by setting up political action committees. This allows corporations significant say in the outcome of elections.

Also, citizens at large have the right to petition the government; when this is done in the halls of the legislature, it is called *lobbying*. In the past, lobbying meant such unethical practices as bribery; today, it more typically involves providing information to legislative aides—information that may prove influential in future votes. Since 1946, lobbyists must register with Congress and file quarterly statements that reveal their expenses and sources of funding. Since the Foreign Agents Registration Act passed in 1938,[4] lobbyists representing other governments must register with the United States government as well.[5]

Legal System

Individual voices, in fact all manner of individual liberties, are protected by the county's supreme legal document: the United States Constitution. Under the Constitution, every aspect of governmental action is codified. Laws are deduced from the principle of rights— rights of the people, rather than rights of the government. Thus, the government's actions as well as the actions of its citizens are regulated under the rule of law. The rule of law, rather than the rule of people with their whimsies or hereditary privilege, even protects the rights of what the country considers to be the smallest possible minority: that of individuals.

The legal system in the United States protects its citizens' rights through three main entities. The *military* protects the country from outside invaders. *Police forces* protect from domestic criminals. The *court system* settles legal disputes and sentences criminals to punishment according to predefined laws and interpretations thereof. The United States Supreme Court serves as the ultimate arbiter.

Public relations functions in an increasingly legal environment in the United States. Sexual harassment, all forms of discrimination, and abuses of labor are growing concerns. So, too, are issues of the quality and safety of products and of protection of the environment while producing those goods. New communication technology makes organizations increasingly vulnerable to charges that they are violating those norms of safety, quality, and fairness.

Public relations practitioners in publicly traded companies need to understand financial reporting requirements of the Securities and Exchange Commission, established in 1934. Major considerations include the need to prepare and distribute annual reports and to disclose information in a timely way and prohibitions related to issuing prospectuses encouraging investors to buy stock.

One final legal consideration for public relations practitioners in the United States is the copyright statute, originally passed in 1909 and revised in 1976,[6] which protects the

---

[4]The act was amended in 1966 to require disclosure by agents engaged in public relations, politics, financial negotiations, consultancies, or other activities on behalf of other governments (Kennedy, 1966).

[5]Diplomats, officials of other governments, journalists for United States publications, and people involved in charitable or religious activities are exempt from registering.

[6]The revision took into account technological developments such as photocopying, cable television, and videotaping.

original author of a work. Copyright law determines whether others can use not only written materials such as brochures or press releases but music and video clips as well. Fair use of copyrighted work depends on the purpose (nonprofit or commercial), the nature of that work, the amount to be used in relation to the entire work, and the effect of use on the market value of the copyrighted material.

Economic System

The motto of the United States democracy is "In God we trust." A typical sign displayed in small enterprises plays on this motto: "In God we trust; everyone else pays cash." Indeed, capitalism is a dominant feature of the U.S. infrastructure. (As with democracy, Toth, 2002, argued that postmodernists dismiss the possibility of any dominant ideology such as capitalism.)

Most U.S. means of production and distribution are privately owned. Indeed, capitalism is a social as well as economic system based on the principle of individual rights. Contemporary capitalism, in the United States and elsewhere, is characterized by privatization, employee ownership, and industry. Enterprises are operated for profit, under competitive conditions for the most part. In 1997, the U.S. gross domestic product was $7,824,008 million.

Capitalism has been consistent with the U.S. political ideal of achieving the common good (Gianaris, 1996; Greenberg, 1985). Increasingly, however, activists are questioning the moral justification for capitalism (van Parijs, 1997). In particular, they challenge the globalization of capitalism (Maitra, 1996). As we were developing this chapter, for example, protestors were massing in the nation's capital, Washington, DC, to demonstrate against the International Monetary Fund and the World Bank.

Activism

Sam Adams and his daring band of revolutionaries were among the earliest activists in what would become the United States of America. The Sons of Liberty formed an activist group determined to change the government from outside its structure. Since then, grassroots activists have prospered under the country's democracy and its free press. The country's individualistic culture, too, has contributed to the sense here that the work of each individual can help change a system that is not working. However, public relations practitioners have been accused of co-opting environmental activists, in particular, "under the veil of grassroots democracy" (Holtzhausen, 2002, p. 258).

For a very current analysis of the growing social activism in the United States, see Crespo (2002). This photojournalist brought together his own experience as well as essays from organizers of such actions as the Million Mom March and protests against the death penalty, the World Trade Organization, Haitian immigration, and logging of the country's redwood forests.

Lerbinger (2001) explored the relationship between contemporary public relations and these types of activism, concentrating on the period that began in the 1960s when social movements such as civil rights, environmentalism, and feminism became better organized than ever before. As a result of concurrent regulation of big business (and media coverage thereof), corporations relied heavily on public affairs to monitor their socio/political environment. Lerbinger credited this development with leading to increased appreciation for and sophistication of public relations practice.

The Excellence project (L. A. Grunig et al., 2002) found much the same thing: One characteristic of effective public relations is the ability to deal with activist groups. Those external constituencies push the organization to improve, to become more competitive, and—in short—to excellence.

MEDIA ENVIRONMENT

As described in chapter 1, one of the first attempts to link the mass media (radio, television, and newspapers) with society and its political system was Siebert, Peterson, and Schramm's (1963) *Four Theories of the Press*. The United States fell under what they called the *libertarian theory*,[7] also known as the *free press*. The idea is that individuals should be free to publish whatever they want. Thus, attacks on government are common, even encouraged. The media are thought to play a watchdog role over government.

Since then, the work of Siebert and his colleagues (1963) has been widely studied, accepted, and critiqued. For example, Skjerdal (1993) condemned these four normative theories used to illustrate the press' position relative to its political environment as outdated and overly simplistic. Altschull (1984) attempted to improve on the four theories by reducing them to three and adding a development component; in his view, journalism throughout the First World (including, of course, the United States) corresponds to the liberal system.[8]

Hachten (1992) added one kind of media system, identifying a total of five types found throughout the world. They are authoritarian, Communist, revolutionary, developmental, and Western. The latter is the system people in the United States and Western Europe[9] have come to equate with freedom of the press. Ownership of broadcast and print media is private, and the government cannot interfere with reporting. In this system, journalists have the right to "talk politics" (p. 19). In return, they are expected to report responsibly.

However, the press in general has been accused of keeping U.S. citizens in the dark and impotent because of growing concentration and commercialization of our mass media. Pseudoevents like Media Democracy Day have been designed to promote an alternative system, one that informs and empowers all members of society. Media Democracy's web site (http://www.communicationism.org/mediademocracyday.org/home) "prioritizes diversity over monopoly, citizen control over corporate choice, cultural development over company profit, and public discourse over public relations."

Despite these and similar criticisms, the notion of the "free press" of the United States is touted worldwide. We put "free press" in quotation marks because the reality, as Skjerdal (1993) pointed out, is that even the U.S. media system contains elements of authoritarianism. He cited Kamen's (1991) analysis of coverage of the Gulf War as evidence of U.S. reporters being required to run battlefield stories past government censors before being dispatched. Nevertheless, the Constitution guarantees the right to free speech,[10] and the government rarely controls the media directly. At the same time, any number of influences shapes media coverage. Public relations is prominent among them.

Most introductory textbooks in the field point out to student readers that nearly one half of the mainstream media's daily content comes from public relation sources. That

---

[7]The other three theories are *authoritarian*, in which the state controls the media; *Soviet*, closely tied to Communist ideology; and *social responsibility*, which emphasizes the media's obligations to (a diverse) society.

[8]Other prominent media scholars who took on the four theories include Lowenstein and Merrill (1990), Martin and Chaudhary (1983), McLeod and Blumler (1989), and McQuail (1987).

[9]Hachten considered this Western concept rare; it exists in few countries outside the United States and Western Europe.

[10]Exceptions include some cases of speech that interferes with war effort (e.g., troop movements in times of war), false statements of fact, incitement or provoking others to violence (including speech advocating crime), threats, appropriation of speech owned by others, invasion of privacy, child pornography, and obscenity.

content, of course, is not necessarily neutral. Like Skjerdal (1993) before him, Cutlip (1995) provided this instance: "The United States military's control of the news of the Gulf War with Iraq in 1991 was a perfect example [*sic*] how news sources, guided by public relations officials, can control and shape the news with the truth a casualty" (p. 283).

This spin on the news provided by public affairs or public relations sources determined to influence public opinion is played out in all forms of media, print and broadcast. Cutlip (1995) alluded to what he called "talk show democracy" (p. 283) in the U.S. news radio.

What about media access? Daily newspaper circulation at the turn of the recent century was 212 per 1,000 people; there were 806 television receivers per 1,000 inhabitants at that same point. (*World Statistics Pocketbook*, 2001).[11] It is hard to imagine any limits. Nearly 10 years ago, even before the information superhighway had ventured into every hill and vale of the country, Cutlip (1995) wrote the following:

> Today's Washington is wired for quadrophonic [*sic*] sound and wide screen video, swamped by fax, computer messages, 800 numbers, and CNN to every citizen in every village in the nation. Its every act or failure to act to [*sic*] blared to the public thanks to C-Span, open-meeting laws, financial disclosure reports, and campaign spending rules, and its every misstep is logged in a database for use of future opponents. (pp. 283–84)

Like radio, saturation of television has important implications for public relations and, for one recent critic (Sanders, 2002), for democracy itself. In Sanders' view, deregulation and ownership by corporate conglomerates have changed television from an information to an entertainment medium in this country. Hollihan (2001) went so far as to suggest that democracy is facing a crisis in light of television's effects on political campaigning: increased cost, higher level of entertainment, more ethical issues, greater cynicism on the part of the public, and decreased political participation.

Even in this era of specialized and online publications, most people in the United States get their news from the mass media such as television and newspapers. Furthermore, what citizens learn from electronic news sources is questionable. In the context of political communication, for instance, sound bites provide little fodder for deep discussion of critical issues. For this reason, groups such as the University of Maryland's Center for Political Communication and Civic Leadership are experimenting with different approaches to mediated campaign information. The center, for example, recently hosted a "Recovering Democracy Forum," wherein gubernatorial candidates were invited to join a range of citizens (including community activists, students, and political leaders) for facilitated and meaningful dialogue. Even so, one founder of the center explained, traditional broadcast media still attract viewers to political news: "It's like gladiators. You want to see who's going to get bloodied up" (Parry-Giles, quoted in Sherman, 2002).

The United States has been at the forefront of the information revolution. Television and Internet consumption and their concomitant influence on social and cultural habits have been attributed to Americanization. However, sages (Nye, 2002) emphasize that correlation is not causation; the United States simply introduced computers at a faster rate than did many other countries. Given today's worldwide immersion in this information medium, the United States influence on culture is likely to diminish.

---

[11]Compare these numbers from the *World Statistics Pocketbook* (2001) with Slovenia, for just one example, where newspaper circulation in 1999 was 199 per 1,000 people and—strikingly different from U.S. figures—television receivers were 356 per 1,000 people.

SOCIETAL CULTURE

Many U.S. practitioners of public relations work in multinational companies. They must be able to understand and interpret cultures other than their own. As retired French practitioner Jacques Coup de Frejac (1991) said, most important, multinational communicators need:

> A new "intelligence" of other cultures. I consider the building blocks of culture to be all the historical, religious, ideological, social and human elements which constitute the heritage of individuals, tribes and people. There cannot be any good Public Relations without a careful appraisal of others in order to be in harmony with their culture. (p. 23)

Societal culture, what Hofstede (1984) called "the collective programming of the mind which distinguishes the members of one human group from another" (p. 21), is based on what he considered mental programs. Hofstede explained that individuals organize what they know, believe, and expect into these mental programs. When groups of individuals share the programs, he added, we call them a culture.

Organizations as well as societies have cultures; organizational culture can have a strong effect on how public relations is practiced. Adler (2002) pointed out that many managers of multinational organizations believe, therefore, that organizational culture will "moderate or erase the influence of national culture" (p. 67). This would mean that managers could ignore the cultures outside a multinational organization as long as they create and maintain a strong internal culture. Research, Adler said, shows otherwise: "Employees and managers *do* bring their ethnicity to the workplace" (p. 67).

Tixier (1993) found also that culture affects public relations. She studied 40 companies in 11 countries and found that different cultures see the role of communication differently. For less developed countries, she found, communicators often simply copy models of public relations from more developed countries. But cultures, she said, "play an increasingly obvious role as countries reach a greater degree of development" (p. 30).

Language also is an integral part of culture. Anyone who wants to be a global public relations practitioner should learn at least one language other than his or her own, even though English has become essentially the language of international relations. Wouters (1991) expressed the importance of language well:

> Command of other languages for Americans is undeniably increasing in importance as an international mentality spreads . . . willingness to learn other languages shows a sophistication and appreciation of other cultures that is still desperately needed in the United States. Even if the language is not essential to the transaction of business, it has always been an asset. (p. 98)

Although it is important for global public relations practitioners to understand the cultures in which they work, the task would be impossible unless a way is found to identify similarities among cultures that can be classified in some way. It may help to understand the need for such a classification by comparing the numbers of cultures with the numbers of individuals affected by an organization. Practitioners cannot deal with every individual affected by an organization, so they group them into types of publics that respond to organizational consequences in different ways. We must do the same with cultures: Look for types of cultures that require different applications of the generic principles of excellence.

For many years, anthropologists have identified different dimensions of cultures. However, the Dutch organizational researcher Geert Hofstede (1984) developed a set of dimensions of culture that have been used widely by management scholars—including public relations scholars—to study the effect of culture on behavior in organizations. He developed these dimensions by studying theories of anthropologists. Then he tested the concepts by using them to measure cultural differences among employees of a U.S.-based multinational corporation—which he called HERMES—in 39 countries. These dimensions explicate cultural effects on public relations. The dimensions and their implications for public relations are discussed in the following sections.

Individualism or Collectivism

Societies range on a continuum from highly individual to highly collective. This dimension describes how individuals relate to larger groups such as extended families, tribes, or organizations. In individualistic cultures, people define their self-worth by their personal achievements and individual welfare. In collectivist cultures, people define their worth in relationship to larger groups. Individualistic societies value competition; collectivist societies value collaboration and teamwork.

In his study of HERMES employees, Hofstede (1984) found that the United States was the most individualistic of the 39 countries. In his reanalysis of the original data, Hofstede (2001) found that the United States still ranked first out of the 50 countries and 3 regions included in that second calculation. He pointed out that individualism correlates with the extent of economic development.

Given the logic of this dimension, the generic characteristics of excellent public relations—especially symmetrical communication and social responsibility—would seem more likely to be adopted in collectivist cultures. This may explain why asymmetrical models of public relations continue to be popular in the United States, for example, and why the symmetrical model may be valued more in Europe and Asia. Practically, it also may mean that public relations practitioners may have to explain the value of symmetrical communication and social responsibility in individual terms in individualistic countries—that communicating symmetrically and being concerned about others also is good for the self-interest of the organization and the people in it.

Power Distance

This dimension describes how cultures deal with inequality. Some cultures are more likely than others to accept an inequitable distribution of power, prestige, and wealth among different classes or groups. In cultures with high power distance, employees are more likely to accept a centralized work arrangement where superiors make all decisions. When power distance is low, management is decentralized and subordinates make more of their own decisions. Hofstede (1984) found the United States ranked just below the midpoint. That ranking changed little in his (2001) reanalysis; the United States ranked 40th out of the 50 countries and 3 regions in terms of power distance.

The greater the power distance, the more difficult it would be to implement the generic principles of public relations. Senior management, for example, would seem less likely to treat public relations managers as equals—thus relegating public relations to a technical support function and excluding it from strategic management. Symmetrical communication works best when power distance is low—especially a symmetrical system of internal communication. Tayeb (1988), for example, found that employee commitment to the organization and the level of interpersonal trust were lowest when power distance is high. Likewise, organizations would value both diversity and social responsibility less when power distance is high.

The generic principles can be applied when power distance is high, but they must be introduced slowly—as Verčič, L. A. Grunig, and J. E. Grunig (1996) found practitioners were doing in Slovenia. If introduced in small increments, the generic principles then can help gradually to lower the power distance in organizations where societal culture accepts high-power distance.

Uncertainty Avoidance

This dimension of culture refers to the extent to which people in a society can tolerate uncertain, ambiguous situations. When uncertainty avoidance is high, people tend to be dogmatic and authoritarian. They also formulate many rules to reduce uncertainty. They are likely to stay in one job for their lifetime. When uncertainty avoidance is low, people are more open to new ideas, new situations, and diversity. According to Hofstede's (1984) initial study, the United States (along with Canada and the United Kingdom, the countries included in the Excellence study) were ranked in the bottom third of all countries studied on this dimension. As with the first two dimensions, the U.S. ranking changed little with Hofstede's (2001) recalculation: The United States was 43rd out of the 53 countries and regions ranked.

Also like the first two characteristics, high-uncertainty avoidance makes application of the generic principles difficult. Diversity introduces uncertainty. As part of strategic management, public relations introduces requisite variety—uncertainty. Symmetrical public relations brings organizational change—more uncertainty. In these situations, public relations practitioners again must introduce uncertainty in small doses and must research their proposals for change as thoroughly as possible to reduce the uncertainty of what they propose. If they do, practitioners still should be able to introduce gradual change in societies that avoid it.

Masculinity and Femininity

Masculine cultures value assertiveness, making money, and acquiring possessions. Feminine cultures value relationships, concern for others, and quality of life. In addition, women occupy fewer managerial roles in masculine cultures than in feminine cultures. According to Hofstede's (1984) original study, the United States was about one third of the way from the highest level of masculinity. It ranked 15th out of 53 in his (2001) reanalysis.

Obviously, the generic principles such as symmetrical communication, diversity, and social responsibility fit better with feminine than masculine cultures. Again, however, they can be introduced incrementally in masculine cultures to change them gradually.

In the second edition of *Culture's Consequences*, Hofstede (2001) reanalyzed his data for 50 countries (rather than the initial 39) and 3 regions. Thus, the new rankings place each country in relation to 52 other areas. Hofstede also added a fifth dimension of culture— long-term orientation (LTO) versus short-term orientation (STO).

LTO Versus STO

Like the initial four dimensions, LTO versus STO was empirically found and validated (Hofstede, 2001). It reflects a choice of focus for people's efforts: future or present. LTO reflects Confucian values of persistence, thrift, personal stability, and respect for tradition. Not surprising, it was found in answers to questions to the Chinese Value Survey of 1985 (samples came from 23 countries, including the United States). Also not surprising, East Asian countries scored highest; Western countries generally scored on the low side. More specifically, the United States ranked 17th out of the 23 countries (cited in Hofstede, 2001).

Implications for U.S. public relations practice are found primarily in the area of relationships. According to Hofstede (2001), low LTO is associated with the expectation of quick results and the sense that the most important events in life have occurred in the past or occur at present. One key difference between it and high LTO is, in business, short-term results: what Hofstede (2001, p. 366) called "the bottom line" so important to cultures with short-term orientation. By contrast, LTO is associated with the sense that most important events will occur in future and—most significantly—with the building of relationships and market position in business. Thus, public relations practitioners in the United States, with its emphasis on short-term results, may face an uphill battle in convincing top management of the importance of relationship building because cultivating relationships is an inherently long-term process.

We looked at each of Hofstede's (2001) five dimensions individually, but they do interact. Some cultures may have characteristics favorable to the generic concepts on some dimensions but not on others. The United States—with its high individualism; moderately low power distance, uncertainty avoidance, and LTO; and moderately high masculinity—does not have a culture particularly conducive to the generic principles, which may explain why so many U.S. practitioners favor an asymmetrical model and a technical role, do not value diversity, and frequently have lapses in ethics and social responsibility.

Culture shapes public relations, but public relations can help to change culture. To do so, however, the generic principles from the Excellence project must be introduced slowly so that they are perceived as fitting within a range of what is acceptable in a particular culture.

Mass communication and modernization have failed to wipe out the idiosyncrasies of local cultures. Even globalization does not necessarily mean homogenization of culture. Nye (2002) offered historical proof in the example of 17th century Japan, which had deliberately isolated itself from attempts at globalization on the part of European seafarers. By the mid-19th century, when Japan became the first Asian country then to embrace globalization, it borrowed innovations successfully from countries throughout the world yet retained its unique culture.[12] Thus, it makes sense to explore any uniqueness of U.S. culture or cultures even in this era when antiglobalization protestors attack transnational corporations. At the same time, we must keep in mind that culture—including U.S. societal culture—is not static. Its customs, values, rituals, and even language can change as it borrows from other cultures.

U.S. PUBLIC RELATIONS

Harold Burson, co-founder of what remains one of the world's largest and most respected public relations firms, Burson-Marsteller, described the evolution of the field this way: With the boom of post-World II, clients knew what they wanted to do and merely asked

---

[12]Globalization and the information revolution actually may reinforce rather than homogenize culture, according to Nye (2002). He explained that the Internet, for example, allows customers to come together in niche markets and geographically dispersed voters to establish political communities.

their public relations agents, "How do I say it?" With the extensive activism of the 1960s, executives became less sure of themselves and asked, "What do I say?" With more and more public relations professionals coming to the decision table by the 1980s, their bosses then asked, "What do I do?"[13]

There is no question that U.S. public relations has become more strategic over time. However, describing the actual history of public relations in the United States is beyond the scope of this chapter. We say this not because of the time span involved—slightly more than 1 century. Rather, that history is contested[14] and—because we are not historians—we choose not to enter the dispute. We do acknowledge that along with history of the field in this country comes considerable baggage. Our earliest practitioners were press agents or publicists at best. Thus, the field is rooted in less-than-effective and –ethical practice. Instead, then, we date the ensuing description of public relations theory and practice from the mid-1980s—the point at which Burson (quoted in Frank, 2000) credited public relations with gaining a seat at the management decision-making table.

Profile of Contemporary Practitioners

From the 1980s to 2000 (projected), the number of practitioners in the United States grew from 126,000 to 197,000 (U.S. Department of Labor, 1998).[15] This rapid growth is likely to continue, with a 55% increase predicted by 2006, according to the "Best Jobs" issue of *U.S. News & World Report* (1997). Cutlip, Center, and Broom (2000) figured[16] that most of these practitioners work in the corporate sector (40%); followed by agencies (27%); associations, foundations, and educational institutions (14%); health care (8%); government (6%); and nonprofit organizations (5%). More than 90% of all practitioners in the United States have college degrees. Nearly 25% of them have some graduate education, a full 25% have master's degrees, and 2% have doctorates (Cutlip et al., 2000).

The most recent and comprehensive salary survey ("Profile 2000," 2000), conducted jointly in 1999 by the International Association of Business Communicators (IABC) and Public Relations Society of America (PRSA), breaks out some figures by country (United States, Canada, and outside the United States and Canada). Average pay for U.S. communicators was $72,000. Consultants' salaries were significantly higher ($110,000) than those with corporate jobs ($63,000). Geographical location in the country also affected pay. Practitioners in the mid-Atlantic region earned the highest ($113,000 on average) and those in the mountain region earned the least ($56,000 on average).

In 1998, 65.7% of those the government (U.S. Department of Labor, 1998) considered to be in public relations were women. About 14% of U.S. practitioners are minorities—primarily of African and Hispanic origin (U.S. Department of Labor, 1998). Minorities comprise about 25% of the U.S. population. Further evidence of the lack of diverse

---

[13]Many in the U.S. public relations industry have heard versions of this story, either from Burson himself or secondhand. We thank Frank (2000) for writing it down.

[14]In addition to the dispute about where contemporary public relations got its start—The United States or Germany—there is the question of whether the field developed as the four models (J. E. Grunig & Hunt, 1984) suggest (from publicity or press agentry through stages of public information and two-way asymmetrical and, ultimately, to two-way symmetrical) or whether all four models have existed since public relations' inception in the late 1800s.

[15]Cutlip et al., (2000) pointed out that this figure undoubtedly is low, because the U.S. Department of Labor's categories of "public relations specialists" and "managers: marketing, advertising and public relations" excludes many others (e.g., graphic designers, lobbyists, and researchers) who work in the field.

[16]Based primarily on PRSA and IABC membership profiles and descriptions.

representation in public relations is the fact that people of Color make up only about 7% of the membership of U.S. professional societies (Cutlip et al., 2000).

What do these practitioners actually do? The Universal Accreditation Board of the PRSA recently surveyed 1,147 members and learned that, overwhelmingly, 89% of them spend their time in strategic planning and implementing. (Of course, we on the Excellence study team learned that strategic planning and management means different things to different people.) The PRSA study used the term strategic planning to encompass working with members of the dominant coalition "to discuss what kind of image the company wants to project and how to go about it" (Frank, 2000, p. 9). After strategic planning, survey respondents described what they spend "a great deal of" or "some time" doing (in decreasing order) as program planning (88%); project management (86%); media relations (78%); account–client management (67%); special events, conferences, and meetings (66%); internal relations (65%); community relations (60%); issues management (55%); relations with special audiences (54%); and crisis management (45%).

The most recent survey[17] of job satisfaction among U.S. practitioners (cited in "Job insecurity," 2002) established that IABC members,[18] at least, are happy with their work. Respondents cited access to technology, benefits, and flexible hours as the most satisfying aspects of their jobs. Mentoring, working from home, and lack of promotion were least satisfying.

Throughout the last 30 years, public relations practice in the United States has been marked by boom times and busts. For example, downsizing characterized the early 1990s. Then, with the emergence of start-up dot coms, practitioners found lucrative work helping attract investment capital. With the economic recession that followed, many practitioners were out of work once again.[19] The bottom line of the recent IABC study (cited in "Job insecurity," 2002) was that communicators see little job security in their field. However, with rampant charges of managerial malfeasance on the part of some of the country's major companies, industry leaders suggest that expert public relations counselors will once again be in great demand (Edelman, 2002). Already, 82% of the IABC members surveyed said they have unlimited or at least weekly access to senior management.

A Generation of Changes in the Field, Explored Through the Lenses of the Excellence Study and Contemporary Practitioners

By 1983, the premier trade publication in public relations had celebrated its first quarter century. In the 26th anniversary issue of *pr reporter*, Editor Pat Jackson listed the four changes he considered "elemental" since his newsletter's inception in 1958: (a) the field had moved steadily from publicity to policy; (b) practice expanded from applied communication theory to behavioral science; (c) the objective went from influencing opinion to motivating behavior; and (d) research, both qualitative and quantitative, formal and informal, became a major (what Jackson speculated might be "*the*" major) factor.

Articulating these shifts might reflect Jackson's (*pr reporter*, 1983) well-known bias toward behavioral change. However, taken together they suggest what he considered the

---

[17]IABC surveyed 1,349 members in the spring of 2002. For more information on the study, contact IABC at www.iabc.com.

[18]Most IABC members are from the United States, although this association includes a broad geographical base of membership.

[19]In spite of the weak economy, women executives in all fields—including public relations—may be inching up the corporate ladder, according to a recent survey by the women's advocacy group, Catalyst (cited in "Items of interest to professionals," 2002).

"scientifically oriented practitioner" (p. 1) whose work is accountable—linked to the organizational bottom line. At the same time, an increasing number of women were reaching the top in public relations; 20% of the people listed in *O'Dwyer's Directory of Public Relations Executives*, cited in that same issue of *pr reporter*, were women (up from 13.7% just 3 years earlier). This profile of the emerging professional in the 1980s is consistent with results of the Excellence project (Dozier et al., 1995; J. E. Grunig, 1992; L. A. Grunig et al., 2002), which began at that same time.

In 1985, we were part of a team[20] that received a major grant from the Research Foundation of the IABC to study excellence in public relations. The Excellence study, as it came to be called, represented the largest support for research in the field until the turn of this new century. One highly respected professional, former head of the Institute for Public Relations, referred to the Excellence study in a memo to institute board members as "the foundation piece of much of our thinking about corporate PR today" (W. W. White, personal communication, May 8, 2002).

Of course, this research has enjoyed its share of critics from all sides. Conservatives with a strictly business bent regard the Excellence theory, with its emphasis on balancing the concerns of the self-interest of the company with the collective interests of society, as idealistic. Liberals see its authors as pawns of the establishment, working to enhance the effectiveness of a function that empowers capitalists at the expense of unempowered publics. Criticisms notwithstanding, the Excellence study has resulted in an unprecedented development in the scope and substance of what we know (and thus can teach) about public relations from the previous generation of knowledge.

We use *generation* here not in the traditional sense of the interval of time between the birth of parents and that of their children (typically 30 years or three generations per century).[21] We do not use the term as in *spontaneous generation*, because that would deny the years of planning, collecting, and analyzing data and reporting of results and implications from the Excellence study that we undertook. Instead, we use *generation* as a stage of development—as in types of computers. We will conclude this section of the chapter by projecting the next generation of theory and practice in the United States—what we predict but has not been realized to date.

In 1985, the year in which the grant for the Excellence study was awarded, eminent public relations professional for Reynolds Metals, Joseph Awad, identified trends that have only increased in this generation of practice. He also made forecasts that have come about at least in part. For example, Awad predicted that public relations would enjoy a growth surge—largely in reaction to mounting external pressures. This has happened both in terms of numbers of public relations students and practitioners in this country and in the responsibility practitioners have taken on in strategic management.

Like Jackson before him, Awad (1985) also believed that public relations would become more accountable—not only to clients and employers but to society. He cited the trend toward the field's efforts being directed at concrete, measurable objectives rather than toward such vague concepts as public image or goodwill. As a result, he prophesied that public relations would become more effective—largely as a result of the increasing emphasis on emerging issues and the participation of the field in issues management. A concomitant shift would be toward greater reliance on research for both planning purposes and

---

[20]Additional members of the team of principal investigators were David M. Dozier, William P. Ehling, Fred Repper (deceased), and Jon White. We were assisted by a number of graduate students, other colleagues, and IABC members.

[21]Collins and Zoch (2002) used this 30-year span for their generational analysis of public relations educators. Their Delphi study encompassed the period from 1960 to 1990.

benchmarking evaluation of results. Today, we applaud the existence of the Measurement Commission, sponsored by the Institute for Public Relations. Members of the Measurement Commission represent the best in both practice and scholarship, working together to determine both the value of measuring effectiveness and the best methods for doing so. However, we decry the field's continuing emphasis on such poorly defined (and perhaps irrelevant) concepts as image and goodwill.

In what seems somewhat comical in this new century, Awad (1985) also speculated that new communication techniques such as computers would become as commonplace as the typewriter and the telephone. In a still-cogent argument, however, he urged practitioners to avoid the pitfall of mere gadgetry and rely on electronic communication to improve understanding between publics and organizations. Kornegay and L. A. Grunig (1998) described cyberbridging as a process wherein women, especially, could benefit from using the information superhighway to scan the environment and thus make the transition from communication technician to manager. Through this interactive process, of course, organizations would come to understand the legitimate concerns of their stakeholders as well. Indeed, J. E. Grunig and his students (described in Burch, 1997) used the Internet effectively to monitor public opinion of selected organizations—part of the scanning process. Results have established that there is much to be gained from the analysis of groups' responses to particular situations. Implications suggest that by using online discussion groups and establishing their own interactive web sites, organizations can carry out truly two-way and symmetrical public relations programs.

Awad (1985) expressed a further concern that resonates more than 20 years later: The profession's top managers, some of whom are or were pioneers in the field, are retiring or dying. This concern has led a number of U.S.-based associations to initiate professional development programs designed to enhance the capabilities of those who report directly to those senior managers. For example, the Institute for Public Relations and the San Francisco Academy offer several such seminars each year. Both the IABC and the PRSA sponsor extensive professional development sessions at every annual conference. Commercial operations, such as Ragan Communications, conduct similar programs. Distance-learning graduate programs, based in universities such as Syracuse, also help to educate midlevel practitioners for greater responsibility.

To fill the void in top-level leadership of the field, Awad (1985) also suggested that education in public relations would expand (although he predicted the emergence of coursework in the curricula of business management schools, a goal yet to be realized but discussed ad nauseum in professional settings; e.g., Pincus, 2002). He further expected that more practitioners would seek and gain accredited status, which remains as elusive as public relations courses in the business school.

All in all, this concern for senior executives in public relations remains. According to Ogilvy Public Relations Chief Executive Officer (CEO) Bob Seltzer, a shortage of qualified people is the biggest issue facing agencies (cited in Frank, 2000). As a result, the Council of Public Relations Firms[22] has developed methods for recruiting midlevel executives from other fields into ours.

---

[22]The council also studied public relations salaries for their competitiveness. It found that in 2000, top executives were earning an average $250,000 per year and general managers were earning $170,000. Top executives in firms received annual bonuses of 36%, which is in line with other industries. However, baseline salaries are significantly lower than those of, say, business consultants and attorneys. Furthermore, Seltzer (cited in Frank, 2000) predicted that higher salaries in U.S. public relations would help achieve diversity of all kinds in public relations practice.

Awad (1985) went on to predict the coordination of all activities involved in public relations, and he did not mean the integrated marketing communication touted so frequently in the 1990s. Instead, he emphasized the importance of coordinating public relations strategy because its numerous specialties, in his view, are less effective when fragmented. As with Awad's previous projections, the Excellence study also emphasized the need to place public relations functions under an umbrella that would allow for the reallocation of resources within communication as publics became more or less strategic.

Awad (1985) may have been most prescient when describing the trend toward increased responsibility and ethics. Changing value systems—coming to the United States as a result of greater diversity at home and among global competitors, suppliers, and customers— challenge public relations professionals here with supporting the large, complex organization as well as its pluralistic publics. As Awad put it, "Public relations can become the voice & defender of the human, the individual, the personal in a world dominated by quantitative or technocratic thinking" (p. 2).

Over the years of the Excellence study, the research team came to focus more and more on the importance of ethics and integrity; we acknowledged the importance of personal integrity on the part of practitioners and on an ethical norm that combines elements of the deontological and the teleological. That is, we emphasized the value of professional standards or rules—such as disclosure—that would help govern practice; at the same time, we also highlighted the relevance of utilitarian or consequence-based ethics. We reasoned that publics are strategic for the organization because they have consequences on it, or vice versa. As a result, one of us[23] (L. A. Grunig) established what we believe to be at least among the first of its kind: a graduate-level seminar in the philosophy and ethics of public relations. It explores ethical concerns reflected in the professional literature: advocacy, accountability, solicitation of new business, whistle blowing, spin, confidentiality, social and public responsibility, diversity issues, concealment versus disclosure, lying, accuracy, codes of ethics (including global ethics), ethics of research and education, professionalism, logical arguments, dealing with the press, front groups, and divided loyalties between the organization and its publics.

Amplifying the voice of publics in the process of organizational decision making demands more of a communicator than technician's skills. It requires someone at the management level who can function as a peer professional among other members of the organization's dominant coalition. Inclusion in that power elite, or at least a direct reporting relationship to the C-suite (with the other chief executives), is a major premise of the Excellence study. It has been a concern among U.S. practitioners at least since the mid-1980s.

In 1987 ("Public relations pros are counselors, not just tactical communicators"), *pr reporter* highlighted the need for counselors rather than technicians. It pointed out that pioneers such as Edward L. Bernays, Arthur Page, Ivy Lee, and Pendleton Dudley considered themselves policy consultants. However, after World War II and the explosion of the communication industry, more and more of the jobs for practitioners in this country were tactical.

So, where do we stand in 2002? To begin to answer, we quote a handful of pundits in the field. We also cite students, who represent the future of public relations.

---

[23]The other of us, J. E. Grunig, revising the textbook *Managing Public Relations* (J. E. Grunig & Hunt, 1984), is substituting a lengthy chapter on ethics for the scant page or so in the original edition. Most current textbooks in the field include substantial discussion of ethics (Hutchison, 2002).

One good measure comes from the final editorial written by the outgoing editor of *PR Week*, another major trade journal in public relations. Bloom (2002) called this "PR's golden era" (p. 6). He explained that public relations has never been so vital than in this time of helping organizations and society at large cope with massing threats. He added, "Nor has PR ever been so valuable to corporate marketers who seek more cost-sensitive ways of reaching consumers against the backdrop of a fragmented media and increasingly cynical public" (p. 6). Bloom also highlighted problems that continue to plague the field: (a) confusion between public relations and marketing, (b) lack of determination (and the ability) to measure public relations outcomes as well as outputs, (c) mere lip service paid to the importance of a diverse workforce in public relations, and (d) too few professionals who understand how to establish good relationships with journalists.

Another editor of the trade press has a different, less optimistic take on the state of affairs of U.S. public relations. On his *O'Dwyer's PR Daily* website, O'Dwyer (2002) offered advice to students that reflects not a golden age but a time when the term *public relations* has been so discredited in the English language that he urged students to call themselves anything but public relations people or communicators. He cited a 1999 study financed by the PRSA and the Rockefeller Foundation[24] that, he claimed, the PRSA was too embarrassed about to publicize. Why? The research showed "PR specialist" ranking 43rd out of 45 public figures[25] as "believable sources of information."

One student (Pulgar, 2002) who responded to O'Dwyer's (2002) piece questioned the desirability of changing the name of the field—surely a tired argument by now. As Pulgar said, "It's a lot easier to discard an idea rather than rebuild it." His suggestions echo those of many professionals and many textbooks in the field: "Let's work to correct all the mistakes the field's forefathers have made. The reason PR practitioners are expendable is because we are not organized. Put together a board, make an association and license our members so not just anyone can do what we do. Only then will people take us seriously."

Since the 1980s, however, public perception of this field may have changed for the better—at least from students' perspectives. In the mid-1980s, one of us routinely began to ask her undergraduate students in the introductory public relations class what public relations meant. With no formal knowledge of the subject, they said "devious," "lying," "propaganda," "superficial," "snow job," and "covering up." Their most benign labels included "publicity," "image," and "packaging." By 1988, students' comments shifted: They still said "propaganda" and "image" but also added "liaison," "mediator," "representation," "communication," "interaction," and "networking." In 1996, their list included "consulting," "management," "media," "promoting," "communications," "information," "link," "liaison," "writing," and "working with people." In our view, these labels suggest a clear trajectory from the unethical to a more accurate representation of what public relations people most probably do today.

Throughout the history of public relations, practitioners and scholars have attempted to identify and name a single concept that defines the value of public relations. Early in public relations' history, publicity by itself sufficed as the answer—"there is no such thing as bad publicity." When public relations people recognized that publicity had to have some effect on a public before it had value, they adopted one faddish term after another. First, it was "image," then "identity" and "image" together. Now the popular terms are "reputation" and "brand."

---

[24] A political scientist at Columbia University conducted the project.

[25] Only famous entertainers and television or radio talk show hosts ranked lower than public relations people.

With the exception of "identity," most of these terms describe essentially the same phenomenon: what publics think of an organization. "Identity" describes what an organization thinks of itself. Subtle differences can be found in the professional and academic literature among reputation, image, brand, and impressions; but all basically describe cognitions that publics hold about organizations. Jeffries-Fox Associates (2000) conducted a content analysis of 1,149 articles in 94 trade and academic publications to compare the use of the terms "reputation," "brand equity," and "good will" and found that "reputation" and "brand equity" were the most frequently used terms. Jeffries-Fox Associates concluded that "the same component ideas are associated with brand equity and corporate reputation" and that the terms are "used interchangeably" (p. 6). At the same time, they concluded that public relations managers are more likely to use the term "reputation" and marketing managers to use "brand equity." As a result, they recommended adopting the term "reputation" to distinguish public relations from marketing.

In spite of the fact that the term "reputation" means essentially the same thing as older, discredited concepts, the public relations profession in the United States is vigorously attempting to associate reputation management with public relations. The "next challenge," according to an editorial in *PR Week* ("Reputation Name Must Be Pushed," 2000), "is to mobilize support for the phrase 'corporate reputation'" first among "PR agencies and in-house practitioners" so that "there is a better chance that the second audience—clients and journalists—will understand and use the phrase themselves" (p. 10). These public relations professionals promoting the concept of reputation have been joined by business scholars (e.g., Fombrun, 1996) eager to enter the intriguing new research area of reputation, marketing experts promoting the concept of branding, and public opinion research firms eager to capitalize on the popularity of reputational evaluative surveys such as those that produce the annual *Fortune* magazine index of corporate reputations.

J. E. Grunig and Hung (2002) reviewed a substantial portion of the literature on reputation and its reputed role in explaining the value of public relations. They provided evidence that the attempts to show an association between expenditures on public relations and reputation and between reputation and financial performance are methodologically and statistically unsound. They argued that a more logical connection could be shown among public relations activities, relationships, and value to an organization.

The Excellence study (L. A. Grunig et al., 2002) showed that public relations makes an organization more effective when it identifies an organization's most strategic publics as part of strategic management processes and conducts communication programs to develop and maintain effective long-term relationships between organizations and those publics. As a result, public relations professionals can determine the value of public relations by measuring the quality of relationships with strategic publics more accurately than by measuring reputation. In addition, they can evaluate communication programs by measuring the effects of these programs and correlating them with relationship indicators.

J. E. Grunig and Hung's (2002) review of the literature and survey research showed the critical effect of management behaviors on both reputation and the type and quality of relationships. They defined reputation as cognitive representations—what collectivities of people think about organizations. They found that the most important cognitive representations consisted of the recall of either good or bad behaviors of organizations. The recall of behaviors, in turn, had the most significant effect of any type of cognitive representation on the way research participants viewed the type and quality of relationships with an organization.

J. E. Grunig and Hung's (2002) research showed that public relations professionals who are interested in protecting or enhancing the reputations and the relationships of the organizations they serve should do so by participating in the strategic management processes of the organization so that they can have a potential influence on the organizational behaviors chosen by management. The traditional public relations approach of putting out strategic messages after decisions are made would have little effect on either reputation or relationships.

By 2002, the field—as indicated by scholarly research and professional development sessions at conferences of such groups as the PRSA—is moving toward the management of relationships. Skilled technicians will always be in demand, but people with knowledge of strategic management and two-way symmetrical communication must work to identify strategic publics and then establish and maintain good relationships with them (L. A. Grunig et al., 2002). Holtzhausen (2002) called the focus on public relations as a management function "the biggest contribution to establish public relations as a serious field of study" (p. 254).[26]

However, because of the well-documented glass ceiling for professional women and people of Color in the United States (Cline et al., 1986; L. A. Grunig et al., 2000; Toth & Cline, 1989), nontraditional employees in public relations have an especially difficult time transcending the technician's role and ascending to management. This is a problem not only for those practitioners but also for the companies that discriminate against them. Recall that Weick's (1979) principle of requisite variety established that organizations need as much diversity inside as exists in their environment. Excellent public relations, then, requires women and men in all roles as well as practitioners of diverse racioethnic backgrounds (L. A. Grunig et al., 2002). We believe that higher education will help overcome the field's perception of low status and the reality of lingering discrimination (L. A. Grunig, 1992).

Education

The first course in public relations in the United States was taught by Bernays at Cornell University in 1923. He began what has become the noble tradition of using his own textbook (in this case, *Crystallizing Public Opinion*) in the class. Since then, more than 300 extensive courses of study have developed in U.S. universities. The most recent ranking of these programs by *U.S. News & World Report* ("America's best graduate schools," 1996) listed the University of Maryland first, followed by Syracuse University and the University of Florida. In addition, professional bodies have designed continuing education programs and some campuses now offer distance learning. One contentious issue continues to be where the public relations program should be situated: journalism? communication? English? business?

There is no question, however, that the body of knowledge has been growing (even though it remains insufficient for any true profession). One of us recalled that when he began teaching at the University of Maryland in 1969, "It took me about six weeks to tell the students everything I knew and everything that was in the literature" (quoted in Burch, 1997). Five years ago, *Books in Print* listed more than 600 titles on public relations—most of them published in the United States. This literature establishes a firm—if not rock-solid—basis on which to teach.

The most commonly assigned textbooks for courses in public relations principles (Hutchison, 2002) are Baskin, Aronoff, and Lattimore's (1997) *Public Relations: The*

---

[26]To the postmodern scholar Holtzhausen (2002), this is not a plus. She condemned both the management and excellence foci as metanarratives that have "drowned out" (p. 256) other discourses she considered equally valid.

Profession and the Practice (4th ed.); Cutlip et al.'s (2000) *Effective Public Relations* (8th ed.); Newsom, Turk, and Kruckeberg's (2000) *This Is PR: The Realities of Public Relations* (7th ed.); Wilcox, Ault, Agee, and Cameron's (2000) *Public Relations: Strategies and Tactics* (6th ed.); and Seitel's (2001) *The Practice of Public Relations* (8th ed.). Similarly, U.S. educators have considerable choice when assigning texts for classes in public relations writing, techniques, campaigns, and cases.

Since 1956, the PRSA (among other organizations) has been studying public relations education in this country. In 1981, close to the starting point of our analysis in this chapter, it established its Commission on Education, which subsequently published a model curriculum consisting of a minimum of five courses in public relations (Ehling & Plank, 1987).

The most recent Commission on Education report (PRSA, 1999) shows a surprising congruity between what practitioners and what scholars believe is critical to the public relations curriculum at this point. It includes recommendations for both undergraduate and graduate education. Curricular models are based on these assumptions: grounded in the liberal arts, theory based, writing across the curriculum, and emphasis on courses rather than departments where those courses are housed. The report recommended that coursework in the public relations major should comprise 25% to 40% of an undergraduate student's total program. Of those courses, at least half should be identified clearly as public relations courses in these topics: principles, case studies, research, writing and production techniques, planning and management, campaigns, and supervised internship. For the 30- to 36-hr master's degree, the Commission on Education report emphasized public relations management and an advanced understanding of the body of knowledge, culminating in a thesis and exam or capstone project (or both). Since 1989, the PRSA has offered a certification program for institutions of higher education that offer public relations courses and degree programs that meet these standards.

A recent study (Collins & Zoch, 2002) identified the U.S. academics who have made the greatest contributions to the theoretical understanding of public relations from 1960 to 1990 in this country. They are (in alphabetical order) Glen Broom, Scott Cutlip, David Dozier, James E. Grunig, Larissa A. Grunig, Robert Heath, Dean Kruckeberg, and Elizabeth Toth. The top four are, first, J. E. Grunig, followed by Cutlip, and—tied for third place—Broom and Heath. Scholar–participants in the Delphi research credited these men with the following: J. E. Grunig, conceptualizing the first deep theory of public relations (situational theory), contributing the four models of public relations, and bringing a scientific approach to the study of public relations; Cutlip, laying the groundwork for public relations theory, studying the history of the field, and bringing together theory and practice in this textbook; Broom, conceptualizing the four roles of public relations and contributing to the Cutlip and Center books; and Heath, adding to our understanding of issues management and risk communication and applying rhetorical principles to public relations.

These educators both publish in and are informed by the two major scholarly journals in public relations published in the United States: the *Journal of Public Relations Research (JPRR)*[27] and the *Public Relations Review*. Several trade publications exist as well: the PRSA's *The Public Relations Strategist* and *Tactics*, the IABC's *Communication World*, *PR News*, *Ragan Report*, *pr reporter*, *PR Week*, and *O'Dwyer's PR Services Report* among them. Such publications help lay the groundwork for establishing the field as a true profession, one with a published body of knowledge.

---

[27]*Public Relations Research and Education*, begun in 1984 by J. E. Grunig, provided the impetus for the subsequent *Public Relations Research Annual* (1989–1991, edited by J. E. and L. A. Grunig), which begat the *JPRR*.

Professionalism

Several professional groups exist for practitioners in the United States. The PRSA—established in 1948 and headquartered in New York—is the largest, with almost 20,000 members. The IABC has more than 13,000 members; it was founded in 1970 and is headquartered in San Francisco. The PRSA sponsors a student membership organization, the Public Relations Student Society of America. In addition to these major bodies, there are numerous specialized, regional, and local associations. They include the Black Public Relations Society, the Arthur Page Society, Women Executives in Public Relations (WEPR), the National School Public Relations Association, the Council for the Advancement and Support of Education, the Florida Public Relations Association, the Public Relations Seminar, and the Wise Men—to name just a few.

One recent development worthy of attention is the effort of 14 such groups to work together on "PR for PR," as David Drobis (chairman of Ketchum Public Relations) put it in his 2002 Distinguished Lecture to the Institute for Public Relations. Drobis, long-term supporter of research and education in the field, described an effort to provide industry positioning on what he and others in such groups as the Page Society, the PRSA, the IABC, the National Investor Relations Institute, the Public Affairs Council, and WEPR consider three critical issues: disclosure, transparency, and ethics.

All of these professional groups emphasize the importance of ethics. A code of ethics is a norm for any such society. Enforcement of a code of professional standards in public relations, however, has been a major problem. The PRSA revised its code in 2000, removing any enforcement mechanism and reducing its 12 standards to 6 provisions. Despite this ongoing commitment to educate about and to encourage ethical behavior, practitioners in the United States have had to acknowledge the problem of their many colleagues who do not belong to any professional society and, thus, are not governed by any stated norms.

In the absence of state licensing, accreditation of public relations practitioners is a central issue to many of these professional societies. The PRSA's program, Accredited Public Relations (APR), may be the best known. The IABC has its Accredited Business Communicator program. However, the goal of developing a single accreditation program (referred to as universal accreditation or UA) has proven elusive for its proponents within the United States, who contend that a single, strongly supported program would move the practice toward professionalism.

Also, at least the PRSA's accreditation efforts have become increasingly controversial. APR status is required for representation in the National (voting) Assembly, as it is for holding any office at the national level. As a result, the 80% of the PRSA's nonaccredited members have expressed a sense of disenfranchisement recently. However, at the most recent assembly meeting (2002), a proposal to decouple accreditation from the assembly was defeated. In addition, the APR program is frequently criticized for its high cost and low passing rate.

Since the heyday of Bernays, often considered the father of U.S. public relations, some practitioners have called for the licensing of communicators.[28] This restriction into

---

[28]One of the most recent proponents of restricting practice responded to the O'Dwyer (2002) web site piece on advice for students. Rather than licensing, however, JM (2002) recommended requiring new practitioners to take the PRSA's APR exam. Without the added credibility of accreditation, he argued, the field could look forward to being regulated as real estate, law, and accounting are now in the United States.

the field, they believe, would help establish public relations as a profession. Professional status, in turn, would enhance its credibility. However, professionalism has been called the Achilles heel for practitioners in this country (Collins & Zoch, 2002). U.S. practitioners and scholars agree for the most part that public relations is not yet a profession. Collins and Zoch (2002) determined that it was a "quasi-profession" (p. 1), after providing a thorough review of the literature in professionalism and applying criteria such as licensing, status, social responsibility, serving the public interest, codes of ethics and standards, specialized knowledge and skill, a body of knowledge, professional values, and autonomy to public relations practice.

Collins and Zoch's (2002) determination that U.S. public relations fails to qualify as a profession is based largely on the fact that licensing[29] is not required. In addition, they cited Cutlip et al.'s (2000) assertion that research in the field contributes little to building and testing theory and, as a result, that the body of knowledge is inadequate for professional status. The country's largest professional body, the PRSA, began to codify that BOK in 1986—close to the time we begin this look at U.S. practice. The project continues to this time. In addition, professional groups such as the PRSA, the IABC, and the Institute for Public Relations have established foundations to support scholarly and applied research.

The PRSA, beginning at its 2000 conference in Chicago, took the lead in establishing what it called the Global Alliance. This coalition of public relations associations from throughout the world, now headed by Italian professional Toni Muzi Falconi, has begun to meet to tackle global issues that include ethics, education, and accreditation. In the United States, most large firms are concerned about their international practice—especially integrating their operations. Daniel J. Edelman (2002), founder and chairman of Edelman Public Relations Worldwide, explained the difficulty of operating dozens of geographically dispersed companies as a single-service unit. He described twin goals of establishing international standards for practice and assuring clients of equivalent quality of work in every office of the firm. He also cited the need to import programs to the United States from other parts of the world (rather than originating programs solely from this country) and to generate programs for domestic companies within their own countries.

As in many countries, practitioners in the United States grapple with nomenclature—what to call ourselves. Over the last generation, substitute terms for public relations have developed; they include "corporate communication," "corporate relations," "communications," "public affairs," and "corporate affairs" (O'Dwyer, 1981). However, like many of our professional and academic colleagues, we prefer "public relations" rather than some euphemism. It reflects our purpose in building relationships with the publics on which organizations have consequences, or vice versa.

FUTURE CHALLENGES

Future challenges for United States practitioners include what may seem obvious: exploiting the potential of constantly changing technology, especially communication technology; growing the theoretical body of knowledge, so the field may move from its careerist

---

[29]These constitutional issues seem to preclude licensing, or permission granted by the state to practice public relations: freedom of expression and people's right to pursue occupations without undo interference from the state.

status; hiring bright, well-educated practitioners (and educators) who embrace professional norms and can take the place of the aging leadership of this field;[30] encouraging aspiration for the strategic managerial role, without selling the field's skill base short; globalizing practice in light of growing economies and privatization around the world; working to eliminate any remaining discrimination against women or people of Color, whether they be practitioners of public relations, employees, customers, or suppliers; raising the ethical bar; increasing professionalism among all practitioners, regardless of whether they join professional societies; enhancing research skills and, thus, helping make public relations more accountable to the organizational bottom line; and legitimizing the concerns of all publics of the organization—internal and external—by dealing with them with balance and sensitivity. Then, the work of U.S. practitioners will have impact beyond their own bottom line; they may affect other individuals, publics, and other organizations in a positive way.

Are we there yet in the United States? By no means. Press agentry remains the most common approach to public relations, despite the wealth of educational programs available, the research base, and the drive toward professionalism. Are we on the way? Yes, but as Kanter (1998) said, "Everything looks like a failure in the middle" (p. 94). We are at some midpoint in the United States—well beyond our rudimentary beginnings yet well short of our goal of truly global, truly professional, truly strategic, truly empowered, truly responsible, truly ethical, and truly effective public relations practice.

Case Study of Public Relations Excellence in a United States Chemical Corporation

In the Excellence study, Larissa A. Grunig, James E. Grunig, David Dozier, and graduate students at the University of Maryland and San Diego State University conducted qualitative interviews of heads of public relations, members of the dominant coalition, and midlevel public relations personnel at 25 organizations that had scored either at the top or bottom of an index of public relations excellence that was calculated from 20 variables. These case studies focused on why the dominant coalition valued public relations; how the public relations function was structured and its role in strategic management; and how the function became, or failed to become, excellent.

One of these case studies, of a U.S. chemical corporation, provides an excellent example of a near-excellent public relations function and how it became excellent. For ethical reasons, the Excellence researchers guaranteed confidentiality to all organizations studied; so we refer to this organization only as Chemical Corporation. For this case study, interviews were conducted in person with the director of corporate communications; the vice-president for strategic planning, investor relations, and public affairs (a member of the dominant coalition); and a midlevel communication specialist assigned to internal communication.

Chemical Corporation had a score on the Excellence factor higher than three fourths of the organizations included in the quantitative portion of the Excellence study. It reached this level of excellence in large part because of the senior communicator's knowledge of two-way communication and of public relations as a strategic management function. The corporation's public relations function did not reach the highest level of excellence, however, because senior management did not perceive public relations to be part of strategic management. After the quantitative questionnaires were completed, the communication

---

[30]One new wrinkle is the defection of high-level public relations counselors to management consulting firms.

department began to report to a new vice-president of strategic planning, investor relations, and public affairs. His background was in strategic planning. The vice-president recognized and made use of the knowledge of two senior communicators—one in corporate communication and one in marketing communication—and the public relations function became part of strategic management.

As a result, this case study provides a profile of an organization that meets most of the standards of excellence in communication management identified by the Excellence study research team. Public relations was involved in strategic planning, it gradually changed the perception among senior managers of the importance of communication, it worked effectively with counterparts in other departments such as human resources, it practiced a symmetrical model of public relations (including elements of both advocacy and negotiation), it tried to create opportunities for women to move into communication management, and it incorporated diversity into the public relations function.

The Value of Public Relations to the Corporation.   One of the two major purposes of the Excellence study was to explain the value of public relations and to estimate that value in monetary terms. The member of the dominant coalition who completed the quantitative questionnaire had assigned a cost–benefit ratio of 200% to public relations and 300% to the communication manager. During the qualitative interviews, however, the vice-president said he "could not begin to 'dollarize' the function. In some respects it's an infinite value. In some respects, it's like throwing money in a hole."

Nevertheless, the vice-president described relationships with two publics—employees and the financial community—for which he said communication had an important role. For employees, he said:

> I could not cite an explicit example for you, but to the extent that we're getting all of our employees, through employee communication, oriented around our strategy, which is, number one, to root out work that we do that wastes money, by definition communication is saving us money. It's saving us money by better enabling the people who should be saving us money to go out there and get the job done. Ultimately, that loops around and helps us make money.

For financial relations, he said:

> All I can tell you is that the director of investor relations walked in the door 10 minutes before you did and said: "You might be interested to know our stock just hit an all-time high today." Now, do I believe we accomplished that without the benefit of communication? No, of course not, communication in every respect . . . in causing the underlying performance, in getting out there and making sure that the investment community knew what we were doing, but for those two things our stock would not be at an all-time high today. Now, do I believe that today somehow we got some leverage from the few million dollars we spend on communication each year? Damn right, I do!

Structure of the Communication Function.   In one sense, Chemical Corporation did not meet the criterion of excellence in public relations by having its communication function integrated into a single department. In addition, the director of corporate communications, according to both questionnaires, was not a part of the dominant coalition. Nevertheless, Chemical Corporation achieved integration through its vice-president of strategic planning, investor relations, and public affairs, who was a member of the dominant coalition. The vice-president was responsible for strategic management; the directors of corporate communication, marketing communication, and investor relations reported to him. In addition, a director of government relations and state relations reported to the general counsel and secretary of the company.

At the time the quantitative questionnaires were completed, Chemical Corporation did not have a director of marketing communication. According to both the vice-president and director of communication, marketing communication activities then were dispersed throughout the business units of the corporation. These activities now have been brought together in a single function that reports to the vice-president but not to corporate communication. The director said that the company does not practice integrated marketing communication. In fact, he said the company "does not have a staff function devoted to marketing." Instead, each business unit handled marketing. In the chemical industry, according to the director, marketing typically is not a part of the dominant coalition. Instead, the manufacturing function generally has more power. In consumer product companies such "as an IBM," in contrast, he said "marketing more often is in the dominant coalition. It has to do with the culture of the industry and the specific company."

The corporate communications department, therefore, had responsibility for employee communication, relations with "major media," and "corporate advertising if there is a need for it," according to the director. Corporate communications also communicated with shareholder groups by producing annual reports and earnings announcements and by working with the financial media. The investor relations department, in contrast, "deals directly with analysts and institutional shareholders," the director said.

The director of corporate communications said that it would be better to have all communication functions under one department but that integration in Chemical Corporation was achieved through the vice-president. The communication function was structured as it was, he added, for "political and pragmatic reasons." Nevertheless, he said, there was informal collaboration among the communication functions. The critical factor, the director said, is "not who you report to but rather whether you have access. As a communicator, I have direct access to any of the officers at will. Yesterday, for example, we had a meeting with analysts; and I was there with all of the officers of the company."

The communication function, therefore, achieved integration informally. Importantly, it did so through the strategic management function of the corporation.

Public Relations and Strategic Management. The quantitative questionnaires had shown that the director of corporate communications believed he was heavily involved in strategic management of the company but that the member of the dominant coalition did not. In the qualitative interviews, both the vice-president and the director of communication were asked for an explanation. According to the director: "It may be a semantic thing. From a business perspective, I'm not involved in day-to-day business planning. [The vice-president] is more involved in that. If there are strategic issues that require planning, however, I'm involved." The director provided an example of disclosing and discussing "worst-case scenarios" in communities where chemical plants were located. He said he was involved in planning stages for this issue along with people from health, safety, and the environment; legal; and the businesses. He said, "We're not just waiting for it to hit the fan."

The vice-president also reported that the discrepancy had narrowed since he replaced his predecessor. The current vice-president previously had been vice-president for strategic planning and still is responsible for strategic management. He said: "[The communication director] has been given the opportunity to be more involved. What we discuss over lunch gets him involved in strategic planning . . . more than my predecessor could."

The vice-president emphasized the importance of viewing communication as a strategic function: "Some people scratch their heads and say, 'Why in the world does a strategic planning guy have anything to do with public affairs?'" He answered:

> Most people perceive strategic planning over here at this end of the corporation and if you get through R&D [research and development], marketing, and manufacturing and all these things somewhere at the other end you have someone worrying about public affairs and public relations. My answer is that they have a linear view of a corporation. If you view a corporation as being a work process and those work processes are cyclical, then you take that linear view of the corporation and bend it around into a circle, then it's funny what comes together in the circle—strategic planning and public affairs.
>
> In fact, everything you do strategically in a company has to do with relations with the outside world. It has to do with your relationship to the customer, your competitors, your suppliers. And, of course, public affairs isn't just a transmitting function; it's a two-way function. So, in fact, it's perfectly logical for the public relations function to be directly tied to the strategic function. What do people most want to know about a corporation? They want to know your strategy. So the things really fit together.

The director of corporate communications used a copyrighted flow chart to explain how his department "moved from being order takers to strategic planners." Previously, other departments would give the department a "request to communicate," such as human resources asking for a videotape or the health, safety, and environment department asking for an environmental report. After the change in orientation, that request was not honored until the head of public affairs or his designee did an "alignment check." The alignment check asked whether the request to communicate fit the company's strategic goals: "Is the message consistent with key messages? Has the audience been identified? Has desired behavior been defined? What is the 'requestor's' expected timing? What are resources expectations? What is the benefit of the message to the intended audience?"

The employee communication specialist explained that the communication department benefited from reporting to a strategic planner because he imposed a strategic view on communication. She said, "We now have a methodical, planned way to do work that is tied into the business side of things." In addition, she said, senior management began to "pay more attention to communication because [the vice-president] has opened their eyes." Communication staffers at her middle-management level became involved in strategic planning through teams formed by the vice-president—including teams devoted to the media, employee communication, and financial communication.

How Did the Communication Department Become Excellent?   The senior communicator described the evolution of the department as "a confluence of forces in which I know I played a role . . . something I take a lot of personal pride in." The senior communicator's knowledge of strategic management appears to have been the necessary condition that made it possible for three other factors to have an effect: (a) crises that sensitized senior management to the importance of public relations, (b) a mediating vice-president who understood public relations and had valuable connections in senior management, and (c) business and communication knowledge of the senior communicator.

"Gradually," the vice-president said, "the function evolved to what we have today. It [excellence in public relations] started with the fact we had some good people. If I hadn't had a couple of talented communication managers, I couldn't have done anything." Then, he mentioned the second and third factors: "Without a couple of senior managers, our chairman and COO [chief operating officer], who wanted to treat communication strategically, I couldn't have done it. I was a nice linkage between those two things [competent communicators and strategic management]."

Crises and company performance then played a role, according to the vice-president: "The job of the communication function is to get you the reputation you deserve. Until not too long ago, we probably were getting the reputation we deserved, and everyone wanted to blame the communication function for it. One of things that's helped is that we've had a good message to deliver; the company has been performing better." Since the 1984 tragedy in Bhopal, India, he added, the chemical industry has "been more willing to be open to the public."

After the quantitative questionnaires for the Excellence study had been completed, the communication department held an all-day seminar for senior managers on communication during which a member of the IABC Excellence study research team made a presentation that especially emphasized the importance of public relations in strategic management. Both the communication manager and the vice-president mentioned this presentation as an important factor that helped to change the thinking of senior management about public relations.

The vice-president from strategic planning was a valuable link between the communication function and senior management. His background played a part. Although trained as a chemist, he said he appreciated the importance of communication because a parent and relatives had worked in journalism.

In addition to these factors, the senior communicator pointed out the importance of his own knowledge of the chemical business in addition to his knowledge of communication:

> If the communicator doesn't understand the business of the organization, he or she is never really going to get ahead. That took me a long time to understand. I'm not a chemist by training. I don't have an interest in that, but I have an interest in the chemical industry that I did not have five or 10 years ago. That's important whether you're in the auto industry or the computer industry or in government and whatever industry or business people are in. I think that's a tremendous weakness of professional communicators.

The knowledge base of the communication director and of the communication department about communication itself also explains how the public relations function became excellent at Chemical Corporation and how the director gained access to the dominant coalition. Interviews with both the communication director and employee communication specialist showed that they did not formally study public relations but that both gained their knowledge from the IABC, research journals and professional publications, and experience. The communication director did not have a degree in public relations and he had not taken courses in the subject. The director said he gained his knowledge from professional organizations, especially the IABC. He also said he "learned from the world around him." In addition, the director said he reads communication journals regularly, including *Communication Research* and the *Journal of Communication*.

The Need for International Communication. As is typical in many U.S. corporations, this otherwise excellent public relations function did not conduct its international public relations well. Both the director of communication and the communication specialist identified communication at Chemical Corporation's international sites as a problem to which that the department needed to devote more attention. "For all practical purposes, we have no professional communication opportunities outside headquarters," the director said. He explained that the company had some human resources activities—internal communication—at major sites: "One of the problems we have is trying to ensure that site activities are aligned with what we're doing here." In addition, he said the company did not use public relations firms abroad unless there is a crisis. In that case, he added, it used a network of firms.

The communication specialist reiterated that some international subsidiaries have communication specialists, but "nothing major." She said: "Just last week I met with all the international human resources managers. Part of the vision the employee relations strategic work team has is to have communication strategies and plans in place within five years for all of the major locations, including international locations. In the past, we have not focused on the international communication function."

REFERENCES

Adler, N. J. (2002). *International dimensions of organizational behavior* (4th ed.). Cincinnati, OH: South-Western.

Altschull, J. H. (1984). *Agents of power: The role of the news media in human affairs*. New York: Longman.

America's best graduate schools: 1996 annual guide. (1996, March 18). *U.S. News & World Report*.

Awad, J. (1985). *The power of public relations*. Westport, CT: Praeger.

Baskin, O., Aronoff, C., & Lattimore, D. (1997). *Public relations: The profession and the practice* (4th ed.). Dubuque, IA: Brown.

Bernays, E. L. (1923). *Crystallizing public opinion*. New York: Boni & Liveright.

Best jobs. (1997, October 27). *U.S. News & World Report*, 20–28.

Bloom, J. (2002, September 23). One year, many chats, a few lasting thoughts. *PR Week*, 6.

Books in print. (1996). New Providence, NJ: R. R. Bowker.

Broom, G. M. (1982). A comparison of sex roles in public relations. *Public Relations Review, 8*(3), 17–22.

Burch, D. (1997, Summer). A marriage of ideas: Jim and Lauri Grunig and the give-and-take of effective public relations. *College Park, 8*(3), 20–25.

Cline, C. G., Masel-Walters, L., Toth, E. L., Turk, J. V., Smith, H. T., & Johnson, N. (1986). *The velvet ghetto: The impact of the increasing percentage of women in public relations and business communication*. San Francisco: IABC Foundation.

Collins, E. L., & Zoch, L. M. (2002, August). *PR educators—"The second generation": Measuring and achieving consensu*s. Paper presented at the meeting of the Public Relations Division, Association for Education in Journalism and Mass Communication, Miami.

Coup de Frejac, J. (1991). The importance of north–south relations in a multicultural world. *International Public Relations Review, 14*(4), 23–25.

Crespo, A. (2002). *Protest in the land of plenty*. Miami: Center Lane Press.

Cutlip, S. M. (1995). *Public relations history: From the 17th to the 20th century*. Hillsdale, NJ: Lawrence Erlbaum Associates.

Cutlip, S. M., Center, A. H., & Broom, G. M. (2000). *Effective public relations* (8th ed.). Upper Saddle River, NJ: Prentice-Hall.

Dozier, D. M., & Broom, G. M. (1995). Evolution of the manager role in public relations practice. *Journal of Public Relations Research, 7*, 3–26.

Dozier, D. M., with Grunig, L. A., & Grunig, J. E. (1995). *Manager's guide to excellence in public relations and communication management*. Mahwah, NJ: Lawrence Erlbaum Associates.

Drobis, D. (2002, November 7). Distinguished lecture to the Institute for Public Relations. New York.

Edelman, D. J. (2002, Fall). A challenging time, a bright future. *The Public Relations Strategist, 8*(4), 46–48.

Ehling, W. P., & Plank, B. (Eds.). (1987). *The design for undergraduate public relations education: The report of the 1987 Commission on Undergraduate Public Relations Education*. New York: Public Relations Society of America.

Farber, D. A. (2002). *The first amendment* (2nd ed.). New York: Thomson.

Fombrun, C. J. (1996). *Reputation: Realizing value from the corporate image*. Boston: Harvard Business School.

Frank, J. (2000, November 6). The industry booms as PR jobs shift focus. *PR Week*, 9.

Gianaris, N. V. (1996). *Modern capitalism: Privatization, employee ownership, and industrial democracy.* Westport, CT: Praeger.

Greenberg, E. S. (1985). *Capitalism and the American political ideal.* Armonk, NY: M. E. Sharpe.

Grunig, J. E. (1984). Organizations, environments, and models of public relations. *Public Relations Research and Education, 1*, 6–29.

Grunig, J. E. (Ed.). (1992). *Excellence in public relations and communication management.* Hillsdale, NJ: Lawrence Erlbaum Associates.

Grunig, J. E., & Grunig, L. A. (2001, May 21). Auditing a pr function through theoretical benchmarking: Jim & Lauri Grunig's research. *pr reporter* (Suppl.), *12*, 1–4.

Grunig, J. E., & Hung, C. J. (2002, March). *The effect of relationships on reputation and reputation on relationships: A cognitive, behavioral study.* Paper presented at the meeting of the Public Relations Society of America's Educator's Academy 5th Annual International, Interdisciplinary Public Relations Research Conference, Miami.

Grunig, J. E., & Hunt, T. (1984). *Managing public relations.* New York: Holt, Rinehart & Winston.

Grunig, L. A. (1992). Toward the philosophy of public relations. In E. L. Toth & R. L. Heath (Eds.), *Rhetorical and critical approaches to public relations* (pp. 65–91). Hillsdale, NJ: Lawrence Erlbaum Associates.

Grunig, L. A., Grunig, J. E., & Dozier, D. M. (2002). *Excellent public relations and effective organizations: A study of communication management in three countries.* Mahwah, NJ: Lawrence Erlbaum Associates.

Grunig, L. A., Toth, E. L., & Hon, L. C. (2000). *Women in public relations: How gender influences practice.* New York: Guilford.

Hachten, W. A. (1992). *The world news prism: Changing media of international communication* (3rd ed.). Ames: Iowa State University Press.

Hofstede, G. (1984). *Culture's consequences: International differences in work-related values* (abridged ed.). Newbury Park, CA: Sage.

Hofstede, G. (2001). *Culture's consequences: Comparing values, behaviors, institutions, and organizations across nations* (2nd ed.). Thousand Oaks, CA: Sage.

Hollihan, T. A. (2001). *Uncivil wars: Political campaigns in a media age.* New York: Bedord/St. Martin's.

Holtzhausen, D. R. (2002). Towards a postmodern research agenda for public relations. *Public Relations Review, 28*, 251–264.

Hutchison, L. L. (2002). Teaching ethics across the public relations curriculum. *Public Relations Review, 28*, 301–309.

Items of interest to professionals. (2002, December 2). *pr reporter, 45*, 4.

Jeffries-Fox Associates. (2000, March 3). *Toward a shared understanding of corporate reputation and related concepts: Phase I. Content analysis.* Basking Ridge, NJ: Report Prepared for the Council of Public Relations Firms.

JM. (2002, September 23). MuddPR@earthlink.net. *O'Dwyer's PR Daily.* Retrieved from http://www.odwyerpr.com, September 25, 2002.

Job insecurity. (2002, December 2). *pr reporter, 45*, 3.

Jordan, T. L. (2002). *The U.S. Constitution and fascinating facts about it* (7th ed.). Naperville, IL: Oak Hill.

Kamen, J. (1991, March). CNN's breakthrough in Baghdad: Live by satellite (censored). *Washington Journalism Review, 13*(2), pp. 24–27.

Kanter, R. M. (1998). Small business and economic growth. In J. J. Jasinowski (Ed.), *The rising tide* (pp. 87–99). New York: Wiley.

Kennedy, Jr., H., (1966). What you should know about the Foreign Agents Registration Act. *Public Relations Quarterly, 11*, 17–18.

Kornegay, J., & Grunig, L. A. (1998). Cyberbridging: How the communication manager role can link with the dominant coalition. *Journal of Communication Management, 3*(2), 140–156.

Lerbinger, O. (2001). *Corporate power strategies: Getting the upper hand with interest groups.* Newton, MA: Barrington.

Lowenstein, R. L., & Merrill, J. C. (1990). *Macromedia: Mission, message, and morality.* New York: Longman.

Maitra, P. (1996). *The globalization of capitalism in third world countries.* Westport, CT: Praeger.

Martin, L. J., & Chaudhary, A. G. (1983). *Comparative mass media systems.* New York: Longman.

McLeod, J. M., & Blumler, J. G. (1989). The macrosocial level of communication science. In C. R. Berger & S. H. Chaffee (Eds.), *Handbook of communication science* (pp. 271–322). Newbury Park, CA: Sage.

McQuail, D. (1987). *Mass communication theory: An introduction*. London: Sage.

Newsom, D. A., Turk, J. V., & Kruckeberg, D. (2000). *This is PR: The realities of public relations* (7th ed.). Belmont, CA: Wadsworth.

Nye, Jr., J. S. (2002, October 6). In the global age, America's not such a big cheese. *The Washington Post*, p. B3.

O'Dwyer, J. (1981, August). Special report: Fewer major corporations have "public relations" departments. *Jack O'Dwyer's Newsletter*, 1–3.

O'Dwyer, J. (2002, September 17). Students should train as writers. *O'Dwyer's PR Daily*. Retrieved from http://www.odwyerpr.com, September 25, 2002.

Pincus, J. D. (2002, Fall). Expanding the MBA. *The Public Relations Strategist*, p. 4.

Reputation must be pushed. (2000, October 2). *PR Week*, p. 10.

pr reporter. (1983, September 26). [No title] *26*, p. 1.

Profile 2000: A survey of the profession. Part II: Compensation survey. (2000). (International Association of Business Communicators) *Communication World, 13*.

Public relations pros are counselors, not just tactical communicators. (1987, April 20). *pr reporter, 30*, 1–4.

Public Relations Society of America. (1999). *Public relations education for the 21st century: A port of entry: The report of the Commission on Undergraduate Education*. New York: Author.

Pulgar, D. (2002, September 24). Senior, Florida International University. *O'Dwyer's PR Daily*. Retrieved from http://www.odwyerpr.com, September 25, 2002.

Sanders, A. (2002). *Prime-time politics*. Glen Allen, VA: College.

Seitel, F. P. (2001). *The practice of public relations* (8th ed.). Upper Saddle River, NJ: Prentice-Hall.

Sherman, C. (2002, September 24). UM group seeks alternatives to Md. candidates' debates. *Daily Record*. Retrieved from http://www.inform.umd.edu/campusInfo/De. . . s/InstAdv/newsdesk/Clips/200210924.htm, September 24, 2002.

Siebert, F. S., Peterson, T., & Schramm, W. (1963). *Four theories of the press*. Urbana: University of Illinois Press.

Skjerdal, T. S. (1993). *Siebert's four theories of the press: A critique*. Retrieved from http://www.geocities.com/CapitolHill/2152/siebert.html, September 25, 2002.

Tayeb, M. H. (1988). *Organizations and national culture: A comparative analysis*. London: Sage.

Tixier, M. (1993). Approaches to the communication function in France and abroad. *International Public Relations Review, 16*(2), 22–30.

Toth, E. L. (2002). Postmodernism for modernist public relations: The cash value and application of critical research in public relations. *Public Relations Review, 28*, 243–250.

Toth, E. L., & Cline, C. G. (Eds.). (1989). *Beyond the velvet ghetto*. San Francisco: IABC Research Foundation.

Toth, E. L., & Grunig, L. A. (1993). The missing story of women in public relations. *Journal of Public Relations Research, 5*, 153–175.

U.S. Bureau of the Census. (2000). *Statistical abstract of the United States: 2000* (120th ed.). Washington, DC: U.S. Government Printing Office.

U.S. Department of Labor, Bureau of Labor Statistics. (1998, January). *Employment and earnings*. Washington, DC: U.S. Government Printing Office.

van Parijs, P. (1997). *Real freedom for all: What (if anything) can justify capitalism?* Cary, NC: Oxford University Press.

Verčič, D., Grunig, L. A., & Grunig, J. E. (1996). Global and specific principles of public relations: Evidence from Slovenia. In H. M. Culbertson & N. Chen (Eds.), *International public relations: A comparative analysis* (pp. 31–65). Mahwah, NJ: Lawrence Erlbaum Associates.

Weick, K. E. (1979). *The social psychology of organizing* (2nd ed.). Reading, MA: Addison-Wesley.

Wilcox, D. L., Ault, P. H., Agee, W. K., & Cameron, G. T. (2000). *Public relations: Strategies and tactics* (6th ed.). New York: Longman.

World Statistics Pocketbook (22nd ed.). (2001). New York: United Nations Publishing.

Wouters, J. (1991). *International public relations*. New York: Amacom.

Public Relations in Brazil: Practice and Education in a South American Context

Juan-Carlos Molleda
Andréia Athaydes
Vivian Hirsch

When public relations arrived in Brazil in the 1910s it had a Canadian influence, but has since acquired the strong flavor of the largest South American country. This unique Brazilian flavor is enhanced by a combination of a nascent scholarship and a young democracy that emphasizes voluntarism and partnerships to overcome great social inequalities. The national iron and steel company (Companhia Siderúrgica Nacional) in Rio de Janeiro founded the first authentic public relations department in 1951 (Kunsch, 1997). The strong influence of Portuguese language and culture have isolated Brazil from its neighbors. This isolation has created a rich and unique rainbow of artistic, culinary, and social expressions. At the same time, that isolation has motivated Brazil to strive to reach out to the international community. The welcoming attitude of Brazilians is rooted in its history. This is a country that had peaceful transitions from Portuguese colonialism to independence and from military dictatorship to democracy.

Even though the country has grown inward, today Brazilians are open and eager to learn from, and share with, the world in every field of knowledge and professional activity, including public relations. As the largest country in Latin America with the eighth largest economy in the world, Brazil is a fertile environment for the growth of public relations. Brazil legalized the public relations profession in 1967 and created the most formal regulatory structure that is known worldwide. Regulating the public relations industry has its supporters and critics. Federal and regional councils seek to control the practice and set ethical and professional standards. This chapter seeks to introduce the reader to the complexity of public relations in this giant South American nation.

HISTORY AND DEFINITIONS OF PUBLIC RELATIONS

According to Dall'Agnol (1998), the evolution of public relations in Brazil can be divided into four periods: the pioneers, the professionals, the academics, and the researchers. The first period started on January 30 of 1914, when a Canadian corporation called The São Paulo Tramway Light and Power Company Limited created a public relations department (Kunsch, 1997; Peruzzo, 1986; Wey, 1986). Eduardo Pinheiro Lobo, considered as the father of the profession in Brazil, headed the first department. From the 1920s to the end of the 1940s, Brazilian public relations developed primarily in the government sector.

The second period of *professionals* began in the 1950s with a series of public relations classes offered at Getulio Vargas Foundation and the University of São Paulo. In both institutions, public relations courses and seminars were closed linked with business administration (Wey, 1986). In 1953, Getulio Vargas Foundation hired American professor Eric Carlson to carry out the first formal public relations program. Carlson worked with Sylla Chaves as translator and a couple of professors and professionals from various parts of Brazil (Chaves, 1963). Large organizations began expecting professionals to possess technical knowledge and skills, a change for a field that until then was considered a job for people with well-known family heritage who could easily develop influential contacts and friendships in cocktail parties (Wey, 1986).

The Brazilian Association of Public Relations (ABRP) was founded in 1954. A group of professionals from the private and public sectors in São Paulo sponsored its creation. According to Sharpe and Simões (1996), many of the founders of the association were related to the Institute for the Rational Organization of Work and the Institute of Administration of the University of São Paulo. The aim was to increase the strategic implementation of public relations in public administration.

The third period, referred to as *academics* by Dall'Agnol (1998), was characterized by the creation of social communication programs in the '60s and '70s expanding the traditional focus on journalism education to other communication disciplines as well. Among the prominent scholars who represent this academic stage are Cândido Teobaldo de Souza Andrade from the University of São Paulo, the first to graduate from a doctoral program in Brazil and author of one of the first books entitled *How to understand public relations* that was published in 1962. Another scholar was Marta D'Azevedo from the Federal University of Rio Grande do Sul (UFRGS), who wrote the book *Public relations theory and process* in 1971. Eugênio Wenhausen, also from UFRGS, coauthored with Roberto Porto Simões the publication entitled *An introduction to public relations* in 1974. Other notable educators were Nemercio Nogueira and Nei Peixoto doVale (Dall'Agnol, 1998). During this period, public relations programs were created in several institutions of higher education all over the country.

The fourth period is led by Simões who is considered, after Andrade (1986), as one of the first Brazilian scholars to theorize the objectives of public relations. His book *Public relations: Political function* has been considered one of the most influential publications in the field since its publication in 1984. The Superior Council of Communication and Public Relations of Spain published the book in Spanish in 1993. Simões is one of the few, if not the only, Brazilian scholars of public relations who has published academic work in the United States (Sharpe & Simões, 1996; Simões, 1992). Some other scholars and professionals who have contributed to the study of public relations are Margarida K. Kunsch, Cecília Peruzzo, Sidinéia Freitas Gomes, Fábio França, Marcos Fernando Evangelista, Martha Geralda D'Azevedo, Walter Ramos Poyares, Hebe Wey, and Waldyr Gutierrez.

Brazil has one of the largest collections of public relations publications and research papers in Latin America. An impressive number of educators and researchers discuss issues concerning the profession and direct master's and doctoral theses. The Brazilian Society of Interdisciplinary Studies of Communication offers an online database with papers presented in its different congresses (Banco de papers, n.d.). Many universities with public relations programs have their own academic journals to publish studies or commentary papers primarily produced by their professors and graduate students.

The federal and regional councils offer comprehensive lists of publications in the field. The Website of the Regional Council of Public Relations Professionals (Rio Grande do Sul and Santa Catarina) has identified more than 500 publications in Portuguese and Spanish, including more than 100 books with an emphasis on public relations (Livros, n.d.).

DEFINITIONS OF PUBLIC RELATIONS

Official definitions of public relations have been offered by several institutions such as the Inter-American Confederation of Public Relations (CONFIARP), the national Federal Council of Public Relations Professionals (CONFERP), ABRP, as well as a group of scholars. Brazil is a founding member of CONFIARP, created in Mexico in 1960 (Molleda, 2001). Today, Brazilian Antonio-Carlos Lago is the president of the confederation and ABRP. His country is an active participant of the confederation and will host the 25th biannual Inter-American Congress in 2004.

In 1963, at the conclusion of the IV Inter-American Conference of Public Relations in Rio de Janeiro, the first official definition of public relations was approved and adopted by CONFIARP (known at that time as the Inter-American Federation of Public Relations, FIARP) and ABRP. The definition reads:

> Public relations is a socio-technical and administrative discipline with which the opinion and attitude of a public are analyzed and evaluated. Public relations is carried out through a planned, continuous program of reciprocal communication destined to maintain a beneficial affinity with and comprehension of the public. (Pérez-Senac, 2000, p. 22)

This definition emphasizes the influence of social and management sciences for the strategic use of public relations based on two-way symmetrical communication between an organization and its publics. This definition is compatible with those found in the United States body of literature (J. Grunig, 1992; J. Grunig & Hunt, 1984).

At the national level, the 1967 law (details in the legal section below) considers public relations activities as consisting of the following: the diffusion of information of institutional character from an entity to the public through the mass media; the coordination and planning of public opinion research with an institutional purpose; the planning and supervision of the use of audiovisual media for institutional means; the planning and execution of public opinion campaigns; and the teaching of public relations techniques according to norms to be established in the regulation of the law in 1968 (Congreso Nacional do Brasil).

From the legal and professional to the academic sector, public relations has acquired a distinctively Brazilian flavor. Simões (1992) defined public relations as a political function. He stated that an organization needs to convey "that it exists, with permission from a granting power (government) in order to produce something or provide some service to society.... [I]t must act in benefit of all of its partners in society. Its action must be geared toward the common good and never to its own interests. There must be an integration interest" (p. 196). The "integration" theme is present as a key element of the conception of public relations in Latin America (Molleda, 2001).

Additionally, Simões described six common public relations approaches in Brazil and South America:

1. the communication approach includes publicity and internal communication;

2. the marketing approach emphasizes product and organizational promotions;

3. the organizational legitimacy approach focuses on explicit ethical actions;

4. the motivational approach is carried out in conjunction with human resources;

5. the interpersonal approach concentrates on social, technical and political networking; and

6. the event organization approach includes the coordination of social and cultural activities as ends in themselves.

With a distinctive approach, Cicilia Peruzzo (1993) explained the social function of public relations by defining communitarian or popular public relations as "those committed with society transformation toward a stage of higher social equality" (p. 133). Peruzzo (1986, 1993) stated that it implies a new conception of the world and human beings, which includes building a fair and free society; seeking to defend the rights of citizens; seeing civil society as a promoter of change; encouraging the exchange of knowledge between disciplines of study to further political education among citizens, stimulating collective actions, autonomy and the sharing of decision-making power in social movements and other types of organizations.

The study of public relations in undergraduate and graduate programs is producing many master's thesis and doctoral dissertations. The wealth of research is constantly progressing and redefining the scope of the discipline. The next section focuses on public relations education in Brazil.

PUBLIC RELATIONS EDUCATION

In 1965, the International Center of Higher Studies of Communication for Latin America (CIESPAL) conducted four regional seminars to promote the redirection of journalism careers in communication or science institutes of "collective communication" (Meditsch, 1999). At a seminar in Rio de Janeiro, CIESPAL introduced the concept of a "polyvalent communication professional," a professional who could acquire a holistic knowledge of the mass media as well as perform scientific research, public relations and advertising. According to Meditsch, by 1970, a third of the schools in the continent had changed their names from "journalism" to "communication." By 1980, 85% of schools had made this change. The notion of "polyvalent journalists" evolved into the concept of "social communicators." However, it is significant to note that while the name was accepted, the idea of a "polyvalent communicator" was not accepted by educators. Brazil was the pioneer in defending the legitimacy and need for specialized studies in journalism, advertising, political propaganda, and public relations in Latin America. The emphases were offered under the umbrella of social communication.

In 1967, the University of São Paulo's School of Communication and Arts offered the first four-year public relations program. Since then, significant strides have been made in public relations education in the country. According to the Regional Council of São Paulo and Parana, public relations is currently being taught in 78 undergraduate programs and 24 graduate programs across the nation (Cursos de Graduação, 2002; Pós-Graduação, 2002).

In the past decade, under President Fernando Henrique Cardoso, the management and operation of higher education in Brazil has undergone significant changes. The Brazilian education department (Ministério de Educação), under the aegis of its higher education division (Secretaria de Ensino Superior or SESu), has established a rigorous system for evaluating graduate programs nationwide, with the goal of ensuring a minimum level of quality for both new and existing programs. Among the many evaluation instruments established for this purpose are curricular guidelines and quality standards.

To develop these documents, SESu formed committees of education specialists consisting of university professors from across the nation and solicited their input. Although these committees have existed in Brazil since 1985, when José Sarney was president, we have chosen to focus our attention in this chapter on the 1990s because it was during this decade that important changes were made in the teaching of communication, particularly public relations.[1] Based on Regulation Law 146/97 a Committee of Specialists in Communication Education (CEE-COM) was formed. The development of curricular guidelines was the main challenge faced by this committee. Many of the demands of public relations professionals, which were represented in the document developed by the National Parliament of Public Relations, were included in the curricular guidelines for communication.[2] This allowed the narrowing of the gap between educational and professional performance, obviating the need for a judicial-legal solution for the inappropriate practice of public relations by professionals in other areas.

The goal was to ensure that the demands of public relations professionals were addressed through higher education if not by legal means. The document emphasizes the specific abilities, in addition to the ones required for communication in general, that public relations professionals must possess regarding the development of relationships with key stakeholders, establishment of needs assessments and plans, development of strategies for improving relationships; implementation of integration instruments and programs; conduct of activities related to communication strategies; dialog between the typical functions of public relations and the other professional managerial functions that exist in the area of communication or other areas with which it interacts; and, finally, all other activities that common sense or public relations organizations may deem specific to this discipline.

Although the curricular guidelines for communication were not approved by the Higher Education Council until July 4, 2001 (through CES Resolution 16/2002), the final document had already been provided to the division of higher education. Based on this document, members of the newly formed committee developed quality standards for all areas of specialization.

The committees of education specialists completed its term in July 2002. The responsibility to evaluate and recognize graduate education programs in Brazil has been passed on to the National Institute of Statistics and Educational Research, the organization that oversees the national university examinations (known as "Provão"), using the quality

---

[1] The Committees of Education Specialists are made up of professors from different universities to provide assistance to the higher education division in the analysis of different activities within its jurisdiction.

[2] A national discussion regarding the attributes and functions of public relations professionals, which resulted in the development of a document, by CONFERP, aimed at revising the law that regulates the public relations profession in Brazil: Law 5.377/69.

standards developed by the committees.[3] The institute also is responsible for developing the Manual of Evaluation of Education Conditions, with 70% of criteria being common to all disciplines, and only 30% specific to each discipline.

From supranational to national definitions as well as academic and professional initiatives, public relations continues its development in Brazil. In particular, the profession faces a distinctive legal framework that is not found in any other country of Latin America. This regulatory framework has been blamed for excluding the term "public relations" from most private organizations (Kunsch, 1997).

LEGAL STATUS

According to Kunsch (1997), Brazil was the first country in the world to adopt a public relations legislation (Congresso Nacional do Brasil Law 5,377, December 11, 1967). Similarly, Panama has regulated the profession since 1980. Other Latin American countries, such as Costa Rica and Peru, have tried to pass laws to regulate public relations without success.

Federal and regional councils were created to enforce the law and to penalize those who did not comply with it. Professionals must have a public relations degree and be licensed by their states' regional councils to practice public relations legally. Despite the longevity of the law and the work carried out by the regulatory bodies, licensing has been difficult to enforce, especially at times when the scope of public relations has expanded and diversified (Molleda, 2002a).

The government recognized that under the 1967 law, public relations professionals could be licensed if they were practicing public relations since 1965 and they were ABRP members. Professionals must have practiced public relations for more than two years and received their main source of income from this practice. This provisional condition (provisionados) was accepted until 1969 when only professionals with a university degree in communication and an emphasis on public relations from a recognized institution or a foreign degree properly revalidated in Brazil in the Ministry of Education could obtain the professional license. Even though the government itself has gotten involved with law enactments, public relations agencies cannot be hired by government entities unless bids are solicited through advertising agencies. Moreover, public relations firms need to be subcontracted by advertising agencies for work to be directly provided to government. In some cases, public relations can comprise 70% of the marketing mix but will still have to be channeled via an advertising agency for government projects.

The law has lasted without modification for more than three decades and some scholars blame it as being a "serious obstacle for the growth and consolidation of the area" (Kunsch, 1997, p. 22). Public relations associations and councils have repeatedly addressed the nation's political, social and economic advances as a justification for updating the legislation. In 1998, at the conclusion of the four-year National Parliament of Public Relations sponsored by the Federal Council (CONFERP), changes to the law were drafted.

The national debate coordinated by the Federal Council produced a document named "Conclusions of the National Parliament of Public Relations," which was presented at the

---

[3]A national qualifying examination for 24 university programs. The students are submitted to this exam at the end of their graduating course in order to evaluate and measure knowledge and abilities acquired along the course. In the field of communication, only journalism has been included in this system since 1998. No date has been set for the inclusion of the other communication areas in this evaluation system.

XV ABRP Congress in Salvador, Bahia, in August 1998 (Conselho Federal, 1998). The decisions of the Parliament have not been made legally binding through the modification of the two first paragraphs of Law 5.377/69. As a result, CONFERP, under the direction of Flávio Schmidt, is working toward finalizing the document so it can be put into practice. Federal Council Secretary General Jorge Eduardo Caixeta, in an interoffice memorandum to the regional counsels dated August 20, 2000, noted that:

> In all regulated professions, it is the respective Federal Council that establishes what society should consider in order for concepts, behavior standards, and professional stance to be defined. ... It seems that we suffer from a chronic problem: all of us know what public relations is, what it does, what its specific activities are. And yet, when asked to define these concepts, we stumble, choke, and ... let time go by. Time has gone by and now it is past the time for us to assume the responsibility for doing so.

To achieve this objectives, in early 2002, the federal and regional counsels, in consultation with professionals in their respective states, drafted a resolution proposal that defines public relations professional activities in Brazil. This proposal is based on the original document developed by the Parliament. In August 2002, CONFERP's deliberative group met in Belo Horizonte, in the state of Minas Gerais, to further develop this proposal. The group has had difficulty in achieving consensus on two issues:

1. The definition of the concepts used in the field of public relations such as institutional, corporate, organizational, public, or civic communication. This issue is problematic because existing theories in Brazil regarding these themes include different terminology. Public relations professionals often use these terms interchangeably in their daily work and may also incorporate additional ones.

2. The fact that, because the existing law does not precisely identify the types of activities that are specific to public relations, many of them are currently recognized as appropriate for professionals such as administrators, marketers, journalists, and others. Claiming that these activities and functions belong to public relations will certainly lead to conflicts, perhaps even legal challenges, from these other professions.

Regarding this matter, França (2001) noted:

> It is difficult to determine, thinking ahead to 2000, which directions public relations professional activities will take. The practice of public relations seems fragmented, lacking a strategic positioning and favoring organized, integrative and systemic action. If it were strong enough to elevate the stature of public relations in the market along with those who dedicate themselves to it and the organizations who greatly need it. (p. 3)

Although the situation has improved significantly in the past five years, public relations in Brazil, although guaranteed a legal status, has not yet acquired legitimacy in the eyes of society. To achieve this legitimacy, CONFERP is focusing its efforts on obtaining a clear and objective definition of the functions and activities of public relations professionals, guaranteeing them defense subsidies, even if these are applicable only to legal matters.

The resolution proposal was approved in October of 2002. Highlights include: (1) The definition of the main concepts used in the field; and (2) the definition of varied public relations activities including those related to public relations education, which reflect the curricular guidelines approved in 2002 through State Council of Education Resolution 16/2000.

CONFERP realizes that the existence of the law in and of itself will not guarantee the recognition of public relations professionals by the Brazilian society. This will only occur if public relations graduates demonstrate that they are competent to practice the public relations activities described under the law. In addition to tackling legal aspects, which is its main function, CONFERP has created committees (coordenadorias) that work with higher education institutions to ensure that public relations professionals receive high-quality education.

The recognition of the public relations field by the different segments of Brazilian society is being promoted by the legal redefinition of the profession along with its unification with the national and international education sectors, thus ensuring that it has the theoretical and practical bases required for the full exercise of professional public relations activities.

TRENDS IN THE INDUSTRY

Duarte (2001) stated that despite efforts to regulate the public relations profession, encroachment has persisted over the decades. Journalists frequently perform public relations functions calling themselves "institutional journalists" (jornalismo empresarial). Such journalists see public relations as just the production of corporate publications and the diffusion of information on behalf of the organization. Another trend is the introduction of terms such as endomarketing, institutional marketing, social marketing, relationship marketing, and media training, which incorporate strategies and tactics historically associated with public relations. Professionals of other areas are gaining enormous visibility in the market and now present those approaches as novelties.

Other associations unite those professionals who have a broader view of corporate communication practices, which respond to the trend in integrated or marketing communication in Brazil. For instance, the Brazilian Association of Business Communication (ABERJE) claims to be the major entity representing social communication in Brazil (O que é a Aberje, n.d.). Its objective is to discuss and promote communication as an instrument linked to the strategic management of organizations and strengthening the citizenry. Founded in 1967, ABERJE claims to have a membership of more than 1,000 private and public companies and institutions from five administrative regions (O que é a Aberje, n.d.).

Nevertheless, and despite all these associations and legalities, any journalist in Brazil can open a small firm and call himself/herself a public relations practitioner. Brazilian business executives take these "media relations boutiques" into consideration and solicit bids from these firms also along with large global firms such as Edelman. There is a widespread misunderstanding in Brazil regarding the role of public relations. Most business executives regard public relations as mere media relations and measurement of success is determined by media advertising equivalency. The global messaging strategies and tactics are not yet recognized in Brazil. Instead, business marketing executives and CEOs engage a public relations firm to "put the product or executives in the media" with a positive spin—obviously at 1% or less of the cost of advertising.

According to the most recent association in Brazil inaugurated in 2001—Brazilian Association of Communication Agencies (Associação Brasileira das Agências de Comunicação, ABRACOM)—the size of the public relations market in the country is about US$ 50 million. If true, this would prove once again that the only recognition for public relations is still in its value as a tool of basic media relations activities.

INFRASTRUCTURE AND PUBLIC RELATIONS

This section summarizes the nature of the Brazilian infrastructure as it relates to public relations practices. Relevant aspects of the political and economic spheres as well as the extent of activism embedded in society are addressed.

Political System

Since winning independence from Portugal in 1822, Brazil has been a federal republic, with a new constitution that was promulgated in 1988. The president is popularly elected to no more than two 4-year terms. The 1994 elections marked the second presidential suffrage since the end of military rule. Fernando Henrique Cardoso won that election and won reelection in 1998. Labor Party candidate Luís Inácio "Lula" da Silva was elected president with 61% of the vote on October 27, 2002. This is the first time that a left-wing Workers' Party candidate has been elected President in Brazil's history.

Brazil experienced dramatic changes especially in the '80s and '90s (Ortiz, 1991; Santos & Silveira, 2001). Today, Brazilians enjoy the benefits of a young, vibrant democracy, despite its imperfections. Political rights improved substantially between 1984, when the military was still in power, and the early 1990s. According to Mainwaring, Brinks, and Perez-Linan (2001):

> In 1984, the last of the military presidents was still in office; citizens in state capitals and a number of other cities were not able to elect their own mayor; one-third of the federal senate had been elected indirectly in rules designed to guarantee majorities for the military government; communist parties were outlawed; and the left still faced sporadic repression. (p. 54)

These vestiges of authoritarian rule had been eliminated by 1990. As a result, there are many different political parties in Brazil. "[I]ndividuals are given significant freedom in expressing their beliefs ... this notion dates back to Brazil's founding, where different groups were not forced to assimilate fully to the Portuguese culture" (Gannon, 2001, p. 116).

Government institutions have realized the power of communication in a modern democratic society. In 1997, the Federal Senate created a large-scale communication operation with the purpose of promoting political education among the Brazilian citizens and motivating their participation in the nascent democratic process (Testa, 1999). The mission of the newly founded Secretary of Social Communication was based on the Brazilian Constitution, which emphasizes that citizens actively participate in grassroots democratic traditions. Access to information regarding the Senate, its members and actions, as well as open channels of communication between senators and citizens, were considered fundamental. One of the apparent outcomes of this initiative of the Brazilian Senate, which includes journalists in residence and mass media productions, has been an increase in political coverage by local and national media outlets and an increase in public awareness of the political system. It has motivated more inquiries from citizens about senators and legislation, which has been recorded by the "Voice of the Citizen," a "hotline" of the Department of Public Relations. Such democratic advancements have partly contributed to economic growth and the organization of increasingly active civil societies. A Code of Defense of the Consumer was enacted in 1991. According to Sorj (2000), the advances in consumers' rights have also become a channel of expression for the defense of the rights of citizens.

As democracy advances, Brazilian organizations have endured a hard fight for public recognition. The emerging society is much more oriented toward results. Quality of products and services, environmental protection, and social responsibility have become relevant matters for organizations. Since 1985, the advancement has empowered citizens. The democratic process has also challenged government officials. They are advised and assisted by public relations or social communication professionals who build bridges of participation between ministries and other governmental dependencies, organized groups, and common citizens.

Once a radical leftist, the newly elected president of Brazil portrays a renovated image of moderation and has been building linkages with industrialists, bankers, and stock exchange officials. As a consequence "many business leaders have moved to his side, seizing the opportunity to open an unprecedented dialogue with the leftist candidate [now elected president] and his team" (Lula's historic victory, 2002).

The young but vibrant Brazilian democracy, and the great inequalities the Brazilian population faces are pressuring organizations to increase their community involvement through partnerships with employees, other organizations, community groups, and local and federal government agencies. Nevertheless, Molleda's (2002b) study indicated that Brazilians continue to mistrust their government, which is characterized as being bureaucratic and inefficient. The study focused on the social role of public relations professionals including partnership with the government in developing social and educational programs. The "partnership with government" items created a distinctive dimension of the external social role but those statements were reported to have the lowest mean scores. Molleda (2002b) concluded that despite these results "[i]t is possible that progress toward participative democracy, voluntarism, and a stronger civil society will increase organizations' involvement with government and community initiatives" as a key dimension of the social role of public relations in Brazil (p. 21). This process may be accelerated by Lula's administration despite some skepticism on this issue in some circles.

Economic System

With an estimated 170 million inhabitants in 2000, Brazil has the largest population in Latin America and sixth largest in the world (World Bank, 2002). Eighty percent of Brazil's population lives in the south-central urban area. Whereas this fast growth in urban population has positively influenced economic development, it has also created serious social, environmental, and political problems for large cities.

Possessing large and well-developed agricultural, mining, manufacturing, technology, and services industries, Brazil's economy outweighs that of all other South American countries and is expanding its presence in world markets. In the information technology realm, Brazil is considered one of the 30 leading exporters of high-tech products. It occupies the 27th place in the world, according to United Nations.

However, since the 1960s, Brazil has ridden a roller coaster of high and low economic performance. The late '60s and early '70s were years of double-digit annual growth. In the '80s, however, its performance was poor in relation to its potential (World Bank, 2002). The adoption of a new Constitution in 1988 did not help much to improve the situation. Lack of flexibility was the result of the introduction of major rigidities in budgeting and public expenditure. In the early 1990s the Real Plan motivated economic recovery. The main goal of this plan was to reduce inflation and keep it low, which it did to the appreciation of the masses. The inflation rate before 1994 was four digits but was only a single digit in 1998. Despite the success of the economic program, the country faces the problem of poverty.

The new Brazilian democracy and the social equality challenges are also much more demanding of private organizations. There have been major changes in Brazil's emergent economy as well. During the 1980s, Brazilian companies went trough a process of economic adjustments and improvements that made them less dependent on being favored by the State and more suitable to compete in a world market. Brazilian "[c]onglomerates . . . don't have much more room to expand locally, yet they face increasing international competition at home," Adese says (2002, p. 29). Such is the case of Metalúrgica Gerdau S.A. which is located in the extreme south and is one of the fastest growing steel producers in the world (Rohter, 2001).

Environmental awareness among Brazilians has increased with the noticeable involvement of the private sector and civil society at large in discussions about taking actions to save the environment. While Brazil still has not approved genetically modified organisms (GMOs), the country requires labeling of the few imported products containing genetically modified products so that consumer can choose whether to buy them. Brazil has made significant progress in human development since 1975, which is a comprehensive measure of economic development (United Nations Development Programme, 2001). The state of São Paulo has produced a new index reflecting both human development and social responsibility.

Activism and Social Movements

In general, Latin American citizens, especially the lower strata of the population, are becoming more active and outspoken. The new unionism in rural Brazil, for example, is a consequence of the country's democratic transition during the 1980s. The unionism trend could increase in the administration of Luis Inacio "Lula" da Silva who was a former factory worker and trade union leader. The participation of civil society in the construction of a democratic system entails individual and collective involvement. Herbert de Souza, a.k.a. Betinho, was the principal leader of the Action Movement of Citizenry against Hunger, Misery and for Life (Movimento da Ação da Cidadania contra a Fome, a Miséria e pela Vida). Founded in 1993, this movement responded to the need of motivating citizens to participate in reducing the level of social fragmentation and exclusion (Plasencia, 2001). During its best years of 1993 and 1994, the movement had more than 5000 committees in different regions of the country. Three main campaign themes guided its actions: food for the hungry, work to eradicate the misery of the unemployed, and democratization of land ownership.

According to Plasencia (2001), the movement was inspired by the global promotion of democratic ideals and, paradoxically, the ever-increasing inefficiency of democratic regimes to facilitate ample participation of the people in political activity and public life. Democracy becomes not only the responsibility of political parties and the state, but also of every citizen as well, according to the principles of the Action Movement of Citizenry. It is necessary to discourage indifference and awaken the conscience of people for abandoning the culture of resignation. Even with this enhanced social conscience, Brazilians has yet to follow the steps of more developed nations and it is very difficult to form public interest groups to discuss matters of interest such as medical diseases or to protest against urban violence.

Social movements constitute a space to develop education programs in democracy. State and private organizations have developed partnerships with community groups, philanthropic institutions, and small businesses, creating new forms of solidarity. However, there appears to be more talk than action, especially in the hectic urban centers.

The growth of volunteerism in Brazil is evidence of "the seemingly intractable nature of Brazil's social ills such as the heightened concern over how to solve those problems and the growing impatience with government's ability to address them," according to Buckley (2001, p. A01). "It also is evidence of how the power of democracy . . . can go beyond free elections and fair trials to affect a society in ways that are subtler but no less profound."

The World Social Forum, the counter to the World Economic Forum, took place for the third time in Porto Alegre, capital of Rio Grande do Sul, in January 2003. Bruno (2001) stated that the United Nations has ranked Porto Alegre as Brazil's best metropolis in terms of quality of life: "For 12 years, Porto Alegre's budget has been decided by hundreds of well-organized community and worker groups" (p. 25). The city's mayor and its left-wing coalition from his Worker's Party (PT) have made progress in housing, public transportation, the health system, infrastructure, education, and legal system. This has attracted the attention of urban planners worldwide.

With the assistance of 100,000 activists from 156 nations and more than four thousand journalists, the forum, as one of its best events, had a protest rally against the creation of the Free Trade Area of the Americas (FTAA). Romero (2002) reported the view of Mark Ritchie of the Institute for Agriculture and Trade Policy in Minneapolis: "I was amazed at how the concept of corporate responsibility has grown in Brazil."

The democratization of Brazil and the difficulties of the economy have contributed to the birth of a more active society. A large number of nongovernmental organizations (NGOs) emerged during the 1990s dedicated to the issues of ethics and social responsibility. In this context, a large number of public relations programs have been implemented to support these organizations. The level of development, perhaps, is the aspect that impacts the evolution and practice of public relations in Brazil the most. This largest South American country is rapidly changing because of a vibrant democracy and an emerging economy while struggling to reduce the gap between different socioeconomic classes. This struggle is more pronounced in the large urban centers located primarily in the southeastern zone. The government sector is aware of the struggle and has increased its own internal and external communication activities. The private sector is also in tune with this fact and has contributed to ease the crisis with nonprofit initiatives such as the Ethos Institute of Business and Social Responsibility (Instituto Ethos de Empresas e Responsabilidade Social).

Ethos conducted research in the largest urban areas of Brazil and reported that a more demanding consumer is emerging who stresses the need for socially responsible organizations (Responsabilidade, 2001). Nevertheless, the government is still seen as the most responsible entity for dealing with crime and health problems. Private organizations are seen as a second force capable of contributing to employment and effective social transformation. The active and complex nature of Brazilians was dormant during the military oppression, but those cultural dimensions have always been embedded in the culture.

CULTURAL DIMENSIONS

The most common Brazilian greeting is "tudo bom?" meaning "is everything well?" This optimism is present in social interactions, making Brazilians a very friendly people. Gannon (2001) explained, "Brazilians have tremendous spirit in the face of adversity. . . . The well of this spirit is continually replenished by the Brazilians' passion for life" (p. 113). Brazilian society is very diverse given contrasting European, African, and Asian roots. The Brazilian population is made up of five major ethic groups: the indigenous full-blooded natives who mainly live in the upper Amazon basin and in the northern and western border regions; Portuguese who initiated intermarriages with natives and slaves since colonization in the 1500s; Africans brought as slaves; and, various other Europeans, Middle Eastern, and Asian immigrants who entered the country mainly between 1875 and 1960. Since the mid-nineteenth century, about 5 million Germans, Italians, Spaniards, and Poles have settled in the southern states of Paraná, Rio Grande do Sul, Santa Catarina, and São Paulo. The largest Japanese community outside of Japan is in São Paulo.

Mainly the white elite have cherished the myth of a racially balanced democracy in the country. But, since 1995, when President Cardoso brought the issue to the political arena, discriminatory cases and a different reality has been uncovered (Affirmative action, 2001). Rohter (2002) explained that "[o]fficially, less than half of Brazil's 175 million people are classified as black. But in a nation that likes to consider itself a racial democracy, 70 percent of those living below the poverty line are black, as are 80 percent of those who are illiterate, and some studies indicate that on average, whites live longer than blacks and earn twice as much" (p. A4). Being black seems to be a stigma in Brazil. Forty percent of Brazilians called themselves brown (i.e., mestizo) and only 5% called themselves black. According to the Brazilian Institute of Geography and Statistics, 5.6% of the northeastern population is reported black and 64.5% mixed race (parda) (Distribuição da população, 1999).

In September 2001, Brazilian officials attending the United Nation's antiracism conference in South Africa agreed to support quotas for blacks in universities and the civil service. Already, the State Assembly of Rio de Janeiro has voted to implement the proposal in the two universities it sponsors. Thus, the race issue is complicated. "There is a good amount of income inequality, and much of it is concentrated among those with darker skin pigmentation, even though Brazilians of all types tend to interact more easily in daily life than their American counterparts," wrote Gannon (2001, p. 116).

Brazil is the only Portuguese-speaking nation in the Americas. National identity is strong in spite of the variety of ethnic groups and class distinctions. This multiracial society or "Brazilian rainbow" has been isolated from its Spanish-speaking neighbors on the border regions of the Amazon rainforest and the Parana basin as a consequence of language, geography, and history. "Isolation has bred introversion. That partly reflects Brazil's vast size, self-sufficiency and fairly peaceful history. . . . Its legacies include ugly everyday violence and deep-rooted social inequalities" (Brazil's 500 years of solicitude, 2000, p. 15).

About 80% of the population professes to follow Roman Catholicism, with most others being Protestants or followers of practices derived from African religious cults. "As late as the 1990s, Brazil was recognized as the largest Catholic country in the world," according to Birman and Leite (2000, p. 271). These authors argued that it is not clear whether this is true today: "Doubts abound as we now witness the rapid proliferation of alternative religious movements (led by a burgeoning number of Pentecostal churches and sects), which has led the Catholic Church to adopt measures intended to recapture lost ground." In a strong uncertainty avoidance society such as Brazil, "we find religions which claim absolute truth and which do not tolerate other religions" (Hofstede, 1983, p. 83).

According to Hofstede's (1983) cultural dimensions, Brazil is a culture that strongly avoids uncertainty: "there will be a higher level of anxiety in people, which becomes manifest in greater nervousness, emotionally, and aggressiveness" (pp. 81–83). Nevertheless, Brazilians live in uncertainty because, especially in the political and economic arena, the future is unknown. Therefore, Brazilians seem to find ways to escape their reality with a great passion for life and optimism to overcome the anxiety that unstable scenarios cause.

On two other of Hofstede's dimensions, Brazilians are collectivistic with high power distance embedded in their society. This combination is defined by Triandis (2002) as vertical collectivism. That is, vertical cultures accept hierarchy as a given which is enhanced by the fact that collectivistic cultures are higher in conformity. Societies with high power distance let inequalities such as physical and intellectual capacities "grow over time into inequalities in power and health" (Hofstede, 1983, p. 81). "The latter may become hereditary and no longer related to physical and intellectual capacities at all," according to Hofstede. These aspects seem to be causing struggles within the population that, since 1985, is in the process of overcoming the repression of dictatorships.

According to Hoftede (1983), Brazil is considered a moderately feminine society. The feminine feature could be related to a peaceful transition from colonialism to a federative republic and from dictatorship to democracy. In general, Brazilians put relationships with people before money and appreciate the preservation of the environment (Gannon, 2001). This fact has been emphasized since the World Environmental Summit in 1992, when Brazil became the center of promotion and conservation of biodiversity.

Using Hofstede's (1991) fifth dimension of culture, Confucian work dynamism later described as long-term orientation (Hofstede, 2001), Brazil can be categorized as a short-term orientation society. The fact that the future is always unknown by Brazilians could in part explain this categorization.

Triandis (2002) elaborated on the dimensions of cultures, which could be easily interpreted to explain the complexity of Brazilian society. Subgroups with different interests, beliefs, and attitudes concerning a wide array of issues can be found in Brazil. In the southeast, where the major economic centers are located, the gap between the rich and the poor is great. "Affluence is shifting most rich cultures toward individualism," Triandis wrote (2002, p. 27). "Affluence has the consequence of making people independent of their groups." This reality is overwhelming sociologists.

More specific aspects can be analyzed when focusing on communication behavior and the impact of cultural dimensions. Brazilians as "[c]ollectivists use indirect and face saving communications. . . . This means that e-mail will be less satisfying to collectivists, since they will not have access to the context" (Triandis, 2002, p. 38). Taking into consideration the vertical collectivistic nature of Brazilian society, they limit the information they send to only some "important" people. Dealing with high- or low-status individuals, face-to-face communication will produce higher levels of cooperation among Brazilians. This assumption applies to media relations strategies, in which media owners, editors, and journalists should be approached both personally and through formal channels, with the former being a common and effective practice.

The cultural aspects of Brazil have an impact on public relations practices in the country. People orientation is a must in developing media, community, government and employee relations strategies. Human communication is a primary component of ongoing relationship efforts. Personal contacts, typified by the personal influence model, are essential to develop solid interactions with journalists, editors, and government officials. In public organizations and government agencies, a primary function of public relations is "protocol and ceremonial," which is the consequence of a culture characterized by high power distance.

In their pursuit of high and immediate impact, Brazilian and transnational corporations frequently opt for special events that attract a gathering of the masses. Nationalism and diversity (the Brazilian rainbow) are especially emphasized. This has been enhanced by a campaign promoting voluntarism among common citizens, organized groups, and a variety of institutions. One limitation for public relations planning is the short-term orientation found in Brazilian society whereby most of the strategic public relations programs focus on immediate and reactive actions.

MEDIA INFRASTRUCTURE

Media Control

The emergence of a commercial model of broadcasting in Brazil began in the 1920s. Magazine publishers, press agencies, advertising agencies, and radio and television broadcasters have pressed hard for a commercial media (Herman & McChesney, 1997). The Brazilian government did not establish a public broadcasting system for its propaganda efforts. Instead, it censored the media and tried to exert control over them. The influence of the government on the development of the media infrastructure in Brazil is summarized in the following paragraph:

> The Globo system was rewarded by the generals with huge subsidies in the form of a taxpayer-financed telecommunications network and satellite system, a very large flow of government advertising, discrimination against rival networks, which helped sink several of them. . . . The Globo network absorbs some 80 percent of TV advertising revenue and 60 percent of all Brazilian advertising, and it also controls vast interests in other media sectors (including *O Globo*, the [third] largest newspaper in Brazil, news and advertising agencies, record, printing and publishing companies, and all kinds of radio stations). . . . The ending of the military regime in 1985 did not curb the expansion of the Globo empire; the weak civil liberties that followed did not have the incentive or power to intrude. (Herman & McChesney, 1997, p. 165)

Brazil's largest newspaper is *Folha de São Paulo*, and the second largest is O *Estado de São Paulo*. *O Globo* is the third-largest daily. Nevertheless, the expansion of the Globo conglomerate continues in Brazil, Latin America, and the Spanish-speaking United States. Globo accorded a long-term strategic alliance with News Corporation considered as one of the largest global media oligopolies (Herman & McChesney, 1997). A more recent business partnership has been consolidated between AOL-Time Warner, Banco Itaú, and Globo to create AOL Brasil, which has moved forward the era of media convergence in Brazil.

Like many other Latin American countries, Brazil's media environment is considered to be *partly free* by the *Press Freedom Survey 2002* (Freedom House, 2002). A 1967 press law prescribes prison terms for libel, but this provision is rarely enforced. A 1999 law would penalize prosecutors, judges, and government attorneys for leaking information to the press about ongoing cases. The press is privately owned and newspapers have played a central role in exposing official corruption. There are dozens of daily newspapers and numerous other publications throughout the country. In recent years TV Globo's near monopoly on the broadcast media has been challenged by its rival, Sistema Brasileiro de Televisão (STB). A federal judge ordered the closure of 2000 community radio stations in São Paulo in January 2002 because the stations allegedly interfered with airplane flights! A number of journalists reported incidents of intimidation, including assaults and death threats. In the Ramo Branco electoral zone, media were prohibited from reporting on municipal elections by a local judge.

New information technology is helping to diversify the Brazilian media infrastructure and practices. Brazil has experienced an impressive growth in the number of Internet hosts from 268,000 in 1995 to 1,203,100 in 2000 (United Nations Development Pro-gramme, 2001). Between 1998 and 2000, Internet users have increased from 3.8 million to 16.9 million, displaying what a powerful channel of communication this new medium has become.

Brazil has a very sophisticated media infrastructure; some analysts say that the system is more advanced that the level of education of the population. Satellites are used for both the print (e.g., *Gazeta Mercantil*) and the broadcasting industry. Each corner of the vast country can be reached with any combination of media mix.

The sophistication of the media industry makes "media relations" an essential public re-lations function in Brazil. New information technologies are increasing the use of Internet communication between media and public relations professionals. Public relations profes-sionals are conscious of the power of the media in mobilizing public opinion. Primarily, "information subsidies" or communication activities are oriented toward obtaining a fa-vorable coverage of the organization, hiding unfavorable aspects that could be negative for the organization's reputation and "framing" organizational positions to influence positive responses when perhaps focusing on solving eventual conflicts (Penteado, 2002).

Former and current journalists (converted into public relations practitioners) dominate the media relations function (Penteado 1996, 2002). According to Penteado (1996):

[P]ublic relations departments are usually divided between the "journalists," who are the press agents, and the mediators in a two way situation that usually deal with external environments; and the "public relations," practitioners who take care of the internal environment and of most events, and also responsible for most of the research. Journalists who, later covert to public relations may be those who tend to use one-way publicity and two-way publicity communication in Brazil. (p. 124)

CONCLUSIONS

To sum up the relationship between the Brazilian environment and public relations in Brazil, it is clear that the country has achieved a significant degree of professionalism and scholarship in public relations. "The profession as an institution is an unquestionable reality by the action of its professionals in several segments of society, in companies, universities" and by professional councils, associations, and labor unions (Dall'Agnol, 1998, p. 9). The legal status of the profession has its supporters and detractors. It is clear that Brazilian professionals can be separated into three camps: members of the regional councils, members of the business communication association, and many others that do not belong to either group.

Public relations is a constantly changing industry but in regions such as Latin America, these changes are much quicker and intense due to a series of socioeconomic factors. For example, one issue is devaluation of national currencies. Because the "recognition" of public relations in Brazil is basically limited to media relations, public relations fees which in the developed world would be of US$ 10,000 per month are only about 10,000 reais in Brazil, which at best be the equivalent of US$ 2800. Moreover, the slowdown of the United States and world economy, recent corporate scandals, and high oil prices are having serious effects on Latin America's economies.

Changes and trends have forced companies to act in a more socially responsible manner. Changes in the public relations industry have clients investing more in other areas of the communication mix that were previously ignored such as promotions and relationship marketing. They are also taking advantage of new technologies such as the mobile internet.

Despite economic difficulties, the public relations industry has grown in Brazil and Latin America over the last five years. The main differences are in the perceptions among executives of large national and multinational corporations regarding the use of communication as tools to pursue business objectives. Although a majority of clients still do not understand the full scope of public relations and insist in believing that media relations is what public relations is all about, some people do understand that public relations can be an effective way to manage organizational communication.

Public relations agencies have felt the effect of these changes such as a growth in the request for proposals, more demanding clients, better acceptance of specialized services and opinions, as well as increased confidence of those who hire their services. But, on the other hand, agencies too have had to strive to consistently provide better services, proactive attitudes and constructive criticism.

That said, agencies still face situations where clients have no idea of what they can do for their company, and still have the expectation of securing results comparable to those of their latest advertising campaign (for 1% of the price). Therefore, the trends we see for the near future are pretty much an evolution of what is already in place. Currently, we observe an explosion of niche publications clearly indicating a segmentation of the market, targeting new or emerging consumer groups. Along with that come the new forms of communicating with these publics. The use of e-publicity (or online media relations) is gradually but consistently replacing the old press-conference/press-kit format. Journalists today go to the Internet not only to find out if anyone has written the story they want to write, but also to analyze and discover new topics to write about.

In summary, an overview of public relations in Brazil and the environmental variables that influence its development allow us to make various assumptions. More democracy and economic complexity in a large nation positively influences the development of public relations as a professional practice and discipline of study. As the Brazilian economy stabilizes and its political system strengthens, public relations will continue to develop in Brazil, positively influencing the rest of the South American nations. A closer relationship between government, the private sector, community groups, media outlets, activists, and social movements may achieve the integration that seems to be the core of the Latin American school of public relations.

CASE STUDY: COCA-COLA AND THE PARINTINS FOLKLORIC FESTIVAL

Founded in 1886, Coca-Cola produces more than 230 brands in nearly 200 countries. Headquartered in Atlanta, Georgia, the corporation's first international bottling plant was opened in Canada in 1906 (Around the world, n.d.). Almost 50 years after it foundation, Coca-Cola arrived in northeastern Brazil in 1942 (A pausa que, n.d.).

The first bottling plants were located in the cities of Recife and Natal. They were called the "Victory Corridor" because this operation was part of the war efforts determined by the then-president of Coca-Cola, Robert Woodruff. During World War II, the corporation promised the United States military servicemen that, wherever they were, they would continue drinking cold Cokes at the same price of 5 cents. The outsourced Brazilian plants supplied the finished product to cargo ships heading toward Europe from the country's northeast coast.

Today, Coca-Cola Brazil is very much engaged in community initiatives. The page named "Example of Citizenship" of the company's Website in Brazil is introduced by these statements:

Citizenship means the consistent exercise of the rights and responsibilities of a citizen with the State. This is the commitment of Coca-Cola since almost 60 years of activities in Brazil, in which it has always tried to play an active role in social development of the communities where it operates in the country. At the end, our success is a fruit of a strong interaction with the public, the partnership between the corporation and the Brazilian society. (Exemplo de cidadania, n.d.)

Among the various social programs Coca-Cola has developed in this giant South American nation are environmental protection and conservation actions, educative programs, sport activities, and cultural programs. The best-known cultural program is the Folkloric Festival of Parintins; an event in which only Parintins residents can parade and participate in the professional choreographies that include themes concerning endangered species and environmental protection.

Legends, music, and complex dances are combined with blue and red colors in a unique jungle carnival. The annual Festival of Parintins, in Parintins, city of the Tupirambarana Island in the Amazon State, has been sponsored by Coca-Cola since 1995. The global beverage corporation partners with local and federal governments as well as community, environmental groups, other corporate sponsors, and the mass media to make this three-day event at the end of June possible. The promotional rights of the arena (bumbodromo) have been licensed to TV A Crítica, a company of the Brazilian System of Television (SBT), which is the main competitor of the largest broadcasting system Globo.

The estimated cost of this folk festival with cattle ranching roots is US$ 3 million (Nogueira, 2002). The Atlanta-based corporation has gradually increased its economic and promotional support from US$ 1 million in 1999, US$ 1.5 million in 2000, to US$ 2 million in 2001 (Coca-Cola, 2001). The festival is based on the rivalry that has divided Parintins in two camps: Garantido Boi (Guaranteed Ox) and Caprichoso Boi (Capricious Ox) supporters. The Garantido Boi supporters built their houses and businesses, which were painted red in one half of the town, while fans of the Caprichoso Boi built their house and business in the other half of the town and painted them blue. According to Darlington (2000), "even Coca-Cola has had to adapt. After Caprichoso supporters refused to buy Coke because of its red cans, the multinational Goliath created huge blue advertising banners, traditionally the trademark color of its rival Pepsi." As a corporate video says, "Coca-Cola wins over a city maintaining impartiality in the use of the red and blue colors" (Coca-Cola Parintins, 1999). The corporation had to invent a new logo for Parintins (Lengsfeld, n.d.).

The legend tells the story of a pregnant wife of a farmer who asked her husband to slaughter a prized ox, which symbolizes love and wealth, so she could eat its tongue. The angry owner searched for the farmer and caught him. The farmer was saved when a shaman (witchcraft doctor) revived the bull. This evolved into a century-old folk rivalry between the Capricious Ox and the Guaranteed Ox. As far as 1913, bands of singers in animal costumes have danced in the streets while improvising lyrics.

The Parintins festival started as an official competition between the Caprichoso and Garantido "bumbás" (groups of dancers) in 1964 (O festival, n.d.). Each group of around 3500 dancers and drummers stage this "Amazon Opera" for three nights, with three hours of spectacle each night. It combines the artistic beauty of the Carnival of Rio de Janeiro and the happy atmosphere of the Street Carnival of Bahia, all captured in the wilderness and density of the rainforest. The unique festival captures and promotes not only local legends but also scenes of daily life in the Amazon homeland.

Coca-Cola brought international attention to Parintins. "The festival has gradually reinvented the poor riverside community, showcasing the beauty and creativity of the far-flung region better known for environmental destruction and lawlessness," Darlington wrote. "But some critics are beginning to wonder if all the attention is helping erode decades-old traditions."

Celso Schvartzer, manager of institutional relations, explains that "Coca-Cola's main goal is to spread the festival in the regions where it still is not known. Here in the Amazon region it is already acclaimed, not just known" (Coca-Cola Parintins, 1999). The Amazon Secretary of State for Culture, Sports and Tourism estimates that approximately 100,000 visitors have attended the event in the last three years (Nogueira, 2002). It is expected that the number of visitors will increase this year because of the promotion of the festival in the Carnival of Rio.

After five years of logistic and financial support, the success of the festival is a concern for the main sponsor. As a consequence, Coca-Cola has limited the number of their national and international guests, which include media personalities, journalists, intellectuals, and opinion makers in general. Darlington (2000) quotes Tim Haas, president of Coca-Cola for Latin America, when he says: "You have to strike a balance between growth and traditional values. You have to be very careful you don't exploit this."

"Today Parintins has a new format, a business format," the Amazon Secretary of Culture, Robério Braga says (Coca-Cola Parintins, 1999). "Both an institutional and business relationship that consolidates the government, Coca-Cola [and] Kuat [aim] to promote the legitimate cultures making the Amazon people proud of their indigenous roots, their natural roots, for Brazil's 500 years we're going to have a green and yellow bull." These are the colors of the national flag.

The public relations efforts of Coca-Cola in Parintins go beyond publicity and media relations. They have nurtured long-term relationships with government officials and community groups as well as celebrities and tourists. The special attention to local political and community leaders is key in a country that is characterized by a vertical collectivistic culture, in which both the hierarchy and integration of society are interlinked.

The sponsoring organization is involved in operative and logistic efforts through its front-runner brand Kuat, called the guaraná of the Amazon. More than 700 workers from Parintins were hired to build and maintain a 200-guest balcony (glass box) inside a 35,000-set arena, or bumbodromo, where the festival takes place, and 50,000 square feet of social and sports club space. All the raw materials needed for the construction of these facilities are from the Amazon region as well as arts and crafts exhibits, furniture, and decorative accessories.

Brazilians enjoy large public gatherings, in which music, colors, and cultural expressions are combined. It seems the global giant has capitalized on that fact as other transnational corporations have done, such as America Online Brazil and its "Rock in Rio" music festival in January 2001. Any corporate engagement that promotes cultural values, concentrates large numbers of participants and spectators and reaches out to communities, celebrities, and government officials is likely to succeed and resonate through time.

REFERENCES

Adese, C. (2002, March). Corporate Brazil goes global: Latin America's largest competitors seek to buy and build international market share. *Latin Trade, 10*(3), 29–35.

Affirmative action in Brazil; I'm Black, be fairer to me; Brazil may adopt quotas, in education and jobs, for the darker-skinned. (2001, October 18). *The Economist,* p. 66.

Andrade, C. T. (1986). *Curso de relações públicas* (3rd ed.). São Paulo: Atlas.

A pausa que refresca 1942/1945. (n.d.). Coca-Cola Brazil Website. Retrieved March 12, 2002 from http://www.cocacolabrasil.com.br/quemsomos/historia/historia.asp

Around the World. (n.d.). Coca-Cola Website. Retrieved March 12, 2002, from http://www2.coca-cola.com/ourcompany/aroundworld.html

Banco de papers. (n.d.). Sociedade Brasileira de Estudos Interdisciplinares da Comunicação. Retrieved September 15, 2002, from http://www.intercom.org.br/papers/indexbp.html

Birman, P., & Leite, M. P. (2000). Whatever happened to what used to be the largest Catholic country in the world? *Daedalus, 129*(2), 271–290.

Brazil's 500 years of solicitude; It's time for South America's giant to shake off its inferiority complex. (2000, April 22). *The Economist*, p. 15.

Bruno, K. (2001). This is what democracy looks like. *Earth Island Journal, 16*(2), p. 25.

Buckley, S. (2001, January 9). Volunteerism is blossoming in Brazil. *The Washington Post*, p. A01.

Chaves, S. M. (1963). *Aspectos de relações públicas*. Rio de Janeiro: DASP.

Coca-Cola Parintins 99; Versão Inglês [English version]. (1999). (Videocassette produced for Coca-Cola in Brazil by AV Produções).

Coca-cola y el festival Parintins bailan nuevamente en el 2001. (2001). Coca-Cola Colombia's Website. Retrieved March 13, 2002, from http://www.cocacola.com.co/cocacolamundo/coca_col_sala_eventos.php#a

Congresso Nacional do Brasil. (1967, December). Law No. 5,377.

Congresso Nacional do Brasil. (1968, September). Decree No. 63,283: Regulation of Law No. 5,377.

CONRERP-SP. (2002). Conselho Regional de Profissionais de Relações Públicas 2ª Região—Retrieved September 15, 2002, São Paulo/Paraná: www.conrerp-sp.org.br

Conselho Federal de Professionais de Relações Públicas. (1998). *Conclusões do parlamento nacional de relações públicas* [Brochure]. Brasilia, Brazil: Comissão Redactora.

Cursos de Graduação. (2002). CONRERP—2ª Região São Paulo/Paraná. Retrieved September 16, 2002, from http://www.abrpsaopaulo.com.br/guiabrasileiro/cursos/gradua_rp.htm

Dall'Agnol, P. (1998). *The historic trajectory of the public relations profession in Brazil*. Paper presented at the First International Interdisciplinary Research Conference of the Public Relations Society of America's Educators Academy. College Park, MD.

Darlington, S. (2000). Brazil parties in the Amazon; festival celebrates Brazil's cattle ranching roots. *Reuters*. Retrieved March 6, 2002, from http://abcnews.go.com/sections/travel/DailyNews/brazilfest000719.html

Distribuição da população por cor ou raça. (1999). Instituto Brasileiro de Geografia e estadística (IBGE). Retrived September 15, 2002, from http://www.ibge.gov.br

Duarte, J. A. (2001). Assesoria de imprensa, o caso brasileiro. In A. T. Barros, J. A. Duarte, & R. E. Martinez (Eds.), *Comunicação: Discursos, Prácticas e tendencias* (pp. 1–14). Rideel: Brazil.

Exemplo de cidadania. (n.d.). Coca-Cola Brazil's Website. Retrieved March 12, 2002, from http://www.cocacolabrasil.com.br/empresa/cidadania/cidadania.asp

França, F. (2001). Relações públicas: visão 2000. In M. M. Kunsch (Ed.), *Obtendo resultados com relações públicas* (pp. 3–17). São Paulo: Pioneira.

Freedom House. (2002). *The annual survey of press freedom 2002*. Retrieved on October 14, 2002 from http://www.freedomhouse.org/pfs2002/pfs2002.pdf

Gannon, M. J. (2001). *Understanding global cultures: Metaphorical journeys through 23 nations* (2nd ed.). Thousand Oaks, CA: Sage.

Grunig, J. E. (Ed.). (1992). *Excellence in public relations and communication management*. Hillsdale, NJ: Lawrence Erlbaum Associates.

Gruning, J. E., & Hunt, T. (1984). *Managing public relations*. New York: Holt, Rinehart and Winston.

Herman, E. S., & McChesney, R. W. (1997). *The global media: The new missionaries of corporate capitalism*. London: Cassell.

Hodess, R., Banfield, J., & Wolfe, T. (Eds.). (2001). *Global corruption report 2001*. Berlin: Transparency International.

Hofstede, G. (1983). The cultural relativity of organizational practices and theories. *Journal of International Business Studies, 14*(2), 75–89.

Hofstede, G. (1991). *Cultures and organizations: software of the mind*. London: McGraw-Hill.

Kunsch, M. M. (1997). *Relações públicas e modernidade: Novos paradigmas na comunicação organizacional.* Brazil: Summus.

Lengsfeld, R. (n.d.). Parintins: A city divided into blue and red. TAM Airline. Retrieved March 6, 2002, from http://www.tamgetaways.com/city.html%BFaction=grt& rtid=15& city_id=9.html

Livros. (n.d.). Conselho Regional de Relações Públicas—4ª Região. Retrieved on September 15, 2002, from http://www.conrerprssc.org.br/

Lula's historic victory. (2002, October 28). Economist Intelligence Unit. Retrieved November 3, 2002, from EIU viewswire database.

Mainwaring, S., Brinks, D., & Perez-Linan, A. (2001). Classifying political regimes in Latin America, 1945–1999. *Studies in Comparative International development, 36*(1), 37–65.

Meditsch, Eduardo. (1999). CIESPAL: progreso y problema del comunicólogo. *Chasqui, 67,* 70–74.

Molleda, J. C. (2001). International paradigms: The Latin American School of public relations. *Journalism Studies, 2*(4), 513–530.

Molleda, J. C. (2002a, March). *The legal status of public relations in Brazil: The views of professionals.* Paper presented at V International, Interdisciplinary Public Relations Research Conference of the Public Relations Society of America Educators Academy. Miami, FL.

Molleda, J. C. (2002b). *International paradigms: The social role of Brazilian public relations professionals.* Paper presented at the 85th Annual Convention of the Association for Education in Journalism and Mass Communication. Miami, FL.

Nogueira, W. (2002, February 26). Bumbás planejan investir R$7,5 milhões no festival. *Investnews-Conteúdo Online Gazeta Mercantil, www.gazetorio.com.br.*

O festival folclórico do parintins. (n.d.). Retrieved March 6, 2002 from http://parintins.com/docs/festival.ph3

O que é a Aberje. (n.d.). Associação Brasileira de Comunicação Empresarial. Retrieved September 15, 2002 from http://www.aberje.com.br/

Ortiz, R. (1991). *A moderna tradição brasileira—Cultural brasileira e indústria cultural.* São Paulo, Brazil: Editora Brasiliense.

Penteado, R. (1996). *Effects of public relations roles and models on quality committed Brazilian organizations.* Unpublished master's thesis, University of Florida, Gainesville.

Penteado, R. (2002). Assesoria de imprensa na era digital. In J. Duarte (Ed.), *Assesoria de imprensa e relacionamento com a mídia; teoria e técnica* (pp. 340–362). Brazil: Editoral Atlas.

Pérez-Senac, R. (2000). Desarrollo y aportes de una corriente Latinoamericana de relaciones públicas. *Alacaurp, 1,* 21–26.

Peruzzo, C. K. (1986). *Relações públicas no modo de produção capitalista.* São Paulo Brazil: Summus.

Peruzzo, C. K. (1993). Relaciones públicas y cambio social. *Chasqui, 46,* 111–114.

Pinheiro, P. S. (1996, September/October). Democracies without citizenship. *Nacla Report of the Americas, 30*(2), 17–23.

Plasencia, J. R. (2001). *Cidadania em ação.* Brazil: DP&A editora.Wey, Hebe. (1983). *O processo de relações públicas.* Riode Janeiro, Brazil: Summus.

Pós-Graduação. (2002). CONRERP–2ª Região São Paulo/Paraná. Retrieved September 16, 2002, from http://www.abrpsaopaulo.com.br/guiabrasileiro/cursos/posgradua.htm

Responsabilidade social das empresas: Percepção do consumidor Brasileiro. (2001). Instituto Ethos. Retrieved March 5, 2002, from http://www.ethos.org.br/pri/open/publicacoes/index.asp

Rohter, L. (2001, August 30). From Brazil, an emerging steel giant. *The New York Times,* p. C1.

Rohter, L. (2002, August 17). The Saturday profile; from maid to Rio governor, and still fighting. *The New York Times,* p. A4.

Romero, S. (2002, February 7). Brazil forum more local than worldly. *The New York Times,* p. A18.

Santos, M., & Silveira, M. L. (2001). O Brasil: Território e sociedade no início do século XXI. Riode Janeiro, Brazil: Editora Record.

Simões, R. P. (1992). Public relations as a political function: A Latin American view. *Public Relations Review, 18*(2), 189–200.

Sharpe, M. L., & Simões, R. P. (1996). Public relations performance in South and Central America. In H. M. Culbertson and N. Chen (Eds.), *International public relations: A comparative analysis* (pp. 273–297). Mahwah, NJ: Lawrence Erlbaum Associates.

Sorj, B. (2000). *A nova sociedade brasileira.* Riode Janeiro, Brazil: Jorge Zahar Editor Ltda.

Testa, A. F. (Ed.). (1999). *Marketing politico e comunicação; o Senado e a opinião pública.* Brasilia, Brazil: Senado Federal Secretaria de Comunicação Social.

Triandis, H. C. (2002). Generic individualism and collectivism. In M. J. Gannon and K. L. Newman (Eds.), *The Blackwell handbook of cross-cultural management.* pp. 16–45.

United Nations Development Programme. (2001). *Human development report 2001.* New York: Oxford University Press.

Wey, H. (1986). *O proceso de relações públicas (3a edição).* São Paulo, Brazil: Summus Editorial.

World Bank. (2002). ICT at a glance: Brazil. Retrieved on October 14, 2002 from http://www.worldbank.org/ cgi-bin/sendoff.cgi?page=%2Fdata%2Fcountrydata%2Fict%2Fbra_ict.pdf

18

Public Relations in Chile: Searching for Identity Amid Imported Models

Maria Aparecida Ferrari

Seventeen years of military rule have had a severe impact on the culture and behavior of the Chilean people. Under the military regime, few were willing to participate in public issues, because they were afraid of reprisals rather than because of lack of interest or creative ideas. Today's Chilean society is more concerned with daily problems and difficulties and appears indifferent to political and social issues. The legacy of the military has resulted in a striking lack of solidarity among Chileans, who appear to have become more individualistic and self-centered. Paradoxically, the social, economic, and cultural legacy created by the military, which was subsequently adopted by the new democratic regime, attempted to sell Chile as a *jaguar* or as a winner. As a result, the Chilean cultural and communication system has been based on a mystified concept of reality which is a mix of nationalism, leadership, competitiveness, success, and innovation.

Despite the first manifestations of public relations during the 1950s, it wasn't until the 1990s with the reinstatement of democracy and the globalization of the economy, that business expansion made possible the development of public relations in Chile. Notwithstanding the existence of seven university-level public relations programs, the profession is not fully understood and is confused with the activities practiced by journalists. This chapter will examine the impact of historical events on the freedom of expression, the media system, and in the practice of public relations among Chile's private and public organizations.

THE BEGINNING OF PUBLIC RELATIONS IN CHILE

As a profession, public relations formally began in Chile with the founding of the first public relations department at the Braden Copper mining company in 1952, with Mario Illanes Peñafiel as manager. In 1953, Ramón Cortez Ponce, a journalist and professor at the School of Journalism at the University of Chile, founded the first public relations agency in the country. Together with Uruguay, Argentina, and Bolivia, Chile was one of the last countries to integrate public relations to the formal structure of public and business organizations in Latin America (Becerra, 1983). Like the majority of Latin American countries, Public Relations accompanied foreign copper companies into Chile, soon to be followed by companies from the machine sector. Slowly, companies with 100% indigenous ownership such as Cristalerias de Chile, CMPC (Compañía Manufacturera de Papeles y Cartones de Puente Alto), and Compañía de Petróleos de Chile (COPEC) also adopted public relations functions. These companies hired the Ramón Cortez Ponce agency to advise them in designing and implementation of their public relations efforts.

EARLY PUBLIC RELATIONS EDUCATION

The history of Public Relations in Chile is closely linked to the evolution of Journalism. The first School of Journalism was founded on May 28, 1953 at the University of Chile. The school also administered short courses on public relations and advertising. Dr. Juan Gómez Millas, Rector of the University of Chile, declared at the time that public relations and advertising courses were "an indispensable complement to Journalism" (Délano, 1990). Ramón Cortés Ponce became the first director of the School of Journalism at the University of Chile. He designed and taught the first course on public relations with the intent of demonstrating how "the similarities and differences between the theoretical and practical training of both professionals augment each other" (Délano, 1990). During the 1960s, several courses and seminars were conducted in other schools of journalism such as the Pontifícia Universidad Católica de Chile (in Santiago), and Universidad de Concepción (in the city of Concepción).

It was also during the 1960s that Carlos Aracena Aguayo wrote the first Chilean document addressing public relations as a formal discipline. The 114-page book, *Las Relaciones Públicas en Acción* (Public relations in action), is an unpretentious document presenting the history of public relations in the country together with proprietary course materials and information collected by the author during his participation in seminars and conferences held between 1958 and 1961.

A significant event in the development of public relations in Chile is the official ruling issued by the Controller General of the Republic in 1959. The ruling stated that "Journalists should also be responsible for the discharge of the Public Relations profession." Because they possessed legal recognition, journalists easily became public relations managers in public, state-controlled or municipal organizations. The private sector, however, was not bound by this official ruling. The ruling had great repercussions on the society because at that time, the state owned and controlled 70% of the economy.

El Mercurio, the most influential daily newspaper in Chile, published an article that categorically stated that journalism and public relations were incompatible professions. Despite the fact that each profession is well respected independently, combining the two posed grave risks to the application of ethical standards in public information. The newspaper emphasized that students interested in studying these two disciplines should choose to study only one and be convinced of the fact that both professions are incompatible (Délano, 1990). This early manifestation was the harbinger of the clash in prestige between the two professions where the greater prestige for journalism in Chilean society lowered the standing of public relations in the society in the years to come.

BIRTH OF A PROFESSIONAL ASSOCIATION

The Chilean Institute of Public Relations Professionals (ICREP) was founded on January 25, 1960 with the objective of promoting the professional development and the diffusion of public relations in Chile. ICREP offered a 150-hour, three-level, professional development program to its members. This program was subsequently recognized by The Interamerican Confederation of Public Relations Associations (CONFIARP).

The Chilean Institute for the Rational Administration of the Business Organization (ICARE) was another organization that played an active role in training public relations professionals in the country. ICARE also offered courses in the areas of marketing, finance, and human relations. The first intensive course on public relations was administered by ICARE in 1977. Oddly enough, public relations was the only area that declined in acceptance and did not perpetuate itself.

CLASS ORGANIZATIONS AS A MOBILIZING FORCE FOR PUBLIC RELATIONS

The emergence of national public relations associations in Brazil (1954), Mexico (1955), Venezuela (1956), Argentina and Panama (1958), and Peru and Chile (1960) resulted in the creation of Interamerican Federation of Public Relations Associations (FIARP) in 1960. FIARP was founded with the basic mandate of creating affiliated public relations associations in every Latin American country. The founding members of FIARP were Argentina, Brazil, Chile, Colombia, Cuba, the United States, Mexico, Panama, Peru, Puerto Rico, and Venezuela. The principal objective of FIARP was to defend and consolidate the profession through the organization and promotion of seminars and conferences, and to oversee the ethical practice of the profession. In 1985, FIARP made the transition to become a formally organized confederation currently known as CONFIARP (Interamerican Public Relations Confederation). CONFIARPs principal mandate is to maintain the integrity and identity of public relations in Latin America.

As noted earlier, the ICREP (the Chilean Institute of Public Relations Professionals) was created in 1960 with the objective of integrating public relations professionals, and to provide opportunities for professional development through formal courses and training programs. On May 26,1983, the Council of Public Relations Professionals Chile was founded with the purpose of integrating public relations practitioners and to replace ICREP. The principal motivation for founding this Council was to restate the role of public relations and to legitimize public relations practitioners' roles in society. This was necessitated by the fact that many public relations practitioners did not have formal training in public relations, and, in fact, many did not have formal training in any field of endeavor whatsoever.

However, the strategy of bringing legitimacy to the profession failed to come to fruition. Flanagan (1992) reported based on her research that "62.8% of Chilean executives did not know about the council or any other professional association. This shows that Public Relations does not have the social visibility required for an acceptable professional activity." For the past 19 years, the council has been the only formal representative of Chilean Public Relations professionals. Since there is no legal requirement for affiliation, its members have demonstrated a timid lackluster expression that has not led to an effective diffusion and legitimization of the profession. In September 2002, the council had approximately 500 members and is engaged in the promotion of public relations programs designed for small and medium-size organizations.

THE BIRTH OF PUBLIC RELATIONS EDUCATION IN CHILE

Until the 1970s, the Chilean university system was recognized as one of the best in Latin America. Chilean universities led intellectual developments in the field of modernization, Marxism, and free-market economy and provided the forum for the open discussion of these concepts. The failure of the Chilean socialist experiment and the demise of the Left precipitated the emergence of a right-wing dictatorship and the onset of conservative policies and neoliberal thinking in the economy. With the purpose of achieving structural change, a new higher education system was implemented in 1980. The implementation of the system led to the creation of technical education centers, professional institutes, and private universities. According to Eyzaguirre (1993), "the spirit of the new legislation was to increase the response to the demand for education and to make available resources more in keeping with the geographical and social realities where the new institutions were located." By 1983, Chile had 24 centers of higher education.

As a result of the new university system, professional level public relations programs began in 1980 at the National Public Relations School and at INACAP (National Training Institute). In 1985, public relations courses began to be offered at IPEVE (Professional Teaching Institute). Subsequently, public relations was also offered at the Instituto del Pacífico and DUOC (University Department for Farmers and Workers), which is affiliated with the Catholic University of Chile (Pontifícia Universidad Católica de Chile).

The emergence of professional institutes that offered operational and tactical-level public relations education benefited journalists. The formal requirement of a five-year university-level education allowed journalists to acquire the responsibility (to this day) for the management of communications in public and private organizations. Major political and economic transformations, that began at the end of 1980s, brought about a process of modernization and internationalization of the economy attracting many prestigious and experienced foreign business organizations to Chile.

This process of modernization and internationalization also brought new management styles to the country. The first major achievements became visible during the early 1990s, under the democratically elected government of President Patrício Aylwin. The stable economy was the result of free-market policies implemented during the previous decade. As a result, the potential for the field of communications was indeed extremely positive. Many public and private organizations began to organize their public relations and communications departments with a free-market perspective that needed to be sensitive to the challenges of globalization.

Flanagan (1992) reported that in her analysis of 100 Chilean business organizations, she found that journalists managed 49% of the public relations/communications departments. In the remaining 51%, 12% of professionals were self-taught, 32% had university training in areas such as economics, business administration, law, or engineering, and only 7% had university-level degrees in public relations from foreign universities. Flanagan's findings reveal that public relations has failed to achieve the stature of journalism and other professions. One of the reasons for this lack of acceptance is the delayed recognition of university-level public relations education by the Ministry of Education. It was only in 1992 that the Ministry approved public relations as a field of study, which meant that prior to 1992, most practitioners held public relations positions without the required credentials as well as specific knowledge and skills. Délano (2000) concluded that, "the fact that the managerial and strategic role of Public Relations in Chile was never exercised by a professional specifically trained in Public Relations corroborates Flanagan's conclusions. Exceptions occur when the professional has been trained outside of Chile. In general, professionals in Public Relations positions are either lawyers, sociologists, engineers, or journalists."

The Ministry of Education officially recognized the first university-level public relations program offered by Universidad de Viña del Mar in 1992. In 1993, the programs offered by Universidad Santo Tomás, Universidad de Las Américas, and Universidad de Artes, Ciencias y de Comunicación (UNIACC), all located in the capital of Santiago, were also granted official recognition. In 1995, Universidad del Pacífico began to offer Public Relations education.

The quality of the Public Relations program offered by Universidad de Viña del Mar is noteworthy. The curriculum was reorganized in 1992, with a strategic managerial focus closely aligned to Chilean culture and values, by this author. Students also are required to plan and execute a supervised public relations campaign for the client organization. The education offered by this program, that takes four and one half years to complete, is considered to be the best suited for the requirements of the Chilean market (M. A. Salazar, personal communication, August 2000).

In 1992, the Extension Center of the Catholic University of Chile began to offer short training programs in Public Relations Planning, Corporate Image, Planning of Events, and Protocol. In addition, the concerted efforts of public relations educators made possible the organization of seminars and training programs with the participation of renowned international researchers and academics such as Margarida M. K. Kunsch (Brazil) and Otto Lerbinger (United States) in 1992, Melvin Sharpe (United States) and Roberto Porto Simões (Brazil) in 1993, and James Grunig and Larissa Grunig (United States) in 2000. Today, six private universities offer public relations programs.

In Chile, there is a noticeable difference between the teaching and reputation of public and private universities. Public universities (Universidad de Chile, Universidad de Santiago, and Universidad de Concepción) and the three traditional private universities (Pontifícia Universidad Católica de Chile, Universidad Técnica Frederico Santa Maria, and Universidad Adolfo Ibañez) have been in existence longer and boast of many former students who currently hold important public positions. The private universities, on the other hand, aren't as rigid in the selection of their students and do not have an alumni body comparable to "traditional" universities. The fact that the majority of the faculty has a social sciences or journalism background has given a certain "journalistic" bias to the education of the new public relations professionals. This bias, which is not totally pertinent to the requirements of the public relations market, will cease to exist when university public relations programs have faculty with comprehensive training in public relations, and who are less concerned with "informative" aspects and more with the strategic and managerial aspects of the profession.

Currently, there are no public relations graduate programs in Chile. Graduate-level professional education programs known as "diplomados" are offered in organizational communication by Universidad Diego Portales, Pontifícia Universidad Católica de Chile, and Universidad del Desarrollo (initially in the city of Concepción and currently in Santiago). In general, the curriculum totals 372 hours of class time and requires candidates to present evidence of completion of an undergraduate degree before gaining admission to the program. The programs were not designed to prepare researchers or academics but to train qualified professionals in the area of strategic organizational communication.

BIBLIOGRAPHY AND THEORY BASE

There are four public relations textbooks written by Chilean authors. In 1960, Carlos Aracena Aguayo wrote the first book titled *Las Relaciones Públicas en Acción* (Public relations in action). The second book, *Las Relaciones Públicas en Chile: fundamentos prácticos y teóricos* (Public relations in Chile: theory and practice), was written by Bárbara Délano Alfonso in 1990. This book presents the personal biographies and professional history of three early Chilean thinkers in the area of public relations. Délano also details the active principles of public relations and, in the latter chapters of the book, discusses the importance of protocol for the public relations professional. In 1993, Pablo Eyzaguirre Chadwick wrote *Manual de Relaciones Públicas* (Public relations manual) discussing a number of operational definitions and process requirements for public relations, and detailing the importance of protocol and etiquette in the organization of events. Eyzaguirre also wrote a fourth textbook called *Relaciones Públicas* (Public relations) in 1997.

The remaining textbooks used in Public Relations programs are mainly translations of books written by James E. Grunig and Todd Hunt (*Dirección de Relaciones Públicas*, 2000), John Pavlik (*La investigación en Relaciones Públicas*, 1999), Philip Lesly (*Manual de Relaciones Públicas*, 1973), and Scott Cutlip and Alan Center (*Relaciones Públicas*, 1963). The only exception is the book written by Roberto Porto Simões (*Relaciones Públicas: función política*, 1993) which was translated from Portuguese. There are two dissertations that address the practice of public relations in Chile. The first is the doctoral dissertation written in Spain by Catalina Flanagan Simonsen, in 1992. The second is the master's dissertation written by Carmen Gloria Ortega in 1993 at California State University, Hayward. The limited number of Chilean publications on the subject, together with a highly abstract theoretical base from abroad, is one of the principal impediments to the development of research and practice that conforms to local cultural requirements and idiosyncrasies (Ortega, 1993).

The absence of indigenous research and the ensuing lack of dissertations in public relations have made Chile totally dependent on foreign concepts and theory that bear no relationship to Chilean culture and identity. The main question for public relations researchers and academics is whether to follow North American or European models or to develop a unique Latin American identity that is free of foreign influence. This issue is closely linked to the legitimization of university-level public relations programs that have existed for a decade. Similar to what occurred in other Latin American countries, the Council of Public Relations Professionals Chile was unable to achieve a representative stature and to legitimize public relations practice in Chilean society.

There is no available data either on the number of private and public organizations that have a public relations department, or on the number of professionals who have graduated from university-level public relations programs. One of the explanations given to justify this situation is the fact that there is no legislation regulating the practice of public relations (as in Brazil, Panama, and Peru). Further, there exist no additional registration requirements, beyond a university diploma, to monitor the public relations professional.

B. J. A. Délano (personal communication, August 2000) addressed this issue when she emphasized, during her interview with the author, that "universities and professional institutes which provide Public Relations education are not interested in publicizing the true number of graduates. The statistics would reveal that the number of graduates far exceeds available work positions. A number of Public Relations professionals estimate that there are approximately 6000 graduates. Approximately 1000 graduates have achieved placement in the Public Relations job market. Of these placements, about 120 can be found in strategic organizational roles."

CHILE AS A NATION: DEMOGRAPHICS AND A BRIEF HISTORY

From its independence in 1818 until the military coup of 1973, Chile suffered three brief interruptions from civilian democratic rule. During the twentieth century, specifically from 1932 until the fall of Allende in 1973, Chilean constitutional rule had remained intact. Two thirds of the population of (15,050,341) (as of September 2002) live in cities. Since the 1992 census, the population of Chile has increased by 12.8%. After Cuba and Uruguay, Chile has the third lowest population growth in Latin America, with Argentina in fourth place. Due to the accelerated growth of the population aged over 60 years, the base of the demographic pyramid is undergoing a profound change. Chile is one of the more urbanized and industrialized countries in Latin America, and boasts a literacy rate of 95%. The country possesses a sophisticated social security system that is funded by individual capitalization mechanisms. The system has been operated since 1983 by a number of Administrators of Pension Funds (AFP), and requires the participants to deposit part of their monthly income in a savings account that is used to float the pension fund. The ethnic composition of the country is mainly derived from immigrant Europeans with indigenous inhabitants constituting a small percentage of the total population.

CONTEXT OF THE CHILEAN ECONOMIC AND POLITICAL SYSTEM

The main issue for Latin America is the definition of the role of government in promoting development, political stability, and social order. Today, Latin American governments are at the mercy of world markets and the pressure groups, while facing a chronic lack of financial resources. Besides the efforts of the government, Chilean society has met the challenge of addressing the new realities of political power and the pressure to increase public expenditure. Over the past 10 years, new political strategies have led to a political and social consensus that has substantially reduced the social conflict seen in most Latin American nations.

Historical events have had a profound effect on the development of public relations in Chile. The beginning of industrialization of the country occurred during the nineteenth century with the often-dubious support of the British Empire. In 1879, the Chilean bourgeoisie drew the country into a war with Peru and Bolivia over the control of nitrate extraction. The arrival of multinational companies such as Guggenheim converted nitrate mining as the principal source for the economic well-being of the country. After the decline of nitrate, Braden Copper arrived during the 1930s to initiate the massive extraction of copper. International Telephone & Telegraph (ITT) arrived shortly thereafter operating telephone communication services, and later making substantial investments in the hotel sector.

Between 1945 and 1946, the United States and Chile entered into an agreement to strengthen the foundations of a continental defense system. The fragile economic situation experienced by many Latin American countries after World War II was one of the principal motives for establishing such military assistance agreements. In 1950, the Economic Commission for Latin America and Caribbean (CEPAL) was established to assist the region with economic and social development. The history of CEPAL can be divided into five distinct phases. When it was founded, CEPAL provided direct support for the industrialization required to help Chile depend less on imported products. In the 1960s, CEPAL's objective was the facilitation of reforms required for industrialization. During the 1970s, CEPAL provided orientation for the implementation of development strategies and the diversification of exports. In the 1980s, the issue of external debt was tackled through the promotion of structural adjustments coupled with economic growth. The 1990s were devoted to the equitable transformation of production processes.

The great merit of CEPAL was to seek and integrated perspective of development based on an objective interaction with regional governments. The goal was the development of an identity capable of defending regional interests, which would facilitate the implementation of structural change. The main idea was the modernization of the economy based on the adoption of first world technologies that would serve to break economic dependence on the United States that the majority of Latin American nations experienced during the second half of the twentieth century.

The 1960s witnessed the first signs that the Chilean economic system was wavering. The pace of economic growth was unable to induce an equitable distribution of wealth. Unions and left-wing political parties emerged to address the contradictions and injustice of the prevailing economic structure. The Chilean economy exhibited two distinct structural characteristics at this time: the concentration of the means of production in the hands of a reduced number of national and foreign investors, and a substantial foreign debt. Beginning in 1965, there was agrarian reform to diversify ownership that had hitherto been cornered by a minority. By 1970, a substantial number of agricultural estates had been expropriated. In addition, legislation was introduced to allow the Chilean government to acquire a part of foreign capital holdings. This led to the emergence of hybrid, state-controlled organizations that were able to receive foreign investments resulting, for example, in the "Chileanization" of copper mining. As a result, the Chilean government acquired control of 51% of the shares in largest copper mine in the country that was formerly owned by Braden Copper.

During the 1970s, a number of United States, European, and Japanese firms, established themselves in Chile in the areas of food processing, automotive technology, and petro-chemicals. Nevertheless, United States influence continued to play a dominant role in the formulation and implementation of Chilean economic policy. From 1973 to 1990, Chile lived through a military government commanded by General Augusto Pinochet Ugarte. Ideologically, the Pinochet government was a right-wing, anticommunist, conservative dictatorship with a paradoxical vision for progressive economic policies. Nonetheless, the Pinochet government has been singled out as one of the cruelest Latin American dictator-ships, and has earned the dubious reputation of being responsible for the dismantling of state economic intervention implemented during the 1930s.

Despite recent economic crises in different regions of the world (Mexico in 1994, Asia in 1998, and Argentina during 2001), Chile continues to demonstrate the macroeconomic stability that was implemented during the Pinochet government. Chile's financial system has been stable requiring no external economic assistance. Compared to its neighbors, Chile has a privileged economic situation, thereby offering opportunities for investment that are more optimistic than in other Latin America countries.

The Chilean political transition, together with a neoliberal market economy, has af-forded the country a democracy of opportunities ranging from an efficient and respected State through a society with pluralistic perspectives, to organizations which are beginning to be concerned with their publics. Despite the existence of a sound productive structure and a robust economic system, Chilean culture is still attached to the values and behavior of an outdated social model. In this context, business organizations seeking to expand their market share have given special attention to the intangible perceptions of the publics such as their image, reputation, and credibility.

Public relations has been slowly incorporated into organizations, either as an internal department or as an external communication agency. The practice of public relations has not been legitimated by executives, and is still confused with the press agentry practiced by journalists. The combination of economic growth and the consolidation of university level public relations programs could lead to increased participation of public relations in public and private organizations. Societal pressure for a better quality of life will probably force organizations to rethink their mission, objectives, and relationship with their publics. In this context, it will be easier perhaps to demonstrate the importance of public relations practice on business performance.

CULTURE AND POWER IN CHILE: VALUES AND IDIOSYNCRASY

To understand Chilean culture, it is necessary to review the Spanish colonization and its relationship with indigenous inhabitants. From the mixture of these two races, there emerged the mestizo who, because of their desire to be part of the Hispanic world, reneged their native heritage. According to Castellón & Araos (1999), the cultural identity of Chile was the result of three factors: (1) the Spanish language imposed by the conquerors; (2) national boundaries that were determined by distinct geographical features ranging from the desert in the north to the frozen glaciers of the south; (3) interpretation of the world through a hybridization of European Catholicism and the mystic relationship with nature that was native to the land.

Bassa (1996) further developed these concepts by revealing that "from colonial times when the Spaniard longed to return to the homeland, the Creoles wished that they had been born in Europe, the 'mestizos' who did not understand the ambiguities of the past and the Indian who longed for pre-Hispanic times. Even today, each segment of Chilean society hides its true identity and wishes to be the other" (p. 44). The political transition of the past decade and the adoption of a successful economic model reveals that the principal components of the power structure of Chilean society are the state, political parties, businesses, the Catholic Church, the armed forces, emerging ecological and feminist groups, and mass media. The critical boundaries are those that separate civilian society from the state and, within the state, the boundary that separates political power, political parties, and the armed forces.

Traditionally, the Catholic Church had been the leading mouthpiece of Chilean society. During the 1960s, the church was the driving force for social reform. It also played an important role in the area of human rights during the Pinochet regime. Today, the church has withdrawn from the political arena, dedicating itself to issues pertaining to moral order and social values. Nevertheless, the influence of the church is far greater in Chile than in any other Latin American nation.

Three examples serve to illustrate the influence of the Chilean church and its conservative outlook toward world issues. Chile is the only country in Latin America that does not have a law permitting divorce. The implementation of government policies regarding the use of condoms for the prevention of AIDS, proposed by CONASIDA (National AIDS Commission) have been curtailed by the strong negative pressure of the Church. Official discussion of clinical abortion is forbidden in the country. A number of analysts argue that the Catholic Church has "a lobby that is so effective that no one can notice it or be aware of its existence." Because of pressure by the Church, public relations campaigns designed to address these issues have been totally ineffective.

Contemporary Chilean history can be divided into three distinct phases: before, during, and after the military regime of Pinochet. Until 1970, Chile was an extremely conservative and traditional country where interpersonal relationships were closely aligned with family and friends and maintaining group solidarity—similar to the cultural dimension of collectivism that Hofstede (1984) identified. After the military coup in 1973, social relations were severely affected leading to the weakening of personal relationships and a conflict of ideologies. Since the coup, Chile has been divided between those who are "for" or "against" the Pinochet regime. With the return of democracy in 1989, Chile became an active player in the globalization process that led to concomitant cultural changes to which the society had to quickly adapt.

Currently, Chilean culture is in the middle of a transition between a religious paternalistic model characterized by insecurity and improvisation of work tasks, and a new model based upon technology, work rationalization, and the depersonification of social relationships. Researching public relations practice of Chilean organizations, Ferrari (2000) concluded that the public relations model adopted in this country was closely linked to organizational culture, and to the process of political and economic development of recent years. Of the 13 organizations that were studied, 6 could be characterized as having an authoritarian culture. The decision making in these stratified organizations was highly centralized and was made based on traditions. Four organizations studied were undergoing the transition from authoritarian to participative culture. Only three organizations in this study displayed a participative cultural model, where employee participation in organizational decision making was reinforced by the dominant coalition. The predominant organizational values of these organizations were: commitment, honesty, efficiency, and individualism. The stress placed on tangible rewards has intensified individualism and redefined the relationship between employees and the organization.

Another interesting finding of the study (Ferrari, 2000) was with regard to the model of public relations practiced by these organizations. Six Chilean organizations practiced the two-way asymmetric model based on reactive programs operating within an authoritarian cultural framework. Six multinational organizations practiced the symmetrical model, where negotiation and mediation were used to address the highly dynamic environment they faced because they belonged to the vulnerable economic sector that obligated them to a proactive stance with their publics. Only one company practiced the public information model. The study also revealed that 9 of the 13 organizations had former journalists as the public relations manager. Three public relations managers had a university education, but in a different discipline. The public relations manager of only one organization had formal training in public relations. Senior executives of these 13 organizations generally associated public relations practice with organizing events, and arranging parties or cocktails.

These results were confirmed by a study on the "The Best Places to Work" by Levering and Moskowitz (2001). According to this study, of the 10 best companies to work for, 8 were subsidiaries of a multinational corporation with headquarters in the United States, Germany, France, or Australia. The majority of the CEOs interviewed for this study declared that there was a "headquarters culture" that the subsidiaries attempted to reproduce. These CEOs felt that 50% of an organization's success is due to organizational culture. Twenty-five percent of the success of a subsidiary is due to the unique characteristics of the country. The remaining 25% is due to the team spirit that managers are able to achieve. An interesting finding was the paternalistic attitude that Chilean workers expect from their companies. This is different to what normally occurs at headquarters, and closely reflects the existence of a traditional relationship between the superior and a protected loyal subordinate.

PUBLIC RELATIONS AGENCIES

The Chilean communications scene changed during the 1990s as a result of the influx of multinational public relations such as Edelman, Porter Novelli, Ketchum, Burson Marsteller, and Hill & Knowlton. These organizations made a commitment to the development of public relations in Latin America and began work on improving the images of private corporations with the government, the media, and various other publics. Except for Burson Marsteller which operates independently, the remaining agencies have local affiliates. There are approximately 10 Chilean public relations agencies. Both multinational and Chilean agencies have been forced to provide a wide range of services because public relations has not been widely accepted as an independent profession. The majority of these agencies work with journalists who act as public relations professionals. Until the arrival of multinational agencies, Chilean professionals based their activities on a very limited tactical focus. Globalization and the liberalization of the economy have forced many Chilean companies to demonstrate more transparency in their operations. Multinational companies, mainly from the telecommunications, mining, and financial sectors, contract the services of international public relations agencies. Most Chilean public relations agencies, on the other hand, have restricted their activities to managing internal and external communications and press relations. It is quite common for a Chilean company to hire a press agent to transform a company executive into a newsworthy commodity.

PUBLIC OPINION AND THE INFLUENCE OF MASS MEDIA: CENSORSHIP AND FREEDOM OF SPEECH

Despite the new press law of May 2001, limitations to freedom of speech continue to exist in Chile. This is true for a diverse number of mass media vehicles, notwithstanding the efforts made to reimplement and improve the open democratic system that had ceased to exist during the military regime. A change in mentality to end the widespread self-censorship, a vestige of the military regime, which affects freedom of speech and the pluralistic development of mass media, is long overdue. Self-censorship has a great deal to do with the desire to not create problems or trouble for anyone. The journalist practices self-censorship because the effects of causing discomfort to certain interests may be personally disastrous to the journalist (Krohne, 2002).

Public decree no. 3.621 of 1981 transformed all professional councils into associations that had no power to control ethical practices or to require mandatory registration. The return of democracy has been unable to restore to the councils the rights that were withdrawn by this decree instituted during the military regime. This situation affects Chilean society as a whole bacause there are no means to ensure the quality and credibility of the communication professional. Chile is the only Latin American country where censorship of the cinema is enshrined in the Constitution (article no. 19). The long-overdue approval of the motion picture qualification law on December 9, 2002 will require the reexamination of 380 films that were censored during the military regime (1974 to 1990).

From the mass media perspective, the changes of the past had dual consequences. First, there was a demand for greater information on the status of the economy. Second, there was the requirement for improving the technical expertise of journalists and mass media communicators. The ever-increasing demand for high-quality information has forced the media to become a proactive player in the development of a more ethical relationship with society.

Many Chileans regard the press as the fourth power, because of its tremendous influence on public opinion. Others, however, prefer to see the press as an instrument of publicity, which is dominated by market forces. In Chile, television audiences are extremely large. Ninety five percent of Chilean homes possess a television set. Despite the outstanding technical quality achieved by Chilean television, this medium has not become an important element in tailoring public opinion. One of the reasons for the lackluster quality of TV programming includes the fact that public relations and communications professionals are not involved in designing and implementing institutional and issue-focused campaigns.

To summarize the media environment in Chile, one can say that television is primarily an entertainment medium and the press is the principal vehicle for mobilizing public opinion. These facts explain the importance of press agentry in the activities of agencies and communication consultancies. Chileans consider exposure in the printed media as powerful and it is an important means for achieving social prestige. Public relations campaigns focused on strategic public or minority issues have not achieved adequate exposure in the national press. In fact, there is more concern for information which favors the interests of social and economic groups than public issues. The reason for this may well reside in the individualism which permeates all segments of Chilean society, a legacy of the difficult years of military rule, as already stated.

NEWSPAPERS AND MAGAZINES

The open political environment that existed in Chile until 1973 contributed to the emergence of a free press which often resulted in the politicized and controversial behavior of the printed media. With the arrival of the military regime, the situation changed radically and there was severe control of the press for seventeen years. Under the strict control of the military regime, the only exceptions emerged at the end of the seventies with the weekly magazine *Hoy* that was followed by other alternative media. According to Krohne (2002), "these alternative media which included the *Apsi*, *Análisis*, *Cauce*, and *Hoy* magazines and the newspapers *Fortín Mapocho* and *La Epoca* did not survive the end of the military regime" (p. 24).

Some analysts are of the opinion that during the 1980s, the media adapted to the market and its cruelties. The revitalized newspaper conglomerates had a distinct right-wing orientation. For example, the *El Mercurio* group (which in 1973 represented one third of national newspaper circulation) consolidated its market share and during1988 became the main proprietor of more than 50% of newspapers with national circulation (Krohne, p. 22).

Television took over the market that previously belonged to the print media. Journalism had to modernize to correctly interpret the new national scenario. Today there are few newspapers, magazines, or television channels that are dedicated to politics or that defend a specific ideology, as had been the case in the past. Today, business ideology permeates radio and television because to survive in a neoliberal economy, it is necessary to secure revenue through advertising.

There seems to be public apathy, mainly due to the fear that has persisted since the Pinochet government. In summary, this phenomenon has led to a crisis of values. This crisis, which has been affected by globalization, has led to individualism, the disinterest among the younger generation in politics, and to a disorganized citizenry. Another important effect of the crisis was the weakening of regional printed media that compete with the dominant national press. There are seven national and one state daily newspaper. Six of the dailies have a distinct right-wing orientation. They compete with 42 regional newspapers that have limited technological infrastructure, and practically no access to international news sources.

The *El Mercurio* group, that owns the largest daily in the country, dominates the printed media. The editorial policies of *El Mercurio* are directed to the dominant social coalition with a notable neoliberal orientation to the economy, a conservative stance to moral and ethical issues, and right-wing orientation on politics. The *El Mercurio* group also publishes an afternoon daily, *La Segunda*, which is characterized by a very agile editorial policy that is well in tune with the moral and political agenda of the country.

Copesa is the second print media conglomerate. It is responsible for the publication of *La Tercera* which is directed to the professional sector, and to the emerging groups associated with economic modernization. Third behind these leaders is the state-owned La Nación group that publishes the daily *La Nación*. The newspaper *Ultimas Notícias* targets the middle class. *La Hora* is a free newspaper. *La Cuarta* has a distinct place with the humbler segments of the population with an essentially sensationalist content. *La Época* dedicates itself to economic and political issues. The newspapers *El Diário* and *Estratégia* specialize in financial journalism. Two magazines, *Cosas* and *Caras* cater to women. The *¿Qué Pasa?* is an influential weekly magazine that is characterized by an inquisitive and direct editorial policy.

TELEVISION AND RADIO

Since its creation in 1922, radio has always been managed by businesspeople with clear commercial objectives, unlike the print media. The linking of radios to political parties occurred in the beginning of the 1970s, largely due to the prevailing political conflict. The 1980s saw a structural mutation of Chilean communication media. According to Tironi (1998), until the 1980s there persisted an organizationally primitive and relatively elitist system of print media that was highly dependent on the state, with marked political, cultural, and educational pretensions.

Today, there exist a total of 1264 radio stations (FM and AM) of which 220 are community radio stations. Many radio networks such as Chilena (belonging to the Catholic Church), Cooperativa, and Agricultura have a strong orientation toward news. The rest are dedicated to music and entertainment. In 1973, the formerly subsidized television stations were forced by the government to seek private funding through the procurement of paid advertising and sponsorships. The effects of this policy can be seen today in the quality of the programming aired on Chilean television. Since the 1980s, there has been a massive shift to privatize the ownership of TV stations giving them a strong market orientation and information and entertainment focus. Between 1970 and 1983, the number of television sets increased sixfold. In 1974, there were 53 television sets per 1000 people; in 1980 the figure was 205, and in 1982 there were 302 sets per 1000 people. The massive utilization of satellite technologies also benefited the creation of new FM stations. In contrast, there was a decline in newspaper circulation, partly because of the economic crisis between 1982 and 1984, as well as President Frei Montalva's educational reform on reading habits.

Today, commercial Chilean television is privately owned. There are six stations of which three have national coverage. The Catholic University of Chile owns channel 13. TVN is state-owned. Megavisión belongs to the Televisa/Mexico communications conglomerate. American Media Partners own Chilevisión. La Red belongs to Compañía Chilena de Television S/A. Canal 2 is owned by Compañía Chilena de Comunicaciones. The globalization of communication has induced Chileans to prefer the content of the media of neighboring countries. The lack of domestic cultural television programming has greatly harmed the country.

It is obvious that globalization and new technologies have created an ideal environment for the expansion of communications in Chile. Among the principal characteristics of this expansion are the creation of monopolies and the adoption of North American programming strategies. Radio, because of its closeness to local language and national sentiment, has achieved a stronger cultural bond with its audience. Television, on the other hand, is seen as a privately administrated mass medium which is focused on imported entertainment and news programming.

One of the more noticeable features of the present-day Chilean is the absolute absence of interest in politics, which is made explicit through individualistic behavior. Group participation generally occurs when there is a threat to public safety or to personal and family integrity. As a result, public relations is commonly practiced in the context of internal communication or through press-agentry activities. Public relations is generally not involved in designing and implementing institutional television and radio campaigns for large audiences. Until the present day, over the air television is a mass medium which has not implemented programming oriented to the structuring of issue-conscious publics. In Chile, there is a consensus that the principal mission of television is to entertain whereas the role of the print media is to influence and mobilize public opinion. It is clear that the beginning of the twenty-first century brought market forces to the media.

THE PARTICIPATION OF THE CITIZENRY IN NATIONAL AFFAIRS: NONGOVERNMENTAL ORGANIZATIONS

Like other Latin American nations, Chile does not have a philanthropic culture and a proactive stance on issues of concern to its citizens. As a result, predominantly during the military regime, a number of nongovernmental organizations (NGOs) were founded, with links to left-wing scholarly organizations. Initially, these organizations were funded from abroad and hosted banned political groups that were to ultimately launch the political platform leading to the return of democracy and the first Concertación government. After the return to democracy, these organizations lost external funding, which reduced their political visibility. They engaged in movements for other domestic causes such as defending small businesses, advancing the feminist movement, and advocating environmental issues.

Until 1996, feminist groups received more support than the "green" groups. After 1996, the number of environmental NGOs grew substantially. Some of their initiatives were highly publicized and served to retard the financing of many mega projects that endangered the environment. In summary, these "green groups" will be among the principal social and political forces of the country. To achieve this stature, the "green" NGOs will have to seek alliance with political parties.

The protection of the indigenous Mapuche community reached its heyday during the military regime when activists challenged the illegal occupation of native lands. However, during the political transition (after the end of the military regime), the significance of these activists was substantially reduced. Since the 1990s new activist groups have manifested to protect the rights of indigenous people. Most observers agree that the changes in the behavior of the population were due to the rapid social transformation that was forced by the new economy. Family and work relationships, together with personal friendship, have suffered affecting Chilean culture. The most prominent feature of this change is the individualism caused by fierce personal competition and reduced work opportunities. This individualism is also noticeable in the declining participation of the younger generations in politics, national issues, and in the formation of activist groups. Despite the existence of groups concerned with the defense of natural resources and individual freedoms, it is apparent that many Chileans have lost their cultural identity and their willingness to participate in deciding urgent social and national issues.

With the rapid growth of NGOs in the country, it is believed that there will appear in the near future a solidarity movement capable of implementing structural and social projects. Presently, few NGOs have a permanent communications and public relations department whose principal focus is the design of communication campaigns for disseminating goals and policy objectives. The principal obstacle is the lack of financial resources to invest in planned communication.

Another factor that has hampered the growth of NGOs is the worldview that society expects the state to provide all necessary basic services. The absence of solidarity and citizenship, a legacy of the 1970s and 1980s, are dominating factors in Chilean culture. National and international NGOs that receive foreign financial support are the most visible. Chile—despite the existence of relevant issues such as AIDS, discrimination of women, and the destruction of the environment—has not been able to realize the importance of NGOs.

PUBLIC RELATIONS IN CHILE: THE PAST AND THE FUTURE

From the first public relations department founded by the Braden Copper Company in 1952 until the present day, the evolution of public relations has been hampered by the strong presence of journalism and by the low status the profession enjoys in Chilean society. In addition, at least until the 1980s, multinational companies merely replicated the public relations strategies and tactics dictated from their headquarters. Most often, these practices had no relevance to the organization's environment in Chile, further hampering the growth of the profession. The government sector has established public relations departments to maintain sustained relationships with its diverse publics including the use of mass communication media. Only large Chilean organizations, such as Corpracion Nacional del Cobre (CODELCO) and Empresse Nacional dedistuguj de energie SA (ENDESA), have an in-house public relations department, who often rely on the professional services of public relations agencies. Few medium and small organizations currently have a public relations department.

Senior managers often consider themselves to be the public relations professionals of the company regarding public relations purely as a social endeavor, dedicated to maintaining personal contacts with politicians, society and the media (Ferrari, 2000). This is typical of the personal influence model that has been written about in the last decade (Huang, 1990). The difficulty in identifying the principal events in the history of public relations in Chile is due to the absence of a suitable knowledge base. Délano (1990) dedicated her research to an analysis of the importance of three early Chilean thinkers and their personal and professional history. Eyzaguirre (1993) explained the history of public relations education in Chile.

The history of public relations as a professional activity was largely influenced by the political context of Chile during the 1970s and 1980s. This is consonant with the framework used in this book that proposes a country's political system as a key variable in the development and status of the public relations profession. There are two schools of thought on the nexus between the recent political history of Chile and the public relations profession. First, some believe that the military regime (1973–1990) had a positive influence on the public relations profession by legitimizing it, which was a result of the encouraging globalization and privatization of businesses (Délano, 2000). The second point of view argues that the military regime actually hampered the development of the mass media as well as public relations. Public relations, this school of thought holds, was restricted to the organization of parties and cocktails (Ruiz-Velasco, 1995). During the military regime, many public relations posts were in the hands of individuals close to the military. Censorship was also widespread because there was a public office that decided what could and could not be published in the media. This situation lasted until the beginning of the 1990s.

According to many public relations professionals, the current professionalization of public relations is a result of the combination of two unique factors: the return of democratic rule and the implementation of a neoliberal economy. The international exposure of many Chilean companies forced them to become more transparent, not only with their shareholders, but also with their clients, suppliers, the media, and stakeholders. This trend was accelerated largely as a result of privatization, globalization of the companies and the development of mass communication media. Currently, approximately 15 national and international agencies provide integrated communication services including public relations. The more widely known agencies are multinationals. A number of local agencies work in alliance with foreign partners.

There is no reliable record of the number of Chilean organizations that have public relations/communication departments. The Council of Public Relations Professionals, the national body that represents Public Relations professionals, is not considered relevant by businesses. Journalists, who are affiliated to their own professional associations, occupy the vast majority of public relations positions. The number of professionals who have graduated from university public relations programs is still very small given that the first graduates only came to the market in 1995.

According to Veragua (2001), past president of The Council of Public Relations Professionals "the PR professional has an important role in the administration of internal and external communication processes. Without communication there is no organization, and without communication there is no coordination. This is the main reason why PR professionals need to collaborate with the creation of an organizational climate that contributes to the improvement of individuals and the organization."

CASE STUDY MCDONALD'S LETTUCE[1]

In April 1991, following an outbreak of cholera in Latin America, the government of Chile and its Ministry of Public Health prohibited lettuce and other raw vegetables from being served in restaurants. The prohibition presented a significant challenge to McDonald's, whose signature sandwiches such as the Big Mac could not be served with this essential ingredient. Chile was the only country of the 83 in which McDonald's operates where its sandwiches did not include lettuce. Focus group testing demonstrated consumer dissatisfaction with a sandwich without lettuce. But the government was apprehensive about changing the restriction for reasons of public health and politically motivated criticism. Burson-Marsteller Santiago was hired by McDonald's to develop and implement a strategic PR program to address the issue.

---

[1] This case study was furnished by Mr. Ramiro Prudencio, CEO Burson Marsteller Brazil, and Ms. Claudia Adriasola, CEO Burson Marsteller Chile.

Target Audiences and Their Perceptions

There were two primary target audiences. The first was government health officials, who perceived a public health risk to lifting the prohibition. Perceptions dictated that no restaurant had the infrastructure, know-how, or food safety expertise to properly produce and serve lettuce. The sense of risk was compounded by a concern that any outbreak in enteric disease could be used against the ministry for political purposes. Concerns were further heightened by ongoing political conflicts between the Health Ministry and medical worker unions. The second target audience was consumers, who for years had consumed lettuce in restaurants and, after the prohibition, were consistently receiving public health messages concerning the proper handling of raw vegetables and risk of cholera.

Despite the public health messages, consumers felt that a sandwich without lettuce was less satisfying. Moreover, they expressed underlying concerns about the risk that eating improperly handled lettuce might present. Once official approval for serving lettuce was given, the program objective was to reintroduce the consumption of this leafy vegetable in a manner that managed possible consumer concerns and emphasized improved product taste.

Strategy & Implementation

The core concept was to demonstrate McDonald's recognized leadership and expertise in food safety, and to demonstrate that an outright ban on serving lettuce was unnecessary to assure public health. Activities included:

- Development of collateral materials that fully explained McDonald's food safety expertise and its proposed program to control the entire lettuce process from seeding in the field to serving in the restaurant

- Meetings with key public health officials at the ministerial and civil service levels

- Ally development with suppliers, restaurant association, United States Embassy, and others

- Tours of lettuce processing facilities with health officials and media

- Internal communications strategies and activities to prepare staff to address consumer concerns in restaurants or at McDonald's offices

- Media relations activities to underscore McDonald's food safety expertise and lettuce processing and to highlight reintroduction of lettuce on McDonald's sandwiches

Results

On August 18, 1995, McDonald's was the first restaurant to serve lettuce in Chile since April 1991. Sales jumped more than 15% in the days following the announcement, which was carried on every television news program in Chile. McDonald's held this advantage over other competitors, less prepared for the removal of the prohibition, for several weeks.

REFERENCES

Bassa, I. A. D. (1996). *Bases culturales para la formulación de un modelo de gestión estratégica de empresas chilenas* (Cultural bases for a development model of strategic management of Chilean companies). Unpublished master's thesis, Pontifícia Universidad Católica de Chile, Santiago, Chile.

Becerra, N. A. P. (1983). *Perfil das Relações Públicas na América Latina* (Profile of Public Relations in Latin America). Unpublished master's thesis, Universidade de São Paulo, São Paulo, Brazil.

Castellón, L., & Araos, C. (1999). Medios de comunicación e identidad cultural: una reflexión desde la prensa escrita (Levels of cultural identity: A reflection from the printed media). *Anuário Unesco/Umesp de Comunicação Regional, II*(2), 91–107.

Cutlip, S. M. & Center, A. H. (1963). *Relaciones Públicas*. Barcelona, España: Ediciones Rialp S.A.

Délano, B. J. A. (1990). *Las Relaciones Públicas en Chile—fundamentos prácticos y teóricos* (Public Relations in Chile: Theory and practice). Santiago, Chile: Universitaria.

Eyzaguirre, P. C. (1993). *Manual de Relaciones Públicas* (Public relations manual). Santiago, Chile: Los Andes.

Eyzaguirre, P. C. (1997). *Relaciones Públicas* (Public relations). Santiago, Chile: Calicanto.

Ferrari, M. A. (2000). *A influência dos valores organizacionais na determinação prática das Relações Públicas em organizações do Brasil e do Chile* (The influence of organizational values in the practice of public relations in Brazilian and Chilean organizations). Unpublished doctoral dissertation, Universidade de São Paulo, São Paulo, Brazil.

Flanagan, C. S. (1992). *Relaciones Públicas: concepto, evolución y practica actual en Chile* (Public Relations: Concept, evolution and current practice in Chile). Unpublished doctoral dissertation, Universidad Complutense de Madrid, Madrid, Spain.

Grunig, J. E. & Hunt, T. (2000) *Dirección de Relaciones Públicas*. Barcelona, España: Ediciones Gestión 2000 S.A.

Hofstede, G. (1984). *Culture's consequences: international differences in work-related values*. London: Sage Publications.

Huang, Y. (1990). *Risk communication, models of public relations and anti-nuclear activism: A case study of a nuclear power plant in Taiwan*. Unpublished master's thesis, University of Maryland, College Park.

Krohne, W. (2002). *La Libertad de Expresión en Chile bajo la Atenta Mirada de La Crítica* (Freedom of expression in Chile as seen by the attentive eye of the media). Santiago, Chile: Fundación Konrad Adenauer.

Lesly, P. (1973). Manual de *Relaciones Públicas*. Barcelona, España: Ediciones Martínez Roca S.A.

Levering, R., & Moskowitz, M. (2001, November 16–29). Los mejores lugares para trabajar (The best places to work). *Revista Capital, Negocios y Mundo*, (73), 120–124.

Ortega, C. G. (1993). Growth and development of public relations in Chile. U.S.A. Unpublished master's thesis, California State University, Hayward.

Pavlik, J. V. (1999). *La Investigación en Relaciones Públicas*. Barcelona, España: Ediciones Gestión 2000 S.A.

Ruiz-Velasco, L. (1995, July). Relaciones peligrosas (Dangerous relationships). *Revista America Economia*, (97), 22–24.

Simões, R. P. (1993). *Relaciones Públicas: función política en la empresa y en la institución pública. 3ª edición*. Barcelona, España: Editorial El Ateneo.

Tironi, E. (1998, April). Los medios y el poder (Power and the media). *Revista Capital, Negocios Y Mundo*, Special Issue: El Poder, 76–79.

Veragua, M. (2001, January). Relaciones Públicas: por un mundo mejor (public relations: for a better world). Retrieved January 21, 2001 from *http://www.dirigible.cl*.

PART

V

INTERNATIONAL PUBLIC RELATIONS: KEY
DIMENSIONS AND ACTORS

19

TRANSNATIONAL PUBLIC RELATIONS BY FOREIGN GOVERNMENTS

MICHAEL KUNCZIK

DEFINITION OF PUBLIC RELATIONS AND STATUS OF RESEARCH

The focus of this chapter will be the field of international public relations with particular reference to the issue of image cultivation by nations. Taking the quantity of publications as an indicator, one has to conclude that the body of research on this topic has large gaps. Even the relationship between news media and images of nations is not well researched and for this very reason the following discussion cannot be treated as complete. The main reason for this gap in research can be seen in the often highly sophisticated methods that states adopt to influence world opinion. Among others, public relations agencies and even the secret service units play a decisive role in these activities, which very often take place far from public view (Kunczik, 1997). Public relations is often perceived as the art of camouflaging and deceiving and it is assumed that for public relations to be successful, target groups (those to be influenced) not notice that they have become the "victims" of public relations efforts.

Because credibility is a decisive variable in the communication process, attempts are constantly being made to influence media reporting by covert means to avoid the impression of manipulation. The aim of such activities is chameleonlike: to adapt to the surroundings while remaining submerged. Attempting to identify the instigators of public relations by nations is often like trying to nail pudding to a wall. Therefore, there is very little literature on this theme. One cannot, after all, do a representative survey of the former KGB (or its successor organization) or the Central Intelligence Agency (CIA), although the United States Information Service (USIA) has been the subject of a published empirical study (Bogart, 1976). The borders between secret services and news agencies are often blurred, as evident from the example of TASS, the former Soviet news agency

(Kruglak, 1962). But besides that, most industrialized as well as developing countries either have created special organizations (e.g., USIA, the British Council, Maison Française, Goethe Institute, and so forth) to improve their country's image abroad or have commissioned public relations agencies to do so on their behalf.

For the nation-state, public relations implies the planned and continuous distribution of interest-bound information by a state aimed (mostly) at improving the country's image abroad. Trying to distinguish between advertising, public relations, and propaganda in foreign image cultivation is merely a semantic game. In Lasswell's (1942) definition of *propaganda* as "the manipulation of symbols as a means of influencing attitudes on controversial matters" (p. 106), one could easily substitute *public relations* for *propaganda.* I treat propaganda and public relations as synonyms following the tradition of one of the founding fathers of modern public relations Edward L. Bernays who stated: "the only difference between 'propaganda' and 'education,' really, is the point of view. The advocacy of what we believe in is education. The advocacy of what we don't believe in is propaganda" (1923, p. 212).

So, public relations for the nation-state comprises persuasive communicative acts directed at a foreign audience. But a famous comment by Walter Lippmann applies also to the changeability of images: "For the most part we do not first see, and then define, we define first and then see" (1922, p. 81). In other words, from the wealth of events and information available, we select those that conform to the already existing image (selective perception) in our minds. Furthermore, can information in which one is not interested in be ignored? For example, in September 1947, a six-month propaganda campaign to promote the United Nations was begun in Cincinnati whose slogan was: "Peace begins with the United Nations—the United Nations begin with you." It was largely unsuccessful because those who paid attention to the message were primarily individuals who already had an interest in, and were informed about, the United Nations. As Star and Hughes (1950) observed, "The conclusion is that the people reached by the campaign were those least in need of it and that the people missed by it were the new audience the plan hoped to gain" (p. 397).

Donsbach (1991) published an extensive study on the selective perception of West German newspaper readers that clearly confirms the phenomenon of *de facto* selectivity. In the precommunicative phase, recipients chose those media that they assumed followed an editorial line as close as possible to their own political persuasions. This implies humans are more likely to select information that confirms their preexisting views than information that challenges preexisting views. Of course, this logic holds water only where there is a choice of free media. Donsbach was able to prove that newspaper readers prefer to read those articles that they expect will confirm their existing opinions. But, and this is very important, the selection rule applies only when positive information is offered. When negative information is offered, both supporters and opponents of a certain position have similar reactions: they heed it. In other words, the protective shield of selective perception works against information that might result in a positive change of opinion, but not against information that might produce a negative change of opinion. Churchill may have been right when he stated: "To build may have to be the slow and laboring task of years. To destroy can be the thoughtless act of a single day" (Howard, 1986/1987).

HISTORICAL OUTLINE OF IMAGE CULTIVATION BY GOVERNMENTS

The following short review of early image cultivation by states makes no claim to completeness but is meant merely to underscore that image cultivation did not begin with the age of the mass media. The Bible contains examples that prove that the character of a nation and its image has concerned humanity from the beginning of its history. As reported in *Genesis* (18:32) if God had found even 10 innocent people in Sodom, he would not have destroyed the city in order to save them. The Apostle Paul, in his letter to Titus (1:12), wrote the following about the Cretans: "It was a Cretan himself, one of their own prophets, who spoke the truth when he said, 'Cretans are always liars, wicked beasts, and lazy gluttons'." Further examples were gathered by Duijker and Frijda (1960, 1):

> Herodotus discusses the characteristic habits of the Scythes, the Phrygians, the Libyans and many others. Vatsayana, in the Kama-Sutra, notices striking differences in the sexual behaviour of the human female, and one of his classifications is based on region of origin. Tacitus presents, in his famous Germania, an elaborate description of the attitudes, customs and morals of the Germans. Juvenal speaks rather sarcastically about the little Greeks in imperial Rome, and makes it quite clear that he considers them a rather contemptible bunch of spineless good-for-nothings.

Alexander the Great (356 BC–323 BC) created what can be described as the first war reporter unit. Reports written to serve his objectives were sent to the Macedonian court, reproduced there, and disseminated with propagandistic intent. Callisthenes of Olynthus (c. 360 BC–328 BC), appointed to accompany Alexander as historian on his Asiatic expedition, spread the claim that the king was the son of Zeus, the supreme god. The sacred oracle of Didyma confirmed the story—surely under the influence of Alexander's "Public Relations department," which probably made skillful use of the oracle's utterance: It is very difficult to fight the son of so powerful a god!

The invention of the printing press by Gutenberg (about 1445) was the point of departure for a new kind of international public relations practice. Emperor Maxmillan I (1493–1519) was the first German leader (and to the best knowledge of this author the first leader of any nation) to manipulate the predecessors of the modern newspaper—then called "new newspapers" (*newe zeytungen*), as an instrument to influence public opinion. With biased war reports, he tried to influence the mood of the public in his empire. Maximilian also tried to communicate with the population of the enemy state, for example, the commoners of the Republic of Venice. In repeated appeals, he tried to incite them to insurrection against the finance aristocracy promising them liberation and a share of the city-state's government and the possessions of the rulers.

In 1576, Rudolf II was elected emperor of the Holy Roman Empire of the German Nation by the Reichstag in Regensburg. The Turks were Rudolf's main opponent as it was their leader Sultan Murad III who had declared war on the German nation. To mobilize support, Rudolf used the instruments of propaganda such as leaflets, coins, medals, festivities, political acts of symbolic value, art, and architecture (e.g., triumphal arches). In 1593, when the Turks attacked, the emperor started his propaganda campaign, including atrocity propaganda. Detailed accounts of Turkish atrocities (e.g., disemboweling a pregnant woman and smashing the foetus against the wall) were published in leaflets and newspapers.

Cardinal Richelieu (1585–1642) the leading minister who asserted absolutism in France, had a press office that used pamphlets to fight France's foreign opponents, especially the Habsburgs. *La réputation* was the political keyword for the cardinal, a master in public relations. Richelieu also established a press department and had a minister for "Information and Propaganda." From the beginning of his career, Richelieu hired writers to produce leaflets that justified his policies and attacked his political opponents. The most important instrument of his press policy was the *Gazette*, a weekly. In 1635 Richelieu established the Académie Française to which leading literati were appointed. Its main task was to standardize French language and influence long-term public opinion. Richelieu also distributed publications, biased appropriately to suit his purpose, in foreign countries. Rome was the center of the world in those days and he who had a good reputation in Rome had a good reputation in the world (i.e., Europe). According to Richelieu, the best way for a sovereign to get a good reputation in Rome was to govern decently. France wanted to become the "Arbitre de la Chrestiente" (Arbiter of Christendom), and in order to achieve this aim, even negative information about other countries was disseminated. Without a doubt, Richelieu was a master of public relations for France's image and can be regarded as a pioneer in public relations for nations.

Public relations for France reached a high point during the reign of Louis XIV. The, "Sun King," who reigned for 54 years (1661–1715), was a master of image construction. His personality, life, and body were put on stage and Louis le Grand was created. To polish the king's image, newspapers were founded, academies were established, castles were built, and birthdays and battle victories were celebrated. Numerous statues of Louis XIV were errected as part of a statue campaign in the 1680s (Burke, 1992). Triumphal arches were built in abundance. The palace at Versailles was imitated all over Europe. Every utterance of the king was recorded by secretaries. Dozens of painters were kept busy. Among those employed to polish the image of the king were the painter Lebrun, the musician Lully, and the poets Corneille, Racine, and Jean-Baptiste Roquelin (Molière). These extravagant activities, however, ruined France. In 1715 when the king died, France, the richest country of Europe, was on its way to ruin.

Louis XIV used publicity to defend France, whose incarnation he believed himself to be ("L'état c'est moi!"), against hostile public opinion in Europe. Burke (1992) examined the parallels between modern publicity agents and the "glory enterprise" of Louis XIV. He analyzed "the selling of Ludwig XIV" (p. 4). According to Burke *gloire* (glory) was a keyword of the time. Louis XIV was a master of impression management. He played the part of the king, living the life of a living image. As Burke pointed out, Louis XIV's image projection was aimed not only at the domestic public: "The foreign public for l'histoire du roi was considered no less important than the domestic one. In 1698, for example, the petite académie was [. . .] to draw up a list of medals suitable for presentation to foreigners" (p. 158). France had practical reasons for image cultivation in, for example, the Ottoman Empire because both had a common enemy in the Holy Roman Empire of the German Nation. But the main target of Louis XIV's image policy were the other courts of Europe: "The ambassadors formed a substantial part of the audience for the court festivals, plays, ballets and operas. They were very often presented with gifts, which would enhance the king's name abroad—medals and tapestries of the events of the reign [. . .] and jewelled portaits of Louis himself" (Burke, 1992, p. 162).

Texts glorifying Louis IV were published in foreign languages. For example, Latin was used to reach the educated people in Europe. Burke (1992) labeled Louis XIV's image policy as "theatre state" and described the life of the king as a grand spectacle. Statecraft became stagecraft. Burke concluded that the main difference between modern image shaping and Louis' image building is technological. Louis was presented by means of print, statues, and medals, whereas twentieth-century rulers have relied on photography, cinema, radio, and television. Burke wrote that "Long before the cinema, the theatre affected perceptions of politics. For his contemporaries the sun-king was a star" (p. 199). Louis used the grandiosity of official architecture and sculpture to dwarf the spectator, to make them conscious of his power.

It is pertinent to mention here that the "founding fathers" of the United States also made use of the media to achieve their foreign policy objectives during times of conflicts or war. James Truslow Adams (1927) who compared World War I propaganda activities with those used by the founding fathers came to the conclusion that the widely held view that propaganda was an invention of thr First World War was inaccurate. He argued that the propaganda activities of the anti-British American revolutionaries were comparable to those mounted between 1914 and 1918. The 1776 revolution had been set in motion by Samuel Adams and a number of other agitators living in Massachussetts. Generally speaking, American public opinion was against the federalists who tried to portray the British as an enemy. Incidents such as the Boston Tea Party were arranged partly for the purpose of attracting public attention through media coverage. Samuel Adams argued: "Put your enemy in the wrong and keep him there" (Baldwin, 1965, p. 8).

PROFESSIONAL INTERNATIONAL IMAGE CULTIVATION

The birth of professional international image cultivation took place during World War I (Kunczik 1998). The first step in this development was the fight for America's neutrality. A commentary in *The New York Times* (September 9, 1914) carried the headline: "The Press Agents' War," whose author argued: "The present European war [. . .] deserves to be distinguished as *first press agents* war" (p. 8). The Germans wanted the Americans to stay neutral and the British wanted to create the impression that there was a fight between the forces of good and evil and that the British cause was America's too. The first British act of war was to cut Germany's overseas cables on August 5, 1914. Germany was cut off from the world's most important neutral country at the very moment when the American public opinion was being formed on the question of responsibility for the outbreak of the war. William Gibbs McAdoo (1931), Secretary of the Treasury and Wilson's son-in-law, reported that because of cable control: "Nearly everything in the newspapers which came from Europe during the war was censored and colored in the Allied interest" (p. 322). Unbiased news simply disappeared out of the American papers about the middle of August, 1914. British intellectuals and the Oxford University took part in the propaganda effort against "Frankenstein Germany" (Kunczik, 1997, p. 179). The authors of the Oxford Pamphlets were able "to give a patriotic bias to the apparent objective presentation of material" (Squires, 1935, p. 17). The British handled journalists perfectly. American correspondents were invited to visit the front and later they were wined and dined in the headquarter chateau. The Neutral Press Committee had the task of influencing foreign journalists. With the Help of *Who's Who* a mailing list of about 170.000 American opinion leaders was compiled. They were bombarded with propaganda material, which was sent by private persons and not by official institutions to increase credibility. Needless to say, these materials received wide press coverage. Even years after the war ended, there lingered the impression that before America entered the war, there had been no British propaganda.

One clever move of British propaganda was to arrange for the translation, printing, and distribution in the United States of works of extreme German nationalists, militarists, and exponents of the "Machtpolitik" (power policy). These nationalistic individuals who had little influence in Germany were created to be the representatives of the terrible character of the German population as worshippers of power and might. According to Millis (1935) "the stupefied Germans discovered themselves convicted before world opinion on the evidence of a few writers whom the vast majority of Germans had never read or never even heard of" (p. 77).

Although the Germans lost the public relations battle in the United States, they weren't really as bad as portrayed. The first step taken to advance the German cause was the establishment of the German Information Bureau. The Germans, like the British, preferred to use interpersonal channels ofcommunication to distribute their point of view. According to Wilke (1998), the German Embassy had a list of 60,000 names (p. 16). The Germans, like the English, made use of the third-party approach and tried to influence public opinion through the publication of books written by Americans. Millis (1935) reported that authors Frank Harris and Edwin J. Clapp were on the German payroll (p. 203). In December 1914, the services of William Bayard Hale, a leading American journalist and former advisor to President Wilson, were secured by Dernburg to wage a publicity campaign (Viereck, 1930).[1] Grattan (1929/1969) elaborated: "He was put in immediate charge of the news sheet, and was detailed to prepare pamphlets and other publicity materials for distribution to the general public. His salary was to be $15,000 a year and he apparently continued in active service for almost precisely a year, although his contract did not expire until the middle of 1918" (p. 87). Among other things, Hale established contacts with the League of American Women for Strict Neutrality, who claimed to have gathered 200,000 signatures for a petition to Congress (Millis, 1935, p. 203). Germany, after having tried in vain to buy *The New York Sun* and *The Washington Post*, bought *The New York Evening Mail* (for $1.5 million) with sole the purpose of reaching a large metropolitan audience (Doerries, 1989).

The Germans had no success in this publicity war, because the British "paper bullets" gradually had already changed public opinion in their favor. On April 6, 1917, President Wilson declared war against Germany. Recognizing public opinion as a major force in the war, on April 14, 1917, President Wilson established the Committee on Public Information (CPI) headed by journalist George Creel to conduct propaganda abroad and in the United States. The task was the "whole business of mobilizing the mind of the world" (Creel, 1920, p. XIII). That is, America should be represented not merely as a strong man fully armed, but as a strong man fully armed and believing in the cause for which he is fighting— for ideas and ideals. According to Creel (1920), the CPI's charter was to carry "to every corner of the civilized globe the full message of America's idealism, unselfishness, and indomitable purpose" (p. 4).

The CPI was able to build on the experience gained in the commercial sector. Creel (1920) described the fight for the minds of men, for the "conquest of their convictions" (p. 4): "In all things, from first to last, without halt or change, it was a plain publicity proposition, a vast enterprise in salesmanship, the world's greatest adventure in advertising" (p. 4). He avoided describing the activity as propaganda because "that word, in German hands, had come to be associated with deceit and corruption" (p. 4). Eric Goldman (1948) characterized America's entry into the war as "brilliant publicity for publicity" (p. 12). Creel (1920) contended that one of his most effective ideas was to bring to the United States, delegations of foreign newspaper men periodically so they might "see with their own eyes, hear with their own ears" (p. 227), and on their return be able to report fully on America's morale and effort. According to Creel, "these trips were of incalculable value in our foreign educational work" (p. 227). Mexico was selected for the initial experiment, the Swiss came next, then Italian journalists, and finally a group from Scandinavia.

---

[1]Hearst was not informed about his correspondent's second job (Doerries, 1989). How close the connections between Wilson and Hale was documented by Josephus Daniels (1944), Secretary of the Navy in Wilson's cabinet. He pointed out that early in the campaign that put Wilson in the White House, the Democratic Party circulated a number of copies of William Bayard Hale's *Woodrow Wilson: The Story of His Life*: "It was the *vade mecum* of all Democratic speakers. It was the best story of Wilson before he became President, that had been written" (p. 76). In 1913 Wilson sent "his personal friend and biographer" (p. 181) Hale to Mexico to make a firsthand study and report on the situation over there; Hale was entrusted with an important and confidential mission in the critical days of Watchful Waiting (Daniels, 1944).

After the end of World War I the character of diplomacy slowly changed. The mediation of foreign policy intensified and today nearly every act in the (open) conduct of foreign policy takes public relations (the effect on the respective image), into account.[2] Immediately after World War I, Carl Byoir and Bernays conducted public relations for Lithuanian groups in the United States. They were agitating for an independent Lithuania, which, like the other Baltic states, had previously belonged to Russia (Bernays 1965, p. 188ff.). From the beginning, the firm Carl Byoir & Associates accepted every client it could get. In 1931, a contract was signed with the Cuban government of General Machado, a ruthless dictator, whose character was very hard to sell positively to the American public. In 1933, this relationship ended when the general was toppled. That same year Byoir opened business relations with the German Tourist Information Office whose links with the Nazis was obvious.

In 1927, in an address on "International Communications," Ivy L. Lee, one of the most influential public relations counsels in the United States, argued that the nations of the world must get matters of importance into print in the newspapers. To accomplish this, Ivy felt nations needed to create an appetite among the reading public by humanizing stories (Hiebert, 1966, 255ff.). Even more important was a lecture Lee gave on July 3, 1934 in London on "The Problem of International Propaganda" in which he developed the idea that international propaganda should be a kind of two-way communication. The motto of Theodore Roosevelt "Speak softly, but carry a big stick" was labeled as old-fashioned. Lee believed that nation states should speak clearly and loudly and without hiding a stick. He argued that complete knowledge of the truth would make people understand each other. Each government should become aware of press relations and understand, that "correspondents of foreign newspapers were there to ascertain facts and facts alone, and to ascertain them promptly and accurately" (Hiebert, 1966, p. 261). According to Lee, the wisest and most enlighted government is the one which effectively assists the press. Lee considered it to be a mistake for governments to rely on the printing presses of other countries to tell their stories for them. Lee proposed to the Soviet Union, which had a bad image due to its refusal to pay Czarist debts, to use paid advertising instead. According to Lee, the Soviet Union had to establish a reputation of good faith, and a desire to comply with every international obligation. Because of his role as counselor to Russia, Lee was attacked as a traitor who worked against American interests. Hiebert (1966, 283) wrote: "Upon notification of American recognition, one of the first things done by Maxim

---

[2]It has become self-evident that foreign policy has to take the media into consideration. Manheim (1994) examined the head-of-state visits of Prime Minister Benazir Bhutto of Pakistan (1989) and of President Roh Tae Woo of Korea (1989) to the United States in the context of public diplomacy. He analyzed how each visit was planned, orchestrated, and conducted with United States and their home country media, elite, and public opinion in mind. Bhutto, for instance, had signed a contract with lobbyist and political consultant Mark Siegel, who waged a campaign with the theme of democratic partnership. Siegel laid emphasis on the political elite and tried to create the impression that Bhutto was the guarantor for democracy. Manheim wrote: "The centerpiece of the visit was Bhutto's address at the Harvard University commencement, where she called for the creation of an association of democratic nations, one in which the richest democracies would aid the poorest and through which economic and political sanctions might be applied against those nations moving away from the democratic ideal" (p. 85). According to Manheim the visit was a complete success. Wooing the mass media, international and domestic, was the primary purpose of the 1994 visits to the beleaguered Bosnian city of Sarajevo by Benazir Bhutto and Turkish Prime Minister Tansu Ciller. The two leaders as "women, mothers and spouses," wanted to show their solidarity with the courageous women of Sarajevo. Before Bhutto went to Sarajevo her main political opponent, former prime minister Nawaz Sharif, had visited Bosnia and made a $3 million personal donation. The press in Pakistan glorified this as a heroic deed, so Bhutto was forced to counter to win the upcoming March 1994 elections.

Litvinov, Soviet Foreign Minister, was to send a cable to Ivy Lee expressing appreciation for the part he had played in paving the way for a closer Russian-American relationship."

Ivy Lee had connections to Nazi Germany also. He worked for the German Dye Trust. Although he had no formal relationship with the Nazi Government he conceded that the advice he offered his client was ultimately intended to guide the German government in its public relations in the United States. Among other things, he made suggestions for German statements on disarmament: "Germany does not want armament in itself. It is willing to destroy every weapon of war if other nations will do the same. If other nations, however, continue to refuse to disarm, the German government is left with no choice except to demand an equality of armament. The German people are unwilling to believe that any people will deny them this right today" (Hiebert, 1966, p. 289). Lee also proposed that Joachim von Ribbentrop, the special commissioner for disarmament, should visit the United States to explain Germany's position to President Roosevelt and also to enlighten the Foreign Policy Association and the Council on Foreign Relations on the issue. Lee testified before a committee of the House of Representatives that he had disseminated no German propaganda in the United States, but that he only acted as adviser. He argued that his advice included the repeated suggestion that "they could never in the world get the American people reconciled to their treatment of the Jews and that Nazi propaganda in the United States was a mistake" (Hiebert, 1966, p. 290).

Regarding Lee's handling of the negative image of Hitler's storm trooperss, Hiebert (1966) reported: "Lee advised that the government issue a frank statement on this subject, including in the information that the storm troops number about 2,500,000 men, were 'between the ages of 18 and 60, physically well-trained and disciplined, but not armed, not prepared for war, and organized only for the purpose of preventing for all time the return of the Communist peril" (p. 289). This was an unimaginable masterpiece of ethical and moral elasticity because simultaneously Lee worked for the recognition of the Soviet Union.

ACTORS IN THE FIELD OF INTERNATIONAL PUBLIC RELATIONS

It is almost impossible to make a clear distinction between the nature of international public relations activities of nation-states, international social/economic organizations (e.g., the World Bank, Greenpeace), international political organizations (e.g., United Nations, NATO, etc.), and multinational corporations (MNCs). Furthermore, the same public relations agency often counsels nation states and MNCs. The following discussion proceeds from the premise that the economy cannot be regarded as a subsystem equal in importance to others. Rather, economics is assumed to be a basic social factor that also decisively influences other subsystems. In particular, this chapter argues that economy and policy are inseparable. All too often, people overlook the fact that MNCs are quite active in moulding foreign policy and interact with states for this purpose. Bernays (1965), working as PR counselor for United Fruit, wrote, "I was struck by the thought that although I was advising a banana company, I was actually fighting in the Cold War" (p. 766).

Nations' worry over their image gives power to such organizations as Amnesty International. Founded in 1961 by British jurist Peter Benenson, Amnesty International seeks to obtain the release of political and religious "prisoners of conscience" through international protest. Benenson was moved to act in 1961 when two Portuguese students were sentenced to 7 years' imprisonment each for uttering a toast to freedom. In January 1989, Amnesty International focused on violations of human rights in Turkey. This may be one reason why in June 1989 the Turkish government hired Saatchi & Saatchi, the well-known advertising agency, to improve the country's image.

A simple classification of those who use international public relations can be developed using two dimensions: for-profit versus nonprofit and public versus private.

	Public	*Private*
For-profit	State-owned airlines	MNCs
Nonprofit	Governments, international organizations	Foundations

This is only a rough classification. Other actors are also in the field such as individual international influence brokers (e.g., former diplomats and government officials such as Henry Kissinger) and international public relations agencies (e.g., Interpublic, Omnicom Group, Wire & Plastic Products), who often give advice and influence, or at least try to influence, world politics. Walter Isaacson (1992) argued that Kissinger's comments on the crackdown of the democratic movement in China in June 1989 were based on commercial interests, because Kissinger had clients (among them, Atlantic Richfield, ITT, and an investment partnership called China Ventures) with strong business interests in China. After the Tiananmen Square crackdown, Kissinger recommended, in a television interview on ABC, that the United States should maintain good relations with China instead of imposing economic sanctions, as an indication of America's political maturity. Isaacson maintained, that "if the American reaction to the Tiananmen had been mild, as Kissinger urged, China Ventures would have proceeded, and Kissinger would have made a significant amount of money" (p. 749). According to Isaacson, Kissinger's trip to China in November 1989 was staged to show the world that the time to ostracize China had passed. Kissinger met Deng Xiaoping, among others, and later reported on his meetings and the atmosphere within China to President Bush and other top American leaders.

The close interconnections between nations and MNCs are demonstrated by another example involving the Mobil Corporation. In October 1981, an advertisement appeared in *The New York Times*: "Saudi Arabia: Far More Than Oil" (Grunig & Hunt, 1984, p. 521). In 1986 Mobil waged a campaign in the United States for the sale of missiles to Saudi Arabia, which, Mobil argued, would serve America's interests:

This week, the Senate will attempt to override President Reagan's veto [of the resolution by the Congress to block the sale of missiles to Saudi Arabia], and kill the sale. When the crucial roll call is taken, members should remember a simple fact: They *aren't* voting on just an arms bill for Saudi Arabia. They *are* voting on an arms bill for American interests. Against such a yardstick, we trust the presidential veto will be sustained. (Onkvisit & Shaw, 1989, p. 148)

Mobil also referred to the Red Menace emphasizing Soviet involvement in the Middle East.

The Ford Company also fought against communism. In 1951 Henry Ford took part in the Crusade for Freedom. According to Cutlip (1994), Henry Ford II identified himself with that crusade "making an imaginative, constructive and dramatic effort to fight Communism. Use of Ford-Lincoln-Mercury dealerships throughout the United States as focal points for Crusade collections magnified this identity" (p. 698). In 1953, close to the 50th anniversary of Henry Ford, the film *The American Road* was produced to show that Ford was an American success story. Furthermore, a 50th anniversary book was published with a foreword in the name of Henry Ford II written by the public relations agency of Earl Newsom. The book said, among other things, that "the growth and achievements of Ford Motor Company have been made possible by the kind of world we live in, by American democracy, and the economic opportunity to seek change and progress freely" (Cutlip, 1994, p. 698).

The German DEMAG (Deutsche Maschinenbau AG), which built the steel factories in Rourkela, India, waged a three-year campaign in which the industrialization policies of the Indian government were praised as was the efficiency of German industry. During this period, the Soviet Union built another steel plant in India. The Soviets then waged a campaign against Germany and its industry, alleging that Germans were capitalists who were tyring to colonize India and exploit it by selling German products of poor quality. This fight for Indian public opinion was called "West German-Russian steel battle" (Darrow, Forrestal, & Cookman, 1967, p. 523). DEMAG countered with its own campaign distributing pamphlets to journalists, members of the parliament, and educators. Twenty thousand copies of a picture poster explaining the processes of steel production were donated to schools and universities. Radio Ceylon, popular among the Indian public, aired programs sponsored by DEMAG. Advertisements were published in Indian newspapers and journalists of the most important Indian dailies were visited by the press secretary of DEMAG.

Even rates of exchange can become the target of public relations campaigns of MNCs as was the case with Eastman Kodak (Dilenschneider & Forrestal, 1990). The company knew that its competitive position in the world marketplace was hurt by the then strength of the United States dollar. Kodak's communication division suggested that a public relations program be targeted at this issue. Fact-finding meetings with President Reagan, high-level administration officials, and key national economic and trade groups were arranged. According to Dilenschneider and Forrestal, the company funded a $150,000 study by the American Enterprise Institute, a conservative think tank (18 members of the Institute joined the Reagan Administration in 1981), to research the relationships between the strength of the dollar and the federal budget deficits. The Institute found a relationship between high interest rates required to finance the huge deficits and the dollar's strength. Dilenschneider and Forrestal wrote:

> Kodak believed a public affairs program could play a major role in persuading the government to pass legislation to eliminate federal budget deficit and intervene in currency exchange markets to stabilize the overvalued dollar. Kodak developed a 12-month communications program to reach members of Congress, the administration, and others in a position to influence economic policy. The message was that the overvalued dollar and escalating budget deficits were so damaging to manufacturers that a decisive action was needed (p. 679).

The program, which received a Silver Anvil Award in the 1986 competition sponsored by the Public Relations Society of America (PRSA), included a mailing to Kodak's shareholders, a "Write to Congress" campaign, consultations with leading politicians including Treasury Secretary Baker, and visits by Kodak executives to members of Congress and Cabinet members. According to Dilenschneider and Forrester the campaign played a direct role in changing the government's position and furthermore set the stage for two historic events: the September 1985 Group of Five communiqué pledging dollar stabilization, and the Gramm-Rudman-Hollings Act, aimed at eliminating federal budget deficits by 1991.

MEDIATION OF FOREIGN POLICY

Public relations for states is closely connected to the mediation of foreign policy. Hertz (1982) asserted: It is perhaps no exaggeration to say that today half of power politics consists of image making. With the rising importance of publics in foreign affairs, image making has steadily increased. Today, hardly anything remains in the open conduct of foreign policy that does not have a propaganda or public relations aspect . . . (p. 187).

Kepplinger (1983) concluded that the mass media, originally located outside the political system, have taken over a place within the political system. The media have become a political force which no longer just react, but also act. The functional dependencies of political institutions and the mass media in parliamentary democracies are seen as a matter of both domestic and foreign politics. Through their mediating function, the mass media hold a key position in the political process. The media have the power to put themes on the agenda hitherto ignored by politics and can help establish contacts not possible at the level of diplomacy thereby becoming instruments of foreign policy.

On the significance of the mass media in foreign policy, Karl (1982) wrote: "The media are increasingly a part of the process (if not the entire process) in the communication between governments and publics about international politics" (p. 144). Indeed, governments can come under pressure from what is already on media record. Thus, in the event of a potential or actual conflict, negotiated solutions could become more difficult if it appeared that such a new conciliatory approach might involve a loss of face. Karl wrote: "In an age of media diplomacy, statecraft may have become the hostage—if not the victim—of stagecraft. Only the media have a first-strike capability on both national and international levels" (p. 155).

The mass media of communication have broken into the traditionally exclusive sphere of diplomacy and have themselves become an instrument of international conciliation and mediation as also of conflict. The mass media, by serving in the diplomatic sphere as a source of international information, can contribute to international orientation by establishing a common fund of knowledge that enables or facilitates negotiations, for example. But as to the quality of this common basis of information, many countries (especially developing countries) believe that their positions are not receiving due attention in the world or in a certain region because of the current lop-sided structure of the global information system. Such a situation can be defined as an image crisis when the political elite of a state believe that they do not have a fair and adequate image in a foreign country and believe that they are not given adequate and unbiased media attention.

According to Signitzer and Coombs (1992), the field of diplomacy is shifting from traditional diplomacy toward public diplomacy. They wrote that "the actors in public diplomacy can no longer be confined to the profession of diplomats but include various individuals, groups, and institutions who engage in international and intercultural communication activities which do have a bearing on the political relationship between two or more countries" (p. 139). The authors made a distinction between the tough-minded and the tender-minded schools of public diplomacy:

> The tough-minded hold that the purpose of public diplomacy is to exert an influence on attitudes of foreign audiences using persuasion and propaganda. . . . The tender-minded school argues that information and cultural programs must bypass current foreign policy goals to concentrate on the highest long-range national objectives. The goal is to create a climate of mutal understanding. (p. 140)

The authors argued that neither school is correct, but have to be synthesized. They also made a distinction between political information, usually administered by a section of the foreign ministry or by an embassy, and cultural communication, usually administered by a cultural section of the foreign ministry, cultural institutes abroad, or some semiautonomous body (e.g., the British Council). Two types of cultural communication were identified by the authors. The first, cultural diplomacy, refers to the creation of cultural agreements in a formal sense aimed at presenting a favorable image of one's own culture abroad. The second, cultural relations, does not have unilateral advantages in mind but has the goal of information exchange in order to present "an honest picture of each country rather than a beautified one" (p. 140).

The shifting from traditional diplomacy toward public diplomacy implies that politicians are trying to instrumentalize the mass media. Adaptation of foreign policy to the mass media implies that politicians are accepting public relations counsel. The dominating motive of political action is no longer the substantial quality of policy, but the creation of newsworthy events, and public relations practitioners know how news is selected by journalists. Bernays (1923) argued in his famous *Crystallizing public opinion*: "The counsel on public relations not only knows what news value is, but knowing it, he is in a position to make news happen. He is a creator of events" (p. 197). In his memoirs (1965) Bernays described how he advised the exiled Czech politician, Tomás Garrigue Masaryk, who had been elected president of the Czechoslovak National Council, to issue his country's declaration of independence on a Sunday for public relations reasons because it would get more space in the media, Sunday being a slow news day.[3]

Important to image building are "pseudoevents" (Boorstin, 1961) that are deliberately staged to gain attention or create a certain impression. There are hundreds if not thousands of examples which demonstrate that the staging of pseudoevents has become routine. These make up much of media coverage. Mahatma Gandhi staged pseudoevents in his struggle for India's liberation from British rule. In 1930 he organized the famous march on the salt works of Dharasana (popularly knowns as Dandi March) in violation of government orders against marches, which resulting in the police caning several thousand demonstrators with long sticks with steel nails embedded in the end. More than 2,000 newspapers throughout the world reported this bloodbath. World public opinion condemned the British for this barbaric action and an American senator read a UPI report on the incident in Congress. Physically, the police had been the victors, but morally they had been vanquished.

THE STRUCTURAL NECESSITY OF INTERNATIONAL PUBLIC RELATIONS

Mass media reporting of foreign affairs often governs what kind of image of a country or culture has in another country. International news is selected by criteria similar to those used for national news or local news. Higher ranking (superpower) or geographically and/or culturally close states are most likely to be reported on by the media of a country. Economic alliances and ideological relations also generate more intensive coverage of another country. In the Foreign Images Study for the United Nations Educational Scientific and Cultural Organization (UNESCO), the selection of international news in 29 countries was examined (Sreberny-Mohammadi, 1985). According to this study, selection is done by universally valid criteria, with particular emphasis on the unusual such as disasters, unrest, and coups. Regionalism is particularly pronounced in all media systems. Hence, one cannot speak of a clear predominance of the world centers over the periphery. But negativism (civil war, natural disasters, debt crisis, human rights violations, electoral frauds, etc.)

---

[3]Reading Masaryk's *The Making of a State: Memoirs and Observations, 1914–1918* (New York: Howard Fertig; original work published 1927) is like reading a guide to efficient international public relations.

often remain the only important news factors dominating the coverage of developing countries by the media of developed nations. Aside from this aspect, the media of the Third World do not themselves measure up to the demands made by their representatives at the international level, for they select news according to the same criteria as the Western media. Accordingly, the media of the Third World are noted for using a high proportion of nonpolitical bad news from industrialized nations. The crisis-oriented reporting on the Third World by the Western media corresponds to the bad picture of the Western nations in the press of developing countries. Overall, the cynical journalists' adage, "Bad news is good news," applies to the reporting of international events.

A replication of the Foreign Images Study conducted in 1995 by Robert Stevenson and Annabelle Sreberny-Mohammadi but not yet completely published (Kunczik and Zipfel, 2001, 429ff.) seems to confirm this pattern of news flow. Wu (1998) investigated the determinants of international news flow and concluded that "the everyday representation of the world via news media is far from a reflection of global realities" (p. 507). Recent research on the international flow of television news demonstrates that some countries are in a central position (United States, Great Britain, Russia, France, and Germany) and many countries are in a peripherical position concerning the flow of news (Kim and Barnett, 1996). The flow of television news has a similar structure. The global market of television news is dominated by APTV (Associated Press TV), Reuters Television and WTN (World television News) (Boyd-Barrett 1998).

Given the structural conditions of the international flow of news, countries which need to have a positive image in a certain geographical region for economic or political interests (including those nations that are at a disadvantage from the outset because of the standard processes of gathering and reporting by mass media), must mount active publicity campaigns. Although by definition, public relations for states is always interest-bound communication, it can offset communication deficits resulting from the deficiencies of media structures. This form of public relations activity for states, meant primarily to compensate for structural communication deficits, aims mainly to adapt the image to news values by trying to influence mass media reporting. *Structural* international public relations helps in correcting the "false" images previously created by mass media. *Manipulative public relations*, on the other hand, tries to create a positive image that in most cases does not reflect reality and includes lying and disinformation. The AIDS campaign of the KGB[4]

---

[4]The AIDS disinformation campaign began in 1985 whereby the United States was blamed worldwide for the outbreak of the disease. This report, although dismissed as absurd by all experts, including Soviet medical scientists, met with much positive response, especially in African countries. For example *Afrique Nouvelle*, a weekly newspaper very close to the Catholic church, reported: "According to an authorized scientific source, the AIDS virus was developed in the research center at Fort Detrick, Maryland, where it was grown at the same time as other viruses to be used in biological weapons. It was then tested on drug addicts and homosexuals" (United States Department of State, 1987, p. 71). In August 1986 a study conducted by biophysicist Professor Jakob Segal, his wife Dr. Lilli Segal, and Dr. Ronald Dehmlow of Humboldt University in East Berlin became public. The study claimed that at Fort Detrick in 1977, the United States had synthetically manufactured the AIDS virus by combining two naturally occurring viruses, VISNA and HTLV-I. Experts agree that this hypothesis is untenable, but it circulated nonetheless in the media of Africa, South Asia, and the Soviet Union. Indeed, it was discussed extensively at the eighth conference of the Nonaligned Movement at Harare in September of that year. Both *Pravda* and *Izvestiya* have repeatedly printed articles alleging that AIDS was created in laboratories at Fort Detrick as part of alleged attempts by the United States to create new biological weapons (Walker, 1988). The Soviet media later warned against American soldiers spreading AIDS in other countries. The obvious intention of such reports was to spread mistrust of the American military, but it also affected tourists, businesspeople, and so forth. Indeed, the newspaper *Sovyetskaya Rossiya* reported on January 23, 1987 that in Western Europe AIDS was most prevalent in places where United States troops were based.

and the disinformation campaign of the Reagan administration against Muammar Qaddafi are good examples of this.[5]

IMAGES OF NATIONS AND THE INTERNATIONAL SYSTEM

In literature there is no clear definitive distinction between such concepts as attitude, stereotype, prejudice, or image. We agree with Boulding (1956) that the conception of an image involves not only present image but also aspects of its past as well as future expectations. Therefore, *national image* can be defined as the cognitive representation that a person holds about a given country—a person's beliefs about a nation and its people. Of special importance to political action is the benevolence or malevolence imputed to other nations in images as well as the historical component of the image. Feelings about a country's future are important too.

Boulding (1969) defined *image* as "total cognitive, affective, and evaluative structure of the behavior unit, or its internal view of itself and the universe" (p. 423). Whether our perceptions of the world are real or fictional does not play a large part in our daily lives. One behaves as if one's perception of the world were "true." Boulding (1967) localized an image sphere, which he described as a "world of literary images" (p. 5). In this world the test of reality is the least pronounced. That is, the elimination of errors either does not take place at all, or occurs only at enormous cost. It is in this world that the images of the international system are localized and international decision makers mainly move. Indeed, Boulding regarded the international system as by far the most pathological and costly part of the world system (e.g., costs of military, foreign ministries, diplomatic corps, secret services, and wars).[6] Boulding wrote (1967):

> On the whole the images of the international system in the minds of its decision makers are derived by a process that I have described as "literary"—a melange of narrative history, memories of past events, stories and conversations, etc., plus an enormous amount of usually ill-digested and carelessly collected current information. When we add to this the fact that the system produces strong hates, loves, loyalties, disloyalties, and so on, it would be surprising if any images were formed that even remotely resembled the most loosely defined realities of the case. (p. 9).

Manheim (1991) took the same position, arguing that for top decision makers in the United States, "the likelihod is that most people in our government and others, even at the highest level, received at least as much information about the June 1989 massacre

---

[5]On August 25, 1986, a report appeared in the *Wall Street Journal* claiming that Qadaffi was planning new attacks, that the United States and Libya were again headed for collision, and that the Pentagon was preparing plans for another bombardment of Libya. The report was described as "authoritative," that is, as being reliably sourced, by the spokesman for the White House, Larry Speakes. Other newspapers followed with reports that Libya was sponsoring terrorist activities and that there was the possibility of renewed confrontation with the United States According to Hedrick Smith (1988), George Shultz, the Secretary of State, said: "Frankly, I don't have any problems with a little psychological warfare against Qaddafi" (p. 448), then recalled Churchill's justifying deceptions against Hitler during World War II: "In time of war, truth is so precious, it must be attended by a bodyguard of lies".

[6]In fact, decision makers are usually aware that they are living in a world of images. As the famous French statesman Talleyrand pointed out, in politics what is believed to be true is more important than truth itself. Ronald Reagan knew that "Facts are stupid things" (*Time*, August 29, 1988, p. 52). Kissinger (1969) stated: "Deterrence above all depends on psychological criteria" (p. 61).

in Beijing's Tiananmen Square from media reports as from diplomatic or intelligence sources. They know little more than we know. We are vulnerable" (p. 130). For politicians (foreign ministers, for example), the success of their career has not been dependent on the ability to estimate correctly the images of foreign nations but to meet the demands and stereotypes of their voters. If people believed that the Soviet Union was an "empire of evil" (as Ronald Reagan stated), one can win elections only if one is of the same opinion or at least gives that impression. Although they often refuse to believe it themselves, politicians are as prone to distorted perceptions as anyone else. When such distorted perceptions flow into political decision making, there can be very negative consequences.

ESTABLISHMENT OF TRUST AS THE MAIN AIM OF INTERNATIONAL PUBLIC RELATIONS

The main objective of international public relations is to establish (or maintain existing) positive images of one's own nation or to appear trustworthy to other actors in the world system.[7] Trust is no abstract concept. In the field of international policy, trust is an important factor in mobilizing resources such as receiving political and/or material support from other nations, for example. In other words, if other actors in the world system place their trust in a nation and her future because of her reliability, then trust becomes the equivalent of money. Put simply: trust is money and money is trust. The positive image of a country's currency reflects confidence in that country's future. International business and currency exchange rates are not determined simply by pure economic facts (like currency reserves and gold reserves, deficit or surplus in balance of trade or balance of payment). The image of a nation, the solvency rating of its businesses, the credibility of its politicians and their reliability to tame inflation by tight fiscal and monetary policies are some factors that are of decisive importance. Indeed, a country's reputation for solvency is more important to the stability of her currency than some short-term economic fluctuations.

In 1926 French economist Albert Aftalion published his theory (Théorie psychologique du change) based on the hypothesis that the exchange rate of a country's currency is determined mainly by trust in the future of that country. A deficit of the balance of payments will not cause a devaluation of the currency as long as the belief in the future of the currency attracts foreign capital thus balancing the deficit. There is one main reason for the use of a certain currency as key currency: trust in that currency. Monetary policy is image policy. Money is an illusion, nothing more than the trust people have in their respective currency.

Public relations counselor Ivy Ledbetter Lee certainly was aware of the importance of trust when he argued: "Those who handle a loan must create an atmosphere . . ." (Hiebert, 1966, p. 266). Lee knew that simple statistics were not enough to market a loan. Lee handled loans for Poland, Rumania, France, and other countries, but considered Hungary a difficult case because too many people in America "had a mental picture of the [Hungarian] people

---

[7]Sometimes some countries seem to be interested in having a negative image in certain target groups. In 1991 Austria's Home Secretary, Franz Löschnack, published an advertisement in the Romanian newspaper *Romania Libera*. Romanians wanting to emigrate to Austria were warned against trying to enter Austria. Foreigners were not allowed to work in Austria without official permission and for Romanians no permission would be given. Romanians also had no prospects for asylum in Austria: "There are no more shelters for people asking for asylum." The last sentence of the advertisement was: "You don't have the slightest chance." The compositor of *Romania Libera* protested in a subtle way: Below the Austrian ad was placed an ad for the Bucharest center for disinfection, which fought against rat infestations and rounded up stray dogs.

as a wild, Bohemian lot, instead of the agricultural, sane, and highly cultivated people that they really are" (Hiebert, 1966, p. 267). His advice to Hungary was to create the image that their country was stable and civilized. Argentina had problems attracting investors because of its image of social instability. Lee advised them to send a polo team to the United States to compete with American teams contending that "polo is not played except where there is a very high degree of civilization and a stable society. . . . The galloping gentlemen would tell the story more convincingly than any amount of statistics or mere statements as to the true conditions" (Hiebert 1966, p. 267).

Some examples of attempts by countries to gain trust with the international community:

1. On July 1, 1994 Banco do Brasil advertised in the leading German daily *Frankfurter Allgemeine Zeitung* that Brazil now had a new and stable currency: the *real*. This monetary reform was called the most decisive turning point in the history of Brazil's economy. Brazil now offered investors more opportunities than ever before urging them to have confidence in the new currency, to overcome memories of the old currency that was plagued by inflation. The advertisement closed with the slogan: "BANCO DO BRAZIL. Good for you. Good for Brazil."

2. Estonia published in *Time* (July 4, 1994) a country profile as an advertisement: "ESTONIA: Rebirth of a Nation." The advertisement claimed that after years of quiet opposition to Soviet rule, Estonia had seized the opportunity of the failed coup of August 1991 in Moscow to declare full independence. "Swift and decisive actions underwrote this move: a new constitution was drawn up, free elections held, monetary reform (including a new currency) was initiated, and a fast-track policy of economic renewal was implemented," the advertisement declared. Estonia characterized itself as the champion of free trade and exuded confidence that it could withstand the shock of competition. Information about the economic climate and new opportunities in the Baltics was provided, especially concerning the progress of privatization: "New ownership structures are the single most important aspect of the marketization of economic life."

3. Peru, which had a poor image around the world due to the outbreak of cholera in 1991 and the guerrilla movement Shining Path in 1993, published a special advertising section in the *International Herald Tribune* on November 24, 1993. President Alberto Fujimori emphasized in an interview the "dramatic moves his government has made to improve the country's economic and business climate." One article dealt with the economic comeback of the country. Privatization was described as generating cash and competition. Peru was characterized not only as a country of ancient culture but also as a nation of opportunities.

Many nations have published similar advertisements. Sometimes nations are interested in projecting a negative image strategically, at least to a target group. Mexico became the first country to practically declare itself insolvent by an ad in *The International Herald Tribune* (June 8, 1989). Luis Tellez, the general director of financial planning in the Mexican ministry of finance, signed the text in which the chairman of the Citicorp bank, John Reed, was attacked. The banker was accused of having too restricted a view of things:

> For Mexico, the debt crisis is much more than a discussion of swaps or of the return of flight capital. It is a story of adjustment, of an extraordinary effort to transform an economy and of the hopes of millions of Mexicans for an opportunity to increase their standards of living. All parties involved should begin to look at the situation from both sides. We created the debt

problem together; therefore it is up to both debtors and creditors to find a way out. . . . We should all realize that there is much to gain by acting together. If banks insist on keeping their eyes closed to economic realities there will be no winners.

THE TACTIC OF WITHDRAWAL

Many countries (especially developiong nations) make considerable efforts and spend vital and often scarce resources to cultivate their images abroad (especially in developed countries) principally to attract foreign aid. No precise linkage between commissioned public relations activities and what appears in the mass media as a result of these activities can be traced. Typically, one can do little more than guess at what suggestions were made, which were accepted, and how they were implemented. The precise nature of the intervention remains a mystery. Manheim and Albritton (1984) studied the influence of the activities of public relations agencies on the images of nations. In particular, they examined the coverage by *The New York Times* of six countries (the Republic of Korea, the Philippines, Yugoslavia, Argentina, Indonesia, and Rhodesia), which had hired public relations agencies in the United States.[8] The major service the public relations firms had offered was to improve their client's access to American journalists. In addition, they wrote press releases, did direct mailings, and sent out newsletters and brochures. In some cases, embassy personnel were trained on how to speak about sensitive issues such as terrorism or human rights. Field trips for the press, visits with editors, and lunches with business groups were organized. One of the main effects of this public relations activity was that with the exception of Indonesia, the media coverage of each country was reduced. This corresponds to research findings on the effects of mass communications where the image of a country that makes negative headlines and also has a negative image in public opinion cannot be changed by the sudden appearance of positive reporting because this would be perceived as incredible. Withdrawal from public attention makes people forget, providing an opportunity to build a positive new image more slowly.

Nevertheless, some of the emphases of the public relations activities can be illustrated (Cutlip, 1994; Kunczik, 1997; Manheim, 1994; Manheim & Albritton, 1984), such as visits by heads of state, the release of political prisoners, press junkets organized by the respective governments or by transnational corporations, establishment of information offices, cosmetic redistribution of power within a country, scheduling of elections, sporting events, and so on. These events have a high likelihood of coverage by the news media. It is useful to adopt some hypotheses that have been developed in mass media research to guide research on public relations conducted on behalf of nations. For example, one hypothesis could be that the more a country depends on trade exports, the more likely and the more intensely it will mount campaigns of image cultivation abroad. Further, a state may be more likely to mount a public relations campaign in another region if the reporting in that region is biased due to the structures of news selection. Another hypothesis could be that the more important (economically and/or politically) an entity (whether country or union such as the European Community), the more likely it is that foreign countries will mount campaigns in that country (e.g., most campaigns are waged in the United States and Western industrialized countries). So far, public relations and/or advertising campaigns for

---

[8]Coverage of Mexico, which had no contract with any agency, was also monitored. *The New York Times* was chosen because it is the newspaper most widely read by the American elite, is most frequently quoted by political decision makers, and is known from previous research to have a strong agenda-setting effect on public opinion, and provides more foreign coverage than comparable American daily newspapers.

tourism have been the focal point of activities in the area of international public relations (Kunczik & Weber, 1994).

PUBLIC RELATIONS DURING WAR: THE NECESSITY
TO MANIPULATE THE NEWS MEDIA

In times of war, the manipulation of the news media is often considered a necessity. The first military theoretician to recognize this was the Prussian general, Carl von Clausewitz (1780–1831). In his *Vom Kriege* (On War), published posthumously in 1832, von Clausewitz argued that Napoleon's military success was due mainly to the enthusiasm of the French people. According to von Clausewitz, war is an act of violence aimed at forcing the enemy to accept one's will. The central aspect of warfare, he suggested, is not physical force but morale. The goal of war, then, is to break the enemy's morale. The von Clausewitz theory of war takes the following factors into consideration: (1) the government that defines the war's aims, (2) the army that is fighting, and (3) the people.

Important to understanding the theoretical foundation of censorship is the environment in which military actions take place. This environment is characterized by danger, the highest physical strain, and confusion. Von Clausewitz (1832/1873) called this *friktion*, which means all plans developed during practice maneuvers have to be changed during real war. Camouflage and deception are the norm in war. Most intelligence is not secure and very often is wrong. Indeed, von Clausewitz argued, in war most news is false. Secrecy becomes most important because the enemy has to be deceived.

According to von Clausewitz (1832/1873) lying and deceiving are necessities of war. Mastery of deceit and hypocrisy is decisive for successful military actions because the aim has to be to surprise the enemy. The German sociologist Simmel (1920) argued that during war, the basis of social life must be undermined. The enemy must be confronted with unexpected situations. Simmel made the assumption that "all relationships between people are self-evidently based on their knowing something about each other" (p. 256). People have expectations regarding the behavior of others and know that those they are dealing with also have such expectations. Stable social relations are based on the formation of "expectations of expectations," which makes social behavior predictable. During war, one has to deceive the enemy's expectations of one's behavior and undermine the foundations of human coexistence.

In times of war, communication with the enemy requires that we try to pass false intelligence to the enemy even when the enemy is aware that this is our intention. It is a situation of paradoxical communication (Watzlawick, 1976). Decision making in war, then, means making paradox predictions. The higher the probability of a certain action, the lower the chance the enemy will mount it. The lower the probability of an action, the higher the probability the enemy will act that way. The art of disinformation assumes highest importance for survival in times of war. Successful disinformation means the enemy treats false information as credible. The logic of disinformation is as follows: What does the enemy think, about what I think, about what he thinks, and so on (Watzlawick, 1976). Reporting the truth of war might not only give the enemy advantages but also weaken the morale of one's own population and/or troops. Lying and propaganda are important instruments of warfare. If journalists can be instrumentalized and manipulated as tools of propaganda, then they are useful. But reporting the truth in most cases is dangerous for the successful achievement of the aims of war.

Three more reasons for manipulating the media and institutionalizing censorship during war are (1) the morale of the soldiers, (2) the morale of the population, and (3) world public opinion. Any nation waging war has to find stories that justify and ennoble its cause. These are the stories to be disseminated, whereas those that tell of the horrors of war from the soldiers' point of view should be suppressed. The German sociologist Ferdinand Tönnies (1922) argued that when a country is at war, its people believe in the just cause of the war, which was forced upon them by the enemy. To stabilize belligerent public opinion, the government stigmatizes the enemy as aggressor or as a nonhuman monster. President Bush, who characterized Saddam Hussein as another Hitler, argued that "Saddam tried to cast this conflict as a religious war, but it has nothing to do with religion *per se*. It has, on the other hand, everything to do with what religion embodies: good vs. evil, right vs. wrong" (*Time*, March 11, 1991, p. 24).

During war it is of vital interest to the supreme command or the government to control the mass media in order to hinder shifts in public opinion. It can be argued, for instance, that the United States was drawn into the quagmire in Somalia by the influence of television. But television was also probably responsible for America's subsequent withdrawal from Somalia. As Considine (1994) put it:

> The pictures of Michael Duran and other soldiers brutalized in Somalia set off a media and public clamour for American withdrawal. The frenzy prompted Secretary of State Warren Christopher to say that however useful television coverage was to national understanding, edited highlights and pictures taken out of context could not become the driving force for determining American foreign policy. (p. 11)

But Considine maintained that "State Department sources had confirmed that news coverage was driving United States foreign policy" (p. 11). At least the quality of foreign policy has changed under the influence of television; possibly not a turn for the better. There are indications that even warfare is being affected by media coverage. A NATO officer explained why the Allied forces declined to shoot down Serbian helicopters that were violating the no-fly zone: "Even if they were carrying arms, we worried that someone would stick civilian bodies in the wreckage just in time to be filmed by CNN" (*Newsweek*, March 14, 1994). Further, NATO commanders decided not to use napalm or cluster bombs, capable of clearing large swaths of terrain, in Bosnia because: "Bad TV. Napalm leaves it victims shrivelled and charred. Cluster bombs tear them into shreds. The West is worried how they might look on the nightly news" (*Newsweek*, April 25, 1994, p. 13).

The Gulf War (II)

Hill & Knowlton, belonging to Wpp, played a major role in the preparations for the Gulf War.[9] Shortly after the invasion of Kuwait in August 1990, Hill & Knowlton signed a contract with a lobby group called Citizens for a Free Kuwait (CFK). CFK was financed with US $17,861 in contributions from individuals and US $11,852,329 from the Government of Kuwait (MacArthur, 1992; Trento, 1992). Its relationship with CFK brought the agency an estimated US $10 million to 12 million. According to MacArthur, H&K organized a Kuwait Information Day on United States college campuses on September 12. September 23 became a national day of prayer, and September 24 was declared by the governors of

---

[9] Wpp (Wire and Plastic Products) is one of the most important transnational advertising and public relations networks. Besides Hill & Knowlton, Burson Marsteller and Cohn & Wolfe belong to wpp. Ogilvy & Mather; Young & Rubicam and J. Walter Thompsonare advertising agencies owned by Wpp. The gross income of Wpp in 2000 was about $7.97 billion; Kunczik and Zipfel 2001, 450*ff.*)

13 states as a national Free Kuwait Day. Thousands of media kits extolling the virtues of Kuwaiti society were distributed. Media events featuring Kuwaiti "resistance fighters" and businesspeople were organized. Meetings with newspaper editorial boards were arranged. Video news releases from the Middle East were produced. According to Trento (1992), H&K arranged a press conference with a Kuwaiti "freedom fighter" in early September to offset the view that Kuwaitis were fleeing their country and to outline the activities of Kuwaiti resistance. According to Trento, press conferences were arranged to present the image of a strong, gallant Kuwaiti resistance to counter reports of young Kuwaitis partying the war away in the discos of Cairo.

Hill & Knowlton tried to remind members of Congress that Kuwait was a democracy by showing copies of its constitution (Roschwalb, 1994). There is no doubt that Kuwait had certain problems with its image in the United States. H&K also used "atrocity propaganda." MacArthur (1992) emphasized that of all the accusations made against Saddam Hussein, none had more impact on the American public than the one about Iraqi soldiers removing 312 babies from incubators and letting them die on the cold floor in order to steal the incubators. According to Cutlip (1994), Robert Keith Gray, then head of Hill & Knowlton sent a memo to Citizens for a Free Kuwait requesting atrocity stories (p. 771). In October 1990, the Congressional Human Right's Caucus held a public hearing on conditions in Kuwait under Iraqi occupation. Trento (1992) reported that George Hymel of H&K and his staff "provided witnesses, wrote testimony, and coached the witnesses for effectiveness. The PR staff produced videotapes detailing the atrocities and ensured that the room was filled with reporters and television cameras" (p. 381). Nayirah, a 15-year-old Kuwaiti girl, whose last name was kept secret supposedly to protect her family in Kuwait, testified:

> I volunteered at the al-Addan hospital. . . . While I was there, I saw the Iraqi soldiers come into the hospital with guns, and go into the room where 15 babies were in incubators. They took the babies out of the incubators, took the incubators, and left the children on the cold floor to die. (MacArthur, 1992, p. 58)

None of the members of Congress knew that Nayirah in fact was the daughter of the Kuwaiti ambassador to Washington! As Cutlip (1994) commented:

> H&K sent its own camera crew to film this hearing that it had helped cast and direct. It then produced a film that was quickly sent out as a video release used widely by a gullible media. Too late some alert reporter unmasked the story as a hoax and revealed that Nayirah was the Kuwaiti Ambassador's daughter living in Washington. Once more the press served as patsies for the public relations staged event[10] (p. 771).

H&K also ensured that the video was aired by about 700 TV stations. On October 10, 1990, about 53 million Americans watched the tearful testimony on ABC's *Nightline*.

---

[10]Cutlip (1994) was referring to Susan B. Trento's (1992) *The Power House: Robert Keith Gray and the Selling of Access and Influence in Washington* and to John R. McArthur's *Remember Nayirah, Witness for Kuwait?* (in *The New York Times* op-ed page, January 6, 1992), but in the meantime some new evidence has been published and Cutlip's argument has to be modified. (For H&K's version of the Kuwait account, see Pratt, 1994). Roschwalb (1994) pointed out that the story of Iraqi soldiers removing hundreds of babies from incubators "was shown to be almost certainly false by an ABC reporter, John Martin, in March 1991 after the liberation of Kuwait" (p. 271). MacArthur emphasized that Nayirah was the daughter of the Ambassador, had been brought to the Committee by H&K, and that H&K did not respond to the question whether she was in Kuwait in August and September 1990 when the alleged atrocities took place.

According to H&K, the substance of Nayirah's testimony was true and using her as a witness was a stylistic move. The Ambassador verified that Nayirah indeed had been in Kuwait. Kroll Associates, a private investigative company, inquired on behalf of the Kuwaiti government about the alleged atrocities and concluded "that multiple incubator atrocities had taken place and that Nayirah was a witness to one of them" (Pratt, 1994, p. 289). MacArthur (1992) argued that the main result of the investigation was that Nayirah did not work in the hospital, came to the hospital by accident, and did not see babies taken out of incubators.

According to Roschwalb (1994), the atrocity story "seriously distorted the American debate about whether to support military action. Seven senators cited the story in speeches backing the January 12 resolution authorizing war" (p. 271). Decisive in supporting the credibility of the baby incubator story was the fact that on December 19, 1990 Amnesty International published a report on human rights violations in occupied Kuwait. The report included the baby incubator story: "In addition over 300 premature babies were reported to have died after Iraqi soldiers removed them from incubators, which were then looted. Such deaths were reported at al-Razi and al-Addan hospitals, as well as the Maternity Hospital" (MacArthur, 1992, p. 66). President Bush too made frequent use of the atrocity story. On October 15, 1990 he said: "I met with the Emir of Kuwait. And I heard horrible tales: newborn babies thrown out of incubators and the incubators then shipped off to Baghdad" (MacArthur, 1992, p. 65). MacArthur also quoted a speech of Bush to the troops, which he characterized as Bush's best imitation of an H&K press release: "It turns your stomach when you listen to the tales of those that have escaped the brutality of Saddam the invader. Mass hangings. Babies pulled from incubators and scattered like firewood across the floor" (p. 65).

When questioned whether the testimony of Nayirah was decisive in mobilizing support for the war, Frank Mankiewicz, vice-president of H&K, answered that he had been against the war from the beginning and the decision for war was the President's (*Der Spiegel*, No. 40, 1990). But Mankiewicz also called Kuwait a success for his company. Because the White House, Pentagon, and State Department controlled all information they gave to the media and the public, Trento (1992) argued that it remains a question whether or not H&K's effort on behalf of Kuwait was technically necessary or effective. But it is important to note that it did demonstrate that a public relations firm behaved like a warmonger by distorting facts, distributing atrocity propaganda, and presenting violators of human rights as democrats.

TERRORISM AS INTERNATIONAL PUBLIC RELATIONS

Attracting attention is another aim of international public relations. Certain forms of terrorism, namely, those designed to reach the public through media coverage, are specifically staged for the mass media (Schmid & de Graaf, 1982; Weimann, 1990). Terrorists, normally labeling themselves as freedom fighters, know that journalists tend to regard dramatic and violent events as news. Weimann (1990) quoted a Palestinian terrorist/freedom fighter after the 1972 Munich Olympic Games incident (Palestinian terrorists captured Israeli olympic competitors, resulting in nine Israeli and five Palestinian deaths): "We knew that people in England and America would switch their television sets from any programme about the plight of the Palestinians if there was a sporting event on another channel. . . . From Munich onwards nobody could ignore the Palestinians or their cause" (p. 16).

The "theatre of terror" (Weimann, 1990) evolved by adjustment to the modes of news selection and international terrorism became a media event and eventually international public relations. Responding to the stigmatization as terrorist, Yasser Arafat argued in a 1988 interview:

> George Washington was called a terrorist by the British. DeGaulle was called a terrorist by the Nazis. What can they say about the P.L.O., except to repeat this slogan? We are freedom fighters, and we are proud of it. According to international law and the United Nations Charter, I have the right to resist Israeli occupation. I don't want to harm anybody. But look how they are treating my people. These savage, barbarian, fascist practices against our children, our women! (*Time*, November 7, 1988)

In the Algerian War, which began in 1954 and lasted 8 years, the Algerian insurgents used the media instrumentally. Abane Ramdane, the FLN liberation movement leader, asked rhetorically: "Is it better for our cause to kill ten of the enemy in the countryside of Telergma, where no one will speak of it, or one in Algiers that will be mentioned the next day in the American press?" (Schmid & de Graaf, 1982, p. 19). In this interplay, symbiotic relationships developed between the freedom fighters and the mass media. Robert Kleinmann of CBS, reporting on the final phase of the Algerian War, said: "If the photographer wanted to be sure to get a picture, it was very useful for him to find out when an assassination was going to take place. Many of the most startling pictures of assassinations in Algeria were obtained in that fashion.... There is a very fine line here between reporting and instigating murder.... There are competitive pressures on reporters and cameramen in the field" (Schmid & de Graaf, 1982, p. 141).

CONCLUSION

An overarching conclusion that can be drawn from this review of literature on transnational public relations by governments is that there still exist large gaps in research on this topic. Furthermore, there are many aspects of international public relations that have not been discussed here such as the formation of images. Edward W. Said (1978) pointed out that the Orient was almost a European invention since antiquity as a place of romance, exotic beings, haunting memories and landscapes, and remarkable experiences. This contrived Orient helped define Europe (or the West) as its contrasting image. Such images are extremely difficult to change by means of public relations. One finds Japan and India as good examples of this. Suvanto (2002) demonstrated how ancient stereotypes about Japan (geisha, temples, cherry blossom, Mt. Fuji) have survived in Western travel literature. The literature written for Western businessmen has created the image of the Japanese as "sariiman" (e.g., they all look the same in their dark suits, they work in big companies all their lives, they work long days in their offices, their company is a community, etc.). The image of India in the "West" is still influenced by the so-called Alexander-novel (Kunczik, 2000), a work of fiction published about 1.700 years ago. This novel, which was translated into 35 languages, met the demand for entertainment and mysteries. It became a bestseller with the second largest distribution of all books during the Middle Ages with only the Bible having a higher circulation. A content analysis of German schoolbooks found that India still is presented in a way that reflects those very old stereotypes (Kunczik, 2002b). The "Imperatives of Intercultural Education" developed by Gordon W. Allport (1954) in his study about the origin and nature of stereotypes *The Nature of Prejudice* should not be forgotten. Allport calls attention to the decisive role of the school in learning prejudice. Such stereotypes are extremely difficult to change by using public relations.

There is always the danger of the self-fulfilling prophecy. Images can have a dramatic influence on the destiny of whole nations. The famous comment by Thomas and Thomas (1928) is still valid: "If men define situations as real, they are real in their consequences" (p. 572). The image of a country as one in permanent crisis or as economically unreliable, generated perhaps by continuous negative reporting, can influence economic decision-making processes and discourage investments, which in turn can create, or exacerbate, future crises. Barnett et al. (1999) examined monetary and trade networks as part of the process of globalization. Kunczik (2002a) has begun research on the influence of images of nations on the flow of international capital with special reference to the role of the rating agencies (esp. Standard & Poor's and Moody's). Credit rating agencies evaluate financial claims according to their creditworthiness. Sovereign credit ratings are the risk assessments assigned to the obligations of central governments. Sovereign risks consist of three different risks: economic, political, and social. In this context, image policy (public relations) can become quite important, because the rating agencies use "Western" (especially American) criteria to evaluate foreign countries. S. Narenda, "Principal Information Officer of the Government of India" and "Information Advisor to the Indian Prime Minister" emphasized in 2001: "If Standard & Poor say we are poor, we frown." Y. V. Reddy, one of the directors of the Reserve Bank of India, pointed out: "Unquestionably, Indian economy is far stronger now. In view of this unblemished record and current economic strength, it becomes difficult to explain the CRAs' (Credit Agencies') delay in upgrading India's credit rating to investment grade. The ratings of India by these two agencies would appear to convey that India in 1998 is no better off than it was in 1991." Due to globalization one of the main problems for so-called developing countries and/or emerging markets will be their image in the world of international investors. The better the image the easier will be the access to the international capital market. If this assumption is correct, there will be a more intensive image-fight between nations with image polishing becoming a functional equivalent to investor relations.

The Gulf War and the wars in Yugoslavia demonstrated a new trend: the "privatization" of war and atrocity propaganda by public relations firms. Hill & Knowlton's work during the Gulf War is no individual case. Cutlip (1994) pointed out, that "tiny Kosovo, threatened by Serbian aggression after Yugoslavia's break up" asked the American public relations firm Ruder-Finn to wage an intensive public relations campaign in the United States (the firm also worked for Croatia and Bosnia-Herzegovina). The president of Ruder-Finn emphasized: "We helped to formulate the message in a way that Americans could understand." Cutlip (1994) commented like a prophet: "Again the objective is to move public opinion to embroil America in that fratricidal conflict" (p. 771*ff.*).

As my final remark I emphasize the simple wisdom that image cultivation begins at home, in one's own country, in the way one deals with one's people and one's journalists. The best image cultivation is observance of human rights, establishment of a democratic form of state, and a free press.

REFERENCES

Adams, J. T. (1927). *New England and the Republic 1776–1850*. Boston: Little, Brown.

Aftalion, A. (1926). Théorie psychologique du change, In: Revue d'économic politique (p. 945–986).

Allport, G. W. (1958). *The nature of prejudice*. Garden City, NY: Doubleday. (Original work published 1954)

Baldwin, W. H. (1965). History of persuasion. *Public Relations Quarterly, 10*.

Barnett, G. A., et al. (1999). Globalisation and international communication. An examination of monetary, telecommunications and trade networks. *Journal of International Communication, 6*(2), 7–49.

Bernays, E. L. (1923). *Crystallizing public opinion*. New York: Boni & Liveright.

Bernays, E. L. (1965). *Biography of an idea: Memoirs of public relations counsel Edward L. Bernays*. New York: Simon & Schuster.

Bogart, L. (1976). *Premises for propaganda: The United States Information Agency's operating assumptions in the Cold War*. New York: Free Press.

Boorstin, D. (1961). *The image: A guide to pseudo-events in America*. New York: Harper & Row.

Boulding, K. E. (1956). *The image*. Ann Arbor: University of Michigan Press.

Boulding, K. E. (1967). The learning and reality-testing process in the international system. *Journal of International Affairs, 21*.

Boulding, K. E. (1969). National images and international systems. In J. N. Rosenau (Ed.), *International politics and foreign policy*. New York: Free Press.

Boyd-Barrett, O. (1998). Global news agencies. In O. Boyd-Barrett, and T. Rantanen (Eds.), *The globalization of news* (pp. 19–34), London: Sage.

Burke, P. (1992). *The fabrication of Louis XIV*. New Haven, CT: Yale University Press.

Clausewitz, C. P. G. von (1873). *On war*. (J. J. Graham, Trans., Vols. 1–3). London: N. Trübner. (Original work published 1832)

Considine, D. (1994). Media literacy and media education. *Telemedium: The Journal of Media Literacy, 40*.

Creel, G. (1920). *How we advertised America*. New York: Harper.

Cutlip, S. M. (1994). *The unseen power: Public relations. A history*. Hillsdale, NJ: Lawrence Erlbaum Associates.

Daniels, J. (1944). *The Wilson era: Years of peace, 1910–1917*. Chapel Hill: University of North Carolina Press.

Darrow, R. W., Forrestal, D. J., & Cookman, A. O. (1967). *The Dartnell Public Relations Handbook* (rev. ed.). Chicago: Dartnell.

Dilenschneider, R. L., & Forrestal, D. J. (1990). *The Dartnell public relations handbook* (3rd ed.). Chicago, IL: Dartnell.

Doerries, R. R. (1989). *Imperial challenge: Ambassador Count Bernstorff and German-American relations, 1908–1917* (C. D. Shannon, Trans.). Chapel Hill: University of North Carolina Press.

Donsbach, W. (1991). *Medienwirkung trotz Selektion. Einflußfaktoren auf die Zuwendung zu Zeitungsninhalten*. Cologne, Germany: Böhlau.

Duijker, H. C., J. & Frijda, N. H. (1960). *National character and national stereotypes*. Amsterdam: North-Holland.

Goldman, Eric. F. (1948). *Two-way street: The emergence of the public relations counsel*. Boston: Bellman.

Grattan, C. H. (1969). *Why we fought*. (K. L. Nelson, Ed.). New York: Bobbs-Merrill. (Original work published 1929)

Grunig, J. E., & Hunt, T. (1984). *Managing public relations*. New York: Holt, Rinehart & Winston.

Hertz, J. H. (1982). Political realism revisited. *International Studies Quarterly, 25*.

Hiebert, R. E. (1966). *Courtier to the crowd: The story of Ivy Lee and the development of public relations*. Ames: Iowa State University Press.

Howard, C. M., (1986/87, Spring). How to Say "No" Without alienating reporters. *Public Relations Quarterly*.

Isaacson, W. (1992). *Kissinger: A biography*. London: Faber & Faber.

Karl, P. M. (1982). Media diplomacy. In G. Benjamin (Ed.), *The communications revolution in politics. Proceedings of the Academy of Political Science, 34* (4).

Kepplinger, H. M. (1983). Fuktionswandel der Massenmedien. In M. Rühl & H. W. Stuiber (Eds.), *Kommunikationspolitik in Forschung und Anwendung*. Düsseldorf, Germany: Droste.

Kim, K., & Barnett, G. A. (1996). The determinants of international news flow: A network analysis. *Communications Research, 23*, 323–353.

Kissinger, H. (1969). *American foreign policy: Three essays*. New York: Norton.

Knorr, K. D. (1980). Die Fabrikation von Wissen. In N. Stehr & V. Meja (Eds.), *Wissenssoziologie. Kölner Zeitschrift für Soziologie und Sozialpsychologie, Sonderheft 22*. Opladen, Germany: Westdeutscher Verlag, 226–295.

Kruglak, T. E. (1962). *The two faces of TASS*. Minneapolis: University of Minnesota Press.

Kunczik, M. (1997). *Images of nations and international public relations*, Mahwah, N.J: Lawrence Erlbaum Associates.

Kunczik, M. (1998). *British and German Propaganda in the United States from 1914 to 1917*. In J. Wilke (Ed.), *Propaganda in the 20th century. Contributions to its history.* Cresskill, NJ: Hampton Press, 25–55.

Kunczik, M. (2000). Indian Identity and India's image in historical perspective. Paper presented at the IAMCR Conference, Singapore.

Kunczik, M. (2002a). Globalization: News media, images of nations and the flow of international capital with special reference to the role of rating agencies. *Journal of International Communication, 8* (1), 39–79.

Kunczik, M. (2002b). The image of India in German schoolbooks. An explorative study of textbooks in geography, religion, German lessons and history, Paper presented at the IAMCR conference, Barcelona, Spain.

Kunczik, M., & Weber, U. (1994). Public diplomacy and public relations advertisements of foreign countries in Germany. *The Journal of International Communication, 1*, 18–40.

Kunczik, M., & Zipfel, A. (2001). *Publizistik*, Cologne, Weimar, and Vienna: Böhlau Verlag.

Lasswell, H. D. (1942). Communications research and politics. In D. Waples (Ed.), *Print, radio, and film in a democracy.* Chicago: University of Chicago Press.

Lippmann, W. (1922). *Public opinion.* New York: Harcourt Brace.

MacArthur, J. R. (1992). *Second front: Censorship and propaganda in the Gulf War.* New York: Hill & Wang.

Manheim, J. B. (1991). *All of the people all the time: Strategic communication and American politics.* Armonk, NY: M. E. Sharpe.

Manheim, J. B. (1994). *Strategic public diplomacy and American foreign policy: The evolution of influence.* Oxford, UK: Oxford University Press.

Manheim, J. B., & Albritton, R. B. (1984). Changing national images: International public relations and media agenda setting. *American Political Science Review, 78.* 47, 641–657.

McAdoo, W. G. (1931). *Crowded years: The reminiscences of William G. McAdoo.* Boston: Houghton Mifflin.

Millis, W. (1935). *Road to war: America 1914–1917.* New York: Houghton Mifflin.

Olasky, M. N. (1985, Spring). A reappraisal of 19th-century public relations. *Public Relations Review, 11.*

Onkvisit, S., & Shaw, J. J. (1989). *International marketing. Analysis and strategy.* Columbus, OH: Merrill.

Pratt, C. B. (1994). Hill & Knowlton's two ethical dilemmas. *Public Relations Review, 20.* 3, S.277–294.

Roschwalb, S. A. (1994). The Hill & Knowlton cases: A brief on the controversy. *Public Relations Review, 20* 3, 267–267.

Said, E. (1978). *Orientalism,* New York: Pantheon Books.

Schmid, A. P., & de Graaf, J. (1982). *Violence as communication: Insurgent terrorism and the Western media.* London: Sage.

Signitzer, B., & Coombs, T. (1992). Public relations and public diplomacy: Conceptual convergences. *Public Relations Review, 18*, 137–147.

Simmel, G. (1920). *Soziologie* [Sociology] (2nd ed.). Munich, Germany: Duncker & Humblot.

Smith, H. (1988). *The power game: How Washington works.* New York: Random House.

Squires, J. D. (1935).*British propaganda at Home and in the United States. From 1914 to 1917*, Cambridge, MA.: Harvard University Press.

Sreberny-Mohammadi, A. (1985). *Foreign news in the media. International reporting in 29 countries.* Paris: UNESCO.

Star, S. A., & Hughes, H. M. (1950). Report on an educational campaign: The Cincinnati plan for the United Nations. *American Journal of Sociology, 55*, 389–400.

Suvanto, M. (2002). *Images of Japan and the Japanese. The Representations of the Japanese Culture in the Popular Literature Targeted at the Western Worls in the 1980s–1990s,* Jyväskylä, Finland: University of Jyväskylä.

Thomas, W. I., & Thomas, D. S. (1928). *The Child in America.* New York: Knopf.

Tocqueville, A. de (1946). *Democracy in America*, Vol. II, London 1946: Oxford University Press.

Tönnies, F. (1922). *Kritik der Öffentlichen Meinung.* Berlin: Springer.

Trento, S. B. (1992). *The Power House: Robert Keith Gray and the Selling of Access and Influence in Washington.* New York: St. Martin's Press.

United States Department of State (1987, October). *Soviet Influence Activities: A Report on Active Measures and Propaganda.* Washington, DC: United States Government Printing Office.

Viereck, G. S. (1930). *Spreading Germs of Hate*. New York: H. Liveright.

Walker, F. E. (1988, May). Recent changes in the Soviet propaganda machine. *Journal of Defense & Diplomacy*.

Watzlawick, P. (1976). *How Real is Real? Confusion, Disinformation, Communication*. New York: Random House.

Weimann, G. (1990). "Redefinition of image": The impact of mass-mediated terrorism. *International Journal of Public Opinion Research, 2*, 16–29.

Wilke, J. (Ed.) (1998). *Propaganda in the 20th century. Contributions to Its History*, Cresskill, NJ: Hampton Press.

Wilke, J. (1998). German foreign propaganda in the United States during World War I: The Central Office of Foreign Services.

Wu, H. D. (1998). Investigating the determinants of international news flow. In *Gazette, 60*, 493–512,

20

Public Information in the UNESCO: Toward a Strategic Role

Vincent Defourny

The United Nations Educational, Scientific and Cultural Organization (UNESCO) was created in 1946 in response to the emerging needs of the end of World War II and to address the urgent necessity to build peace around the world, develop mutual understanding among people and cultures, and structure international co-operation in specific areas such as education, science, and culture. Although communication is not mentioned at the same level as other disciplines, it has been important to the organization since its inception, as indicated in its constitution:

> ... To realize this purpose the Organization (UNESCO) will: (a) Collaborate in the work of advancing the mutual knowledge and understanding of peoples, through all means of mass communication and to that end recommend such international agreements as may be necessary to promote the free flow of ideas by word and image ... (UNESCO Constitution, article 1) (UNESCO, 2000)

At its inception, the founders hesitated between making UNESCO a purely intellectual organization or an intergovernmental body. They finally adopted a compromise, combining the best of both structures. As a result, the organization has organic links with member state governments, academics, and intellectuals through national commissions, and with what is now called the civil society, with representatives of a large spectrum of international nongovernmental organizations. These constituencies, as well as the Secretariat comprised

---

The views or opinions expressed in this chapter are the author's and do not necessarily represent those of UNESCO.

of approximately 2000 international civil servants based mainly in Paris led by a director-general, have shaped UNESCO's unique profile over more than five decades.

The purpose of this chapter is to propose some milestones and historical references that will be useful, it is hoped, in understanding how UNESCO envisages its international public relations and how these contribute to shaping the actual organization and, thus, to identify emerging organizational patterns. One of the major ideas addressed in this section is that long-lasting difficulties to define and embrace the nature of UNESCO's organizational communication have led to hesitating conceptions and practices of public information and public relations with consequences on UNESCO's image and international influence.

REACHING THE WORLDWIDE MASSES

Founded with the idea that international specialists in education, science, and culture would enlighten national and international policies with their recognized knowledge and moral authority, UNESCO grew with great emphasis being placed on mass communication and other means of communication as major amplifiers for its programs. The first General Conference in 1946, stated the following objectives for the Mass Communication section: "to publicize the program of UNESCO as much as possible and to initiate a program of mass education, in the broadest sense" (UNESCO General Conference, 1st session, Paris, 1946).

As a consequence, the daily publication *UNESCO Monitor* was established. In addition, a weekly 15-minute radio program on education, science and culture—"UNESCO World Review"—was produced in 18 languages for dissemination by stations in 47 countries that agreed to broadcast these programs. In parallel, a survey of technical needs in the press, radio, and film was carried out in 12 countries. National and linguistic adaptations of common universal messages were at the heart of UNESCO's concerns from the beginning. Rapidly, member states realized that such activities were very demanding and two years later the report of the debates of the General Conference stated: "The Committee was emphatic in its assertion that adequate public information services are essential to the success of UNESCO. More than any of the other Specialized Agencies, UNESCO is dependent upon public understanding. The Committee noted with surprise the small staff available for public information services. . . ." (UNESCO, 1948).

The dissemination of the Universal Declaration of Human Rights, very recently adopted by the United Nations, was a major concern. It is also worth noting that the same governing body commissioned two in-depth studies on the origin of Fascism and National Socialism. But the publication of these studies soon became problematic since some countries dismissed the idea of producing them under UNESCO's imprint. The researchers' academic skills were probably not an issue. Rather, the ideological dimensions of these subjects were such that it became almost impossible to obtain universal coverage. In the end, only the analysis of National Socialism, entitled *The Third Reich*, was published by an intellectual partner nongovernmental organization (NGO) with UNESCO's assistance. Its circulation was very limited (Lacoste, 1994, p. 36).

Although political problems such as the former were arising, the prevalent organizational communication culture at that time can be easily compared with the "professional model" of Mintzberg's theory (1979). This model, similar to that usually found in the academic world, is characterized by the separation of intellectual thinking from support services. There is "knowledge" on one side, and on the other the channels by which to transmit it to those who are "ignorant." The communication process is linear and one-way and definitely not far from the "press agentry" model proposed by J. Grunig (1992).

Nevertheless, already at that time one observes that the focus on communication was subject to discussion and debate. According to L'Etang, (1999) John Grierson, the first UNESCO Director of Mass Communications and Public Information, left the Organization after only one year, criticizing the perception that public information entailed acting as "an advocate with a brief for the defense; showing up only the good points, suppressing the weak and, in fact, giving a prejudiced and false picture of the work in hand." For the same reason, he deplored UNESCO's practice of employing former journalists in the division, which he thought inevitably led to a biased approach and an overemphasis on the print media. With a visionary perspective on modern public relations, he wrote: "we need at UNESCO an almost new type of information man with powers of academic and organizational reference as well as skill in one or other of the various forms of public presentation. Such men are obviously rare" (Grierson Archive, G5: 4: 5, p. 4). There is no clear idea of what Grierson had in mind. He was probably seeing the public information officer more as a manager of communication projects than just a good copywriter. We can deduce that the organization has not been capable of drawing the lessons of this departure nor of understanding his rough definition of this new professional profile for UNESCO public information.

SEARCHING FOR THE RIGHT SKILLS

Writing has been the most important skill sought when recruiting public information officers as a result of which numerous former journalists have been recruited over the past 50 years. As a consequence, these former journalists have often had difficulties in defining their roles and positions inside the organization. They tend to believe that writing stories about UNESCO's action in line with organizational strategies is incompatible with their journalistic independence. They perceive it as unprofessional journalism.

This reflects a typical worldwide demarcation between communication specialists and journalists. Public information and public relations are perceived as perverted "journalistic" activities. The situation might find some explanation in some epistemological references. It is the author's view that this conception is directly inherited from a Cartesian understanding of reality in which there subsists the myth of a complete and objective representation of the world. Educated in such a paradigm, journalists consciously or unconsciously pretend to be in that external position from which it seems to be possible to objectively report about real facts. They feel they are in position they can reveal the unbiased truth. Despite its international statute and the multiple origins of its personnel, UNESCO is still strongly influenced by that French classical school of thinking. One reason could be because it is located in Paris. Many of Descartes's and other positivists' ideas are behind a number of UNESCO decisions. However, modern philosophy has demonstrated how reality can be seen as a social construct and how actors are embroiled in the reality they intend to depict. Therefore, a strategic understanding of the role of communication in organizational development is required to give a chance to a less negative approach to public relations activities. It is part of the shared views underlying this volume and one of the key arguments developed later in this chapter. Perhaps Grierson had the intuition that a good UNESCO communication professional would better articulate intellectual, political, and strategic capacities with technical writing skills than with journalistic ones.

In 1948, the *UNESCO Courier* partially replaced the *UNESCO Monitor* before becoming an illustrated magazine in 1954. It had its hours of glory when it was published in 35 different languages, with an overall distribution of more than 1.5 million copies, renowned authors, and largely referreed articles. Its evolution is interesting because it reflects, over the decades, the search for a journalistic identity inside UNESCO's Public Information services. For many years, the magazine was not an institutional publication, but an opinion journal tackling topics covered by UNESCO's mandate but with little reference to activities carried out or official points of view. Journalists were proud of their independence. In 2001, the decision to discontinue the *UNESCO Courier* created such emotion among member state representatives that the director general had to find a compromise in the form of a biannual publication with a new format but with the old title. In fact, the organization was supporting, at high cost, an independent internal magazine. Although its title does not make it clear, this magazine was not the organization's bulletin. This function had to be covered by other magazines such as *UNESCO Monitor* (1948–1955), *UNESCO Chronicle* (1955–1980), *UNESCO Newsletter* (1979–1987), and *UNESCO Sources* (1989–2001). Lines of authority for these periodicals were always subject to discussions and debates, as well as the journalists' administrative status. Now, they are integrated in an editorial team and their role as public information officers appears to be difficult to accommodate with their former professional identity.

In line with what was happening to similar organizations around the world, the development of UNESCO in the fifties and sixties led to the reinforcement of a bureaucratic model with numerous rules and procedures. With a sophisticated administrative manual and code of conduct, UNESCO officials anticipated every situation. There was no room for uncertainty and this led, for example, to the formal adoption of the UNESCO emblem in 1954, although it had already been used the previous year. The UNESCO logo looking like a Greek temple was communicating the greatness and ambition of the organization.

Similarly, in 1958, member states inaugurated a brand new headquarters in Paris. This modernist building, conceived by famous architects, appears as another symbol of the organization's golden age. At this point, UNESCO was well settled and ready to welcome the recently decolonized states. This strength permitted it to become engaged in a type of "pharaoh's work," such as the relocation of the Abu-Simbel Temple in Egypt to preserve it from the rising backwaters of the Aswan dam. The success of this enterprise was the result of an impressive international public campaign led by UNESCO. In March 1960 UNESCO launched an international appeal that invited the world to give financial and technical assistance for the safeguarding of the Nubian monuments. Awareness was raised obout the need and urgency to safeguard the antique heritage in the Egyptian cradle of civilization. UNESCO's *public information* model was at its best during this campaign. Similar to the experiences of the government of the United States some decades earlier in mobilizing its population for World War I through public information campaigns, UNESCO managed to have real impact on a critical situation by using communication deftly. As J. Grunig and L. Grunig (1992) stated, the public information model, although related with truth, accuracy and honesty, is still an asymmetrical model because practitioners selectively disseminate information and do not truly engage in dialogue with the public. Although this model is obviously efficient in certain situations such as this, it cannot solve all types of crises. In other periods, UNESCO has had to face situations of great political and ideological complexity in which it was no longer possible to adopt a high and uncontested profile. To be efficient, public information requires this type of asymmetrical relationship between the organization and its audiences.

After this era of successes and achievements, the Cold War context of the sixties and seventies contributed to the freezing of UNESCO's actions. Organizational and political factors simultaneously contributed to the development of stereotyped attitudes and actions in the organization. System theory demonstrated that redundancy and lack of uncertainty inevitably lead to more stable states of a system. That is the reason why bureaucracies slowly evolve to reach the point where the system becomes paralyzed. Considered with some historical distance, a number of UNESCO's positions and activities during that period corresponded to an axiology where no unforeseen events could intervene. For example, it is well known that UNESCO meetings and conferences were among the few where scientists and intellectuals from the Eastern and Western blocs could meet and exchange ideas. There were some other symbolic communication activities that corresponded to this situation such as the direct television link-up between American and Soviet secondary-school children organized under the auspices of UNESCO in the early sixties.

Similarly, the *UNESCO Courier* was one of the rare periodicals authorized to cross the Iron Curtain. For both sides, it provided articles and images from unknown parts of the planet. It was a little window on the outside world. For Nelson Mandela, during his incarceration in South Africa, the *UNESCO Courier* was the sole reading material and contact with the outside world. These bridges across borders were highly appreciated by the individuals who benefited, while for the dominating powers it was a less dangerous way of staying "politically correct," at least in the short run. The public information staff at UNESCO had definitely acquired an art of writing texts that did not disturb the powerful. To prevent any problem, administrative rules very precisely defined who had and who did not have the right to speak to the media.

DIVERGENT OPINIONS

During the Cold War period, UNESCO's conference rooms progressively became an arena for the conflict between Western democratic and Eastern socialistic blocs. In the early 1980a, UNESCO was involved in the debate over the *New World Information and Communication Order* (NWICO). The question, mainly raised by Third World countries, referred to the then-domination of reporting on world issues by media from a few developed countries. Third World countries strongly felt that their views were clearly underrepresented or misinterpreted and they considered the situation unacceptable. The debate pitted two worldviews: one based on free entrepreneurship and marketplace of ideas and the other on state-controlled and planned activities aimed at development. UNESCO's role in this debate is best summed up in its *World Communication Report* (1997):

> The discussions which took place on the subject within UNESCO were extremely stormy. Tension reached a climax in the mid-1980s when the United States (1984) and the United Kingdom (1985) withdrew from the Organization. For their part, a number of international organizations representing professional media circles put all their weight into the balance in order to isolate UNESCO and to make the international community understand that the New World Information and Communication Order constituted an intolerable assault upon press freedom and the free flow of information. (UNESCO, 1997, p. 214)

The crisis about NWICO weakened the position of UNESCO because its credibility had been strongly attacked and its universality questioned. The public information efforts to remedy this situation have not yielded expected results. Instead, they have often been perceived as propaganda for theses advocated by Socialist or Third World countries. Major European newspapers attacked and criticized the director general of UNESCO, at that time, Amadou Mahtar M'Bow of Senegal. The withdrawal of important member states over this debate resulted in massive budget reduction and the resulting morale crisis almost paralyzed UNESCO. Consultative working groups were established to study ways of improving staff management, programming, budgeting, and public information. Such attempts to reform a bureaucratic system hit by a crisis repeatedly occurred in succeeding years, but outcomes and effective results appear to have been very limited. Possibly, the reason may have been that the underlying purpose of these efforts was to restore or readjust the broken system. Staff members who wanted to take initiatives and continue pursuing the original ideals had to invent, as Mintzberg (1979) put it, an *adhocracy*—a system which no longer works with rules and procedures but with personal relationships and inventiveness to bypass the blocking points.

The burial of the NWICO, which was followed by *perestroika* and the falling of the Berlin Wall, as well as the election of a new director-general, Federico Mayor Zaragoza of Spain, in 1987, created the conditions for the renewal of UNESCO. For example, after the NWICO failure, a new strategy for communication was conceived and presented to the General Conference in 1989. The purpose of the new program in the area of "communication in the service of humanity" was to "render more operational the concern of the Organization to ensure a free flow of information . . . and its wider and better balanced dissemination, without any obstacle to the freedom of expression and to strengthen communication capacities in the developing countries, so that they may participate more actively in the communication process." Press freedom continued to be the keystone of the program, entailing not only freedom of expression, but also "independence, pluralism and diversity of the [public, private and other] media." The first 600-page World *Communication Report* (UNESCO, 1997), published that year, served as the underpinning for this new policy. It reviewed recent developments in all aspects of communication throughout the world.

Applying to itself the principles of freedom of expression, diversity, and pluralism, the *UNESCO Courier* underwent a radical change. In 1989, it became an independent magazine with 56–58 pages in full four-color printing and with an editorial policy intended to systematically take an intercultural approach to world issues. It also contained interviews with leading public figures, thinkers, and creative artists. Because the editorial team was not dealing with UNESCO activities but with global issues, there was a proposal to create a new monthly called *UNESCO Sources*, to reflect day-to-day work and improve visibility among partners and the media.

REFOCUSING

Because many friends of UNESCO, including many heads of states such as Vaclav Havel and Nelson Mandela, were rediscovering the preamble of the organization's constitution and mission statement, Director-General Mayor chose to reform the Secretariat not by reorganizing its structures but by rallying energies around a new flagship—the Culture of Peace.[1] As such, this specialized UN agency on education, science, culture, and

---

[1]UNESCO's constitution states: ". . . since wars begin in the minds of men, it is in the minds of men that the defences of peace must be constructed . . ."

communication celebrated its 50th anniversary by paying tribute to the founding fathers who had given UNESCO its clear mandate: to build peace in the minds of people.

Although the United Kingdom rejoined UNESCO in 1997, and UNESCO's image improved, slowly recovering some of its lost prestige, the economic and pragmatic orientations of the 1990s did not favor the success of Mayor's reform.[2] Considered as a missionary or a preacher by some influential member states that first wanted to improve organizational efficiency, the director-general had a difficult time bringing the majority of stakeholders along with him. Too many press releases and speeches condemning peace violators in the most general terms or defending the most difficult causes with abstract words hindered UNESCO's credibility. Within the Secretariat, the existence of a parallel structure assembled under the principle of loyalty to the director-general, as well as the coexistence, in civil servants' minds, of different organizational models—reminiscent of the original *professional model*, formal rules inherited from the *bureaucratic model*, daily practices of *adhocracy*, and the internal break created by the *missionary model*—indicated the need for deep structural reform.

This reform began at the end of 1999 when the new director-general of UNESCO, Koïchiro Matsuura of Japan, was appointed. Public information was one of the pending issues that called for major changes. In their request to address this question, the governing bodies stressed that UNESCO's visibility depended as much on its ability to establish partnership and cooperation ties with social and professional circles sharing common objectives with it as on its media-oriented information policy. It was believed that UNESCO would be appreciated by public opinion, and by the various sectors of the public concerned by whether it was competent, and by its political partners in member states if they could see the usefulness and relevance of its actions.

Such a comprehensive approach to UNESCO's outside communication was not limited only to the Office of Public Information and other dissemination units but also presupposed secretariat-wide mobilization. The need was not merely to improve the organization's capacity to inform but also to get it to transform its capacities to interact with all sectors of the public. This included imparting information, listening to others, and being able to take part in discussions where and when the issues actually arise.

STRENGTHS AND WEAKNESSES

With a view to building a solid communication strategy, a process of external and internal consultations was held and the new plan approved by the executive board in June 2001. A group of prominent experts in communication met twice and addressed a set of recommendations largely integrated in the strategy.[3] This process led to a wide reorganization

---

[2]United States President George Bush announced to the 57th UN General Assembly in September 2002, that the United States would reenter UNESCO.

[3]The president of the group was Nils Gunnar Nilsson (journalist, Sweden) and its membership consisted of José Joaquín Brunner (communication specialist, Chile), Jean-Marie Brunot (former chairman of a press group, France), Tim Cullen (consultant, United Kingdom), Andrej Gratchev (former spokesperson of the head of state, Russian Federation), Manfred Harnischfeger (corporate communication director, Bertelsman Group, Germany), Hisanori Isomura (former director of NHK, Japan), Katherine Smith (specialist in new technologies, United States), Allister Sparks (journalist, South Africa), Ekwow Spio-Garbrah (former Minister of communication, Ghana), Carmen E. Tipling (Head of the national public information agency, Jamaica), Gebran Tuéni (Director of the independent press group An Nahar, Lebanon), Dejan Verčič (researcher and consultant, Slovenia) and Pere Vicens (chairman of the International Publisher Association, Spain).

of the concerned services as well as to the recruitment of a new director for the Bureau of Public Information. The process is still being implemented and therefore it is impossible to determine its efficacy. The following paragraphs will try to depict more precisely the balance of the situation prevailing before the strategy, as well as the main orientations, which are supposed to tackle the unsatisfactory issues.[4]

When addressing the communication problems of an organization such as UNESCO, two major pitfalls must be avoided. The first is restricting the parameters of communication to only the tools and media of information dissemination. The second is employing the term "communication" indiscriminately so that everything by nature becomes communication. While the first pitfall is indisputably reductive, the second can give rise to great confusion. However, the communication and information strategy must cover the whole gamut of actions ranging from the most sophisticated undertakings requiring the involvement of professionals to the everyday practice of all members of staff in their dealings with the outside public. It is through all these channels that UNESCO displays itself to public opinion, and it is on the basis of the totality of signals it emits that the image of the organization is implanted in the minds of those with whom it interacts.

Before assessing the overall results of UNESCO's visibility, it is necessary to briefly review its publics, the major supports utilized, and the objectives pursued. Afterward, results of enquiries and research about UNESCO's exposure and perception will be presented. Although the organization does not use such a typology, one might find it interesting to group the target public with which the organization maintains relations into three major categories forming concentric circles. The first group comprises all persons—and through them, various institutions—that have a formal link with UNESCO. These would include member states through their permanent delegations, governments, the ministries concerned, and their national commissions; intergovernmental organizations; and NGOs. This first group is in a way the internal audience and UNESCO's immediate partners. It represents several tens of thousands of persons.

The second category covers all persons who are more or less part of UNESCO's target constituencies. These are specialized communities of educators, scientists, artists, journalists, or members of society involved in, or even only potentially concerned by, UNESCO's action. These communities all over the world represent several tens of millions of persons and a great many institutions. The final category is somewhat residual. It encompasses all those not belonging to the first two categories. Because under its mandate UNESCO reaches out to all men and women in whose minds the defenses of peace must be constructed through education, science, culture, and communication, the world population should be seen as the organization's constituency, in the broadest sense.

The traditional tools of communication are essentially books, print, and electronic media. But the digital revolution, which has for some years been radically transforming the communication and information scene worldwide, is offering glimpses of new, unsuspected, and promising ways in which the organization can deploy its action and interact with the world. It is no easy matter to give an outline of UNESCO's communication and information activities. They form a very wide-ranging whole that is variable according to one's standpoint. For example, it may be viewed from the standpoint of the media, those at the receiving end, or the objectives or the Organization's internal structures.

---

[4]Parts of the following paragraphs are borrowed from the Official document presented in May 2001 by the director-general to the 161st session of the Executive Board (document 161 EX/43). The author had the privilege of assisting Georges Malempré, assistant director-general, who was entrusted with the mission of preparing the communication strategy presented in that document.

An analytical approach to the question might be to observe the "outlets" and to measure communication outflows. The table below provides some approximate data for the last two years.

UNESCO Publishing	251 new titles (including 14 CD-ROMs) published 2000 titles in the catalog 6 specialized journals	Average print run per language edition: 3000 copies
Monthly Periodicals	The *UNESCO Courier*: 11 issues per year, published in 27 languages + four co-publications in Braille *UNESCO Sources*: 11 issues per year in 5 languages	Combined circulation of the *Courier*: 160,000 copies Combined circulation of *Sources*: 52,000 copies + 400,000 copies of a Chinese-language monthly supplement
Internet	100,000 Web pages online	93,000 visitors per month in January 1999 1,000,000 visitors per month in December 2001
Press	20 press operations 556 press releases in 1998 and 1999	Media coverage: unquantified
Audiovisual	Coproduction of documentary films Production of 15 institutional subjects	Media coverage: unquantified 400 times on CNN
Cultural events	148 exhibitions 108 concerts, shows, or special events	178 member states involved in organizing cultural events at headquarters

In addition to these traditional means of communication, many documents, brochures, folders, and posters are produced by the secretariat at and away from headquarters, many speeches are made by the organization's representatives at many gatherings, and there are various information exchange facilities.

A third way of presenting UNESCO's communication might consist of highlighting the main objectives of all these efforts. A distinction could thus be drawn between activities designed to impart knowledge, raise awareness, mobilize people, or change certain forms of behavior. There is a gradation in the effects sought, which suggests that means should be made consistent with aims. While common sense, which makes it possible to see approximately where one stands in relation to these objectives, governs many communication choices, it must be agreed that very little or no systematic thought is given to the effects sought. Nonetheless, one could expect this to improve in future since over the last three years, UNESCO has been progressively adopting results-based management.

One variant to the *objectives approach* could be to present the functions assumed by communication and information action. They might include, for example, maintaining (or restoring) trust among the main stakeholders, preparing the organization's transparency, increasing UNESCO's credibility, establishing contact among actors at different levels, and exchanging information. But here too, it must be recognized that systematization is more intuitive than rigorous and it would certainly be appropriate to engage in substantial *a posteriori* rationalization to construct a logic of communication action.

ANALYZING THE IMAGE

In spite of all the efforts and supports used to communicate, for several years, the governing bodies have continued to draw the director-general's attention to the fact that UNESCO suffers from a lack of visibility. Recognition of this fact prompted the recent communication strategy elaboration process. If this served to raise awareness, it must be recognized that the organization's visibility is meaningful only if it helps to deal cogently with the issues UNESCO faces by virtue of its mandate. In fact, nothing is to be gained from promoting UNESCO's name if the substance of its action is neither relevant nor credible. The degree of visibility is one consequence of the performance of its mission, but should never be in itself a yardstick of the effectiveness of its action. If there is a "virtuous" circle that leads through efficacy via credibility to visibility, there can also be an infernal spiral that loops around ineffectiveness and poor reputation, or "bad press," and becomes exacerbated with increased visibility.

Despite a biased methodology including limited sampling, an inquiry into how UNESCO is perceived was conducted at the beginning of 2001, at the request of the Swedish National Commission. The study gathered data from opinion-leaders in four countries (Canada, India, Sweden, and the United Kingdom) and officials within the United Nations system. The findings of this study clearly revealed that there was a broad measure of support for the original principles and mandate assigned to UNESCO, but that there were also many signs of frustration and disappointment vis-à-vis an institution that has embarked upon too many different fields, that does not possess resources to match its ambitions, and that tends to be stultified by a degree of bureaucracy. Comparison with other agencies of the United Nations system was distinctly to its disadvantage. In contrast to other organizations of the system, UNESCO could not illustrate its mission by a simple and instantly understandable image. From its multifarious missions there emerged an image that is complex, abstract, and frequently hazy. Moreover, because its mandate is basically intellectual and not so much operational, UNESCO frequently creates the impression of being a remote bureaucracy.

The mission assigned to UNESCO since its creation has nevertheless enjoyed an undeniable aura for a whole range of different sectors of the public. The same appeared true of several of the topics, which it has determined to be its priorities for some years. Some of these topics are: world heritage, education for all, ethics of science and technology, environmental protection, prevention of natural disasters, and conflict prevention. The major thrusts of its new medium-term strategy are those that deal with the most burning issues facing the world today. Many of the programs are favorably perceived in the professional circles concerned. Nevertheless, UNESCO, like other intergovernmental organizations, was feeling the effects of the general disengagement occurring within the public sector, and the organization is in danger of seeing its impact dwindle in a mood of general indifference if it does not succeed in making its action, and its achievements, sufficiently clear and comprehensible.

Another study in the beginning of 2001, was a retrospective analysis of UNESCO's visibility in about 30 international newspapers over a period of two years (from January 1, 1999 to December 31, 2000). The objective was to discover the media outreach, how the image of UNESCO had been projected in the major international press organs, which have a recognized credibility, and, by extension, how world opinion leaders perceive UNESCO based on the information they gathered from the press. More than 2000 articles were analyzed, providing an interesting picture of media portrayal of UNESCO: the organization's

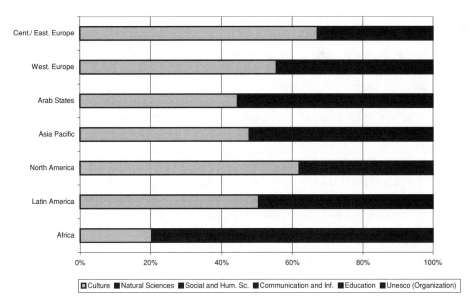

FIG. 20.1.   UNESCO press coverage study 1999–2000. Topics by regions.
(*Note*: From UNESCO.)

name is largely associated with world heritage; education is referred to in less than 10% of
the articles; there are very few (3%) articles that refer negatively to UNESCO; important
UNESCO events such as the Dakar Forum on education, the World Conference on Science,
the inscription of new sites on the World Heritage list, and the election of the director-
general have had a significant impact in the international press. Besides its innovative
methodology, this study showed that the press, according to the geographic region, was
not necessarily reactive to the same topics. For example, African newspapers were propor-
tionally more interested by social sciences and communication issues than those from other
regions of the world. Figure 20.1 excerpted from the study, illustrates these variations.

Surprisingly, in an organization where cultural diversity was proclaimed as a common
wealth, there is no systematic tool to capture and analyze the differences of the reception
contexts, or to tailor messages to suit local cultures. In most cases, the same messages are
produced in different languages (usually English, French, Spanish, Arabic, and Russian)
for different publics around the globe. Experienced journalists from different regions, hired
on a permanent basis by UNESCO, revise the translations and sometimes introduce in the
texts a few adaptations in order to interest journalists from their region. A relatively small
number of national commissions and field offices devote time, skills, and resources to
professionally communicate with their local publics. Those who do something can hardly
count on guidelines, materials or ideas from headquarters.

SEARCHING FOR CHANGE

If the blurred and splintered image projected by the organization has previously been
accentuated by a lack of coordination of its activities as a whole, the services responsible
have also suffered for a number of years from a continuous depletion of their means of
action. Guided primarily by strategies aimed at making savings and optimizing resources,

the organization has been led to undertake structural adjustments of the services concerned, which have not been followed by any clear redefinition of their tasks. By regarding the communication media as a set of program support resources, the tendency has become established, as in most organizations, to reduce communication to the status of a tool and to focus attention too exclusively upon the production and dissemination of information. However, awareness is growing that communication is far more closely bound up with the logic of action. What is the impact produced by such communication media? How do they contribute to achieving the expected results?

Accordingly, if one starts to think about the program in terms of communication and begins to formulate communication in terms of results in relation to set objectives, both communication and public information become strategic components, intrinsically linked to the definition of programs in which the identification, knowledge, and understanding of the target populations always and necessarily precede discussions on the formulation of messages and the choice of means. This change is the linchpin of the communication strategy that the director-general began to implement at the beginning of 2002.

The strategy adopted comprises of 12 major headings that include both strategic principles and practical mechanisms. They are briefly presented hereafter.[5]

- *Anchoring communication activities in the program.* This implies discovering the communication dimension in the substantial activities and managing it in such a way that it directly serves the results that are expected.

- *Distinguishing substantive communication from institutional communication so that they are better coordinated.* The amalgam of the two components of the organization communication has led to confusion and non assumed or badly assumed responsibilities.

- *Establishing a structure to manage communication in a strategic perspective.* Communication and public relations are not just instruments—they require professionals able to adjust them to the overall organizational strategy.

- *Making communication a two-way process through responsiveness to target audiences.* Listening is part of the communication process and gaining the attention to the public is the starting point of a successful communication process.

- *Developing a communication culture inside the secretariat.* Good internal and external communication first requires communicating attitudes and shared values regarding the virtue of openness and dialogue.

- *Spreading the load by involving partners in communication activities.* It is quite obvious that the UNESCO Secretariat cannot support alone the promotion of the organization's objectives. Many partners from the public and private sectors could be involved to disseminate the key messages.

- *Establishing an effective system of editorial and graphic identity (one that is understandable, consistent, and eloquent).* The "temple-like" logo does not communicate what the organization intends to be and its use has been so anarchic that a renewed design is badly needed to graphically deliver key and central messages.

- *Refocusing relations with the press.* Credibility in international public opinion will be gained by good press relations: activities, efforts, and products adapted to media constraints and logic in which UNESCO's views on issues relevantly contribute to public debate.

---

[5]The full document is available online at http://unesdoc.unesco.org/images/0012/001225/122549e.pdf Retrieved January 5, 2003.

- *Publishing a high-quality periodical.* This item originated a number of passionate discussions among the governing bodies because the *UNESCO Courier* was implicitly to be discontinued. Finally, it was decided that a new *UNESCO Courier* would be published twice a year and widely circulated, free of charge, among the far–ranging UNESCO community through the channel of the national commissions.

- *Refocusing publishing activities (printed, audiovisual, and multimedia productions) to reach target groups more effectively.* Since its creation, UNESCO has published almost 10,000 titles, in all its fields of competence, in 70 languages, to be distributed all over the world. Publications should be better articulated with projects and programs so that the principal criteria for UNESCO publishing should no so much be the intent to sell the maximum number of books but to reach the right publics. When targeting large audiences, partnerships with international publishers should be sought.

- *Coordinating Websites and expanding Web communication in the future.* With its growing potential, the Internet is not just a new worldwide medium, but it is also another way to reach and interact with publics. To take full advantage of the Internet is a challenge that starts with the transformation of the present Website, which is an unbalanced patchwork quilt, into a dynamic whole with a greater coherence.

- *Organizing cultural activities, at and away from headquarters, that reflect the creative diversity of UNESCO.* Cultural events use the universal language of art and aesthetics. They say something about the organization as well as contributing to a better understanding of foreign cultures.

UNDERSTANDING UNESCO'S COMMUNICATION ROLE

The historical references evoked different aspects of UNESCO's approach to communication. Simply put, there are three major facets. First, because of the organization's nature, all types of communication practices are central in most of UNESCO's actions. UNESCO does not build roads or hospitals. It is a worldwide forum that brings people together and creates the conditions under which ideas and experiences can be exchanged. The responsibility to facilitate communication crosscuts all entities (headquarters, field offices, central services, and others). Second, UNESCO has a mandate to develop communication in the world. It defends the free flow of ideas and press freedom as well as promoting access for all to information. Communication is one of the major action areas, parallel to education, culture, and science. The Communication and Information Sector is in charge of this dimension with international standard-settings, professional, and academic developments. Third, UNESCO's communication is a permanent process of (re)explaining its institutional dimension, its *raison d'être*. It is the "corporate" communication arm of the organization. Most of the time, this component is internally called "public information" to avoid confusion with the other facets of communication. It principally falls under the responsibility of the Bureau of Public Information, which is supposed to be expert in dealing with the public.

It is relatively easy to make these conceptual distinctions. Most of the examples briefly presented above demonstrate how these three facets are interwoven and overlap. Many of the reforms to improve the effectiveness of UNESCO's communication have had the intention of separating and distinguishing these facets. Public information activities were repeatedly reduced to manage some of the communication instruments used by the organization (books, audiovisual media, press releases, etc.) and intended for the external public. The public information focus has often been "instrumentalized." Over the last 50 years, the promising developments and potentialities in the information and communication area

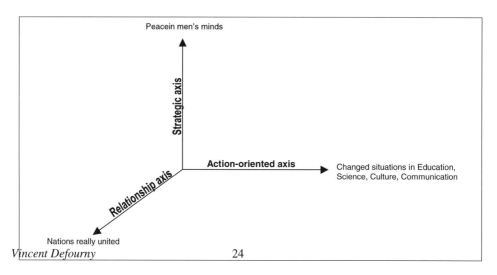

FIG. 20.2.   UNESCO and its three driving forces.

(film, radio, television, Internet, and so on) have misled a number of senior managers and member state representatives. Probably influenced by advertising and marketing success stories, they thought that the use of a particular tool or the technology would almost automatically serve UNESCO's interests. The problem lay not so much in reaching the public at large, but in developing a context favorable to the achievements of the organization's objectives. In other words, the organization had to develop the strategic use of communication. The present author believes that a complex goal such as developing UNESCO's communication strategy requires recognizing and better understanding its complexity. The new communication strategy adopted in 2001 intends to follow these lines and principles, and is to be directly plugged into the medium-term strategy covering the period 2002–2007.

The following representation based on system theory, of what UNESCO as an organization is and what its communication role is, is relevant to visualizing some of the key ideas of this chapter.

First, it is necessary to draw three axes, corresponding to three organizational driving-forces (Figure 20.2): (1) the strategic axis with the guiding principle of UNESCO's mandate (peace in the minds of men); (2) the action-oriented axis leading to the fulfillment of all the expected results of its program (education for all throughout life, sound press freedom, preserved and respected world heritage, etc.); and (3) the relationship axis looking toward the achievement of international solidarity (the real United Nations).

The end points of these dimensions belong to utopia, but they definitely organize and structure the mobilization of resources and ideas. Of course, today's UNESCO is still far from reaching these targets, but it is not difficult to observe that, since its foundation, the organization has made significant strides toward reaching them.

Second, interactions between these three subsystems are interesting to consider. (1) People's aspirations find their way in the projection of the relationship axis toward the strategic axis. National and regional consultations preceding the elaboration of the medium-term strategy and the definition of strategic objectives are good examples of this process through which stakeholders collectively place their aspirations in a common document. (2) It is also well known that concrete action and activities find their inspirations in great ambitions: the strategic axis must feed the action-oriented one. For example, in Bosnia and Herzegovina, the reconstruction of the old bridge at Mostar was much more than a heritage preservation activity. It was a way of building peace and dialogue in a war-torn region.

(3) Lastly, concerted actions are much more effective than any other. The action-oriented axis finds its real deployment through the relationship dimension. This third movement can be called "conspiracy/conspiration." So these three key movements (aspiration, inspiration, and "conspiracy/conspiration") linking the three fundamental dimensions (strategy, action, and relationship) represent the organizational "respiration," the repeated and permanent movement that keeps the organization alive (Figure 20.3).

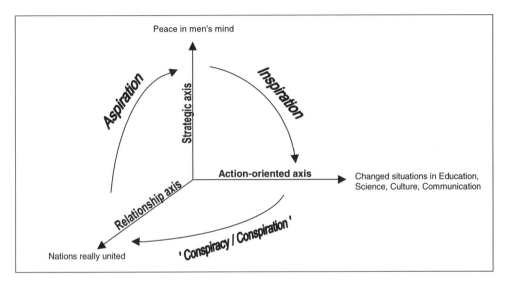

FIG. 20.3.   The organization "respiration."

It is the purpose of communication to stimulate this respiration in such a way that a given situation for the organization—say, the circle joining points A, B, and C placed on the three axes—will be enlarged and improved by a spiral movement produced by the dynamic of strategic communication (Figure 20.4).

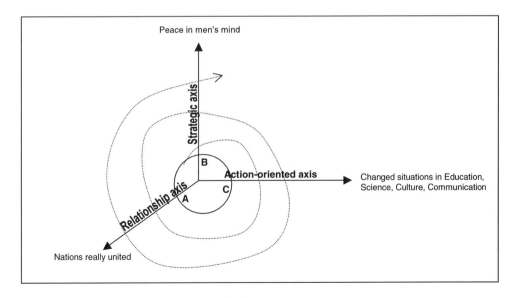

FIG. 20.4.   The role of strategic communication.

In practical terms, this means communicating from the heart of the organization and in line with organizational strategy, objectives and results-orientation by establishing bi-directional communication with constituencies. This should contribute to channeling public aspirations, providing meaning and understanding to large and small-scale projects, as well as consolidating communities. The implementation of the communication strategy during the coming years will be critical and results will have to be carefully analyzed to detect its real strengths and weaknesses.

REFERENCES

Grierson J. Archive, University of Stirling, G5.

Grunig, J. E. (Ed.) (1992). *Excellence in public relations and communications management.* Hillsdale, NJ: Lawrence Erlbaum Associates.

Grunig, J. E., & Grunig, L. A. (1992). Models of public relations and communication. In Grunig, J. E. (Ed.), *Excellence in public relations and communication management* (pp. 285–325). Hillsdale, NJ: Lawrence Erlbaum Associates.

Lacoste, M. C. (1994). *The story of a grand design—UNESCO 1946–1993.* Geneva: UNESCO.

L'Etang, J. (1999). John Grierson and the public relations industry in Britain. In *Screening the Past (electronic journal)*, Melbourne: La Trobe University. Retrieved January 15, 2003, from http://www.latrobe.edu.au/screeningthepast/firstrelease/fr0799/jlfr7d.htm

Mintzberg, H. (1979). *The structuring of organizations: A synthesis of the research.* Englewood Cliffs, NJ: Prentice-Hall.

UNESCO (1997). *World communication report.* Geneva: UNESCO.

UNESCO (2000). Basic Texts, Paris.

UNESCO (1948). Records of the general conference of UNESCO, third session, Beirut, Resolutions.

21

Managing Sustainable Development in Sub-Saharan Africa: A Communication Ethic for the Global Corporation

Cornelius B. Pratt

While industry represents perhaps the single biggest threat to society and the natural world, it can also represent one of our greatest allies in our mission to safeguard it and provide for its sustainable development.

—World Wide Fund for Nature, in Marsden (2000), p. 9

Sub-Saharan Africa faces a litany of developmental challenges, not least its deteriorating environment and ecosystem, its faltering agricultural productivity, its heavy-handed state intervention, its inadequate foreign investment, its improper political governance, its limited public health programs, its narrow business partnerships, and its social strife. Long after the implementation of structural adjustment policies required by the International Monetary Fund (IMF) for its strategic support of teetering African economies and the adoption of investment practices enunciated by both the World Bank and the European Union, those challenges are still far from abating. A statement issued at the conclusion of the U.N. World Summit on Sustainable Development (WSSD), held in Johannesburg, South Africa, August 26-September 4, 2002, underscored the enduring nature of those challenges: "Africa's efforts to achieve sustainable development have been hindered by conflicts, insufficient investment, limited market access opportunities and supply side constraints, unsustainable debt burdens, historically declining ODA [official development assistance] levels, and the impact of HIV/AIDS."

It is against that backdrop that this chapter focuses on the question, How can organizational communication, particularly that undertaken by the global corporation, be used to respond effectively to the challenges of sustainable development in sub-Saharan Africa? It is that question—at the global level—that prompted the Warwick Business School to hold a

Corporate Citizenship Research Conference in July 1998. It explored corporate citizenship and developed an agenda for improving it. Marsden (2000) writes: "Private sector business, particularly . . . [the] large international companies, is increasingly being seen, both by those working inside it as well as outside, as part of the solution to the world's biggest environmental and social problems, rather than just being a part of the problem" (pp. 9-10). More important, however, is the evolving ethic that guides global corporate behaviors: that community involvement, environmental and sustainability initiatives, and stakeholder engagement are gaining momentum (Muirhead, Bennet, Berenbeim, Kao, & Vidal, 2002).

Corporate involvement in communities per se is not new. However, what is refreshing is corporate commitment to (1) a "focus on building bridges between corporations and community" (Vidaver-Cohen & Altman, 2000, p. 145); (2) a recognition of the "mutuality of interests and practices between society and business" (Waddock & Smith, 2000, p. 47); (3) the promotion of "civic engagement . . . to restore neighborhood houses, volunteer in tutoring and mentoring programs, provide impoverished families with . . . vital civic activities" (O'Connor, 2000, p. 142); and (4) the "idea that all those involved in the corporation are potentially members of one community; while they clearly have significantly divergent interests, needs, and values, they also have some significant shared goals and bonds" (Etzioni, 1998, p. 679).

Thus this chapter links three (theoretical) constructs—stakeholder theory, corporate social performance (CSP), and sustainable development—and argues that global organizations apply them *ethically* in their attempt to respond more effectively to the challenges of the societies or nations in which they operate. It argues that business organizations—as harbingers of development in the Third World—apply normative core values of stakeholder theory and those inherent in their social performance to evaluating and responding to community challenges and to collaborating with other organizations and community groups in their contributions to national development. WSSD acknowledged the importance of ethics for sustainable development and emphasized the need to consider ethics in the implementation of "Agenda 21" of the "Rio Earth Summit."

A caveat at this point is necessary: This chapter is neither an add-on to the growing list of strategies for Third World development nor a challenge to the strategies of development agents; rather, it makes the case that stakeholder theory and CSP, as constructs of a communication ethic, frame current programs and extant organizational responses to community challenges.

Understandably, a key principle of effective governance—political, corporate, or organizational—is establishing strong, ethical relationships with one's constituents or publics. The public relations literature is replete with studies that have investigated that principle (e.g., Grunig, 2001; Grunig & Repper, 1992; Ledingham, 2001; Ledingham & Bruning, 1998). Organization-public relationships are all the more critical whenever the principal agent is large or influential globally. For business and major political and community organizations, the emphasis on building firm, dynamic relationships with various publics has morphed into an evolving stakeholder theory, which recognizes the inherent disparate values among an organization's publics. That theory is becoming more relevant today largely because of the social landscape, densely dotted with protest movements, on which major organizations and institutions operate.

THE STAKEHOLDER THEORY

By definition, stakeholder theory has been grounded in functionalist organizational theory (e.g., Freeman, 1984; Freeman & Gilbert, 1988; Freeman & Reed, 1983) and in ethical theory (Argandoña, 1998; Carroll, 1989; Cohen, 1995; Donaldson, 1989; Evan & Freeman,

1988; Phillips, 1997). The former, whose seminal proponent is Freeman (1984), is "about groups and individuals who can affect the organization, and is about managerial behavior taken in response to those groups and individuals" (p. 84). That view defines a stakeholder as "any group or individual who can affect or is affected by the achievement of an organization's purpose . . . [S]ome corporations must count 'terrorist groups' as stakeholders" (p. 53). In general, such groups include shareholders, employees, suppliers, customers, communities in which a firm operates, government agencies, creditors, and competitors. "One of the goals of stakeholder theory," writes Phillips (1997), "is to maintain the benefits of the free market while minimizing the potential ethical problems created by capitalism" (p. 63).

The ethical perspective holds that normative criteria be used by an organization to identify its stakeholders, to allocate rights, and to consider their values in assigning duties (Argandoña, 1998; Donaldson, 1989; Quinn & Jones, 1995); that is, the duty of each stakeholder is to play its part fairly in achieving the organization's common good. An organization should treat its stakeholders as "ends" (Evan & Freeman, 1983).

The stakeholder theory is not without its limitations (e.g., Donaldson & Preston, 1995; Jones & Wicks, 1999). Major issues have been disclosing organizational actions to stakeholders, getting stakeholders' consent, and acting fairly in assigning rights, duties and rewards to stakeholders. Further, Windsor (1998) argued that, because stakeholder theory is at an early stage of development, the identification of stakeholders is very much unresolved. Similarly, Mitchell, Agle and Wood (1997) seek answers to the question, Who or what really counts in a firm's stakeholder environment by using a typology based on one or more of three relationship attributes: power, legitimacy, urgency.

It is argued here that it is the less-than-explicit application of the normative stakeholder theory (Donaldson & Preston, 1995) by the global corporation and its partners that irks anti-globalization activists and spurs protests against business and economic institutions, as routinely occur during annual meetings of the IMF and the World Bank, and as most recently occurred at the WSSD. It is on similar protests that the next section focuses.

PROTESTS AGAINST BUSINESS AND ECONOMIC INSTITUTIONS

Historically, protests are a social movement with which business and government have to contend. They are a tool for exercising citizen rights and for making demands on the power structure. The completion of the first phase of the extensive Lesotho Highlands Water Project early in 1998 attracted the coalescence of several rural and urban environmental groups from both Lesotho and South Africa, to whose governments protests were directed. At issue was the need for further environmental impact analysis, particularly in areas where it was thought that continuing the construction of a dam on the Orange River would cause flooding, damage farmlands and pastures, threaten wildlife and forests, and destabilize rural communities. Even so, the World Bank in June 1998 approved a $45 million loan for constructing the second phase of the dam, further heightening tensions and increasing the call from civic and environmental groups for "environmental justice."

Organizations, particularly those with global operations, confront similar challenges from protest groups. Since 1998, for example, when violent protests rocked the World Trade Organization ministerial conference in Geneva, several protests have been organized against other major global economic institutions—the Group of Eight (Britain, Canada, France, Germany, Italy, Japan, Russia, the United States); the World Bank; the IMF; the World Economic Forum; the European Union—as proxies for attributing blame for Third World poverty and underdevelopment to the perceived failures of the global corporation in protecting and fostering stakeholder interest. Such protests have implications for the perceived failure of global institutions to create broader opportunities for stakeholder input into the governance and policies of global institutions. The criteria for evaluating the social performance of multinational agencies are being expanded to include the human-rights arena. In essence, responsive (global) corporations should *also* be evaluated on their human-rights record, not just on the standard measures of corporate performance. For communication practitioners, that development expands and redefines their boundary-spanning role to relationships with activist groups.

The grievances of activist groups do not have an enduring common theme, but comprise a mixed bag of global issues: labor rights, trade barriers and relations, animal rights, environmental damage (Went, 2000). For the most part, those issues do not frame the traditional discourse on CSP, even though they are the embers over which the fate of the global corporation depends. Yet, they have become the most prominent features of today's economic and political landscape (Held, McGrew, Goldblatt, & Perraton, 1999). For example, November 30 through December 3, 1999, was a watershed in protests against the World Trade Organization, a 135-nation trade group. Protesters got extensive publicity for what they construed as the macabre acts of global corporations—and of their willingness to do business as usual. The sentiments of those protesters rubbed off on the World Economic Forum (January 31-February 4, 2002) in New York City.

WSSD recognized the intersection between development and the environment, as did the Rio de Janeiro Earth summit 10 years earlier. Both summits were fertile grounds for protests. For one thing, the mere mention of "sustainability" attracts the ire of environmentalists worldwide. For the developing nations, that raises gruesome memories of environmental decadence on the rain forests, excessive logging in the Amazon, and the incursions of corporations in pristine homelands. For another, the conferences sought novel partnerships among governments (whose legitimacy is questionable), non-government organizations with competing and sometimes conflicting interests, and foundations and businesses whose investment prospects are narrowly focused on the short term. In the perception of environmental groups a narrow focus translates into a disregard of the concerns and rights of community stakeholders.

CORPORATE SOCIAL PERFORMANCE

Delegates at WSSD reached an agreement on six key issues: water and sanitation, climate change, energy, human and environmental health, sustainable development, and global poverty. The latter is grounded in six issues: that access to markets holds the key to development in many countries; that all export subsidies be phased out; that nations commit to a 10-year framework of programs on sustainable consumption and production; that corporate accountability and responsibility be enhanced; that nations improve their responses to natural disasters; and that a global fund be established to eradicate extreme poverty.

Those agreements suggest a leadership role for business, not least corporate establishments whose headquarters are in the developed nations. For one thing, the economic straits of much of the developing world, particularly sub-Saharan Africa, suggest the presence of economic and political infrastructures that compromise development agendas. For another, it is the ethics-driven global corporation that can serve as a harbinger of, and a vanguard for, development in a complementary mode, assisting national governments and development centers, business roundtables, community groups and other nongovernmental organizations—all in their quest to reverse plummeting economies and stem the incidence of poverty.

WSSD, as it were, set a new tone for global assistance in Third World development, particularly in Africa, where the HIV/AIDS pandemic is robbing the continent of its skilled labor and where political crises and rule by whim are making the region less attractive to global investors. Even so, since the 1990s the region has adopted market-driven economies, most notably by privatizing state-owned infrastructures, and adopting structural adjustment programs by which its economies were liberalized and streamlined.

An earlier summit, the United Nations Conference on Environment and Development held in 1992 in Rio de Janeiro, offered, among other things, a blueprint for sustainable development, the elimination of unsustainable patterns of production and consumption, and the enhancement of the development, adaptation, diffusion, and transfer of technologies.

This chapter argues that corporate governance or CSP is a strategic response to Africa's development problems, particularly those discussed in WSSD. Corporate communicators whose interest should be consistent with those of their key constituents should assist their organizations in framing that response.

CSP, a multidimensional construct (Carroll, 1991; Sharfman, 1996; Wolfe & Aupperle, 1991), has been disaggregated into five most frequently used dimensions: community relations, treatment of women and minorities, product quality, employee relations, and treatment of the environment (Graves & Waddock, 1994; Turban & Greening, 1997; Waddock & Graves, 1997). The last of these dimensions—treatment of the environment—provides a framework for this chapter.

Wood (1991a) defines CSP as the degree to which social responsibility motivates actions taken in behalf of a firm; the degree to which the firm uses socially responsive processes, the existence and nature of policies and programs designed to manage the firm's societal relationships; and the observable outcomes (i.e., social impacts) of the firm's actions, programs, and policies. Thus, that definition integrates three principles: corporate social and ecological responsibility; social responsiveness and issues management, outcomes of corporate social impacts, social programs, and social policies (Bansal & Roth, 2000; Stanwick & Stanwick, 1998; Wartick & Cochran, 1985; Wood, 1991a, 1991b). Corporate social responsibility refers to an organization's legitimacy within a society and its public responsibility; that is, corporations have obligations to groups other than their stockholders and beyond responsibilities required by law or employee unions. "The fundamental idea of 'corporate social responsibility,'" writes Frederick (1986), "is that business corporations have the obligation to work for social betterment" (p. 4). Social responsiveness includes corporate environmental assessment, stakeholder management, and issues management. The third principle investigates the impacts of the corporation on social policies and social programs, Thus, CSP reflects a firm's commitment to its social environment and its ability to adapt to institute changes in that environment that benefit stakeholders.

Studies (e.g., McWilliams & Siegel, 2000) show that CSP can have benefits for organizations; other effects have also been observed. Effects of CSP on financial performance, for example, have been associated with significant excess negative returns to shares of companies that announced divestments of business units in South Africa (e.g., Wright & Ferris, 1997); the effects have been neutral (e.g., Aupperle, Carroll, & Hatfield, 1985; Teoh, Welch, & Wazzan, 1999); and positive (Belkaoui, 1976; Frooman, 1997; McNatt & Light, 1998; Meyerson, 1999; Pava & Krausz, 1996; Posnikoff, 1997; Preston, 1978; Waddock & Graves, 1997; Wood & Jones, 1995). Positive relationships have also been observed between CSP and employee morale and productivity (Solomon & Hanson, 1985), and between CSP and organizational attractiveness to new employees, that is, the development of employment-related images of organizations (Luce, Barber, & Hillman, 2001; Riordan, Gatewood, & Bill, 1997; Strand, Levine, & Montgomery, 1981; Turban &

Greening, 1997). Also, a strong relationship has been observed between profitability and CSP, that is, profitability of a firm allows and encourages managers to implement programs that increase the level of corporate social responsibility (Stanwick & Stanwick, 1998; Waddock & Graves, 1997).

THE ENVIRONMENT-DEVELOPMENT LINK

In the annals of the environment-development literature, two concepts are understandably conjoined. One is the protection of the environment; the other, its sustainability and concomitant development. Those two concepts help explain the evolving corporate interest in ecological responsibility and the consumer interest in corporate "greening." The reasons for the upsurge in that interest have been varied. They include legislation, stakeholder pressures, economic opportunities, ethical concerns, critical events, and corporate values (Bansal & Roth, 2000; Dillon & Fischer, 1992; Lawrence & Morell, 1995; Winn, 1995).

Greening, as a global issue, is at the forefront of the agendas of major environmental and community groups—such as Greenpeace, Earth First! and the Sierra Club, with worldwide presence; and the Network for Environment and Sustainable Development in Africa (NESDA), the Landless People's Movement, Anti-Privatization Forum, Earthlife Africa, Lawyers Environmental Action Team, and Advocates Coalition for Development and Environment, all in Africa. So conjoined are sustainability and conservation that it is a fruitless exercise to attempt to delineate one from the other. However, whenever early ecological discourse referred to conservation, it did so bereft of—if not separated from—the evolving companion discourse on sustainability. But McKee (2001) underscores lucidly the inherent synergy between them:

> When an ecosystem becomes unsustainable and collapses, we imperil nature's services and jeopardize our own resources. . . . One possible solution is conservation. People around the world are making noble efforts to set aside lands in which nature can continue its work. Others have identified particular areas of rich biological diversity, some of which have been targeted for conservation. (p. B20)

Africa's responses to environmental issues took root during the June 1972 United Nations Conference on Human Environment held in Stockholm, where social activists from developing countries raised questions on the effects of affluent countries' operations on the environment. Since then African countries have ratified more than a dozen Multilateral Environmental Agreements, indicating their commitment to sustainable development. And since the 1992 Earth Summit in Rio de Janeiro, where "Agenda 21: The United Nations Program of Action from Rio" was adopted, African countries have made progress toward implementing actions called for in Sweden and Brazil. They have established political and economic groups such as the Lake Chad Basin Commission, the African Timber Organization, the East Africa Wetlands Program, and the Lake Victoria Global Environment Facility Project.

In the nongovernmental realm, NESDA, an African initiative, is helping countries such as Botswana, The Gambia, Côte d'Ivoire, Cameroon, Ghana, and Ethiopia achieve environmentally sustainable development by assisting them in developing strategies for environmental management and in establishing relations between sub-regional initiatives (e.g., the Eastern Africa Biodiversity Support Program, the Nile Basin Initiative, and the Integrated Coastal Zone Management) and the rest of the continent.

In the political-corporate sector, the New Partnership for African Development (NEPAD) collaborates with the developed countries in fostering international trade and foreign investment. In mid-April 2002, for example, a summit, "Partnership with the Private Sector for Financing Africa's Growth through NEPAD," acknowledged business as a key player in addressing Africa's environmental challenges through international trade and foreign investment.

During WSSD, delegates expected the United States to play a leading role in averting environmental scourge and global warming, particularly because of the country's reluctance to approve the Kyoto Protocol on climate change. Nonetheless, the United States has a commendable history of environmental enhancement—and, some argue, a dismal record on the environment. The leadership role of the United States in ecological responsibility is grounded in the 19th century, an epoch during which the federal government regulated forestlands, with Congress in 1831 prohibiting the removal of timber from public lands. In 1862 it passed the Morrill Act, by which it set aside lands that could be used by states for educational purposes. That act also established the Department of Agriculture to provide oversight for agricultural land use. George P. Marsh's *Man and Nature* (1864) provided a fillip to the conservation movement and contributed to reforms during the United States Reconstruction (1865-1877) by arguing that public land management was for usufruct alone, not for consumption; therefore, humans should stop destroying the earth's (natural) resources. Consequently, in 1930, for example, the U.S. government established a Timber Conservation Board, which called for greater cooperation between government and industry in promoting conservation—a collaboration that was a bellwether for much of the free world.

U.S. political interest in environmental protection was demonstrated in the creation of the Bureau of Land Management in 1946, in the enactment of the Forest Pest Control Act of 1947, and in the founding of the Civilian Conservation Corps in 1933, all of which coalesced in bringing to a head conservation and sustainability.

Therefore, it is perhaps not an exaggeration to conclude that the late Rachel Carson's controversial book, *Silent Spring* (1962), a response to "the senseless, brutish things" that were being done to the environment, set the stage and upped the ante for today's global dialogue on sustainable development. Carson's work sought to establish causal links between the use of DDT and other pesticides *and* damage to the environment, to humans, and to animals.

Five years after *Silent Spring* was published, the United Nations Educational, Scientific and Cultural Organization sponsored an Intergovernmental Conference for Rational Use and Conservation of Biosphere, which held seminal discussions on a then-emerging concept: sustainable development.

Shortly thereafter, several forces, including the sometimes disparate activities of environmental and other national groups, coalesced to provide the impetus for global attention to the health and management of our nation's forests and rangelands. Even so, a few milestones can be identified as making far-reaching inroads into pushing forest and rangeland health into the forefront of national governments' agendas.

For example, in 1969 alone, three U.S. organizations, the Natural Resources Defense Council, Friends of the Earth, and the United States Environmental Protection Agency, were created to focus U.S. attention on the environment. On January 1, 1970, the National Environmental Policy Act of 1969 was signed; it established the Council on Environmental Quality in the president's office. Also in 1970, a global event, "Earth Day," saw more than 20 million people in the United States alone demonstrate peacefully in behalf of the environment.

Additional developments quickly provided further fillip to the cause of sustainable development. In 1993, Canada convened in Montréal a seminar of experts on sustainable development of boreal and temperate forests. Its mandate: To respond to a June 1992 United Nations conference on the environment during which a call was issued on global attention to the importance of sustainable forest management as a strategic response to meeting our current need for forest products and services without jeopardizing those of future generations. Consequently, the nations that participated in the seminar developed national criteria for and national indicators of sustainable forest management; they are more succinctly referred to as the Montréal Process. A sequela of that initiative in developing those measures was the founding in Geneva in 1994 of the Working Group on Criteria and Indicators for the Conservation and Sustainable Management of Temperate and Boreal Forests.

On February 3, 1995, the 10 original members—Australia, Canada, Chile, China, Japan, the Republic of Korea, Mexico, New Zealand, Russia, the United States—affirmed the Montréal Process by issuing the Santiago Declaration, which comprises seven criteria for and 67 indicators of sustainable forest management. (Uruguay and Argentina endorsed the declaration in July and October 1995, respectively.)

The seven criteria (and the number of their indicators):

1. Conserving biological diversity (9 indicators)

2. Maintaining productive capacity of forest ecosystems (5 indicators)

3. Maintaining forest ecosystem health and vitality (3 indicators)

4. Conserving and maintaining soil and water resources (8 indicators)

5. Maintaining forest contributions to global carbon cycles (3 indicators)

6. Maintaining and enhancing long-term multiple socioeconomic benefits (19 indicators)

7. Establishing legal, institutional and economic framework for forest conservation and sustainable management (20 indicators)

The key here is that global interest in the health of the environment is not lost on corporations and on other multinational agencies whose activities have been criticized as being unhealthful for the ecosystem. Ecosystem regulations aside, it behooves the multinational organization to adhere voluntarily to practices that, at the minimum, are demonstrably reflective of their governments' commitment to sustainable development within their borders.

Since that historic event of 1995, 11 U.S. federal government agencies have entered into a Memorandum of Understanding (initially signed October 16, 2000), which seeks to resolve federal agency responsibilities related to continually collecting, monitoring, analyzing, reporting, and distributing data on the Montréal Process.

A number of reports and technical documents have been issued by the group; and a number of roundtables have been organized for (a) sharing information and perspectives (community of interests) on the sustainable management of our forests (a community of place); and (b) providing dialogues that will move the United States toward sustainable forest management. Such roundtables will, for example, facilitate communication with stakeholders interested in tracking the roundtables and in fostering participation by key constituents. For example, the Sustainable Minerals Roundtable is identifying the status of minerals in sustainable development and is formulating agreed-upon, nationwide indicators for sustaining minerals. Similar efforts are being undertaken for sustainable rangeland management.

The agendas of those groups—as well as those of several others—suggest areas rife with corporate communication opportunities and challenges. To what extent, for example, do key publics know about, let alone support, sustainable development? How much can a nation—and domestic environmental and interest groups and companies—benefit from both a pervasive public and a systemwide understanding of sustainable development? Both those questions suggest opportunities—as well as challenges.

THE TRIONYM OF SUSTAINABLE DEVELOPMENT

Although there are disparate definitions of sustainability, there is some general agreement on what it means. By definition, sustainable development, as noted above, has been associated with concepts such as environmental sustainability; conservation; corporate, social or national responsibility; general do-gooderism; and ecological sustainability. Even though there is disagreement over the meaning of sustainable development, there is comparatively little disagreement about the implications of sustainable development for national development. One coexists with the other, making any difference between them nuanced.

Perhaps a much-earlier description of sustainability was implied in a 1905 letter written by United States Secretary of Agriculture James Wilson and addressed to Gifford Pinchot, the first chief of the new United States Forest Service, to which authority over 86 million acres of federal forest lands had just been transferred from the Forest Reserves. The letter stressed that "all land is to be devoted to its most productive use for the permanent good of the whole people, and not for the temporary benefit of individuals or companies" (Pinchot, 1974, p. 261). It also stated in part:

> The permanence of the resources of the reserves is therefore indispensable to continued prosperity, and the policy of this department for their protection and use will invariably be guided by this fact, always bearing in mind that the conservative use of these resources in no way conflicts with their permanent value.

The World Commission on Environment and Development (commonly known as the Brundtland Commission) proffered a mantra of sorts on sustainable development: to meet communities' current needs without compromising the ability of future generations to meet theirs. Similarly, the National Research Council Board on Sustainable Development (1999) described it as meshing, in the long run, society's developmental goals with its environmental limits and noting that effective efforts at sustainability require society's collective, uncertain and adaptive behaviors vis-à-vis its goals and modus operandi. Both descriptions indicate the trionym of sustainable development, most commonly referred to as the three E's—economic opportunity, environmental protection, social equity (e.g., Fedkiw, 2001):

- Economic opportunity sustains a healthy economy that will create meaningful jobs, reduce poverty, and provide high quality of life in an increasingly competitive global environment.
- Environmental protection ensures the availability of a healthy ecosystem.
- Social equity ensures that all people have access to justice and have the opportunity to achieve economic, environmental and social well-being.

That trionym is inarguably consistent with the concerns of Africans for healthy economies and environments that meet the dire needs of the present generation, as well as those of the future, while pari passu enhancing the quality of the environment. It also has major ethical implications for the regnant actions of corporations in their midst. Such implications are

even more important when cast in a historical context: At the turn of the 20th century, corporations tended to disregard the public interest willy-nilly. And even as recently as one-half
century ago, corporations had so much power over the marketplace and so little responsibility to society (Bowen, 1953; Eberstadt, 1977; Elbing & Elbing, 1967; Levitt, 1958).

A GLOBAL ETHIC

The Montréal Process, world summits on the environment, and protest movements point
to a ferment in the investigation of corporate behavior vis-à-vis sustainable development.
Stakeholder theory and CSP, together, provide the framework for communicating with multiple audiences. Stakeholder theory has attracted its own debates on its ethical foundation
and the issue of who stakeholders really are. On the one hand, Ulmer and Sellnow (2000)
argue that it lacks a normative foundation. On the other, Donaldson and Preston (1995) argue that the theory is both functionalist and normative and suggest that one way to construct
that foundation is to connect the theory with more fundamental philosophical concepts.

A second criticism is that stakeholders are not always clearly defined. Mitchell, Agle,
and Wood (1997) state that to identify stakeholders and ascertain their salience require a
consideration of their influence, legitimacy of relationship with corporation, and urgency
of their claim on a company. Therefore, the implications of stakeholder theory and of CSP
for fostering an ethic for the global corporation's contribution to sustainable development
are subsumed under five non-discrete elements, as a communication ethic: communitarianism, community engagement, mutuality of interests, the common good, commerce and
citizenship.

Communitarianism

For the African, the very notion of the self is counterproductive to her or his penchant
for communitarianism, which, in turn, explains the African penchant for tribal institutions
and her or his strong loyalty to the tribe in preference to the nation. Moemeka (1997,
1998) distinguishes among individualistic, collectivist, and communalistic cultures and
concludes that in African societies the latter are supreme: "I am because we are." An
African takes action or expresses an opinion based on its implied consistency with norms
and thought patterns in a group (Nwankwo & Nzelibe, 1990). Obeng-Quaidoo (1985)
referred to that phenomenon as the non-individuality of the African.

Communitarianism—what Moemeka (1997) refers to as the supremacy of the community—gives the community pride of place as supreme authority over the individual, who,
whenever necessary, defers to community interest. "The value of such a communalistic
principle," writes Moemeka, "lies in the unity that it sustains, the selfless service that it
generates, and the valor (honor) that it inspires" (p. 174). Similarly, Traber (1997) argues
that communitarian rationale "does not *simply* mean that the community is supreme and
that individuals have to subordinate themselves to it. It does, however, mean that there is
a moral commitment to community, aiming at both civic order and civic transformation"
(emphasis added, p. 339). Preconditions for being-in-community, as Traber (1997) puts
it, are truth-telling, social justice, solidarity, and human dignity.

For a corporation to adopt communitarianism requires that it unify with its stakeholders
who are also community residents; that it seek out areas where its citizenship can be most
creatively accomplished; and that it set itself as a model of exemplary corporate behavior
by telling the truth, engaging in a struggle for equitable social order and embracing the
ethical norm of human dignity. Global corporations that disregard the cultural attributes of

African thought and behavioral patterns or whose management styles run afoul of cultural practices perpetuate hostile work environments and earn the ire of local residents, as was the case with the Shell Petroleum Development Company in Nigeria.

Its parent, the Royal Dutch Shell Company Group, had been a target of environmentalists, particularly Greenpeace and the Movement for the Survival of the Ogoni People in southeastern Nigeria, because its actions were largely antithetical to communitarianism. In 1958 Shell began oil exploration in Nigeria's Niger delta, where the company's pipelines, about 18 inches above ground, crisscrossed the Niger delta. Flames from intense heat at points where gas burns made farming difficult and environmental damage palpable. Oil accounts for 90 percent of Nigeria's export earnings. Yet, compensation to the Ogoni people was low; their homeland had been mired in abject poverty; unemployment was high; and environmental damage on, and raids against, Ogoni communities were pronounced. Shell had colluded with Nigeria's late dictator, Sani Abacha, to amass weapons and ammunitions for the Nigerian police, to despoil the Ogoni people's homeland, and to leave them with nothing more than a pittance in royalties. Citizen protests, arrests, assassination, and intimidation were common. Shell Oil was insular, arrogant, inward-looking, defensive, and uncommunicative (Mirvis, 2000).

In 1995, Shell Company and its supporters in Nigeria's then-military government announced that there would be an environmental survey of the Niger delta. The panel was stacked with people sympathetic to both the Nigerian government and the company. The findings of that survey were fraught with irregularities. There were more protests and a call for an end to decades of environmental pollution and the payment of a fair share of oil revenues to the Ogoni people. Shell conceded, promising to respond more effectively to community demands, building schools, hospitals, community centers, and roads. It was reported that there was an overhaul of its culture into which was integrated citizenship strategies (Mirvis, 2000; Vidaver-Cohen & Altman, 2000). Such changes earned it worldwide admiration, the status of Britain's "most admired company," and the rank of top five in Europe (Vidaver-Cohen & Altman, 2000). However, the company's critics still contend that it was all too little, too late, and that real transformation in Shell's environmental and social performance in the Niger delta is yet to come (Mirvis, 2000).

Other oil companies in the delta were also targets. In July 2002, delta women took more than 700 Chevron Texaco workers hostage for the same reasons that Shell Oil had been under community attack. The women threatened to disrobe before their hostages as a cultural shaming experience for them. Chevron Texaco offered to employ 30 villagers, to build schools, community centers and a water-purification system, and to improve public health facilities in villages.

Community Engagement

Organizations use moral reasoning to arrive at organizational decisions, have cultures that embrace rationality and respect, and are dependent on multiple parties to create and recreate their own cultures and communities. As Christians, Ferré, and Fackler (1993) state, "Organizations are cultures in the sense that their members engage in producing a shared organizational reality" (p. 131). Working with communities entails much more than getting involved in community projects; it requires setting up a system for community input well before major projects are under way; it requires searching for channels by which community views are represented in organizational decision-making; it requires that corporations, as moral agencies, enunciate and share their cultures with their stakeholders; it requires that business and community interests be aligned for their mutual benefit; and it requires the sharing of organizational symbolism with all stakeholders and being influenced by that of the latter. It is a mutual process, one that might suggest that corporations "get more of what they want when they give up some of what they want" (Grunig & White, 1992, p. 39).

Engaging the grassroots is illustrated in Kenya's Green Belt Movement, whose operations fan across the entire continent. Began in 1977 when logging and deforestation were factors in the deterioration of the country's ecosystem, it employs some 100,000 people, mostly women, who have planted more than 20 million trees, which, in turn, supply their planters with fruits, leaves, and branches that are sold occasionally to local manufacturers and retailers. The movement also collaborates with global companies to promote organic farming and sustainable practices. The local women, the business sector and the environment benefit from efforts grounded in the local environment.

Key questions have been raised regarding community engagement. For example, What stakeholders should participate in corporate governance, and what are the ways and means of their representation? (Etzioni, 1998). For community representation, Etzioni suggests that communities be granted a voice in approximate proportion to the size and duration of their respective investments in corporations. And Mitchell, Agle, and Wood (1997) point to stakeholder influence, legitimacy and urgency of claim as criteria for determining stakeholder salience.

Mutuality of Interests

From the preceding section, it is clear that the various audiences who comprise an organization's stakeholders do not have equal rank—and do not communicate with the organization with equal intensity. Even if they do, do they have consistent interests? Do investors have the same community-development interests as short-term employees? Do creditors and community residents have mutual interests? And does the corporation use what Post (2000) describes as the "glocal" approach, in which it works with a local partner or builds a visible local presence through activities in the community, thereby recognizing the importance of integrating global business strategies and local interests?

As noted earlier, in June 1998, the World Bank provided a loan for further construction of a dam on the Orange River, a move that irked environmentalists who wanted impact studies on possible environmental damage before project implementation. Residents on the path of the dam saw the project as potentially hazardous to the ecosystem and as a telltale of economic hardships. Such chasm in expectations and possible outcomes is sometimes apparent between employee interest and the direction of organizational investments.

In 1998, T. Coleman Andrews III, a U.S. citizen, was hired as chairman and president of South African Airways (SAA), the national airline that was competing for passengers with a regional airline, Sun Air, and hemorrhaging financially. He flooded South Africa with cheap fares, running black-owned Sun Air into bankruptcy, but was unable to make SAA profitable. In slightly more than three years on the job, Coleman used an assertive, can-do, streamlined management style in his attempt to get the airline into the black. His management style was not driven by the African value of reaching a consensus, of demonstrating deference to authority or seniority, or of listening intently to employee complaints and acting on them. His greatest stumbling block: employees who did not see their own professional interests and cultural values as consistent with those of upper management. Tensions grew and employees embarrassed Coleman with a long list of grievances, forcing him to resign in March 2002.

As noted at the outset, African communities have development challenges, which may seem far-fetched to, say, a creditor of a multinational corporation. But there are areas in which the interests of all stakeholders intersect: All, in some measure, are investors and have a stake in the well-being of a corporation. An African community invests in a company by offering land or space, building roads and making available its labor. An investor does the same thing by giving up initial capital for future profit. Creditors make short- or long-term investments by providing services or products for future cash settlements.

Thus, to the extent that stakeholder theory accepts the legitimacy of *all* stakeholders as investors of sorts in a corporation, it is important that investors be treated as means, not as ends. Investments are a means toward corporate profitability. Therefore, investors should be treated equitable as principals whose interests are consistent with those of the corporation. One element in the trionym of sustainable development is social equity, which means that all stakeholders should have a shot at communication opportunities for social well-being and self-improvement.

Common Good

This has been defined as "everything that is good to more than one person, that perfects more than one person, that is common to all" (Argandoña, 1998, p. 1095). It is the fulfill-ment of a company's purpose as a company, that is, the creation of conditions that enable its stakeholders achieve their personal goals. The good *for* the individual translates into the good *of* the community. The 1905 letter sent by United States Secretary of Agriculture James Wilson on the transfer of authority over national forestlands to the United States Forest Service noted that "all land is to be devoted to its most productive use for the permanent good of the whole people, and not for the temporary benefit of individuals or companies" (Pinchot, 1974, p. 261). The common good, as a communication ethic, transcends the values and interests of any single group.

It can be argued that stakeholder theory is inherently divisive because it categorizes publics in accordance with their influence and legitimacy and the urgency of their corporate claims. It can be viewed as antithetical to the tenets of sustainable development, principles that have been the armor of protest publics. If those were so, then, it stands to reason that organizational communication of the common good be done in a fair, judicious, equitable manner that does not pit one group against another. Inter-group dynamics can determine what group is ahead of other groups in terms of returns on investment—creating group conflicts.

Commerce and Citizenship

Admittedly, public- and private-sector agencies have different goals: the former operates supposedly in the public interest, the latter in that of their investors, that is, to yield returns on their investment. Perhaps that is where the difference ends. In reality, both sectors have more similarities than differences: to serve as good citizens of the societies in which they operate.

An organization's level of social performance is a key measure of its citizenship. But what is good corporate citizenship? Davenport's (2000) Delphi study identified three key indicators of corporate citizenship: (1) the use of rigorous ethical standards in business dealings; (2) company commitment to all stakeholders—community, consumers, employ-ees, investors, suppliers; and (3) company commitment to the environment, that is, through programs such as recycling, waste and emission abatement, and impact assessment through environmental audits. Participants also identified 20 principles of corporate citizenship—such as invests in communities in which a business operates, respects the rights of consumers, invites and engages in genuine dialogue with stakeholders, engages in responsible human-resource management, and engages in fair trading practices with suppliers.

It is critical, then, that global organizations communicate with their stakeholders about their commitment to (1) ethical principles in business conduct, (2) all stakeholders, and (3) to the environment. That communication can be enabled by corporate participation in events or the use of innovative ideas that project activities grounded in ethics and in stakeholder and environmental commitment.

I present here two architectural illustrations of environmental sensitivity. First, in 2001, the United States Department of Agriculture Forest Products Laboratory, in collaboration with the Southern Forest Products Association, the Engineered Wood Association, and the Advanced Housing Research Center, completed a four-bedroom, 2,200-square-foot research demonstration house that showcases moisture-resistant construction techniques, proper building practices for moisture control, the use of recycled materials in home-building, resource sustainability, and energy efficiency. The building sits on a property that adjoins the campus of the University of Wisconsin, Madison. It demonstrates how the use of advanced technologies and alternative methods for home-building can improve energy efficiency, affordability, durability, environmental performance, disaster resistance, and the overall safety of housing.

Second, the use of similar technologies is being planned for urban renewal in South Africa, where Earthlife Africa in 1993 conceived the Greenhouse People's Environmental Center Project. Indigenous technologies and materials will be used to build the house at Joubert Park, in Johannesburg. The house, like that in Wisconsin, will be an epitome of green values and practices. Research on sustainable technologies and materials that will be used in the building is being done at the University of Witwatersrand.

CONCLUDING REMARKS

This chapter is based on the notion that two theoretical constructs—stakeholder theory and corporate social performance—be used as key elements in developing a communication ethic for managing sustainable development in sub-Saharan Africa. Both constructs have ethical underpinnings. In communicating the "good news" about corporate involvement in sustainable development, it is important that communication strategies used acknowledge the shift from information distribution (which, at heart, is publicity or outputs) to organizational positioning and relationship management, the ideals of symmetrical organizational communication.

That shift can symbolize the overarching importance of impressions or images that are often sought, cultivated and influenced by organizational actions. It can also be an indicator of a corporation's deliberate attempt to regulate and control information—and its presentation—so that it is consistent with the mutual interest and common good of all stakeholders. That shift, then, seems well suited to a two-pronged analysis. The first is at the corporate or organizational level, the second at the interpersonal (or individual) level.

ORGANIZATIONAL LEVEL

Communication at the corporate level requires the interplay of three dimensions: (1) visibility, that is, how prominent a corporation is in a community; (2) valence, that is, the tone in which, or the extent to which, a corporation is perceived (or portrayed) in a generally positive or negative light; and (3) public salience, that is, whether it is perceived (or portrayed) as relating directly to the common good of stakeholders.

INTERPERSONAL LEVEL

The corresponding dimensions at the *interpersonal* level, that is, the employee-villager or employee-supplier dyad, are as follows: (1) familiarity, that is, the extent to which a community resident is aware of the commitment of a corporation to the environmental; (2) favorableness, that is, a villager's evaluation of corporate activities; and (3) personal salience, that is, the extent to which corporate activities identify with the well-being or common good of community residents.

All six dimensions—at both organizational and interpersonal levels—bear on a corporation's three goals:

- To generate, through information-sharing, awareness of ethical corporate activities among all of its stakeholders.

- To better position the corporation as a major player in improving ecosystem health, —that is, brand-positioning of its "green" activities.

- To build and strengthen relationships between the corporation and all stakeholders.

RECOMMENDATIONS

The preceding analysis leads to two recommendations. The first is that the application of stakeholder theory and CSP be grounded in a communication ethic that emphasizes ethical relationship-building as necessary for communicating the "good news" of tangible corporate contributions to sustainable development in Africa. It is also advisable that attempts be made to extend that communication to the ideal two-way symmetrical process in which organizations use communication to manage conflict and improve understanding among stakeholders and to promote organization-stakeholder change.

The second is that corporations in sub-Saharan Africa engage in a culture-balancing act by co-opting indigenous cultures into their practices in ways that will foster the common good of all stakeholders, in ways that are consistent with the principles of sustainable development, and in ways that will ensure "the permanent good of the whole people, and not for the temporary benefit" (Pinchot, 1974, p. 216) of those corporations. Such corporate actions will assuage the activist groups, engender better relationships between the global corporation and its stakeholders, demonstrate sensitivity to the environmental impacts of corporate actions, enable a number of global organizations to rise well above their occasional disreputable status, and, above all, foster and sustain a region's much-needed development.

REFERENCES

Argandoña, A. (1998). The stakeholder theory and the common good. *Journal of Business Ethics, 17*, 1093–1102.

Aupperle, K. E., Carroll, A. B., & Hatfield, J. D. (1985). An empirical investigation of the relationship between corporate social responsibility and profitability. *Academy of Management Journal, 28*, 446–463.

Bansal, P., & Roth K. (2000). Why companies go green: A model of ecological responsiveness. *Academy of Management Journal, 43*, 717–736.

Belkaoui, A. (1976). The impact of the disclosure of the environmental effects of organizational behavior on the market. *Financial Management, 5*, 26–31.

Bowen, H. R. (1953). *Social responsibilities of the businessman*. New York: Harper & Brothers.

Carroll, A. B. (1979). A three-dimensional conceptual model of corporate social performance. *Academy of Management Review, 4*, 497–505.

Carroll, A. B. (1989). *Business and society.* Cincinnati, OH: Southwestern.

Carroll, A. B. (1991). Corporate social performance measurement: A commentary on methods for evaluating an elusive construct. In J. E. Post (Ed.), *Research in corporate social performance and policy: A research annual, Vol. 12* (pp. 385–401). Greenwich, CT: JAI Press.

Carson, R. (1962). *Silent spring.* New York: Houghton Mifflin.

Christians, C. G., Ferré, J. P., & Fackler, P. M. (1993). *Good news: Social ethics and the press.* New York: Oxford University Press.

Cohen, S. (1995). Stakeholders and consent. *Business & Professional Ethics, 14*, 3–16.

Davenport, K. (2000). Corporate citizenship: A stakeholder approach for defining corporate social performance and identifying measures for assessing it. *Business and Society, 39*, 210–219.

Dillon, P. W., & Fischer, K. (1992). *Environmental management in corporations.* Medford, MA: Tufts University Center for Environmental Management.

Donaldson, T. (1989). *The ethics of international business.* New York: Oxford University Press.

Donaldson, T., & Preston, L. (1995). The stakeholder theory of the modern corporation: Concepts, evidence, implications. *Academy of Management Review, 20*, 65–91.

Eberstadt, N. (1977). What history tells us about corporate responsibilities. In A. B. Carroll (Ed.), *Managing corporate social responsibility* (pp. 17–22). Boston: Little Brown.

Elbing, A. O., Jr., & Elbing, C. J. (1967). *The value issue of business.* New York: McGraw-Hill.

Etzioni, A. (1998). A communitarian note on stakeholder theory. *Business Ethics Quarterly, 8*, 679–691.

Evan, W. M., & Freeman, R. E. (1988). A stakeholder theory of the modern corporation: Kantian capitalism. In T. L. Beauchamp & N. E. Bowie (Eds.), *Ethical theory and business* (pp. 97–106). Englewood Cliffs, NJ: Prentice-Hall.

Fedkiw, J. (2001, March-April). *Sustainability and the pathway hypothesis.* Paper presented at the American Society for Environmental History/Forest History Society Joint Annual Meeting, Durham, NC.

Frederick, W. C. (1986). *Theories of corporate social performance: Much done, more to do.* Working paper, Joseph M. Katz Graduate School of Business, University of Pittsburgh.

Freeman, R. E. (1984). *Strategic management: A stakeholder approach.* Boston: Pitman.

Freeman, R. E., & Gilbert, D. R. (1988). *Corporate strategy and the search for ethics.* Englewood Cliffs: Prentice-Hall.

Freeman, R. E., & Reed, D. L. (1983). Stockholders and stakeholders: A new perspective on corporate governance. *California Management Review, 25*, 88–106.

Frooman, J. (1997). Socially irresponsible and illegal behavior and shareholder wealth: A meta-analysis of event studies. *Business & Society, 36*, 221–249.

Graves, S. B., & Waddock, S. A. (1994). Institutional owners and corporate social performance. *Academy of Management Journal, 37*, 1035–1046.

Grunig, J. E. (2001). Two-way symmetrical public relations: Past, present and future. In R. L. Heath (Ed.), *Handbook of public relations* (pp. 11–30). Thousand Oaks, CA: Sage.

Grunig, J. E., & Repper, F. C. (1992). Strategic management, public, and issues. In J. E. Grunig (Ed.), *Excellence in public relations and communication management* (pp. 117–157). Hillsdale, NJ: Lawrence Erlbaum and Associates.

Grunig, J. E., & White, J. (1992). The effect of worldviews on public relations theory and practice. In J. E. Grunig (Ed.), *Excellence in public relations and communication management* (pp. 31–64). Hillsdale, NJ: Lawrence Erlbaum and Associates.

Held, D., McGrew, A., Goldblatt, D., & Perraton, J. (1999). *Global transformations: Economics, politics and culture.* Cambridge: Polity Press.

Jones, T. M., & Wicks, A. C. (1999). Convergent stakeholder theory. *Academy of Management Review, 24*, 206–221.

Lawrence, A. T., & Morell, D. (1995). Leading-edge environmental management: Motivation, opportunity, resources, and processes. In D. Collins & M. Starik (Eds.), *Research in corporate social performance and policy, supplement 1* (pp. 99–126). Greenwich, CT: JAI Press.

Levitt, T. (1958). The dangers of social responsibility. *Harvard Business Review, 36*, 41–50.

Ledingham, J. A., & Bruning, S. D. (1998). Relationship management in public relations: Dimensions of an organization-public relationship. *Public Relations Review, 24*, 55–66.

Ledingham, J. A. (2001). Government-community relationships: Extending the relational theory to public relations. *Public Relations Review, 27*, 285–295.

Luce, R. A., Barber, A. E., & Hillman, A. J. (2001). Good deeds and misdeeds: A mediated model of the effect of corporate social performance on organizational attractiveness. *Business & Society, 40*, 397–415.

Marsden, C. (2000). The new corporate citizenship of big business: Part of the solution to sustainability? *Business and Society Review, 105*, 9–25.

Marsh, G. P. (1864). *Man and nature; or, physical geography as modified by human action.* New York: Charles Scribner.

McKee, J. F. (2001, January 26). Saving the environment, one (fewer) child at a time. *The Chronicle Review,* p. B20.

McNatt, R., & Light, L. (1998, February 16). Good works—and great profits. *Business Week,* 8.

McWilliams, A., & Siegel, D. (2000). Corporate social responsibility and financial performance: Correlations or misspecification?" *Strategic Management Journal, 21*, 603–609.

Meyerson, A. R. (1999, January 31). Techies discover the joys of giving. *The New York Times,* pp. 1, 11.

Mirvis, P. H. (2000). Transformation at Shell: Commerce and citizenship. *Business and Society Review, 105*, 63–84.

Mitchell, R. K., Agle, B. R., & Wood, D. J. (1997). Toward a theory of stakeholder identification and salience: Defining the principle of who and what really counts. *Academy of Management Review, 22*, 853–886.

Moemeka, A. A. (1997). Communalistic societies: Community and self-respect as African values. In C. Christians & M. Traber (Eds.), *Communication ethics and universal values* (pp. 170–193). Thousand Oaks, CA: Sage.

Moemeka, A. A. (1998). Communalism as a fundamental dimension of culture. *Journal of Communication, 48*, 118–141.

Muirhead, S. A., Bennett, C. J., Berenbeim, R. E., Kao, A., & Vidal, D. J. (2002, July). *Corporate citizenship in the new century: Accountability, transparency, and global stakeholder engagement.* New York: The Conference Board.

National Research Council Board on Sustainable Development. (1999). *Our common journey: A transition toward sustainability.* Washington, DC: National Academy Press.

Nwankwo, R. L. N., & Nzelibe, C. G. (1990). Communication and conflict management in African development. *Journal of Black Studies, 20*, 253–266.

Obeng-Quaidoo, I. (1985). Culture and communication research methodologies in Africa: A proposal for change. *Gazette: International Journal for Mass Communication Studies, 36*, 109–120.

O'Connor, J. (2000, November). Corporate citizenship. *Industrial Distribution, 89*, 142.

Pava, M. L., & Krausz, J. (1996). The association between corporate social responsibility and financial performance: The paradox of social cost. *Journal of Business Ethics, 15*, 321–357.

Phillips, R.A. (1997). Stakeholder theory and a principle of fairness. *Business Ethics Quarterly, 7*, 51–66.

Pinchot, G. (1974). *Breaking new ground.* Washington, DC: Island Press.

Posnikoff, J. F. (1997). Disinvestment from South Africa: They did well by doing good. *Contemporary Economic Policy, 15*, 76–86.

Post, J. E. (2000). Moving from geographic to virtual communities: Global corporate citizenship in a dot-com world. *Business and Society Review, 105*, 27–46.

Preston, L. (1978). Analyzing corporate social performance: Methods and results. *Journal of Contemporary Business, 7*, 135–150.

Quinn, D., & Jones, T. M. (1995). An agent morality view of business policy. *Academy of Management Review, 20*, 22–42.

Riordan, C. M., Gatewood, R. D., & Bill, J. B. (1997). Corporate image: Employee reactions and implications for managing corporate social performance. *Journal of Business Ethics, 16*, 401–412.

Sharfman, M. (1996). The construct validity of the Kinder, Lydenberg, and Domini social performance ratings data. *Journal of Business Ethics, 15*, 287–296.

Solomon, R. C., & Hanson, K. R. (1985). *It's good business*. Atheneum: New York.

Stanwick, P. A., & Stanwick, S. D. (1998). The relationship between corporate social performance, and organizational size, financial performance, and environmental performance: An empirical examination. *Journal of Business Ethics, 17*, 195–204.

Strand, R., Levine, R., & Montgomery, D. (1981). Organizational entry preferences based upon social and personnel policies: An information integration perspective. *Organizational Behavior and Human Performance, 27*, 50–68.

Teoh, S. H., Welch, I., & Wazzan C. P. (1999). The effect of socially activist investment policies on the financial markets: Evidence from the South African boycott. *Journal of Business, 72*, 35–89.

Traber, M. (1997). Conclusion: An ethics of communication worthy of human beings. In C. Christians & M. Traber (Eds.), *Communication ethics and universal values.* (pp. 327–343.). Thousand Oaks, CA: Sage.

Turban, D. B., & Greening, D. W. (1997). Corporate social performance and organizational attractiveness to prospective employees. *Academy of Management Journal, 40*, 658–672.

Ulmer, R. R., & Sellnow, T. L. (2000). Consistent questions of ambiguity in organizational crisis communication: Jack in the Box as a case study. *Journal of Business Ethics, 25*, 143–155.

Vidaver-Cohen, D., & Altman, B. W. (2000). Corporate citizenship in the new millennium: Foundation for an architecture of excellence. *Business and Society Review, 105*, 145–168.

Waddock, S. A., & Graves, S. B. (1997). The corporate social performance-financial performance link. *Strategic Management Journal, 18*, 303–319.

Waddock, S., & Smith, N. (2000). Relationships: The real challenge of corporate global citizenship. *Business and Society Review, 105*, 47–62.

Wartick, S. L., & Cochran, P. L. (1985). The evolution of the corporate social performance model. *Academy of Management Review 10*, 758–769.

Went, R. (2000). *Globalization: Neoliberal challenge, radical responses*. London: Pluto.

Windsor, D. (1998, June). *The definition of stakeholder status*. Paper presented at the annual conference of the International Association for Business and Society, Kona-Kailua, HI.

Winn, M. (1995). Corporate leadership and policies for the natural environment. In D. Collins & M. Starik (Eds.), *Research in corporate social performance and policy, supplement 1* (pp. 127–161). Greenwich, CT: JAI Press.

Wolfe, R., & Aupperle, K. (1991). Introduction to corporate social performance: Methods for evaluating an elusive construct. In J. E. Post (Ed.), *Research in corporate social performance and policy: A research annual, Vol. 12* (pp. 265–268). Greenwich, CT: JAI Press.

Wood, D. J. (1991a). Corporate social performance revisited. *Academy of Management Review, 16*, 691–718.

Wood, D. J. (1991b). Social issues in management: Theory and research in corporate social performance. *Journal of Management 17*, 383–406.

Wood, D. J., & Jones, R. E. (1995). Stakeholder mismatching: A theoretical problem in empirical research on corporate social performance. *International Journal of Organizational Analysis, 3*, 229–267.

Wright, P., & Ferris, S. P. (1997). Agency conflict and corporate strategy: The effect of divestment on corporate value. *Strategic Management Journal, 18*, 77–83.

Krishnamurthy, Sriramesh and Dejan Vercic, ed. The Global Public
Relations Handbook: Theory, Research and Practice.
Lawrence Erlbaum Associates, 2003.

CHAPTER

22

SERVING PUBLIC RELATIONS GLOBALLY: THE AGENCY PERSPECTIVE

AMY RUDGARD

This chapter is designed to provide insight into international public relations (PR) from an agency perspective. To do this, we must recognize the role of international public relations agencies. Despite the fact that in today's marketplace nearly every PR agency includes "international PR" as part of its offering, for the purposes of this chapter, this term refers to those agencies capable of handling an international assignment from conceptualization to implementation, via its network of offices and professionals at local market level. There are nearly two dozen firms today whose network spans every continent. However, some have played a more significant role than others in the evolution of international PR in the realm of agencies.

THE EVOLUTION OF THE INTERNATIONAL PUBLIC RELATIONS AGENCY

Hill and Knowlton is recognized as the first-ever international PR agency and can probably claim to have had the most impact on the development of international PR. In 1927, John Hill founded the agency that would eventually become Hill and Knowlton International Public Relations in Cleveland, Ohio. Instead of working on his own, as was the practice in those days, Hill hired other agents and trained them to work in his "style"—thus becoming, in effect, the founder of the modern-day PR consultancy. In 1933 Hill was joined by Don Knowlton, and Hill and Knowlton was officially born. The firm moved its headquarters to New York in 1934 and, during the 1950s, became the first United States agency to build a European network.

In 1952, Hill and Knowlton became the first American PR consultancy to recognize the business communication implications of the formation of the European Economic Community. The agency established a network of affiliates across Europe and became the first United States PR firm to have wholly owned offices in Europe. In 1980 the company was bought by the advertising agency J. Walter Thompson. Expansion led to the firm's current network of offices and Hill and Knowlton became the first United States PR firm to open an office in Budapest, Hungary. Today, its Europe Middle East & Africa (EMEA) network consists of 28 wholly owned offices in 21 countries, with associates in a further 16 countries. The EMEA region, headquartered in London, boasts that multinational assignments (in two or more markets) account for over half of its business in the region.

After establishing itself in Europe, H&K continued to achieve international dominance by being the first PR firm into new marketplaces such as the People's Republic of China. It has been operating in Asia for more than 30 years and currently has 250 specialists either in its offices or that of its associates in every major business center in the region. It is one of the few agencies to have a substantial wholly owned network of offices in Latin America and claims to be Canada's leading strategic communications company. It remains strong in the United States its home market, where it is ranked third.

Hill & Knowlton has never looked back since it first set foot on European soil. Its acquisition in 1987 by one of the largest marketing communications services groups, WPP, only fueled its growth and international dominance. Today, the firm consists of 2000 employees across 70 offices in 36 countries across Asia, Europe, the Americas, Africa, and the Middle East. Some of the firm's prestigious international clients include Kellogg, American Express, and GE Capital.

The other highly influential agency is Burson-Marsteller, which was created in 1953 with the marriage of two already established businesses—Harold Burson's public relations firm and Bill Marsteller's advertising agency. For about the first 15 years, Burson-Marsteller (B-M) was primarily a business-to-business specialist. But with the 1957 Treaty of Rome and the creation of the European Economic Community, B-M realized the need to expand and redefine its business. One of its first moves was the pursuit of large, multinational clients with communication needs across the globe, and with it, the need to expand beyond business-to-business PR. By 1959, B-M had broadened its capabilities to include consumer, public affairs, and marketing communications.

In the 1960s, B-M could see that Hill & Knowlton, the industry leader, could genuinely claim the territory of serving clients in Europe. With its own expansion into the continent, B-M demonstrated the seriousness of its intentions to challenge the dominance of Hill & Knowlton. Harold Burson successfully established himself as an industry leader in Europe, lecturing on public relations and attracting press interest for the firm. All the effort paid off, helping B-M continue its international expansion and increase revenues from $4.4 million in 1969 to $28.3 million in 1979. At that time, the company had 17 offices in 12 countries with 600 employees and was acquired by Young & Rubicam, retaining its name.

By 1983, B-M became the world's largest PR firm and by 1985, was the first to reach $100 million in revenues. It also continued expanding its offices to 45 in 23 countries. During the 1990s, B-M expanded its expertise to address the emerging technology sector and added a further 16 offices. In 1992, it became the first agency to reach $200 million in revenues. Today, B-M's global revenues stand at approximately $304 million with 1600 employees and a network spanning 34 countries with 24 offices in Asia/Pacific, 35 in the Europe, Middle East and Africa, 19 in North America, and 10 in Latin America.

Both Hill & Knowlton and Burson-Marsteller remain dominant figures in the marketplace today, *PR Week*'s Global Agency rankings for the year 2000 (based on income) puts Hill & Knowlton third, followed by Burson-Marsteller.

As Hill & Knowlton and Burson-Marsteller ploughed forward, other PR visionaries were following not too far behind. Richard Edelman opened his firm in 1952 and established himself as an expert in marketing communications, product launches, and brand-building. In 1965, the firm began its international expansion by opening an office in London. In 2000, Edelman remained sixth in *PR Week's* Top Global Agency rankings, which is particularly worth noting due to the fact that it is one of the few international firms to remain independent, as it has not (yet) been acquired by any one of the major marketing communications conglomerates. In addition, Cooper & Golin (today's Golin/Harris International) expanded to London in the mid-1960s. In 1974, Peter Gummer, or Lord Chadlington as he is now known, created Shandwick Public Relations in London. Today, following several mergers, it is known as Weber Shandwick.

In the late 1980s, Fleishman-Hilliard began its own expansion into Europe. Fleishman-Hilliard is an interesting story considering that it was founded in 1946, had fewer than 60 employees until 1980, but grew by 1990 to employ 600. It opened its doors for business outside the United States in 1987 when it opened F-H Europe. In 2000, F-H is ranked second by *PR Week*, losing its #1 spot to the new Weber Shandwick following its merger with BSMG. F-H has more than 2300 employees in 83 offices. Its revenues for 2001 were $345 million. F-H states its overall approach to international public relations as centred around global capabilities with local practitioners who understand the local market's business and marketing practices, government issues and regulations as well as social customs. F-H explains that its local managers have years of experience in national communications and are able to ensure that clients' international programs are designed and implemented in the most effective and appropriate ways.

However, the creation of international PR agencies was not purely fueled by the expansion of their clients because mergers and acquisitions also played a part. There has been the formation of agencies like Porter Novelli International, created in 1996 when North American PR powerhouse Porter Novelli merged with Countrywide Communications Group, a UK and European firm. Major advertising and marketing conglomerates have acquired many of the top international PR firms in an effort to complement the network of their flagship advertising agencies. These companies offer integrated marketing services utilizing their sister companies' expertise in public relations, media buying, web marketing, and customer relationship marketing. This has proved a successful relationship for both sides, expanding the role of the advertising executive while providing additional financial resources and new business opportunities for the international PR agency.

Perhaps one of the more recent, and interesting, examples of such an acquisition is the story of Shandwick International's acquisition by IPG, the $7 billion advertising and marketing conglomerate. Shandwick was founded in 1974 by Lord Chadlington (known then as Peter Gummer) in London. To form his network, he handpicked many of his associate agencies who often were national specialists in a particular type of communication. As the firm expanded internationally, it became the only real contender on a global level that had its roots in Europe—a truly international marketplace. With headquarters and a real center of excellence in London, it was naturally well positioned to handle and develop regional or even global business for the firm. Shandwick was one of the first international PR agencies to go after European companies that had international interests—showing them that to be competitive with their American counterparts, they needed to consider the benefits of appointing a major PR firm to advise and help implement their communications around the globe.

Unlike Hill & Knowlton or Burson-Marsteller, who had set up their networks primarily to handle communications for American firms that wanted to expand to foreign markets,

Shandwick was advising major European firms that were either expanding internationally or had international interests. Some of Shandwick's international clients included the Dutch overnight courier firm TNT Express Worldwide (now part of TNT) that was competing with UPS, DHL, and Federal Express, and the mobile phone and cordless products division of Siemens, the German conglomerate. One of Shandwick International's first and longest international clients was 3i, upon which Lord Chadlington founded the firm and for whom Shandwick handled communications across Europe for more than 25 years. Over time, the firm began to strengthen its network offering in the United States and brought major American firms such as Compaq into its fold. The acquisition by IPG (like many of the other PR agencies purchased by advertising and marketing conglomerates) provided Shandwick with additional financial resources to acquire more agencies and bolster its network and services around the world. By the early part of 2000, Shandwick had 1,731 staff with a network of 122 wholly owned, associated and affiliated offices in 61 countries.

Lord Chadlington remained chairman for two years before moving on to new endeavors and it was at that point that Weber Shandwick was born. IPG merged Shandwick International with one of its technology PR specialist companies, The Weber Group. Weber Shandwick further increased its size and capabilities when IPG merged it with BSMG one year later. Today, the firm is the number one global PR agency according to the 2000 *PR Week* rankings and is, undoubtedly, the largest PR agency in the world (certainly in terms of fee income and probably staff too—with more than 3000 throughout its network).

No matter how these global agencies evolved, there is no doubt that they have helped transform the landscape of international public relations. The agencies have made international—even global PR—truly possible through their networks and connections to practitioners across the world that has been hard for many companies to afford or recreate in-house. The practitioners throughout their network have helped transfer public relations concepts and skills from one part of the world to the next, even making public relations in some markets more sophisticated. The scale of the assignments and the commitment by world-renowned clients has shown businesses, small and large, the power of public relations. In addition, clients cannot make such an investment without being able to see a demonstrable return on their investments—driving forward the development of PR evaluation methods. All of this has helped to make public relations a more valued and respected marketing tool.

THE AGENCY'S ROLE AND OFFERING TO THE MARKETPLACE

What exactly do international PR agencies offer their clients, what benefits and advantages do they bring to their business? In researching for this chapter, a number of international public relations professionals—both practitioners for multinational clients as well as agency consultants were consulted. A key topic of discussion was what did these professionals believe to be the most popular reasons for organizations to choose an international PR agency and its network?

The reason stated most often by both groups is the need for the organization to *have more control and consistency over its international communication*. Without an internal PR team, an organization will struggle to ensure that its external and internal communication is consistent and timely. Even with an internal PR team, the structure can interfere with consistent and timely communications. For example, the in-house teams are focused solely around the headquarters and do not have the staff to handle local market communications. Another situation might involve local management in charge of local market communication that can often result in no single person being assigned to the function or several different local PR agencies handling it from one country to the next. Either way, the end result is often patchy with different materials, messages and styles of communication.

The second most popular reason given was *a lack of internal resources or expertise within the company*. This can be the result of a company being a start-up, which previously has not needed a formal communications structure or does not need one full time. Alternatively, a firm might have a very established team internally, but this in-house team might lack the appropriate skills. For example, the team may have focused purely on business and financial PR around the globe and not have consumer PR expertise. Another example might be a situation where an organization is looking to make changes to its communications but can't change its structure. A new global head of PR might be appointed to find local staff with varied skills and expertise and without the power to make changes in staff at a local level. The new global executive might find it easier to improve the quality and nature of the firm's communications by appointing an international PR agency to support the local practitioners and enhance their everyday work. Today's international agencies have specialists across many practices and service areas in most of their major offices and are able to provide a great depth of expertise from across the organization—both by practice and geographically.

Rapid business expansion, often with growth into new/unfamiliar markets, was cited as another business driver for hiring an international PR agency. A firm that has been very successful in its home market and decides to embark on an international expansion strategy requires strong communication (as a one-off or on a longer term basis). This can be particularly true of consumer-oriented businesses. Most often such a firm will have an established team of PR professionals handling communication in its home market but they usually have very little experience handling PR in other parts of the world. Alternatively, this situation applies to a start-up organization in a high-growth business such as the technology sector during the 1990s. Such businesses do not have a communications structure and cannot build internal resources fast enough or find enough experienced practitioners to keep up with global growth.

Another reason mentioned included an international firm that is *suddenly facing an international communication need, announcement, issue or crisis and/or the need for impact/results quickly around the world*. Perhaps the organization is facing a major international crisis such as a product recall, or product boycott, or perhaps the organization becomes the subject of a takeover or merger. In both cases, strong international communications is required for a limited time and the organization might simply not have any, or sufficient, resources to handle it. Neither situation would justify the hiring of additional staff as a short-term contract with an agency will do the job. An interesting reason raised by both groups was the situation in which an organization recognizes *the need for an international PR program, but it does not have the support or buy-in of local management*. In such a situation, it can be difficult for senior communications professionals with an international focus to achieve the organization's goals. However, this situation can often be tackled through the appointment of an international PR agency paid and managed directly by the senior communications professional.

A desire for greater cost-savings and cooperation across local PR teams/managers was cited as an advantage to clients. When talking of cost-savings, some agency practitioners might prefer to refer to "better value for money" as the savings resulting from working with an international agency network are not always visible on the bottom line. However, in the most direct manner of obtaining cost savings, some clients negotiate discounts on fees with agencies when they appoint a selected agency to work across a number of markets or an entire region. Clients also can achieve better value for money through less duplication of materials and tools. This can also apply to events or activities such as press launches or media competitions. The time and scale required to make either of these two activities successful is often difficult for an individual market to handle or finance on its own. This also links into better cooperation across local PR teams. This can be particularly important when trying to ensure managers do not work in isolation focusing only on their market with little or no knowledge of other colleagues' activities. An international agency is often hired to handle a coordination role with local markets, gathering and sharing information across all PR managers, producing consistent tools and materials to support all PR managers and running workshops that bring all PR managers together for training, strategic direction, and a common understanding of their roles and responsibilities.

An organization is not able to justify the head count of an in-house international PR team is another practical reason cited for hiring an international agency. Often, the organization is willing to put marketing budget toward PR activities but cannot, or will not, commit a budget to hiring a team internally to oversee strategy and implementation. In this case, one PR professional or even a small team might be created at global or regional level within the organization and they will use an international PR agency as the "arms and legs" across the region.

A slightly worrying but perhaps real reason for hiring an international agency as cited by consultants is that *it provides the means for an international PR head to justify his or her position, gain control, and increase sphere of influence within the marketing department and organization.* An international PR director may find it difficult to justify his or her position if he or she does not have a network of local PR practitioners or an international agency network—as one individual or even a small team—and his or her position may become questionable and unmanageable. In addition, as many PR practitioners can report, PR often comes second or is overlooked by senior management in the marketing mix. Many marketers will state that this is a result of the unpredictable nature and inability for clear evaluation of PR. Either way, the issue remains that senior PR practitioners often struggle within their own organization to gain strong support or commitment to the PR effort—as was already cited as a barrier to success by the practitioners we contacted for this chapter. In such a situation, the appointment of an agency, and the agency's support and professional approach, often enables the in-house manager to deliver better results, build a more effective argument for greater support of PR, and ultimately increase his or her sphere of influence within the marketing team.

The final reason cited was agency practitioners' *knowledge of local media and culture.* It is interesting to note that this reason was not cited more often even though many agencies use this as a selling point when they pitch their service. It appears that these two factors are not deemed important or, perhaps, simply taken for granted.

According to Dominic Shales, Vice President of Marketing, Europe, Middle East and Africa for Hill & Knowlton, "it is important for all our agencies to be as good as the best of the local competition in every market and we do mostly achieve this. That, with the added access to talent, experience, cross-border management expertise and the bank of knowledge and systems, is really why clients want to buy into international networks" (personal communication, June 2002).

In the words of Michael Leyer, director of public relations for Siemens mobile phones, the reasons behind their decision to work with Weber Shandwick was:

> Our organization benefits from Weber Shandwick's strong expertise in consumer public relations. We also value their ability to provide greater consistency–particularly in our messages across all markets, grant a high quality of service to the international media, provide monitoring and evaluation at an international level and therefore providing data on our ROI. (Personal communication, November, 2001)

AREAS OF SERVICE OFFERED BY INTERNATIONAL PR AGENCIES

Some of the common areas of service that a client organization can expect from an international PR agency are:

1. *Coordination.* This is the role of the lead team in liaison with the PR professionals of the local market, whether in-house or agency staff, to ensure that information is gathered and shared in a consistent manner. Usually, this is handled through regular conference calls, dedicated and secure extranet sites, and fax. Most agencies will use a template "report" form to ensure consistency in the type of information gathered as well as a "news bulletin" document to ensure that the information disseminated is accurate and consistent.

2. *Strategy and program development.* This refers to strategic counsel and advice for communication-related matters. Often, many agencies have the luxury of bringing many "heads" together to formulate the best advice or find a creative solution to a client's problem. Many in-house PR staff can rarely draw on the resources, particularly at an international level, or dedicate the time to focus on a problem as an agency can. This is paid for "thinking" time with a multinational cap on. According to Dominic Shales, "the most important thing is a clear and simple strategy which not only pays full attention to local needs, but that also carries a central theme under which a range of local initiatives can be successfully implemented."

3. *Creativity.* Generating ideas and creative thinking is not a new agency service, but within an international agency, the added advantage is that the ideas should be more relevant to the markets where they need to be implemented. Agencies often brainstorm a selection of tactics for which in-house staff or the local market implementation teams can review, discuss, and shape to fit their local market needs. In other cases, the agency's responsibilities might be more centralized, in which they are brainstorming ideas for a regional or global campaign platform that all local market implementation must follow. Either way, their brainstorming process will draw on their international resources and ideas will be tested in the relevant markets to determine which one(s) are the most appropriate.

4. *Tools and materials development.* This is possibly the most common service an international PR agency, particularly the lead team, may offer. Central tools and materials reduce duplication of effort and costs while ensuring consistency of message and style. The lead team will often draft all content and even production, including ensuring that materials are translated into local languages for the relevant markets (particularly if their network is employed as well). Many agencies use a "toolkit" approach—in which ideas brainstormed to support the creative platform are included in the toolkit with materials to support each concept. Agencies often coordinate the distribution of materials (many use a PR intranet or extranet) and handle any additional questions or requests that local market staff might have in relation to the materials.

5. *Fostering best practice.* This is the role of the agency in encouraging all staff (theirs or the client's) to achieve the best PR practice possible. Many agencies provide for client training in areas such as media training for international spokespeople in multiple languages or PR training for in-house PR managers. They facilitate workshops enabling in-house staff to share their problems, best work, and experiences to learn from it and enhance their communications. Another task the agency often undertakes is the creation of guides or policies for handling crises or product launches. This might even extend to specific assignments directly relevant to their business, such as use of a celebrity spokesperson for a cosmetic company or handling communication around a plane crash for an airline. The agency can often remain objective in this role, making assessments and recommendations to a client where there is a need/opportunity for better PR practice.

6. *Quality control.* Ensuring that the public relations service is of the highest quality can be a time-consuming task particularly in an organization with a lot of proactive communication. A thinly resourced team cannot possibly be on top of all communication activities happening across 25 countries. Many lead teams at an international agency are able to stay on top of PR activities worldwide on a weekly basis, providing a status report on a weekly or monthly basis to clients and raising serious concerns as soon as they arise. This might extend to the agency taking a more proactive role in preparing guides to the international PR practitioners as to how PR and media relations should be handled on behalf of the company—the do's and don'ts, for example

7. *Implementation.* This refers to delivering and carrying out PR activities at a local, regional, and/or international level. The agency might operate in a fixed number of markets on retainer or tap into markets as and when they are needed. With many of the online systems and staff training available at top agencies, staff is able to come up to speed on a project or account quickly. In its fullest implementation role, the local agency would usually be responsible for customizing, translating, and preparing all materials for local distribution. They would prepare the media lists and usually handle the follow-up calls with the media, reporting status and results to the local client and central lead team. If there is any media organization that spans borders or is deemed so influential that only "corporate" or regional/global executive management handle interviews/comment, often the agency lead team—when employed to handle media relations—will assign the lead team to take on this type of "international" media. Otherwise, the local agencies handle the country-specific media with local client management as spokespeople. The agency would also provide the human resources to handle the development, logistics, and execution of any events, media promotions/competitions, publicity stunts, etc.

8. *Reporting.* Creating and managing consistent and easy-to-understand methods that can be used by all PR practitioners to report work-in-progress, work planned, work completed, results, issues/problems, etc. This often includes media monitoring and the central collection of media coverage. Many agencies use templates in paper form or online to collect this information in a timely and routine fashion. Online systems often enable quick and easy access and review by the central client and agency team or for easy consolidation into an executive summary report.

9. *Intelligence.* Intelligence includes using PR outcomes and reports, often media coverage, to provide insights across the communications structure and throughout the rest of the organization—for example, sales, marketing, senior management. Many clients will ask agencies to help prepare information that will keep their other communications teams (e.g., a corporate/financial team) in the loop on the consumer PR activities and results. The agency might produce a PR Highlights report, outlining the best work/results achieved internationally, to show relevant management how the company's recent news has been

received and to show off their successes. Some companies' sales staff will use a selection of the best media coverage to send or e-mail to their buyers to aid the sales process. Marketing management might be interested to know how the firm is doing against a major competitor via reports that provide insights and analysis taken from media coverage and comparing product reviews, share of voice, journalist endorsement, and so forth.

10. *Evaluation and Measurement.* Establish and manage methods of measuring and evaluating the PR effort. This usually consists of evaluation against individual PR projects and the annual PR program objectives. Agencies often devise evaluation methods such as a system for analyzing international media coverage, and international journalist audits to ascertain whether they believe a client's communication has improved or what messages they retained from a press conference/briefing. The agency will then create templates and instructions for local practitioners to implement locally and ensure that data is captured consistently. The central team can then analyze all the international data easily, producing a summary report detailing the outcome and insights into that outcome.

11. *Resourcing.* Resourcing includes providing consultants for secondments (the industry term for the practice where a consultancy loans a consultant to a client organization on a short or long-term fixed contract to work as a member of that client organization yet still employed by the consultancy) or providing support in recruitment and hiring of in-house staff. Some international agencies provide their own PR consultants to clients on secondment when additional resource is needed (during a major project, crisis or if an in-house PR executive is on leave for maternity or illness). Some international agencies will also provide resources if a client's in-house executive resigns and a replacement has not yet been found. At the same time, the agency might also help the client find the replacement by helping to prepare the job description, outline the recommended criteria and qualifications and even identify and interview potential candidates.

An agency might be hired to perform one, or all, of the above services, but this usually depends on the nature of the assignment and the structure of the client organization. There are typically three classifications of international accounts as defined within the agency environment.

1. *International lead team.* This typically involves hiring an international "dream team" of consultants from across its network and specialist practices to handle strategic, creative, and centralised functions but they are not involved in any local implementation. This is often the situation when an organization has in-house PR managers in local markets and, perhaps, even some local PR agencies on retainer as well. The international lead team might coordinate across the in-house PR managers and other local PR agencies but would have no direct role in local implementation.

2. *International centralized program management.* This often comprises of an international lead team as well as local market teams to handle implementation. However, the local market teams are not always exclusively part of the same agency as the lead team. For example, the client might insist that agencies that already exist can remain and in countries without an agency, a pitch is held with the "agency of choice" automatically included on the pitch list. Occasionally, in the situation of an organization that has a strong in-house international PR team but very few PR managers at a local level, they might hire an international agency network purely for implementation, without need for the services of an international lead team.

3. *International de-centralized program management.* This tends to be a less common structure in which an international agency is hired to work in multiple markets or regions without a lead agency or team coordinating activities in a centralized way. For example, a client might wish for North America and the different European regions (Northern,

Southern, Eastern Europe, etc.) to have autonomy in their local PR and communications, but hire one agency to work in all areas to secure best practice as well as cost-savings.

It is difficult to say which of the above three structures is best because selecting the appropriate method depends on the client organization's structure and goals. The group of professionals that were interviewed as part of the research for this chapter were asked to choose what they thought was the best of these three structures for achieving consistency in communication and good results in media coverage. An overwhelming majority said the best structure is to appoint one central lead agency and give an incentive to local managers to use the same agency locally. If the relationship should prove unsuccessful, they can choose to look for an independent local agency. According to Dominic Shales of Hill & Knowlton, when delivering a one-agency solution "you have to have the ability to deliver client programmes as effectively in *each* country. H&K has focused on building up a network of offices that are typically top five (one or two in most cases) in every local market, with the corresponding specialist skills required" (personal communication). Of the practitioners interviewed for this chapter, many of those who sit on the "client side" also felt that a good structure is to appoint the central lead agency but leave the local agency selection to the decision of the local management. There was not much support for the idea of imposing one agency centrally as well as locally.

This is not surprising because many clients do not have the authority or are constrained by strong internal politics when trying to impose a "one agency for all" approach. One only has to spend a few minutes with an agency's regional or global account director who has used such an approach to understand why many of them do not support it either. They can recount war stories of clients with unrealistic expectations about using "one agency" or others who held a grudge (counterproductive to the PR effort, no less) as a result of their favorite agency losing out or because they had no say in the final decision. They also will be fair in saying that no agency network is perfect. Every international agency has its strong and weak offices. When the agency is imposed in every market, the local client that gets the weak office is surely losing out—but agency staff is often caught in a difficult situation due to the pressure on them to keep the client's business. Either way, they often get caught up in too many politics, mostly with the client, and are not able to concentrate on conducting productive, results-oriented PR.

At the same time, it is understandable that very few consultants favour the idea of local managers selecting the agency they want. These consultants often are frustrated at trying to run a program across a network of agencies that has been cobbled together. They find it a challenge to deliver the kind of results expected by the client when the agencies selected by the local clients are not up to the job. They also find that these local agencies, that are loyal, first and foremost, to their local client, often ignore the central agency's requests and strategy or do not properly use the tools and materials provided. Unless the central agency has real authority and the local agency is accountable to it, this is too common a scenario faced by international consultants.

BARRIERS TO SUCCESSFUL INTERNATIONAL PR—THE AGENCY PERSPECTIVE

According to Matthew Neale, a director at Weber Shandwick handling international assignments like the global account for Siemens mobile phones:

> having the right account structure is essential to delivering best results for a client. At Weber
> Shandwick, we not only make sure that we have a firm understanding of the client's goals and

expectations but *also* their own internal structure. If we believe their structure could impact on the kind of results they are looking for, we sit down and discuss this with clients in order to find the right solution and approach. (Personal communication, October 2003)

Neale adds:

how a campaign is structured and financed is often a clear indicator of whether the outcome will be successful or not. It comes down to where the authority lies? An international PR campaign—like any "campaign"—depends on leadership, accountability and authority for success. It's not enough to ask nicely and hope that the 40 or 50 practitioners around the world—whether on the agency or client side—will work together to achieve a common goal. The critical thing is to get all of these things clarified at the outset. (Personal communication)

It's no surprise that the group of agency consultants interviewed for this chapter cited "the client having no authority over the local PR team to drive activity and results" as one of the two biggest barriers to successfully running an international program. Dominic Shales explained: "regional offices may be unenthusiastic about working with an international agency, which they themselves have not chosen. "Not invented here syndrome" can often kill an international program if badly managed at the client side."

One way of tackling this, according to Matthew Neale, is how the campaign is financed. "Even if a client does not have direct authority over its local PR managers, control of a centralized global PR budget means that he or she more or less does," explained Neale. "How the campaign is financed can have a real impact on the agency's performance too. Often, if local agencies are paid locally, their loyalty is to their local client first. That's fine if the local client is on side with the regional or global campaign—but problems arise when he or she isn't interested in the bigger picture."

The group of practitioners interviewed for this study were given three different financial arrangements from which to select the one that they believe represented the best arrangement. Both groups were split quite evenly in their choice of the best arrangement. Nearly half the group (approximately 20 practitioners) favored arrangement A in which the HQ pays the lead agency while making budget allocations to local managers who can then pay their local agency. A similar number of practitioners favored arrangement B where the HQ pays the lead agency and the lead agency pays the local agencies as well. Only a few of the practitioners interviewed for this study (although more prevalent from within the client contingent) cited arrangement C in which the HQ pays the lead agency but local managers must find their own budgets to pay local agencies.

It seems that the practitioners who favored arrangement B felt that it offered greater control, particularly to the lead agency. In many agencies, the team selected to lead a particular account have only indirect authority over the staff from the various other offices working on the account. However, when the lead team holds the budget, they have more authority over their own colleagues and can more easily hold them accountable. In turn, the client can hold the lead agency accountable for the performance of the entire agency. Many clients would like a person to talk to when they feel there are issues with their international PR—wherever in the world that might be taking place. Other benefits of this arrangement that were cited were a greater consistency through the control and authority it grants as well as easing the payment process for clients. Often, a client wants one bill in one currency making this arrangement a popular one with the purchasing department.

The practitioners who favored arrangement A held slightly different views on the subject. They were most concerned with ensuring that local management felt empowered and, therefore, are more cooperative and less resistant to an international program. They felt that although HQ still held ultimate responsibility for the budget, they retained overall control, but local management were empowered to make decisions about the services required for their local market situation. One practitioner believed this strengthens the links between the agency and client at all levels by ensuring that the client understands what services they are getting for their money. One consultant felt that this arrangement was better than arrangement B due to the fact that the agency didn't have "control over the local clients." Another consultant pointed out that it is important that budget is assigned according to the market needs not where *the agency* wants it to go. Although it would seem a foolish move by any agency to assign budget from a self-serving point of view as it will only impact on program success and bring forth problems later in the relationship.

One aspect practitioners interviewed seemed to agree on was that selecting the right budget and payment process should be aligned with client objectives and structure. One practitioner pointed out that if a directive to do local PR comes from HQ, then HQ should find the money for the local markets to see this through. According Michael Leyer, Director of PR for Siemens mobile phones (and a Weber Shandwick client), "I find a combination of both suitable. We have established a retainer around the globe, funded by headquarters, to cover central projects and we also ask local managers to find their own budget to finance purely local PR activities."

Andrew Pirie, Co-President of Asia Pacific at Weber Shandwick, stated that he had been exposed to all three scenarios and while he firmly believed that international centralized program management can generate real benefits for clients, it can only work effectively if the client's internal organisation allows for such centralised control. "Despite being 'multinational,' many companies allow their local market businesses to exercise a great deal of autonomy and this often does not sit easily with a centralized communications function." In such cases, the international lead team arrangement often works best—as it does not place the agency in a position where it is expected to achieve local market results without having an effective mandate to do so. According to Pirie, the third option of decentralized program management brought a "lack of coordination, lack of cooperation and each market going off and doing their own thing (without necessarily keeping HQ and the lead agency in the loop)." This seems to defeat the purpose of wanting a centrally coordinated international PR effort.

However, one could argue in favor of arrangement C because local managers are in the best position to choose the best agency in their market, while retaining autonomy and ownership of the agency relationship. However, one might respond that this might be true if purely local PR is the objective, but when the PR is more regional or global in nature, shouldn't the decision be a joint one at best?

According to Pirie of Weber Shandwick:

it is essential to get the right financial commitment and structure in place to ensure success. If the client organization sets international PR objectives and works with an agency to develop a strategy and programme, senior management should be prepared to ensure that (sufficient) budget is committed for local implementation. It is unrealistic to expect local management to suddenly produce enough budget to support a programme they did not design or, in some cases, request.

The above-mentioned scenario, in which a client lacks financial commitment, brings us to the second biggest barrier quoted by agency consultants and in-house clients alike—the fact that "senior management within the client organization are not committed to PR and the agency relationship." One might say that this is not only a barrier to international campaigns but also domestic ones as well. The added difficulty this often brings for international campaigns is linked to the fact that there are more "clients." A domestic program will typically have one client—the PR and/or marketing management that hired the agency. An international program will have regional or global HQ staff as well as all the local marketing or PR managers. Senior management's mindset regarding the international PR program is usually reflected at local level—if senior management are not backing the global PR strategy, how can you expect the local management to do so?

Another barrier to success cited by interviewees was working for an organization whose senior management does not have strategic marketing and communications objectives. An international agency can be appointed without a strategic goal—say only in the interest of cost savings. The client is more committed to reducing costs than to the optimum in communications and, as a result, the client will not always cooperate in a way that is conducive for the agency to deliver its best. As a result, the agency will find it difficult to succeed. Other barriers raised included the fact that clients often held unrealistic expectations (or different expectations) of what the international agency is there to do and able to do. This is often the result of poor internal communication within the client organization as to the role and expectations of the agency appointed. Interviewees also felt that success could be impaired by clients who viewed the agency as implementers and were not willing to take their advice, clients with insufficient budget, too much local client resistance to use an international PR agency associated or chosen by headquarters and, last, agency politics and structures.

Hill & Knowlton seems to have taken the previous comment on board by addressing their own structure as explained by Dominic Shales: "having dedicated global client directors will greatly improve the client experience. With total control and responsibility for the account worldwide, these people are able to cut through the inherent regional structures in place in most traditional agencies, which in turn ensures improved and more consistent delivery and results for the client." Agencies like Hill & Knowlton and Weber Shandwick also try to address the barriers through staff training. Burson Marsteller has even created a "university"—the Burson Marsteller University Learning Centre—for schooling and developing its staff. Very few of the practitioners interviewed, even on the client side, cited poor performance by the agency as a major barrier to success.

Yet, when clients are asked about their previous agency or put an account up for re-pitch, the current agency's performance is often the first explanation given—it seems that, all too often, the agency becomes the scapegoat for "poor results." However, the message from the practitioners we contacted seems to indicate that these dissatisfied clients might also want to look inside their own organizations for clues as to why the relationship wasn't as successful as it could have been. From the feedback of the interviewees, it seems that clients should make sure that they have absolutely communicated their objectives and expectations clearly to internal staff, have their staff's full commitment to the effort, have the right structures in place, and have the appropriate levels and mode of financing to match. Because it is clear that, from an agency perspective, all the training and tools in the world cannot address these issues.

In addition to the above barriers that inhibit the successful implementation of programs, international agencies must face up to criticisms leveled at them from the marketing industry, by clients, and independent and domestic competitors.

A popular complaint, often raised by clients who are using three and four agencies competitively, is a lack of creativity. Clients complain that international agencies can be too formulaic in their approach causing programs to become "dumbed down" to appeal to the lowest common denominator market in terms the level of PR sophistication. According to Dominic Shales of Hill & Knowlton, "creativity should translate across borders and adhere to clear objectives. We have introduced our own Blue Cow creativity workshops to encourage new ways of thinking and creative brainstorming techniques to generate fresh, innovative ideas that can be adapted across borders." Matt Neale of Weber Shandwick explained that his agency avoids work being "dumbed down" by "taking a flexible approach. Whenever possible, we make sure there is a common goal and strategy but some room for local variation in implementation. We try to put the basic building blocks in place for a local program, while providing additional creative ideas and tools that more sophisticated PR markets can use as an 'add-on' or the local markets can use as a model or inspiration for their own creative ideas."

In conjunction with the lack of creativity comes over administration, another popular complaint of international PR agencies. Many clients do not want to pay their agencies to pass papers between one office and another regarding how much budget is left, ascertaining who is responsible for poor results, or trying to foster a better local relationship. They also do not want agencies to spend their time preparing lengthy reports and documents on the status of the global budget, how successful the PR was the previous month, and what each country plans to do next. They want their fees to go toward achieving tangible results. Agencies maintain that international account management brings a certain amount of administration. The issue lies in how well they explain and organize this with their clients. According to Matt Neale, "it is always important to sit down with the client when it comes to programme administration and work out what they are able to handle and what makes sense for them to handle in-house themselves. It is also important to agree with the client what they really need or want. There is no point in producing endless reports because you, the agency, believes they show how great the work is—if no one on the client side bothers to read them."

Another criticism that arises frequently is poor human resource management leading to higher turnover of staff. This is not a problem unique to international PR agencies because it can affect all types of agencies throughout the industry. The impact created by this issue at an international agency is typically connected to the scale of the account. There is often a much greater learning curve for new staff joining a large international account—both in terms of the structure of this particular account, the client's business area, the program(s) past and present, as well as any issues facing the program around the globe—say in a particular market or with a particular agency office. In addition, clients depend on the fact that there will be a high level of knowledge retained within their agency partner, particularly if they have been working together for years across many markets. The process of "training" and passing essential knowledge onto a new team or a new agency can be too much to bear. The bottom line is that if staff turnover at the agency is high, it can be have a detrimental effect on the relationship. With the boom of the late' 90s and increasing difficulty in finding good, quality staff, agencies had to learn to be better at people management and hang on to the staff they valued. Perhaps, this criticism will be less important in 5–10 years' time.

In addition to these issues, there are two major business challenges facing international PR agencies. One is their dependency on large, lucrative international clients. Most of these agencies carry domestic clients as well, but the loss of a client is never so severe as when a multi-million dollar client walks out the door. The impact on the agency's business can be significant not only financially but also in terms of damage to the reputation of the agency. This may also result in the loss of good, quality staff, often not by the agency's choice. In some cases, the newly appointed agency poaches good staff from the incumbent agency or consultants leave of their own accord, no longer interested in the other clients on the books. Many agencies work hard at creating structures to minimize this impact and also try to keep the new business pipeline full of opportunity. But the conversion time for a major international assignment, which is quite infrequent to begin with, is usually much longer than the time it can take for an existing client to reduce their commitment or move on elsewhere. Client retention is always important and ensuring a strong relationship—particularly one that the client has invested in as well—becomes critical to the international agency.

The other business challenge to be tackled is how international agencies demonstrate their value to the client organization. As Dominic Shales explains, "We are still bad as an industry at showing tangible evidence of the value we bring. At Hill & Knowlton, we have been a partner in the development of a PR measurement and evaluation tool with other WPP Group companies called PRecision. It is now essential that we look for such tools which can become standard and that the industry works together to ensure measurement and evaluation services become more sophisticated." Again, this is not just a challenge for international PR agencies but is of greater importance to them because of the scale of their assignments. If a client spends several million dollars with one international agency, that agency absolutely needs to be able to demonstrate to senior management of the client organization that there has been a return on that investment. Many large international tenders have a member of the purchasing department involved in the agency pitch and selection process to ensure this.

Also, while other marketing disciplines have common evaluation methods, more and more clients have been asking the same question of PR agencies in which they expect a common method—accepted across the industry—for measuring the efficacy of PR. Unfortunately to date, PR evaluation has taken many forms, varying from agency to agency, such as an analysis of the quantity and quality of global media coverage, benchmarking share of voice against a major competitor, analysis of agency results against fee spent, and attempts at incorporating PR into other marketing evaluation systems. Creating one common system of evaluation has not proved easy, perhaps because PR agencies are often hired for many different reasons. Advertising agencies are performing a service that is primarily linked to consumer awareness and understanding. This can be measured through consumer surveys. On the contrary, PR agencies, especially those with an international focus, might be hired for a variety of reasons such as product PR, repositioning a brand, and managing or preventing a communications crisis. The fact is that PR assignments, even consumer assignments, can be much more complex in their objectives than advertising assignments and possibly other assignments for marketing services firms. The reality is that having one standard industry tool for measurement (similar to tools used by the advertising industry) is proving difficult. The PR industry needs a range of measurement tools that can be tailored to meet the most common assignments. Yet, even this depends upon the client and agency having a good understanding of the organization's objectives—business and marketing—and setting clear, measurable PR objectives to match. But, as was apparent from the feedback from the practitioners contacted for this chapter, this itself seems to be a challenge. Either way, clients and international agencies will need to collaborate to find a common way of demonstrating how PR adds value to the business for the benefit of both entities.

There is no better way to understand international PR from an agency perspective than to take a first-hand look at a couple of success stories. The following two cases should illustrate to readers some of the points discussed above.

CASE STUDY 1—WEBER SHANDWICK

The first is a case study from the work that Asia Pacific region of Weber Shandwick did on behalf of MasterCard. According to Andew Pirie, Co-President of Asia Pacific, Weber Shandwick:

> this case study is an excellent example of many international client–agency relationships that are long term and are not based purely around a specific task or assignment. We have been working consistently with an overall remit to enhance MasterCard's communication with its cardholders, merchants and member financial institutions throughout the region since early 1995. This programme is also a good example of how we add value not only through our international PR skills and strategy, but also through the use of our regional network and the coordination of campaigns across a dozen markets. We have given the client a flexible approach in the structure whilst still retaining some control and accountability. In ten of the countries, Weber Shandwick owned or affiliated offices are on retainer and the other markets have independent agencies but, irrespective of this, all agencies still report into our regional team based in Singapore.

Objectives

- To position MasterCard as a total payments solution company, not just a credit card company.
- To provide communications support for the full range of products and services—debit, credit, chip, and e-commerce
- To strengthen relationships with all key constituencies

Approach

Weber Shandwick created a regional hub in Singapore to liaise with the regional client team and from which to manage the network. As consistency of tone and message are important to MasterCard, the regional hub developed central communications strategies and PR program templates, ensuring that global and regional business developments became relevant in all markets. The regional team oversaw the roll-out and implementation of these template programs in target markets, providing quality control and feedback to the regional client. They also facilitate best practice and ideas exchange with consultants from the local agencies, which may take on an original "regional" concept and localize this as needed.

To position MasterCard as a total payments solution company and provide effective product communications, the regional team developed template PR programs for:

- Product promotion—supporting new product launches and developments such as microchip-based cash cards and debit cards
- Consumer education—such as appropriate credit card usage
- Leveraging MasterCard sponsorships—such as the Jordan Formula 1 Grand Prix team and their involvement with soccer's World Cup—including MasterCard's global soccer ambassador, Peĺe
- Demonstrating MasterCard's understanding of the Asian consumer and marketplace with the publishing, every six months, of the "MasterIndex" consumer confidence survey and

a complementary survey "Asian Lifestyles " appealing to news media and market analysts alike.

- Supporting MasterCard's annual members meeting
- Addressing business/industry issues such as the growing concern over the increase in consumer debt that appears in official statistics as the credit card market grows. This was tackled through communication to regulators and politicians explaining that it is inevitable that consumer debt would increase as consumers transfer their spending from cash to cashless methods, meaning concerns over debt levels are often overstated. In addition, communication highlighted the economic benefits that come from greater use of more efficient, cashless payment.

Outcome

Evaluation is tailored with each template program, depending on the individual objectives. But in terms of the overall program outcome, Weber Shandwick cites the value it has brought to MasterCard as evident through:

- A superior and improving "share of ink," or media exposure, in absolute terms and relative to major competitors
- Client satisfaction and the long-standing nature of their relationship
- The recognition they have received for award-winning work. In 2000, the team's efforts were recognized in the Singapore Institute of Public Relations Awards when the MasterCard regional communications program won the top award for Best Campaign (Nongovernment Campaign) over $100,000.

CASE STUDY 2–HILL AND KNOWLTON

The second case study is of Hill & Knowlton's seventh Campaign for promoting the Consumption of Olive Oil in the 15 European Union (EU) member states. According to Dominic Shales:

> this case study is a great example of how central strategy coordination teamed with regional input and implementation can ensure coherence and synergy of key messages, whilst allowing for the exploitation of national opportunities. This is only possible through the adaptation of all activities and materials to meet the specific needs and customs of each country. A central strategy was particularly effective for this campaign, as medical issues tend to originate from an international platform. In addition, it ensured large-scale economies made for an effective financial mechanism. Employing an international agency provided the client with an understanding of regional diversity, which meant less adaptation was required as the campaign would already be fine- tuned to meet regional campaign requirements.

Campaign Objectives

- To disseminate to health professionals and science media, scientific information supporting the health benefits associated with the consumption of olive oil
- To develop a central strategy that allowed for effective national implementation in all 15 European markets

- To develop central communications activities to support the consumer campaign to be implemented by a range of agencies

Strategy

- Support the main objective of the nonproducer countries to promote more widespread adoption of olive oil into the diet, through the understanding of its health benefits
- Support the main objective of the producer countries to preserve and reinforce the traditional use of olive oil in the national diet, again through reviving the understanding of its health benefits.

Approach

- Established coordination centres for implementation to address the very different needs of the producer and non-producer countries: London coordinated the nonproducer countries and Milan coordinated the producer countries.
- Central team members handled the planning and management of international activities, advised on and supported local market activities, coordinated the campaign, and organized financial management and central reporting.
- The central team used its understanding of the local markets and feedback from local colleagues to design a strategy that could be easily adaptable to each market's conditions.
- Local market teams, meanwhile, identified key national messages, platforms, challenges, and opinion leaders that were in-line with the central strategy.

Tactical Implementation

- A database of the most important target national and pan-European audiences was researched and established.
- Educational materials were produced, aimed at primary care professionals to help them in their capacity to counsel patients about nutrition and healthier eating habits. These materials were distributed collectively in an "educational kit." In some markets distribution was linked to third-party organizations, willing to lend their endorsement to the materials.
- Consultation aids for doctors were created as a tool to help doctors counsel patients about the health benefits olive oil and of a Mediterranean-style diet. Distributed with educational posters, all materials were produced in the various languages.
- Twenty of Europe's top experts in lipidology, epidemiology, cardiology, nutrition and psychology were invited to debate and agree a Consensus Statement on Olive Oil that summarized the latest scientific knowledge about the health benefits of olive oil and a Mediterranean-style diet. The Consensus Statement on Olive Oil was published as a landmark scientific paper and distributed throughout Europe to media and relevant target audiences.
- A carefully selected group of journalists were invited to International workshops to update them on the most recent scientific information about olive oil and the Mediterranean-style diet. This provided an opportunity to build anticipation among European health correspondents before the international Consensus Statement on Olive Oil was published.

- Two international symposia were organized, one for nonproducer countries and the other for producer countries. Forty six multidisciplinary delegates including medical experts, representatives from primary healthcare professions, health educators, and journalists attended each event. National meeting were also organized.

- Biannual newsletters were produced centrally for local adaptation to secure a continuous and cost effective flow of scientific information

- Active participation and discussion about the Mediterranean-style diet was also negotiated at various other leading scientific congresses at both a national and international level. Press conferences were organized where appropriate.

- A medical information Internet library was established to host all information developed during the campaign.

- The press offices in each market were responsible for collating and distributing all news stories. These were often sourced and written centrally then adapted to suit various national media environments

- Patient handouts were drafted centrally and then adapted to the dietary habits of the various countries

Results

The campaign was effective and well received in most countries creating:

- High levels of media coverage in both medical and lay press
- A 42% sale increase in the European markets
- Effective financial tracking and internal invoicing systems leading to successful EU auditor review
- H&K was selected for the next pan European campaign which started in Spring 1999

REFERENCES

www.bursonmarsteller.com
www.fleishman.com
PR Week Global Rankings, August 2001 (*note that although published in 2001, all figures are based on 2000 PR agency financial performance*)
www.edelman.com
www.golinharris.com/default.asp
www.porternovelli.com/pnwebsite/pnwebsite.ns/index?openpage
www.hillandknowlion.com
www.webershandwick.com

CHAPTER

23

PUBLIC RELATIONS OF MOVERS AND SHAKERS: TRANSNATIONAL CORPORATIONS

DEJAN VERČIČ

Public relations is a managerial function (Cutlip, Center, & Broom, 2000) and public relations theory originates in economics and strategic management (Verčič & J. Grunig, 2000). Business (Pearson, 1989) and its particular form, the corporation (Olasky, 1987), are the paradigmatic subjects of theorizing in what Verčič & J. Grunig called "the American concept of public relations" (2000, p. 12). Further, this concept was identified by Verčič, L. Grunig, and J. Grunig (1995) as the only global concept of public relations currently available.[1] Yet, while "all public relations is global or international" (L. Grunig, J. Grunig, & Dozier, 2002, p. 541) because all companies affect, or are affected by, the world that lies beyond their borders, it is amazing that we have only a few quality publications on the public relations practices of transnational corporations (TNC).[2] As contemporary companies "should globalize unless they can find very good reasons not to" (Yip, 2001, p. 150), so should research and theorizing in public relations. Public relations is an innovative social

---

[1] Only recently has work been initiated on alternative conceptualizations, primarily in Europe; see van Ruler & Verčič (2002a, 2002b) and Verčič, van Ruler, Bütschi, & Flodin (2001), and reflections from Africa (Rensburg, 2002), Asia (Sriramesh, 2002) and Latin America (Ferrari, 2002); for a North American reflection see L. Grunig & J. Grunig (2002). See also Sriramesh, Kim, & Takasaki (1999).

[2] In this chapter we use the term "transnational corporation" (TNC) as a generic term for business (for-profit) entities operating in more than one country as defined by Dicken (1988, p. 177) and quoted in the chapter. Organizational studies and in international management literature use different names, like "transnational corporation," "multinational corporation," "international corporation," "global corporation," etc., to distinguish between different types of international businesses and one such typology is presented in the chapter. Yet, when it is not explicitly specified differently, we use the term "transnational corporation" to cover all types of international businesses. In the same way we use the term "corporation" as a generic term for a large for-profit organization. "Transnational corporate public relations" in that context is used as a generic name for public relations carried in and on behalf of transnational corporations.

technology (Verčič, Razpet, Dekleva, & Šlenc, 2000) and its global diffusion is controlled primarily by TNCs in their transformation into global institutions (Kruckeberg, 2000).

This chapter intends to provide a presentation of "the beast" by first providing a definition of what constitutes a transnational corporation. Next, it provides a rough estimate of the scope of the diffusion of TNCs, lists the largest among them, and presents how they are classified based on the level of their transformation from a domestic to a global business in organizational studies. Then the chapter focuses on currently available information on transnational corporate public relations. Finally, the chapter provides a plea for a theory of transnational corporate public relations by highlighting the peculiarities of corporate public relations in international arena and concludes with a view toward the future.

THE "MOVERS AND SHAKERS"

Peter Dicken (1998), in his best-selling book on the globalization phenomenon, entitled the translational corporations (TNCs) as "the primary 'movers and shapers' of the global economy" (p. 177) and defined them as follows: "A transnational corporation is a firm which has the power to co-ordinate and control operations in more than one country, even if it does not own them" (p. 177).

Dickens sees TNCs as the primary beneficiaries of the present form of globalization that is characterized by economic deregulation and the privatization of state-owned assets around the world. Yet he doesn't believe that these processes make states obsolete or puts their "economic sovereignty at bay" (Vernon, 1968). Besides TNCs and governments there are also nongovernmental organizations that operate transnationally, giving us three major players we need to consider when analyzing the world beyond one's national borders. TNCs are the primary movers and shakers of the global economy, but they do not act in isolation.

Wallace (1982) warned that multinational businesses are not necessarily organized as firms, as limited liability companies, or as corporations, but rather as groups or networks of entities that have been established under different national regimes with different nationalities and legal forms. Early European multinational business enterprises are generally considered to be the forerunners of modern multinational corporations and they appeared on the world map from 1300 to 1700. Gabel and Bruner (2002) listed several of the early European multinational businesses: the Hanseatic League in Germany, the Merchant Adventurers Company in Britain, the Medici family of Italy, the Muscovy Company in Russia, the Dutch East India Company in the Netherlands, and the British East India Company (known to contemporaries simply as "the Company"). UNCTAD (United Nations Conference on Trade and Development) calculated that by the end of the twentieth century, there were approximately 39,000 parent-company TNCs controlling about 265,000 foreign affiliates (Dicken, 1998, p. 43). The largest among them have revenues of over US $200 billion (Table 23.1), employ over 1 million people (Table 23.2), and have profits of over US $15 billion (Table 23.3).

There are many descriptions of the phenomenon of these large firms that co-ordinate and control operations in more than one country. Based on a review of relevant literature, Stohl (2001) developed a typology of organizations to describe "the transformation and convergence of domestic to global forms of organizing" (p. 328). Her description of the five types "are based on the predominance of a single national/cultural identity, the perceived importance of an international orientation and perspective, the legitimacy of multiple voices and authority, the type of structure, the 'ideal' management model, and the interconnected nature of interactions across a diversity of cultural groups" (p. 328). She labeled the five types of organizations domestic, multicultural, multinational, international, and global.

TABLE 23.1

The World's Largest Companies by Revenues in 2001 US $Million

Rank	Company	Revenues ($million)
1	Wal-Mart Stores	219,812.0
2	Exxon Mobil	191,581.0
3	General Motors	177,260.0
4	BP	174,218.0
5	Ford Motor	162,412.0
6	Enron	138,718.0
7	DaimlerChrysler	136,897.3
8	Royal Dutch/Shell Group	135,211.0
9	General Electric	125,913.0
10	Toyota Motor	120,814.4

Note. Retrieved January 14, 2003 from http://www.fortune.com/fortune/Global500

TABLE 23.2

The World's Largest Companies by Employment

Rank	Company	2001 Number of Employees
1	Wal-Mart Stores	1,383,000
2	China National Petroleum	1,167,129
3	State Power	1,162,645
4	Sinopec	937,300
5	United States Postal Service	891,005
6	China Telecommunications	566,587
7	Agricultural Bank of China	500,000
8	Siemens	484,000
9	Industrial & Commercial Bank of China	429,709
10	McDonald's	395,000

Note. Retrieved November 8, 2002 from http://www.fortune.com/lists/G500/g500_topperf_co_bigemploy.html

Stohl (2001, pp. 329–330) noted that these five types of organizations can be placed on a continuum from being purely domestic to being purely global with distinctions based on six dimensions. The first dimension is a predominantly national orientation as seen in domestic organizations that identify with one country and one dominant culture. Multicultural organizations identify with one country with some recognition by management of the cultural diversity of their workforce. Multinational organizations identify with one nationality while doing business in several countries. International organization identify with two or more countries. Global organization identify with the global system.

The second dimension is the perceived importance of international orientation. Domestic organizations have no international orientation while multicultural organizations give it very little importance. International orientation is important for multinational organizations, extremely important for international organizations, and dominant for global organizations.

The third dimension is the legitimacy of multiple voices and authority. Domestic organizations are parochial, multicultural organizations are ethnocentric, multinational organizations are polycentric, international organizations are regiocentric, and global organizations are geocentric.

TABLE 23.3

The World's Largest Companies by Profits

Rank	Company	2001 Profits ($millions)
1	Exxon Mobil	15,320.0
2	Citigroup	14,126.0
3	General Electric	13,684.0
4	Royal Dutch/Shell Group	10,852.0
5	Philip Morris	8,560.0
6	BP	8,010.0
7	Pfizer	7,788.0
8	Intl. Business Machines	7,723.0
9	AT&T	7,715.0
10	Microsoft	7,346.0

Note. Retrieved November 8, 2002 from http://www.fortune.com/lists/G500/g500_topperf_co_highprofit.html

The fourth dimension is the type of structure. Domestic organizations have hierarchical, traditional bureaucratic, and matrix structures. Multicultural organizations introduce teamwork and flattening of hierarchy. Multinational organizations are hierarchically managed from a central location with national subsidiaries, which are miniature replicas and employ teamwork. International organizations have joint hierarchy and international divisions that integrate global activities with teamwork within subsidiaries but not across. Global organizations have decentralized decision making and share responsibilities.

The fifth dimension is the management model. Domestic organizations are monocultural, multicultural organizations favor cultural dominance, multinational organizations cultural compromise, international organizations cultural synergy, and global organizations cultural integration.

The sixth dimension is the level of international interaction. Domestic organizations may import and export goods and services with a few representatives abroad. Multicultural organizations also import and export with some representatives abroad and also have intercultural communication among workforce. Multinational organizations favor intercultural communication among workforce, management, clients, customers, etc. International organizations are internationally loosely coupled. Global organizations are global networks, integrative and tightly coupled.

It is no wonder that international corporate public relations practices operate along two extremes. The first is when domestic public relations practices are extended to other countries with few, or no, modifications and the other is when international public relations practices are unrelated to domestic public relations programs (Wakefield, 2001, p. 641). To bridge the gap between these two extreme positions, Verčič, L. Grunig, and J. Grunig (1995) and L. Grunig, J. Grunig, and Verčič (1998) proposed a normative theory of generic principles and specific applications (based on five environmental variables) in international public relations.

THE PUBLIC RELATIONS OF TRANSNATIONAL CORPORATIONS: GENERIC PRINCIPLES AND SPECIFIC APPLICATIONS

A normative theory of generic principles in international public relations argues that there are some principles of public relations that can be practiced around the world. Verčič, L. Grunig & J. Grunig (1995) proposed the following generic principles borrowing from the findings of the "excellence study" (reported in Dozier, L. Grunig, & J. Grunig, 1995; J. Grunig 1992; and L. Grunig, J. Grunig & Dozier 2002):

1. Public relations is involved in strategic management.
2. Public relations is empowered by the dominant coalition or by direct reporting relationship to senior management.
3. The public relations function is an integrated one.
4. Public relations is a managerial function separate from other functions.
5. The public relations unit is headed by a manager rather than a technician.
6. The two-way symmetrical model of public relations is used.
7. A symmetrical system of internal communication is used.
8. Knowledge potential for managerial role and symmetrical public relations.
9. Diversity is embodied in all roles.
10. An organizational context exists for excellence.

L. Grunig, J. E. Grunig, and Verčič (1998) tested the application of these principles in Slovenia and confirmed the validity of this general model. Rhee (2002) arrived at similar conclusions based on her study of the principles in South Korea. The impact of specific environmental variables on the international application of the generic principles has been discussed in detail by Sriramesh and Verčič (2001) and in Chapter 1 of this book.

The above conceptualizations have laid out the first frameworks to organize empirical research on public relations practices in transnational corporations. Wakefield (1999, p. 34) conducted a Delphi study on the application of the generic principles proposed by Verčič, L. Grunig, and J. E. Grunig (1995) soliciting responses from 23 public relations veterans in 18 countries. He conducted a follow-up study adding another 31 respondents from 15 countries and developed what he labeled as "factors of effectiveness in multinational public relations" that form the foundation for practicing "world-class" public relations.

He suggested that organizations practicing "world-class" public relations would have a global, but not a "central-mandate" philosophy, and value "outside-in" dialogue over "inside-out" communication. Further, in these organizations, the senior public relations managers in every unit report to the senior executive in a country in which they operate but have dual matrix reporting relationship to headquarters public relations which is located in the country of a TNC's origin. The communication efforts of these organizations are coordinated, both at headquarters and internationally and PR cooperates closely with other departments such as marketing and legal, but is not subordinated to them. The author also suggested that the PR officers in every unit of organizations that practice "world-class" public relations are full-time and have proper training. His other suggestions were that:

- Public relations officers operate as a global team with horizontal reporting relationships.
- Public relations staffing represents the diversity of the firm's transnational publics.
- A central person is a team leader, not a mandate giver.
- Communication between public relations people is "multiway," not just two-way.
- Opportunities for interaction are frequent, and both formal and informal.

Although the studies reviewed above have evaluated corporate public relations in international settings, further studies are needed before we can claim the existence of a theory of transnational corporate public relations.

TOWARD A THEORY OF TRANSNATIONAL CORPORATE PUBLIC RELATIONS

Drucker (1994, p. 96) wrote that "[e]very organization, whether business or not, has a theory of the business." This makes assumptions about the environment (which define what an organization is paid for), about the specific mission (what an organization considers to be meaningful results) and assumptions about the core competencies needed to accomplish the mission (where an organization must excel in order to retain leadership).

A theory of the business has relevance on two levels: it applies to public relations client organizations (organizations employing public relations capacities, internally or/and externally) and to the public relations function in/for these same organizations itself. It is beyond the scope of this chapter to elaborate how theories of business differ between domestic, multicultural, multinational, international, and global firms. Notwithstanding any differences, three commonalities remain:

1. "*All* TNCs have an identifiable home base, which ensures that every TNC is essentially embedded within its domestic environment" (Dicken, 1998, p. 193). No corporation is culture-free or nation-free.

2. "The creation of particular types of demand and the shaping of customer tastes and preferences are an intrinsic part of the TNC system" (Dicken, 1989, p. 249). For that very reason, it is interesting to note a parallel between the dominance of TNCs originating in the United States that are at the top of the list of the largest TNCs in the world and the major United States export industry: "The single largest export industry for the United States is not aircraft or automobiles, it is entertainment—Hollywood films grossed more than $30 billion worldwide in 1997" (UNDP [United Nations Development Programme]), 1999, p. 4).

3. "Global business is not, then, just about business: it has cultural, legal, political and social effects as much as economic ones" (Parker, 1996, p. 485). Three books expressing the intellectual spirit at the dawn of the twenty-first century question practices of TNCs exactly because of these "externalities" (Verčič & J. Grunig, 2000): Frank (2001), Hertz (2001), and Klein (2000). Similarly, Plender (2000) warrants the newest unpopularity of capitalism: "Large corporations are the engines of creative destruction. So they make a large target. For their part, politicians need enemies. In the post-cold war world big business fits the bill."

L. Grunig (1992, pp. 72–73) questioned the purpose of the public relations profession: "Are we in the business of persuasion? of information? of negotiation? of co-optation? of co-operation?" The models of public relations first presented by J. Grunig and Hunt (1984, pp. 21–22) answer the question differently (the press agentry model says that public relations is about presentation, the public information model says that it is about information, the two-way asymmetrical model says that is about persuasion, and the two-way symmetrical model says that it is about negotiation). J. Grunig and L. Grunig (1989) summed up those purposes in two general forms: control of the external environment by the focal organization and adaptation of the focal organization to its environment. So far as transnational corporate public relations is related to markets, it is also involved in control. This explains why Wakefield (2000, pp. 199–200) found that submission of public relations to marketing is more common internationally than in the United States corporate world. While White (1997, p. 159) postulated that "[p]ublic relations is a practical management and business discipline, partly because it is also a moral discipline," this maxim still seems to be in the second tier when firms practice public relations internationally.

TABLE 23.4
The Nine Principles

At the World Economic Forum, Davos, on January 31, 1999, UN Secretary-General Kofi A. Annan
challenged world business leaders to "embrace and enact" the Global Compact, both in their
individual corporate practices and by supporting appropriate public policies. These principles cover
topics in human rights, labor, and environment:

Human Rights
The Secretary-General asked world business to:

Principle 1: Support and respect the protection of international human rights within their sphere of
influence; and
Principle 2: Make sure their own corporations are not complicit in human rights abuses.

Labor
The Secretary-General asked world business to uphold:

Principle 3: Freedom of association and the effective recognition of the right to collective bargaining;
Principle 4: The elimination of all forms of forced and compulsory labor;
Principle 5: The effective abolition of child labor; and
Principle 6: The elimination of discrimination in respect of employment and occupation.

Environment
The Secretary-General asked world business to:

Principle 7: Support a precautionary approach to environmental challenges;
Principle 8: Undertake initiatives to promote greater environmental responsibility; and
Principle 9: Encourage the development and diffusion of environmentally friendly technologies.

Note. Retrieved November 8, 2002 from http://65.214.34.30/un/gc/unweb.nsf/content/thenine.htm

Meaningful results in transnational corporate public relations relate above all to the
legitimacy of the system (Jensen, 1997) that enables them to operate (Ruler & Verčič,
2002a, 2002b, Verčič, van Ruler, Bütschi & Flodin, 2001). The 1970s saw a more critical
attitude toward TNCs starting with the notion of a national "economic sovereignty at bay"
(Vernon, 1968) and efforts by many national governments to regulate the activities of
TNCs. The 1980s was a decade of deregulation and increased efforts to attract foreign
investments, while the 1990s "saw a proliferation of corporate codes of conduct and an
increased emphasis on corporate responsibility" (Jenkins, 2001, p. III). Table 23.4 presents
an international framework for self-regulating corporate practices around the world.

Kruckeberg (2000) noted that the corporation has traditionally been "a central institution
in American culture, with a historical pattern of rights and duties, powers and responsibilities" (p. 150). With an increase in the proportion of the world's population taking
part in the global economy from around a quarter to four-fifths in only 25 years (Jefkins,
2001, pp. 6–7), "corporations as global institutions may become far more powerful and
pervasively influential" (Kruckeberg, p. 150)—a central institution in global culture!

Public relations competencies in transnational businesses have a special emphasis in
dealing with multiple publics with conflicting expectations and interests (Verčič, 1997).
The vice president in charge of external affairs of one of the largest TNCs, the Royal
Dutch/Shell Group of companies, commented on the results of their research on international publics:

We found that many rational and intelligent people thought that it was a reasonable proposition
that companies such as Shell should mediate to reduce tensions between different levels of

government, or that they should take positions on social policy matters. At all times we should remember that Shell is a business. Activities as these are not within the normal, legitimate role of a business. Therefore, we cannot meet such expectations. (de Segundo, 1997, pp. 17–18)

The importance of researching factors outside the organization was further emphasized by Drucker (1997): "In fact, approximately 90% or more of the information any organization collects is about inside events. Increasingly, a winning strategy will require information about events and conditions *outside* the institution: noncustomers, technologies other than those currently used by the company and its present competitors, markets not currently served, and so on" (p. 22).

In addition to these general remarks, there is a need to highlight some concrete features of transnational corporate public relations, which is the focus of the next section.

PECULIARITIES OF TNC PUBLIC RELATIONS

There are several features of public relations in and for TNCs that we can only mention here, yet they need further study. In general, we can identify them under the following headings: fewer professionals, more stakeholders, more competitors, and more issue groups.

Fewer Professionals

While normative public relations theory argues for a strategic public relations management function staffed by educated and trained professionals, it is common for the total number of public relations staff in international operations to be well below the total number of business entities they are required to serve and support. In the 1990s, when ABB was among the most admired European TNCs, it comprised of 1000 companies operating in 140 countries with 217,000 employees. These were further fragmented to 5000 profit centers. These 5000 centers in 1000 firms were attended to by a global network of approximately "200 communication specialists (although not all have only communications as their function)" (Robertson, 1997). What is important to understand in this context is that this example is far from extreme—it might well be closer to the norm. It is not uncommon to find some diversified conglomerates that have only a handful of public relations professionals in the HQ being responsible for activities around the world! One may wonder how they succeed and this aspect needs further research.

Downsizing and outsourcing have contributed to the further decrease in the number of public relations professionals working TNCs (Newsom, VanSlyke Turk, & Kruckeberg, 1996, p. 72). Studies that assess collaboration with "global" public relations agencies from a perspective of a "downsized public relations department" are still lacking.

More Stakeholders

There is no doubt that the larger a corporation becomes, the greater the number of stakeholders it needs to contend with. The largest TNCs operating around the globe have more stakeholders than corporations operating within a single country. But that is not all. As Fombrun & Rindova (2000) argued based on the case of Royal Dutch/Shell: "in different settings, the relative importance of stakeholders varies, and the factors that influence reputation are different" (p. 85). In 1995, Royal Dutch/Shell faced two major crises. The first centered on its decision to scuttle its aging offshore drilling platform—the Brent Spar—in the North Sea, which resulted in a vociferous, and successful, opposition from an NGO—Greenpeace (The case study of Brent Spar has been discussed in the chapter on Germany in this book). The other focused on the corporation's human rights record in Nigeria. As a part of its learning experience from these issues, Shell initiated several projects, among which the most interesting from a public relations perspective are the "Assessing Society's Changing Expectations" project and the "Becoming WoMAC (The World's Most Admired Corporation)" project. Fombrun and Rindova noted that "firms that rate well with some evaluators do not always do so well with others" (p. 85). This may open some new questions regarding stakeholder relationship management that is not only complex but qualitatively different in a transnational as opposed to a single-country setting.

TNCs often operate as conglomerates of corporations that have very little in common. They may well have different identities, names and values, and in some cases may be in the process of being bought only to be sold soon after. In recent years, many TNCs have managed "value chains" that have no, or very limited, legal bonds. For example, there may be a link between a Vietnamese textile producer who is outsourced by a branded corporation in the United States who then sells the product via a third legal entity in Europe. The very notions of internal communication and corporate social responsibility need to get completely new meanings under such circumstances. Yet public relations literature is silent on such issues.

More Competitors

Public relations is generally described as being concerned with relations between organizations and their publics. In a single country, it is often the case that corporate public relations opportunities and problems arise out of actions of competitors even if such instances are not so visible. Yet, such instances become much more visible in the international arena. Globalization is about competition, promoting and restricting it, and as such about competitors. Two books that explored the subject of lobbying in the European Union (Pedler, 2002b; Pedler and van Schendelen, 1994) indicated how the lobbying practices TNCs employ in the context of European integration and institutions depend on the practices of their competitors. For example, clean air and the issue of car emissions in Europe pit the interests of car manufacturers and the oil industry, and the interests of the governments of domestic (European, in this case) and foreign countries (e.g., Japan and the United States). Car and oil corporations (with different technologies and interests based on them) play games between themselves and their public relations activities are in that respect both competitive and co-dependent (Pedler, 2002a). Under such circumstances, publics may not be emerging out of issues or problems (J. E. Grunig, 1997), but based on the actions of other corporations.

More Issue Groups

Naomi Klein (2000) introduced counter-corporate activism by stating:

> Dozens of brand-based campaigns have succeeded in rattling their corporate targets, in several cases pushing them to substantially alter their policies. But three campaigns stand out for having reached well beyond activist circles and deep into public consciousness. The tactics they have developed—among them the use of the courts to force transparency on corporations, and the Internet to bypass traditional media—are revolutionizing the future of political engagement. By now it should come as no surprise that the targets of these influential campaigns are three of the most familiar and best-tended logos on the brandscape: the Swoosh,

the Shell and the Arches. (p. 366; the author is referring to Nike, the Royal Dutch/Shell Group of companies, and McDonald's, respectively.)

Not only are there more issue groups around the world than in any single country, but they also perceive themselves as global warriors that are in a global search for causes to oppose. Transnational issues management may well be a different game than one plays domestically.

CONCLUSIONS

Corporate public relations in the world stage is the forerunner of the best in public relations. It demands more work in a more complex environment. Therefore, to study the best in public relations we need to focus on transnational corporate public relations. In the past decade, we have seen the emergence of the first normative theory focusing on corporate public relations at the international level. What we need in this decade are descriptive studies documenting the everyday practice of transnational corporate public relations and analyses of empirical data from individual case studies, cross-sectional and longitudinal surveys, and behavioral data. It is a no-risk strategy to predict that excellent public relations will very soon be only transnational. Global institutionalization of public relations depends on global institutionalization of corporations and their employment of public relations services.

There continues to be little information on the profile of model global corporate public relations practitioner. Are they to be natives in a country in which they are serving or are they to be professional expatriates committed only to their corporations? Are they building lasting relationships with their stakeholders or moving from country to country (as professional diplomats do) so often that this is not possible? Currently, TNCs probably employ the majority of public relations professionals and they will probably employ an even larger share of them in the future. TNCs are public relations' natural environment.

REFERENCES

Cutlip, S. M., Center, A. H., & Broom, G. M. (2000). *Effective public relations*, 8th ed. Upper Saddle River, NJ: Prentice Hall.

Dicken, P. (1998). *Global shift: Transforming the world economy*, 3rd ed. London: Paul Chapman.

Dozier, D. M., Grunig, L. A., & Grunig, J. E. (1995). *Manager's guide to excellence in public relations and communication management*. Mahwah, NJ: Lawrence Erlbaum Associates.

Drucker, P. F. (1994). The theory of business. *Harvard Business Review*, 27(5) September–October, 95–104.

Drucker, P. F. (1997). The future that has already happened. *Harvard Business Review*, 75(5) September–October, 20–24.

Ferrari, M. A. (2002). The Latin American perspective on public relations: The case of Brazil and Chile. In D. Verčič, B. van Ruler, I. Jensen, D. Moss, & J. White (Eds.), *Proceedings of the BledCom 2002: The status of public relations knowledge in Europe and around the world*, (pp. 19–24). Ljubljana: Pristop Communications.

Fombrun, C. J., & Rindova V. P. (2000). The road to transparency: Reputation management of Royal Dutch/ Shell. In M. Schuletz, M. J. Natch, & M. H. Larsen (Eds.), The expressing organization: Linking identity, reputation and the corporate brand (pp. 79–96). Oxford: Oxford University Press.

Frank, T. (2001). *One market under God: Extreme capitalism, market populism, and the end of economic democracy*. London: Secker & Warburg.

Gabel, M., & Bruner, H. (2002).*Global Inc. An atlas of the multinational corporation*. Retreived November 6, 2002, from http://www.globallinksconsulting.com/GIncOnLine.html

Grunig, J. (1992) (Ed.). *Excellence in public relations and communication management*. Hillsdale, NJ: Lawrence Erlabaum Associates.

Grunig, J. E. (1997). A situational theory of publics: Conceptual history, recent challenges and new research. In D. Moss, T. MacManus, & D. Verčič (Eds.), *Public relations research: An international perspective* (pp. 3–48). London: ITP.

Grunig, L. A. (1992). Toward the philosophy of public relations. In E. L. Toth & R. L. Heath (Eds.), *Rhetorical and critical approaches to public relations* (pp. 65–91). Hillsdale, NJ: Lawrence Erlbaum Associates.

Grunig, J. E., & Grunig, L. A. (1989). Toward a theory of the public relations behavior of organizations: Review of a program of research. In J. E. Grunig & L. A. Grunig (Eds.), *Public relations research annual* (Vol. 1, pp. 27–66). Hilsdale, NJ: Lawrence Erlbaum.

Grunig, J. E., & Hunt, T. (1984). *Managing public relations*. New York: Holt, Rinehart and Winston.

Grunig, L. A. (1992). Toward the philosophy of public relations. In E. L. Toth & R. L. Heath (Eds.), *Rhetorical and critical approaches to public relations* (pp. 56–91). Hillsdale, NJ: Lawrence Erlbaum.

Grunig, L. A., & Grunig, J. E. (2002). The Bled manifesto on public relations: One North American Perspective. In D. Verčič, B. van Ruler, I. Jensen, D. Moss & J. White (Eds.), *Proceedings of the BledCom 2002: The status of public relations knowledge in Europe and around the world* (pp. 25–34). Ljubljana: Pristop Communications.

Grunig, L. A., Grunig, J. E., & Dozier, D. M. (2002). *Excellent public relations and effective organizations: A study of communication management in three countries*. Mahwah, NJ: Lawrence Erlbaum Associates.

Grunig, L. A., Grunig, J. E., & Verčič, D. (1998). Are the IABC's excellence principles generic? Comparing Slovenia and the United States, the United Kingdom and Canada. *Journal of Communication Management, 2*(4), 335–356.

Hertz, N. (2001). *The silent takeover: Global capitalism and the death of democracy*. London: William Heinemann.

Jefkins, R. (2001). *Corporate codes of conduct: Self-regulating in a global economy (Technology, Business and Society Programme Paper Number 2)*. Geneva: United Nations Research Institute for Social Development.

Jensen, I. (1997). Legitimacy and strategy of different companies: A perspective of external and internal public relations. In D. Moss, T. MacManus, & D. Verčič (Eds.), *Public relations research: An international perspective* (pp. 225–246). London: ITP.

Klein, N. (2000). *No logo: Taking aim at the brand bullies*. London: Flamingo.

Kruckeberg, D. (2000). Public relations: Toward a global professionalism. In J. A. Ledingham & S. D. Bruning (Eds.), *Public relations as relationship management: A relational approach to the study and practice of public relations* (pp. 145–157). Mahwah, NJ: Lawrence Erlbaum Associates.

Newsom, D., VanSlyke Turk, J., & Kruckeberg, D. (Eds.). (1996). *This is PR: The realities of public relations*, 6th ed. Belmont, CA: Wadsworth.

Olasky, M. N. (1987). *Corporate public relations: A new historical perspective*. Hillsdale, NJ: Lawrence Erlbaum Associates.

Parker, B. (1996). Evolution and revolution: From international business to globalization. In S. R. Clegg, C. Hardy, & W. R. Nord (Eds.), *Handbook of organization studies*, pp. 484–506. London: Sage.

Pearson, R. (1989). Business ethics as communication ethics: Public relations practice and the idea of dialogue. In C. H. Botan & V. Hazleton, Jr. (Eds). *Public relations theory* (pp. 111–131). Hillsdale, NJ: Lawrence Erlbaum Associates.

Pedler, R. (2002a). Clean air and car emissions: What industries and issue groups can and can't achieve. In R. Pedler (Ed.), *European Union lobbying: Changes in the arena* (pp. 104–122). London: Palgrave.

Pedler, R. (Ed.) (2002b). *European Union lobbying: Changes in the arena*. London: Palgrave.

Pedler, R. H. & van Schendelen, M. P. C. M. (Eds.) (1994). *Lobbying the European Union: Companies, trade associations and issue groups*. Aldershot, UK: Dartmouth.

Plender, J. (2000, September 11). Unpopular capitalism. *Financial Times*, p. 18.

Rensburg, R. (2002). The Bled manifesto on public relations: An African perspective and vision. In D. Verčič, B. van Ruler, I. Jensen, D. Moss, & J. White (Eds.), *Proceedings of the BledCom 2002: The status of public relations knowledge in Europe and around the world* (pp. 35–43). Ljubljana: Pristop Communications.

Rhee, Y. (2002). Global public relations: A cross-cultural study of the excellence theory in South Korea. *Journal of public relations research 14*(3), 159–184.

Robertson, M. (1997). How can you possibly think global, act local. In T. R. V. Foster & A. Jolly (Eds), *Corporate communications handbook* (pp. 302–308). London: Kogan Page.

Ruler, B. van & Verčič, D. (2002a). 21st century communication management—the people, the organization. In P. Simcic Brønn & R. Wiig (Eds.), *Corporate communication: A strategic approach to building reputation* (pp. 277–294). Oslo: Gyldendal Norsk Forlag.

Ruler, B., & Verčič, D. (2002b). *The Bled manifesto on public relations*. Ljubljana: Pristop Communications.

Segundo, K. de (1997). Meeting society's changing expectations. *Corporate reputation review, 1*(1–2), 16–19.

Sriramesh, K. (2002). The Bled manifesto on public relations: An Asian perspective. In D. Verčič, B. van Ruler, I. Jensen, D. Moss, & J. White (Eds.), *Proceedings of the BledCom 2002: The status of public relations knowledge in Europe and around the world* (pp. 44–49). Ljubljana: Pristop Communications.

Sriramesh, K., & Verčič, D. (2001). International public relations: A framework for future research. *Journal of communication management, 6*(2): 103–117.

Sriramesh, K., Kim, Y., & Takasi, M. (1999). Public relations in three Asian cultures: An analysis. *Journal of public relations research, 11*(4): 271–292.

Stohl, C. (2001). Globalizing organizational communication. In F. M. Jablin & L. L. Putnam (Eds.), *The new handbook of organizational: Advances in Theory, Research, and Methods* (pp. 323–375). Thousand Oaks, CA: Sage.

United Nations Development Programme (UNPD). (1999). *Human development report 1999*. New York: Oxford University Press.

Verčič, D. (1997). Towards fourth wave public relations: A case study. In D. Moss, T. MacManus, & D. Verčič (Eds.), *Public relations research: An international perspective* (pp. 264–279). London: ITP.

Verčič, D., & Grunig, J. E. (2000). The origins of public relations theory in economics and strategic management. In D. Moss, D. Verčič, & G. Warnaby (Eds.), *Perspectives on public relations research* (pp. 9–58). London: Routledge.

Verčič, D., Grunig, L. A., & Grunig, J. E. (1995). Global and specific principles of public relations: Evidence from Slovenia. In H. M. Culbertson & N. Chen (Eds.), *International public relations: A comparative analysis* (pp. 31–65). Mahwah, NJ: Lawrence Erlbaum Associates.

Verčič, D., Razpet, A., Dekleva, S., & Šlenc, M. (2000). International public relations and the Internet: Diffusion and linkages. *Journal of communication management 5*(2), 125–137.

Verčič, D., van Ruler, B., Bütschi, G., & Flodin, B. (2001). On the definition of public relations: A European view. *Public Relations Review, 27*(4), 373–387.

Vernon, R. (1968). Economic sovereignty at bay. *Foreign Affairs, 47*(1), 110–122.

Wakefield, R. I. (1999). World-class public relations: A model for effective public relations in the multinational. In D. Verčič, J. White, & D. Moss (Eds.), *Proceedings of the 6th international public relations research symposium: Innovation in public relations, public affairs and corporate communication practice* (pp. 30–37). Ljubljana: Pristop Communications.

Wakefield, R. I. (2000). Preliminary Delphi research on international public relations programming: Initial data support application of certain generic/specific concepts. In D. Moss, D. Verčič, & G. Warnaby (Eds.), *Perspectives on public relations research* (pp. 179–208). London: Routledge.

Wakefield, R. I. (2001). Effective public relations in the multinational organization. In R. L. Heath (Ed.), *Handbook of public relations* (pp. 639–647). Thousand Oaks, CA: Sage.

Wallace, C. D. (1982). *Legal control of the multinational enterprise: National regulatory techniques and the prospects for international controls*. The Hague: Martinus Nijhoff.

White, J. (1997). Business and organizational consequences of the moral role of the public relations practitioner. In D. Moss, T. MacManus, & D. Verčič (Eds.), *Public relations research: An international perspective* (pp. 159–169). London: ITP.

Yip, G. S. (2001). Global strategy in the twenty-first century. In S. Crainer & D. Dearlove (Eds.), *Financial Times handbook of management*, 2nd ed. (pp. 150–163). London: Financial Times & Prentice Hall.

CHAPTER

24

NONGOVERNMENTAL ORGANIZATIONS AND INTERNATIONAL PUBLIC RELATIONS

ANA TKALAC

JURICA PAVICIC

FABULA DOCET! (STORY TEACHES US)

The nonprofit sector consists of organized individuals or organizations that wish to create a society as a community of responsible individuals oriented toward personal or family interests as well as toward the interests and development of their local community and global society (Pavicic, 2000). For more than 40 years, the social role of the nonprofit sector has been investigated and documented by various authors (Kotler & Zaltman, 1971; Lazer, 1969; Samuelson, 1970). Social analysts have been intensively researching this area since the late 1950s, determining the field through three main elements of modern society—government, community, and the market (Smith & Lipsky, 1993).

Another topic closely related to this field of research includes the concept of social responsibility—taking care of the community, which is for the most part oriented toward resolving social problems and crises. Solving problems such as war, disease, or hunger and promoting international development should primarily be considered part of the standard "business portfolio" of government/governmental institutions.

However, such problems are often resolved by the actions of community actors that are independent, cooperating, and non-governmental (Bellah, 1985; Pavicic, 2000). Why is this so? Many governments and governmental institutions are usually either not able, not prepared, or not willing to be involved in the resolution of specific social problems— especially in "troublesome" cases like human rights, international democracy, democratic elections, or ecology. The only "Robin Hoods" left to help in such situations are nonprofit organizations. Even though nongovernmental organizations (NGOs) have consistently used public relations as a primary tool to mobilize public opinion in their favor, public relations literature on this subject is rather thin.

INTERNATIONAL NGOs AND SOCIETY/THE INTERNATIONAL COMMUNITY— *IN AEDEM ES NAVI!* (THE SAME DESTINY AWAITS US)

Socially engaged activism, especially at the international level, is mostly organized by NGOs.[1] Charnovitz (1997, p. 186) offered the following description of nongovernmental organizations:

> NGOs are groups of individuals organized for the myriad of reasons that engage human imagination and aspiration. They can be set up to advocate a particular cause, such as human rights, or to carry out programs on the ground, such as disaster relief. They can have memberships ranging from local to global.

People and organizations willing and dedicated to work and achieve the above-mentioned goals are derived from one of the key democratic rights—the right of citizens to organize themselves (Pentikainen, 2000). Although there is no general regulation governing NGOs, the basis for obtaining "nongovernmental" status includes three criteria: (1) NGOs should not be constituted as political parties, (2) they should not have profit as a motive, and (3) they should not be criminal in operation—in particular, they should be nonviolent (Willetts, 2002).

These characteristics are formally articulated in documents such as the European Convention on the Recognition of the Legal Personality of International Non-governmental Organizations (Strasbourg, 1986—Council of Europe) and United Nations Economic and Social Council (UN ECOSOC) resolutions.

There is evidence to suggest that the development of nongovernmental organizations (or bodies that are not part of the state or kingdom), as well as the idea of universal *pro bono* activism, can be traced far back in time. Antonides & Van Raaij (1998) emphasized that in the medieval period some theoreticians such as Aquinas, Luther, and Calvin, insisted on the social responsibility of merchants and bankers and suggested that those who ignored the problems of poor people (hunger, disease, poverty), be socially "excommunicated."

Simmons (1998), Paul (2000), and other authors agreed that ideas on the necessity of acting in an organized way for the good of the community have existed since the early 1800s. According to Simmons (1998), the British and Foreign Anti-Slavery Society were the forerunners and even the initiators of government actions against slavery. Those actions resulted in the World Anti-Slavery Convention of 1840. Other forerunners of international nongovernmental organizations such as the World Alliance of YMCA (in 1855) and the International Committee for the Red Cross (in 1863) were founded relatively soon afterward (Paul, 2000).

---

[1]The term "nongovernmental organizations (NGOs)" is sometimes considered a synonym for "nonprofit organizations" or *vice versa*. In many cases there is no significant difference between these two terms that could affect understanding of these words in essence—the difference may only be lexical. However, "nonprofit organizations" should be considered as a superordinate term because it includes a wider range of organizations and institutions. According to Paul (2000), nonprofit organizations also include institutions like museums, universities, and hospitals focused on services with sporadic engagement in advocacy. In contrast, NGOs are significantly dedicated to advocacy.

The development of numerous local, national and international independent societies or organizations led to the formation of the Union of International Organizations (*Union des associations internationals*) in 1910. This union consisted of more than 130 international organizations (Rice & Ritchie, 1995; Willetts, 2002).

Although the international visibility of nongovernmental organizations of that time was quite developed and at times even officially directed through bodies such as the League of Nations, international NGOs were formally recognized only in June 1946 by the United Nations when the Committee on Non-Governmental Organizations was established as a standing committee of the ECOSOC—Economic and Social Council (Economic and Social Council resolution 3 (II), 1946).

NGOs might sometimes consider themselves as the only real representatives and benevolent protectors of the society, often leading to tensions between NGOs and governments. According to Paul (2000), elected government officials and bureaucrats defend themselves against NGO criticism by pointing out that NGO leaders are not democratically elected. However the mission of NGOs is largely directed at helping society's human development by using their "social capital," the potential to cause or hasten positive social changes (Putnam, 1993).

One of the recent concepts very relevant to NGOs is the concept of *civil society.* Although Judge (1994) emphasized the difficulties caused by the fact that civil society is discussed through a variety of terms such as NGOs, voluntary associations, nonprofit and charitable organizations, etc., it is important to grasp the concept's main characteristics. Because the term "civil society" was rarely used prior to 1989, one could argue that "civil society" gained currency as a concept only at the time of the transformation of the U.S.S.R. (Judge, 1996).

However, the main problem with providing a definition for the term "civil society" is in providing a response to the question: Who are its stakeholders? Cohen and Arato (1992) equate civil society with persons, institutions, and organizations that have the goal of expressing or advancing a common purpose through ideas, actions and demands on governments. According to Agenda 21 of the 1992 Rio Earth Summit (Commission on Sustainable Development [CSD] in Gemill & Bamidele-Izu, 2002), civil society might be classified into eight main groups: women, children and young people, indigenous peoples and communities, *nongovernmental organizations*, workers and trade unions, the scientific and technological community, business and industry, and farmers.

Because the problems that NGOs have to deal with are so diverse and encompass the political, economic, and social aspects of human existence, any generalization of the practical methods, goals or actors might be considered an inappropriate simplification. Instead, it might be useful to consider an analysis of the levels of NGO activities offered by Paul (2000). By using the example of the World Court Project, a network of NGOs opposed to nuclear weapons, Paul suggested the following levels:

1. Micro-policy (getting the World Court to accept the case on the illegality of nuclear weapons),

2. Macro-policy (questioning governments' strategic reliance on such weapons), and

3. Norm-setting (persuading the public(s) that nuclear weapons are dangerous and a threat to real security in the world).

Although there are three levels to the action mentioned above, other initiatives might consist only of one or two levels.

TABLE 24.1
Changes in Terminology Related to NGOs

Level of Organization	From 1946 to the Early 1990s	From the Early 1990s Onward
Local	National NGO, at the UN Not discussed elsewhere	Grassroots, community-based or civil society organization, or local NGO
Provincial (United States—state)	National NGO, at the United Nations Not discussed elsewhere	Civil society organization or local NGO
National	National NGO, at the UN NGO, outside the UN	NGO or national NGO or civil society organization
Regional	International NGO	NGO or civil society organization
Global	International NGO	NGO or major group or civil society organization

Note. From *UNESCO Encyclopedia of Life Support Systems*, by P. Willetts, 2000.

The idea of international NGO activism is confirmed by many institutions worldwide. NGOs cooperate with the UN, governments, parliaments, numerous private organizations, and companies. One of the most important symbolic social honors for international NGOs was the 1997 Nobel Peace Prize given to Jody Williams, Head of the International Committee to Ban Landmines. The recognition she received and other widely publicized statements such as the declaration that the main weapon in her campaign was the e-mail, further increased the popularity of international NGO activism (Knickerbocker, 2000).

There is no doubt that NGO activism is a "developing area." Consequently, since 1946, the social, economic, and political environment has brought changes to the widely used terminology covering the international dimension of NGOs (Table 24.1). NGOs are sometimes not taken very seriously and cannot totally avoid the reputation of being utopian, antagonistic to governments, and potentially obstructionist (Dichter, 1999). However, among all other participants in the contemporary globalization process, NGOs might be considered as the person in the famous quotation by Alphonse de Lamartine: "Sometimes, when one person is missing, the whole world seems depopulated." Why is this so? Probably because of the important social role of NGOs in monitoring and forcing local and world leaders to take care of others and championing worthy causes such as democracy, cultural appreciation, universal education, and the preservation of the ecology.

FIGURES— *PLUS ULTRA!* (YET FURTHER)

The problem of inconsistent criteria that makes it difficult to produce any uniform classification, as well as the constant changes in the activities of NGOs, casts doubt on the reliability of various quantifications (e.g., number of employees/volunteers, number of projects, etc.) of the activities of international NGOs. However, since recognition from the United Nations in 1946, there has been considerable development of international NGOs. The largest growth in the number of international NGOs occurred in the period 1990–2000 as indicated in Table 24.2.

TABLE 24.2
Growth of International NGOs Between 1990 and 2000

Purpose	1990	2000	Growth (%)
Culture and recreation	1,169	2,733	26
Education	1,485	1,839	23.8
Research	7,675	8,467	10.3
Health	1,357	2,036	50
Social services	2,361	4,215	78.5
Environment	979	1,170	19.5
Economic development, infrastructure	9,582	9,614	0.3
Law, policy, advocacy	2,712	3,864	42.5
Religion	1,407	1,869	32.8
Defense	244	234	−4.1
Politics	1,275	1,240	−2.7
Total	31,246	37,281	19.3

Note. From *Human Development Report 2002*, by Anheier, Glasius, and Kaldor, 2001.

CURRENT PROBLEMS AND CRITICISMS OF INTERNATIONAL NGOs VERSUS INTERNATIONAL PUBLIC RELATION—*QUAE CULPARE SOLES, EA TU NE FECERIS IPSE!* (DON'T DO YOURSELF, WHAT YOU USUALLY DISAPPROVE OF)

NGOs and all their relevant stakeholders might be negatively influenced by issues that provoke certain public criticisms and, to some extent, go against the idea of modern non-governmental activism and the important international social role it plays. The most notable problems in such a context are:

- *Sometimes the status of international NGO is abused to achieve some latent political, religious or economic benefits—quite different from the formally declared benefits.* There is always one rotten apple in the barrel. The bad apple can rot the others as well as damage the basic idea of eating apples. In the case of NGOs, the "dangerous apples" could be organizations or networks with unacceptable or controversial missions or methods of operation. The most commonly used international example in this context is al Qaeda (Naim, 2002). A different kind of NGO, but still very controversial, is the organization of the Reverend Sun Myung Moon (Paine & Gratzer, 2001). For instance, the Moon organization is working very hard to achieve a leading role in the NGO community at the United Nations declaring:

  > "The organization of the Reverend Sun Myung Moon is seeking a major role in the NGO community at the UN. . . . The Moon organization has used the UN for conferences and for publicity events. . . . A new Moon-sponsored "umbrella group," known as the World Association of NGOs (WANGO), proposes itself as an authentic voice of the NGO community. . . ." (Paine & Gratzer, 2001, pp. 1–24).

  It is also worrying that there are reports on the Moon organization's systematical violation of United States tax, immigration, banking and other laws (Parry, 1997) or information on the Moon organization's criticism of women for acting as men's equals (Paine & Gratzer, 2001).

- *In some countries and regions, international NGOs with large potential and resources could generate misunderstanding and distorted perceptions regarding the concept of being "nonprofit" (which is one of the most important components of their NGO status).* Although NGOs might have an international focus and outreach, they act locally. Local people working for NGOs in some regions might treat them as "cash cows." Some of them might be able to earn several times more by working for NGOs than by working for local businesses or government. Abramson (1999) cited the example of Uzbekistan where although the average state salary was $120 per year in 1998, local drivers, administrative assistants, or receptionists working for international NGOs were earning between $2,400 and $4,800 annually! Some authors emphasized that in many cases such distorted perceptions of nonprofit status and all related disparities could also be caused by so-called "professional do-gooders" or "professional altruists" who, work for international NGOs advocating altruist causes but live in luxurious houses, have expensive cars, and enjoy many such material benefits. These professionals also typically earn ten or twenty times more than the average local wage (Vaknin, 2002)

- *At some stage of their life cycle, some international NGOs become unproductive and bureaucratic.* Such problems affect all types of organizations in both the profit and non-profit sector (Pavicic, 2000). The problem is obvious in organizations that have an increasingly international impact. Through organizational change and growth, these organizations may begin to lose their flexibility, their established values and their effectiveness (Edwards & Hulme [1992] cited in Uvin & Miller, 1994). On the other hand, there are examples from some African countries where local NGOs might consist of only three people (e.g., a director, a secretary, and a driver) and no members (Onishi, 2002). This also reflects negatively on the general perception of NGOs.

- *Some international NGOs may be involved in misuse of financial and other resources* (Paine & Gratzer, 2001). Although only a few NGOs may be guilty of this, they can tarnish the reputation of all NGOs and have a negative effect on NGOs' publics, especially donors.

- *Sometimes international NGOs are seen only through the spectacles of "fashionable case studies"—like the Red Cross (Judge, 1994), Amnesty International, or Greenpeace.* Such case studies can be informative, interesting and educative for practitioners, but such extremely positive examples could generate a certain level of frustration and demotivation among other, less successful, organizations.

- *Some NGOs could have a conflict of interest.* One of the recent cases that might be perceived in this light is the Cafedirect-Oxfam case. According to Vaknin (2002), Cafedirect is a firm committed to the "fair trade" of coffee. The NGO Oxfam owns a 25% stake in Cafedirect. Oxfam started a campaign against Cafedirect's competitors and accused them of exploiting coffee growers by paying them only a tiny fraction of the final retail price. Such involvement in market competing could lead to conflicts of interest and/or unethical behavior among NGOs. A similar type of conflict may be seen in instances where NGOs are partly financed by governments or government agencies (Pharoah, 2002). In such cases, the key questions are "Can I bite the hand that feeds me?" and "Am I really non-governmental?"

- *"Illegality" is illegality!* Although some authors declare that "illegality" is often a matter of interpretation and environment (Judge, 1994), many international NGOs are caught in a "double measures" trap. They insist on a strict social expulsion of NGOs that are obviously illegal, and those that engage in behaviors such as violence, supporting terrorism, or racial segregation. It is also important to observe here that some NGOs do not register themselves with appropriate authorities in countries where they are active, preferring to work illegally (Judge, 1994).

- *NGOs are considered as important social partners in bringing positive social changes.* Therefore, sometimes NGOs are faced with numerous "missions impossible" thrust upon them by other social partners whose expectations are too high and unrealistic (Lewis, 1998; Pavicic, 1997).

- *Large international NGOs from developed countries sometimes develop standards based on "western" traditions and expect these standards to be universally applicable.* The so-called effect of "westernizing" can be seen as a serious image problem (Toulmin, 1994). Moreover, examples of local acceptance of "westernizing" could even culminate in protests or negative consequences for those local organizations that cooperate with international NGOs. For instance, in Jordan, the editor of an independent weekly magazine was expelled from the local union of journalists because he was accused of accepting foreign donations for his projects (Mekki, 2000). According to Vichit-Vadakan (2001), NGOs in Thailand are perceived by many Thais as agents that aim to undermine local society and the Thai way of life. Sometimes this clash can be put in simple stereotypical terms—wealthy countries and their organizations emphasize ecology and democracy, while underdeveloped countries really need jobs and food (Shikwati, 2002).

- *Large international NGOs could attract large donors who perceive them as the only organizations capable of coping with certain social difficulties.* Such donors could also be interested in having a reliable partner institution. Since the number of donors and their funds are limited, smaller national, regional and even international NGOs could be at a handicap in their fund-raising activities.

- *The effects of NGOs' work could be counterproductive (or perceived as such).* There is evidence that the arrival of NGOs might provoke local social polarizations and other clashes, or that NGOs could be perceived as "irritating" (Vaknin, 2002). Vaknin also emphasized the problem of good intentions but bad effects in the case of footballs stitched by children of Pakistan. Because of the actions of NGOs and the fear of worldwide protests against child labor, Nike and Reebok relocated their workshops and took work away from some 7000 children. The NGOs' intentions were good, but the average family income in these extremely poor families fell by 20 percent (Vaknin, 2002). The result was that child labor was eradicated, but, this also meant that the children had fewer clothes and less food! Unfortunately, in this case, both alternatives could be considered as bad, but the affected families probably think that the decrease in income is the worse option.

NGOs AND PUBLIC RELATIONS—*PER ASPERA AD ASTRA!* (THROUGH A PATH OF THORNS TO THE STARS)

All positive social roles, along with criticism and problems, create space for the implementation of international public relations. Public relations could, in a sense, be considered a catalyst or even generator of positive international NGO practice and an impediment to negative practices. Gemmill & Bambidele-Izu (2002) suggested that civil society, through NGOs, should have one of the most important roles in the following five areas of activities:

- Information collection and dissemination
- Policy development consultation
- Policy implementation

- Assessment and monitoring
- Advocacy for environmental justice

Wilcox, Ault, Agee, and Cameron (2000) stated that traditionally, all nonprofit social agencies were viewed as the "good guys" of society and as high-minded, compassionate organizations whose members were committed to helping people live a better life. This perception has recently been seriously challenged. During the early 1990s different charity organizations came into the center of public attention due, among other things, to extremely high executive salaries and different forms of financial improprieties.

The American Red Cross faced massive public protests over its mismanagement of funds collected after the earthquakes of San Francisco in 1989. The organization collected approximately $52 million and initially distributed only $10 million to those affected by the earthquake. After public pressure, the organization rechanneled the entire amount to the victims (Tate, 2002). After the September 11, 2001 tragedy in New York and Washington, D.C., the Red Cross drew the wrath of the public by announcing that it planned to channel part of the money collected by the Liberty Fund to future projects unrelated to the tragedy. At first, the Red Cross designated only 10% of the fund to the families of victims. After the vociferous public criticism it received, the Red Cross reversed its earlier policy and announced that all the money raised for the Liberty Fund would be distributed to September 11 victims only and not reserved for any future use by the organization (Tate, 2002).

The United Way of America was another NGO that came under public scrutiny for fraud. In one of the most highly publicized scandals, William Aramony resigned in 1992 as president and CEO when he was charged with tax manipulation, misusing huge sums of donor contributions for his own benefit, and filing false income tax returns (Young, 2002). The "United Way of America" story become a topic not only in the news, but also in public relations textbooks (Cutlip, Center, & Broom, 1999; Wilcox, Ault, Agee & Cameron, 2000). Even though the story is now more than 10 years old, the public still remembers it well and this NGO has lost some of its luster.

Such erosion in public confidence has been instrumental in making organizations that depend almost exclusively on the goodwill of people change the way they communicate with the public. Reforms in the way NGOs operate and communicate were aimed at reassuring the public that contributions are being spent for the core charitable mission of these organizations, with minimal spending on administrative costs (Frumkin and Kim, 2001). In the light of these events, public relations has gained new importance assuming responsibility for rebuilding organizational credibility and restoring public confidence.

Modern society is typified by intense media scrutiny in many parts of the world making any attempt to fool the public a fatal proposition. All NGOs are more or less dependent on the support of the public. All are also placed in the middle of various social, political, and economic trends that require high-quality management and good public relations. According to Cutlip, Center, and Broom (1999), the altered climate of the 1990s brought about a significant change in the way that public relations is practiced by NGOs. These authors mentioned five major trends in this area: the introduction of marketing and management concepts in communications strategies; the development of information technology and its implications; the use of advertising in public relations programs; the need for the adaptation of a public relations curriculum; and a constant increase in public relations standards in non-profit organizations.

Marketing concepts and management by objectives are becoming increasingly important to the communication strategies of NGOs. McConkey (1975) claimed that management by objectives was the prominent style of leadership for non-profit organizations. This meant that "association leaders contain their activities in a clearly defined set of organizational goals" (p. 223). Kelly (2000) stated in his article on nonprofit public relations management: "Management by objectives is a central concept in the public relations process, which dictates that activities are planned and implemented in support of functional objectives derived from organizational goals" (p. 90). The challenges that NGOs face in the new competitive and performance-driven world can be met through a better, and more efficient management process. Improving the management of communications, as well as management in general, is seen as a way of raising operational effectiveness.

Technology has widened communication selectivity and reach, but on the other hand, has also raised the question of ethics, privacy and legitimacy. Sanborn (2000) stated: "By using the Web, non-profit groups are beginning to create individual identities and use skills they learned offline to present their message to a new, often global audience" (p. 37). Reis (2000) reported on a recent study from the Mellman Group that showed the vast potential of the Internet in bringing about social change. The study contended that about 50 million Americans over 18 have Internet access and also contribute time and money to charitable or advocacy causes.

On the other hand, the Internet has also proved a crucial tool in organizing activist groups. It has also directly equipped protesters with a powerful weapon. Global Exchange, for example, set up a "virtual activist" tool kit online to protest against Gap's labor conditions. The kit included a standard letter to send to the company, as well as anti-Gap flyers; all documents could be easily downloaded from the Internet site (as quoted by Li, 2001). Another example includes the demonstrations that followed Seattle's 1999 World Trade Organizations meeting that were organized by a coalition of environmental and citizens' groups who had been communicating with each other prior to the demonstrations. About 1500 NGOs signed an anti-WTO protest declaration created online by Public Citizen. The Internet allowed organizers to share ideas and tactics instantly and without much expenditure of scarce resources. Without e-mail, such a massive mobilization would have been impossible (Kettl, 2000).

One of the consequences of the revolution in communication technology is that people are overwhelmed with information overload. The only effective response is a comprehensive and focused strategic communication plan, based on coordinating communication management with the work of public relations professionals (Lauer, 1993).

Paid advertising has become the main communication tactic of NGOs. The American Cancer Society has achieved great success by carefully identifying concerns that people really care about, providing services that connect with major public issues, and communicating its activities effectively through advertising (Gallagher & Vaughan, 2002). Kotler and Andreasen (1996) stated that one of the characteristics of organization-centered nonprofit organizations is that they rely excessively on advertising and promotion to achieve their objectives. The authors added that "this is partly because they have a distorted view of what it takes to change people's behavior" (p. 516).

The need for building coalitions in communities and empowering the people that are being helped requires different skills than those taught in traditional public relations curricula. Ehling (1992) stated that "Although the picture of public relations professionalism has brightened over the years and public relations educational programs have grown and strengthened, all is not well" (p. 456). The principles and specifics of communication in nonprofit organizations have undergone significant transformations in recent years becoming more complex. On the one hand, this increase in complexity needs to be followed by a formalized body of knowledge that is the subject of academic study. On the other, there is a growing need for establishing academic programs that can train professionals to work in this field. Such an education should extend beyond any single traditional discipline encompassing a wide variety of skills instead. Current university public relations programs are not adequately responding to the needs of nonprofit communications specialists or to the requirements of international communicators. To effectively prepare these professionals, specific knowledge and perspectives need to be integrated in educational programs.

NGO Executives have higher expectations for professional public relations providers. Managers of NGOs increasingly recognize how essential public relations is to their success. Cutlip, Center, and Broom (1999) believe that public relations practice in a nonprofit organization includes a wide spectrum of approaches. While a single practitioner may be assisting an NGO by implementing a simple publicity campaign, there may be other instances where NGOs could have a large, professional, public relations department with a strategic plan and an adequate budget.

It is essential to take all these trends into consideration when planning a strategic communication campaign, whether national or international. However, the question that remains is what are the elements of international public relations in the communication strategies of NGOs. Does the development of information technology and the globalization of the media guarantee a place for every "good" cause on the planet?

The process of globalization accentuates the need for the development of international public relations principles. Verčič, L. Grunig, and J. E. Grunig (1996) have identified nine normative generic principles that can be used to describe, and practice, global public relations. These authors also proposed five environmental variables that can be used to construct country specific strategies, which include political ideology, the economic system, the level of activism, culture, and media culture. Sriramesh and Verčič (2001) later reduced these five factors to three: a country's infrastructure, the media environment, and societal culture, which are described in Chapter 1 of this volume. It is easy to see how each of these dimensions influences the public relations strategies of the typical NGO. Taking into consideration the diverse global characteristics and specifics of the different publics around the world, the question is, Are there any universally applicable values?

NGOs AND INTERNATIONAL PUBLIC RELATIONS—*EXTRA MUROS ET INTRA!* (WITHIN AND OUTSIDE THE WALLS)

"Optimistic observers imagine a global meritocracy of suffering in which all deserving causes attract international support" (Bob, 2002, p. 37). Allen L. Hammond of the World Resources Institute recently proposed that the combination of global media, new technologies, and altruistic NGOs may soon empower the "underrepresented" of the world (cited in Bob, 2002). But while there are different groups that have felt the benefits of the globalization of NGOs and the public relations that helps promote their causes, there are many questions in this domain that remain unanswered.

In today's society where the media determine what is "just," NGOs have to struggle to gain public attention among many competing interests while also overcoming indifference of this international audience. They also have to compete with various powerful opponents such as governments, multinational companies, and international financial institutions that are supported by highly organized public relations. In that kind of context the transnational NGO community displays a clear hierarchy of influence and reputation. Large and powerful organizations such as the Human Rights Watch, Amnesty International, Greenpeace, and Friends of the Earth have the resources and expertise to investigate the claims of local groups from distant places and give them legitimacy (Bob, 2002).

"The worldwide reach of media organizations such as CNN [the BBC, and Sky Television] may lead one to think that communication strategies are cross-cultural. They are not. A safe rule of thumb is to simply assume that each time the borders are crossed, the rules of the game change" (Boyer, 1997, p. 485). People live in different countries that often are also culturally distinct. One of the themes of this book (described in Chapter 1) is that every country is a complex system of social relations, religious beliefs, languages, attitudes, and habits, all of which will obviously impact on how communications are received and delivered. It is a basic principle in communications theory that, for any communication to be successful, the sender of the message must understand the frame of reference of the receiver of the message (Schramm, 1954). Obviously, the international NGO must understand the cultural dimensions of its relevant publics in order to be successful, because they may differ substantially from the public of its own home culture.

There are various dimensions of culture such as the degree of traditionalism, the degree of secularism, the degree to which cultures rely on explicit and verbal information (low context cultures) versus implicit and nonverbal information (high context cultures), and the degree to which they are oriented towards the individual rather than being interdependent or relational (Batra, Myers, & Aaker, 1999). For example, many researchers have classified North American and Western European cultures as relatively more secular, low context, and oriented toward the individual, in contrast to Asian cultures, while Hispanic cultures fall somewhere in between (Martenson, 1989). As described in Chapter 1, Hofstede (1980) found that the United States, Great Britain, and Canada represented individualistic cultures, while the United States proved to have low tolerance for ambiguity.

Given these differences across cultures on various environmental variables, it seems logical that the publics in different countries may have different ways of deciding whom to trust, different levels of involvement toward the same cause, and so on. Considering the lack of relevant research in the area of international public relations of NGOs, this question remains unanswered. Despite this lack of empirical evidence, the starting point in formulating the main goals of international public relations for non-governmental organizations should not differ significantly from the objectives NGOs identify for their domestic activities. The objectives that Wilcox et al. (2000) defined for nonprofit organizations (p. 389) can be viewed from an international perspective:

1. *Develop public awareness of the organization's purpose and activities.* All of the trends mentioned earlier, mainly the globalization of media and the fast development of information technology make it possible to communicate globally. Delivering the message to an international public becomes easier in light of those trends, even though the problem of cultural and national differences still remains an issue.

NGOs have become sophisticated communicators and instigators of change in the global marketplace. Wootliff and Deri (2002) reported on a study conducted in the United States, Europe, and Australia which showed that in spite of large differences in size and approach among NGOs, these organizations are "no longer perceived as small brands of activists, but rather as the new 'super brands,' surpassing the stature of major corporations, government bodies and even the media among consumers" (p. 159).

In November 1997, *The New York Times* published a confidential Ernst & Young audit of labor and environmental activists it had conducted for one of Nike's factories in Vietnam. The audit, which was leaked to the newspaper, outlined the bad environmental practices of Nike, generating a series of articles and columns in newspapers across the United States and around the world critical of Nike. The NGO Working Assets Citizen Action followed up on the story and generated 33,000 letters to Nike CEO Phil Knight, urging him to pay workers a living wage and to implement a comprehensive third-party monitoring system.

Pressure was brought upon Nike by NGOs such as Global Exchange and Vietnam Labor Watch who also encouraged universities doing business with Nike to push it into changing its behavior. In 1998 Nike announced its pledge to end child labor, to follow United States occupational health and safety standards, and to allow NGOs to participate in the monitoring of its Asian factories (Wootliff and Deri, 2002).

2. *Induce individuals to use the services the nongovernmental organization provides.* After the public becomes aware of the NGO's purpose, the second and closely related step is connecting with the people at whom the service is aimed. The importance of communication in informing potential users of free medical examinations, clothing, food, counseling, scholarships, and other services is essential. The difficulties in transcending communication barriers are significant even without an international dimension. An example includes health and welfare agencies that need to build a communication bridge between ethnic communities. Traditional programs and communication messages fail to reach various needy publics because of cultural and linguistic differences, limited access to information, and low levels of education (Cutlip, Center, & Broom, 1999).

3. *Create educational materials (especially important for health-oriented agencies).* Again the international factor plays a major role in the formulation of the message but the issue of "speaking the same language" is a problem for NGOs domestically as well as internationally. The main challenge is in understanding the publics with whom the NGO is communicating. For example, in the population control campaigns in many developing countries, a major achievement of public relations campaigns has been to demystify contraception and make it acceptable for public discussion of contraception in general, and specific contraceptive methods in particular (Kotler & Andreasen, 1996).

4. *Recruit and train volunteer workers.* A significant proportion of international nonprofit organizations rely on unpaid volunteers for clerical assistance, fundraising, conducting tours and even volunteer recruitment. This can create two types of problems for the manager of the nonprofit organization. First, the need for a steady inflow of volunteers means that a third public is added to those with whom the manager must communicate. On one hand, programs must be designed to attract paid personnel, while on the other, communicators must be careful about the possible consequences of the proposed programs on existing volunteers, none of which is simplified with the international factor. Second, it is not easy to manage volunteers, because their status allows them to get away with a higher level of unreliability (Kotler & Andreasen, 1996).

Cutlip, Center, and Broom (1999) reported that almost 40 million people volunteer each year in the United States. Because volunteers are an important resource in the life and economy of many NGOs, nongovernmental organizations need to constantly work toward attracting more volunteers. To continue attracting volunteers in the numbers necessary to carry out their programs, organizations need to take innovative approaches in communicating with their publics (Baskin and Aronoff, 1988).

5. *Obtain funds to operate the organization.* The main financial resources of NGOs worldwide consist of large donations from private foundations, large individual public contributions, companies, other NGOs and government/governmental agencies. According to an estimate by Hulme and Edwards (1996), some $5.7–10 billion passes through international NGOs annually. The role of high-quality, transparent international communication strategies in obtaining these funds is crucial.

Finally, one should take into consideration the fact that "communication influences, and is influenced by, culture. Logically, then, culture should affect public relations and, because public relations involves communication, public relations does help alter culture" (Sriramesh & Verčič, 2001, p. 106.). It becomes quite obvious that all the elements of non-governmental operations have significant implications on society as a whole. The changing competitive environments that affect the business world similarly affect NGO which must adapt to the changing social and economic environments. In such a surrounding, "effective communication and public relations strategies will be central to their success" (Boyer, 1997, p. 508).

REFERENCES

Abramson, D. M. (1999). A critical look at NGOs and Civil Society as means to an end in Uzbekistan. *Human Organizations*, Fall, *58*(3), 240–250.

Anheier, H., Glasius, M., & Kaldor, M. (2001). Global Civil Society. Oxford: Oxford University Press. Retrieved October 21, 2002 from http://www.undp.org/hdr2002/ and http://globalpolicy.igc.org/ngos/role/ intro/growth2000.htm

Antonides, G., & Van Raaij, W. F. (1998). *Consumer Behavior*. Chicester: Wiley.

Baskin, O. W., & Aronoff, C. E. (1988). *Public relations: The profession and the practice*. Dubuque, IA: Wm. C. Brown.

Batra, R., Myers, J. G., & Aaker, D. A. (1999). *Advertising management*. New Delhi: Prentice Hall of India.

Bellah, R. N., (ed.) (1985). *Habits of the heart: Individualism and commitment in American Life*. New York: Harper and Row.

Bob, C. (2002). Merchants of morality. *Foreign Policy, 129*, 36–45.

Boyer, R. (1997). Public relations and communications for nonprofit organizations. In C. L. Caywood (Ed.), *The handbook of strategic public relations & integrated communications*. (pp. 481–508). Boston: McGraw Hill.

Charnovitz, S. (1997). Two centuries of participation: NGOs and international governence. *Michigan Journal of International Law, 18*(2), 183–286.

Cohen, J. L, & Arato, A. (1992). *Civil society and political theory*. Cambridge, MA: MIT Press.

Council of Europe (1986). European Convention on the Recognition of the Legal Personality of International Non-Governmental Organisations. Strasbourg.

Cutlip, S. M., Center, A. H., & Broom, G. M. (1999). *Effective public relations*, 8th ed. New Jersey: Prentice Hall.

Dichter, T. W. (1999). Globalization ands its effects on NGOs: Efflorescence or a blurring of roles and relevance?. *Nonprofit and Voluntary Sector Quarterly, 28*(4), 38–58.

Edwards & Hulme (1992). In P. Uvin, & D. Miller (Eds.) (1994). *Scalling Up: Thinking Through the Issues*. The World Hunger Program. Retrieved October 23, 2002 from http://www.globalpolicy.org/ngos/role/ intro/imp/2000/1204.htm

Ehling, W. P. (1992). Public relations education and professionalism. In J. Grunig (Ed.), *Excellence in public relations and communications management* (pp. 439–466). Hillsdale, NJ: Lawrence Erlbaum Associates.

Frumkin, P., & Kim, M. T. (2001). Strategic positioning and the financing of nonprofit organizations: Is efficiency rewarded in the contributions marketplace? *Public Administration Review, 61*(3), 266–275.

Gallagher, M., & Vaughan, S. R. (2002). Internal controls in nonprofit organizations: The case of the American Cancer Society, Ohio Division, *Nonprofit Management and Leadership, 12*(3), 313–325.

Gemmill, B. & Bamidele-Izu, A. (2002). *The Role of NGOs and civil society in global environmental governance*. In Esty D. C. & Ivanova, M. H. (eds.) Global Environmental Governance: Options and Opportunities. Yale School of Forestry and Environmental Studies. New Haven CT.

Hofstede, G. (1980). *Culture's consequences*. Beverly Hills, CA: Sage.

Hulme, D., & Edwards, M. (1996). (Eds.). *NGOs, states and donors: Too close to comfort?* New York: St. Martin's Press.

Judge, A. (1994). NGOs and civil society: Some realities and distortions the challenge of "necessary-to-Governance organizations" (NGOs). Adaptation of a paper presented to a Seminar on State and Society at the Russian Public Policy Center, Moscow, December 6–8, 1994. Retrieved October 21, 2002 from http://www.globalpolicy.org/ngos/role/intro/def/2000/civso.htm

Judge, A. (1996). Interacting fruitfully with un-civil Society the dilemma for non-civil society organizations. Presentation to a World Bank Workshop on Civil Society in the FSU and East/Central Europe, Washington, DC, October 16, 1996. Published in *Transnational Associations, 49*(3), 1997, 124–132. Retrieved October 21, 2002 from http://www.globalpolicy.org/ngos/role/intro/def/2000/un-civ.htm

Kelly, K. S. (2000). Managing public relations for nonprofits. *Nonprofit Management and Leadership, 11*(1), 87–95.

Kettl, D. F. (2000). The transformation of governance: Globalization, devolution, and the role of government. *Public Administration Review, 60*(6), 488–497.

Knickerbocker, B. (2000). Nongovernmental organizations are fighting and winning social, political battles. Christian Science Monitor Website/Nando Media, February 6, 2000. Retrieved October 23, 2002 from http://www.globalpolicy.org/ngos/00role.htm

Kotler, P., & Andreasen, A. R. (1996). *Strategic Marketing for NonProfit Organizations*, 5th ed. Upper Saddle River, NJ: Prentice Hall.

Kotler, P., & Zaltman, G. (1971, July). Social marketing: An approach to planned social change, *Journal of Marketing, 35*, 3–12.

Lauer, L. D. (1993). Achieving an admired organization: The essential elements of communicating nonprofits. *Nonprofit World, 11*(5), 36.

Lazer, W. (1969). Marketing's changing social relationships. *Journal of Marketing, 33* (January), 3–9.

Lewis, D. (1998). Interview with Michael Edwards on the future of NGOs. Retrieved October 21, 2002 from http://globalpolicy.igc.org/ngos/issues/edwards.htm

Li, G. (2001). An analysis: The impact of non-governmental organizations on the practice of public relations. *Public Relations Quarterly, 46*(4), 11–14.

Martenson, R. (1989). International advertising in cross cultural environments. *Journal of International Consumer Marketing, 2*(1), 7–18.

McConkey, D. D. (1975). *MBO for Nonprofit Organizations*, New York: American Management Association (AMACOM).

Mekki, H. (2000). Foreign Funding of NGOs fuels anger in Jordan. Agence France Presse, September 11, 2000. Retrieved October 23, 2002 from http://www.globalpolicy.org/nogs/role/globdem/funding/2001/0410jord.htm

Naim, M. (2002). Al Qaeda, the NGO. *Foreign Policy*, March/April, 129, 99–100.

Onishi, N. (2002). Nongovernmental organizations show their growing power. Retrieved October 12, 2002 from http://globalpolicy.igc.org/ngos/0322ngos.htm

Paine, H., & Gratzer, B. (2001). Rev. Moon and the United Nations: A challenge for the NGO community. Retrieved October 21, 2002 from http://www.globalpolicy.org/ngos/analysis/1101moon.htm

Parry, R. (1997). Dark side of Rev. Moon: Generation Next The Consortium, September 8.

Paul, J. A. (2000). NGOs and global policy-making. Retrieved October 23, 2002 from http://globalpolicy.igc.org/ngos/analysis/anal00.htm

Pavicic, J. (1997). *Mogucnosti primjene marketinga i poduzetnickih aktivnosti u humanitarnim organizacijama*: Magistarski rad. Zagreb. Ekonomski fakultet Sveucilista u Zagrebu.

Pavicic, J. (2000). *Upravljanje strateskim marketingom neprofitnih organizacija*. Doctoral dissertation. Zagreb: Ekonomski fakultet Sveucilista u Zagrebu.

Pentikainen, A. (2000). *Creating global governance—The role of non-governmental organizations in the United Nations*. Helsinki: Finnish UN Association.

Pharoah, C. (2002). Who pays the piper? Bond, September 2002. Retrieved October 23, 2002 from http://www.globalpolicy.org/ngos/role/globdem/funding/2002/0902piper.htm

Putnam, R. D. (1993). *Making democracy work*. Princeton, NJ: Princeton University Press.

Reis, G. R. (2000). Fund raising on the Web: Why having a dot—org Website isn't enough. *Fund Raising Management, 30*(11), 22–24.

Rice, A. E., & Ritchie, C. (1995). Relationships between international non-governmental organizations and the United Nations, *Transnational Associations 47*(5), 254–265. Retrieved October 23, 2002 from http://www.uia.org/uiadocs/unngos.htm

Samuelson, P. A. (1970). *Readings in Economics*. New York: McGraw-Hill.

Sanborn, S. (2000). Nonprofits reap the rewards of the Web. *InfoWorld, 22*(25), 37.

Schramm, W. (1954). *The process and effects of mass communication.* Urbana: University of Illinois Press.

Shikwati, J. (2002). Do Not Need White NGOs to Speak for Me Times, September 3.

Simmons, P. J. (1998). Learning to Live with NGOs. Foreign Policy. Fall. Retrieved October 21, 2002 from http://globalpolicy.igc.otg/ngos/issues/simmons.htm

Smith, S. R., & Lipsky, M. (1993). *Nonprofits for hire: The welfare state in the age of contracting.* Cambridge, MA: Harvard University Press.

Sriramesh, K., & Verčič, D. (2001). International public relations: A framework for future research. *Journal of Communication Management, 6*(2), 103–117.

Tate, C. F. (2002). Enron proof oversight. *Association Management, 54*(8), 85–96.

Toulmin, S. (1994). The Role of transnational NGOs in global affairs. Retrieved October 21, 2002 from http://globalpolicy.igc.org/ngos/role/globalact/state/2000/1122.htm

Tse, D. K., Belk, R. W., & Zhou, N. (1989). Becoming a consumer society: A longitudinal and cross cultural content analysis of print ads from Hong Kong, the People's Republic of China and Taiwan. *Journal of Consumer Research, 15*, 457–472.

United Nations (1946). Economic and Social Council Resolution 3 (II) on the 21st of June. Retrieved October 21, 2002 from http://www.un.org/esa/coordination/ngo/committee.htm

Vaknin, S. (2002). The Self-appointed altruists. Business and Economics Desk in United Press International, September 10, 2002. Retrieved October 23, 2002 from http://www.globalpolicy.org.ngos/credib/2002/1009altruist.htm

Verčič, D., Grunig, L. A., & Grunig, J. E. (1996). Global and specific principles of public relations: Evidence from Slovenia. In H. M. Culbertson & N. Chen (Eds.), *International public relations: A comparative analysis.* (pp. 31–65). Mahwah, NJ: Lawrence Erlbaum Associates.

Vichit-Vadakan, J. (2001). Central role in development for Thai NGOs? Retrieved October 23, 2002 from http://www.globalpolicy.org/ngos/intro/general/2002/12thai.htm

Wilcox, D. L., Ault, P. H., Agee, W. K., & Cameron, G. T. (2000). *Public relations: Strategies and tactics,* 6th ed. New York: Longman.

Willetts, P. (2002). What is a non-governmental organization? Article 1.44.3.7. Non-Governmental Organizations. In *UNESCO Encyclopedia of Life Support Systems.* Retrieved October 21, 2002 from http://www.staff.city.ac.uk/p.willetts/CS-NTWKS/NGO-ART.htm

Wootliff, J., & Deri, C. (2001). NGO's: The new super brands. *Corporate Reputation Review, 4*(2), 157–164.

Young, D. R. (2002). Organizational identity and the structure of nonprofit umbrella associations. *Nonprofit Management and Leadership, 11*(3), 289–304.

25

EPILOGUE
THE MISSING LINK: MULTICULTURALISM
AND PUBLIC RELATIONS EDUCATION

KRISHNAMURTHY SRIRAMESH

Among other things, the preceding chapters have highlighted the fact that environmental factors have a significant impact on public relations practice around the world. Given the extent of globalization that has occurred especially in the past 10 years, a *majority* of public relations practice in the twenty-first century has, and will continue to, become multinational and multicultural in nature. Therefore, it is not only the "international public relations professional" who needs to be aware of the differences in cultures, political philosophies, and economic systems, but this knowledge needs to be a part of the repertoire of every public relations professional. In other words, every public relations professional needs to become a multicultural communicator in an ever globalizing world. Therefore, it is pertinent to ask: Is the current public relations education system adequately equipped to train students to become effective multicultural public relations professionals?

This chapter attempts to respond to this question drawing on experiences and literature from Asia, complementing the information from Asia that has already been presented in this volume. There are several reasons for critiquing public relations education from an Asian perspective. First, existing public relations literature lacks a reasonable representation of Asian experiences despite the size of the continent in area and population and its sociocultural diversity. For decades, multinational corporations as well as nongovernmental agencies such as United Nations Development Program (UNDP), United Nations Food and Agriculture Organization (FAO), United Nations International

---

This chapter was revised from Sriramesh, K. (2002). "The dire need for multiculturalism in public relation education: An Asian perspective," *Journal of Communication Management, 7*(1), pp. 54–70.

Childrens Emergency Fund (UNICEF), and the World Health Organization (WHO) have conducted public communication campaigns in this diverse continent to achieve a variety of objectives. However, the vast pool of information from these experiences (with varying degrees of success) has not been incorporated into the public relations body of knowledge or curricula. Second, Asia is emerging as the fastest growing market, attracting the investment of scores of multinational companies. The professionals of these companies can benefit from such knowledge in designing effective strategies for communicating with diverse Asian publics. Third, an Asian country such as Singapore, has used, and continues to use, public communication campaigns successfully to build a modern state in about a generation. Similarly, China has used communication campaigns to build a novel brand of liberalized capitalism without concomitant political liberalization, and established itself as an economic and military power with increasing global outreach. These, and similar, Asian experiences have not been adequately chronicled or integrated into building a multi-cultural body of knowledge that would contribute to holistic multicultural public relations education and practice. Finally, the author's familiarity with public relations practice and curricula in some Asian countries also contributes to a cogent critique. It is important to note that although Asia is being used as an example in this chapter primarily because of the familiarity of the continent to the author, the themes of the chapter and the issues it raises are undoubtedly relevant to other regions of the world such as Africa, Latin America, the Caribbean, and Eastern Europe, as well. The diversities of these countries have yet to be fully incorporated into existing public relations theorizing and curricula.

With this goal in mind, this chapter begins by highlighting the current American bias in public relations literature as well as curricular content around the world. The chapter cites experiences and examples from Asia to advocate the primary theme: existing public relations literature and educational practices would greatly benefit by incorporating experiences from Asia as well as other regions such as Africa, Latin America, Eastern Europe and the Caribbean that have so far received very little recognition. Finally, the chapter offers some proposals that would help incorporate multiculturalism and holism into public relations education.

CURRENT STATUS OF PUBLIC RELATIONS EDUCATION

Public relations education, as with any branch of education, needs to stand on two principal pillars: a comprehensive body of knowledge and a pool of qualified educators who can impart, and contribute to the building of, this body of knowledge. When we extend this logic to *multicultural* public relations education, it is evident that we need a body of knowledge of *multicultural* public relations and a pool of qualified educators who can impart this *multicultural* knowledge, and contribute to building it as well. There is a dire need for public relations education to identify the characteristics that make for an effective multicultural practitioner, and help impart these to students who, as professionals, will need to operate in multicultural environment.

However, keen observers of public relations education can definitively conclude that there are many chasms in these critical areas of public relations education. Although many books make references (over a few pages) to the need for multicultural public relations perspectives, currently, there are only four books specifically devoted to international public relations (Banks, 1995; Culbertson & Chen, 1996; Moss & DeSanto, 2001; Nally, 1990). Of these, only one (Culbertson & Chen, 1996) has included representative chapters of public relations in a few Asian and African countries. Moss and DeSanto's anthology of international case studies has cases from Europe, the United States, one case from South

Africa, and none from Asia, the Caribbean, Eastern Europe, or Latin America. Although many refereed journals have begun to publish articles on public relations in different parts of the world, there is a scarcity of published literature on international public relations in general and very limited information from Asia, Africa, Eastern Europe, and Latin America, in particular.

This dearth in published empirical studies from several regions of the world is indicative of the current public relations education as a whole, which is dominated by information based on experiences from the United States. European scholars who are currently spearheading the European Body of Knowledge (EBOK) project have contended that public relations education even in European countries is "largely United States centered" (Verčič, 2000; Verčič, van Ruler, Flodin, & Buetschi, 2001). They have remarked that all over Europe, American books have been used to study the concept and practice of public relations. In Asia too, public relations programs exclusively use books written by authors from the United States. These textbooks are presumably aimed at students in the United States, and are based on public relations experiences of professionals in the United States. In a few instances, these books are translated verbatim into other languages without any attempt to align the contents with the environmental contexts of the native country, thus reducing the value of this information to local students.

THE BODY OF KNOWLEDGE OF PUBLIC RELATIONS IN ASIA

Despite the obvious dearth of information on public relations in Asia, public relations has been, and is being, practiced in Asian countries for a long time. Public relations is said to have been practiced in biblical times in the Holy Land (Eshkol, 1992). Kaul (1988) has referred to the rock and pillar edicts set up by Emperor Asoka around 320 B.C. to illustrate the use of public relations in ancient India: "The inscriptions were meant to inform the people about the policies of his [Asoka's] government, to persuade them to carry out certain tasks and to create goodwill amongst them for the establishment. . . ." According to Kaul, Asoka also used these edicts to propagate Budhdhism, a religion to which he had converted later in life. Alanazi (1996) has chronicled numerous examples of public relations practices in the Arabian peninsula since pre-biblical times, noting that "in what today would pass as a 'press release,' a circular handwritten on a crude type of paper told Babylonian farmers, around the year 2000 B.C., how to increase their crop yields." This rich Asian public relations heritage has not been chronicled adequately, or exploited beneficially, by educators in helping students broaden their horizons and become effective multicultural communication professionals.

The body of knowledge of public relations in Asia is young and growing. Most of the empirical studies that have analyzed public relations in Asia have evolved in the last ten years, with contributions predominantly by graduate students from the Asian continent studying in American universities. These, and other, studies have contributed to our understanding of public relations in countries such as Taiwan (Huang, 1990, 2000), India (Bardhan, 2001; Sriramesh, 1992, 1996), South Korea (Jo & Kim, in press; Kim, 1996; Rhee, 1999, 2002), Japan (Cooper-Chen, 1996; Sriramesh & Takasaki, 1999), Saudi Arabia (Alanazi, 1996; Al-Badr, in press; Al-Enad, 1990), Thailand (Ekachai and Komolsevin, 1996), Singapore (Chay, this volume; Tan, 2001), Malaysia (Kaur, 1997); and China (Chen, 1996; Hung, 2002). After obtaining their doctoral degrees, many of these authors have continued their research programs and have continued to build the body of knowledge of Asian public relations using concepts and theories developed in the United States. To this end, one must acknowledge the immense contributions of many American universities in expanding the body of knowledge beyond United States experiences. Many American universities, especially the highly ranked public relations programs, have provided Asian scholars financial help (through fellowships and assistantships), a robust education based on a strong theoretical base, and research and communication skills to enable them to scientifically analyze and report on public relations phenomena in Asian countries. Without the strength of this foundation, one would not have been in a position to contemplate taking public relations education to the next level of making it more multicultural.

Despite these welcome advances, only a few Asian countries are represented in the above list. Whereas these studies are a good foundation on which to build a comprehensive body of knowledge taking into account the complex socioeconomic milieu that is Asia, much more work needs to be done. As already described in earlier chapters of this volume, there is a significant lack of empirical knowledge of public relations practice in Asia (and other regions of the world as already mentioned earlier), including the impact of environmental variables on the profession. This has adversely affected not only students in Asian universities who lack local examples and experiences to which they can relate more readily, but also students in the United States and Europe who can, and need to, expand their horizons in a world that has become much more multicultural and interdependent—which is the central theme of this chapter and book.

What is currently needed are studies that describe the relationship between the complex sociocultural environments of Asia (and the other regions of the world) and public relations practice, with appropriate case studies. These studies should help specify the appropriate communication strategies and techniques for operating in the complex Asian environment. As stated in Chapter 1, currently very few studies exist that have attempted to link public relations practices with environmental variables either in Asia or other regions of the world.

Once established, a comprehensive body of knowledge of Asian public relations would enhance multicultural public relations education in various ways. First, it would help us understand what public relations *is*—the perceived role for the profession in the Asian context and whether it is perceived to serve the same purpose as currently described in the public relations literature. Recent studies (van Ruler, Verčič, Flodin, and Buetschi, 2001; Verčič, van Ruler, Flodin, and Buetschi, 2001) have highlighted the inherent problems of extending United States-based definitions of public relations to Europe. It is not difficult to imagine the problems of exporting these definitions to the even more distant, and diverse, cultures of Asia, Africa, and Latin America. Second, students and practitioners would be able to use this body of knowledge to discern the political, economic, social, and cultural complexities of Asian countries and use appropriate strategies to better relate to their publics in these countries when there is a need to communicate. The need for contextual sensitivity grows with the increasing numbers of foreign organizations entering the emerging markets of Asia and other regions of the world. Third, the importance of interpersonal communication typified by the personal influence model (Huang, 2000; Sriramesh, 1992; Sriramesh, 1996), a key component for success in Asia (and other continents as well), will be made obvious by such a body of empirical knowledge. If public relations involves the management of relationships with key publics through strategic communication (Heath, 2000; Ledingham and Brunig, 2000), interpersonal communication would be an important key in unlocking complex Asian cultures to the outsider and would help increase the efficacy of public relations professionals. Finally, a body of knowledge with relevant Asian case studies would highlight the successes and failures of various communication and public relations strategies and techniques within the complex Asian social and cultural milieu, thereby helping strategic managers to design more efficacious communication programs and campaigns.

CURRENT STATUS OF MULTICULTURAL PUBLIC RELATIONS EDUCATION

Having established the importance of making the public relations body of knowledge multicultural, and emphasized that the existing body of knowledge is predominantly United States-centered, it is pertinent to address the current status of public relations education. There is little doubt that the United States is currently recognized as the leader in providing the most comprehensive public relations education. This reputation has been well earned because many institutions of higher learning in the United States have increased their support for public relations programs, owing among other things, to increased demand at both the graduate and undergraduate levels. Scholars affiliated with public relations programs in the United States have made significant contributions to the development of the body of knowledge of public relations and professional practice. This is the primary reason for Asian students (especially graduate students) to make many sacrifices to study in the United States. As already stated, United States universities, especially those with highly ranked public relations programs, deserve to be lauded for providing the theoretical and methodological foundations for many of these international scholars, thus preparing them to help contribute to building a more multicultural body of knowledge.

Many public relations scholars in the United States have made significant contributions over the past 25 years to building the body of knowledge in this domain. As a result, public relations has achieved recognition as an independent branch of study in many United States universities. Scholars in the United States have also contributed to establishing theoretical concepts specific to public relations such as the models of public relations (J. E. Grunig & L. Grunig, 1992; J. E. Grunig & Hunt, 1984), the roles of public relations practitioners (Broom and Dozier, 1986, Dozier, 1992), the power of the public relations department (L. Grunig, 1992a), the nexus between activism and public relations (L. Grunig, 1992b; Hollahan, 2001), and audience segmentation (J. E. Grunig & Repper, 1992). Several studies have also analyzed the presence of some of these concepts in different cultures (J. E. Grunig, L. Grunig, & Dozier, 1996; J. E. Grunig, L. Grunig, Sriramesh, Huang, & Lyra, 1995; Moss, Warnaby, & Newman, 2000) thereby giving these concepts an international dimension. Despite these significant contributions, it is time for the field to move to the next level and make the body of knowledge of public relations truly multicultural in keeping with the already stated demands of the twenty-first century.

The increasing number of United States students who wish to specialize in public relations, and the almost total reliance in Asia on United States textbooks as well as public relations curricula, compels one to ask whether the United States, as the pioneer and current leader of public relations education, has strong credentials in delivering *multicultural* public relations education as well. Unless the United States education system grows to the next level—by emphasizing multiculturalism in its graduate and undergraduate curricula and delivering such education—it is bound to lose its current international stature as the leader in public relations education. More importantly, it will fail to provide state-of-the-art education to the thousands of eager undergraduate and graduate students in American universities who wish to specialize in public relations. As far back as 1990, a United States public relations professional criticized the ethnocentrism of United States public relations practice (Farinelli, 1990). In 1994, a study noted that of the 119 institutions then offering public relations programs in the United States, only one offered a course on international public relations at the undergraduate level (Sommerness, 1994). There is no empirical evidence on the specific number of universities that currently offer a course in international public relations in the United States but the number does not appear to be very high. Even if a course on international public relations were offered by a significant number of universities in the United States, it will not be sufficient because it is important to go beyond having only *one* course on international public relations. There is a dire need to integrate multiculturalism into other public relations courses as well. Currently, there is very little multiculturalism in United States public relations education as admitted by the Commission of Public Relations Education (CPRE) in its report released in October 1999.

With 48 leading public relations educators and professionals as members, the CPRE was commissioned by the Public Relations Society of America (PRSA) to evaluate the status of education in the United States and make recommendations for improvement. The commission's primary goal was to "determine the knowledge and skills needed by practitioners in a technological, *multicultural and global society* [emphasis added], and then to recommend learning outcomes ..." (CPRE, 1999). The commission rightly recognized the need to prepare students to operate in a globalized environment. Although the goal of the commission explicitly recognized the need for multiculturalism in public relations education, which is laudable, its recommendations fell far short of proposing adequate representation to *multicultural public relations* education. For example, of the 12 "necessary knowledge" factors that the commission contended public relations graduates ought to possess, "multicultural and global issues" was listed 10th. Further, in the list of 20 "necessary skills" that the commission determined public relations graduates must have obtained at the end of their education, only three directly contribute to multicultural public relations education. They were listed far lower in the list—"sensitive interpersonal communication [13], fluency in a foreign language [14], and applying cross-cultural and cross-gender sensitivity [20]."

If one were to make the reasonable assumption that the placement of an item on the these lists correlates with the relative importance accorded that item, multicultural public relations does not appear to have been accorded a high priority in the commission's recommendations despite the stated goal of preparing students to operate in a "multicultural and global society." In fact, "applying cross-cultural ... sensitivity," appeared at the end of the list, almost as an afterthought! The lack of importance to multiculturalism in the committee's deliberations is further affirmed when one studies the list of six specific courses the commission recommended for "the ideal undergraduate major in public relations." There is no mention in this list of a course on multicultural public relations or anything remotely connected to international (global) public relations. Similarly, the commission's recommended list of courses for graduate curricula does not have any international or multicultural public relations courses nor does it contain any courses that contribute to expanding the cultural horizons of students. The commission, it is clear, missed an opportunity to increase the significance for multiculturalism in the public relations curricula of United States universities (thereby taking the lead for the rest of the world as well).

An unscientific, but keen, observation of the universities in the United States confirms this lack of importance accorded to international or multicultural issues in most public relations programs. The current president of the Association for Education in Journalism and Mass Communication and the director of a journalism school where public relations programs are typically housed in the United States, observed that the September 11 terrorism story should compel universities (especially journalism and communication schools) to include greater international content in their curricula. He argued that United States television networks' sparse coverage of foreign news prior to the tragic incidents of September 11, "bordered on malpractice" (Campbell, 2002). This criticism can be extended to public relations curricula also because only a few universities currently offer a course on international or global public relations. Fewer still include international issues in other public relations classes. In the rare instances where a course on international public relations is offered, it is taught only as an "elective," attracting only a small number of students who are interested in international issues for their own reasons. There is a need to rethink the course contents of all public relations courses in an effort to include multicultural issues into other public relations courses such as public relations writing, public relations campaigns, and public relations strategies.

To some extent, the lack of emphasis to multiculturalism is influenced by a lack of resources. There are simply not enough educators who have the interest, or the knowledge/experience base required, to teach courses in global public relations. Twelve years ago two leading public relations educators contended that public relations education in the United States was "terrible"(Wright and Turk, 1990). They commented that "there are some places [universities] where the public relations faculty have never published refereed scholarship, and there are institutions who have hired incompetents to teach public relations" (p. 12). The influx of educators from other communication domains into the ranks of public relations educators continues in the United States. Many are readily absorbed by public relations programs in response to the increase in demand for public relations educators. Many of these "switchovers" have neither the practical experience nor the theoretical background that competent public relations educators ought to possess. Some of them have not even taken a course in public relations. In such an environment, multicultural public relations certainly takes a back seat to the more pressing issues of "servicing" the large number of public relations students by offering basic skills courses.

The need for multiculturalism in public relations education is indisputable because public relations, like communication, is a cultural construct:

> However, we foresee an era in which public relations will undergo fundamental changes and become enriched as a profession . . . to succeed in their effort to communicate to [with] their publics in a global marketplace, public relations practitioners will have to sensitize themselves to the cultural heterogeneity of their audiences. . . . The result will be the growth of a culturally richer profession. (Sriramesh and White, 1992)

Unfortunately, 11 years have elapsed since that statement was made and the public relations education system's progress toward this goal has been painstakingly slow in the United States and around the world. One may ask why this special focus on the United States? Apart from the fact that the United States is considered the *de facto* leader of public relations education, many Asian countries still harbor a "West is best" mentality on many issues including public relations education. They often follow the United States in matters such as curriculum development, course materials, and so forth. To prepare students as multicultural professionals, a comprehensive public relations education should deliver knowledge on the linkage between public relations and the key environmental variables that influence the practice internationally (as already discussed in this volume). The political, economic, legal, media, and cultural factors of a society play a role in the nature of public relations practice, as discussed in Chapter 1. Communication aspects, especially interpersonal communication, need to be addressed as well when one analyzes multiculturalism and public relations. In the next sections, this chapter will review some of these environmental factors giving Asian examples as a prelude to making propositions that would help enhance the multiculturalism of public relations education.

DEFINITION AND NOMENCLATURE ISSUES IN PUBLIC RELATIONS

Having reviewed the predominant American influence on public relations education around the world, it is pertinent to ask whether there are similarities between the United States and the culturally closer European (at least Western European) conceptualizations of the public relations profession and education as a prelude to linking it to Asia, a more distant culture. The ongoing EBOK study did just this, asking "whether public relations is just an Anglo-American concept or whether there is (also) a European authenticity of public relations" (van Ruler, Verčič, Flodin, and Bütschi, 2001). To answer this research question, the authors conducted a Delphi study of 37 public relations academics and professionals from 25 European countries, which led them to conclude that "public relations is not a very widely used name for the field in Europe, not in practice but especially not in science [academe]" (p. 4). The authors also observed that in many European languages, there is no equivalent for the term "public relations." Some of the preceding chapters in this book also have made references to this.

A similar conceptual extension needs to be made regarding the definition and social role of public relations in Asian settings, which are even more distant from United States culture. But how is the definition of public relations in Asia different? Although the term "public relations" itself is widely used in Asian countries, it is often indicative of "spin doctoring" or mere self-serving publicity by the source of the message. Further, it is important to recognize that unlike in some Western European and United States contexts, the *parameters* of public relations practice in Asia are often limited to maintaining good relations between the client/organization and one specific public: the government. Establishing an Asian definition of public relations invariably leads one to recognize the influence of the political system over the public relations profession.

POLITICAL PHILOSOPHY AND PUBLIC RELATIONS IN ASIA

Some Asian examples help illustrate the political system–public relations linkage. We know from chapter 6 in this volume that public relations has often been characterized as *Gong-Bo* (public relations by government) in South Korea, denoting the almost total control the government wields over much of the society's activities including organizational public relations. This situation has required that public relations professionals liaise almost exclusively with the government, thus making the government the only public—contrary to the multiple "relevant publics" approach that United States textbooks recommend. After the liberalization of the economy and democratization brought on by the 1988 Seoul Olympics, the South Korean public relations field has acquired a different name—*Hong-Bo*, which means "disseminating information in a wide coverage" or "make organizations or persons known to the public broadly" (Jo, 2001). Park's study of the coverage of public relations in three major South Korean newspapers led him to conclude that the term *Hong-Bo* is used more frequently than the term "public relations" to refer to the profession, denoting that public relations and publicity are often seen as synonyms in South Korea (Park, 2001). Park also found that regardless of the term used, the public relations profession was viewed negatively by journalists.

Hong-Bo has its roots in, and is indicative of, an authoritarian government and its arm, the *Chaebol* system (Sriramesh, Kim, & Takasaki, 1999). First instituted in the 1960s in South Korea, the *Chaebol* system has its roots in the Japanese *chaibatz* system (see also the chapter 4 in this volume), which disappeared in Japan after World War II when General Douglas McArthur spearheaded the democratization of Japan. The *Chaebol* system consists of a small group of business conglomerates that have dominated the South Korean economy for decades. The underlying philosophy of this system was laudable—to bring the corporate system and the government together to work in unison to build a strong nation. However, in practice, it turned out to be a system that promoted cronyism. After the 1961 revolution led by Park Chung-Hee (who ruled South Korea from 1961 to 1979) the *Chaebol* system rapidly expanded its outreach with Park's express consent. Both sides benefited from this arrangement because the *Chaebol* had a near monopolistic control over different sectors of the economy while the economic development it brought helped Park stay longer in power. The hugely unpopular *Chaebol*s needed *Hong-Bo* to evade, or counter, negative media coverage.

The government was, and to a large extent continues to be, the significant player in India also. Until the economic liberalization of 1991, most of the critical sectors of the economy were controlled by the government through public sector enterprises. The few private sector monopolies that also operated in tandem with public sectors were controlled by rich family-owned firms. These families had close ties to their benefactors in the government, developed through a system of interpersonal friendships and *quid pro quo* personal influence. Eleven years after liberalization, all sectors of the economy have not yet been opened to competition and many industries still trudge on as inefficient public sector enterprises. Indian public relations continues to be oriented toward maintaining a strong relationship with one key public: the government. Public relations, then, becomes a synonym for government relations (Sriramesh, 1996).

The political system in Singapore also has a great influence on the role of public relations in the society. Although Singapore is a democratic republic, many observers take a contrary view of Singapore's version of democracy. In chapter 5 in this volume, Chay has cited Yuen (1999) and Ho (2000) to substantiate this point. Tan (1994) observed that whatever influence corporations have on public policies is derived primarily from their use of the *personal influence* model. A relatively recent example from Singapore also highlights the direct influence that the political system of the country has on media culture. The acting minister for information exhorted the media to play their "social role" as partners in nation building despite the "pressures" of globalization: "Our local media have played an important role in building modern Singapore. By communicating the government's message across to the people, it has [sic] helped to rally support for policies that have brought us progress and prosperity" (*Straits Times*, March 8, 2002).

It is clear from these examples that the definition and scope of public relations is greatly influenced by the political system in these Asian countries. There can be no doubt that establishing robust government relations is crucial to the strategic management of public relations in Asia, unlike the popular United States concept of public relations where the government is but one relevant public with whom the organization has "enabling linkages" (J. E. Grunig and Hunt, 1984) but the organization must also establish strong linkages with many other critical publics in order to maintain an equilibrium with its environment.

Public relations concepts developed in the United States and transported to Western Europe are based on the fact that they will be practiced in an environment that harbors a particular type of democracy—the free marketplace of ideas. Issues management literature (Heath & Causino, 1990; Jones & Chase, 1979) is replete with references to a healthy public debate occurring before governmental policies are enacted. In fact, the *issue lifecycle* that Crable and Vibbert (1985) proposed assumes that multiple players such as political opinion leaders, the media, activist groups, and citizens' groups play an active role in an open public policy making process that ends with public policies being enacted in the "critical stage" of the life cycle. However, the assumptions that form the underpinnings of issues management are often really alien to the political systems of many Asian countries as well as the personal experiences of much of the Asian populace. This brief review of the concept of political system and its impact on public relations is the context for one self-reflective question: Do public relations programs currently provide students information on the world's political systems and the relationship between these systems and public relations?

ACTIVISM

Chapter 1 has conceptually linked activism with political systems. Activism is another area that United States-based public relations concepts have considered as being important to strategic public relations management (L. Grunig, 1992b, Dozier and Lauzen, 2000; Hollahan, 2001). This assertion is indisputable when one considers the pressure that activist groups can impose on organizations from within (e.g., employee unions) and from the outside (e.g., consumer advocacy or environmental groups). In pluralistic democracies, activists wield a lot of power especially when they have the strength of public opinion behind them. When viewed from an Asian perspective, however, activism does not appear to play a major role in determining public relations strategies. Many Asian societies do not value pluralism or tolerate open disagreement with established authority, as a result of which activism is either nonexistent, muted, or orchestrated by established authority for self-serving purposes. In the rare instance that one sees popular activism, it is often crushed mercilessly as happened in Tianan men Square in June 1989. However, there are some instances where activists have had successes against giant multinational corporations in a few Asian countries.

Immediately after economic liberalization in India, for example, many American companies such as KFC, Pizza Hut, and McDonald's rushed into the market. These companies were severely resisted, often through violent means, by nationalistic activists whose slogan was "we want computer chips and not potato chips." More recently, South Korea witnessed massive activist pressure from power industry workers opposed to privatization of the industry. President Kim Dae-Jung, in his final year in office (2002), initiated a massive privatization plan of the utilities industry and other inefficient public sector firms much to the chagrin of organized labor. The reality remains, however, that activism is not very apparent in most Asian societies beyond organized labor movements or isolated instances of pressure directed at multinationals, which are easier targets for populist nationalistic movements. Perhaps this is because of a higher level of tolerance in many Asian cultures. It also may be because of the cultural idiosyncracy of deference to authority. More often, it is an outcome of fear of retribution by established political authority. Empirical evidence is needed to identify the nature of activism in Asia and its impact on public relations.

MEDIA SYSTEMS

Chapter 1 has discussed the significance of the media for public relations professionals as well as the confrontational relationship between the two. The Western notion of the media as "watchdogs" of society is not evident in most Asian countries, even those that claim to be democracies. Illiteracy and poverty, two factors discussed in Chapter 1, play a very big role in the subjugation of media by politicians who govern. Illiteracy makes only the urban educated minority the audiences for print media in Asia. Poverty and a lack of infrastructure (such as lack of rural electrification) limits the outreach of the electronic media, which can substitute or complement the print media. As a result of poor audience, many of the media of Asian countries are rarely self-sustaining and depend heavily on government subsidies. Governments use these and other covert means for keeping the media in line.

In March 2002, the World Association of Newspapers and the World Editors Forum, which represents more than 18,000 publications in 100 countries, complained to Thai Prime Minister Mr. Thaksin Shinawata that the proposed expulsion of two correspondents of the *Far Eastern Economic Review (FEER)* ordered by his government constituted "a breach of the right to freedom of expression." The expulsion was the result of the *FEER*'s reporting of the tensions between the Thai monarchy and Mr. Shinawata's administration, based largely on the public comments of King Bhumibol Adulyadej. After an international furore, the government backed down. In this instance, the *FEER* had the will and financial soundness to oppose the strongarm tactics of the government. However, an indigenous media organization, especially one that is financially weak, would not contemplate such media activism.

We need studies that analyze the media in Asia and provide case studies that illustrate the dynamics of the relationship between organizations, political systems, and media operations, as part of an overall body of knowledge of public relations in Asia. Such knowledge should prove useful to students, scholars, and professionals around the world.

CULTURE AND PUBLIC RELATIONS

Communication and culture have a reciprocal relationship. Because communication is the primary activity of public relations professionals, it behooves us to explore the impact of culture on public relations activities (Sriramesh & White, 1992). Being the largest continent in size and population, Asia is also home to a broad spectrum of very diverse cultures and religions. The public relations body of literature has only started focusing on culture as a relevant variable in the past 10 years. Even after a decade, there are very few studies that link cultural variables with public relations variables. The few existing studies have predominantly attempted to link Hofstede's (1980, 2001) dimensions of culture with public relations practice (Huang, 2000; Rhee, 1999; Sriramesh, 1992). Through his seminal study, Hofstede (1980) provided a thorough foundation on which to build culture-related theories of organizational behavior. But Hofstede himself admitted that he had not been able to discern *all* the dimensions of culture accepting that there are many other dimensions of culture that are often unique to individual countries. These certainly have an impact on public relations practice. The field would benefit from having empirical evidence about the nexus between the specific cultural idiosyncracies of individual countries and public relations practice before we can move toward globalizing some of the cultural principles.

The importance of such delineation is very apparent when one analyzes the diverse cultures in Asia, home to established religions such as Hinduism, Islam, Budhdhism, and Jainism. Even within the same national boundary, Asian countries have several distinctively different cultures. Countries such as Malaysia and Singapore are multiracial in nature and have consistently tried to conduct communication campaigns to foster interracial harmony. A review of the cultural dimensions of Asia helps one understand its complexity, which not only highlights the challenges of conducting multicultural public relations in this region, but also stresses the need to address this complexity in the public relations body of knowledge.

Public relations in China and Taiwan as well as in other countries that have a significant Chinese population (such as Singapore and Malaysia), is influenced by *guanxi*. Just as culture is hard to define (Hofstede, 2001; Kroeber and Kluckhohn, 1952), the term *guanxi* defies easy and ready definition because its practice varies from context to context:

No unchanging, single form of *guanxi* exists. [There are] urban *guanxi*, rural *guanxi*, business *guanxi*, all-female *guanxi*, owner/tenant *guanxi*, class *guanxi*, marriage *guanxi*, comrade *guanxi*, husband/wife *guanxi*, mother-in-law/daughter-in-law *guanxi*, classmate *guanxi*, and more. Each of these relationships carries its own connotations and its own social/historical specificity. (Kipnis, 1997)

Despite its complex manifestation, however, *guanxi* is ultimately about building inter-personal relationships with key publics—typified by the *personal influence* model. This is evident when one examines the origin of the term:

Guanxi is composed of two ideographs, "guan," and "xi." "Guan" functions both as an action-verb ("to close," "to lock up," or "to shut down"), and a noun that describes a physical site (a "gateway," "pass," or "checkpoint"), or a state of affairs ("a barrier"). Traditionally (in China), gateways ("guankou") were found at strategic points along the Great Wall which had historically served as a territory marker for country, culture and creed—for example, it drew a line between insiders (the Han Chinese) and outsiders (the "barbarians" who resided beyond the Great Wall). The high walls built around the ancient Chinese cities had a similar demarcation function: people who lived within the walls were granted the status of insiders, while those who lived outside were not. (Aw, Tan, & Tan, 2002)

Just as *guanxi* is idiosyncratic of Chinese culture, Japanese culture also has its own cultural idiosyncrasies that affect public relations practice in that country (Sriramesh & Takasaki, 1999). As mentioned by Inoue in chapter 4 in this volume, the concept of *wa* (harmony with fellow humans) is valued greatly by the Japanese, who are reticent to disagree publicly so as not to deharmonize society. Pegels, who attempted to link Japanese culture with management philosophy, described the profound influence of this concept on Japanese society: "the quest for *wa* is a national cultural philosophy. . . . Attaining *wa* does not allow for individualism—*wa* demands considerable conformity, and the Japanese are trained to conform from early childhood" (Pegels, 1984). Sriramesh, Kim, & Takashi (1999) linked this cultural trait and the high-context communication that Hall and Hall (1990) had identified to the operation of press clubs in Japan.

The above description of the diversity of Asia based on certain environmental variables helps offer the following propositions that should improve public relations education by making it more multicultural. The resulting holistic and multicultural education system should surely produce more effective public relations professionals who will also be more valued by their organizations.

1. *Building a multicultural body of knowledge.* First and foremost, it is important to establish a *holistic and multicultural* body of knowledge of public relations that truly reflects the political, social, economic, and cultural differences that make regions such as Asia different and challenging environments for public relations practice. Among other factors, this body of knowledge should contain information on three key areas. First, it should chronicle the history and development of the public relations profession in different regions of the world. It is hoped that such descriptions would help improve our under-standing of a *global* definition and scope of public relations. Next, this body of knowledge should present empirical data about the strategies and techniques public relations pro-fessionals operating in different regions of the world employ, especially in response to the diverse environments they face. Finally, this body of knowledge must include case studies explicating the successes and failures of different strategies and techniques around the world. Identifying successes and failures in strategy should contribute to the holistic

development of the public relations industry. These case studies should also analyze the pitfalls of replicating United States (principally) and Western European (to a lesser extent) public relations strategies and techniques in other regions of the world such as Asia. Many multinational corporations have made the mistake of simply replicating their home-country communication strategies in a socially and culturally diverse host country, often with dire consequences.

A comprehensive body of knowledge with this wealth of information would truly help educators around the world in their efforts to train professionals for multicultural public relations practice in the emerging markets of Asia and other regions of the world. As noted earlier in this chapter, public relations theories and constructs developed in the United States have laid the foundation on which to build the body of knowledge of *multicultural* public relations. Now is the time to build on this foundation and establish new, or variations of these, theories and constructs by integrating regional differences and experiences. Such efforts would help reduce, and eventually eliminate, the existing ethnocentricity in public relations theories and education, thereby leading to a holistic and multicultural profession.

For the immediate future at least, much of the theory building of multicultural public relations will continue to originate from international graduate students studying principally in the United States and a few Western countries, as well as from recent graduates some of whom have returned to their home countries. Hopefully, in the future, there will be a sufficient number of strong public relations programs in educational institutions located in other regions of the world such as Asia, Africa, and Latin America where such studies can take place indigenously. Further, one hopes that an increasing number of non-natives will conduct public relations research projects in Asia, Africa, or Latin America, thereby lending an outsider's perspective to such research and further integrating the profession.

2. *Building a multicultural curriculum.* As discussed earlier in this chapter, in addition to the current body of knowledge, public relations curricula around the world need to diversify. The overreliance on curricula based on the United States experience deprives the ever-growing number of public relations majors studying in the United States and around the world from expanding their horizons as future *multicultural* professionals. There is a dire need to remedy this situation by introducing greater international content to public relations curricula at both the undergraduate and graduate levels in all countries. Courses with a multicultural focus, such as courses on international public relations, should not be offered merely as electives for students, or superfluous teaching assignments for faculty, as is often the case currently. Instead, these courses ought to be integrated into public relations curricula as an essential knowledge asset that all students should be required to acquire.

Especially at the undergraduate level, public relations students in the United States and other countries ought to receive a broad liberal arts education that includes courses on the different political, economic, media, and legal systems as well as different religious traditions that one encounters around the world. Many students in the United States have very little exposure to international issues as highlighted by Brownlee (1988) who remarked that the typical American college student "does not seem to know the difference between Nigeria and Nicaragua, doesn't know that Mexico is to the south of the United States and Canada to the north. . . ." Even after 14 years, this situation persists, as evident in the CPRE's report cited earlier in this chapter.

The ethnocentricity of the United States education system, the current leader in the field of public relations education, has a direct influence on public relations students in many other regions of the world including Asia. Most Asian universities look up to the

United States education system as the model in setting their own curricula and frequently invite American professors as visiting fellows (aided often by benefactors such as the Fulbright Foundation) to help set up their public relations programs. Whereas this practice has many benefits, unless public relations education in the United States becomes more holistic and multicultural, the ethnocentricity in the curriculum just gets extended to other continents as well, inhibiting the holistic growth of public relations education around the world. Further, because Asian universities use United States books almost exclusively, the utility of their content to Asian students is limited to the basic principles of public relations and checklists, with little by way of contextual explication tempered by many environmental factors.

Despite the benefits, one has to recognize that there are practical problems in attempting to make public relations curricula more international and multicultural. The practical, but myopic, world view that public relations education ought to meet the demands of students (as "consumers") that they be taught "basic skills" to get an entry-level job, is the principal obstacle. Whereas there can be little argument that "skills" courses ought to be the necessary foundation of a good public relations education, university decision makers ought to recognize that it is equally essential to include multicultural issues in public relations curricula for the holistic development of students. Further, international experience is not valued adequately by administrators, faculty, or students in most universities, a situation that is changing in a few universities in the United States. There are few financial or other incentives to encourage faculty to include multiculturalism in their course content. Faculty members who wish to teach international public relations courses rarely receive enthusiastic support and resources from their supervisors. Many of these supervisors are more interested in, or are pressured to think about, staffing "required" (mandatory) and "service" (core) courses first and then focus on multicultural courses if resources permit. This is particularly debilitating when there is already a low number of faculty who are interested in, or wish to take on, the challenges of conceptualizing a new course such as international public relations.

Another curricular idea that is worth exploring is to have collaboration among two or more faculty of different countries who can jointly teach classes or specific modules of classes either through online computers or by using new technologies such as videoconferencing. The advancement of technology makes this possible as the least expensive and least disruptive option in encouraging dialogue among students and faculty of different countries or even continents. Of course the technology required for such a link has not diffused adequately for this idea to be feasibly applied in most regions of Africa and Asia. But some urban centers of Asia such as Singapore are certainly well equipped technologically for such joint classroom teaching opportunities. Until videoconferencing is within the reach of many more universities, Web-based instruction can be used collaboratively between institutions from different countries or continents. A course designed to be delivered in this manner is also exciting enough to attract larger numbers of students to sign up for international public relations classes whether these are offered as "electives" or core courses.

When establishing public relations curricula, universities in other regions of the world should try to avoid merely replicating the curricula of public relations programs in the United States based on a "West is best" worldview, which remains a widespread practice. These regional programs would do well to judiciously adopt the elements from United States curricula that are useful to their local environment, of which there are many, but also use the body of *multicultural* public relations to build course content specific to their regions and include information from other regions of the world as well. These programs also need to complement imported concepts by including information on the unique local practices and regional public relations issues and cases as well. The next two propositions, although important, may be harder to implement because of the concomitant constraints.

3. *International Experience.* A different society or culture should become a classroom for an increasing number of public relations students in all countries, if their education is to become truly multicultural. Study abroad (and student exchange) programs and international internships are very helpful in providing students this "field" experience and first-hand knowledge of multiculturalism. However, currently, few students in the United States or Asia take advantage of these programs for a variety of reasons. For most, staying for a period of one or two semesters in an exotic culture has psychological barriers. For others, personal factors such as family and friends pose an impediment. Language has always been a matter of concern to students, drastically reducing the choice of countries where one can study.

Financially, it is relatively easier for students from the United States and Western Europe to study abroad than it is for Asian students, because of the disparity in the cost of living as well as differential currency exchange rates. Even students from Singapore, a relatively affluent country (whose per capita income in 2001 was US $20,892), often decline study abroad opportunities citing financial constraints. Cultural or religious barriers often constrain students from foreign travel as in the case of Western Asia and the Middle East. Many bureaucratic impediments also inhibit the few interested students from availing of study abroad opportunities. In Asian countries, which tend to be more bureaucratic, transferring credits of similar courses has often proved problematic as is the issue of swapping credit hours of courses with similar content but different "contact" hours (the number of hours students spend in the classroom per week). As a result of these constraints, fewer students avail the opportunity of experiencing a foreign culture.

4. *Faculty exchange programs.* Many more faculty members should opt to participate in faculty exchange programs to gain, or enhance, their international experience by teaching abroad for one or two semesters. Currently, United States faculty who undertake international teaching and research opportunities do so almost exclusively during their sabbaticals. As a rule, in the United States, only faculty with tenure, and typically those who have been in residence in the same university for at least six years, are eligible for a sabbatical. This situation restricts junior (untenured) faculty and tenured faculty who change employers from engaging in international teaching or research experiences. These factors have greatly reduced the number of public relations faculty who avail themselves of international teaching and research opportunities. Faculty from Asia rarely seek, or receive, opportunities to teach outside of their regions.

CONCLUSION AND THE FUTURE

As an epilogue to this volume, this chapter has argued that there is a dire need for making public relations education and practice multicultural because we operate in a shrinking world that has fewer trade barriers and faster and cheaper communication technology. It has advocated establishing a comprehensive *holistic and multicultural* body of knowledge of public relations. As a first step in expanding the body of knowledge of public relations and making it more multicultural, there is a dire need for anthologies describing public relations experiences in Asia, Africa, Latin America, and the Caribbean. Such anthologies also need to address the issue of how societal factors such as political, cultural, and economic levels of countries influence public relations practice.

After a sufficiently comprehensive knowledge base has been established, cross-national studies of public relations using the same research protocol can be planned and executed to assess similarities and differences in public relations practice, further enhancing the body of knowledge. Such projects will also be appropriate opportunities for scholar educators of different countries to collaborate. The body of knowledge that results from these projects will be useful to public relations educators around the world in building comprehensive public relations curricula that are more multicultural and holistic. Ultimately, these developments in the body of knowledge and curricula should benefit future students, researchers, and professionals. This volume, it is hoped, has provided the first forays into a multicultural body of knowledge of public relations. The proposals made in this chapter, it is hoped, will pave the way for the public relations profession around the world to become truly *strategic* as a result of becoming more multicultural.

REFERENCES

Alanazi, A. (1996). Public relations in the Middle-East: The case study of Saudi Arabia. In H. M. Culbertson & N. Chen (Eds.), *International public relations: A comparative analysis.* (pp. 239–256). Mahwah, NJ: Lawrence Erlbaum Associates.

Al-Badr, H. (in press). Public relations in Saudi Arabia. In K. Sriramesh (Ed.), *Public relations in Asia.* Singapore: Prentice Hall.

Al-Enad, A. (1990). Public relations roles in developing countries. *Public Relations Quarterly, 35*(1), 24–26.

Aw, A., Tan, S. K., & Tan, R. (2002, July 15–19). *Guanxi* and Public Relations: An Exploratory Qualitative Study of the Public Relations-Guanxi Phenomenon in Singapore Firms. Paper presented to the Public Relations Division of the International Communication Association, Seoul, South Korea.

Banks, S. P. (1995). *Multicultural public relations: A social-interpretive approach.* Thousand Oaks, CA: Sage.

Bardhan, N., & Sriramesh, K. (in press). Public Relations in India. In K. Sriramesh (Ed.), *Public relations in Asia.* Singapore: Prentice Hall.

Bardhan, N. (2001). Radicalizing public relations metanarratives: India as a case study. Paper presented to the Public Relations Division at the annual conference of the National Communication Association, Atlanta, GA.

Broom, G. M., & Dozier, D. M. (1986). Advancement for public relations role models. *Public Relations Review, 7*(1), 37–56.

Brownlee, B. J. (1988). Main Street America asks students to give international perspective. *Journalism Educator, 43*, pp. 17–20.

Campbell, D. (2002). Serious business. *American Journalism Review, 24*, 44–47.

Chen, N. (1996). Public relations in China: The introduction and development of an occupational field. In H. M. Culbertson & N. Chen (Eds.), *International public relations: A comparative analysis.* Mahwah, NJ: Lawrence Erlbaum Associates.

Cooper-Chen, A. (1996). Public relations in Japan: Beginning again for the first time. In H. M. Culbertson and N. Chen (Eds.) *International public relations: A comperative analysis.* Mahwah, NJ: Lawrence Erlbaum Associates.

CPRE (1999). Public Relations Education for the 21st century: A port of entry. New York: Public Relations Society of America.

Crable, R. E., & Vibbert, S. L. (1985). Managing issues and influencing public policy. *Public Relations Review, 11*, 3–16.

Culbertson, H. M., & Chen, N. (1996). *International Public Relations: A Comparative Analysis.* Mahwah, NJ: Lawrence Erlbaum Associates.

Dozier, D. M., & Lauzen, M. M. (2000). Liberating the intellectual domain from the practice: Public relations, activism, and the role of the scholar. *Journalism of Public Relations Research, 12*(1), 3–22.

Dozier, D. M. (1992). The Organizational Roles of Communications and Public Relations Practitioners. In J. E. Grunig (Ed.), *Excellence in public relations and communication management* (pp. 327–355). Hillsdale, NJ: Lawrence Erlbaum Associates.

Ekachai, D., & Komolsevin, R. (1996). Public relations in Thailand: Its functions and practitioners' roles. In H. M. Culbertson, & N. Chen (Eds.), *International public relations: A comparative analysis.* Mahwah, NJ: Lawrence Erlbaum Associates.

Eshkol, D. (1992). PR in Israel: An up-to-date overview. *International Public Relations Review, 15*, 5–8.

Farinelli, J. L. (1990). Needed: A new United States perspective on global public relations. *Public Relations Journal, 46* (November), 42, 18–19.

Grunig, J. E., & Grunig, L. A. (1992). Models of public relations and communication. In J. E. Grunig (Ed.), *Excellence in public relations and communication management* (pp. 285–325). Hillsdale, NJ: Lawrence Erlbaum Associates.

Grunig, J. E., & Hunt, T. (1984). *Managing public relations.* New York: Holt, Rinehart, & Winston.

Grunig, J. E., & Repper, F. C. (1992). Strategic management, publics, and issues. In J. E. Grunig (Ed.), *Excellence in public relations and communication management* (pp. 117–157). Hillsdale, NJ: Lawrence Erlbaum Associates.

Grunig, J. E., Grunig, L. A., & Dozier, D. (1996). Das situative model exzellenter public relations: Schlussfolgerungen aus einer internationalen studie' (The contingency model of excellent public relations: Conclusions from an international study). In G. Bentele, H. Steinmann, & A. Zerfass (Eds.), *Dialogorientierte unternehmenskommunikation* (Dialogue-oriented approaches to communication) (pp. 199–228). Berlin: Vistas.

Grunig, J. E., Grunig, L. A., Sriramesh, K., Huang, Y. H., & Lyra, A. (1995). Models of public relations in an international setting. *Journal of Public Relations Research, 7*, 163–186.

Grunig, L. A. (1992a). Power in the Public Relations Department. In J. E. Grunig (Ed.), *Excellence in public relations and communication management* (pp. 483–501). Hillsdale, NJ: Lawrence Erlbaum Associates.

Grunig, L. A. (1992b). Activism: How it limits the effectiveness of organizations and how excellent public relations departments respond. In J. E. Grunig (Ed.), *Excellence in public relations and communication management* (pp. 503–530). Hillsdale, NJ: Lawrence Erlbaum Associates.

Grunig, L., Grunig, J. E. & Verčič, D. (1998). Are the IABC's excellence priniciples generic? Comparing Slovenia and the United States, the United Kingdom, and Canada. *Journal of Communication Management, 2*, 335–356.

Hall, E. T., & Hall, M. R. (1990). *Understanding cultural differences.* Yarmouth, ME: Intercultural Press.

Heath, R. L. (Ed.) (2000). *Handbook of public relations*, Thousand Oaks, CA: Sage.

Heath, R. L., & Causino, K. R. (1990). Issues management: End of first decade progress report. *Public Relations Review, 16*, 6–17.

Hofstede, G. (1980). *Culture's consequences.* Beverly Hills, CA: Sage.

Hofstede, G. (2001). *Cultrue's consequences: Comparing values, behaviors, institutions, and organizations across nations*, 2nd ed.). Thousand Oaks, CA: Sage.

Hollahan, K. (2001). The dynamics of issues activation and response: An issues processes model. *Journal of Public Relations Research, 13*, 27–59.

Ho K. L. (2000). *The politics of policy-making in Singapore.* Singapore: Oxford University Press Pte. Ltd.

Huang, Y. (2000). The personal influence Model and *Gao Guanxi* in Taiwan Chinese public relations. *Public Relations Review, 26*, 216–239.

Huang, Y. H. (1990). *Risk communication, models of public relations and anti-nuclear activities: A case study of a nuclear power plant in Taiwan.* Unpublished Master's thesis, University of Maryland, College Park, MD.

Hung, C. J. (2002). *The interplay of relationship types, relationship maintenance, and relationship outcomes: A dialectical approach on how multinational and Taiwanese companies practice public relations in China.* Unpublished doctoral dissertation, University of Maryland, College Park.

Idid, S. A. (1998). *Beauty, brain and brawn in public relations.* Bangi, Selangor: Universiti Kebangsaan Malaysia.

Jo, S. (2001 May). Models of public relations in South Korea: The difference Between *HongBo* and public relations. Paper presented to the Public Relations Division at the annual conference of the International Communication Association, Washington, DC.

Jo, S., & Kim, J. (in press). Public Relations in South Korea. In K. Sriramesh (Ed.), *Public Relations in Asia: An anthology.* Singapore: Prentice Hall.

Jones, B. L., & Chase, W. H. (1979). Managing Public Policy Issues. *Public Relations Review, 2*, 3–23.

Kaul, J. M. (1988).*Public relations in India.* Calcutta: Noya Prokash.

Kaur, K. (1997). *The impact of privatization on public relations and the role of public relations management in the privatization process: A qualitative analysis of the Malaysian case.* Unpublished doctoral dissertation, University of Maryland at College Park.

Kim, Y. (1996). Positive and normative models of public relations and their relationship to job satisfaction among Korean public relations practitioners. Unpublished master's thesis, University of Florida, Gainesville.

Kipnis, A. (1997). *Producing Guanxi: Sentiment, self, and subculture in a North China Village.* Durham, NC: Duke University Press.

Kroeber, A. L., & Kluckhohn, C. (1952). Culture: A critical review of concepts and definitions. *Papers of the Peabody Museum of American Archeology and Ethnology, 47,* Cambridge, MA: Harvard University.

Ledingham, J. A., & Brunig, S. D. (Eds.) (2000). *Public relations as relationships management.* Mahwah, NJ: Lawrence Erlbaum Associates.

Moss, D., & DeSanto, B. (Eds.) (2001). *Public relations cases: International perspectives,* London: Routledge.

Moss, D., Warnaby, G., & Newman, A. J. (2000). Public relations practitioner role enactment at the senior management level within U. K. companies. *Journal of Public Relations Research, 12,* 277–307.

Nally, M. (1990). *International public relations in practice.* Kogan Page, London.

Park, J. (2001, August). Hong Bo and PR in the Korean Newspapers. Paper presented to the Public Relations Division of the Association for Education in Journalism and Mass Communication (AEJMC), Washington, DC.

Pegels, C. (1984). *Japan vs. the West: Implications for management.* Boston, MA: Kluwer-Nijhoff.

Rhee, Y. (1999). *Confucian culture and excellent public relations: A study of generic principles and specific applications in South Korean public relations practice.* Unpublished Master's thesis, University of Maryland at College Park.

Rhee, Y. (2002, July 16). Culture and dimensions of communication in public relations: An exploratory study of South Korean practitioners. Paper presented to the Public Relations Division, International Communication Association, Seoul.

Ruler, B. van, Verčič, D., Glodin, B., & Bütschi, G. (2001). Public relations in Europe: A kaleidoscopic picture. *Journal of Communication Management, 6,* 166–175.

Sommerness, M. (1994). Back to the future: International education in public relations. *Public Relations Review, 20,* 89–95.

Sriramesh, K. (1992). Societal culture and public relations: Ethnographic evidence from India. *Public Relations Review, 18,* 201–212.

Sriramesh, K. (1992). *The impact of societal culture on public relations: An ethnographic study of south indian organizations.* Unpublished doctoral dissertation, University of Maryland at College Park.

Sriramesh, K. (1996). Power distance and public relations: An ethnographic study of Southern Indian organizations. In H. M. Culbertson & N. Chen (Eds.), *International public relations: A comparative analysis* (pp. 171–190). Mahwah, NJ: Lawrence Erlbaum Associates.

Sriramesh, K., & Takasaki, M. (1999). The impact of culture on Japanese public relations. *Journal of Communication Management, 3,* 337–351.

Sriramesh, K., & White, J. (1992). Societal culture and public relations. In J. E. Grunig (Ed.), *Excellence in public relations and communication management* (pp. 597–614). Hillsdale, NJ: Lawrence Erlbaum Associates.

Sriramesh, K., & Verčič, D. (2001). International public relations: A framework for future research. *Journal of Communication Management, 6,* 103–117.

Sriramesh, K., Kim, Y., & Takasaki, M. (1999). Public relations in three Asian cultures: An analysis. *Journal of Public Relations Research, 11,* 271–292.

Takasaki, M. (1994). *Public relations in Japan.* Unpublished term paper, Purdue University, West Lafayette, IN.

Tan, S. P. (1994). Roles of organized business in public policy making in Singapore: changes and continuities. Academy exercise, department of political science, NUS.

Tan, R. (2001). *The State of public relations in Singapore.* Singapore: Singapore Polytechnic.

Verčič. D. (2000). The European body of knowledge. *Journal of Communication Management, 4,* 341–354.

Verčič, D., van Ruler, B., Bütschi, G., & Flodin, B. (2001). On the definition of public relations: A European view. *Public Relations Review, 27,* 373–387.

Wright, D., & Turk, J. V. (1990). *Public relations education: The unpleasant realities.* New York: Institute of Public Relations Research and Education.

Yuen C. K. (27 Sept 1999). *Leninism, Asian Culture and Singapore.* Available on: http://www.sintercom.org OR www.comp.nus.edu.sg/~yuenck/new.

AUTHOR INDEX

SUBJECT INDEX

A

ABERJE (Brazilian Association of Business Communication), 363
Aboriginals, of Australasia, 130, 135
ABRP (Brazilian Association of Public Relations), 357–358
Academic programs
  professional association with, *see* Public relations education
  as UNESCO's mission, 425, 427, 430–431, 434–435
    communication role for, 436–439, 438*f*–439*f*
Accountability, in United States public relations, 339
Accreditation, for public relations practitioners, 124–126, 150, 304
  in United States, 337–338, 340, 346
Acculturation, organizational, 11
Action-orientation
  of UNESCO, 436–439, 438*f*–439*f*
  during war, media manipulation for, 416–417
Activism
  in Australasian public relations, 128–130, 132
  in Brazilian public relations, 366–367, 446
  challenge to corporate culture, 7, 17, 77
  in Chilean public relations, 391–392
  in Egyptian public relations, 187, 190
  in German public relations, 203
  as global research framework, 2, 6–7, 8*t*
  on HIV/AIDS, 156, 158
  in Japanese public relations, 76–77
  local, *see* Grassroots movements
  in multicultural public relations education, 514
  in Netherlands public relations, 233–234
  by nongovernmental organizations
    criticisms of, 494–496
    growth of, 493, 494*t*, 498
    role of, 491–493, 493*t*
  in Polish public relations, 258, 264, 268, 270–272
  in Russian public relations, 309–310

  in Singapore public relations
    civil sources of, 88, 94–95, 101
    economic factors of, 95–96
    limits to, 97–98, 101
    responding to, 96–97
  in Slovenian public relations, 292–293
  in South African public relations, 156–158
  in South Korean public relations, 111–112
  sustainable development and, 443–444, 446–449, 452
  in Swedish public relations, 250–251
  theocratic, 7
  in transnational public relations, 404, 406–408, 486–487
  in United Arab Emirates public relations, 53
  in United States public relations, 330–332, 336–337
Adams, Samuel, 330, 403
Adhocracy, 430, 431
Administration
  as international agency barrier, 472
  of nongovernmental organizations, 495–497, 501–502
  in United States public relations, 324–325, 334, 340–341
Advertising agencies, 6, 460–461, 473
  nongovernmental organizations as, 497–498
Advertising and advertisements
  in Chinese public relations, 38
  in Egyptian public relations, 182–183
  in Japanese public relations, 71–72
  in Netherlands public relations, 227–229, 237
  by nongovernmental organizations, 498
  in Polish public relations, 258–260, 263, 270
  propaganda vs., 400, 408, 414
  in Russian public relations, 305–306, 310–311
  in Singapore public relations, 89, 101–103
  in South Korean public relations, 107, 111, 116
  in United Arab Emirates public relations, 49–50
Advertising Yearbook, 116, 118, *119*
Advertorials, 71–72

T